A Reappraisal of the Efficiency of Financial Markets

NATO ASI Series

Advanced Science Institutes Series

A series presenting the results of activities sponsored by the NATO Science Committee, which aims at the dissemination of advanced scientific and technological knowledge, with a view to strengthening links between scientific communities.

The Series is published by an international board of publishers in conjunction with the NATO Scientific Affairs Division

A Life Sciences B Physics	Plenum Publishing Corporation London and New York
C Mathematical and Physical Sciences D Behavioural and Social Sciences E Applied Sciences	Kluwer Academic Publishers Dordrecht, Boston and London
F Computer and Systems Sciences G Ecological Sciences H Cell Biology	Springer-Verlag Berlin Heidelberg New York London Paris Tokyo

Series F: Computer and Systems Sciences Vol. 54

A Reappraisal of the Efficiency of Financial Markets

Edited by

Rui M.C. Guimarães

University of Porto, Faculty of Engineering
Rua dos Bragas, 4099 Porto Codex, Portugal

Brian G. Kingsman
Stephen J. Taylor

University of Lancaster, School of Management
Lancaster LA1 4YX, United Kingdom

Springer-Verlag
Berlin Heidelberg New York London Paris Tokyo
Published in cooperation with NATO Scientific Affairs Division

Proceedings of the NATO Advanced Research Workshop on A Reappraisal of the Efficiency of Financial Markets held in Sesimbra, Portugal, April 11–15, 1988.

ISBN-13:978-3-642-74743-4 e-ISBN-13:978-3-642-74741-0
DOI: 10.1007/978-3-642-74741-0

Softcover reprint of the hardcover 1st edititon 1989

2145/3140-543210 – Printed on acid-free paper

PREFACE

The behaviour of market prices is a fascinating subject for researchers. Opinions vary substantially, from the view that prices accurately and quickly reflect relevant information to the other extreme that prices are not rationally determined and are hence to some degree predictable. This diversity of belief about the efficiency of markets is reflected in these proceedings of the NATO Advanced Research Workshop on "A reappraisal of the efficiency of financial markets".

The thirty-one workshop papers cover stock, currency and commodity markets. We are pleased to have contributions on markets in eleven NATO countries: Belgium, Canada, Denmark, France, Germany, Greece, Italy, the Netherlands, Portugal, the United Kingdom and the United States. The workshop papers thus provide a wide-ranging account of contemporary research into financial markets worldwide.

The workshop was held at the Hotel do Mar, Sesimbra, Portugal from April 11th to April 15th, 1988. We record our gratitude to Jose Cabral for ensuring the smooth progress of the workshop.

The generous financial assistance of NATO was supplemented by contributions from:

The Chicago Board of Trade,
Alianca Seguradora,
Banco Comercial Portugues,
Fundacao Luso-Americana Para o Desenvolvimento,
Junta Nacional de Investigacao Cientifica e Tecnologica.

We speak for all the workshop participants in expressing our thanks to all our sponsors.

Rui M. Campos Guimaraes, University of Porto,
Brian G. Kingsman, University of Lancaster
Stephen J. Taylor, University of Lancaster

Table of Contents

Section 3 SEASONAL AND OTHER ANOMALIES

Section 4 INITIAL AND REPURCHASE STOCK OFFERS

Section 9 OPTIONS MARKETS

THE NATO ADVANCED RESEARCH WORKSHOP ON "A REAPPRAISAL OF THE EFFICIENCY OF FINANCIAL MARKETS"

Rui M.C. Guimaraes
GEIN, Department of Mechanical Engineering
University of Porto, Rua dos Bragas
Porto 4099, Portugal

Brian G. Kingsman and Stephen J. Taylor *
Department of Operational Research and Operations Management
School of Management
University of Lancaster
England LA1 4YX.

Keywords/Abstract: efficient markets/workshop summary

Thirty one papers were presented at the Nato workshop on the efficiency of financial markets held at Sesimbra in April 1988. This overview paper by the workshop directors summarises the workshop papers and offers suggestions for further research.

1. Introduction

The first use of the phrase "efficient market" in the context of securities markets has been attributed to Fama, Fisher, Jensen and Roll in a paper published in 1969. An efficient market was there defined as "a market that adjusts rapidly to new information". In the following year Fama published his influential survey of early empirical evidence and within a

* Since October 1988 Department of Accounting and Finance.

NATO ASI Series, Vol. F54
A Reappraisal of the Efficiency of Financial Markets
Edited by Rui M.C. Guimaraes et al.

short time the evidence from many studies was accepted as strongly favouring the efficient market hypothesis. Subsequent work, commencing principally with the volume edited by Jensen in 1978, has however presented less consistent conclusions.

Almost all of the early research was concerned with stock markets. This is still the major area covered with over half the papers in this volume on these markets. Much research is concerned with the apparent detection of anomalies, such as size or earnings anomalies or seasonal effects. The general conclusion here appears to be that anomalies exist but not generally at an exploitable level. Some of the papers concentrate on less widely researched aspects such as new issues and tender offers. Another field covered in the stocks area is the existence of excess volatility in stock prices. In both of these areas the evidence suggests the existence of some amount of inefficiency. However this volume also includes papers researching the existence of efficiency in other important financial markets, such as currencies, commodities and options. The evidence on exploitable market inefficiency appears to be rather stronger in these markets than in stock markets.

The papers are not only diverse with respect to the financial markets covered (stocks, commodities and currencies) but they also cover markets in most NATO nations and consider many types of information. There are papers on markets in Belgium, Canada, Denmark, France, Germany, Greece, the Netherlands, Portugal, the United Kingdom and the United States. The simplest information considered is that to be found in time series of prices. Some authors consider company variables such as earnings and size, others consider aggregate dividends, survey forecasts and supply and demand forecasts. The wide range of markets and information evaluated provide a comprehensive view of contemporary research.

2. Defining market efficiency

A major problem is the precise definition of market efficiency. The early empirical work was based on a somewhat imprecise definition, that stock prices are unbiased in their reaction to information. Market efficiency was seen as an implication of rational, maximising investor behaviour in competitive securities markets. This imprecision has been one of the problems in assessing the evidence presented in favour of or against efficiency. Unless precise definitions are agreed then it is difficult to formulate research designs for testing the efficiency hypothesis whose conclusions will be acceptable. Indeed, it sometimes appears that to some the hypothesis is an unchallengeable article of belief about financial markets.

Although definitions were discussed on several occasions at the workshop a consensus was not attained. Some participants argued for particular definitions whilst others regarded efficiency as a matter of degree or as a state that prevailed at some times but not at others.

The question of defining efficiency is impressively discussed in Ball's review paper. An essential starting point is that the issue at hand is concerned with informational efficiency, the relationship between market information and financial prices, not efficiency of how production is organised nor exchange efficiency in converting production to consumption. A number of alternative definitions have been put forward which broadly split into the 'Chicago school' or 'empirical' view most associated with Fama, and the 'Berkeley school' or 'information economics' view most associated with Rubinstein. Fama defined an efficient market as one "in which prices always 'fully reflect' available information". The sufficient conditions for efficiency are

i) there are no transaction costs in trading securities;

ii) all available information is costlessly available to all market participants;

iii) all agree on the implications of current information for the current price and distributions of future prices of each security.

The formalisation of 'fully reflect' is in terms close to those of equilibrium pricing theory. A market is efficient if the possession of the market information does not alter the expected returns from investing in the market. The unconditional expected return is equal to the conditional (on the information set) expected return, i.e. $E(r_{t+1}|\Phi_t) = E(r_{t+1})$.

Following criticism by Le Roy, Fama revised the above definition to one in which the market correctly uses all available information and thus the joint distribution of future prices established by the market is identical to the "correct" distribution implied by all available information at the time.

The alternative definitions attempted to tighten the specification of the nature of the equilibrium contemplated in "efficiency". Sharpe and Beaver defined it as : "market efficiency with respect to an information item means that prices act as if everyone knows that information".

Ball criticises their definition as essentially defining efficiency in terms of the costs of acquiring information. One would expect that non-public information, gathered privately by an individual at some cost, should allow some reward to the individual. Yet the definition does not allow this. Ball concludes that in the 'Berkeley' definition efficiency is a property of information not markets.

The 'Chicago' school is very influenced by the argument that rational, maximising behaviour is not a necessary condition for markets to behave as predicted by models which assume such behaviour. There is little need to fully understand the process by which market prices are formed. The process of aggregating from the individual to the market is left as a "black box". By contrast, the 'Berkeley' school tends to begin with the individual investor and then model the aggregate in terms of some process or property defined over the set of individuals. In a sense, the 'Berkeley' view is that the market is a collection of individuals whilst the 'Chicago' is that the market is an entity in its own right.

The various definitions discussed are statements of economic theory. They do not directly address the question of a precise testable measure of market efficiency. All require, for empirical research, that the correct distribution of future prices has to be postulated, e.g. the CAPM for characterising a rational, competitive equilibrium. This raises the further difficulty that any empirical research is really testing the particular form of asset pricing model used. The inefficiency detected could be the result of an oversimplified CAPM and not really evidence against the concept of market efficiency. Ball provides an impressive list of the limitations of asset pricing models. He comes close to concluding that these are such that we can really gather no evidence concerning market efficiency from analysis of such models. This appears to shift the argument almost to a theological one that efficiency is a credo of belief and any inefficiency detected a problem of observer malfunction.

An intermediate definition, which attempts to address this problem directly is that of Jensen. This includes the transaction costs.

"A market is efficient with respect to information set Φ_t if it is impossible to make economic profits by trading on the basis of information set Φ_t. By economic profits, we mean the risk adjusted returns "net of all costs".

This is a most attractive definition to many empirical researchers and has been the basis of much published research. One point, often ignored, is that the transaction costs are not just the costs for dealing in the market but the cost of processing the information required to manage the trading rule, e.g. the computer systems, and also logically the research and development effort that was devoted to devising the rule. The latter two aspects are frequently ignored in published work and sometimes even the market costs.

Ball criticises this definition severely, from the sufficiency viewpoint. He states that it is logically possible for a market not fully to reflect information but that trading rules have not yet been devised to exploit this. Such a market would by the definition be efficient. As transaction costs increase, in the limit to infinity, no profitable trading rule can exist. So again such a market would be judged efficient.

This seems to us rather to miss the point. The impossibility of economic profits should be regarded as a necessary condition. If trading profits, net of properly defined transaction costs, can be proved to be generated then that market is not efficient. The problem then becomes one of the acceptability of the proof presented. Applying a trading rule in real practice over a sufficiently long time is one clear test. Unfortunately, if true then it is unlikely to be available as published evidence. The Lakonishok and Vermaelen paper is one of the rare examples of this. If the evidence is derived from a simulation study over past prices, great care has to be taken in designing the experiment to attempt to mirror exactly what would have happened if practically applied.

Given these provisos, Jensen's definition appears to be a fruitful line of attack as a necessary condition, not withstanding Ball's criticisms. It can provide evidence of inefficiency but can never prove that markets are efficient.

Since efficiency implies that prices fully reflect all currently known information the only other line of attack is to attempt to develop models that show that current information can be used to predict future prices better than current prices alone.

3. The workshop papers

The papers have been grouped into nine sections of which the first five are devoted to stock markets. There are three survey papers in the first section. We have already noted Ball's paper on definitions. The other two surveys are firstly by De Bondt and secondly by Ikenberry and Lakonishok.

De Bondt takes up one of the issues raised by Ball, the assumption of rational expectations essentially based on Bayesian assessment of probabilities in the CAPM model. His paper reviews the area of stock price reversals and overreaction to news events. He argues that stock prices behave as if investors systematically "overreact" to new information, particularly as it relates to earnings. He draws attention to the vast body of psychological and statistical research showing that individuals, whether expert or not, exhibit inconsistency in their intuitive predictions. They tend to overweight a specific piece of information and underweight distributional information. They are apparently very willing to make extremely strong inferences from very small amounts of information, acting as if the law of large numbers applies to very small data samples. There appears to be a tendency towards over-optimism about the future particularly as it relates to their individual circumstances and by inference the future values for the stocks they have bought or sold.

De Bondt concludes from his survey that the empirical evidence proves the existence of both short term reactions and, perhaps more surprisingly, long term price reversals over several years. He discusses various possible causes that have been put forward to explain these reversals. These include end of year tax loss selling or locking-in of profits, the small firm size anomaly or time varying risk premia. He finds all of them inadequate. He gives some support to a socio-psychological explanation that investors react to each others' trades rather than 'hard' news per se. This is supported by the results of Shiller's survey of nearly 1000 investors, institutions, wealthy private individuals and stockbrokers. On the basis of this he was unable to identify specific news that led to the stock market crash of October 13th.

The overreactions demonstrated are anomalous relative to the standard evaluation models, e.g. CAPM. Yet they broadly agree with the predictions of the theories of intuitive prediction formulated by psychologists. De Bondt therefore concludes that this is the best line of research to pursue to understand these phenomena. He strongly recommends that these approaches should be used in place of the more common assumption of rational expectations in future research.

Ikenberry and Lakonishok present an excellent review of recent work on seasonal anomalies. They conclude that the empirical evidence for the existence of several classes of anomaly is overwhelming. These are real effects and not merely the result of data mining, possible because of the existence of low cost data bases and cheap computing power, and the newsworthiness of papers disproving a generally accepted theory. Annual, monthly and daily seasonalities plus seasonalities around annual statutory holidays have been identified. This provides strong evidence of some predictable patterns in returns. The main emphasis of the review is on research trying to identify the causes of these anomalies. They conclude that no single causal explanation has yet been determined. The effect is due to investor behaviour rather than the market structure per se. The anomalies are most likely due to a compounding, not necessarily additive, of several factors.

The first type of anomaly is in annual returns. First order serial dependency has been identified in asset returns for horizons of several years. A major strand in this area is the work of De Bondt and others discussed earlier. The anomaly identifed here, however, depends upon the assumption of a constant expected returns model. So the work may be disproving this assumption rather than the inefficiency of the market.

A second class of anomalies is in the monthly returns, most strongly in January. This has been shown to occur in stock markets in several countries besides the US. In the US, this effect has been identified as a monthly seasonal in which smaller firms are traditionally found to perform well relative to larger firms. A popular explanation is the tax loss argument, that it pays to sell securities that have suffered capital losses in December so the capital loss can be recognised and used to reduce the tax bill. A similar argument is the incentive payments for investment fund managers, also judged on a January to December year basis. In January, being the start of their year, there is a strong incentive to establish a good performance by aggressive trading, particularly if last year was not so good. The small company effect is probably because better bargains are more likely to be found in less widely known companies, which tend to be the smaller ones. Once a good investment return is established, then risk avoidance sets in for the rest of the year to preserve the initial gains. However, the existence of the January anomaly in other countries with different tax years casts some doubt on these arguments.

Persistent day-of-the-week effects have also been identified, as far back as the 1930s. Monday returns were found to be significantly negative whilst returns on the last trading day of the week, whether Friday or Saturday, tended to be higher than on other days. A common explanation for this effect is the closure of the market over the weekend, either giving time for individual investors to evaluate their portfolios over the weekend or because bad news may be released at the weekend by companies. However various authors examining prices after holidays have cast doubt on the 'closed market' hypothesis.

Other similar anomalies have been identified at the month-end, possibly due to the timing of the flow of funds into pension funds etc., and just before holidays. Ikenberry and Lakonishok point out that approximately 50% of the capital gains on the Dow Jones index over the last 90 years have occurred on the 10 pre-holiday days of the year.

The second section covers size and earnings anomalies. If the correct model for equilibrium expected returns is the standard capital asset pricing model (CAPM) of Sharpe and Lintner then the expected return for a particular security only depends on the risk-free interest rate, the expected return for a market index and the regression coefficient (beta) of security returns on market returns. Other variables such as size and earnings are irrelevant if the CAPM is applicable. Interactions between potentialy anomalous variables, including seasonal factors, increase the complexity of research into determinants of expected returns.

Keim investigates U.S. monthly returns for a longer period (1951-1986) than in previous studies and to understand better the importance of firm size and the earnings to price ratio he separates January from the rest of the year. He shows the earnings and size effects are significant in January (when returns are generally higher than for other months) but only the earnings effect is significant outside of January.

Hawawini, Michel and Corhay study Belgian monthly returns from 1969 to 1983. They find that unsystematic risk is priced over the entire sample period. Also taking into account size and seasonal effects they conclude that the CAPM cannot explain Belgian stock returns.

Levis looks at four effects for U.K. monthly returns from 1955 to 1983 : size, price to earnings ratio, dividend yield and share price. He does not consider seasonal effects. Disentangling four interacting effects is a formidable task but it appears that the dividend yield and PE effects are more important than the other two effects considered. Related studies of Australian, Canadian and Japanese markets are cited by Levis.

Two conclusions can be drawn from the detailed analyses published here. First, there are many possibe anomalous effects and their interactions have to be assessed. Second, it is difficult (for us at least) to see how the expected returns implied by the empirical results can be linked with a rational interpretation by markets of available information.

There are five papers in the third section on <u>seasonal and other anomalies.</u> We have already commented on the survey of seasonal effects by Ikenberry and Lakonishok. Continuing classification of seasonal phenomena, as in the papers here, helps to clarify the questions thrown up by these intriguing anomalies. Why are Monday returns so poor? Why are returns so high just after Christmas? (for the US). To answer these questions we need further research that goes beyond classification and so is able to test possible explanations (see Ikenberry and Lakonishok for a review of these).

Cadsby reports on Canadian stock prices from 1979 to 1987 and, like the other authors in this section, studies daily prices. Similarities between Canadian and U.S. returns are to be expected and these are discussed by reference to parallel work on the U.S. market. Of particular interest is the seasonality of the CAPM risk premium. This is shown to be significant if Monday returns are excluded and even if "good" returns at the turn-of-the-month and the turn-of-the-year (December 21 to January 5) are also excluded.

Condoyanni, McLeay and O'Hanlon have of necessity created their own series of Greek index stock returns. The indices cover 28 stocks traded at the Athens Stock Exchange from 1978 to 1986. Using three methods, including maximum likelihood estimation for the Student's t distribution, they establish that mean returns are low on Tuesdays and Wednesdays whilst they are high on Fridays.

Jennergren and Sorensen investigate price formation on the Copenhagen Stock Exchange from 1890 to 1900. Comparisons of results for distant years with results for recent years provide insight into possible institutional explanations of anomalies. On this occasion it is shown that there is a marked January effect when taxes were negligible. Thus there is further evidence that tax considerations cannot explain a January or turn-of-the-year effect. Jennergren and Sorensen look at several other anomalies and also evaluate standard random walk tests.

Boyle and William Taylor provide another demonstration that January is different by studying skewness of returns for U.S. portfolios. Such skewness can be diversified away for all months except January. This has immediate applications to any research based on Normal distributions for returns (as is usually assumed for option pricing and tests of the arbitrage pricing theory).

Crato and Lopes describe non-seasonal yet surprising anomalies for the Lisbon stock exchange between 1985 and 1987. Evidence is offered for trends in prices and for profits from filter rules. Their results have to be seen in the context of rapid developments in the liberalization of Portugese markets.

The fourth section is about <u>initial and repurchase stock offers.</u> There are three papers on European public offerings (new issues) and a paper on U.S. repurchase tender offers. Initial public offerings are on average underpriced: a high return is obtained on the first day by successful subscribers.

This does not necessarily indicate inefficiencies as subscribers will obtain a higher percentage allocation for overpriced offerings than for underpriced offerings. Unfortunately it appears to be difficult to obtain data on the magnitude of oversubscription for underpriced issues.

Wessels shows that the magnitude of the expected underpricing at the Amsterdam Stock Exchange depends on the type of offer and the tier of the market (official or parallel). Fixed price offers are more underpriced than tender or rights offers and the effect is more pronounced for the parallel market. He attempts to find predictor variables for underpriced issues without success and concludes that the market for initial public offerings is quite efficient.

Husson and Jacquillat report on the "Second Marche" section of the French equity market. Again the magnitude of underpricing depends on the type of offer and is greatest for tender offers made by existing shareholders. The excess returns obtained by successful subscribers are received rapidly (within three days) although maybe not as fast as at other European markets (only one day).

Uhlir finds greater underpricing for German initial public offerings than for other nations. The median initial return over the first trading day is 10% and hardly any issues are overpriced. Various explanations are explored, particularly information asymmetry between uninformed and informed investors. In the long run cumulative portfolio returns are negative for the sample perhaps indicating a reaction to the high initial returns. Uhlir advises a cautious interpretation of the results - his sample like those of Wessels and Husson and Jacquillat is relatively small.

Lakonishok and Vermaelen consider the reverse offer: a firm repurchasing some of its shares through a tender offer. They evaluate two trading strategies for U.S. companies. First, they consider tendering when the market price is at least 3%

below the tender price. This looks a good bet theoretically and empirically it is a tremendous success. The rule returns more than 9% on average over a week with negligible risk. Abnormal profits were certainly possible during the sample period. This new anomaly deserves more research. Second, they consider buying and holding shares after the tender opportunity. This is not successful.

Section five has five papers on excess price volatility. The issue of excessive price volatility in stock markets was first raised in 1981 by LeRoy and Porter and by Shiller. A rational expectations model implies that, in an efficient market, prices should be equal to the expectation of the perfect foresight price, defined as the discounted sum of the infinite future expected dividends. Variance bounds for the variance of the actual prices were determined. Analysing US annual data for a 100 year period it was shown that these variance bounds were violated. Similar conclusions have been reached by the use of regression tests of the present values against actuals. A lively debate on this work and its assumptions and implications has continued.

Shiller presents a new approach, an application of vector autoregressive time series models including a variable related to price in the vector, to meet many of the criticisms made of the original conclusions. This, he claims, is an effective way to deal with the nonstationarity problem and with the possibility that market participants may observe relevant information not observed by the modeller. The approach is to estimate what the dividend-price ratio and returns should be, if the market is efficient, and compare this with the actual dividend price ratio and returns. Since the period return is not linear in price and the present value formula is not linear in interest rates, Shiller works in terms of a linearised return of the natural logarithm of the dividend and the dividend-price ratio. Shiller finds that dividend price ratios seem to show substantial volatility unrelated to the predictions of the efficient market model. Further, returns on stock prices appear to be about two to four times as volatile as they should be under the efficient market model.

Bulkley and Tonks point out that the excess volalility tests are really a joint test of three hypotheses, the model of equity prices as the discounted future expected dividends, that agents efficiently process the information available and that agents know the true model generating future dividends. Previous work has only considered the first of these. They construct a simple trading rule using the market index to buy or sell if the index is more than a certain percentage outside the estimated long run trend or move into bonds at the end of the year. Each year the efficient market price is estimated by fitting a simple time trend to the price logarithm from 1919 to the current date. The rule yielded a profitable excess return of 1.61% above the buy and hold strategy. However no confidence intervals can be provided to assess the significance of this result. A series of artificial prices were generated based on the price trend model fitted for the whole period, 1919-1985, with autocorrelated error terms, to generate confidence limits for the trading rule performance. They found that on 49% of the simulated series the buy and hold strategy beat the trading rule. From this they concluded that their actual result was not significant evidence of exploitable excess price volatility.

Shea attempts to show that the statistical reliability of the tests of the present value hypothesis are adversely affected by the approximations to ex-post rational stock prices that have been used. He identifies the problems arising as a mixture of the wrong variance measure and the incorrect design and interpretation of test statistics. He presents an alternative approach to producing test statistics based upon a cointegration, error correction, model using a nonparametric bootstrapping method, the repeated sampling of estimated residuals with replacement. He advocates this method not only for producing standard errors but also for checking the finite sample behaviour of statistics whose population character can only be understood via analytical means. He then shows that on his revised test statistics, that results by Mankiw, Romer and Shapiro are not inconsistent with the present value hypothesis, contrary to their conclusions.

Shea makes the same point concerning Campbell and Shiller's work, that the assumption of covariance stationarity is incorrect if the ex-post rational price approximations depend upon a fixed terminal date. Using his ergodic ex-post rational price variables as regressands, he finds that the correlation with actuals are much closer to 1 and to the values expected under the null hypothesis than .the values found by Campbell and Shiller.

Uselton and Fraser, unlike previous research study individual firm data. The hypothesis is that actual prices are noisy estimates of the true value. They attempt to study the distribution of the ratio of perfect foresight values to market prices. The perfect foresight values for almost 400 firms are calculated for 1966, by discounting the dividends and the final price over the 20 year period to 1986. Companies were ranked by the perfect foresight-to-price ratio and the value to price ratio for 1966 using calculated capitalisation rates. Rank correlation tests showed that the ratios were positively correlated for utilities, financials and industrials. This lends strong support to the notion that noise traders fail to take full advantage of the information contained in the recent earnings record of a firm. A weighted portfolio based on the estimated value to price ratios for each sector, industrials being split into fourteen categories using SIC codes, was produced. Neglecting transaction costs, all the portfolios had a significant appreciation value, their combined perfect foresight values were greater than the cost of the portfolio. This further confirms that earnings in 1965 did contain information not fully reflected in the prevailing prices.

Verga studies efficiency and price formation in the Italian Stock Market, analysing annual, quarterly and monthly data.

He develops a model using co-integration techniques showing that in the long term prices relate to dividends. However there are also short term bubbles, which he shows are most probably due to naive infrequent traders entering the market after a prolonged positive upward price movement. He shows that the standard simple trading rules fail to beat the buy and hold strategy once transaction costs are considered. The contrast between this and the predictability given by his model, he argues, is that during the bubbles the risk increases so that risk-averse traders do not bring the market back to its "normal" equilibrium level. He shows that, whilst there is a positive correlation between his naive traders' bubble variable each month and the stock index growth over the subsequent quarter, during the extended bull market from 1976 to 87, the price variability is particularly high. This supports the conclusion that the market requires a higher risk premium than usual in such periods. His overall conclusion is that the behaviour of the Italian stock Market is quite consistent with the EMH.

Section six has two general papers, on stock markets by Keane and on futures markets by Catania.

Keane considers the implications of the efficient market literature for practitioners in the investment, corporate finance and financial reporting areas. He argues that the tendency to view the efficiency debate in simple true or false terms is unhelpful. Instead efficiency is a matter of degree and he offers four levels of efficiency.

Catania defends the futures industry against allegations that futures trading was implicated in the market crashes of October 1987. He notes that futures contracts are not well understood by those who wish to regulate the industry. He concludes with a number of research topics of particular interest to the U.S. futures markets.

Three papers covering <u>currency markets</u> are grouped together in the seventh section. Currency markets are highly liquid and the transaction costs are very low. It is therefore appropriate to investigate weak-form efficiency by evaluating trading rules. Any rule will involve some risk and it is necessary to know if profits earned merely reflect time-varying risk premia. The first two papers cover spot and futures speculation respectively, followed by a paper on forward market risk premia.

Sweeney and Surajaras discuss technical rules for several currencies traded at spot rates from 1978 to 1986. They report results for Alxander's filter rule and for the single and double moving average rules favoured by many dealers. A portfolio approach is adopted with currency weights determined by the timing of buy and sell signals. A major concern is the stability of trading profits : can rules successful until 1980 continue to earn profits in subsequent years? Apparently profits do continue for the simple rules evaluated. Sweeney and Surajaras also discuss the best amount of data for parameter selection and the value of parameter revisions.

Taylor and Tari provide new results for three currency futures series from 1982 to 1987. Their trading rule makes use of optimal time series forecasts predicated on an assumption that there are trends in prices. Using parameters obtained from pre-1982 prices they find profits after transaction costs for their six year evaluation period. Risk is discussed by reference to a portfolio invested in bills, stocks and the futures trading strategy. Results are also given for commodity futures traded in London and these too provide evidence against efficiency. The authors find the evidence for inefficient pricing compelling, however Ball (the discussant) offers a different interpretation.

Pope and Peel study the difference between forward exchange rates and current expectations of the future spot rate. This difference provides speculators with a premium for bearing risk. Published exchange forecasts provide monthly expectations three months ahead for nine currencies from 1984 to 1987. Pope and Peel use their new source of survey data to show that the consensus expectation of a large number of foreign exchange analysts does not display the properties of rational expectations. Furthermore there is evidence for time-varying risk premia.

Section eight contains four papers on agricultural and mineral commodity markets.

Labys, Thomas and Gijsbers discuss recent developments in econometric modelling of commodity price behaviour. Their assumption is that the fluctuations due to several years of real crop deficits and surpluses have been vastly amplified by general monetary and economic factors. These include factors such as accelerating inflation, high interest rates, instability of major currency rates, synchronisation of business cycles in major industrial countries and futures markets activity. A general theoretical model is specified treating demand as comprising consumption, pipeline and speculative inventories. Assuming that futures and forward prices are rational expectations prices and a dynamic price adjustment model, the authors derive a single reduced form equation for empirical estimation. An important advance is that they fit the model to individual commodity data, rather than some general index. Fourteen commodities on the London and New York markets are analysed for quarterly data for 1970-83. Preliminary assessment of the results appears to confirm the validity and value of the approach.

Kingsman examines directly for commodity prices, the semi-strong form of the efficiency hypothesis that the current prices contain all the current knowledge of the state of supply and demand factors. He discusses the development of econometric models for forecasting soyabean prices on the Chicago market over the period 1964 to 1977, to assist users' purchasing decisions. These are based on expectations of supply and demand factors either freely circulating in the market or estimated from known information. The performance in using the models to forecast in practice over 1978-80 is analysed and compared to the use of the futures prices as predictors. The usual forecasting criteria demonstrate that the final model gives forecasts superior in every regard to the futures or cash prices alone. He concludes that neither the current futures nor cash price take fully into account the current publicly available market information and thus that the soyabean market is thus inefficient to some degree.

Cabral and Guimaraes continue research into strategies for purchasers based upon the time series forecasts of Taylor's price-trend model. They consider the task of purchasing U.S. maize futures during a fixed period and aim to buy a given amount of futures at less than the average market price. Results for 1963 to 1976 are encouraging and the present paper prepares the way for a study of prices from 1977 onwards. Their paper refines a successful purchasing strategy and takes into account the risk aversion of purchasers.

Lopes also makes use of Taylor's price forecasts and provides comparisons with Kalman filter techniques for daily copper prices. Further research is required to assess the relative value of the forecasting methodologies.

The final section of the proceedings covers options markets. It was surprising that only two papers were available in this area considering the recent growth in options contracts and trading volumes.

Kemna studies transactions prices for European Options Exchange stock options for four months in 1984. These prices are used to assess the joint hypothesis of the standard option pricing model and efficient markets. The results reject the joint hypothesis. Differences between market and model prices are analysed by computing implied volatilities, with adjustments for bid-ask spreads and dividend payments.

Gemmill reports on Euromarket issues of bonds with warrants by Japanese companies. Analysts have held the view that such warrants are undervalued and thus are inefficiently priced. These issues are explored by making use of arbitrage tests and a relevant pricing model which Gemmill develops himself because of the character of Japanese warrants. Arbitrage bounds are frequently broken showing some inefficiency. Implied volatilities decline significantly as time to maturity increases. Further research on volatility models and hence efficiency is recommended.

4. Towards a reappraisal of market efficiency

Any attempt to summarise the evidence on market efficiency is inevitably subjective and what follows is our own interpretation rather than the collective view of the workshop participants. Of course we have been influenced by the remarks of the participants and we hope this is fairly reflected in what follows.

The evidence against efficient markets has accumulated on many fronts during the last ten or so years. There is evidence for seasonal anomalies, for price over-reaction, for excess volatility, for exploitable trends in prices and for many other situations where prices do not fully reflect information. Much of the evidence is statistical and without theoretical foundations. Sometimes tests of significance are performed but even then several assumptions can be required. Thus there is considerable scope for different interpretations of the evidence.

The lack of agreement on a precise definition of market efficiency hampers a conclusive assessment of this evidence. Thus any re-appraisal of market efficiency reflects prior views and the definition adopted for an efficient market. At one extreme with a prior strongly in favour of efficiency most of the empirical evidence can be disregarded because of inadequate research designs and tests. At the other extreme with a vague prior and a definition in terms of markets correctly using all information the evidence can be taken as very much against efficiency. Our preferred position is a Jensen-style definition that takes account of costs whilst our prior views have always been highly tolerant of the idea that markets are inefficient to some degree. We are much influenced by the scientific approach, that for any general theory to be true, it must be presented in the form of an operationally testable and falsifiable definition.

A major contribution of the workshop was to bring together evidence and research from a wider variety of financial markets than is normally the case. Further, evidence from European stock markets can be compared alongside North American markets, where most work to date has been carried out.

We find the evidence in this volume interesting but inconclusive. For stocks much of the anomalies literature can be reconciled with an efficient market, however results for monthly seasonals, over-reaction and excess volatility point towards exploitable inefficiencies. Commodity and currency markets offer plenty of scope we believe for successful trading using publicly available information. Markets are certainly highly efficient but it is likely that profitable decisions can still be made if sufficient effort is expended. This would suggest tentatively that commodity and currency markets are less efficient than stock markets. Perhaps this is due to more frequent and discontinuous changes in the market information or that information on the actual current state of affairs is less reliable than for stock markets. Clearly further research in non-stock financial markets is required.

In general, research either assumes a given model structure and then tests for efficiency or assumes efficiency and then tests alternative model structures. One view, with which we have some sympathy, is that much of the evidence against efficiency reflects the naivety of the models proposed and tested. Development of better models of market behaviour is thus a priority. Various such ideas are put forward in the different papers. Those of De Bondt, of abandoning the assumption that market participants assess probabilities on a rational Bayesian basis, look to be a fruitful line of research.

The efficient market paradigm has provided a valuable framework for many years for understanding financial markets. It has stood up surprisingly well to the test of time, since in general the inefficiencies detected are relatively small. Perhaps one should think in terms of markets being 'near efficient' and that the size of the inefficiency is a measure of the maturity and sophistication of the market. Although small, the inefficiencies detected are exploitable for trading in many circumstances. Future research should aim to explain why the paradigm in its purest form fails in many circumstances although it may be too much to hope for a better paradigm. Future research should also be directed towards rigorous tests that are powerful for discriminating between efficient and inefficient pricing. Empirical knowledge needs to be supported by theoretical models and here, as mentioned earlier, much remains to be done. We trust these proceedings make clear that there are plenty of stimulating problems remaining for researchers into the efficiency of financial markets.

References

Beaver W.H. (1981). Market efficiency. The Accounting Review. 56, pp23-37

Fama E.F., Fisher L., Jensen M.C. and Roll R. (1969). The adjustment of stock prices to new information. International Economic Review. 10, pp1-21

Fama E.F. (1970). Efficient capital markets: A review of theory and empirical work. Journal of Finance. 25, pp383-417

Jensen M.C. (1978). Some anomalous evidence regarding market efficiency. Journal of Financial Economics. 6, pp95-101

LeRoy S.F. and Porter R.D. (1981). The present value relation: Tests based on implied variance bounds. Econometrica. 49, No 3, pp555-574

Shiller R.J. (1981). Do stock prices move too much to be justified by subsequent changes in dividends? American Economic Review. 71, pp421-436

Shiller R.J. (1987). Investor behaviour in the October 1987 stock market crash: Survey evidence. Cowles Foundation Discussion paper No. 853 (November)

WHAT DO WE KNOW ABOUT STOCK MARKET "EFFICIENCY"?

Ray Ball

William E. Simon Graduate School
of Business Administration

University of Rochester
Rochester, NY 14618
USA

KEYWORDS/ABSTRACT: anomalies / capital asset pricing model / efficient markets / research design / review / stock prices

This paper surveys the development of the term "efficiency" in the context of security prices and reviews the principal definitions of "efficiency" that have been proposed, in terms of their likelihood of forming a basis for guiding and evaluating empirical research on the relation between information and prices. It asks what is presently knowable about efficiency, including the conclusions that can and cannot reliably be drawn from the evidence, given the present state of our knowledge about equilibrium security prices. It concludes with a cautious view on the limited reliable evidence concerning "efficiency".

Financial support was provided by the Managerial Economics Research Center at the University of Rochester and the John M. Olin Foundation. Helpful comments were provided by Andrew Christie and Jerold Zimmerman.

NATO ASI Series, Vol. F54
A Reappraisal of the Efficiency of Financial Markets
Edited by Rui M. C. Guimaraes et al.

In the two decades since the term burst upon the financial economics literature, the "efficient market hypothesis" has stimulated interest and controversy among both researchers and practitioners. The subsequent outpouring of research on the "efficiency" of financial markets (and stock markets in particular) has produced some startling evidence -- both for and against "efficiency." It has become an area of strong but conflicting views.

The early empirical work purported to show that stock prices are unbiased in their reaction to information[1]. This property (unbiased reaction to information) formed the basis of the early, imprecise definitions of "efficiency," which was seen as an implication of rational, maximizing investor behavior in competitive securities markets. The early evidence seemed unexpectedly consistent with the theory. Within a short time of Fama's (1970) influential survey, the growing body of evidence in favor of the efficient market hypothesis had emerged as one of the most consistent and influential empirical areas in economics.

Subsequent work has not reached such consistent conclusions. For example, there is impressive evidence that stock prices systematically under-react to earnings announcements[2]. However, there also is impressive evidence that extreme price changes are in part reversed, which is interpreted by the researchers involved as implying that prices systematically *over*-react to variables such as earnings announcements[3]. Taken at face value, these findings seem difficult to reconcile. Furthermore, the evidence in each case is relatively uncomplicated and readily discernible to investors, so the apparent inefficiencies imply a relatively disingenious use of information. Yet we have accumulated equally impressive evidence -- unimaginable before the late 1960s -- that stock prices respond in apparently ingenious ways to some categories of information[4].

---

[1] Notably, Fama, Fisher, Jensen and Roll (1969) [FFJR] in relation to stock splits and Ball and Brown (1968) in relation to earnings announcements.

[2] See the evidence on earnings and dividend announcements surveyed in Ball (1978).

[3] See the evidence of De Bondt and Thaler (1985, 1987), including their (1987, sec. II) analysis of earnings reversals.

[4] There is a variety of convincing evidence, some examples of which are given here. (1) Foster (1981) and Clinch and Sinclair (1987) show that earnings announcements are associated with changes in stock prices of other firms in the announcing-firm's industry. (2) Ball (1972) reports evidence that prices do not respond to earnings changes that have been induced by changes in accounting techniques, in the same manner as Ball and Brown (1968) show that prices respond to earnings changes in general. (3) Schipper and Thompson (1983) provide evidence that can be interpreted as prices responding to corporate strategy announcements, rather than waiting until the implementation of the strategy is announced, in the form of acquisition bids. (4) We believe we have learned, from the unexpectedly negative stock price response to new issues, that managers tend to possess private information and to announce new issues when the information suggests that their stock is over-priced. Further, "the market" does not automatically interpret new issues as good news and appears to understand managers' incentives [this evidence is surveyed in Smith (1986)]. These types of results would have been almost unthinkable to even the most market-oriented "pre-efficiency" researcher.

Reconciliation of the "efficiency" evidence has been complicated by the emergence of extensive "anomalous" evidence in return behavior. The range of evidence is well-known and generally takes the form of uncovering variables (for example, size, day-of-the-week, dividend yield) that are significantly but inexplicably related to security returns. While not directly related to the manner in which prices respond to information (and therefore to "efficiency"), most of this evidence has seemingly defied rational economic explanation and appears to have fundamentally altered researchers' views on stock markets. Taken in its totality, the evidence seems a puzzle.

The "efficiency" literature has produced disagreement in areas other than the evidence. It has produced a variety of research designs, ranging from FFJR's "market model" to Shiller's variance-bounds tests, with some heated debate on their relative merits. The very term "efficiency" has engendered controversy: there is a modest literature, surveyed at length below, on precisely what efficiency means. There even are formal proofs -- whose relevance is disputed by the more empirically-minded researchers -- to the effect that markets cannot be informationally efficient, *a priori*.

What can we make of all this? *Are* securities markets efficient? How does one attempt to resolve the now-voluminous body of conflicting evidence? Can conflicting results be explained in whole or in part by differences in research design? What is currently *knowable* about market efficiency? What *is* "efficiency"?

My objective is to provoke discussion of these and other questions. I first survey, from an historical perspective, the development of the term "efficiency" in the context of security prices. I evaluate the principal definitions of "efficiency" that have been proposed, in terms their likelihood of forming a basis for guiding and evaluating empirical research on the relation between information and prices. I then focus upon the question of what is presently knowable about efficiency -- that is, what conclusions can and (perhaps more importantly at this point) cannot reliably be drawn from the evidence, given the present state of our knowledge about equilibrium security prices. I conclude with my own views on the efficient markets hypothesis.

1. Development of the Term "Efficient Market"

The term "efficient" has been used to describe securities markets in a variety of ways over the past two decades[5]. This section discusses the various definitions which have been proposed, with the objective of settling upon a definition that will be used in subsequent sections, which

---

[5] The term consistently has referred to "informational" efficiency, which is a property of the relation between information and securities prices. It has not referred to "production" efficiency (a property of how production is organized) or "exchange" efficiency (a property of consumption markets). See Stiglitz (1981, pp. 236-37) for a distinction.

review what is knowable about "efficiency". The discussion is organized on a primarily historical basis.

1.1 Early Use of the Term. The term "efficient market" was first used in the context of securities markets by FFJR (1969, p.1), who defined it as "a market that adjusts rapidly to new information." The literature on the time series of prices that preceded FFJR had increasingly but heuristically connected its random walk models with competitive markets. Evidence of statistical dependence in security returns was interpreted by this literature as suggesting the existence of unexploited "excess returns", which would be inconsistent with rational investor behavior in competitive markets. Thus, Roberts (1959, p.7) tentatively reasoned:

> ... there is a plausible rationale [for the random walk model]. "If the stock market behaved like a mechanically imperfect roulette wheel, people would notice the imperfections and by acting on them, remove them." This rationale is appealing, if for no other reason than its value as counterweight to the popular view of stock market "irrationality," but it is obviously incomplete.

FFJR continued the trend in analyzing the securities markets in terms of models that were increasingly economics-based. They cited Mandelbrot (1966) and Samuelson (1965) in linking random walks with "efficiency", they implemented the "market model" with its obvious (but unstated) links with the Sharpe-Lintner capital asset pricing model (CAPM), they extended the information set studied, and they coined (but did not define) the phrase "efficient market". While FFJR pushed empirical research on securities markets significantly closer to mainstream economic theory, they nevertheless provided no explicit development of the "efficient market" theory. The early empirical work thus was increasingly conducted under the belief that it was researching the implications of competitive equilibrium in stock markets, in the context of information use, but it did so without any formal model of this equilibrium.

1.2 Spirit of the Early Work. In extending the information set beyond past prices, to include publicly-available information, FFJR introduced an ingenious research design. As a theoretical *construct*, "publicly-available" information is that which is accessible to all investors at precisely zero cost. No such thing exists in reality, of course, but a significant subset of all information approximates it. In empirical research, the construct is proxied by announcements in (say) the *Wall Street Journal* or on the NYSE ticker tape which, while not precisely costless to acquire and process subsequent to announcement, are close to being so.[6] Simple models of competitive equilibrium imply that average revenue from an activity equals its marginal cost. A testable implication of such models is that, if the cost of reproducing public information is zero, then so are the expected gains. Security prices therefore should adjust to information at the first trade after it becomes publicly-available; the gains and losses should be experienced entirely by owners of securities at the time of the announcement; none should be experienced by those who seek to trade on the information.

In contrast, a competitive information market would allow private gains from producing private information and tests of competition would require estimates of the cost of private information production. The central role of public information in the early empirical research on market efficiency thus is easy to explain: the cost of information production is known to be zero, thus allowing a simple and unique test of some of the most basic reasoning in economics. This is the spirit in which I believe the early work was conducted: researchers were simply testing whether the investment world is competitive. However, none of the early researchers chose to go beyond this basic intuition and model the economics involved.

1.3 Fama's Models. Fama (1970) continued the process of formalization. He noted (p. 384) that "to a large extent the empirical work in this area preceded the development of the theory". He defined (p.383) an efficient market as one "in which prices always 'fully reflect' available information" and stated (p.389) the *sufficient* conditions for efficiency as being: "(i) there are no transactions costs in trading securities, (ii) all available information is costlessly available to all market participants, and (iii) all agree on the implications of current information for the current price and distributions of future prices of each security." His clear intent was to formalize the "fully reflect" notion in terms closer to those of equilibrium pricing theory. Fama was saying that a market is called "efficient" if investors who possess information nevertheless earn a competitive

---

[6] Information processing costs are included because they are part of the costs of reproducing public information. Information acquisition and processing costs should be scaled relative to the value of a stockholding, for comparison with rates of return. For typical "public" information such as announced earnings, any competitive return on such costs would be small relative to (and difficult to detect in) observed rates of return, and is typically assumed away.

expected return from investing: that is, the information does not alter expected returns. This is the basis of his $E(r_{t+1}|\phi_t) = E(r_{t+1})$ definition, equating securities' conditional (on the information set) and unconditional expected returns.

Fama distinguished three nested information sets (past prices, publicly-available information and all information) and correspondingly distinguished the "weak", "semi-strong" and "strong" forms of efficiency. The distinction was not explicitly based on differences in costs of producing information. While it was the first recognition that efficiency must be defined with respect to a particular information set, this approach was not couched in terms of a competitive equilibrium in the market for information about securities. It possibly distracted attention away from the important issue of the costs of obtaining and processing information and from the fundamental economics involved. It also led to ambiguities. Most notably, in Fama's (1970, p.109) introduction he defined efficiency in terms of prices always fully reflecting "available information"; does "available" mean "publicly-available" or does it include information available only to individual investors?

Fama's (1970) modelling seems loose in hindsight, but it served the purpose of early empirical researchers well: they took it for granted that this was a precise enough statement of what they were looking for in the data. I am not aware of any of the important early researchers who thought that further formalization was necessary. It also served to stimulate a definitional debate that has continued for almost two decades. Thus, the modelling and even the concept of "efficiency" began to attract criticism, possibly fueled by: (i) the emergence of information economics as an important field, populated by researchers placing more emphasis upon logical coherence than did the "empiricists"; (ii) the logical scrutiny of the "efficiency" construct that arose naturally from researchers seeking explanations for the early empirical anomalies; and (iii) reactions to Fama's paper. In historical sequence, Rubinstein (1975), Beja (1976), Le Roy (1976), Fama (1976), Grossman (1976), Jensen (1978), Grossman and Stiglitz (1980), Beaver (1981), Jordan (1983) and Latham (1986), among others, have contributed to the debate.

Le Roy criticized Fama's definition on the grounds that it was empty/tautological, because it allowed any feasible set of return distributions to be consistent with "efficiency": the equality of conditional and unconditional expected returns is logically feasible in a market that gets them both wrong. In my view, this criticism missed the spirit of Fama's original definition, which intended the unconditional expected return to be its "correct" value[7]. However, Le Roy's criticism demonstrated that the definition could be tightened. Fama (1976, p.143) responded with a revised definition in which "the market correctly uses all available information" and thus the joint distribution of future prices established by the market is identical to the "correct" distribution implied by all available information at the time. This definition requires empirical researchers to state or imply something about the "correct" distribution of future prices (that is, to have some way of characterizing a rational, competitive equilibrium, using the CAPM for example), but it is difficult to see how empirical research under any definition of "efficiency" could do otherwise. This revised definition embodied the spirit of Fama's earlier definition and, I believe, of most of the empirical work in the area.

1.4 Further Formalization. At around the same time, a sequence of related works attempted to give even tighter specification to the nature of the equilibrium being contemplated in "efficiency". These works shared a common ancestry. They increasingly framed the efficiency construct in the language, logic and assumptions of the information economics literature.

Rubinstein (1975) canvassed several alternative definitions and commented on their various properties. Sharpe suggested a development of one of these to Beja (1976, p.7) and this in turn was further refined by Beaver (1981, p.28) as: "market efficiency with respect to an information

---

[7] This can be seen in terms of the empirical work at the time. The "correct" expected return was measured by the regression function prediction ($\alpha + \beta r_m$) of the "market model", which researchers associated, however loosely, with the CAPM. The market model residual (or prediction error) was the difference between the observed return (which by sample construction was conditional upon the information set being studied) and this "correct" return. The efficient-market prediction was a zero sample average post-announcement residual. The discovery of significant non-zero sample average residuals, post-announcement, was taken as evidence that prices had incorrectly responded to the sampled information and that returns had therefore been "incorrect". My interpretation therefore is that Fama intended to model a research process by which observed returns, conditional upon information announcements, were compared with some economically "correct" value, with the market model providing the empirical proxy for "correct" returns. The lesson from this episode is that one can conduct meaningful empirical research in the absence of watertight definitions.

item means that prices act *as if* everyone knows that information"[8]. More formally, Beaver (p.28) stated:

> A securities market is efficient with respect to a signal y_t' if and only if the configuration of security prices $\{P_{jt}\}$ is the same as it would be in an otherwise identical economy (i.e., with an identical configuration of preferences and endowments) except that every individual receives y_t' as well as [that individual's own information].

Beaver also provided a more comprehensive definition of efficiency, defined with respect to the system that produces the observed signal and thus with respect to the set of all feasible signals. He termed it "information system efficiency", as distinct from "signal efficiency".

Latham (1986) observed the logical feasibility of information that leads to offsetting revisions in individual investors' portfolios, without any net effect on excess demand and therefore on prices. For example, information feasibly could cause two investors to make precisely offsetting buy and sell decisions. He therefore defined efficiency relative to some information set "if revealing it to all agents would change neither equilibrium prices nor portfolios" (p.40). The potential advantage of this definition is not this refinement *per se*, but that it encompasses trading volume and in principle allows a linkage with the empirical work in that area. However, this is of limited use at this point because of our limited insights into the equilibrium determinants of volume (that is, we currently have no way of empirically implementing the "thought experiment" of asking what volume would look like in an "efficient" market, in order to compare it with what we see in the actual markets).

1.5 <u>Comparison of the "Empirical" and "Information Economics" Approaches</u>. The Rubinstein-Sharpe-Beja-Beaver-Latham sequence develops the efficiency construct down a different intellectual path than Fama's. Most noticeably, Fama (and much of the empirical literature) speaks of *the market* using information, or of *the market* establishing prices, whereas the more formal definitions are expressed in terms of individual investors' actions and their relation to prices (and, in Latham's case, volumes). Fama's approach not surprisingly is closer to the empirical traditions of what is sometimes referred to as the "Chicago school" or the "empirical" view; the Rubinstein-through-Latham sequence of definitions is closer to the theory-oriented traditions of what is sometimes referred to as the "Berkeley school" or the "information economics" view.

The "Chicago" tradition is frequently described as "pragmatic empirical". It is strongly influenced by the argument, developed in Alchian (1950) and Friedman (1952) among others, that rational, informed, maximizing behavior by all individuals is not a necessary condition for markets to behave as predicted by models which assume such behavior. Under this school of thought, we do not need to fully understand the process by which market prices are formed, in order to build models which successfully "explain" those prices. Accordingly, the process of aggregating from the

---

[8] Beaver (1981, footnote 11) also attributes the definition to Sharpe, who did not publish it.

individual to the market is likely to be left as a "black box" under this tradition.[9] In contrast, the "Berkeley" tradition is more disposed to commence with the individual and then model prices in terms of some aggregation process or property defined over the set of individuals. Thus, Latham (1985, p. 39) motivates his work in part by the observation: "Fama's revised definition, that the market correctly uses all relevant information in determining security prices, is unclear if investors have heterogeneous information, since Fama did not explain what 'the market uses ... the information' would mean in such a case." Yet I am sure that the phrase seems clear enough to researchers operating under the Chicago tradition, certainly when they study prices rather than volumes. Under this tradition the market is personified and is studied in its own right; the market process of aggregating heterogeneous beliefs is not an important issue.

In comparing these approaches, I am biased by my origins toward the empirical viewpoint. I do not believe that the more formal approaches have provided a positive contribution to our understanding of market efficiency, for the following reasons.

First, from an empirical perspective, there is no obvious advantage of the more formal definitions over Fama's (1976) version. It is difficult to see what their definitional refinements contribute to the estimation and interpretation of an "average post-announcement market model residual" in an event study, for example, or to our understanding of the puzzling day-of-the-week seasonals in returns[10]. Researchers never observe the "otherwise identical" world that is central

---

[9] Rational, calculating, maximizing behavior by all investors is necessary in the more formal theory. In the "empirical" tradition, results are expected to be robust with respect to many violations of this assumption. One version of the argument addresses the very meaning of maximizing behavior. For example, Friedman and Savage (1948, p. 298) employ the metaphor of the billiards player. To "explain" or "predict" the player's behavior, a physicist might assume that the player rationally calculates angles, mass, friction coefficients etc. and processes this information through some physical model of how the ball behaves. But the player need not be a rational physical man in order to succeed: the player acts *as if* rationally calculating and processing information. Another version of the argument stresses the difference between the marginal and the average investor. Here, the marginal investor determines price and is assumed to maximize and to be informed; uninformed or non-maximizing investors are assumed to be inframarginal and to have an insignificant effect on price.

Treating the process of aggregating from individuals to the market as a "black box" has the advantage that the resulting theory is robust with respect to the foibles of individuals. Conversely, it has the disadvantage of being able to say little about episodes such as October 19, 1987.

[10] I disagree with Beaver's (1981, pp.23-24) introductory comment: "Providing a precise definition is a prelude to ... an interpretation of empirical research offered as tests of market efficiency. ... It is difficult to interpret empirical evidence as a test of market efficiency in the absence of a definition of what the concept means". Yet researchers were happy with Fama's (1970) definition, however imprecise it may have been, for some time. They lived with what seems in hindsight an even worse state of affairs before his definition appeared. The reasons, in my view, are twofold. First, researchers had a relatively precise idea of what to expect in the data, even if they did not have an elaborate definitional structure to back their research process up:

(continued...)

to the refinements that have been proposed by this school of thought; on the other hand, they *can* attempt to implement a research design that asks whether prices were "correct" with respect to information, by using the post-announcement return predictions of an acceptable model of asset pricing. Being unable to observe the "otherwise identical" world, the practicing empirical researcher has no alternative but to assume that security prices in that world would behave in a "correct" fashion, as predicted by the CAPM for example, and thus is forced to accept a research design that is more directly implied by Fama's (1976) definition. From the viewpoint of empirical research, it is difficult to see what the "otherwise identical world" approach buys us.[11]

Second, from a theoretical viewpoint the more formal models seem to suffer from a confusion between the properties of information and the properties of markets. Consider their treatment of "publicly-available information". As a construct, this refers to information that is available to all investors at exactly zero cost. The efficiency concept of Latham and predecessors therefore makes all feasible markets tautologically efficient with respect to all genuinely publicly-available information. How would prices ever differ in the "otherwise identical world", in which all investors receive "publicly available" information, which by definition is already costlessly available to them all in the "real" world? Tautologically, prices cannot differ between these worlds: with exactly zero cost of being informed, all investors in the real world become fully informed about "public" information, by construction. In reality, of course, not all investors can be expected to be costlessly and fully informed about any piece of information, however simple to understand; but this merely says that there is no exact proxy for the construct of public information. Correctly interpreted, it is a statement about information, not market efficiency.

---

[10](...continued)
they were looking for evidence that (1) the market responded in an apparently rational fashion to the event being studied; and (2) post-announcement sample average residuals were insignificantly different from zero. Thus, researchers *de facto* defined "efficiency" in terms of these two properties. Second, the issue of logically coherent definitions was low in priority, relative to getting the empirical work done, and any logical shortcomings in definitions only became apparent later. It appears that the interpretation of evidence is not simply an explicit logical process and that one can collect valuable evidence in the absence of watertight theory. This is not to say that definitional refinement is in any sense unnecessary or counter-productive. The point is that from an empiricist's perspective Beaver's claim is overstated: one can interpret empirical evidence in the absence of a logically refined and coherent set of constructs. See also footnote 7.

[11] For purposes of assessing efficiency, the most fruitful area of theoretical research therefore would seem to lie in the development of equilibrium asset pricing models that are capable of explaining some of the more puzzling results that have been observed, rather than in modelling efficiency *per se*. Since tests of efficiency implicitly or explicitly rely upon such models in order to implement empirical proxies for the notion of a "correct" price distribution (or parameters thereof, such as expected return), empirical work on efficiency seems more likely to be prejudiced by failure in asset pricing models than by not refining the existing definitions of the term. These tasks are not independent, however.

Conversely, it seems difficult to see under this definition how any market could logically be efficient with respect to any non-public (i.e., privately costly) information. In the spirit of efficiency as a statement about competitive equilibrium, one would expect the construct of "efficiency" to be defined in such a manner as to allow private rewards for private investments in information, including those made by investors, security analysts and corporations themselves. Yet the definition of Latham and his predecessors does not allow this. Private information, if made public in the hypothetical "otherwise identical world", could lead to different prices and perhaps different portfolios, because the supply price of information has been reduced for a set of investors. The "real world" markets thus would be judged "inefficient" with respect to that information -- but only because the information is privately costly to produce, not because of properties of the markets themselves.[12]

Observe that this definition does not allow the real world and the "otherwise identical" world to differ in their market mechanisms (e.g., transactions costs, institutional arrangements such as the quotation mechanism or the dealer system) or in investors' capacities to process information (e.g., tendency to over-react or to react slowly). The worlds are identical except that information is rendered costlessly in the hypothetical world. The comparison is not of real markets with "ideal" markets; it is of information in the real world with costless dissemination of information in an alternative world. The comparison asks the equivalent questions: "Is what we believe to be public or costless information truly costless? Would we change the world if we made it truly costless? Is our proxy for costless information in fact a good one?" This approach therefore amounts to an enquiry into the properties of information, not of markets. The alternative approach, taken in Fama's definitions, is to compare actual with ideal markets.

In sum, the Rubinstein-through-Latham sequence seems to have emphasized logical coherence at the expense of usefulness. It has produced a structure that offers no immediate promise of assisting or even interpreting empirical work on efficiency. It also has defined "efficiency"-- which I believe is almost universally interpreted by scholars as a property of markets -- in terms of properties of the cost of information production. This contradicts the spirit of the original "efficiency" concept and of the mainstream empirical literature.

1.6 <u>The Existence of Market Efficiency</u>. Grossman (1976), Grossman and Stiglitz (1980) and Jordan (1983), among others, sought an alternative "efficiency" construct. Grossman and Stiglitz (1980, p.404) cited and rejected Fama's (1970, p.383) definition, that in an efficient market "at any time prices fully reflect all available information". They demonstrated that in such a market there would be no incentive for any individual to produce information, because trading upon it would

---

[12] Owners of valuable private information will not necessarily trade upon it immediately. For example, they might attempt to mingle their trades with those of uninformed liquidity traders, as analyzed in Admati and Pfleiderer (1988). Alternatively, they might have strategic reasons for not risking disclosure of their information.

costlessly reveal it to others. They offered a reformulation of "efficiency" as a noisy rational expectations equilibrium, the supply-induced noise interfering with investors' ability to infer information from prices.[13] Prices then cannot "fully reflect all information": without noise, no information is produced, due to lack of incentive; and with noise, prices cannot fully reflect information, because there are uninformed traders. Hence, Fama's definition could not possibly describe any real or hypothetical market. Grossman and Stiglitz thereby highlighted the ambiguity in Fama (1970), referred to in sec. 1.3 above. Whereas Fama referred to prices reflecting "all available information", the fundamental competitive economics predicts only that prices reflect all *publicly*-available information. Even though there clearly is no incentive to reproduce information that already is publicly-available, there do remain incentives to produce private information in a competitive world.[14] Part of the confusion appears to be due to Fama's (1970) statistically-based classification of information sets. If the classifications had been based upon the cost of production of information (zero in the case of the so-called "weak" and "semi-strong" forms of the EMH and positive in the so-called "strong" form), then the subsequent confusion might not have arisen. Grossman and Stiglitz' argument thus points out once more the inadequacy of Fama's (1970) original definition, though in fairness to Fama it should be noted that his 1976 revision was by then free of these problems.

Grossman-Stiglitz raises similar issues to those discussed in the previous subsection. An important value espoused by the "empirical school" is that market participants do not need to individually understand the working of a market for it to function well economically. Under this view, observed securities markets could reflect information sufficiently well for researchers to judge them "efficient," yet those same researchers could *expect* prices to not fully reveal information to *all* investors.

1.7 Why Does Public Disclosure Occur? Information is revealed to all investors in Grossman-Stiglitz through trading by informed investors and its effect on prices. Informed investors act independently, making individual information production decisions. They disclose information to the public only indirectly (and with noise), through their trading. This model omits important institutional solutions to the disclosure incentive problem.

---

[13] In their model, noise takes the form of random per capita supply of the risky asset. This seems highly artificial, particularly in the context of many securities. It seems highly unlikely that there is significant variation in the per capita supply of risky assets (i.e., the market portfolio) between trades of an individual stock, and that this is a significant source of short-term variation in individual stock prices. Subsequent approaches, including Admati and Pfleiderer (1988), introduce liquidity-motivated trading.

[14] This can be seen empirically. For example, it is clear from Ball and Brown (1968) that there are gains from obtaining private information on earnings before "the market" does -- that is, before it becomes publicly-available.

First, firms voluntarily undertake to engage in information production and disclosure to the public, including both actual and potential stockholders. Such undertakings have been included in corporate charters, and thus are a part of their contracts with their stockholders, for six centuries.[15] Second, stock exchange listing requirements, which are a contract between firms and the exchange and thus also are part of listed firms' contracts with stockholders, typically require firms to disclose important information to the market as a whole (i.e., the public), in a timely fashion. Third, directors have fiduciary responsibilities to stockholders that encompass disclosure, and these also form part of the contract between firms and stockholders. There appear to be no first-order "free-rider" incentive problems under any of these institutional solutions: (1) provided the market is efficient as in Fama (1976), the response of the firm's own stock price to the disclosed information will be captured entirely by its existing stockholders, since all post-disclosure buyers will pay a "fully reflecting" price; and (2) existing stockholders incur the per-share costs of information production and disclosure. Fourth, disclosure laws require firms to produce and disclose information.[16] These institutional arrangements overlap; for example, disclosure laws regulate what would otherwise be a contract between the firm and its stockholders. None of this rich institutional detail is captured in the Grossman-Stiglitz model, which allows no role for institutions (including firms) and only allows information production to be distributed atomistically and independently among individual investors. Hence, their demonstration that Fama's (1970) efficiency definition fails, due to lack of individual-investor incentives to produce and disclose public information, is not convincing. Public disclosure *does* occur, but not as a consequence of individuals acting independently.

1.8 <u>Role of Transactions Costs</u>. Jensen (1978, p.96) invokes transactions costs in defining efficiency:

> A market is efficient with respect to information set ϕ_t if it is impossible to make economic profits by trading on the basis of information set ϕ_t. By economic profits, we mean the risk adjusted returns *net of all costs*. (emphasis added)

A similar definition is implied whenever authors reason along the lines: "the post-announcement excess returns are less than transactions costs, and therefore the market is efficient".[17] In my view, this definition is deficient relative to Fama's in several respects.

---

[15] See Watts and Zimmerman (1983).

[16] One can argue whether disclosure laws are opportunistic wealth transfers by the political process or attempts to deal with second-order externalities in information production (e.g., the information revealed in one firm's earnings concerning the values of other firms in its industry, as reported in Foster (1981)).

[17] An early example of this reasoning is Ball and Brown (1968, pp.173-74), attempting to explain away the first documented "anomaly" in the modern literature: post-earnings-announcement excess returns.

First, defining efficiency in terms of properties of trading rules rather than properties of markets addresses one of the interesting implications of competitive markets, but it does not address the core issue of how the markets themselves behave. For example, it is logically possible for a market to not "fully reflect" information and that trading rules have not been devised to exploit this, or that investors are subject to regulation that prevents them from trading (this is a different issue than transactions costs, discussed below). To call such a market "efficient", as would Jensen's definition, cuts right across what I believe to be the spirit of the enquiry: that is, that we are investigating whether securities markets work well as competitive, economic institutions. Under this definition, the efficiency of a market is an *increasing* function of regulatory barriers to the implementation of trading rules, which hardly captures the spirit of the efficiency construct.[18]

Second, I do not see how Jensen's treatment of transactions costs is consistent with the spirit of either the central empirical work in the area or the fundamental motives for studying efficient markets. Consider the following implication of this definition: as the level of transactions costs rises, so does the likelihood that a market will be judged "efficient". In the limit, under this definition, there could be no feasible inefficient market in a world of infinite transactions costs (in the case of sellers, 100% would suffice), because there could be no trading rules that would generate positive after-cost profits.[19] This seems absurd: surely we would want to judge no market as efficient in such a world. In my view, the whole point of efficient-markets

---

[18] The current political scrutiny and restriction of program trading" in the U.S. is a case in point. A less extreme example is Indonesia, which has a stock market in which the government establishes prices and approves trades. Prices are revised infrequently and turnover is low. The Indonesian Government reportedly will not permit arbitrage trading (with regulated prices, one is not surprised, since arbitrageurs would defeat the Government's objective of controlling both prices and the identities of shareholders). I cannot imagine that we would want to label this market "efficient". Yet under the Jensen definition, the impossibility of trading rules would make it an "efficient" market.

[19] To make sense of the definition, it must be read as referring to the absence of *positive* after-cost profits. It is trivial in any market to generate negative after-cost profits, simply by increasing the trading frequency. But this creates another problem for this definition. Suppose short selling is banned, as it is in many countries, and a long trading strategy produces negative profits, before transactions costs, suggesting prices that are "too high". Yet, under this definition, the absence of positive profits would cause the market to be labelled "efficient".

research is to determine whether securities markets act as if they were free of frictions such as transactions costs.

Third, this approach in principle can produce as many definitions of efficiency as there are investors. Transactions costs vary substantially in cross-section. At one extreme, most stockmarkets have brokers or specialists who face negligible costs of transacting. At the other extreme, one can imagine many classes of people who face "large" transactions costs.[20] Whose transactions costs are to be used in judging *the market* to be efficient?

Fourth, the correct benchmark for security returns in tests of efficiency is costs of information production, not costs of transacting. A competitive market in the traditional sense acts *as if* transactions costs are zero. It does not act as if information is a free good. Even published information in reality is not precisely costless, so there will be "small" returns to its use. The issue is whether the returns from information are consistent with its costs.

1.9 Appropriateness of the Term "Efficiency". I know of no evidence that the term "efficiency" was carefully thought out and selected from among alternatives at the outset. It appears to have "caught on" in part because of its convenient juxtaposition with the commonly-held view at the time, that share price behavior was not in any important sense systematic, or capable of orderly economic description.[21] The term "efficiency" suggested the opposite.

In spite of these origins, the term is curiously appropriate. If prices adjust instantaneously to public information, then at any point in time there will be no future price reaction to old information. Thus, of all feasible prices, those established in such a market offer the minimum-variance distribution of future returns, conditional on public information. In contrast, an "inefficient" market at any point in time need not have completed its price reaction to public information (it might have over- or under-reacted) and hence there would be a component of

---

[20] Examples: elderly, incapacitated people; foreign investors; elderly, incapacitated foreign investors; prisoners; elderly, incapacitated foreign prisoners.

[21] For example, when we commenced the research in Ball and Brown (1968), we were confidently advised by our colleagues in other schools and by most of our colleagues in accounting that we should not expect to find any systematic relation between prices and earnings. One accounting practitioner opined that we were "mad". The share market was generally viewed as exhibiting little economic order whatsoever. See also Roberts (1959), quoted above.

future price variation that is response to old information. Present prices then would not be minimum-variance, or "efficient", with respect to public information. The term thus dovetails nicely with its traditional use, connoting the property of minimum-variance. In this sense, the term "efficient" was selected appropriately (if fortuitously or intuitively).

1.10 Conclusions on Definitions. There have been many attempts to find a suitable definition of market "efficiency".[22] Each characterizes market equilibrium with respect to information. One source of difference lies in the type of equilibrium that they characterize. The definitions specify that either:

1. prices are in competitive equilibrium with respect to information; or
2. prices and portfolios are in competitive equilibrium with respect to information; or
3. trading rules defined over a set of information are not profitable, after deducting trading costs.

Most of the more formal literature falls into the first category, commencing with Fama (1970), whereas empirical researchers frequently imply the third type of definition. Research on trading volume increasingly attempts to link with the second approach.

A more striking source of difference in definitions is between the approaches of what I have described as the "empirical" and "information economics" schools. The latter contributions appear to confuse the properties of information with the properties of markets and provide little or no additional guidance to empirical researchers, over and above the former contributions.

It would be preferable to work with constructs that both: (1) are embedded in a well-developed, coherent body of theory; and (2) assist in conducting and interpreting a substantial body of coherent empirical research. The second criterion seems more important for the purpose of the following section, which is to discuss the limitations of current empirical methods. Consequently, I shall work with Fama's (1976) definition, which links well with the important empirical literature on efficiency.

---

[22] Kuhn (1970, p. 71): "Proliferation of versions of a theory is a very usual symptom of crisis".

2. Limitations on Our Knowledge of Efficiency

The previous section argues that Fama's (1976) definition of market efficiency is preferred for present purposes over the alternatives in the literature: a market is efficient with respect to particular information if it uses that information "correctly" in setting prices. Implementing that definition requires a theory of, and an empirical measure of, "correct" prices.[23] This section explores the limitations of our knowledge of what "correct" prices should look like and discusses what these limitations imply for research on market efficiency.

The limitations of available asset-pricing models discussed below are: (1) they address only properties of the exchange of securities, ignoring properties of supply; (2) they are partial-equilibrium models and can only address efficiency relative to microeconomic variables; (3) being partial-equilibrium models, they only allow the assessment of the "correctness" of security prices relative to each other, and thus are susceptible to deficiencies in sampling from the population of assets; (4) they assume that it is sufficient to study a parsimonious number of parameters from continuous density functions of future prices; (5) they tend to assume homogeneous beliefs; and (6) they do not address the costs of producing non-public information and therefore do not permit research on efficiency with respect to such information.

Two features of the following discussion should be kept in mind. First, the existence of limits to our knowledge does not in itself imply that insightful research on "efficiency" cannot be conducted. Rather, the implication is that in evaluating the conclusions from any one piece of research, it is essential to examine the sensitivity of those conclusions to imperfections in our understanding of how "correct" prices behave. Second, much of the discussion in this section is uncomfortably intangible and incomplete. If it were possible to formalize the limitations of existing asset-pricing models in a well-developed and coherent fashion, then the ingredients would be available to eliminate the deficiencies. At best, this discussion offers some loosely-connected

---

[23] This well-known result sometimes is expressed in terms of empirical work being a joint test of efficiency and a particular asset pricing model. Strictly speaking, this is not quite correct. Since the asset pricing models assume perfect markets, which in turn imply efficiency, empirical work involves testing efficiency as modelled by a particular view of asset pricing. It therefore is not a joint test of two hypotheses, but a test of a model of an hypothesis.

observations about our existing knowledge, to assist in interpreting the expanding body of evidence on efficiency.

2.1 Pure Exchange Models. Essentially all of the techniques of modern Finance address only pure exchange, assuming supply to be determined exogenously. Thus (in historical sequence):

> 1. The Present Value model addresses the present price of a given future amount, at a given market rate of interest. It is merely an implication of rational investor behavior in perfect securities markets and it does not address the (supply) issue of how the future amount (e.g., a project cash flow) is determined.
>
> 2. The Miller-Modigliani theorems address the valuation of firms, given their investment policies and therefore their net cash flows. They also are logical implications of rational investor behavior in perfect securities markets and do not address the (supply) issue of how firms' investment policies and cash flows are determined.
>
> 3. The CAPM addresses the valuation of risky securities, given the joint density function of their future values. It also is an implication of rational investor behavior in perfect securities markets and does not address the (supply) issue of how securities' return density functions are determined.
>
> 4. The Black and Scholes option pricing model takes pure-exchange reasoning one step further, dealing with securities that are in identically zero aggregate supply and using a purely demand-driven (arbitrage) valuation procedure under the assumption of rational behavior in perfect securities markets. It does not address (nor can it predict the existence of) the supply of traded options.
>
> 5. The Arbitrage Pricing Model (APT) is a further extension of pure exchange reasoning. It not only ignores supply; it also seeks to reduce the set of necessary assumptions concerning demand.

The literature has followed a tradition of (and has made its most important breakthroughs by) modelling pure exchange. Failure to model the supply of securities quite possibly is the greatest deficiency in modern Financial theory.[24]

One consequence of not explicitly modelling supply is the implicit assumption that supply parameters are constant. For example, consider the notorious day-of-the-week seasonal in stock returns.[25] Evidence of time-varying average returns so startled researchers, raised on a diet of constant expected returns, that a voluminous literature quickly developed. The particularly startling result has been significantly negative average returns on weekends. When supply factors are considered, it is not clear that these results should be surprising. In a competitive world, market returns should equal the marginal efficiency of investment (MEI) over every interval, no

---

[24] The efficient market hypothesis itself is a pure-exchange approach: it asserts that, given the supply of information, rational behavior in perfect securities markets will have certain implications. It does not address the supply of information.

[25] For example, see Cross (1973) and Rogalski (1984). The argument in this paragraph is expanded in Ball and Bowers (1988).

matter what its length. This holds for days, nights and weekends. However, we possess no supply-side theory of how the MEI varies over time (e.g., how Mondays differ from Thursdays). Casual observation does suggest that the MEI on weekends is lower than on weekdays, and possibly is negative (assets are idle and incur positive holding costs).[26] Mondays are said to have higher work absenteeism than other weekdays, with possibly lower MEI. Nights presumably are less productive than days (though in an international market, the notion of a night is not well-defined). These are no more than stylized facts, but they serve to illustrate the point: observed returns feasibly could exhibit any seasonal pattern, in the absence of theory that places bounds on supply seasonals. In pure-exchange models, which by construction cannot impose such bounds, what seasonal pattern of returns could possibly surprise us *per se*? What possible implications concerning market efficiency can we draw from observed day-of-the-week seasonals? If the best knowledge we have is stylized facts rather than theories, surely our priors must be influenced by those stylized facts and we must *expect* daily seasonals in a competitive market.

A second example is provided by our lack of theory on the determinants of CAPM parameters. The CAPM is a very simple pure-exchange model and takes the market portfolio variance, the market risk premium and individual assets' betas as exogenously given. These parameters certainly will not be time-series constants, and in the simple world of the CAPM they could feasibly exhibit any pattern of variation over time. What level of variance in the observed market index could we possibly accept as evidence of efficiency or inefficiency, using pure-exchange logic?[27] What variation over time in the index variance is acceptable? Our theories of asset pricing are silent on these issues, the implication being that we cannot reliably test market efficiency in any research design that is sensitive to substantial variation in asset pricing parameters. This seems to rule out many research designs, especially those using data over an extended period. In particular, I cannot see what logical inference concerning market efficiency can be reliably drawn from Shiller (1981) and related designs. His data certainly present an

---

[26] There is no feasible arbitrage across time that forces returns in any low-MEI interval toward some time-series mean. In particular, it is incorrect to argue that prices always adjust to yield a positive expected return, because there is no guarantee of a natural, positive discount rate at all points in time. Note that the above argument refers to the *marginal*, not average, efficiency of investment and does not require, for example, that all investment assets be idle on weekends. Marginal productivity seems likely to exhibit more seasonal variability than average productivity.

This reasoning shifts the anomaly to the seasonal in the risk premium, since it does not explain positive weekend interest rates. See Ball and Bowers (1988).

[27] For example, consider a perpetuity of expected real cash flows. Let the real riskless rate be zero, which is close to its historical average. An increase in the risk premium (which here equals the real discount rate) from 6% to 8% will reduce the perpetuity's price by 25%, holding expected cash flows constant. If expected real cash flows are negatively correlated with the real discount rate, then the fall in price will be greater than 25%. Is this magnitude of price change too large for "efficiency"? Too small? How can we tell from the models we use?

intriguing puzzle, but I do not see how they relate to the efficiency of markets, unless one is prepared to accept his extraordinary assumption (1981, p. 292) that the nominal discount rate is a time-series constant over the sample period 1871-1979.

To illustrate the limitations involved when supply is ignored, consider the following conjecture. Investors are risk-averse and hence the expected market return on risky assets is an increasing function of the aggregate supply of risk (measured by the standard deviation of future wealth). The aggregate supply of risk is the product of the quantity of risky assets and the uncertainty of the rate of return on risky assets. Uncertainty is a random variable, perhaps following a moving-average process, determined by investors' perceptions of political and economic stability. The supply of risky assets is less elastic in the short term than the long, because it takes time to create new assets and for existing assets to become economically obsolete. There then will be sequences in which, especially over long periods, returns are not stationary. For example, a period of unexpected stability will be associated with increases in equity prices, and thus with positive *ex post* returns, as the discount rate falls. Until supply adjusts, *ex ante* returns will be relatively low, reflecting decreased uncertainty. Supply then will increase over time, as firms create new investments in response to the lower cost of capital (i.e., increased "confidence"). Supply increases will cause yields to rise, because risk-averse investors now bear an increased aggregate supply of risk. The rate at which this occurs depends upon the speed with which new investments can be created. The sequence of high-low-increasing returns will be an equilibrium response to the unexpected reduction in uncertainty. (An equivalent sequence will occur in response to increases in uncertainty). The point of this conjecture is to illustrate that supply characteristics influence the sequence of returns that one would expect in an "efficient" market. Without supply-side theory (i.e., in a pure exchange framework), it is difficult to see how we could be surprised by *any* observed sequence of market returns. It also is difficult to see how we could use the observed sequence to judge any market to be efficient or inefficient.

Similarly, pure-exchange theory is silent on how betas vary in cross-section and across time. What observed betas and what temporal variation in observed betas will we accept as consistent with efficiency?[28] For example, the betas of the fifty extreme "losing" stocks in De Bondt and Thaler (1987) can be expected to be large (relative to the betas of the firms' assets and of other firms' stocks) and highly variable (relative to the betas of successful firms' stocks), the reason being the extreme increase in their market-valued debt/equity ratios. In general, the beta of a firm's equity, given the beta of its assets, is a function of its debt/equity ratio, which varies with

---

[28] These parameters could exhibit seasonals also: there is no reason in principle why aggregate risk and securities' relative risks cannot vary with (say) day-of-the-week. Consider a firm that routinely makes its major announcements -- earnings, dividends, investments, acquisitions -- on Thursdays, perhaps because it schedules board meetings on that day. Thursday returns then will exhibit higher variance and, possibly, covariance.

every realization of the historical return on equity. Equity betas therefore vary every period, given asset betas.[29] Conventional methods of parameter estimation tend either to assume stationarity over extended periods (measured relative to the periodicity of the feasible non-stationarities) or to restrict the allowable non-stationarities. It is not clear that they can capture the non-stationarities one would expect in the data.

Overall, empirical work in securities markets tends to use models that say little about where to expect non-stationarities, and use data and estimation techniques that could easily disguise them. In the circumstances, I am not convinced that we can reliably conclude much about "efficiency" *as an empirical fact* whenever we use research designs that are sensitive to non-stationarities. This applies particularly to analyses of returns over long periods.[30]

2.2 Partial-Equilibrium Models. The available asset pricing models not only ignore supply: they are incomplete statements about demand. The CAPM is a simple extension of the Present Value model to a mean-variance world. As such, it is a pure-exchange statement about the pricing of securities relative to each other: it simply adjusts the "equal rate of return" rule, which is the present value model, for differences in securities' (exogenously-given) risks. The partial-equilibrium characteristic of the CAPM is manifested in the role of the market portfolio, or index: each security is priced relative to the index, the expected return on which is taken as exogenous. Consequently, tests of efficiency currently cannot be conducted in a CAPM framework on information that is correlated with the market index; we have no model of the "correct" expected return on the index itself.

Consider, for example, the information that the central bank will double the money stock one year hence, with probability one. At what level would an efficient market establish the index today? The answer to that question lies in macroeconomic theory, which is not unanimous. It is tempting to answer that prices immediately rise in full anticipation of the money stock doubling, but that assumes that the nominal discount rate is independent of changes in the money stock. At the other extreme, if the real discount rate is to remain constant instead, then the index does not change now: it changes one period hence, and the nominal discount rate over the next year increases instead. Intermediate solutions are feasible: if money influences real variables, then both the nominal and the real rates change, and the index immediately changes to some intermediate point. Which of these three responses occurs in an efficient market depends upon what one's

---

[29] See Cox and Rubinstein (1985, pp.185-196) for a discussion that applies to the case of risky debt. De Bondt and Thaler (1987, p.564) recognize the varying-leverage problem, but do not provide a convincing procedure for detecting the short-run variation in equity betas that the Black and Scholes analysis predicts. Note that, due to leverage, betas and therefore expected returns are a decreasing function of realized past returns -- which is consistent with the negative serial correlation observed in Fama and French (1988).

[30] Fama and French (1988) report evidence relevant to the issues discussed in this subsection.

theory of a "correct" price response to variation in the money stock. The point of the example is that the CAPM provides no insights in this context, because it takes the market return as exogenously given.

In the context of the CAPM and the "market model", we therefore can obtain at best a partial assessment of efficiency with respect to information that is correlated with the market index, because the index itself contains part of the market's reaction.[31]

2.3 Limitations of Available Data. Most tests of market efficiency have been conducted on prices and returns for listed securities, due to limited availability of reliable data for other assets. The tests exclude or substantially under-represent investments in small businesses (sole proprietorships, partnerships, private corporations), human capital, personal property (houses, land, cars), corporate debt and public assets. It is well-known that these data limitations can lead to distorted estimates of important parameters, at least in the context of the CAPM.[32] They therefore are capable of distorting estimates of excess returns and, in turn, of market "efficiency". This is not a simple problem of a non-representative sample of assets; because we rely upon partial-equilibrium models which attempt to describe the pricing of assets relative to each other, it is a problem of evaluating a non-representative sample against a non-representative benchmark. Any resulting biases would most likely be strongest for small stocks, since they are where the benchmark (in the CAPM, this is the "market index", which is the sample average listed stock) is least representative. Most large, private assets are listed and thus the index, which is dominated by such assets, is an effective control group for individual members of this class. In contrast, the smallest listed stocks are the closest substitutes for unlisted assets that are omitted from the market portfolio, and the index is a poorer control group. Their "true" betas could be substantially different than those estimated from indexes of listed stocks. In general, the benchmark used in implementing a partial-equilibrium model, such as the CAPM, is most likely to be deficient in evaluating excess returns on the stocks which are the least comparable to it. We thus seem least able to reliably infer efficiency, or inefficiency, in relation to the smallest stocks.

2.4 Distributional Assumptions. The notion that securities can be described in terms of a small number of parameters of a continuous, joint probability density function of future values, is an intellectual abstraction. Useful as it may be, it is an abstraction. Tests of efficiency are limited by the extent to which the abstraction is valid.

For example, typical market model "event studies" assume a mean-variance world. How frequently is a sample average residual dominated by a small number of outliers, in cross-section

---

[31] This explains why Ball and Brown (1968) orthogonalized their EPS variable with respect to an "market" index of firms' EPS, prior to investigating the relation between EPS and security prices.

[32] Roll (1977, 1978) first demonstrated this problem.

or in time? How will future researchers handle the data from 19 October 1987 and the surrounding high-volatility days, which will dominate conventional parametric estimators? The choices include: (1) allow that subperiod to dominate the results; or (2) adopt a procedure that has the effect of throwing away much of the information contained in that episode, such as excluding it as an outlier, or using estimators that reduce its relative weight, or using non-parametric estimators; or (3) attempt models that incorporate such episodes.

The CAPM provided a major insight into the pricing of risky securities. Nevertheless, it is a very simple model, assuming that investments differ only in risk and that risk can be described in terms of second moments of continuous density functions. It thus provides a limited benchmark for assessing whether the market "correctly" sets prices.

2.5 Heterogenous Beliefs. Available asset-pricing models typically assume homogeneous beliefs, which also is an abstraction. This issue was discussed in 1.5 above; its implications for tests of efficiency, including possible volume tests, are not clear.

2.6 Costs of Producing Non-public Information. There are no developed models of private information production which permit tests of whether that activity in general is competitive. For example:

1. If a security analyst specializes in 10 stocks at an average annual cost of $20,000 (including salary and overheads) each, for clients with an aggregate investment of $20 millions, the expected increase in private return is in the order of one-tenth of one percent. Can we reliably detect such a low number in stock returns?

2. If 1,000 professors of Finance worldwide incur costs of $50,000 each (including salary and overheads) in searching for anomalies, should the expected value of the private return from discovering pricing errors in the market be in the order of $50 millions per year? This is equivalent to 5% per year on a $1 billion portfolio. If they have been incurring search costs for 20 years, what is the expected private return?

3. Why have some researchers published their anomalous evidence? Why have we not all used the information for private gain?

4. What is the predicted size of gains from "inside information"?

These are interesting questions, but we have no well-developed insights into their solution. To date, we understandingly have relied upon publicly-disclosed information, which by definition is privately costless, for our tests of efficiency.

2.7 Summary. It is well-known that tests of efficiency rely upon particular implicit or explicit assumptions concerning equilibrium asset pricing. This section has discussed a range of possible limitations of the available models of asset pricing, together with their possible effects on tests of efficiency. The range of limitations is impressive, to the point where it is tempting to conclude that we can gather little, if any, reliable evidence concerning market efficiency. But that would be too pessimistic. What *can* we conclude?

3. Are Stock Markets Efficient?

The "efficient market hypothesis" now is approximately two decades old, the expression having been coined and the initial empirical work having been completed in the late 1960s. Its second decade has been remarkably different than the first, having been plagued by anomaly and uncertainty. Can we conclude from the evidence that stock markets *are* (or are not) efficient? What is the future of the hypothesis?

There is no doubting that the early empirical literature on market efficiency has had an enduring impact. "Efficiency" was seen from the outset as a property of competitive securities markets. In the late 1960s and early 1970s this was an unusually successful area for empirical research in economics. It was one of the few areas in which a very large amount of data could confront a simple, testable hypothesis that derived from the competitive economic paradigm.[33] And the paradigm appeared to work: stock markets consistently seemed to be efficient. Because this evidence tended to contradict priors, which seem to have been based on prejudice and casual observation of the markets rather than on systematic research, academic attention was quickly drawn to it.[34] Furthermore, the early work on "efficiency" coincided with the emergence of interest in and respect for markets in general among economists. The early empirical work therefore assumed importance and attracted interest beyond its direct implications for stock markets. It influenced the worldwide move toward "liberalizing" financial and other markets.

There also is no doubting the subsequent accumulation of a variety of anomalous evidence, directly or indirectly calling "efficiency" into question. The documented anomalous price behavior included apparent under-reaction, apparent over-reaction and puzzling variation of prices with day-of-the-week, size, dividend yield, earnings yield and other variables that have been difficult to rationalize economically.

Why did the evidence appear to change so drastically? One reason is that the earlier researchers tended to "sweep the evidence under the rug", until its accumulated weight could not be ignored. Perceptions of the existing evidence then changed almost overnight.[35] A second

---

[33] The data were unusually plentiful. In the case of the New York Stock Exchange, the world's largest, CRSP provided comprehensive data on the universe of stocks -- an almost unheard-of luxury among economists. In addition to being plentiful, the data were essentially error-free and came in machine-readable form, which was rare at the time.

[34] Harry Roberts' (1959, p.3) musings seem well-justified in hindsight: "What slight departures from the chance [random walk] model are detectable? Perhaps the traditional academic suspicion about the stock market as an object of scholarly research will be overcome ... ."

[35] Kuhn (1970) describes this as a normal initial response to anomaly. Personal experience is consistent with this response: the survey of earnings anomalies in Ball (1978) took over two years to get published; and even then publication awaited the accumulation of enough anomaly to fill a special issue of the journal. While the anomalous evidence had been quietly accumulating for a decade, researchers were reluctant to confront it until it was abundantly clear.

reason is that our research techniques have progressed. We now have: larger data bases (covering more securities and longer time periods); improved statistical techniques; and computational costs that are orders of magnitude lower than in the first decade of the EMH. Consequently, previously-undetected anomalies now are more likely to be observed. In addition, the nature of the research conducted has shifted systematically over time, into areas where anomaly is more likely *a priori*. The early empirical studies investigated stocks and events that were less extreme than in the studies that followed. Earnings changes, for example, are "normal" events: every NYSE firm experiences one earnings change, every quarter. Investigating the relation between stock prices and simply the sign of earnings changes -- without regard to the magnitude of the change, the size of the corporation, the day or month of the announcement, etc. -- involves studying normal events for normal firms. The market portfolio (i.e., the average firm) thus provides a reasonable control for a portfolio of firms that experience earnings increases, or for a portfolio of earnings-decreasing firms. The control is not perfect, but it is effective; there is not much anomalous return behavior. After the more common information sources such as earnings have been exhausted, researchers have turned to increasingly uncommon phenomena in search of new topics. As time has progressed, researchers have tested "efficiency" (and, therefore, explicit or implicit models of price equilibrium) against progressively more-extreme phenomena, investigating such things as returns on the very smallest stocks on the very first trading day of the year, or on the most extreme "losers" in the market over an interval in time, or on the most extreme stocks in terms of earnings performance or earnings yield. These research designs presumably are more sensitive to misspecifications in our models of market equilibrium. However, models of asset pricing have not kept pace with the requirements of this research, which increasingly finds them breaking down. All factors considered, one should *expect* increasing problems.

Testing a paradigm in successively more-rarified circumstances is "normal" behavior in the progress of science: we first "sharpen" our expectations upon the more routine research designs and we then try them against the extremes.[36] It is here that we are most likely to discover novel insights. But where will this lead us? Will we abandon the "efficient market hypothesis", as some commentators have suggested?

Kuhn (1970, p.84) states that scientific communities have three generic responses to repeated anomaly:

---

[36] Kuhn's (1970, pp.86-87) description fits the "efficiency" literature well: "Faced with an admittedly fundamental anomaly in theory, the scientist's first effort will often be to isolate it more precisely and to give it structure. Though now aware that they cannot be quite right, he will push the rules of normal science harder than ever to see, in the area of difficulty, just where and how far they can be made to work. Simultaneously he will seek for ways of magnifying the breakdown, of making it more striking and perhaps also more suggestive than it had been when displayed in experiments the outcome of which was thought to be known in advance."

> [A]ll crises close in one of three ways. Sometimes normal science ultimately proves able to handle the crisis-provoking problem despite the despair of those who have seen it as the end of an existing paradigm. On other occasions the problem resists even apparently radical new approaches. Then scientists may conclude that no solution will be forthcoming in the present state of their field. The problem is labelled and set aside for a future generation with more developed tools. Or ... a crisis may end with the emergence of a new candidate for paradigm and with the ensuing battle over its acceptance.

Response to the barrage of "efficiency" anomalies depends in part upon the nature of the evidence presented. To evaluate the evidence, one in turn must evaluate the models, techniques and the data employed.

Tests of "efficiency" are well-known to be tests of particular models of equilibrium pricing with respect to information. They therefore are limited by our meager understanding of what an equilibrium in the securities markets would resemble. We saw in sec. 2 that the available models of equilibrium security pricing tend to: describe pure exchange, ignoring supply (e.g., tell us nothing about "betas" and how they might vary across time, including short intervals); be silent about seasonality (e.g., not state or imply anything to distinguish days of the week from each other); describe a partial equilibrium only (e.g., treat as exogenous all "macro" parameters, such as the expected return on the "market" portfolio); assume homogeneity of beliefs; assume that return distributions are continuous and described by a small number of parameters; and ignore costs of private information production. They thus have major inherent limitations in describing the world and in forming the basis for deciding whether markets *are* "efficient". Leaving aside the Present Value model, our models of pricing equilibrium began with the CAPM and thus have an accumulated history of only 25 years. With such a limited tradition in asset pricing, we could hardly expect to have a strong basis for concluding that security prices do (or do not) immediately restore equilibrium, conditional upon information flows, particularly when they are taken to the extreme.

In addition, it is worth examining the nature of the data that are available for estimating parameters of these models. In sec. 2.3 above, we discussed some effects of the data limitations, as first observed by Roll (1977, 1978). These effects are likely to be strongest among small stocks, implying that on data availability grounds alone we might not be able to draw reliable conclusions concerning efficiency from small-stock returns.

A problem that lies at the intersection of theory and data is non-stationarity. There is nothing in the asset-pricing models that bounds the degree of non-stationarity that can be expected in their parameters. We can only search for it in the data, without theory to guide us. This applies to CAPM parameters such as the variance of the return on the market portfolio, the risk premium and stocks' betas. Non-stationarities can be short-term as well as long term, and thus can be difficult to observe from time-series data. They severely restrict the range of reliable research on market efficiency.

Bearing all these limitations in mind, I personally believe that much of the evidence on stock price behavior does not and cannot reliably address the issue of "efficiency" at this point in time: our models of price equilibrium and our data are too limited.[37] Conversely, the most reliable evidence for evaluating "market efficiency" is that which relies less upon particular models of price equilibrium and precise pricing benchmarks such as the market index. It therefore is research that does not involve extreme securities, events or time periods.

Returning to Kuhn's three generic responses to repeated anomaly, my bet is on the first or the second. I expect to see some of the anomalies being resolved after further research and some of them being shelved. I do not envisage theories built around market inefficiency receiving widespread support, for several reasons. First, stock markets must rank highly among markets on *a priori* likelihood of being competitive: there are no entry barriers; there are many buyers and many sellers, who by and large appear to be greedy, avaricious, inventive people; and transaction costs are low. Second, as outlined above, limitations of our models of "correct" pricing and of the available data seem the most likely sources for the impressive range of anomalies that have been documented over the last decade. In the earlier research, where the designs were less sensitive to model and data imperfections, "efficiency" performed relatively well. Third, I personally went

---

[37] This is not to say that empirical research cannot be informative under these circumstances. We have learned a considerable amount from the "anomaly chasing" of the last decade; and there are enough puzzles and clues to work on for some time. However, I do not believe that we can reliably learn much *about efficiency* from these results.

through the transformation from the pre-EMH view of securities markets, and I am still impressed by how well prices respond to information, *relative to what we expected two decades ago.*

4. Conclusions

Conclusions from a selective review of this kind inevitably reflect one's biases. My personal views can be summarized as: (1) the efficient market hypothesis was an audacious and welcome change from the ignorance of stock markets that preceded it; (2) *a priori*, stock markets are paradigm examples of competition and thus of "efficiency" in using information; (3) there are binding limitations in our knowledge of what price behavior to expect in an "efficient" market, so in turn there is limited reliable evidence on "efficiency"; (4) the evidence collected over the past twenty years must have shifted a reasonable person's beliefs toward "efficiency"; (5) to a large degree, the anomalous evidence shows up where one would expect it: where research designs are most sensitive to limitations in our knowledge of asset pricing; (6) the anomalous evidence provides an intriguing set of puzzles for researchers to solve; and (7) given the priors expressed in (2) above, I expect many (though certainly not all) of the anomalies to be resolved in favor of efficiency.

References

Admati, A.R. and P. Pfleiderer, 1988, A theory of intraday trading patterns: Volume and price variability, Review of Financial Studies, forthcoming.

Alchian, A., 1950, Uncertainty, evolution, and economic theory, Journal of Political Economy 58, 211-221.

Ball, R., 1972, Changes in accounting techniques and stock prices, Empirical Research in Accounting: Selected Studies, supplement to Journal of Accounting Research, 1-38.

Ball, R., 1978, Anomalies in relationships between securities' yields and yield-surrogates, Journal of Financial Economics 6, 103-126.

Ball, R. and J. Bowers, 1988, Daily seasonals in equity and fixed-interest returns: Australian evidence and test of plausible hypotheses, in: Stock market anomalies, ed. E. Dimson (Cambridge University Press).

Ball, R. and P. Brown, 1968, An empirical evaluation of accounting numbers, Journal of Accounting Research 6, 159-178.

Banz, R.W., 1981, The relationship between return and market value of common stocks, Journal of Financial Economics 9, 3-18.

Beaver, W.H., 1981, Market efficiency, The Accounting Review 56, 23-37.

Beja, A., 1976, The limited information efficiency of market processes (University of California, Berkeley).

Black, F. and M. Scholes, 1973, The pricing of options and corporate liabilities, Journal of Political Economy 81, 637-654.

Clinch, G.J. and N.A Sinclair, 1987, Intra-industry information releases: A recursive systems approach, Journal of Accounting & Economics 9, 89-106.

Cox, J.C. and M. Rubinstein, 1985, Options markets (Prentice-Hall, Englewood Cliffs).

Cross, F., 1973, The behavior of stock prices on Fridays and Mondays, Financial Analysts Journal 29, 67-9.

De Bondt, W.F.M. and R.H. Thaler, 1985, Does the stock market overreact?, Journal of Finance, 793-805.

De Bondt, W.F.M. and R.H. Thaler, 1987, Further evidence on investor overreaction and stock market seasonality, The Journal of Finance 42, 557-581.

Fama, E.F., 1970, Efficient capital markets: A review of theory and empirical work, Journal of Finance 25, 383-417.

Fama, E.F., 1976, Foundations of finance (Basic Books, New York).

Fama, E.F., L. Fisher, M.C. Jensen and R. Roll, 1969, The adjustment of stock prices to new information, International Economic Review 10, 1-21.

Fama, E.F. and K.R. French, Permanent and temporary components of stock prices, 1988, Journal of Political Economy 96, 246-273.

Fama, E.F., and M.H. Miller, 1972, The theory of finance (Holt, Rinehart and Winston, New York).

Foster, G., 1981, Intra-industry information transfers associated with earnings releases, Journal of Accounting and Economics 3, 201-232.

Foster, G. C. Olsen and T. Shevlin, 1984, Earnings releases, anomalies, and the behavior of securities returns, Accounting Review 59, 574-603.

Friedman, M., 1952, The methodology of positive economics, in: Essays in Positive Economics (University of Chicago Press, Chicago).

Friedman, M. and L.J. Savage, 1948, The utility analysis of choices involving risk, Journal of Political Economy 56, reprinted in: Readings in price theory, American Economic Association (Richard D. Irwin, Inc., 1952, Chicago) 57-96.

Grossman, S.J., 1976, On the efficiency of competitive stock markets where traders have diverse information, Journal of Finance 31, 573-585.

Grossman, S.J., and J.E. Stiglitz, 1980, On the impossibility of informationally efficient markets, American Economic Review 70, 393-408.

Jensen, M.C., 1978, Some anomalous evidence regarding market efficiency, Journal of Financial Economics 6, 95-101.

Jordan, J.S., 1983, On the efficient markets hypothesis, Econometrica 51, 1325-43.

Kuhn, T.S., 1970, The structure of scientific revolutions (The University of Chicago Press, Chicago).

Latham, M., 1986, Information efficiency and information subsets, Journal of Finance 41, 39-52.

Le Roy, S., 1976, Efficient capital markets: A comment, Journal of Finance 31, 139-141.

Lintner, J., The valuation of risk assets and the selection of risky investments in stock portfolios and capital budgets, Review of Economics and Statistics 47, 13-37.

Miller, M.H., and F. Modigliani, 1961, Dividend policy, growth and the valuation of shares, Journal of Business 34, 411-433.

Roberts, H.V., 1959, Stock market 'patterns' and financial analysis: Methodological suggestions, Journal of Finance 14, 1-10.

Rogalski, R., 1984, New findings regarding day of the week returns over trading and non-trading periods: a note, Journal of Finance 39, 1603-1614.

Roll, R., 1977, A critique of the asset pricing theory's tests; Part 1: On past and potential testability of the theory, Journal of Financial Economics 4, 129-176.

Roll, R., 1978, Ambiguity when performance is measured by the security market line, Journal of Finance 33, 1051-1069.

Rubinstein, M., 1975, Securities market efficiency in an Arrow-Debreu economy, American Economic Review 65, 812-824.

Samuelson, P.A., 1965, Proof that properly anticipated prices fluctuate randomly, Industrial Management Review 6, 41-49.

Schipper, K., and R. Thompson, 1983, Evidence on the capitalized value of merger activity for acquiring firms, Journal of Financial Economics 11, 85-119.

Sharpe, W.F., 1964, Capital asset prices: A theory of market equilibrium under conditions of risk, Journal of Finance 19, 425-442.

Shiller, R.J., 1981a, The use of volatility measures in assessing market efficiency, Journal of Finance 36, 291-304.

Shiller, R.J., 1981b, Do stock prices move too much to be justified by subsequent changes in dividends?, American Economic Review 71, 421-436.

Smith, C., 1986, Investment banking and the capital acquisition process, Journal of Financial Economics 15, 1/2, 3-29.

Stiglitz, J.E., 1981, The allocation role of the stock market: Pareto optimality and competition, Journal of Finance, 235-51.

Watts, R. and J. Zimmerman, 1983, Agency problems, auditing and the theory of the firm: Some evidence, Journal of Law and Economics 26, 613-634.

STOCK PRICE REVERSALS AND OVERREACTION TO NEWS EVENTS: A SURVEY OF THEORY AND EVIDENCE

Werner F.M. De Bondt*
Graduate School of Business
University of Wisconsin-Madison
1155 Observatory Drive
Madison, Wisconsin 53706
U.S.A.

KEYWORDS: Bayesian Decision-Making, Heuristics, Noise Trading, Overreaction, Rational Arbitrage, Stock Price Reversals, Time-varying Risk Premia

ABSTRACT: Stock price reversals may be due to short-term overreactions to news, waves of unjustified optimism or pessimism about future earnings, fear and normatively "excessive" risk premia, or other causes. This paper reviews [1] the psychological literature on Bayesian decision-making and intuitive prediction; [2] the arguments that overreaction by individuals is likely to matter at the market level; [3] the evidence on short-term and long-term price reversals. The research findings are compared with the predictions of standard theories of asset pricing and market efficiency.

*I thank Ray Ball, Mary Bange, A. De Ridder, Richard Thaler and seminar participants at the University of Minnesota for helpful comments. Some of the research for this paper was done while I completed my Ph.D. dissertation at Cornell University. Financial support from the C.I.M. Doctoral Fellowship Program (Brussels, Belgium) and from the Graduate School of Business at the University of Wisconsin-Madison (Summer 1987) is gratefully acknowledged.

NATO ASI Series, Vol. F54
A Reappraisal of the Efficiency of Financial Markets
Edited by Rui M. C. Guimaraes et al.

1. INTRODUCTION

Over recent years, our understanding of stock valuation has been greatly influenced by three related developments: [i] the continuing failure of standard frameworks such as the Capital Asset Pricing Model (CAPM), the Consumption Capital Asset Pricing Model, or the Arbitrage Pricing Theory to account for actual stock price movements in a way that is credible and non-tautological; [ii] the emergence of a large "anomaly" literature; and [iii] the re-opening of the "efficient markets debate" with the work on excess volatility, the apparent predictability of two-to-five year returns, and short-term stock price reversals.

All three empirical developments have created a new urgency for the finance profession to come up with better theories of asset valuation. Of course, with respect to standard valuation models, it may reasonably be argued that "market efficiency imposes few restrictions on the behavior of expected returns" (Fama and French [1986, p. 2]) and that, as a consequence, time-varying risk premia may still account for the evidence. Also, the rational agent perfect-market model may be salvaged by introducing information costs and other institutional complexities (Merton [1986]). However, it appears that the more innovative work in the area now focuses on the implications for asset pricing of the presence of non-rational behavioral "noise" traders (see e.g., Campbell and Kyle [1986], Shefrin and Statman [1986], and DeLong, Shleifer, Summers and Waldman [1987]).

The purpose of this paper is to review and re-evaluate the theoretical basis and the empirical evidence relating to a simple behavioral model first suggested by myself and Thaler [1985]. There it is argued that stock prices behave as if the representative agent systematically "overreacts" to new information, particularly as it relates to earnings. The empirical work uses the magnitudes of initial price run-ups or price declines, adjusted for risk, as proxy variables to measure "excessive" market optimism or pessimism. Consistent with overreaction bias and the profitability of contrarian investment strategies, De Bondt and Thaler report predictable long-term stock price reversals for prior (extreme) stock market "winners" and "losers." While investor overreaction easily agrees with our intuition, the cognitive psychological micro-foundations of the theory largely consist of experimental work by Kahneman and Tversky on heuristics and biases, intuitive prediction, and Bayesian updating.

The paper starts in section 2 with a brief review of the psychological evidence on overreaction bias in intuitive judgment. Section 3 discusses the economic question as to whether we should expect overreaction behavior by individual investors to affect prices in financial markets. Section 4 reviews the empirical evidence relating to stock price reversals, both short-term and long-term. Because of space limitations, I do not attempt to summarize either the empirical asset pricing anomaly literature or the work on speculative bubbles and volatility tests (see Keim [1986], Reinganum [1987], Camerer [1987] and West [1987] for useful reviews). Section 5 concludes the paper with a discussion of the implications of price reversals and overreaction for modern finance.

2. DO INDIVIDUAL INVESTORS OVERREACT?

According to the overreaction hypothesis, asset prices overrespond to new information. Obviously, the hypothesis stands or falls with the evidence on the relative sophistication of man as an intuitive statistician.[1] In view of the enormity of the literature on intuitive judgmental processes and heuristics and biases, I focus here on recent research that I think to be most relevant to business and financial decision-making. For more general surveys, I refer the reader to Nisbett and Ross [1980], Hogarth [1981], Kahneman, Slovic and Tversky [1982] and Bazerman [1986]. A broad discussion of the relevance of aggregate psychological variables to financial markets appears in Adler and Adler [1984] and Schachter, Hood, Andreassen and Gerin [1986]. An even broader discussion of the relevance of psychology to economics is found in Hogarth and Reder [1987].

Much of the psychological research on intuitive prediction has produced quite discouraging results. For example, simple regression models, which capture a subject's weighting policy for major predictor variables and which apply it consistently, lead to better predictions than the subject himself. This "bootstrapping" phenomenon, which applies to experts as well as amateurs, builds on the fact that any misconception that the subject has is less detrimental to performance than his inconsistency in applying the decision rule (Dawes [1979]). Contrary to the intuition of most economists, outcome feedback does not necessarily enhance prediction accuracy (see e.g., Brehmer and Kuylenstierna [1978]). The reason is that feedback often induces

---

[1] In this section, I interpret overreaction strictly in the sense of De Bondt and Thaler [1985, 1987], i.e., "overreaction-to-earnings" and systematic bias in investors' expectations of future cash flows. However, overreaction behavior and nonrational subsequent price reversals may also occur, [1], if investors are vulnerable to fashions-and-fads or market momentum unrelated to earnings, or [2], if investors violate the axioms underlying expected utility theory in ways that make their decisions (as in prospect theory) overly sensitive to low probability events, in effect requiring normatively "excessive" risk premia. See section 4.C.

response inconsistency. Neither does it appear that prediction accuracy always improves with experience, incentives, or the amount of available information. Subjects with "expertise" are less likely than amateurs to admit to (or perhaps to understand) their use of heuristics (Northcraft and Neale [1987]). Experts further tend to falsely believe that they can beat decision rules which are known to yield the correct decision in a large proportion of cases. In addition, highly motivated subjects easily grow impatient. They find it difficult to tolerate errors without resorting to a strategy shift (Arkes, Dawes and Christensen [1987]). Finally, the primary effect of extra information is often to make the subjects feel more confident, without clearly improving the quality of their judgment (Oskamp [1965]).

Experiments conducted by Kahneman and Tversky, Grether [1980] and others demonstrate that man can hardly be viewed as a Bayesian decision-maker (for a long list of references, see Kahneman, Slovic and Tversky [1982]). It appears that, contrary to Bayes' Rule, when revising beliefs, subjects systematically overweight singular information about the specific case at hand and underweight distributional or base-rate information. People take, so-to-speak, an "internal" approach to intuitive prediction. Their acquaintance with the problem, their emotional involvement, the immediate availability in memory of numerous vivid details -- all these factors lead people to generate predictions according to a simple matching rule: "the predicted value is selected so that the standing of the case in the distribution of outcomes matches its standing in the distribution of impressions" (Kahneman and Tversky [1982], p. 416). This rule-of-thumb, an instance of the "representativeness" heuristic, violates a basic statistical principle, namely, that the extremeness of predictions must be moderated by considerations of predictability.

Consistent with representativeness and a tendency to ignore base rate information, people have little appreciation of the statistical principle summarized in the "law of large numbers." The willingness of the layperson to make strong inferences based on small amounts of data leads Tversky and Kahneman [1971] to argue that people act as if the law of large numbers also applies to small numbers. Gilovich, Vallone and Tversky [1985] illustrate how common misconceptions of the laws of chance, explained by representativeness, underlie "the hot hand" fallacy in basketball.

In the context of accounting and finance, some of the most detailed work on intuitive prediction and time series extrapolation has been done by Eggleton [1976, 1982] (see Slovic [1972] and Hogarth [1975] for a review of older studies). He reports how subjects "impute a lawfulness to random series" ([1982], p. 90). Again, the "compulsive structuring" of random walk data is attributed to the representativeness heuristic. In a similar vein, Andreassen and Kraus [1987] and Andreassen [forthcoming] show how the "salience of change" influences investors' tendency to discover trends in stock prices. Depending on whether subjects focus on price levels or on changes in levels, their predictions are regressive or extrapolative.

In a different set of experiments, Andreassen [1986, 1987] also suggests that subjects' beliefs as to whether security price changes will persist or regress to previous levels may depend on whether causal attributions are provided to explain recent changes. If such attributions are provided, then any tendency to make regressive predictions (as, e.g., in the case of the gambler's fallacy) is diminished and subjects become more likely to project recent changes into the future. Andreassen argues that the news media provide causal attributions and that we can expect the news accounts to be selective. For example, to present a coherent explanation of a market rise, newspeople are prone to report good news: searching for those stories from the many available that support a rise, and ignoring those that do not. Thus, the argument goes, the media may encourage trading by leading investors to extrapolate recent events into the future.

Further time-series experiments conducted by Schmalensee [1976] reveal undue optimistic bias and overconfidence. Unrealistic optimism about future life events is also reported by Weinstein [1980]. People rate their own chances to be above average for positive events (e.g., the chances that the value of their home doubles in five years) and below average for negative events. The bias increases with the perceived controllability of the outcome (see also Langer [1975]). Both motivational and cognitive factors are to blame. Consistent with representativeness, Weinstein emphasizes people's tendency to focus on their own circumstances and their failure to adopt the perspective of others.

It may be thought that, in view of the fallibility of human judgment, people would exhibit appropriate caution concerning their judgmental abilities. However, many studies show this is false. Subjects are prone to experience confidence in highly fallible judgments, a phenomenon that Einhorn and Hogarth [1978] refer to as the "illusion of validity." The contradiction between the problem solver's self-confidence and his poor performance raises new questions with respect to the link between learning and experience.

Numerous factors restrict our ability to learn and I will only mention a few. It is well-known that prior expectations of relationships can lead to faulty observation and inference, or "illusory correlation" (Chapman and Chapman [1967]). Because of hindsight bias, outcomes often fail to surprise people as much as they should (Fischoff [1975]). People also tend to attribute success to skill and failure to chance.

In decision problems involving both skill and chance, e.g., the selection of securities for superior short-term performance, they feel inappropriately confident and the task structure induces an "illusion of control" (Langer [1975]). Finally, there are "outcome irrelevant learning structures" which reinforce poor heuristic decision rules with positive outcome-feedback. As a consequence, the validity of the rules is not questioned (Einhorn [1980]).

3. SHOULD WE EXPECT FINANCIAL MARKETS TO OVERREACT?

If we accept the notion that many investors have a propensity to overweigh dramatic, unanticipated news events, then the theoretical question arises whether, as financial economists, we should worry about it. Even though economic analysis is frequently applied in non-market settings (see e.g., Becker [1976]), finance consists for the most part of the theory of (perfect) financial markets. Grether [1980] raises a familiar point when he states that, perhaps, "the repetitive nature of market interactions, together with the reinforcement provided by the profit system .. render single observations on individual behavior irrelevant" or "..a relatively few individuals sensitive to arbitrage may make markets work as predicted.." ([1980], p. 555).[2]

One way to rephrase the issue is to ask for the minimal set of restrictions on heterogeneous beliefs and information sets that, even in frictionless markets, remains necessary to allow for the existence of rational, arbitrage-free equilibrium prices. The analysis of Jarrow [1983] indicates that two conditions are necessary. First, in an economy where a generic asset z is identified by an exogenous cash flow z(w) which depends on the state of the world w, all investors must always be in agreement on the value implications of any conceivable state. That is, while they may have different viewpoints on the likelihood of a particular event, they agree on $z: \Omega \rightarrow R$. Secondly, all investors must agree on relevant zero-probability events.

Since Bayesian and non-Bayesian investors are thought to form different opinions on the basis of the same substantive information, overreaction models consider economies where these minimal requirements are not met. However, as pointed out by Russell and Thaler [1985], rational prices may still prevail if it is

[2]Camerer [1987] addresses the issue of whether bias in probability judgment matters in experimental markets. His experimental design is based on procedures laid out by Grether [1980]. Camerer finds that prices and asset holding patterns tend toward Bayesian predictions, even though there is evidence of bias caused by (exact) "representativeness." He rejects a number of competing hypotheses, including overreaction.

assumed that [1], at some future time, the true mapping is revealed to all, i.e., both rational and non-rational investors, and [2], that, in the meantime, only rational investors go short. But, clearly, neither of these assumptions applies in any obvious way to the stock market.

Institutional factors -- such as short-sales constraints, capital gains taxes and transaction costs -- are likely to change the situation for the worse, rather than for the better. In a world with non-trivial trading costs and heteogeneous beliefs, every individual not only chooses the size of his holdings in each asset, but also in which assets to invest. Equilibrium involves the simultaneous determination of asset prices and the identity of the investors trading in each asset (Mayshar [1983]). Some agents never reveal their private information via trade, except by abstaining. As a consequence, market prices cannot reflect it. In general, prices depend in a complex manner on the structure of trading costs and beliefs across investors. Full information efficient prices, however, ought to be independent of the distribution of private information among investors. Under specific circumstances, it may even happen that only the information held by "marginal" investors matters. Miller [1977] presents a model in which the traders who are most optimistic about a company's prospects determine its market value. In other words, stocks appear to be systematically "overpriced."

As argued before, a pure arbitrage opportunity simply does not exist unless it is certain that share prices will eventually revert to their "fundamental" underlying value. However, apart from institutional impediments, there are further economic reasons to doubt that rational arbitrageurs prevail in markets and thereby guarantee full information efficiency.

First, as investors with superior forecasting ability or inside information purchase (sell) undervalued (overvalued) stock, they assume increasing amounts of diversifiable risk, since their portfolios become more and more unbalanced.

Second, as was pointed out by Keynes long ago, it may be rational strategy for traders with superior competence to ride on the trend rather than to go against it. Harrison and Kreps [1978] present a model where, in the presence of short-sales restrictions, some investors rationally bid up the price of a stock in anticipation of the opportunity for selling it at a higher price than they themselves think it is worth. It then follows that, if a self-fulfilling equilibrium is to be found, the price must exceed what any investor is willing to pay for the asset if obliged to hold it forever. DeLong, Shleifer, Summers and Waldman [1987] present a simple overlapping generations model with two assets (a riskless asset and a risky asset) and with two types of two-period lived investors: sophisticated traders and noise traders. Both types of agents maximize expected utility but noise traders misperceive the price of the risky asset in the second period. It turns out that noise traders (i) affect prices so that they become more volatile than can be justified on the basis of the underlying fundamentals; (ii) earn higher returns than rational investors; and (iii) create additional risk and, thereby, higher expected returns. The reason for (iii) is that sophisticated investors dislike bearing the risk that noise traders may be irrationally pessimistic in the future.

Third, it is well-known that the market may rationally launch itself onto a speculative bubble with prices being driven by an arbitrary self-confirming element in expectations (see e.g., Tirole [1982] or Cass and Shell [1983]). But there is nothing that rational arbitrage can do to prevent such bubbles. In fact, there is no choice-theoretic rationale for singling out equilibrium price paths that do not suffer from this "extrinsic" uncertainty.

Of course, irrespective of any arbitrage argument, we may still hope that the non-rational investors will somehow "learn" over time. This is essentially a psychological, not an economic, argument and it is contradicted by the evidence reviewed in Section 2. Its importance is further tempered by the observation that -- since the market is composed of successive generations of participants -- there is a continual in-flow of "inexperienced" and out-flow of "experienced" traders.

A final non-arbitrage rationale for efficient markets is a Darwinian weeding-out process by which, over time, wealth is gradually redistributed from investors with poor forecasting ability to those with superior information or competence. Figlewski [1978, 1982] shows, however, that neither in the short nor in the long run does such a process lead to full information efficiency.

I conclude that there are few if any convincing theoretical reasons to expect that either the competitive process or rational arbitrage can correct market prices for the persistent overreaction of non-Bayesian investors to dramatic news events.

4. DOES THE STOCK MARKET OVERREACT?

Evidently, the "overreaction hypothesis" does not represent an entirely new idea. In *The General Theory*, Keynes argued that "day-to-day fluctuations in the profits of existing investments, which are obviously of an ephemeral and non-significant character, tend to have an altogether excessive, and even an absurd, influence on the market" ([1936], pp. 153-154). Williams notes in his *Theory of Investment Value* that "prices have been based too much on current earning power, too little on long-run dividend paying power" ([1938], p.19). Similar arguments may also be found in, e.g., Taussig [1921], Macaulay [1938] and Graham and Dodd [1951].

More recent empirical findings with respect to the price-earnings ratio (P/E) anomaly also suggest stock market overreaction. It appears that stocks with comparatively low P/E-ratios -- or, equivalently, high earnings yields (E/Ps) -- earn larger CAPM risk-adjusted returns than high P/E stocks.[3] The so-called "price-ratio hypothesis" motivates the work of Basu [1977]. Companies with high (low) P/Es are thought to be temporarily overvalued (undervalued) because the market gets inappropriately optimistic (pessimistic) about current or future earnings. Eventually, however, actual earnings growth differs predictably from the growth rate impounded in the price. Price corrections and the P/E anomaly follow inevitably. Also consistent with the hypothesis, earnings yields affect the association between annual income numbers and share prices (Basu [1978]). During the twelve months that lead up to the announcement date, unanticipated increases (decreases) in earnings cause larger positive (negative) residual returns to securities with low (high) P/Es that to securities with high (low) P/Es.

Alternatively, the P/E-effect may follow from misspecification of the CAPM (Reinganum [1981]). Ball [1978] emphasizes possibly omitted risk factors. If price-earnings ratios are correlated with the omitted variables, then their tendency to proxy for these variables permits P/Es to "explain" differences in securities' rates of return which are not predicted by the simple CAPM. In particular, Reinganum [1981] claims that the small firm effect (for a review, see Schwert [1983]) subsumes the P/E-anomaly and that both are related to the same set of missing factors. However, papers by Basu [1983] and Cook and Rozeff [1984] show a significant P/E-effect even after controlling for firm size. Both effects appear to have strong January components.

If stock prices systematically overshoot, then, (i), their reversal should be predictable from past return data alone. Also, (ii), the more prices are initially out of line, the stronger they should bounce back later on. The moving force is not so much rational learning, or rational arbitrage, as it is extreme expectations later refuted by economic reality. Finally, (iii), the shorter the duration of the initial price move-

---

[3]A related phenomenon is the "dividend-yield" effect. Fama and French [1987] study nominal and real returns on equal- and value-weighted portfolios of all NYSE stocks between 1927 and 1986. Dividend yields often explain more than 25 percent of the variances of 2- to 4-year returns.

ment, the stronger the subsequent price response (per unit of time). Brown and Harlow [1988] refer to (i), (ii) and (iii) as, respectively, the "directional", the "magnitude," and the "intensity" effects. All three hypotheses imply return forecastability and specific violations of weak form market efficiency. The directional and magnitude effects follow from any divergence between market and fundamental values that is eliminated beyond some limit. The intensity effect bears on the economic importance of rational risk arbitrage. If these forces are at work, then non-rational price movements that are concentrated in time -- presumably, in immediate response to specific news events -- should, on average, "be corrected sooner and more fully."

Prior to 1985, there were, at best, only a few hints in the empirical finance literature that foreshadowed the price reversals that have been documented since. In spite of a large body of research on excess return volatility, the possible logical link between the violation of variance bounds tests, stock price reversals, and overreaction was left unexplored (see, however, Campbell and Shiller [1987]). Shiller's [1984] survey article is an exception. Among other evidence (including, e.g., the P/E-effect), Shiller presents regression tests, based on annual data, showing that aggregate real stock prices appear to overreact to real dividends and to real earnings. He also argues -- as does Summers [1986] -- that standard random walk and "event study" tests of market efficiency have little power against "fashions and fads"-type alternative hypotheses.

Simulation evidence presented by Poterba and Summers [1987] indicates that recent variance ratio, regression, and likelihood ratio tests checking for transitory components in stock prices (e.g., Fama and French [1988], French and Roll [1986], Lo and McKinlay [1987], Poterba and Summers [1987]) also have limited power, even with data spanning a sixty-year period. Papers that specifically address overreaction have often dealt with this issue by focusing, for selected stocks, on brief episodes of extreme price gains or losses that, presumably, are associated with the release of firm-specific information. Thus, relatively "calm" periods -- during which any given company's share price tends to move in ways that are suggested by standard valuation models -- are not considered and do not dilute the power of the tests. In addition, the use of residual returns controls for market-wide news and underlying risk factors.

Most tests are based on variants of the following procedure: (1) find (residual and/or cumulative residual) returns for every individual stock in a given population over an initial "formation" period; (2) rank the stocks by the (cumulative residual) return earned over the formation period and form portfolios of winners and losers; (3)

test for average (cumulative residual) return differences between the winner and loser portfolios during a "test period" that follows upon the formation period.

Stock price reversals have been observed over varying time periods ranging between one day to two-to-five year returns. Below, I review the empirical literature classifying papers somewhat arbitrarily as documenting either short-term or long-term price reversals. In order to avoid lengthy reviews of the exact methods used in each study, I only report results that appear robust to obvious manipulations in the testing procedures.

A. Short-Term Price Reversals

Dyl and Maxfield [1987] select at random 200 trading days between January 1974 and January 1984. Each day, they choose the three NYSE or AMEX stocks with the largest percentage price gain (on average, 16.3 percent) or loss (on average, -12.2 percent). On average, over the next 10 trading days, prior winners (losers) earn CAPM risk-adjusted excess returns of -1.8 (3.6) percent.

Brown, Harlow and Tinic [1988] consider all one-day (market model) residual returns above 2.5 or below -2.5 percent for the 200 largest firms in the S&P 500 index. The sample period runs between July 1963 and December 1985 and, in total, there are 4,806 positive and 4,319 negative events. On average, over the next 10 trading days, prior winners earn (insignificant) CAPM risk-adjusted excess returns of 3 basis points (t-statistic: 0.18); prior losers earn about 37 basis points (t-statistic: 7.63).

Bremer and Sweeney [1988] study all Fortune 500 and S&P 500 companies with one-day returns below -10.0 (-7.5; -15.0) or above 10.0 percent. For the period between July 1962 and December 1986, there are 1,305 price declines of this magnitude and 3,218 increases. Five trading days after the price "jump," the cumulative average excess return (CAER) for losers -- with excess returns, for each individual stock, computed relative to the average return of the stock over the sample period -- equals an extraordinary 3.95 (2.84; 6.18) percent. On the other hand, for winners, CAER is (statistically) significant but (economically) irrelevant at minus 4/10 of one basis point (t-statistic: -9.82).

Concerned with stock return volatility during trading and non-trading hours, French and Roll [1986] test, among other hypotheses, whether the process of trading introduces noise into stock returns, as if "investors overreact to each other's trades"

(p. 6).[4] French and Roll's first test is based on daily autocorrelations in returns for all NYSE and AMEX stocks between January 1963 and December 1982. If pricing errors are corrected over time, negative autocorrelations are expected. Secondly, French and Roll compare daily return variances with variances for longer holding periods. If daily returns are affected by noise trading, the longer holding period variance should be less than the cumulated daily variances within the period (i.e., the "implied variance"). The findings are generally consistent with the "noise trading hypothesis." For at least 10 trading days, small but significantly negative autocorrelations in returns persist. After six months, the average actual-to-implied variance ratio for all stocks in the population (for the smallest quintile) equals 0.88 (0.73). These results imply that, on average, between 4 to 12 percent (5 to 27 percent) of the daily return variance is caused by mispricing.

The previous studies -- all based on daily return data -- are vulnerable to the critique that, even in efficient markets, thin trading and price movements between the bid and asked prices may give the appearance of negative serial correlation in returns. Howe [1986] therefore examines the weekly return patterns of NYSE and AMEX stocks that rise or fall more than 50 percent within one week. For the period between 1963 and 1981, the good news and bad news samples comprise, respectively, 385 and 131 observations. During the ten weeks that follow the initial price change, prior winners underperform the market by 13 percent. Prior losers outperform the market by 13.8 percent. Most of the reversal occurs early on. For example, one week after the portfolios are formed, the winners (losers) lag (lead) the market by 7.7 (10.2) percent.

Lehmann [1988] also works with weekly returns. He studies the profitability of a return reversal strategy which finances its purchases of short-term losers (the stocks that underperformed the market over the previous week) by selling winners short (the stocks that outperformed the market). Lehmann's research does not focus on extreme performers. For the 1962-1986 period, almost all securities listed on the NYSE and AMEX are considered. However, the dollar amount invested in each

---

[4]Ohlson and Penman [1985] are also concerned with return volatility. They find a perplexingly robust average increase of about 30 percent in the return standard deviation of NYSE and AMEX stocks following the ex-dates of stock splits. It appears to these authors that "the concept of an informationally efficient market .. is obviously inconsistent with an essentially "arbitrary" increase in return variances" ([1985], p. 264). Forced to look for "folklore explanations," Ohlson and Penman suggest that "..overreaction to information is more likely to occur for relatively low-priced (per share) stocks.." ([1985], p. 265).

security is proportional to its (absolute) weekly excess return, i.e., extreme performers carry more weight in the arbitrage portfolio. Typically, there are more than 2,000 round trip transactions per week, generating weekly volume of about three dollars per dollar long in the portfolio.

The strategy is extraordinarily successful. Net of 10 basis points one-way costs per dollar transacted, portfolios which are long $100 million of losers and short $100 million of winners earn average six-month profits of $38.77 million, with about 2/3 of the profit generated by the losers. The winners have negative returns only in the week subsequent to portfolio formation. However, since their returns are strongly negatively correlated with the returns on the losers, the profits of the arbitrage portfolio are positive for about nine out of every ten weeks. Consistent with the magnitude effect, the winners and losers that gained or lost the most experience the largest reversals.

For various periods starting in May of 1973, Rosenberg and Rudd [1982] and Rosenberg, Reid and Lanstein [1985] report on a one-month "specific return reversal" strategy purchasing an equal-weighted portfolio of stocks whose previous month's specific returns (found relative to a multifactor model) were negative and selling short a portfolio whose previous month's specific returns were positive. Between January 1981 and October 1984, the strategy earns on average 136 basis points per month, with most of it coming from prior losers. The exclusion of stocks with (extreme) prior monthly residual returns below -10 or above +10 percent reduces the profit to 105 basis points.

Jegadeesh [1987] presents regression evidence for NYSE stocks indicating that, between 1945 and 1980, Sharpe-Lintner residual returns for any given month are negatively related to raw returns for the previous month and, reflecting seasonality, positively related to returns for the same month one, two and three years earlier. When decile portfolios are formed on the basis of "one-month-ahead" forecasts of excess returns, the average difference between the risk-adjusted excess returns on the extreme portfolios is about 2.5 percent per month (6.0 percent in January). Adding a size-variable -- measured as the natural logarithm of the market value of equity at the end of the previous month -- to the equation leaves the results largely unchanged. For January excess returns, the size-coefficient is significantly negative; otherwise, it is insignificant.

Brown and Harlow [forthcoming] study the returns of securities with an initial abnormal performance adding up to between 20 (-20) and 65 (-65) percent over periods that range between one to six months. They consider all stocks trading on the NYSE between January 1946 and December 1983. For "negative events," the evidence is consistent with the directional, magnitude and intensity effects. For example, in the first month (month +1) following a 60 to 65 percent price drop, the average price rebound is 6.2 percent. It is only 48 basis points for an initial fall between 20 and 25 percent. Also, for the combined samples of all negative events (i.e., excess returns between -20 and -65 percent) that occurred within one month, the average residual for the following month is 2.7 percent. But, for the same range of negative excess returns, the average rebound is 56 basis points if the initial drop occurred over a six-month period.

For "positive events," the test period excess returns are negative in month +1. However, in agreement with the asymmetry reported by other studies, the price correlation is smaller (in absolute terms) than for losers. It further appears that the magnitude of the price drop is not significantly related either to the amount of the initial rise or to the length of the period over which it occurred. Brown and Harlow document a second asymmetry, relating to the long-term price response to positive and negative events. There is, on average, a further 56 (31) percent price decline between months +2 and +36 of the test period for "prior losers" that already fell between 60 and 65 percent in value over one (six) month(s). This observation, suggesting inertia (rather than overreaction), does not apply to winners.[5]

B. Long-Term Price Reversals

De Bondt and Thaler [1985] study the relative test period performance of (35 stock, 50 stock or decile portfolios) of "long-term" winners and losers. They use monthly return data for NYSE stocks between December 1925 and December 1982. Initial performance is measured over formation periods ranging between one and five years. Typically, the formation periods start in January and end in December. Even though there are always significant differences in the January excess returns of the extreme portfolios, the price reversals become much more pronounced as the formation period lengthens beyond two years. In that case, an "arbitrage" strategy

[5]Further evidence of inertia or underreaction to news events is suggested, among other studies, by the work of Rendleman, Jones and Latane [1982]. After controlling for CAPM-risk, roughly half of the adjustment of stock returns to unexpected quarterly earnings occurs over a 90-day period after earnings are announced. Lo and MacKinlay [1987] and Poterba and Summers [1987] also report positive serial correlation in stock returns over short intervals. Positive autocorrelation is consistent with stock prices slowly gravitating towards their underlying intrinsic values, as well as with "inertia."

that buys losers by selling winners short earns average annual returns ranging between 5 and 8 percent, with most the returns occurring in (the successive months of) January.[6] Vermaelen and Verstringe [1986] and Dark and Kato [1986] both use De Bondt and Thaler's [1985] empirical methods to document overreaction on the Belgian and Japanese stock markets, respectively. For the period between 1964 and 1980, Dark and Kato find that the three-year returns for decile portfolios of extreme prior losers exceed the comparable returns of extreme prior winners by, on average, 69.7 percent (t-statistic: 4.6).

In the U.S. market, Fama and French [1988] also observe long-horizon price reversals which they interpret as being consistent with temporary disparities between market prices and fundamental values, as well as with time-varying equilibrium expected returns. Fama and French test whether (the natural logarithm) of stock price P(t), p(t) = lnP(t), moves through time as if the permanent change from each news shock is less than one. For example, let p(t) = q(t) + z(t), where the "permanent" component q(t) follows a random walk process with drift μ, q(t) = q(t-1) + μ + u(t), and where the "temporary" component z(t) follows an AR(1) process, z(t) = ϕz(t-1) + e(t). Also, let b(T) be the slope of a regression of r(t,t+T) on r(t-T,t), where r(t,t+T) equals [lnP(t+T)-lnP(t)]. In that case, if changes in the random walk and the stationary component are uncorrelated, b(T) measures the proportion of the variance of T-period returns that is explained by the mean reversion of the decaying price component z(t). If prices do not have a random walk component, then, for large T, b(T) tends toward -1/2. If prices move as hypothesized, then, for large T, the variance of the random walk component eventually dominates. As a result, b(T) is

[6]Chan [1987], Jones [1987] and Zarowin [1988] computationally replicate De Bondt and Thaler's [1985] results for three-year formation periods. Chan [1987], De Bondt [1985], De Bondt and Thaler [1987], Fama and French [1986], Jones [1987], and Zarowin [1988] check the findings' robustness. All studies use virtually identical empirical methods. Even though the debate is not closed as yet, it appears that [1] the results do not greatly change depending on whether the residual returns are defined as size-adjusted excess returns, market-adjusted excess returns, market model residuals, or Sharpe-Lintner residuals; [2] the results do not depend on the different methods that can be used to estimates CAPM-betas (see, however, Chan [1987]); [3] the results do not depend on whether December or any other month is the last month of the formation period; [4] the excess returns earned by the extreme portfolios are not explained by unusual attrition (say, because of merger or bankruptcy) during the test period; [5] the extreme portfolios do not contain unusually small firms; [6] the extreme portfolios do not systematically differ through time in terms of average dividend yield, size, or financial leverage.

negative but close to zero for small T, close to -1/2 for intermediate T, and negative but close to zero for large T.

Fama and French study monthly returns between 1926 and 1985 for two market indices, 17 industry portfolios, and decile portfolios of NYSE-listed companies ranked on the basis of market value of equity. The regression slopes are significantly negative when T varies between 3- and 5 years; the slopes suggest that between 25 to 45 percent of the variation in returns over a 3- to 5 year horizon is predictable. However, the stationary component is largely captured by one common factor: the return process of small companies' stocks. Fama and French also find little evidence of firm-specific stationary components, an observation which is "heartening for proponents of parsimonious equilibrium pricing models" ([1987], p. 19).

Poterba and Summers [1987] confirm Fama and French's findings. They apply variance ratio tests to the 82 firms on the CRSP monthly return files that have no missing data between 1926 and 1985, to market returns for the U.S. over the 1871-1985 period, and to market indices for 17 other countries over the 1957-1986 period. Poterba and Summers consistently find evidence that stock returns are positively autocorrelated over short horizons (see also Lo and MacKinlay [1987]) and negatively autocorrelated over long horizons. The results suggest that transitory components in stock prices account for more than half of the variance in monthly returns.

C. Explaining Price Reversals: Where Are We?

Fama and French [1988] and Poterba and Summers [1987] do not explicitly discuss the extent to which their findings are influenced by the unusual behavior of the stock market in January. However, the price reversals of extreme winners and losers largely occur in that month and they continue as late as five Januaries after portfolio formation (De Bondt and Thaler [1987]; Fama and French [1986]). The most obvious interpretation of the January seasonal for losers is that it reflects the size-anomaly. But losers are not unusually small firms (De Bondt and Thaler [1987]) and there is a January winner-loser effect, even after experimental control is exercised over firm size (Fama and French [1986]; Zarowin [1987]). One possible reason for the January seasonal involves tax-motivated portfolio rebalancing behavior. Numerous empirical papers suggest short-term tax-loss selling pressure for losers (see, e.g., Reinganum [1983]) and a capital gains tax "lock-in" effect for winners.[7] While rational tax trading predicts a relation between January returns and short-term losses (but no link with long-term losses), Chan [1986], Jones [1987] and De Bondt and Thaler [1987] all observe how the January reversals are driven in large part by prior long-term performance (see also Branch and Chang [1987]). These findings are consistent with overreaction but they may also follow from (non-rational) tax-loss selling explained by investor reluctance to realize losses (Shefrin and Statman [1985]).

The price reversals and the winner-loser effect are often interpreted as evidence of rationally time-varying expected returns. Factor risk premia may contain a January seasonal (Rogalski and Tinic [1985]) and/or they may vary with certain business cycle variables (see, e.g., Keim and Stambaugh [1986]). Also, the relevant factor loadings could be changing, e.g., when stock prices decline, debt-equity ratios increase, leading to an increase in CAPM-betas (Vermaelen and Verstringe [1986]; Chan [1987]).[8]

While these arguments have a solid theoretical basis and are hard to refute empirically, I doubt their economic significance with respect to most of the studies reviewed above. In particular, the changing-risk argument seems totally incapable of explaining price reversals that occur within a few days or weeks unless the "risk premia" are redefined to reflect flimsy return perceptions and (rationally) unjustified hope and fear. For example, on the assumption that the market risk premium equals 10 percent per year, Bremer and Sweeney [1988] calculate that, on the first day after a negative "jump" in excess of 10 percent, the CAPM-beta of the average loser company would have to suddenly rise to about 50! With respect to long term

---

[7]Ritter [1988] offers an interesting new twist on the tax-loss selling hypothesis, which he calls the "parking-the-proceeds" effect. It appears that the buy/sell ratio for individual investors is below normal in late December and above normal in early January. The phenomenon most clearly occurs following bear markets. Thus, the difference in January performance between small and large companies may not only reflect a "rebound" from December selling pressure (Reinganum [1983]) but also buying pressure that results from delayed portfolio rebalancing behavior by individual investors (who are known, in the aggregate, to prefer low-capitalization stocks).

In addition, price pressures resulting from "window dressing" and portfolio rebalancing behavior by institutional investors -- who, as suggested by Haugen and Lakonishok [1987], may turn contrarian in early January -- could be responsible for the January effect. But, at this time, there is no empirical evidence either to support or to reject that view.

[8]Brown, Harlow and Tinic [1988] present a third line of reasoning. They argue that for rational risk-averse utility-maximizing investors the conditional certainty equivalent value of a stock will always be less than the corresponding conditional expected value. As a consequence, the initial price reaction to uncertain information will, on average, be insufficient. This view -- called the Uncertain Information Hypothesis -- leads to predictions that are observationally equivalent to overreaction to "bad" news and underreaction to "good" news.

price reversals and the test period performance of on "arbitrage" portfolio that buys losers by selling winners short, Chan [1987] admits that the excess returns cannot be explained by the CAPM unless there is positive correlation between the market risk premium and time-varying betas (say, because both are responding to common state variables). However, as explained in De Bondt and Thaler [1987], the dependence of the arbitrage portfolio beta on market movements makes it difficult to interpret that measure as a risk-index.[9] Finally, Poterba and Summers [1987] directly investigate what variability (standard deviation) of expected returns is necessary to account for the observed mean reversion in prices. The estimates are very large relative to the mean of ex post returns; they imply that ex ante returns must frequently exceed 20 percent.

Even though much energy has been spent to distinguish long-term price reversals from mere compensation for risk, tax-induced turn-of-the-year effects, and the size anomaly, relatively little has happened in the way of further testing its original cognitive bias interpretation.[10] The "overreaction to earnings" hypothesis starts from the claim that there are temporary mean-reverting components in company earnings (see, e.g., Brooks and Buckmaster [1976]), particularly with respect to extreme winner and loser portfolios. Such mean-reversion -- which, like the price reversals, is the strongest for losers -- is documented by De Bondt and Thaler [1987] and Zarowin [1987]. But investors either perceive all earnings changes to be permanent or, worse, they detect "trends." Either way, as the original expectations (too optimistic for prior winners; too pessimistic for prior losers) get disappointed, stock prices adjust and move towards their underlying "fundamental values." Thus, mean

[9]The arbitrage portfolio has a CAPM-beta of .395 in bull markets and -.323 in bear markets. In January, the bull (bear) market beta is .748 (-.848). Therefore, the arbitrage portfolio is profitable no matter which direction the market takes. If the market is up, the loser portfolio moves more strongly with it than the winner portfolio does, and the arbitrage portfolio earns excess profits on the long side. If the market is down, the arbitrage portfolio earns profits on the short side. These findings further suggest that losers are initially "undervalued" and winners "overvalued."

[10]If deviations between market price and intrinsic value get corrected over time, negative serial correlation in returns follows inescapably. Any fashion or fad will do. However, price reversals may still be consistent with rational time-varying risk premia. Therefore, the arguments against the efficient market hypothesis stand to gain the most from specific "speculative fad models" that explain the observed mean-reversion in terms of variables which do not relate to "fundamentals" and which ought to be irrelevant -- such as earnings forecast errors. "Overreaction to earnings" may be thought of as precisely one such model.

reversion in stock prices and the associated profitability of contrarian strategies may reflect no more than mean reversion in earnings which the representative investor fails to recognize.

Klein and Rosenfeld [1987] attempt to explain the P/E-anomaly from this perspective. For the period between 1977 and 1984, they analyze financial analysts' earnings predictions on IBES, a data base marketed by Lynch, Jones & Ryan in New York. The quality of analysts' predictions deserves our attention because it represents a natural upper bound on the quality of the earnings-per-share (EPS) forecasts of less sophisticated agents.[11] Klein and Rosenfeld observe that analysts, on average, underestimate the actual EPS of the firms with the lowest dollar level of expected earnings. Using the same data base, Dowen and Bauman [1987] find that, on average, the forecasts for stocks with high P/E-ratios are too large relative to stocks with low P/E ratios. However, neither study succeeds in accounting for the P/E-anomaly.[12]

Zarowin [1987] tests the overreaction-to-earnings hypothesis directly by forming portfolios on the basis of a company-specific "earnings performance measure" (EPM) that is defined as the change in earnings from one year to the next divided by the standard deviation of the company's earnings changes over the previous five years. Between 1971 and 1981, the yearly samples contain 551 to 788 firms (listed both on the Annual Industrial COMPUSTAT and the monthly CRSP return tapes). Zarowin finds that, over the next three years, the 20 percent of the companies with the lowest EPM outperform the top quintile by, on average, 16.6 percent (t-statistic:

---

[11]The debate about the quality of analysts' EPS forecasts remains largely unresolved (see the survey by Givoly and Lakonishok [1984]), particularly as it relates to stocks that we may reasonably believe to be subject to fashions and fads. While there is evidence of bias, analysts' predictions, on average, seem to beat naive time-series extrapolations. However, this comparison is skewed in favor of the analysts since they benefit from larger amounts of (and more timely) information than is captured by time-series models.

[12]De Bondt and Thaler [forthcoming] also use IBES expectations data to test whether, for extreme winners (losers), 8-, 13- and 21-month EPS forecasts are on the average revised downwards (upwards) as time elapses. Their preliminary findings go against overreaction bias for EPS forecasts over 1- and 2-year horizons. However, in the spirit of a well-known Wall Street aphorism -- that the market at times not only discounts the future but also the hereafter -- expectations of long-term EPS growth may be more relevant.

2.9), with the largest part, 13.4 percent, occurring in January.[13] Further evidence on overreaction-to-earnings is provided by Ou and Penman [1987]. For the period between 1973 and 1983, these authors draw numerous accounting data items for the Annual COMPUSTAT files in attempts to measure, for about 1,600 companies per year, "future earning power" and to predict the probability of an EPS-increase in the subsequent year (p). Every year, portfolios are formed and stocks are assigned either to a "long" position (if p>.60) or to a "short" position (if p<.40). Two years later, the average return difference on the positions is a highly significant 14.53 percent (9.08 percent when size-adjusted returns are used). Interestingly, Ou and Penman find that the stocks with large (small) p have typically experienced substantial price decreases (increases) over the previous five years. Also, in the last year before portfolio formation, these companies report very substantial declines (rises) in earnings-per-share relative to other firms. Ou and Penman conclude that "financial statements capture fundamentals that are not reflected in prices" (p. 34). In addition, extreme values of p may be interpreted as "identifying cases where stock prices have previously moved away from fundamentals as well as subsequent reversion to fundamentals" (p. 19).

Apart from non-rational earnings expectations and normatively "excessive" risk premia, a third socio-psychological interpretation of the price reversals involves investors overreacting to each other's trades rather than to news per se (see Black [1986] and French and Roll [1986]). Shiller and Pound [1987] and Shiller [1987] conduct broad-based surveys of institutional investors, wealthy individual investors and stockbrokers in order to study their investment strategies and reaction to news events. On the basis of nearly 1000 responses, Shiller [1987] is unable to identify specific news breaks that led to the October 19 stock market crash. He is sympathetic to the view that the stock market "may have a life of its own to some extent, unrelated to economic fundamentals" (p. 22). Overall, however, we have little evidence directly related to the trading process that allows us to judge, at this time, the relevance of socio-psychological explanations of overreaction.

---

[13]When Zarowin controls for firm size by comparing the test period returns of earnings-based winners and losers with roughly the same market value of equity, the results become much weaker. However, this result is to be expected if, say, for small firms, both "winners" and "losers" (in Zarowin's definition, based on one-year earnings changes) are "long-term" losers in the sense of De Bondt and Thaler [1985], i.e., based on long-term return performance.

5. CONCLUSION

This paper summarizes theoretical and empirical work suggestive of overreaction in stock prices. The empirical evidence is "anomalous" relative to standard valuation models and notions of market efficiency but it is broadly consistent with predictions made by theories of intuitive judgment formulated by psychologists. Yet, many puzzles remain. These puzzles include the extreme seasonality of "price corrections" and their asymmetry in response to "good" or "bad" news events. Overreaction behavior may be driven either by normatively "excessive" risk premia, non-rational expectations of future cash flows (i.e., fashions and fads), or investors overreacting to each other's trades. At this time, the empirical findings do not allow us to clearly distinguish between these hypotheses. Neither do they allow us to reject the view that mean-reversion in asset prices reflects, at least in part, rationally time-varying risk premia. Since, in any event, none of these interpretations are mutually exclusive, the old saw "that much work remains to be done" clearly applies.

Nevertheless, the research that is summarized above already has profound implications for finance. For example, it can no longer be assumed (as it is in event studies) that the reaction of market prices to important news breaks is instantaneous and unbiased. It would be interesting to compare the observed changes in market value with independent estimates of the "correct" change (for a rare attempt -- and results consistent with overreaction -- see Jarrell and Peltzman [1986]).

On a more basic level, our task is to invent better theories of stock valuation. If economic fundamentals cannot account for the volatility of asset prices (Cutler, Poterba and Summers [1987]), what does? It is important that we model how the consensus opinion of market participants evolves through time. The results on overreaction may be helpful in this regard. In many ways, the field of finance is in a state similar to its position at the birth of the efficient market hypothesis. In his classic review article on efficient markets, Fama comments on that period as follows [1970, p. 389],

> ...research on security prices did not begin with the development of a theory of price formation...Rather...faced with the evidence [that speculative prices could be well approximated by a random walk], economists felt compelled to offer some rationalization...there existed a large body of empirical results in search of a rigorous theory...

In this paper, I have suggested that, in the search for better theories of asset valuation, the introduction of findings of behavioral science represents a reasonable (and an empirically promising) modeling strategy. Apart from the fact that numerous empirical anomalies plague the standard models, this is also sensible because there is so much doubt about the descriptive validity for individual behavior of the assumptions underlying these theories (such as expected utility maximization, risk aversion, or Bayesian updating). Yet, in the economics and finance literature, it often seems as if there are no modeling alternatives. For example, with respect to the assumption of rational expectations, Barro and Fisher ([1976], p. 163) argue,

> ...The ... assumption may be excessively strong...but it is a more persuasive starting point than the alternative of using a rule of thumb for expectations formation that is independent of the stochastic properties of the time path of the variable about which expectations are formed. A fundamental difficulty with theories of expectations that are not based on the predictions of the relevant economic model ... is that they require a theory of systematic mistakes..

As described in section 2, the groundwork for a behavioral theory of systematic expectation bias -- or other deviations from "rationality," narrowly defined -- presently exists. Furthermore, it is unlikely that a class of "fully rational" traders can remove such bias at the market level. A willingness to assume more than mere consistency in behavior -- in short, a "richer" behavioral model -- may therefore be useful in tackling such little understood phenomena as the week-end effect, the turn-of-the-year effect, etc. In his review paper on the small firm effect, Schwert argues that ([1983], p. 10, my emphasis):

> ...to successfully explain the "size effect," new theory must be developed that is consistent with rational maximizing behavior on the part of *all* actors in the model..

I believe instead that a promising topic for future theoretical and empirical work is to characterize the "quasi"-equilibria that prevail in markets where a substantial number of economic agents are less than fully rational.

REFERENCES

Adler, P.A. and P. Adler (eds.), 1984, *The social dynamics of financial markets* (JAI Press, Greenwich, Connecticut).

Andreassen, P.B., 1986, On the relationship between excess trading and excess price volatility in security markets, working paper, Department of Psychology, Harvard University (November).

Andreassen, P.B., 1987, On the social psychology of the stock market: Aggregate attributional effects and the regressiveness of prediction. *Journal of Personality and Social Psychology* 53, forthcoming.

Andreassen, P.B., 1988, Explaining the price-volume relationship: The difference between price changes and changing prices, *Organizational Behavior and Human Decision Processes*, forthcoming.

Andreassen, P.B. and S.J. Kraus, 1987, Intuitive prediction and the salience of change: The stock market, exponential growth, and divorce, working paper, Department of Psychology, Harvard University (September).

Arkes, H.R., R.M. Dawes and C. Christensen, 1986, Factors influencing the use of a decision rule in a probabilistic task, *Organizational Behavior and Human Decision Processes* 37, 93-110.

Ball, R., 1978, Anomalies in relationships between securities' yields and yield-surrogates, *Journal of Financial Economics* 6 (August-September), 103-126.

Barro, R. and S. Fisher, 1976, Recent developments in monetary theory, *Journal of Monetary Economics* 2, 133-176.

Basu, S., 1977, Investment performance of common stocks in relation to their price-earnings ratios: A test of the efficient market hypothesis, *Journal of Finance* 33 (June), 663-682.

Basu, S., 1978, The effect of earnings yield on assessments of the association between annual accounting income numbers and security prices, *The Accounting Review* 53 (July), 599-625.

Basu, S., 1983, The relationship between earnings' yield, market value and return for NYSE common stocks: Further evidence, *Journal of Financial Economics* 12 (June), 129-156.

Bazerman, M.H., 1986, *Judgment in managerial decision making* (John Wiley and Sons, New York).

Becker, G.S., 1976, *The economic approach to human behavior* (University of Chicago Press, Chicago, Illinois).

Black, F., 1986, Noise, *Journal of Finance* 41 (July), 529-543.

Branch, B. and K. Chang, 1987, Low-priced stocks and the January effect, working paper, University of Massachusetts-Amherst (July).

Brehmer, B. and J. Kuylenstierna, 1978, Task information and performance in probabilistic inference tasks, *Organizational Behavior and Human Performance* 22, 445-464.

Bremer, M.A. and R.J. Sweeney, 1988, The information content of extreme negative rates of return, working paper, Claremont McKenna College (February).

Brooks, L.D. and D.E. Buckmaster, 1976, Further evidence on the time-series properties of accounting income, *Journal of Finance* 31 (December),1359-1373.

Brown, K.C. and W.V. Harlow, 1988, Assessing the magnitude and intensity of stock market over-reaction, *Journal of Portfolio Management*, forthcoming.

Brown, K.C., W.V. Harlow and S.M. Tinic, 1988, Risk aversion, uncertain information, and market efficiency, working paper, University of Texas at Austin (January).

Camerer, C.F., 1987, Bubbles and fads in asset prices: A review of theory and evidence, working paper, Wharton School, University of Pennsylvania.

Camerer, C.F., 1987, Do biases in probability judgment matter in markets? Experimental evidence, *American Economic Review* 77 (December), 981-997.

Campbell, J.Y. and A.S. Kyle, 1986, Smart money, noise trading and stock price behavior, working paper, Princeton University (September).

Campbell, J.Y. and R.J. Shiller, 1987, Stock prices, earnings and expected dividends, working paper, Princeton University (December).

Cass, D. and K. Shell, 1983, Do sunspots matter?, *Journal of Political Economy* 91 (April), 193-227.

Chan, K.C., 1986, Can tax-loss selling explain the January seasonal in stock returns?, *Journal of Finance* 41 (December), 1115-1128.

Chan, K.C., 1987, On the return of the contrarian investment strategy, working paper, Faculty of Finance, Ohio State University (June).

Chapman, L.J. and J.P. Chapman, 1967, Genesis of popular but erroneous psychodiagnostic observations, *Journal of Abnormal Psychology* 72 (June), 193-204.

Cook, T.J. and M.S. Rozeff, 1984, Size and earnings/price ratio anomalies: One effect or two?, *Journal of Financial and Quantitative Analysis* 19 (December), 449-466.

Cutler, D.M., J.M. Poterba and L.H. Summers, 1987, What moves stock prices?, working paper, Massachusetts Institute of Technology (December).

Dark, F.H. and K. Kato, 1986, Stock market overreaction in the Japanese stock market, working paper, Iowa State University.

Dawes, R., 1979, The robust beauty of improper linear models in decision-making, *American Psychologist* 34, 571-582.

De Bondt, W.F.M., 1985, *Does the stock market overreact to new information?* Ithaca, New York: Ph.D. Dissertation, Cornell University (January).

De Bondt, W.F.M. and R.H. Thaler, 1985, Does the stock market overreact?, *Journal of Finance* 40 (July), 793-805.

De Bondt, W.F.M. and R.H. Thaler, 1987, Further evidence on investor overreaction and stock market seasonality, *Journal of Finance* 42 (July), 557-581.

De Bondt, W.F.M. and R.H. Thaler, 1988, Stock price reversals and analysts' expectations of earnings-per-share, working paper, Graduate School of Business, University of Wisconsin-Madison (work in progress).

De Long, J.B., A. Shleifer, L.H. Summers and R.J. Waldman, 1987, The economic consequences of noise traders, working paper, University of Chicago (September).

Dowen, R.J. and W.S. Bauman, 1987, The relation of earnings surprise to the E/P ratio effect, working paper, Department of Finance, Northern Illinois University (October).

Dyl, E.A. and K. Maxfield, 1987, Does the stock market overreact? Additional evidence, working paper, University of Arizona (June).

Eggleton, I., 1976, Patterns, prototypes, and predictions: An exploratory study, *Studies on Information Processing in Accounting*, Supplement to *Journal of Accounting Research*.

Eggleton, I., 1982, Intuitive time-series extrapolation, *Journal of Accounting Research* 20 (Spring), 68-102.

Einhorn, H., 1980, Learning from experience and suboptimal rules in decision-making, in: T. Wallsten, ed., *Cognitive processes in choice and decision behavior* (Lawrence Erlbaum, Hillsdale, New Jersey).

Einhorn, H. and R.M. Hogarth, 1978, Confidence in judgment: Persistence of the illusion of validity, *Psychological Review* 85, 395-416.

Fama, E.F., 1970, Efficient capital markets: A review of theory and empirical work, *Journal of Finance* 25 (May), 383-417.

Fama, E.F. and K.R. French, 1986, Common factors in the serial correlation of stock returns, working paper, Graduate School of Business, University of Chicago (October).

Fama, E.F. and K.R. French, 1987, Dividend yields and expected stock returns, working paper, Graduate School of Business, University of Chicago (July).

Fama, E.F. and K.R. French, 1988, Permanent and temporary components of stock prices, working paper, Graduate School of Business, University of Chicago (February). *Journal of Political Economy, (*forthcoming).

Figlewski, S., 1978, Market efficiency in a market with heterogeneous information, *Journal of Political Economy* 86 (August), 581-597.

Figlewski, S., 1982, Information diversity and market behavior, *Journal of Finance* 37 (March), 87-102.

Fischhoff, B., 1975, Hindsight # foresight: The effect of outcome knowledge on judgment under uncertainty, *Journal of Experimental Psychology, Human Perception and Performance* 1 (August), 288-299.

French, K.R. and R. Roll, 1986, Stock return variances: The arrival of information and the reaction of traders, *Journal of Financial Economics* 17 (September), 5-26.

Gilovich, T., R. Vallone and A. Tversky, 1985, The hot hand in basketball: On the misperception of random sequences, *Cognitive Psychology* 17 (July), 295-314.

Givoly, D. and J. Lakonishok, 1984, The quality of analysts' forecasts of earnings, *Financial Analysts Journal* (September/October), 40-47.

Graham, B. and D.L. Dodd (with C. Tatham, Jr.), 1951, *Security analysis* (McGraw-Hill, New York).

Grether, D.M., 1980, Bayes' rule as a descriptive model: The representativeness heuristic, *Quarterly Journal of Economics* 95 (November), 537-557.

Harrison, J.M. and D.M. Kreps, 1978, Speculative investor behavior in a stock market with heterogeneous expectations, *Quarterly Journal of Economics* 92 (May), 323-336.

Haugen, R.A. and J. Lakonishok, 1987, *The incredible January effect* (Dow Jones Irwin, Homewood, Illinois).

Hogarth, R.M., 1975, Cognitive processes and the assessment of subjective probability distributions, *Journal of the American Statistical Association* 70, 271-289.

Hogarth, R.M., 1981, *Judgement and choice: The psychology of decision* (Wiley, New York).

Hogarth, R.M. and M.W. Reder, 1986, *Rational choice: The contrast between economics and psychology* (University of Chicago Press, Chicago).

Howe, J.S., 1986, Evidence on stock market overreaction, *Financial Analysts Journal* (July/August), 74-77.

Jarrell, G. and S. Peltzman, 1986, The impact of product recalls on the wealth of sellers, in P.M. Ippolito and D.T. Scheffman (editors), *Empirical Approaches to Consumer Protection Economics* (Federal Trade Commission, Washington, D.C.).

Jarrow, R., 1983, Beliefs, information, martingales, and arbitrage pricing, working paper, Johnson Graduate School of Management, Cornell University (November).

Jegadeesh, N., 1987, Evidence of predictable behavior of security returns, working paper, Columbia University (May).

Jones, S.L., 1987, Reaction to the overreaction hypothesis, working paper, Graduate School of Management, Purdue University (May).

Kahneman, D. and A. Tversky, 1982, Intuitive prediction: Biases and corrective procedures. Reprinted in Daniel Kahneman, Paul Slovic and Amos Tversky. *Judgment under uncertainty: Heuristics and biases* (Cambridge University Press, New York), 414-421.

Kahneman, D., P. Slovic and A. Tversky, 1982, *Judgment under uncertainty: Heuristics and biases* (Cambridge University Press, New York).

Keim, D.B., 1986, The CAPM and equity return regularities, *Financial Analysts Journal* (May/June), 19-34.

Keim, D.B. and R.F. Stambaugh, 1986, Predicting returns in the stock and bond markets, *Journal of Financial Economics* 17 (December), 357-390.

Keynes, J.M., 1936, *The general theory of employment, interest and money* (Harcourt Brace Jovanovich, London).

Klein, A. and J. Rosenfeld, 1987, P/E ratios, earnings expectations and abnormal returns, working paper, Graduate School of Business, New York University (December).

Langer, E., 1975, The illusion of control, *Journal of Personality and Social Psychology* 32, 311-328.

Lehmann, B.N., 1988, Fads, martingales, and market efficiency, working paper, Hoover Institution, Stanford University (January).

Lo, A.W. and A. C. MacKinlay, 1987, Stock market prices do not follow random walks: Evidence from a simple specification test." NBER working paper no. 2168 (February).

Macaulay, F.R., 1938, *Some theoretical problems suggested by the movement of interest rates, bond yields and stock prices in the United States since 1856* (National Bureau of Economic Research, New York).

Mayshar, J., 1983, On divergence of opinion and imperfections in capital markets, *American Economic Review* 73 (March), 114-128.

Merton, R.C., 1987, A simple model of capital market equilibrium with incomplete information, *Journal of Finance* 42 (July), 483-510.

Miller, E., 1977, Risk, uncertainty and divergence of opinion, *Journal of Finance* 32 (September), 1151-1168.

Nisbett, R. and L. Ross, 1980, *Human inference: Strategies and shortcomings of social judgment* (Prentice-Hall, Englewood Cliffs, New Jersey).

Northcraft, G.B. and M.A. Neale, 1987, Experts, amateurs, and real estate: An anchoring-and-adjustment perspective on property pricing decisions, *Organizational Behavior and Human Decision Processes* 39, 84-97.

Ohlson, J.A. and S.H. Penman, 1985, Volatility increases subsequent to stock splits, *Journal of Financial Economics* 14 (June), 251-266.

Oskamp, S., 1965, Overconfidence in case-study judgments, *Journal of Consulting Psychology* 29 (June), 261-265.

Ou, J.A. and S.H. Penman, 1987, Financial statement analysis and the prediction of stock returns, working paper, Santa Clara University (June).

Poterba, J.M. and L.H. Summers, 1987, Mean reversion in stock prices: Evidence and implications, National Bureau of Economic Research working paper no. 2343 (August).

Reinganum, M.R., 1981, Misspecification of capital asset pricing: Empirical anomalies based on earnings' yields and market values, *Journal of Financial Economics* 9 (March), 19-46.

Reinganum, M.R., 1983, The anomalous stock market behavior of small firms in January, *Journal of Financial Economics* 12 (June), 89-104.

Reinganum, M.R., 1987, The collapse of the efficient market hypothesis: A look at the empirical anomalies of the 1980s, working paper no. 87-3, Capital Markets Research Institute, University of Iowa (November).

Rendleman, Jr., R.J., C.P. Jones and H.A. Latane, 1982, Empirical anomalies based on unexpected earnings and the importance of risk adjustments, *Journal of Financial Economics* 10 (November), 269-288.

Ritter, J.R., 1988, The buying and selling behavior of individual investors at the turn-of-the-year, *Journal of Finance* 43 (July), forthcoming.

Rogalski, R.J. and S.M. Tinic, 1986, The January size effect: Anomaly or risk measurement?, *Financial Analysts Journal* (November/December), 63-70.

Rose, A.M., 1951, Rumor in the stock market, *Public Opinion Quarterly* 15 (Fall), 461-486.

Rosenberg, B. and A. Rudd, 1982, Factor-related and specific returns of common stocks: Serial correlation and market inefficiency, *Journal of Finance* 37 (May), 543-554.

Rosenberg, B., K. Reid, and R. Lanstein, 1985, Persuasive evidence of market inefficiency, *Journal of Portfolio Management* 11 (Spring), 9-16.

Russell, T. and R.H. Thaler, 1985, The relevance of quasi-rationality in competitive markets, *American Economic Review* 75 (December), 1071-1082.

Schachter, S., D.C. Hood, P.B. Andreassen and W. Gerin, 1986, Aggregate variables in psychology and economics: Dependence and the stock market, in: B. Gilad and S. Kaish (eds.), *Handbook of behavioral economics* (JAI Press, Greenwich, Connecticut).

Schmalensee, R., 1976, An experimental study of expectation formation, *Econometrica* 44 (January), 17-41.

Schwert, G.W., 1983, Size and stock returns, and other empirical regularities, *Journal of Financial Economics* 12 (June), 3-12.

Shefrin, H. and M. Statman, 1985, The disposition to sell winners too early and ride losers too long: Theory and evidence, *Journal of Finance* 40 (July), 777-792.

Shefrin, H. and M. Statman, 1986, Market models in behavioral finance: Part I: prospect theory, CAPM and APT, working paper, Leavey School of Business, Santa Clara University (November).

Shefrin, H. and M. Statman, 1987, A behavioral finance solution to the noise trading puzzle, working paper, Leavey School of Business, Santa Clara University (December).

Shiller, R.J., 1984, Stock prices and social dynamics, *Brookings Papers on Economic Activity* (2), 457-510.

Shiller, R.J., 1987, Investor behavior in the October 1987 stock market crash: Survey evidence, Cowles Foundation Discussion Paper No. 853 (November).

Shiller, R.J. and J. Pound, 1986, Survey evidence of diffusion of interest among institutional investors, National Bureau of Economic Research, working paper No. 1851 (March).

Slovic, P., 1972, Psychological study of human judgment: Implications for investment decision-making, *Journal of Finance* 27 (September), 779-799.

Summers, L.H., 1986, Does the stock market rationally reflect fundamental values?, *Journal of Finance* 41 (July), 591-601.

Taussig, F.W., 1921, Is market price determinate?, *Quarterly Journal of Economics* 35 (May), 394-411.

Tirole, J., 1982, On the possibility of speculation under rational expectations, *Econometrica* 50 (September), 1163-1181.

Tversky, A. and D. Kahneman, 1971, The belief in the law of small numbers, *Psychological Bulletin* 76 (August), 105-110.

Vermaelen, T. and M. Verstringe, 1986, Do Belgians overreact?, working paper, Catholic University of Louvain, Belgium (November).

West, K.D., 1987, Bubbles, fads and stock price volatility tests: A partial evaluation, working paper, Princeton University (December).

Williams, J.B., 1956, *The theory of investment value* (North-Holland, Amsterdam, reprint of 1938 edition).

Zarowin, P., 1987, Does the stock market overreact to corporate earnings information?, working paper, Graduate School of Business Administration, New York University (December).

Zarowin, P., 1988, Size, seasonality, and stock market overreaction, working paper, Graduate School of Business Administration, New York University (January).

Comments on De Bondt's "Stock Price Reversals and Overreaction to News Events: A Survey of Theory and Evidence"

by Adri De Ridder.

This paper explores and summarizes the evidence of the overreaction anomaly. The main questions which the author tries to answer are:

a) Do individual investors overreact?

b) Should we expect financial markets to overreact?

c) Does the stock market overreact?

The first issue is discussed in the spirit of the human behavior literature. I have nothing to add to the conclusion that reactions on different kinds of stimuli do not tend to be perfectly balanced. I prefer discussing the second questions in the light of market efficiency, thus the price performance should accurately reflect the true implications of the information on the value of the share. Consequently, there should be no subsequent price corrections. On the other hand, we know that the price we observe on a specific stock not inevitably reflects the consensus price set by the market. Instead, the price reflects the most optimistic investors' valuation of the security. Nevertheless, the results by De Bondt and Thaler (1985) support the overreaction hypothesis i.e. the poorest performing stocks in the beginning of the period outperform the market in the latter period (the opposite results for the best performing stocks). Is this what we would expect? We know that

NATO ASI Series, Vol. F54
A Reappraisal of the Efficiency of Financial Markets
Edited by Rui M.C. Guimaraes et al.

most of the excess returns on shares occur in January and that this month is the only month which gives a positive trade-off between the beta of a stock and the realized return (Ticnic and West, 1984). So the overreaction symptoms may be another evidence of the January effect. In any case, we should be aware of how we estimate and interprete risk for stocks under these circumstances.

In my opinion, the paper meets the authors' objectives. Whatever the course of future empirical research on anomalies will take, I would like more attention to be focused on the discussion of basic things like sample, size, risk, leverage, classification of events, excessive risk premia etc. I fully agree with the author that more evidence would be useful.

Reference

TICNIC, S M and WEST, R: Risk and Return: January vs the Rest of the Year, Journal of Financial Economics, 1984

Seasonal Anomalies in Financial Markets: A Survey

David Ikenberry and Josef Lakonishok

Department of Finance
University of Illinois Urbana-Champaign
1206 South Sixth Street
Champaign, Illinois 61820

Keywords:
Anomalies / Seasonal Anomalies / Annual Anomalies / Monthly Anomalies / Daily Anomalies / January Effect / Day-of-the-week Effect / Turn-of-the-month Effect / Over Reaction / Tax-loss selling / Noise / Data Snooping / Market Efficiency / (Unexpected) Returns in Financial Markets

Investigation into the patterns of returns in the stock market is extensive. This paper reviews and integrates much of the published research in this broad area. Some concern for data snooping and the reporting of noise exists over empirical anomaly research. Yet this does not account for the careful research findings of many authors. The over reaction and negative first-order serial correlation in annual returns is discussed. The January effect is reviewed along with the tax-loss and performance incentive hypotheses as rationale. The day-of-the-week anomaly and other anomalies such as the holiday effect are also presented and various possible explanations are discussed.

1. Introduction

Research into market anomalies has blossomed in recent years on many fronts including, for example, the size effect, the P/E effect, the January effect and so on. This paper surveys a subset of this literature regrading seasonal anomalies in the return patterns of various financial assets, with a focus on stocks. These seasonalities have received significant attention in the literature and can be identified on annual, monthly and daily basis. Much of the research on seasonal anomalies concentrates on U.S. equities. However, similar results have been

NATO ASI Series, Vol. F54
A Reappraisal of the Efficiency of Financial Markets
Edited by Rui M. C. Guimaraes et al.

documented on non-U.S. equities as well as other financial assets. The literature reveals that these anomalies, in general, have consistently been present for as long as we have recorded asset prices.

Given this long history of return anomalies, the interesting question comes to mind of why is it that research into return anomalies, after a long absence, has only come to light in the last decade. How is it that the late 1970's and the 1980's have lead us to discover what many argue to be a long standing phenomena?

One rather common response might be that the technology employed in financial economics research has only recently evolved to the point where seasonal anomalies can be uncovered. The availability of high speed computers along with electronic documentation of time series data, especially daily data that became readily available about ten years ago, has enabled researchers to delve much deeper into the historical asset return patterns than was possible in the past. Statistical procedures have also advanced in recent years, perhaps enabling more powerful analysis than was available to earlier researchers.
Merton (1985) has suggested that a "boredom" factor in recent years may be plaguing the literature with respect to this type of research. The profession's support of market efficiency has created a norm whereby an empirical study verifying the absence of anomalies would not add to the accepted knowledge base of the profession. Thus an article presenting supporting research of market efficiency runs the risk of boredom on its way to publication, perhaps never seeing the light of day. Articles with "exotic" findings may be easier to publish.

For those studies which are performed, Merton points out that any stable stochastic process may provide observations leading one to reject the null hypothesis given that it is true. In conventional tests, conclusions from the data are often made knowing that the possibility of a type I error always exists. Suppose, though that we have a multitude of studies in this area.

Some of this research, through the course of random events will show anomalous patterns. This research has an associated excitement level with the ability to attract academic interest. Thus, a small percentage of research on asset return patterns may, by random occurrence, be "non-boring" and receive attention and publication even though the null hypothesis of the work is indeed true. This implies that the literature as a whole is essentially being subjected to the flaw of ex-post statistical inferencing.

Data snooping is a third explanation for the recent volume of anomaly research and is associated with the enhancement in computing power. Data snooping is the practice of both discovering an hypothesis and testing that discovered hypothesis on the same data. The statistical tests routinely used in financial economics are usually interpreted as if they were being applied to new data. But the data available to the researcher are seldom new. We, as a profession, are commonly moved to exploit low cost computing power using common data bases such as the CRSP and COMPUSTAT tapes. In situations such as these, the dangers of data snooping are immense. This occurs not only individually, but also collectively as the empirically explored hypotheses of published research is circulated. Researchers who follow, then begin data snooping by refining the earlier hypotheses and testing these hypotheses with the advantage of hindsight on essentially the same data set. Given the talent that people have for arriving at "stories" of perceived patterns in random sequences, one may more readily find rejection of a random walk hypothesis (Gilovich, Vallone and Tversky 1985).

Black's 1986 presidential address (Black, 1986) concerned the role of noise in the return generating process. Anomalies will be difficult to identify in a world of highly varying returns. But if the degree of noise in returns is underestimated, arbitrary seasonal return patterns will have greater chances of being uncovered while the research has only confronted noise.

A final explanation for the arrival of anomaly studies in the 1980's may well be indicative of a change in attitude with regard to market efficiency. We, as a profession, started with a very strong prior belief about market efficiency. But the evidence which has gradually expanded has shaken the belief of many concerning "extreme" market efficiency. The consequence of this change is that we are becoming more open to seriously considering various deviations from market efficiency. The events leading up to and subsequent to that of October 19, 1987 may perhaps foster further studies questioning the applicability of market efficiency.

Regardless of how or why anomaly studies have arrived, evidence of seasonal patterns in rate of returns mounts as time passes. This paper does not attempt to review all the evidence with regard to anomalies, but rather to review the research identifying or clarifying the nature of seasonal anomalies (seasonal patterns) and the subsequent research which has been conducted in attempting to explain the empirical findings. The authors have attempted to be as complete as possible in their review, yet the tremendous volume of literature precludes a sweeping commentary of all seasonal anomaly research.

Section 2 of this paper reviews the recent literature uncovering seasonal anomalies using annual (multi-year) holding returns. Section 3 discusses the evidence concerning monthly seasonal anomalies. Section 4 is directed toward one of the more concerning anomalies which has perplexed the profession, the seasonal returns in daily data or the day-of-the-week effect. Section 5 discusses other additional seasonal patterns such as the turn-of-the-month and holiday effects. Section 6 provides a summary of the research presented in this paper and the general implications to the profession from seasonal anomaly works.

2. Annual Return Anomalies

Recently, evidence of return irregularities has surfaced for returns of longer time horizons, longer referring to several years. Researchers are finding that using longer time horizons, first-order serial dependency is identifiable in asset returns as the horizon length is varied.

Prior market efficiency studies have generally been conducted under a different methodology. The common approach was to calculate autocorrelations of single period holding returns over changing lags. These studies, in general, failed to find meaningful correlation and provide the primary evidence used to substantiate market efficiency. Current studies differ in methodology by using return horizons longer than a single period and then identifying only first-order serial autocorrelations. Rather than use monthly returns, these studies use holding periods from one to ten years in length to identify any pattern in first-order serial correlations.

DeBondt and Thaler's (1985) work on the overreaction hypothesis lead to much of this research. Their hypothesis suggests that prices tend to follow a reverting or "correcting" pattern. They substantiate their hypothesis on investor behavioral foundations which argue that investor expectations are not unbiased, but that investors tend to overly responded to both positive and negative information. To explore this hypothesis, they developed a test methodology which identifies securities on the CRSP database having 3 years of returns available prior to a given date. From this set of securities, the extreme high and low return securities are labeled as winners and losers and are placed into two separate equally weighted portfolios.

Returns to the portfolios are then calculated up to 60 months after the formation of the two portfolios at the end of each December. The authors find that the loser portfolios produce significantly positive returns, adjusted for the return to the market, several months after the portfolio is formed. They also find the winner portfolios lose money with respect to the market, although the movement is not as large in magnitude.

The "correction" process DeBondt and Thaler observe continues not only for a holding period of 12 months, but for 24 and 36 months after the original formation period. Interestingly, they find the correction to the overreaction being compressed primarily into the month of January while the remaining 11 months of a given year provided little correction.

The DeBondt and Thaler work on overreaction provided a stimulus to advance work in this area. For loser portfolios to consistently garner positive market adjusted returns while winner portfolios falter or fall, indicates that a correction in individual asset returns occurs. If a consistent pattern exists in this correction process over time, then on average, a negative serial correlation of some type must exist and be identifiable. The fact that single-period holding returns of short horizons do not show negative serial correlation has lead research into analyzing much longer return horizons.

Fama and French (1986 and 1987) have provided precisely this type of evidence. Fama and French replicated the DeBondt and Thaler work using a slightly different methodology and verified the overreaction phenomena of loser portfolios achieving market adjusted returns while winner portfolios earn negative adjusted returns. They differ from DeBondt and Thaler, though, in regard to the method in which the correction is observed. Fama and French find that winner portfolios tend to suffer statistically significant negative returns while loser portfolios have positive returns which do not statistically differ from zero, a slightly different twist from the DeBondt and Thaler results.

The primary contribution of the Fama and French papers, though, is the negative first-order serial correlations they identify for various return horizons. The authors use continuously compounded returns calculated over the period 1926 to 1985 from the CRSP tapes using one-, two-, three-, four-, five-, eight- and ten-year return horizons. They then calculate separately, the serial correlations from OLS regression for each holding period. Table 1 shows a "U" shaped structure in the first-order serial correlations.

Table 1[a]

OLS First-Order Serial Correlations

Return Horizon	1Yr.	2Yr.	3Yr.	4Yr.	5Yr.	6Yr.	8Yr.	10Yr.
Mean	-.02	-.18	-.31	-.39	-.37	-.22	-.14	-.17
Small	.00	-.17	-.33	-.51	-.51	-.29	.02	.09
Large	-.03	-.22	-.34	-.27	-.15	.02	.10	-.07

[a] Reproduced from Fama and French (1986)

The first line of Table 1 shows mean serial correlations calculated over their entire data set. The serial correlation of one-year returns is practically zero, not a surprising result. But as the holding period expands, a decrease in correlation occurs with minimum serial correlation found in return horizons of three to five years. Afterward, the serial correlation moves towards zero. In other words, the strongest multi-year return reversals are occurring with three to five-year holding periods.

Fama and French also create 10 portfolios ranked according to size. The correlations from the smallest and largest decile portfolios are presented the second and third lines of Table 1. The results show the small firms more prominently displaying the "U" shaped pattern, with the strongest correlations occurring in years 4 and 5 at -.51.

This constitutes strong evidence that long horizon return patterns have some degree of predictability. Such findings are generally not considered consistent with market efficiency. But, another possibility which is consistent with market efficiency is that the expected returns change over time and produce this unique pattern. (Many, including the authors of this survey, are quite skeptical of this second possibility.)

In a similar vein, Poterba and Summers (1987) have independently verified, using variance ratio tests, the pattern of serial correlations that might arise from mean reverting asset returns. The authors raise issue with the power of tests relying on serial correlation and suggest that a more powerful test of the random walk hypothesis versus a mean reverting return process is to analyze the variances of returns across differing holding periods. If returns follow a random walk, the variance of two-year holding period returns should be twice that of the one-year returns, and likewise the five-year return variance five times larger than the one-year return variance. After normalizing the longer return variances by the length of their return horizons, the presence of a mean reverting process in the return series would force the adjusted long-term variances to be <u>less</u> than the corresponding one-year variance. Therefore, Poterba and Summers test for the ratio of the normalized long-term variances to the one-year variance being less than 1.0. The authors find evidence of mean reverting behavior not only in U.S. equity markets for various indices and for individual stocks, but also document international evidence by examining the capital gain returns from 17 additional foreign equity markets.

In summary, the evidence in these papers is concerning with regard to market efficiency. In defense of market efficiency, one must remember that all of the above tests assume a constant expected returns model. Should a non-constant, expected returns process operate in the market place, these studies will not necessarily reflect inefficient markets.

3. Monthly Return Anomalies

The monthly return anomaly known as the January effect, was first casually observed by Wachtel (1942) and more fully revealed by Rozeff and Kinney (1976). The January effect concerns the abnormal returns which accrue during the month of January and generally surpass those of any other month, particularly for smaller capitalization firms. Rozeff and Kinney identified this phenomena, but could only conjecture as to its origin. For most of the time period they study, their data consisted of an equally weighted index which fortuitously placed emphasis on smaller firms allowing them to detect the January anomaly.

The January effect has received a tremendous degree of attention, not only for its unexpected arrival, but also for the magnitude (and economic significance) of the returns that small capitalization companies (the bottom 20 percent of companies ranked by market value of equity) earn over the S&P 500 index. These small firms, over the years 1926 to 1986, have on average outperformed the index by 5.5 percent in the month of January. Small firms have earned inferior returns in only seven out of these 61 years.

The January effect has also been documented on an international scale, for example by Gultekin and Gultekin (1983). To some extent, world evidence of January excess returns might be expected given the natural arbitrage conditions enforcing the law of one price and the international linkage of financial markets.

The effect has also spanned beyond equity markets. Smirlock (1985) finds evidence of a January seasonal in low grade corporate bonds but not in high grade corporate or U.S. government bonds. Using data from 1953 to 1978, he finds the average January return for low grade corporate bonds of 1.44% to be twice as great as the January return for high grade bonds and to be significantly greater than the average (low-grade bond) monthly return.

The source of the January effect has been linked to tax-loss selling arguments and to the institutional considerations of investment managers. The tax-loss argument, first mentioned in the Wachtel (1942) paper, has been followed by Dyl (1977) and in a related vein by Haugen and Wichern (1973). The argument is that it pays to recognize security losses early and gains late. Thus, December should be a month when securities which have suffered capital losses during that tax year should be considered for sale so that the capital loss can be recognized and used to shield income from taxation. The hypothesis then follows that funds generated by these December sales are re-invested into the market at the beginning of the new year which also represents a new tax year.

Schultz (1985) explored the tax-loss hypothesis by observing data surrounding the implementation of U.S. income taxes. Schultz finds that from 1900 to 1917, when income taxes were essentially not economically significant, January did not provide excess returns for small firms, while the years 1918 to 1929 provided significant January effects for smaller firms.

Jones, Pearce, and Wilson (1987) reject the tax-loss hypothesis using a longer pre-tax period and different estimation techniques from Schultz. They find, in the pre-tax period, a January effect of significant magnitude in the returns to small firms, but not in those of large firms.

Reinganum and Shapiro (1987) using data from the London Stock Exchange do find tax effects in the returns of financial assets. The British tax year-ends on April 5th for individuals while corporations typically choose December 31 for their tax-year end. Furthermore, capital gains, generally, were untaxed prior to 1965. Their data show a significant net return (3.08 percent) in April for the most likely tax-loss candidates over the least likely candidates. Yet contrary to their expectations, they also record similar responses in the January data. Thus, they find that tax-loss selling does influence asset returns, but does not provide a complete explanation of the January effect.

Ritter (1987) presents evidence supporting the tax-loss hypothesis by suggesting that buying and selling behavior of individual investors differs on a calendar basis. Using buying and selling transaction statistics provided by Merrill, Lynch from 1977 to 1985, Ritter documents that selling pressure from individual investors prevails in the month of December relative to annual norms. This selling pressure presumably is a result of an attempt to capture tax-loss shields available only until the last trading day of the year. Buying pressure, though, takes a discrete jump during the first trading days of the new year.

Ritter's hypothesis is that year-end bonus proceeds that investors receive from employment along with the "parked" proceeds from security liquidations in December provide funds sufficient for January's buy side pressure on security prices. Individual investors apply these investment funds to small cap firms (generally less popular with institutional investors) and thus a January effect is manifested in small firms.

Rozeff (1985a, 1985b) presents evidence in support of the tax-loss argument as well. Rozeff documents the share purchases and sales of five types of security investors. Rozeff documents that in December investors outside the exchanges essentially sell securities to those inside the exchange (specialist, members on the floor, and exchange members off the floor) who absorb the shares. The pattern then reverses in January as exchange members' inventories are reduced and shares flow back to institutional and individual owners. Rozeff argues that this behavior is linked to tax-loss capture strategies. He provides evidence showing high tax-loss candidates are subject to strong December losses, yet relatively higher January price rebounds. Rozeff also finds size effects in the return patterns of high and low tax-loss candidates. He concludes that the evidence of tax-loss selling is quite strong, yet he also finds that tax-loss selling does not fully explain the January anomaly.

As compelling as some of the evidence might appear, it does not deny the criticism that the tax-loss argument has received as an explanation for the January anomaly. Constantinides (1984) and Lakonishok and Smidt (1986) raise various conceptual problems with the tax-loss selling argument. For example, there is no compelling reason, after realizing losses in December, to "park" the proceeds until January to buy shares. Why not reinvest the funds immediately in other (attractive) equities? Lakonishok and Smidt (1987) address this point in more definitive terms, showing that many of the implications of tax-loss selling do not hold up under scrutiny. The international evidence also posses problems for the tax-loss selling argument. The January effect is found in countries in which there is no capital gain tax for example, Japan and Canada (before 1972). In addition, there is a January effect in Australia although the tax-year ends in June.

A second rationale to explain the January effect is rooted in the incentive contracts of portfolio managers and is discussed by Haugen and Lakonishok (1987). A substantial percentage of the U.S. equity (and debt) market is under the auspicious of professional investment managers. Many of these investment managers are compensated according to the performance of the capital they manage. It can be argued that the incentive to "risk" the investment capital of a portfolio increases during the month of January, but then decreases throughout the remainder of the year. Because January in general represents a new evaluation period for investment managers, these managers are anxious to establish superior investment performance which will eventually be linked to their compensation. Bargains may be easier to find among the smaller, lesser known companies.

After the managers meet their investment goals, there is a significant reluctance on the part of the managers to rebalance the portfolio in search of any remaining gains. Any further gains from aggressive investments may not yield a significant increase in income, but could result in a reduction of the manager's income by losing previously earned returns in risky assets. As a result, the incentive to search for and take positions in undervalued firms dwindles throughout the year as individual agents meet their goals. But, the first weeks of January represent the beginning of a new performance year and thus encourage managers to aggressively invest in profit opportunities.

In addition, there is a widely held belief that portfolio managers are dressing up their portfolios toward the end of December when a "family portrait" is being taken. In dressing up their portfolios, managers remove lesser known stocks, especially if they decreased in price during the year. These stocks are then replaced by stocks of well established companies.

It should be emphasized that the month of January in the U.S. is not exceptional for large stocks (see Lakonishok and Smidt (1987)). If one observes a value weighted index such as the S&P 500, or the Dow Jones Industrial Average (containing some of the largest U.S. firms), the return in January is not significantly higher than in a typical month and there are other months with returns as high as the January month.

4. Daily Return Anomalies

The day-of-the-week effect has been categorized as one of the more damaging anomalies to the efficient markets hypothesis. The persistence and consistency of this anomaly has provided piling evidence contrary to the hypothesis. There exist perhaps two possible a priori expectations one would have for the pattern in daily returns. One would be that the returns to each day of the week should be similar creating a level return pattern across the week. A second a priori pattern might be that we expect the rate of return earned by financial assets to be constant across all the days with the exception of Monday. The rate of return on Monday could be expected higher than on other days because of the longer holding period (3 days from Friday's close to Monday's close). The evidence to date is not cooperative with either of our two expectations.

The day-of-the-week effect was documented in a number of earlier papers: Fields (1931 and 1934), Osborne (1962), and Cross (1973). It was rediscovered more recently by French (1980) followed closely by Gibbons and Hess (1981) and Lakonishok and Levi (1982). In these studies, Monday returns were found consistently, significantly negative while the returns on the last trading day of the week, Friday or Saturday, tend to be higher than for a typical day. Tuesday through Thursday returns tend to vary across authors, but most authors find Wednesday's return largest of the three days.

Lakonishok and Smidt (1987) examined the day-of-the-week effect using the most extensive time span; the Dow Jones index from 1897 to 1986. Table 2 summarizes some of their results. Monday's rate of return is negative for the total period as well as for the two sub-periods. The magnitude of the Monday rate of

Table 2[a]
Daily Rates of Return of the DJIA by Day of the Week (in Percent)

1887-1986	Monday	Tuesday	Wednesday	Thursday	Friday Before[b] Trading Saturday	Friday Before[b] No Trading Saturday	Saturday
Mean	-0.144	.029	.045	.025	.050	.070	.052
Median	-0.079	.035	.056	.021	.094	.079	.074
% of Days Positive	45.4	51.9	52.6	51.0	54.4	54.6	56.6
1897-5/30/52							
Mean	-0.145	.035	.032	.012	.050	.115	.052
Median	-0.050	.056	.050	.012	.094	.052	.074
% of Days Positive	47.0	50.3	52.2	50.3	54.4	53.6	56.5
6/1/52-1986							
Mean	-0.142	.020	.064	.040		.067	
Median	-0.050	.056	.050	.012		.090	
% of Days Positive	47.0	50.3	52.2	50.3		54.7	

[a] Reproduced from Lakonishok and Smidt (1987).
[b] Prior to May 1952, trading occurred Saturday mornings.

return is .144 percent for the total period. This rate of return is worthy of note because there are 52 Monday's per year. Therefore, the cumulative decrease on Mondays is around 7.5% per year.

Jaffe and Westerfield (1985) examined daily stock market returns for the U.S., U.K., Japan, Canada and Australia. They found that the Monday rates of returns were negative in each country, although, in the Japanese and Australian stock markets, the lowest mean rates of return occur on Tuesdays. They conclude that foreign investors confront a day-of-the-week effect in their respective countries independent of the effect which exists in the U.S.

Following the lead of Gibbons and Hess (1981), Flannery and Protopapadakis (1988) document daily seasonal anomalies not only in the equity market, but also in the U.S. government debt market. The authors, after carefully controlling for institutional clearing mechanisms, record the familiar negative Monday response. They also record negative Wednesday returns, contrary to that of equity returns, although the return is not statistically significant. Interestingly, they find that debt instruments of greater durations tend to exhibit the seasonal influences differently than short-term debt securities.

To gain further understanding into the day-of-the-week effect, some researchers have used intra-day data. Rogalski (1984) obtained open and close values for the Dow Jones Industrial Average and the Standard and Poors Composite Index. He concluded that the Monday effect is actually a non-trading weekend effect. The negative rate of return reported from Friday's close to Monday's close actually occurs from Friday's close to Monday's open. He finds that the rate of return on Monday, from open to close, is similar to other days of the week.

Harris (1986) studied the weekend effect using transaction by transaction data for all NYSE companies for a period of 14 months starting December 1, 1981. He found that for large firms, the negative rate of return from Friday's close to Monday's close also accrues over the non-trading period between Friday's close to Monday's open. This conclusion confirms Rogalski's findings because the indices used by Rogalski are dominated by the largest firms. However, for small firms, Harris found that the negative weekend rate of return accrues during the Monday trading day. The limitation of the study is that less than 300 trading days or less than 60 Mondays were available, a very short time span.

The day-of-the week effect has also been documented in the

stock index futures markets. Dyl and Maberly (1986) and Cornell (1985) use data on S&P 500 Stock Index Futures contract, however the data exists for a relatively short period of time. The results reveal strong negative futures price changes on Monday followed by positive (but insignificant price changes) over the remaining four days of the week.

A possible explanation for the day-of-the-week effect is that negative information is held for release until after the security markets have closed on Fridays. Penman (1987) explores these issues and finds that the release of corporate earnings reports may be advanced or delayed by firms depending on the nature of the release. He confirms results from prior studies that firms with bad news tend to delay disclosing their results while firms with unexpected good news tend to deliver the news on or before the date expected. Penman finds that firms tend to release good information early in the month of a reporting period, and also finds that firms also have a propensity to release bad news after the markets close on Fridays. To the extent that the market does not properly incorporate the timing of information release, this may provide a partial explanation for the turn of the month effect and the day of the week effect.

Miller (1987), in analyzing the daily effect, presents the hypothesis that net buying and selling of shares may not be evenly distributed across the days of the week. This imbalance is caused by the presence of the weekend which, he suggests, permits individual investors the additional opportunity to analyze portfolio rebalancing decisions. Because brokers often do <u>not</u> initiate sell decisions, Miller suggests individuals must initiate this activity on their own time and that they have more time to arrive at such decisions over the weekend. Institutional investors analyze information, in general, during business hours. Therefore, their transactions should be evenly balanced across the week and should not concentrate on one day. Miller suggests that individual buy transactions are to a large extent initiated by brokers and tend to be evenly distributed over the week. The result is that on Monday, because of individual investors, there is an excess of sell orders creating downward price pressure for the day.

Other authors have offered the explanation that the effect being witnessed is a "closed market" effect which induces a negative price reaction following the event. This has been tested by French (1980) and later by Rogalski (1984) by observing the price patterns following holidays. French concludes that the price pattern is not due to a closed market, given that the rate of return on days following mid-week holidays was positive.

Keim and Stambaugh (1984) tested whether the day-of-the-week effect is not due to systematic differences between "true" prices and the actual closing prices recorded on the NYSE and AMEX exchanges. On the exchanges, the last transaction often involves a specialist thus, the closing price often represents a bid or ask price rather than the "true" price. Keim and Stambaugh took a sample of stocks traded over the counter and used bid to bid prices to compute rates of return. Their results, free of the bid-ask noise problem, confirmed the day-of-the-week effect; rates of return were negative on Monday's and large on the last trading day of the week.

One possible explanation of the day-of-the-week effect revolves around the settlement procedures and was proposed by Lakonishok and Levi (1982). They note that stocks purchased on business days other than Friday give the buyer eight calender days before losing funds in exchange for the securities. However, payment for stocks purchased on Friday will, in general, occur on the second Monday following the trade, or ten calendar days latter. Therefore, buyers are willing to pay more on Fridays than on other days by the amount of two days interest, thus forcing up prices. When Monday's trading opens, a price reversal will occur due to the absence of the two extra settlement days. This argument does fit the pattern of the observed data, however even after adjusting the data for interest rates there is still a day-of-the-week effect.

A completely different approach to investigating the weekend effect was used by Coursey and Dyl (1986). They used a laboratory market experiment and introduced interruptions in the trading process. The results, from the laboratory experiment were consistent with the weekend effect. The prices on days before trading was interrupted were significantly higher than on other days.

5. Additional Seasonals in Stock Returns

Quite a number of additional seasonal patterns have recently received attention in the literature. We will review some of these seasonals. Early on in anomalies research, Fields (1934) found a high frequency of price increases before holidays. Later, Roll (1983) observed a high rate of return on the last trading day of December and Lakonishok and Smidt (1987) found high rates of return around Christmas. Ariel (1985) and Lakonishok and Smidt (1987) conducted an extensive investigation of rates of return before holidays (the holiday effect). They find very high rates of return on the last trading day before a holiday. For example, Lakonishok and Smidt based on 90 years of Dow Jones data found that the pre-holiday price increase is 23 times greater than the price increase on a typical day. Over the last 90 years more than 50 percent of the capital gains on the Dow Jones index occurred on the 10 pre-holidays (approximately 10 per year).

Another interesting finding is the turn-of-the-month effect. Ariel (1985), for the period 1963-1982 divided the month into two parts and compared the cumulative returns. The results were startling. The rate of return in the first part of the month was positive and in the second part of the month negative. All the monthly rate of return was compressed in the first part of the month. Lakonishok and Smidt (1987) sharpened Ariel's results. Using Dow Jones data for a period of 90 years, they found that the price increase for four days around the turn of the month, starting with the last day of the prior month, is .47 percent. The average monthly price increase in their sample was .35 percent (ignoring dividends). Therefore, the Dow Jones index goes up around the turn of the month and falls during the remaining period.

An entertaining anomaly, with an explanation, is discussed in a recent paper by Kolb and Rodriquez (1987). They examine whether the returns on Friday the Thirteenth differ from the returns of other Fridays. From previous studies, we know that the returns on Friday are high relative to a typical day. They find that the return on Friday the thirteenth is negative and significantly lower than for other Friday's; if Friday falls on the thirteenth, it then becomes a Monday! The authors uncovered the frightening "Friday the Thirteenth" effect. The explanation in this case is very simple and provided by the authors,

> "Superstition has a long history as an influential and deep-rooted force in many societies. Stories concerning sorcery, black cats, witches, Halloween, and other such topics continue to attract the interest of the general public, as witnessed by the popularity of recent books and movies, such as Friday the Thirteenth Part I, Part II, ..., Part VI (so far!). Given these scary facts, it seems natural to ask whether superstition may play a role in the performance of the securities markets."

Based on Kolb and Rodriquez's study, the answer is yes!

However, Kolb and Rodriquez's research may be indicative of the noise problem referred to earlier in this paper. Kolb and Rodriquez relied on CRSP value-weighted and equally-weighted indices limited to the time period of 1962 through 1985 to arrive at their results. Dyl and Maberly (1988) expand this time period to capture the S&P 500 index from 1940 through 1987. They document a strong negative Friday the thirteenth effect for the decade of the 1970's. Yet for the decades of the 1940's, 50's, 60's and the partial interval 1980-1987, the mean returns were positive, though not statistically different from zero.

6. Conclusions

In this survey, we focused on seasonal anomalies in the return patterns of various financial assets, with an emphasis on stocks. We explored annual, monthly, and daily seasonalities and seasonalities on special days such as holidays. The existing empirical research provides strong evidence of various predictable patterns in returns. Specifically, predictable return patterns have been identified in long horizon returns. A mean reverting behavior was observed, especially for holding periods between 3 to 5 years. The January effect was identified as a monthly seasonal in which smaller firms are traditionally found to perform exceptionally well relative to large firms. The day-of-the-week effect was extensively documented as well; stock returns tend to be negative on Monday and relatively high on the last trading day of the week. Returns were also found to be particularly high on the last trading day before a holiday and around the turn of the month, the holiday and turn-of-the-month effects respectively.

Seasonal patterns have been identified in an overwhelming number of papers using different time periods, applying various statistical techniques, using equity and non-equity assets not only in the U.S. but also across world markets. The fact that seasonal patterns continue to appear in such diverse data sets provides indication that some form of investor behavior is the underlying cause. The volume of evidence appears to reject the possibility of spurious fit in the data. Hence, we should take these anomalies seriously and look for explanations.

Several papers have searched for an understanding of why such predictable patterns in returns do occur. It is hard to imagine that any single factor can explain all of these effects. However several factors seem worthy of investigation and form the basis of the avenues being explored in current research.

DeBondt and Thaler's overreaction hypothesis is a possible explanation for the long time horizon seasonalities. Their hypothesis, subsequently explored by others, suggests that prices follow a reverting pattern. In support of this finding, experimental psychology research has found that people do tend to overreact to dramatic news. Further support of overreaction is contained in the literature concerning excess volatility in the stock market by Shiller (1981). If, as suggested by DeBondt and Thaler, overreaction by investors occurs, we would expect to identify excess volatility in asset returns.

Tax-loss selling appears to be a partial explanation for the January effect. Individual investors, who, as a group, own a greater proportion of their wealth in smaller firms than others, are motivated for tax reasons to become active in the market at the end of the year. Accordingly, evidence on the ratio of buy to sell orders for individual investors is shown to be low in December, yet reverses and become unusually high in January.

Performance evaluation and the incentive structure of professional portfolio managers may also explain some of the January seasonal. It is widely perceived that portfolio managers toward the end of the year "dress up" their portfolios by getting rid of "embarrassing" holdings. In particular, small, obscure companies, especially if they did not perform well in the past, are strong candidates to be dumped toward year's end. The evidence shows that these firms do have higher trading volume at year end and also receive the benefits of the January effect.

The turn-of-the-month effect may very well be affected by the flow of funds into financial markets. The flow of funds into the markets, for example pension reinvestments and bonuses or wages of investors, may not be evenly distributed across the month. Ogden (1987) argues that a preferred habitat for investors occurs toward the end of the month because of standardized payment systems. Buying (selling) pressure from uneven timing of the flow of funds may explain some of the seasonalities such as the turn-of-the-month effect. Documentation of the flow of funds for institutional and individual may well be revealing.

Several authors have offered various explanations for the day-of-the-week effect. One explanation currently being explore is related to the arrival of news. There are systematic timing differences between the arrival of good and bad news. Evidence on unpleasant disclosures shows that it is not evenly distributed; disclosures of bad news are more frequent after markets are closed on Fridays.

Many of the daily seasonalities, when translated to price changes, are, in general, within one tick, or 12.5 cents. This leads to the suspicion that inventory adjustments by specialists and short sellers can potentially provide at least a partial explain for some of the anomalies.

The mystery of the anomalies has inspired a great deal of research into documenting the unexpected return patterns evident in asset prices. We have only reviewed those pertaining to seasonal return patterns. Many of the anomalies, including the seasonals, are intertwined with effects which are not necessarily additive in the direction one might expect. The reader is encouraged, with this paper as an introduction, to explore these interrelationships further.

The fact that the returns were originally referred to as "unexpected" derives from our profession's adherence to the principles of market efficiency. Given that enhanced statistical procedures, boredom, and data snooping are not accountable for the anomalies, we may be more inclined to acknowledge the fact that return irregularities do indeed exist. Yet for as strong as the evidence becomes, none completely nullifies the theorems of market efficiency. As a profession though, a new era in redefining what market efficient behavior is may well be upon us.

Ariel, R., 1987, High Stock Returns Before Holidays, Unpublished working paper (Department of Finance, Massachusetts Institute of Technology).

Ariel, R., 1987, A Monthly Effect in Stock Returns, Journal of Financial Economics 18, 161-174.

Black, F., 1986, Noise, Journal of Finance 41, 529-543.

Constantinides, G.M., 1984, Optimal Stock Trading with Personal Taxes, Journal of Financial Economics 13, 65-89.

Cornell, B., 1985, The Weekly Pattern in Stock Returns, Cash vs. Futures, Journal of Finance 40, 583-588.

Coursey, D. and E. Dyl, Price Effects of Trading Interruptions in an Experimental Market, Unpublished working paper (University of Wyoming).

Cross. K., 1973, The Behavior of Stock Prices on Fridays and Mondays, Financial Analyst Journal 29, 67-69.

DeBondt, W. and R. Thaler, 1985, Does the Stock Market Overreact?, Journal of Finance 40, 793-805.

Dyl, M., 1977, Capital Gains Taxation and Year-End Stock Market Behavior, Journal of Finance 32, 165-175.

Dyl, M. E. Maberly, 1986, The Weekly Pattern in Stock Index Futures: A Further Note, Journal of Finance 41, 1149-1152.

Dyl, E.A., and E. Maberly, 1988, Friday the Thirteenth: The Anomaly That Isn't There, Unpublished working paper (University of Arizona).

Fama, E., and K. French, 1986, Common Factors in the Serial Correlation of Stock Returns, Unpublished working paper No. 200 (University of Chicago).

Fama, E., and K. French, 1987, Permanent and Temporary Components of Stock Prices, Center for Research in Security Prices, (University of Chicago).

Fields, M.J., 1931, Stock Prices: A Problem in Verification, Journal of Business 7, 415-418.

Fields, M.J., 1934, Security Prices and Stock Exchange Holidays in Relation to Short Selling, Journal of Business 4, 328-338.

Flannery, M. and A. Protopapadakis, 1988, From T-Bills to Common Stocks: Investigating the Generality of Intra-week return seasonality, Journal of Finance forthcoming.

French, K., 1980, Stock Returns and the Weekend Effect, Journal of Financial Economics 8, 55-69.

Gibbons, M. and P. Hess, 1981, Day of the Week Effects and Asset Returns, Journal of Business 54, 579-596.

Gilovich, T., R. Vallone, A. Tversky, 1985, The Hot Hand in Basketball: On the Misperception of Random Sequences, Cognitive Psychology 17, 295-314.

Gultekin, M. and N. Gultekin, 1983, Stock Market Seasonality, International Evidence, Journal of Financial Economics 12, 469-481.

Harris, L., 1986, A Transaction Data Study of Weekly and Intradaily Patterns in Stock Returns, Journal of Financial Economics 16, 99-117.

Haugen, R. and J. Lakonishok, 1987, The Incredible January Effect: The Unsolved Mystery of the Stock Market, (Dow Jones Irwin, Homewood, Illinois).
Haugen, R. and D. Wichern, 1973, The Diametric Effects of the Capital Gains Tax on the Stability of Stock Prices, Journal of Finance 28, 987-996.
Jaffe, J., and R. Westerfield, 1985, The Weekend Effect in Common Stock Returns: The International Evidence, Journal of Finance 40, 433-454.
Jones, C., D. Pearce, J. Wilson, 1987, Can Tax-Loss Selling Explain the January Effect? A Note, Journal of Finance 42, 453-461.
Keim, D. and R. Stambaugh, 1984, A Further Investigation of the Weekend Effect in Stock Returns, Journal of Finance 39, 819-840.
Kolb, R. W. and R. J. Rodriquez, 1987, Friday the Thirteen, 'Part VII' - A Note, Journal of Finance 42, 1385-1387.
Lakonishok, J. and M. Levi, 1982, Weekend Effects on Stock Returns: A Note, Journal of Finance 37, 883-889.
Lakonishok and Smidt, 1984, Volume and Turn-of-the-Year Behavior, Journal of Financial Economics 13, 883-889.
Lakonishok and Smidt, 1988, Are Seasonal Anomalies Real?, A Ninety Year Perspective, Unpublished working paper, (Cornell University).
Merton, R., 1985, On the Current State of the Stock Market Rationality Hypothesis, Unpublished working paper, #1717-85.
Miller, E., 1987, Why a Weekend Effect, Unpublished working paper, (University of New Orleans).
Ogden, J., 1987, The End of the Month as a Preferred Habitat: A Test of Operational Efficiency in the Money Market, Journal of Financial and Quantitative Analysis 22, 329-343.
Osborne, M.F.M., 1962, Periodic Structure in the Brownian Motion of the Stock Market, Operations Research 10, 345-379.
Penman, S.H., 1987, The Distribution of Earnings News Over Time and Seasonalities in Aggregate Stock Returns, Journal of Financial Economics 18, 199-228.
Poterba, J. and L. Summers, 1987, Mean Reversion in Stock Prices: Evidence and Implications, NBER Working Paper No. 2343.
Ritter, J., 1987, An Explanation of the Turn of the Year Effect, Unpublished working paper (University of Michigan).
Reinganum, M., and A.C. Shapiro, 1987, Taxes and Stock Return Seasonality: Evidence from the London Stock Exchange, Journal of Business 60, 281-295.
Rogalski R., 1984, New Findings Regarding Day of the Week Returns of Trading and Non-Trading Periods, Journal of Finance 39, 1603-1614.
Rozeff, M., 1985, The December Effect in Stock Returns and the Tax-Loss Selling Hypothesis, Unpublished working paper No. 85-18 (University of Iowa).

Rozeff, M., 1985, The Tax-Loss Selling Hypothesis: New Evidence From Share Shifts, Unpublished working paper No. 85-16 (University of Iowa).
Rozeff, M., W. Kinney, 1976, Capital Market Seasonality: The Case of Stock Market Returns, Journal of Financial Economics 3, 379-402.
Shiller, R.J., 1981, Do stock Prices Move too much to be Justified by Subsequent Changes in Dividends?, American Economic Review 71, 421-436.
Schultz, P., 1983, Transaction Costs and the Small Firm Effect: A Comment, Journal of Financial Economics 12, 81-88.
Smirlock, M., 1985, Seasonality and Bond Market Returns, Journal of Portfolio Management, 42-44.
Wachtel, S., 1942, Certain Observations on Seasonal Movements in Stock Prices, Journal of Business 15, 184-193.

David Ikenberry and Josef Lakonishok "Seasonal Anomalies in Financial Markets : A Survey"

Comments by John O'Hanlon

Ikenberry and Lakonishok (IL) are to be commended for producing a thorough review of the now voluminous "Stock Market Seasonality" literature. In my discussion I propose to refer to some of the non-U.S. studies which were not referred to by IL but which I feel deserve consideration in a forum of this sort.

IL's preliminary discussion centres on possible causes for the high volume of seasonality research in recent years and refers to a number of potential pitfalls for researchers in this area. Computing power and improved quality and availability of data have enabled previously unrecognisable patterns to be discovered. However, with all this computer power, patterns can always be found, even in random series. Maybe the only studies that appear in print are the ones that commit Type I errors. Also many of the U.S. studies may be based on overlapping series from the same data sets and may not therefore constitute independent corroboration of each other. These points invite discussion of the evidence on stock market seasonality in non-US markets. Tests based on national equity markets which have attracted relatively little empirical research are less vulnerable to the accusation that they are using the same data as that used in previous studies to produce apparently "new" results. Thus they are more convincing as corroborative evidence of the existence of phenomena such as weekend and turn of the year effects than additional U.S. studies would be. Non-US markets are also attractive to researchers because they provide differing institutional and fiscal environments in which hypothesised explanations for seasonal patterns can be tested. However, researchers of such markets face considerable problems. They do not generally benefit from the quality of data and ease of access, particularly to daily data, that researchers of the U.S. market enjoy. Also the results of studies on some markets may have to be treated with some caution because of the relatively small number of frequently traded shares. As a result of these problems many of the analyses of non-US markets have been conducted on the basis of stock market indices, which may themselves be suspect, rather than on the basis of

NATO ASI Series, Vol. F54
A Reappraisal of the Efficiency of Financial Markets
Edited by Rui M.C. Guimaraes et al.

company level data. Thus, many of the hypotheses regarding seasonality remain to be tested in those markets.

So far as they go, the non-US results suggest that the seasonal patterns observed in the US are present elsewhere. I have seen "day of the week" tests of varying levels of sophistication for a large number of countries. In some cases the hypothesis of equality of mean returns is not rejected but it is very rare to find a set of results that do not convey the impression that returns are low early in the week and high on the last trading day of the week. In addition to the Jaffe and Westerfield study referred to by IL, one could cite Ball and Bowers (1988) (Australia), Condoyanni, McLeay and O'Hanlon (1988) (Greece), Frantzmann (1987) (West Germany), O'Hanlon and Papaspirou (1988) (Australia, Singapore, Japan, Hong Kong, France, West Germany, U.K., Canada), Santesmases (1986) (Spain) and Theobald and Price (1984) (U.K.). These studies have not generated any complete explanation for the day of the week effect, though some of the evidence suggests that settlement procedures are a contributory factor in markets where the settlement period is a fixed number of trading days. Although they may have failed to find a complete answer to the puzzle, the recurrent patterns that these studies reveal have certainly done something to confirm the belief that the "day of the week" effect is more than the result of a Type I error. Studies of Australian, Far Eastern and European data reveal the interesting finding that in many of the markets where closing prices are recorded before Wall Street opens a negative Tuesday effect is observed. There is thus some suggestion that the pattern of daily seasonality in those markets is Wall Street driven although Ball and Bowers' Australian results suggest that the lagged weekend effect in such markets may be due to discontinuous trading.

International studies of monthly seasonality again provide further evidence on the turn of the year effect. The Gultekin and Gultekin paper shows that, of 16 non-US markets, 13 have their highest mean return in January and, in addition to the Reinganum and Shapiro (U.K.) paper, cross-sectional studies by Brown, Keim, Kleidon and Marsh (1983) (Australia), Levis (1985) (U.K.), Santesmases (1985 (Spain), Van den Bergh and Wessels (1985) (Netherlands) all show January seasonals. The evidence from Australia and the U.K., both of which have tax year ends other than December, suggests a seasonal both in

January and in the first month of the tax year. In the Netherlands, where the tax system is such that a significant seasonal due to tax loss selling is not predicted, a strong January seasonal is found. The existence of non-January seasonals which coincide with non-January tax year ends and of January seasonals which do not seem to be tax generated confirm that, whilst tax loss selling is a significant cause of monthly seasonality, it is not the only significant cause. The argument that the January seasonals in non-US markets may be due to international arbitrage of the tax induced January seasonal in the U.S. is countered by Brown, Keim, Kleidon and Marsh who observe that ".... it seems difficult to reconcile an integrated capital market, that functions so well that a U.S. tax-induced January seasonal shows up in even penny stocks in Australia, with simultaneous mispricing of securities to create the original U.S. January seasonal"

A related area to which non-US studies have contributed is seasonality in risk premia, a phenomenon observed in the U.S. by Tinic and West (1984, 1986). Corhay, Hawawini and Michel (1987) (U.S., U.K., France and Belgium) confirm that, in the U.S., January is the only month with a significantly positive risk premium. In the case of Belgium, significantly positive premia are found for January and April only. For France, although the average value of the January slope coefficient is not significantly different from zero, it is the highest of the year. The only month for which the U.K. exhibits a significantly positive risk premium is April which is the first month of the tax year. Additionally, the European markets seem to have negative non- January risk premiums. Risk premium seasonality is also observed in the West German market by Frantzmann (1987).

<u>References</u> (where not cited by IL)

Ball, R. and J. Bowers, 1988, "Daily seaonsals in equity and fixed interest returns : Australian evidence and tests of plausible hypotheses", in E. Dimson (Ed.) <u>Stock Market Anomalies,</u> Cambridge University Press, 1988.

Brown, P., D. Keim, A. Kleidon and T. Marsh, 1983, "Stock Return Seasonalities and the Tax-Loss Selling Hypothesis : Analysis of the Arguments and Australian Evidence", <u>Journal of Financial Economics,</u> 12, pp.105-128.

Condoyanni, L., S. McLeay and J. O'Hanlon, 1988, "An Investigation of Daily Seasonality in the Greek Equity Market", published in this volume.

Frantzmann, H., 1987, "Return and Pricing Seasonalities in the German Stock Market" presented at the conference of the European Finance Association, Madrid, 1987.

Levis, M., 1985, "Are small firms big performers?" The Investment Analyst, 76, April 1985, pp.21-26.

O'Hanlon, J. and P. Papaspirou, 1988, "The Daily Behaviour of National Equity Markets : Seasonal Patterns and Inter-relationships", forthcoming in The Investment Analyst, 1988.

Santesmases, M. 1986, "An investigation of the Spanish Stock Market Seasonalities" Journal of Business Finance and Accounting, 13(2), pp.267-276.

Theobald, M. and V. Price, 1984, "Seasonality Estimation in Thin Markets", Journal of Finance, 39, pp.377-392.

Tinic, S., and R. West, 1984, "Risk and Return : January versus the rest of the year", Journal of Finance, 13, pp.561-574.

Tinic, S. and R. West, 1986, "Risk Return and Equilibrium : A Revisit", Journal of Political Economy, 94, pp.126-147.

Van den Bergh, W. and R. Wessels, 1985, "Stock Market Seasonality and Taxes : An examination of the tax loss selling hypothesis", Journal of Business Finance and Accounting, 12 (4), pp.515-530.

Earnings Yield and Size Effects:
Unconditional and Conditional Estimates

Donald B. Keim
Finance Department
The Wharton School
2300 SH/DH
University of Pennsylvania
Philadelphia, PA 19104

This paper reexamines the interrelation between the E/P and size effects over a substantially longer period (1951-1986) than previously examined, and estimates the unconditional magnitude of the effects for comparison with similar results reported elsewhere. Given the increasing evidence that the magnitude of these effects is time period specific, we also estimate the effects conditional on an ex ante observable variable that is intended to capture changing expectations about future returns. The results indicate that the ex ante variable reliably predicts the expost magnitudes of the E/P and size effects--especially in January.

Keywords: Conditional Returns; Earnings/Price Ratios; Equity Markets; Seasonality; Size Effect; Unconditional Returns.

NATO ASI Series, Vol. F54
A Reappraisal of the Efficiency of Financial Markets
Edited by Rui M. C. Guimaraes et al.

1. Introduction

Some of the most enigmatic empirical findings in finance concern the anomalies of firm size (Banz (1981)) and the earnings to price ratio (Basu (1977)). Despite repeated efforts, researchers have not been able to disentangle the two effects.[1] The inability of the existing literature to unravel the two effects may be attributed, in part, to the use of relatively short periods of analysis and to the failure to separate January from the rest of the year. Use of the Compustat files for retrieval of earnings limits most studies to the twenty-year window of historical data supplied by Compustat,[2] a relatively short period when compared to the sixty years of CRSP monthly data that are used to document the size effect. The recent release by Compustat of post-1950 data, for both currently-covered and deleted companies, substantially lengthens the available period.

This study has two parts. The first part reexamines the unconditional relation between the size and E/P effects with: (a) a substantially longer sample period, 1951-1986; (b) data that have no significant survivor biases; and (c) analysis of portfolio returns with an emphasis on the important

---

[1]For example, Reinganum (1981), Basu (1983), Cook and Rozeff (1984) and Banz and Breen (1986) examine the size effect and the earnings to price ratio (E/P) effect jointly. Reinganum concludes that the E/P effect vanishes when size is simultaneously considered. Basu argues that the earnings to price effect subsumes the size effect when both variables are jointly considered. The results of Cook and Rozeff are different still, with stock returns being jointly related to both size and the E/P ratio. Banz and Breen find a market value effect but no independent E/P effect across all months, a result similar to that of Reinganum. Only Cook and Rozeff investigate January and non-January months separately. Their research suggests that both the size and E/P effects are significant, both in January and in the rest of the year.

[2]Reinganum (1981), Basu (1983), Cook and Rozeff (1984) and Banz and Breen (1986) examine 14, 17 3/4, 13 3/4, and 7 3/4 years, respectively. As a result, documentation of the interaction between the E/P and size effects has been limited to the 1963-1983 period. Basu (1977), who examines only the E/P effect, uses the 1956 to 1971 period.

differences between January and other months. Over the entire period, the earnings yield effect is apparent in both January and the other eleven months. Conversely, the size effect is observed in the data only in January.

Jaffe, Keim and Westerfield (1988) reexamine the findings of previous researchers with the data used here and their analysis suggests that the results of prior studies (see footnote 1) conflict because the magnitude of the two effects is period-specific. That is, in some periods the size effect dominates the E/P effect, and vice versa in other periods. In response to these findings, the second part of this paper examines the conditional nature of the size and E/P effects. In particular, we use one of the ex ante observable variables proposed by Keim and Stambaugh (1986) to examine the extent to which size- and E/P-related portfolio returns change predictably with changes in the ex ante variable. The results indicate that the ex ante variable used here, which proxies for the level of (small market value) asset prices, reliably predicts the ex post magnitudes of these effects--especially in January.

Data collection and portfolio selection procedures are described in section 2. Section 3 contains portfolio evidence for the unconditional estimates of the size and E/P effects and their interaction. Regression models for conditional mean returns are examined in the penultimate section. The paper concludes with a brief summary.

2. Data

Research on the E/P effect is subject to two potential biases associated with the use of earnings data from Compustat files such as the Primary-Supplementary-Tertiary (PST) data file used here. Banz and Breen (1986) refer to these biases as the ex post selection bias and the look-ahead bias. The ex post selection bias arises for two reasons. First, the PST file excludes nonsurviving firms. Second, when entering a firm, Compustat provides its full accounting history. The look-ahead bias occurs when the researcher uses data not yet available to the investor, i.e., using December net income in January when it is not available to investors until several months later.

Banz and Breen find that estimation of the E/P effect is not very sensitive to the ex post selection bias but quite sensitive to the look-ahead bias. Their analysis (e.g., see their Table III) suggests that much of the measured E/P effect is due to the failure to account for the look-ahead bias. They conclude that the look-ahead bias can be avoided with the annual Compustat data by limiting the sample to Dec. 31 fiscal closers and by computing E/P ratios using year-end earnings and March 31 prices.

Data collection and portfolio selection procedures used here are chosen to minimize these biases. Data on returns, price and shares outstanding are taken from the University of Chicago Center for Research in Security Prices (CRSP) monthly stock return and master files for the 1951 to 1962 period and from the CRSP daily return and master files for the 1963 to 1986 period. Use of the daily tapes over the latter period permits inclusion of AMEX firms, thereby substantially increasing the number of sample firms. During this latter period, daily stock returns are linked together within the month to compute a monthly return.

Earnings per share are obtained from the Compustat PST files (currently active firms) and the complementary Research file (firms that "disappeared") for the 1967 to 1986 period and from the "Backdata" versions of these two files for the 1950-1966 period. We define earnings per share as the annual net income in the calendar year (exclusive of extraordinary items) divided by the number of shares outstanding. A merged file is generated which includes all firms that appear both in the CRSP and PST files. Since Compustat's PST file contains only the annual earnings reported at the most recent fiscal year end, we avoid "stale" earnings information by considering only those firms with fiscal years ending December 31. The number of firms meeting these criteria ranges from 352 in 1950 to 1309 in 1974.

To provide a basis for comparison with previous studies and to motivate the discussion below on the interaction between the size and E/P effects, we first present evidence on the (unconditional) size and E/P effects separately. Panels A and B in Table 1 present summary statistics for portfolios created on the basis of market value of equity (size) and the ratio of earnings to price (E/P). To maintain consistency with the results presented later, the sample of firms used here includes only firms that end their fiscal year on December 31. Ranking of securities and portfolio composition is performed each March 31, and equal-weighted returns for each of the portfolios are computed monthly over the next twelve months.

The now-familiar size (Panel A) and E/P (Panel B) effects are evident in Table 1. The smaller is the average market value of equity of the securities in a portfolio, the higher are the average returns. Likewise, the higher is the average E/P of a portfolio, the higher are the average returns. Interestingly, the average size and E/P columns indicate that small (large) firms tend to be high (low) E/P firms, and vice versa. The next section addresses the question of whether the size and E/P effects are two separate phenomena or, alternatively, whether they both are the manifestation of the same underlying phenomenon. In regards to the latter conjecture, note the strong association between both size and E/P and average price per share in the rightmost column in both panels. Perhaps a single underlying phenomenon, for which price per share is a good proxy, may in fact be at work.

Table 1

A. Size Effect

Average Monthly Returns, Market Values of Equity, E/P Ratios and Prices for Ten Market Value Portfolios of NYSE and AMEX Stocks for the period from April 1951 to December 1986[a]

Market Value Portfolio	Monthly Returns (%) Mean	Monthly Returns (%) Std. Error	Mean Market Value[b] ($ Million)	Mean E/P (%)[c]	Mean Price/Share
Smallest	1.79	(0.32)	$10.2	1.76	12.72
2	1.53	(0.28)	23.3	5.74	18.65
3	1.22	(0.28)	39.8	7.41	22.65
4	1.35	(0.26)	64.2	8.89	27.08
5	1.25	(0.24)	103.2	8.76	30.89
6	1.21	(0.23)	164.7	8.74	34.38
7	1.22	(0.23)	272.9	8.60	38.01
8	1.17	(0.22)	457.7	8.27	42.88
9	1.03	(0.21)	801.1	8.49	53.37
Largest	0.99	(0.20)	3604.7	7.89	69.60

B. E/P EFFECT

Average Monthly Returns, Market Values of Equity, E/P Ratios and Prices for Eleven Earnings/Price Portfolios of NYSE and AMEX Stocks for the Period from April 1951 to December 1986[a]

E/P Portfolio	Monthly Returns (%) Mean	Monthly Returns (%) Std. Error	Mean E/P (%)[c]	Mean Market Value[b] ($ Million)	Mean Price/Share
Highest E/P	1.59	(0.25)	17.71	$365.6	$26.05
2	1.59	(0.24)	13.18	428.0	28.90
3	1.50	(0.22)	11.65	557.0	30.78
4	1.36	(0.22)	10.47	474.5	32.07
5	1.17	(0.22)	9.48	582.0	34.15
6	1.14	(0.22)	8.56	705.4	35.84
7	1.05	(0.22)	7.64	679.7	36.74
8	1.10	(0.24)	6.59	669.6	39.57
9	1.11	(0.25)	5.33	792.2	44.40
Lowest E/P	1.19	(0.28)	3.17	874.8	55.11
Negative Earnings	1.39	(0.39)	-21.18	80.8	11.86

a. The sample includes December 31 fiscal closer only; portfolios are rebalanced at March 31 in each year.

b. Market value of common equity is measured at the end of March in each year.

c. E/P is measured by year-end earnings divided by the common stock price at the end of March in each year.

3. Interaction between Size and E/P Effects: Portfolio Evidence

The size-E/P portfolios used in this section are created using two separate ranking procedures:

<u>Procedure I</u>. Firms are ranked on the ratio of year-end earnings to share price at the end of March in each year and placed into one of six groups. Group 0 includes all securities with negative earnings and groups one to five contain securities with positive earnings. Stocks with the lowest E/P ratios are placed into Group 1, and those with the highest E/P are in Group 5. Next, the stocks in each E/P group are ranked on the March 31 market value of their common stock outstanding. Each E/P group is then divided into five subgroups on the basis of size. Subgroup 1 includes the smallest stocks and subgroup 5 includes the largest stocks. This procedure results in thirty subgroups or portfolios, each of which is updated annually.[3]

---

[3]Note that the 5 portfolios formed from securities with negative earnings are of equal size. Similarly, the 25 portfolios formed from securities with positive earnings are of equal size. However, the number of securities in each of the first 5 portfolios differs from the number in each of the last 25 portfolios.

Reinganum's (1981) procedure ranks all stocks by market value and divides the sample into quintiles. Quintile one contains the smallest stocks, and quintile five includes the largest stocks. All stocks are then reranked by their E/P ratios and divided into quintiles. Quintile one contains the stocks with the lowest earnings to price ratio (negative earnings to price ratios are excluded). A portfolio is formed by collecting all stocks which are in both quintile 1 when ranked on size and quintile 1 when ranked on E/P. This procedure is repeated until 25 groups were formed.

Basu (1983) ranks stocks first on E/P, creating five quintiles. For the securities within a given E/P quintile, he then ranks on size, creating five size quintiles. One of the above twenty-five portfolios can be denoted as portfolio (i, j), indicating it has the ith ranking among E/P quintiles and the jth ranking among the size quintiles within the ith E/P quintile. At this point, his methodology is similar to our Procedure I. He then creates the jth "randomized" size portfolio by combining each of the five portfolios with the same jth size ranking. This procedure yields five size quintiles. The entire procedure is reversed to create five randomized E/P quintiles.

Cook and Rozeff use several grouping procedures. Banz and Breen (1986) rank securities into five size quintiles. Within each quintile, securities are ranked according to E/P ratios.

Equal-weighted returns for each of the 30 portfolios are computed monthly during the year, starting on April 1 and ending on the following March 31. We begin tracking portfolio returns in April since firms do not generally release annual earnings numbers immediately following year end. Thus, our procedure should avoid the look-ahead bias. Both Basu and Cook-Rozeff also begin tracking portfolio returns in April. However, Reinganum starts the return period in January, immediately after the grouping period.

Procedure II. This procedure is identical to procedure I except that firms are ranked on market value first and then ranked on E/P. Since the results from the two procedures are quite similar, all reported results are from procedure I unless otherwise stated.

We first present average characteristics for the 30 portfolios for the period from March 31, 1951 to December 31, 1986. Average monthly returns and beta estimates are reported in Table 2, and Table 3 contains average market values and E/P ratios.

For the subset of stocks with positive earnings, two relations between the ranking variables and returns emerge in Table 2. First, returns are negatively related to market value. This relation is nearly monotonic in each of the 5 columns of positive earnings stocks. The bottom row of the table, which contains the mean difference in return (and standard error of the difference) between the smallest and largest firms within each E/P category, reports that the difference between the extreme portfolios (i.e., the size effect) is significantly positive across all E/P categories. Second, average returns tend to be positively related to the E/P ratio. The mean difference in return between the highest and lowest E/P portfolio, reported in the rightmost column, indicates a positive and significant E/P effect in each size classification. The lowest (but positive) E/P portfolios appear to be an

Table 2

Average Monthly Percent Returns (Standard Errors) <Betas>[a] for 30 Portfolios of NYSE and AMEX Firms Ranked first by E/P Ratio and then Size over the Period from April 1951 to December 1986

	Earnings to Price Ratio[b]						
Size[c]	≤ 0	Lowest	2	3	4	Highest	Highest-Lowest
Smallest	1.52 (0.56) <1.32>[d]	1.62 (0.34) <1.27>	1.36 (0.30) <1.18>	1.52 (0.27) <1.09>	1.68 (0.27) <1.08>	1.90 (0.29) <1.09>	0.28 (0.08)
2	1.08 (0.43) <1.29>	1.14 (0.31) <1.29>	1.15 (0.27) <1.19>	1.13 (0.24) <1.04>	1.42 (0.25) <1.06>	1.62 (0.27) <1.10>	0.48 (0.18)
3	1.13 (0.39) <1.29>	1.12 (0.28) <1.28>	0.99 (0.24) <1.08>	1.09 (0.22) <1.02>	1.44 (0.22) <.95>	1.52 (0.25) <1.06>	0.40 (0.18)
4	0.72 (0.39) <1.49>	1.02 (0.26) <1.20>	1.01 (0.22) <1.05>	1.10 (0.21) <.97>	1.43 (0.22) <.98>	1.47 (0.25) <1.08>	0.45 (0.18)
Largest	1.21 (0.43) <1.60>	0.89 (0.24) <1.11>	0.90 (0.21) <1.02>	0.97 (0.21) <.98>	1.24 (0.21) <.98>	1.43 (0.23) <1.03>	0.54 (0.18)
Smallest-Largest	0.31 (0.54)	0.73 (0.28)	0.45 (0.21)	0.56 (0.19)	0.44 (0.18)	0.47 (0.18)	

a. OLS betas are computed with the value-weighted CRSP index.

b. E/P is measured by year-end earnings divided by the common stock price at the end of March in each year.

c. Size is measured by the market value of common equity at the end of March in each year, and reported in millions of dollars.

d. In several of the earlier years, the number of negative earnings firms in our sample is insufficient to create 5 portfolios with multiple securities. Thus, beta estimates for the negative earnings portfolios are reported for the 1969-1986 period only.

Table 3

Average E/P Ratios and Market Value of Equity (Size) for 30 Portfolios of NYSE and AMEX Ranked First by E/P Ratio and then Size Over the Period from April 1951 to December 1986.

A. Average E/P Ratio (in percent)[a]

	Earnings to Price Ratio					
Size	≤ 0	Lowest	1	2	3	Highest
Smallest	-27.39	3.77	7.11	9.08	11.15	15.94
2	-25.31	4.18	7.13	9.07	11.10	15.97
3	-18.76	4.39	7.17	9.01	11.13	15.48
4	-12.10	4.44	7.14	9.01	11.07	15.61
Largest	-16.84	4.47	7.10	9.02	11.03	14.94

B. Mean (Median) Market Value of Equity[b]

	Earnings to Price Ratio					
Size	≤ 0	Lowest	2	3	4	Highest
Smallest	4.76 (4.56)	20.18 (19.34)	25.10 (24.15)	25.09 (24.66)	19.95 (19.96)	16.16 (15.68)
2	10.31 (9.79)	74.29 (68.21)	83.96 (81.11)	77.14 (73.41)	56.60 (53.74)	46.88 (45.11)
3	19.96 (19.13)	211.26 (203.83)	205.24 (197.50)	175.23 (165.90)	136.26 (130.02)	107.35 (103.82)
4	43.52 (40.07)	538.71 (506.54)	466.73 (445.43)	419.50 (402.65)	333.16 (320.11)	259.33 (244.53)
Largest	262.43 (148.19)	3095.43 (1682.18)	2454.79 (1278.26)	2306.09 (1102.24)	1897.22 (989.00)	1463.64 (820.38)

a. E/P is measured by year-end earnings divided by the common stock price at the end of March in each year.

b. Size is measured by the market value of common equity at the end of March in each year, and reported in millions of dollars.

exception, however, as the returns in this column are greater than or equivalent to the average returns for portfolios in E/P category 2. The beta estimates for the lowest E/P portfolios tend to be the highest in the table, however, indicating that risk-adjusted "excess" returns may be linearly related to the E/P ratio. Surprisingly, stocks with negative earnings outperform many of the positive earnings portfolios in the other five columns.

Panel A of Table 3 contains the average E/P ratio for each of the 30 portfolios and Panel B presents the mean (median) market value for each of the portfolios. These data reveal two related phenomena. First, market values appear lower in the higher E/P columns, suggesting correlation between the two variables. This finding, which has been pointed out in earlier studies, leads one to question whether the results in Panel A can be explained by one or two independent effects. For example, the smallest firms with the lowest E/P ratios tend to have higher average returns than several higher E/P portfolios in that row, but these firms on average have lower market capitalizations than portfolios 2 or 3 in that row.[4] Second, firms with negative earnings appear to have the lowest market values. Thus, the unusual results in the first column of Table 2 might be explained by a market value effect and not by a separate negative earnings effect.

3.1 Size and E/P Effects: January vs non-January Months

Keim (1983) finds that the size effect is much more pronounced in January relative to the other months. Cook and Rozeff find similar results for the

---

[4]Although high E/P firms tend to be small firms, and vice versa, not all low E/P firms are large firms. In fact, detailed examination of the lowest E/P firms reveals, year-after-year, a heterogeneous mix of very large (IBM, Std. Oil of Calif.) and very small firms. Such a mixture is conspicuously absent in the other levels of E/P since larger firms occupy the intermediate E/P levels while smaller firms dominate the higher E/P categories.

E/P effect. Thus, in Table 4, I report average portfolio returns, as well as differences in mean returns between extreme portfolios in the rightmost and bottom row of each panel, separately for January and for February-December. The same general pattern that was evident in Table 2 is also evident in both panels of Table 4, although the January means in Panel A are larger than the non-January returns in Panel B by a factor of ten. If one accepts the difference in mean between extreme portfolios in a particular row or column as a measure of the E/P and size effect respectively, we can make the following observations: (1) the January size effect is significant in each E/P category, although it tends to be larger for lower E/P's; (2) the January E/P effect is nonexistent among the smallest firms, and is of approximately equal magnitude (and is significant) in the remaining four size classifications; (3) there is a positive and marginally significant E/P effect in the smaller and the largest size categories during non-January months; and (4) consistent with the results of Blume and Stambaugh (1983) there is no size effect outside of January. Thus, while both the E/P and size effects are significant in January, only the E/P effect appears important during the remainder of the year. Further, the results are qualitatively and quantitatively the same when portfolios are formed by first ranking on size and then E/P (i.e., Procedure II in the previous section).

3.2 Size and E/P Effects: Results from Regressions

Most previous attempts to disentangle the E/P and size effects have used portfolio returns like those in Tables 2 and 4 as the basis for their tests. For example, Cook and Rozeff (1985) use ANOVA to test for equality of the mean portfolio returns and Banz and Breen (1986), as well as Tables 2 and 4, test for significance of the difference in return between extreme E/P portfolios. Such tests have shortcomings though. ANOVA may reject equality of mean

Table 4

Average Monthly Percent Returns (Standard Errors) for January and Non-January Months for 30 Portfolios of NYSE and AMEX Firms Ranked first by E/P Ratio and then Size over the Period from April 1951 to December 1986

A. January

Size[b]	Earnings to Price Ratio[a] ≤ 0	Lowest	2	3	4	Highest	Highest-Lowest
Smallest	11.32 (2.53)	8.65 (1.83)	6.46 (1.63)	5.87 (1.36)	6.79 (1.43)	7.46 (1.41)	-1.19 (0.81)
2	9.59 (2.42)	3.94 (1.36)	4.16 (1.27)	4.32 (1.22)	5.77 (1.17)	6.28 (1.34)	2.35 (0.69)
3	8.49 (1.87)	2.02 (1.20)	2.48 (1.12)	2.95 (1.05)	3.86 (1.11)	5.79 (1.29)	3.77 (0.78)
4	7.85 (2.14)	0.86 (1.04)	1.55 (1.03)	2.17 (1.06)	3.64 (1.09)	4.66 (1.22)	3.80 (0.70)
Largest	10.86 (2.15)	0.10 (0.95)	0.90 (0.89)	1.44 (0.96)	2.14 (1.00)	3.59 (1.16)	3.49 (0.83)
Smallest-Largest	0.46 (1.79)	8.55 (1.44)	5.56 (1.01)	4.43 (0.80)	4.65 (0.68)	3.87 (0.68)	

B. February-December

Size	Earnings to Price Ratio ≤ 0	Lowest	2	3	4	Highest	Highest-Lowest
Smallest	0.63 (0.55)	0.98 (0.32)	0.89 (0.28)	1.13 (0.26)	1.21 (0.26)	1.39 (0.27)	0.41 (0.17)
2	0.31 (0.40)	0.90 (0.31)	0.88 (0.27)	0.84 (0.23)	1.03 (0.24)	1.20 (0.26)	0.30 (0.18)
3	0.46 (0.37)	1.04 (0.29)	0.86 (0.24)	0.93 (0.22)	1.22 (0.21)	1.13 (0.24)	0.09 (0.18)
4	0.07 (0.36)	1.04 (0.27)	0.96 (0.23)	1.00 (0.21)	1.23 (0.22)	1.18 (0.24)	0.14 (0.18)
Largest	0.33 (0.39)	0.97 (0.24)	0.90 (0.22)	0.92 (0.21)	1.16 (0.21)	1.23 (0.23)	0.27 (0.17)
Smallest-Largest	0.30 (0.56)	0.01 (0.24)	-0.01 (0.19)	0.21 (0.18)	0.06 (0.18)	0.16 (0.17)	

a. E/P is measured by year-end earnings divided by the common stock price at the end of March in each year.

b. Size is measured by the market value of common equity at the end of March in each year.

returns even in the absence of a clear relation between returns and the ranking variables. Examining only the returns on the extreme portfolios ignores the information in the returns on the intermediate portfolios.

In response to these shortcomings, Jaffe, Keim and Westerfield (1988) use seemingly unrelated regression analysis to simultaneously adjust for portfolio risk and test for significance of the size and E/P effects. The interested reader is referred to Jaffe, Keim and Westerfield for details. Suffice it to say that the conclusions they draw based on their exhaustive analysis are in agreement with those drawn in Section 3.1.

4. Predicting Portfolio Returns with ex ante Observable Variables

A simple rational valuation model suggests that stock price variability may arise from changing expected cash flows and/or changing discount rates. The discount rate depends, at least in part, on expected holding period returns for subsequent periods. Keim and Stambaugh (1986) argue that if expected returns change over time, then variation in price can reflect variation in expected returns (through the discount rate). Therefore, Keim and Stambaugh construct several variables that reflect levels of asset prices and find that these predetermined variables predict monthly returns on common stocks of firms of various sizes, long-term bonds of various default risks, and default-free bonds of various maturities.

In this section, we use one of the variables proposed by Keim and Stambaugh to examine the extent to which the size- and E/P-related portfolio returns change predictably with changes in the ex ante observable predetermined variable. The ex ante variable used here captures aggregate price changes in small firm stocks. Keim and Stambaugh (1986, p. 362) hypothesize that "when expected risk premiums on all assets change, the expected risk premiums on small stocks change the most, thereby producing the highest ex post sensitivity. This argument also suggests that the level of small stock prices may provide a sensitive ex ante barometer of expected future risk premiums." To capture the variability in small stock prices, Keim and Stambaugh use the negative value of the mean log price of all stocks in the smallest quintile of size on the NYSE.

4.1 Predicting Returns for the Size and E/P Deciles

We begin by estimating the following regression for the size and E/P deciles described in Section I:

$$R_{pt} - R_{Ft} = a_0 + a_1(\overline{-\log P_{Q1}})_{t-1} + e_{pt} \qquad p = 1, \ldots, 10 \qquad (1)$$

where R_{pt} is the monthly return for portfolio (decile) p in month t, R_{Ft} is the monthly return on the shortest-term Treasury bill with at least one month to maturity, and $(\overline{-\log P_{Q1}})_{t-1}$ is the small firm price variable at time t - 1. The regressions are estimated using weighted least squares, where the weight used in each regression is the reciprocal of the within-month standard deviation of the daily S&P composite. See Keim and Stambaugh for more details on this series and its use in regressions like these.

Table 5 reports for each regression estimated over the 4/1951 to 12/1982 period the coefficient estimates and t-values, the adjusted R-squared and the first-order autocorrelation of the residuals. Consistent with the results of Keim and Stambaugh, the slope coefficients are all positive and tend to decrease with size, and also increase with E/P. The t-values range from 0.65 to 2.34. The evidence is consistent with the hypothesis that expected risk premiums change over time and the level of small firm prices contains information about expected returns.

Since the coefficients on the small firm price variable tend to increase with E/P and decrease with size, the regression results suggest that the

Table 5

Regressions of Monthly Excess Portfolio Returns on the Small-Firm Price Variable[a]

$$R_{pt} - R_{Ft} = a_0 + a_1(\overline{-\log P_{Q1}})_{t-1} + e_t$$

A. Market Value Portfolio	a_0	$t(a_0)$	a_1	$t(a_1)$	Adjusted R^2	$\rho_1(e)$
Smallest	.0487	(2.18)	.0119	(1.34)	.002	.195
2	.0554	(2.71)	.0158	(1.95)	.007	.144
3	.0562	(2.81)	.0174	(2.19)	.010	.135
4	.0490	(2.65)	.0140	(1.92)	.007	.131
5	.0489	(2.93)	.0147	(2.23)	.010	.138
6	.0478	(2.91)	.0145	(2.22)	.010	.146
7	.0431	(2.70)	.0127	(2.01)	.008	.075
8	.0337	(2.20)	.0092	(1.53)	.004	.057
9	.0311	(2.04)	.0091	(1.51)	.003	.048
Largest	.0178	(1.20)	.0038	(0.65)	-.002	.004
B. E/P Portfolio	a_0	$t(a_0)$	a_1	$t(a_1)$	Adjusted R^2	$\rho_1(e)$
Highest	.0492	(2.68)	.0136	(1.87)	.007	.136
2	.0503	(2.91)	.0142	(2.07)	.009	.104
3	.0522	(3.18)	.0152	(2.34)	.012	.107
4	.0405	(2.55)	.0110	(1.75)	.005	.126
5	.0396	(2.50)	.0117	(1.85)	.006	.112
6	.0370	(2.34)	.0106	(1.69)	.005	.097
7	.0388	(2.40)	.0117	(1.83)	.006	.122
8	.0390	(2.28)	.0113	(1.67)	.005	.129
9	.0308	(1.72)	.0082	(1.16)	.001	.100
Lowest	.0365	(1.83)	.0094	(1.19)	.001	.112

a. Regressions are estimated using weighted least squares. The weight used in each equation is $1/\sigma_{sp}$, where σ_{sp} is the within-month standard deviation of daily returns on the S&P Composite. Both the adjusted R^2 and the first-order autocorrelation of the residuals ($\rho_1(e)$) are based on weighted residuals.

magnitudes of the size and E/P effects are conditional on the level of the small firm price variable.[5] To demonstrate this visually, Figures 1 and 2 plot the estimated regressions for all size and E/P deciles, respectively, over the range of small firm price variables observed for the 1951 to 1982 period. Notice that for very low values of the small-firm price variable (i.e., high prices) the size and E/P effects are negligible. On the other hand, the size and E/P effects are quite apparent at high values of the price variable (i.e., low prices). The average value of the small firm variable over the 1951-1982 period is -2.44, which, when substituted into the estimated regressions, produces the familiar size and E/P effects.

4.2 Predicting Returns for the 25 E/P-Size Portfolios

In this section we estimate equation (1) for each of the 25 E/P-size portfolios described in Section 3. The weighted least squares estimates for the 4/51 to 12/82 period are reported in Table 6. As expected, the slope coefficients tend to increase with E/P and decrease with size, resulting in a pattern of increasing coefficients as one moves from the southwest corner of the table (large firms with low E/P ratios) toward the northeast corner (small firms with high E/P ratios). The t-values range from .01 to 2.61. However, the magnitude of the conditional size effect is not independent of the level of E/P, and the magnitude of the conditional E/P effect is not independent of firm size. Using the difference in return between small and large size (high and low E/P) firms as a measure of the magnitude of the size (E/P) effect, the entries in the rightmost column and bottom row represent estimates of the extent to which the expected value of the E/P or size effect changes predictably with changes in the value of the small firm price variable

---

[5]Keim and Stambaugh present such evidence for the size effect.

FIGURE 1
SIZE EFFECT, CONDITIONAL ON -LOG(P)

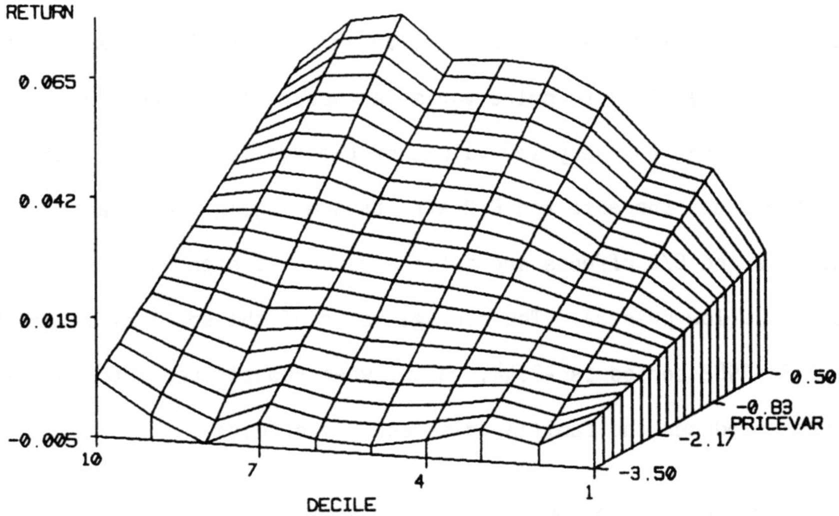

Fitted regressions of excess returns on the small-firm price variable for each of ten size categories

FIGURE 2
E/P EFFECT, CONDITIONAL ON -LOG(P)

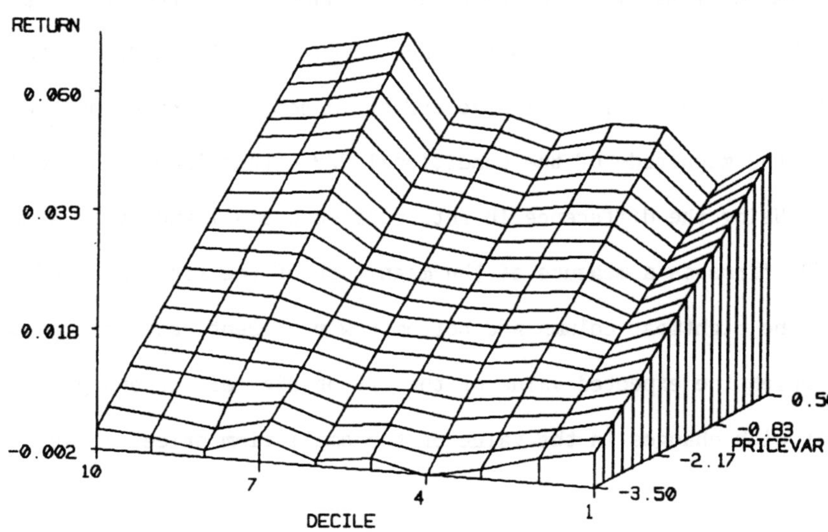

Fitted regressions of excess returns on the small-firm price variable for each of ten E/P categories

Table 6

Regressions of E/P-Size Portfolio Monthly Excess Returns on the Small-Firm Price Variable[a]

$$R_{pt} - R_{Ft} = a_0 + a_1(-\overline{\log P_{Q1}})_{t-1} + e_t$$

Size	Earnings Yield					Highest-Lowest
	Lowest	2	3	4	Highest	
	.0617	.0450	.0458	.0486	.0575	-.0042
	(2.46)	(2.08)	(2.30)	(2.43)	(2.81)	(-0.31)
Smallest	.0176	.0123	.0123	.0125	.0156	-.0020
	(1.77)	(1.44)	(1.56)	(1.57)	(1.93)	(-0.36)
	.006/.137	.003/.155	.004/.130	.004/.182	.007/.143	-.002/.009
	.0459	.0503	.0364	.0502	.0503	.0044
	(2.05)	(2.60)	(2.09)	(2.73)	(2.57)	(0.32)
2	.0134	.0157	.0103	.0143	.0140	.0006
	(1.51)	(2.05)	(1.49)	(1.97)	(1.80)	(0.11)
	.003/.109	.008/.120	.003/.141	.008/.101	.006/.101	-.003/.116
	.0379	.0330	.0437	.0534	.0486	.0107
	(1.88)	(1.97)	(2.68)	(3.40)	(2.61)	(0.75)
3	.0105	.0093	.0136	.0163	.0134	.0029
	(1.32)	(1.41)	(2.11)	(2.61)	(1.81)	(0.51)
	.002/.141	.003/.160	.009/.154	.015/.125	.006/.113	-.002/.065
	.0165	.0387	.0357	.0425	.0503	.0338
	(0.90)	(2.42)	(2.34)	(2.57)	(2.74)	(2.46)
4	.0029	.0119	.0105	.0117	.0146	.0117
	(0.40)	(1.88)	(1.75)	(1.79)	(2.01)	(2.14)
	-.002/.048	.007/.045	.005/.028	.006/.066	.008/.094	.009/.118
	.0080	.0270	.0312	.0376	.0435	.0356
	(0.48)	(1.80)	(2.04)	(2.41)	(2.54)	(2.75)
Largest	.0001	.0079	.0093	.0107	.0124	.0123
	(0.01)	(1.32)	(1.54)	(1.74)	(1.83)	(2.40)
	-.003/.025	.002/.046	.004/.018	.005/.029	.006/.068	.012/.121
						KEY:
	.0537	.0180	.0146	.0110	.0139	a_0
	(2.61)	(1.19)	(1.04)	(0.77)	(1.05)	$t(\hat{a}_0)$
Smallest-Largest	.0175	.0045	.0030	.0018	.0033	a_1
	(2.15)	(0.74)	(0.54)	(0.31)	(0.62)	$t(\hat{a}_1)$
	.010/.117	-.001/.131	-.002/.162	-.002/.099	-.002/.030	Adj. $R^2/\rho_1(e)$

a. Regressions are estimated using weighted least squares. The weight used in each equation is $1/\sigma_{sp}$, where σ_{sp} is the within-month standard deviation of daily returns on the Standard and Poor's Composite Index. Both the adjusted R^2 and the first-order autocorrelation of the residuals ($\rho_1(e)$) are based on the weighted residuals.

(LP_{sm}). The size-related pattern in the regression coefficients is significant only in the lowest E/P category and the E/P-related pattern is significant only in the larger size categories. Stated somewhat differently, small firms (high E/P firms) receive large coefficients regardless of their E/P ratio (size).

The results in Table 6 are interesting in that the pattern of coefficients suggests different conditional size and E/P-related return effects in response to a particular level of LP_{sm}. For example, the highest value of LP_{sm} (i.e., lowest price) in the 1951-1982 period was -1.09 (in December 1974). Figure 3 presents a plot of the estimated regressions for each of the 25 E/P-size portfolios for LP_{sm} = -1.09. The plot suggests a strong E/P and size effect which coincides with the ex post average effects in 1975. Similarly, the estimates of the effects conditional on LP_{sm} = -3.28--the lowest value of LP_{sm} over this subperiod, occurring in December 1968--anticipate the flat and insignificant effects that actually occurred in 1969 (Figure 4).

Of more interest, of course, are out of sample predictions. One example is for the preceding 1927-1951 period when the average value of LP_{sm} was -1.76. The plot of the estimated regressions shown in Figure 5 displays a size effect that is apparent for all E/P levels and consistent with the unconditional averages reported by other researchers. An interesting, and yet to be tested, out of sample prediction for this earlier period is the E/P effect that is apparent only for larger firms. Finally, the December 1982 value of -2.36, when substituted into the estimated regressions, gives the (relatively) flatter pattern of returns across the size and E/P categories that has been characteristic of the data over the recent 1982 to 1987 period (Figure 6).

FIGURE 3
E/P-SIZE EFFECT, CONDITIONAL ON -LOG(P) = -1.09

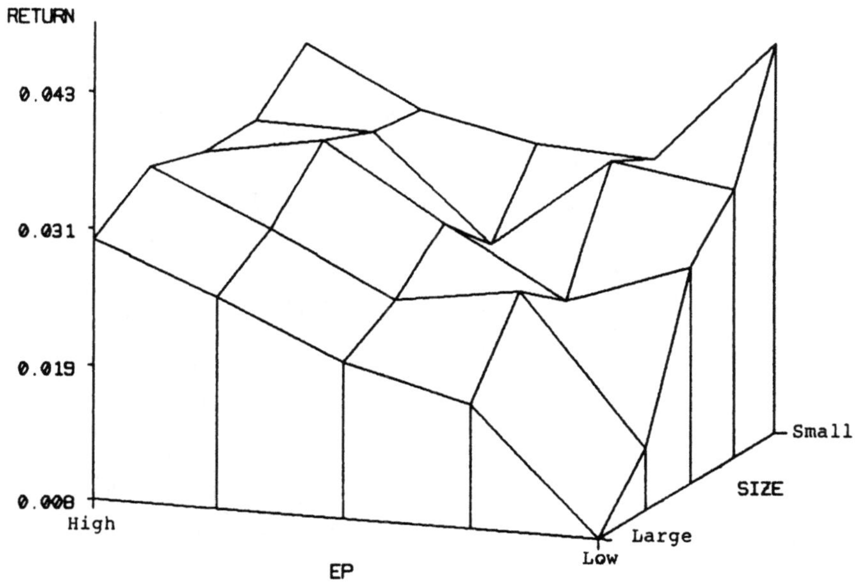

FIGURE 4
E/P-SIZE EFFECT, CONDITIONAL ON -LOG(P) = -3.28

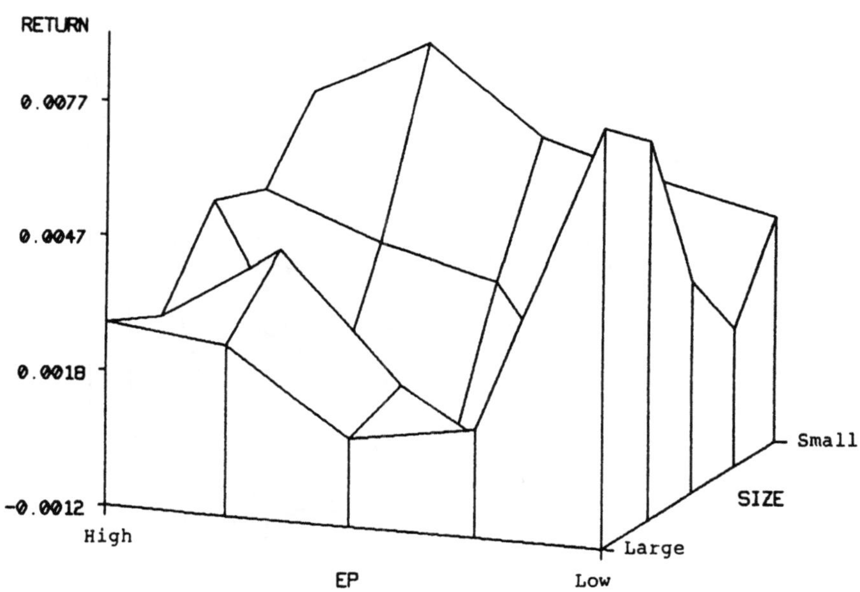

Figure 5
E/P-SIZE EFFECT, CONDITIONAL ON -LOG(P) = -1.76

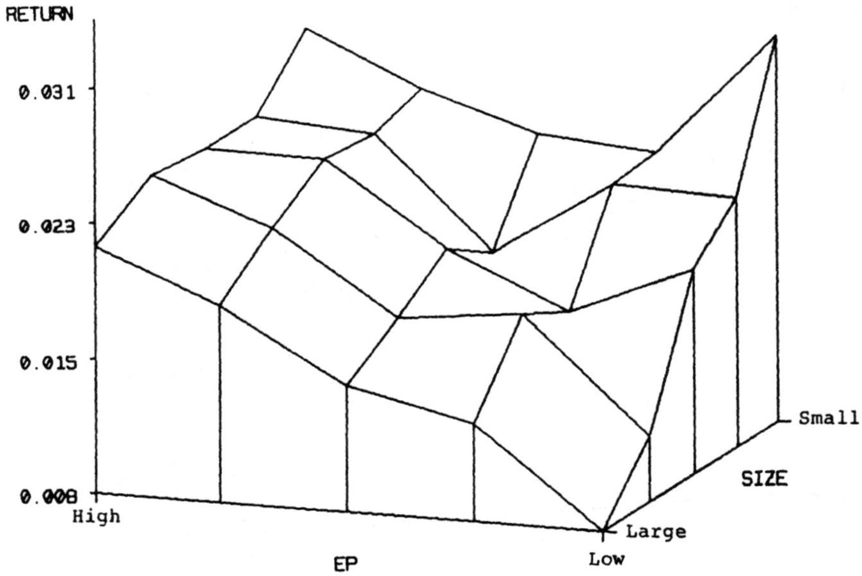

FIGURE 6
E/P-SIZE EFFECT, CONDITIONAL ON -LOG(P) = -2.36

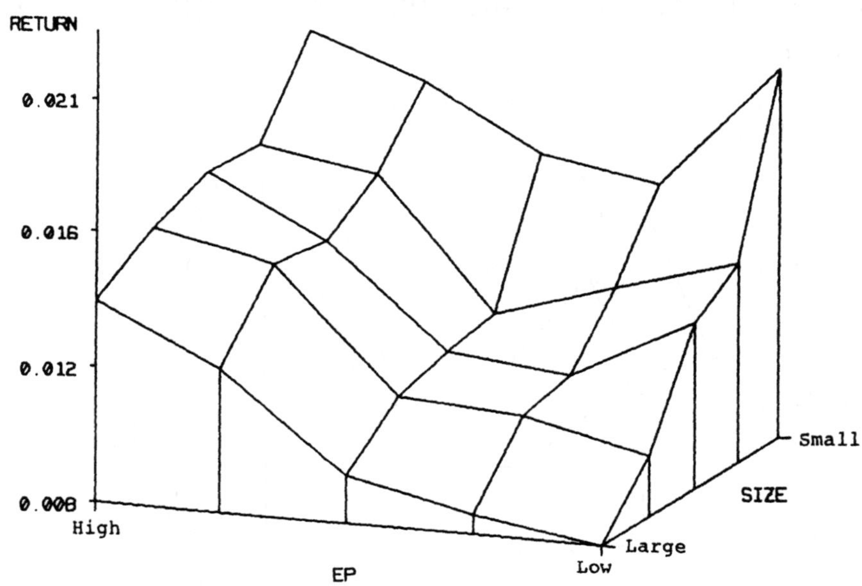

4.3 January Seasonality and the E/P-Size Portfolio Regressions

Keim and Stambaugh find that the coefficient on the small-firm price variable in equation (1) is significantly larger in January than in the other months. Table 7 reports the results for E/P-size portfolio excess return regressions where the coefficients are estimated separately in January and in non-January months (again using weighted least squares). Also reported in the rightmost column and the bottom row are regression results where the dependent variable is the difference between the extreme portfolios in the respective row or column.

The non-January coefficients in Table 7 are not significantly different than zero, but the January coefficients are large and generally significant (t-values range from 1.96 to 5.79) and tend to increase as one moves up the columns (decreasing size) and across the rows (increasing E/P). As a result, the t-value for the difference between the January and non-January coefficients, $t(a_{1J} - a_{1R})$, tends to increase as one moves up the columns and across the rows, and equality of the coefficients is generally rejected.

The rightmost column and bottom row present evidence on the conditional E/P and size effects. The regression results in the bottom row for the difference in returns representing the size effect are consistent with those reported in Table 6 of Keim and Stambaugh: the slope coefficients are significantly positive in January but not in non-January months, resulting in rejection of equality of the coefficients in all but the highest E/P category. On the other hand, the regression results in the rightmost column portray a conditional E/P effect where both the January and non-January regression coefficients on LP_{sm} tend to increase with increasing size and have t-values ranging between 1.33 and 3.39 in the two largest size categories. Also, in contrast to the size-related results, the E/P-related January coefficient is

Table 7

Regressions of E/P-Size Portfolio Monthly Excess Returns on the Small-Firm Price Variable[a]

$$R_{pt} - R_{Ft} = a_{0j}D_{jt} + a_{0r}(1-D_{jt}) + a_{1j}D_{jt}(-\overline{\log P_{Q1}})_{t-1} + a_{1r}(1-D_{jt})(-\overline{\log P_{Q1}})_{t-1} + u_t$$

$$\text{where } D_{jt} = 1 \text{ if month t is January}; \quad = 0 \text{ otherwise}$$

Size	Earnings Yield: Lowest	2	3	4	Highest	Highest-Lowest
	.1717	.1483	.1032	.1269	.1178	-.0540
	(5.79)	(5.72)	(4.23)	(5.32)	(4.79)	(-3.15)
Smallest	-.0010	-.0037	.0013	-.0014	.0030	.0041
	(-0.10)	(-0.44)	(0.17)	(-0.18)	(0.38)	(0.72)
	5.53	5.57	3.96	5.11	4.43	-3.22
	.198/.154	.169/.153	.146/.123	.212/.180	.208/.153	.027/.012
	.1089	.1059	.0988	.0887	.1087	-.0002
	(3.90)	(4.42)	(4.61)	(3.96)	(4.60)	(-0.10)
2	.0025	.0053	-.0001	.0050	.0023	-.0002
	(0.28)	(0.67)	(-0.02)	(0.68)	(0.30)	(-0.04)
	3.62	3.99	4.39	3.55	4.28	0.00
	.079/.100	.099/.125	.120/.147	.165/.110	.178/.111	.040/.137
	.0837	.0838	.0650	.0870	.0947	.0110
	(3.29)	(4.01)	(3.17)	(4.46)	(4.17)	(0.63)
3	.0026	.0010	.0077	.0080	.0033	.0007
	(0.31)	(0.14)	(1.14)	(1.25)	(0.45)	(0.12)
	3.03	3.77	2.65	3.85	3.82	0.56
	.065/.138	.083/.156	.075/.154	.148./133	.169/.115	.086/.052
	.0578	.0672	.0724	.0713	.0871	.0292
	(2.50)	(3.33)	(3.79)	(3.46)	(3.82)	(1.73)
4	-.0027	.0059	.0037	.0046	.0059	.0086
	(0.36)	(0.90)	(0.59)	(0.69)	(0.79)	(1.56)
	2.49	2.88	3.42	3.08	3.39	1.16
	.046/.045	.064/.045	.082/.028	.121/.071	.128/.099	.092/.119
	.0413	.0593	.0531	.0691	.0953	.0540
	(1.96)	(3.12)	(2.74)	(3.52)	(4.48)	(3.39)
Largest	-.0040	.0025	.0046	.0043	.0030	.0070
	(-0.58)	(0.41)	(0.72)	(0.67)	(0.42)	(1.33)
	2.04	2.84	2.38	3.14	4.12	2.80
	.039/.024	.051/.043	.049/.017	.090/.030	.123/.078	.092/.131
						KEY:
	.1305	.0890	.0501	.0578	.0225	a_{1J}
	(5.55)	(5.07)	(2.95)	(3.41)	(1.38)	$t(a_{1J})$
Smallest-Largest	.0030	-.0063	-.0033	-.0057	.0001	a_{1R}
	(0.39)	(-1.09)	(-0.59)	(1.03)	(0.02)	$t(a_{1R})$
	5.16	5.15	2.99	3.56	1.31	$t(a_{1J} - a_{1R})$
	.228/.116	.197/.127	.120/.155	.157/.076	.094/.002	Adj. $r^2/\rho_1(u)$

a. Regressions are estimated using weighted least squares. The weight used in each equation is $1/\sigma_{sp}$, where σ_{sp} is the within-month standard deviation of daily returns on the Standard and Poor's Composite Index. Both the adjusted R^2 and the first-order autocorrelation of the residuals ($\rho_1(e)$) are based on the weighted residual.

significantly larger than the non-January coefficient only in the largest size category. Finally note that the regressions estimated in Table 7 explain nearly 23% of the variation in the size-related difference in returns, but only 9% of the variation in the E/P-related difference in returns.

5. Concluding Remarks

Earlier evidence concerning the relation between stock returns and the effects of size and E/P is not clearcut. Reinganum argues that size dominates E/P, while Basu concludes that E/P dominates size. Cook and Rozeff attach approximately equal significance to both factors. Banz and Breen can find no separate E/P ratio effect. This paper attempts to resolve some of the differences of opinion.

Our research finds significant E/P and size effects when estimated across all months during the 1951-1986 period. This is consistent with Cook and Rozeff but inconsistent with Banz and Breen, Basu and Reinganum. The findings also indicate a difference between January and the rest of the year; <u>both</u> the E/P and size effects are significant in January but only the E/P effect is significant outside of January.

Finally, the paper examined the conditional means of these effects as measured by estimated regressions of portfolio excess returns on an ex ante observable variable that was found by Keim and Stambaugh to reliably predict returns on a wide variety of assets. The results indicate that the ex ante observable variable is able to predict ex post returns on the size and E/P portfolios--especially in January. Further, the magnitude and significance of the estimated coefficients on the ex ante variable are larger, the smaller is firm size and the larger is E/P. Thus, the ex post size and E/P effects, and the interaction between them, take on different shapes conditional on the level of the ex ante observable variable.

References

Banz, R.W., 1981, The Relationship between Return and Market Value of Common Stocks, Journal of Financial Economics 9, 3-18.

Banz, R.W., and W. Breen, 1986, Sample-Dependent Results Using Accounting and Market Data: Some Evidence, Journal of Finance 51, 779-793.

Basu, S., 1977, Investment Performance of Common Stocks in Relation to Their Price-Earnings Ratios: A Test of the Efficient Market Hypothesis, Journal of Finance 32, 663-682.

Basu, S., 1983, The Relationship between Earnings' Yield, Market Value and Return for NYSE Common Stocks: Further Evidence, Journal of Financial Economics 12, 129-156.

Blume, M., and R. F. Stambaugh, 1983, Biases in Computed Returns: An Application to the Size Effect, Journal of Financial Economics 12, 387-404.

Cook, T., and M. Rozeff, 1984, Size and Earnings/Price Ratio Anomalies: One Effect or Two? Journal of Financial and Quantitative Analysis 19, 449-466.

Jaffe, J., D. B. Keim and R. Westerfield, 1988, Earnings Yields, Market Values and Stock Returns, Unpublished working paper (University of Pennsylvania).

Keim, D. B., 1983, Size Related Anomalies and Stock Return Seasonality: Further Empirical Evidence, Journal of Financial Economics 12, 13-32.

Keim, D. B., and R. F. Stambaugh, 1986, Predicting Returns in the Stock and Bond Markets, Journal of Financial Economics 17, 357-390.

Reinganum, M. R., 1981, Misspecification in Capital Asset Pricing: Empirical Anomalies Based on Earnings' Yields and Market Values, Journal of Financial Economics 9, 19-46.

A LOOK AT THE VALIDITY OF THE CAPM IN LIGHT OF EQUITY MARKET ANOMALIES: THE CASE OF BELGIAN COMMON STOCKS

Gabriel Hawawini
INSEAD, Fontainebleau, France
and
The Wharton School of the
University of Pennsylvania

Pierre Michel
Albert Corhay

Université de Liège, Belgium

Keywords

Stock Market Anomalies / Seasonality / Size Effect / Capital Asset Pricing Model / Equity Pricing / Belgian Stock Market

Abstract

We re-examine the pricing of common stocks on the Belgium Stock Exchange in light of two related phenomena recently reported in the literature: the size effect and risk-premia seasonality. When these two phenomena are ignored we cannot reject the hypothesis that the behavior of common stock prices conform to the CAPM. However, when size and seasonality are accounted for in the stochastic process that generates stock returns, the hypothesis that the CAPM describes (and explains) the pricing of common stocks must be rejected, even during the month of January despite the presence of a positive systematic risk premium and the absence of an unsystematic risk premium during that month.

1. INTRODUCTION

In a recent study of the price behavior of Belgian common stocks, Hawawini and Michel (1982) (HM hereafter) examined the relationship between the average return and the risk of a comprehensive sample of 200 securities which traded continuously from 1966 to 1980 on the Brussels Stock Exchange

NATO ASI Series, Vol. F54
A Reappraisal of the Efficiency of Financial Markets
Edited by Rui M. C. Guimaraes et al.

(BSE) and concluded that the pricing of common stocks in the BSE conforms to the standard Capital Asset Pricing Model (CAPM) of Sharpe (1964) and Lintner (1965). Using the testing methodology designed by Fama and MacBeth (1973), HM (1982) could not reject the hypothesis that, over their sample period, there exists a positive and linear relationship between the return on securities and their corresponding level of systematic risk. They also showed that no reward is received for bearing unsystematic or non-market related risk on the BSE (Hawawini (1984)).

In this paper we re-examine HM's evidence in light of two recent phenomena reported in the literature. The first is the size effect discovered by Banz (1981). The second is the reported seasonality in both the monthly returns of common stocks (Gultekin and Gultekin (1983)) and the monthly estimates of the risk premium based on the CAPM (Tinic and West (1984), (1986) and Corhay, Hawawini and Michel (1987a,b)).

Using a comprehensive sample of common stocks traded on the New York Stock Exchange (NYSE), Banz (1981) has shown that a portfolio containing the stocks with the smallest market value (capitalization) outperforms, on average, a portfolio containing the stocks with the largest market value, even after adjusting returns for differences in the systematic risk of portfolios. Rozeff and Kinney (1976) have shown that U.S. common stock returns are, on average, larger in January than during the rest of the year. And Tinic and West (1984), (1986) have shown that the relationship between average common stock returns and systematic risk is significantly positive only in January in the United States. That is, January is the only month of the year during which the estimated systematic risk premium earned by common stocks is positive.

We find that common stocks traded on the BSE exhibit a behavior similar to that of common stocks traded on the NYSE despite the considerably smaller size of the BSE compared to the NYSE. We show that there is a size effect on the BSE and that stock returns and estimated risk premia are seasonal. We also report evidence that seasonality and size effect are two related phenomena (for the U.S. evidence see Roll (1983) and Keim (1983)). We conclude that the price behavior of common stocks traded on the BSE does not conform to the CAPM.

The rest of the paper is organized as follows. In the next section we summarize our major results. In section 3 we describe the sample properties and the methodology we employ to perform our empirical work. We report evidence of risk-premia seasonality in section 4 and evidence of a size effect and its relationship to seasonality in section 5. In section 6 we re-examine the pricing of common stocks when both seasonality and size are taken into account. The last section contains concluding remarks.

2. Summary of major results

The results listed below are based on 20 portfolios of common stocks which traded continuously on the BSE from January 1969 to December 1983 (see section 3 for details):

2.1. The relationships between portfolio returns and systematic risk is, on average, negative over the entire sample period. It is positive only during the month of January and negative during the late summer months of August and September (section 4.1 and table 2).

2.2. Unsystematic risk is priced over the entire sample period as well as during August and September. In January only systematic risk is priced but the relationship between portfolio returns and systematic risk is concave (section 4.2 and table 4).

2.3. There is a negative relationship between portfolio returns and portfolio size over the entire sample period. This relationship is particularly pronounced during the month of January. During the month of December the size effect is positive (section 5 and tables 5 and 6).

2.4. The portfolio containing the smallest firms with the highest systematic risk achieved an average return of 10.31 percent in January alone (the average monthly return over the entire sample period for the equally-weighted market portfolio is 0.84 percent) (section 5 and table 8).

2.5. When size, unsystematic risk and seasonality are accounted for in the stochastic process that generates stock returns, the hypothesis that the CAPM describes (and explains) the pricing of common stock on the BSE must be rejected, even during the month of January despite the presence of a positive systematic risk premium and the absence of an unsystematic risk premium during that month (section 6 and table 9).

3. Sample properties and methodology

3.1. The data

The sample contains the 170 common stocks for which monthly returns were available continuously from January 1969 to December 1983 (a total of 180 monthly returns for each common stock in the sample). These 170 stocks represent 86 percent of all shares listed on the BSE. Returns are measured as percentage monthly price changes adjusted for dividends.

Two market indexes were constructed. An equally-weighted index and a value-weighted index. In the latter, market values were updated yearly (last trading day of December).

3.2. Seasonality in the monthly returns of the market indexes

The statistical properties of the two indexes are reported in table 1. Over the sample period (January 1969 to December 1983) the equally-weighted index (EWI) achieved an annualized rate of return of 10.08 percent and the value-weighted index (VWI) a return of 8.52 percent. The higher return of the former is a reflection of a size effect since small firm are given more weight in the EWI than in the VWI. Note that the EWI exhibits slightly less variability than the VWI despite its higher historical average return. The standard deviation of monthly returns is 3.10 percent for the EWI and 3.75 percent for the VWI.

Both indexes exhibit a similar pattern of return seasonality. Most of the annualized average monthly return is earned on the months of January (about one half of the total) and April (about one quarter of the total).

TABLE 1

Characteristics of the two market indexes based on 170 stocks from January 1969 to December 1983

Monthly Return Over	EQUALLY-WEIGHTED INDEX			VALUE-WEIGHTED INDEX		
	MEAN	MAX	MIN	MEAN	MAX	MIN
All months of the year[a]	0.84% (3.66)[b]	12.10%	-7.43%	0.71% (2.53)[b]	19.08%	-9.12%
JANUARY[c]	4.29% (4.48)[b]	10.91%	-2.78%	4.19% (4.43)[b]	12.10%	-0.69%
FEBRUARY	1.95% (2.95)[b]	9.58%	-0.01%	1.03% (1.63)	4.47%	-3.12%
MARCH	0.51% (0.71)	6.68%	-5.51%	0.09% (0.09)	8.27%	-8.74%
APRIL	2.04% (3.00)[b]	6.62%	-2.26%	2.45% (2.62)[b]	7.64%	-2.49%
MAY	0.16% (0.26)	3.15%	-4.28%	0.05% (0.07)	2.98%	-5.33%
JUNE	0.74% (1.27)	5.31%	-3.97%	0.65% (0.93)	6.22%	-4.82%
JULY	1.56% (2.55)[b]	5.49%	-1.78%	1.37% (2.32)[b]	4.69%	-2.20%
AUGUST	0.50% (0.68)	4.95%	-5.45%	-0.98% (1.10)	5.55%	-9.12%
SEPTEMBER	-1.06% (-1.40)	3.66%	-6.18%	-1.76% (1.99)[b]	3.24%	-8.86%
OCTOBER	-1.39% (-2.52)[b]	2.63%	-5.23%	-1.25% (1.50)	5.79%	-6.70%
NOVEMBER	-0.82% (-1.21)	2.73%	-7.43%	0.28% (0.28)	6.07%	-8.57%
DECEMBER	1.65% (1.71)	12.10%	-3.59%	2.36% (1.70)	19.08%	-5.78%

a. based on 180 monthly observations

b. t statistics in parentheses below average value. Framed returns are statistically significant at the 0.05 level.

c. based on 15 monthly observations

Finally, we could not reject the hypothesis that the returns of EWI are normally distributed. The returns on the VWI, however, deviate slightly (but significantly) from normality. The returns on both indexes are highly correlated (correlation coefficient of .88) as shown by the regression:

$$\text{Ret(EWI)} = - .0020 + 1.067 \text{ Ret(VWI)}$$
$$(1.44) \quad (25.14)$$

with an R-square of .7803. We could not reject the hypothesis that the slope of the regression line is equal to one. We performed our tests with both indexes. Results were qualitatively the same but generally more significant when the EWI was used. The results we report below are all based on the equally-weighted index.

3.3. Methodology

The methodology employed to estimate the relationship between monthly returns, risk and size is similar to that described in Fama and MacBeth (1973) and Banz (1981). It involves three steps. First, an initial period of one year is used to construct 20 portfolios on the basis of size and risk (construction period). The following year of monthly data is then employed to estimate the risk of the portfolios (estimation period). The third and final step is the estimation of the risk premia and the examination of the size effect over the third year of monthly data (test period). The entire procedure is then repeated after dropping the first year of data and moving forward until we reach December 1983.

Portfolio Construction. We used the first 12 months of returns (1969) to construct five equally-weighted portfolios ranked according to their market value (size) as of the last trading day of December 1969. The first and fifth contain 37 securities and the middle portfolios contain 32 securities. Each of these five size-related portfolios were then divided into four subportfolios ranked according to the magnitude of their beta coefficients estimated over the 12-month construction period using a single-index market model (Sharpe (1963), Fama (1976)). When the size portfolio has 37 securities, the subportfolio with the highest beta has 13 securities and the other three have 8 securities. When the size portfolio has 32 securities each subportfolio has 8 securities. This procedure led to <u>twenty</u> equally-weighted subportfolios constructed on the basis of both size and systematic risk (beta).

<u>Risk estimation</u>. We used the second 12 months of returns (1970) to estimate the risk of each stock in the sample. Two measures of risk are considered in this study: systematic risk (the beta coefficient) and unsystematic risk (the standard deviation of the residual of the single-index market model). The risk of a portfolio is then computed as the arithmetic average of the risk of the securities that make up the portfolio.

<u>Model testing</u>. Finally, the third 12-months of returns (1971) are used to estimate the monthly risk-premia according to the following set of regressions:

$$R_{Pt} = \gamma_{ot} + \gamma_{1t}\cdot\beta_{P,t-1} + \mu_{Pt} \tag{1}$$

$$R_{Pt} = \gamma'_{ot} + \gamma'_{1t}\cdot\beta_{P,t-1} + \gamma_{2t}\cdot\beta^2_{P,t-1} + \gamma_{3t}\cdot SE_{P,t-1} + \mu'_{Pt} \tag{2}$$

$$R_{Pt} = \gamma''_{ot} + \gamma_{4t}\left[\frac{V_p - V_m}{V_m}\right]_{t-1} + \mu''_{Pt} \tag{3}$$

$$R_{Pt} = \gamma^s_{ot} + \gamma^s_{1t}\cdot\beta_{P,t-1} + \gamma^s_{4t}\cdot\left[\frac{V_p - V_m}{V_m}\right]_{t-1} + \mu^s_{Pt} \tag{4}$$

$$R_{Pt} = \gamma^*_{ot} + \gamma^*_{1t}\cdot\beta_{P,t-1} + \gamma^*_{2t}\cdot\beta^2_{P,t-1} + \gamma^*_{3t}\cdot SE_{P,t-1} + \gamma^*_{4t}\left[\frac{V_p - V_m}{V_m}\right]_{t-1} + \mu^*_{Pt} \tag{5}$$

where :

R_{Pt} = the realized return of portfolio p in month t,

$\beta_{P,t-1}$ = the beta of portfolio estimated over a 12-month estimation period ending on the calendar year preceding month t and updated yearly,

$SE_{P,t-1}$ = the unsystematic risk (standard error of the market model's residuals) of portfolio p estimated over a 12-month estimation period ending on the calendar year preceding month t and updated yearly,

$\left[\frac{V_p - V_m}{V_m}\right]_{t-1}$ = the relative market value (size) of portfolio p (Vm= market value of all stocks) measured on the last trading day of the calendar year preceding month t and updated yearly,

γ_{1t} = the systematic risk premium in month t,

γ_{3t} = the unsystematic risk premium in month t,

γ_{4t} = the size premium in month t.

Regression (1) assumes that securities' returns are generated by a two-factor model (Black (1972) and Fama (1976)). Regression (2) assumes a four-factor return-generating model (Fama (1976)). If prices behave according to the CAPM then the regression coefficient of systematic risk (the systematic risk premium) should be positive and the estimated regression coefficient of the squared value of systematic risk should be zero (implying linearity). Also, the estimated coefficient of unsystematic risk should be zero (implying no reward for bearing diversifiable risk). Regression (3) is run to test for a size effect. If small firms outperform large firms, the estimated regression coefficient of relative size should be negative. Regression (4) and (5) are run to examine the pricing of common stocks when both risk and size are accounted for. Note that the five regressions are cross-sectional regressions. They are run each month of the calendar year yielding 12 estimates of the regressions' coefficients, one for each month of the year.

The entire procedure just described is repeated after dropping the first year of data. The second year of data is used to construct portfolios, the third to estimate risk and size and the fourth to test the models. We keep on dropping one year of data and moving forward until we reach the year 1983. This approach provides a total of 156 monthly estimates (12 months x 13 years) for each regression coefficients (risk premia and size premia). Finally, note that the variables in the regressions (1) to (5) are not contemporaneous. Risk and size are measured over the calendar period preceding the month over which returns are realized. Hence, the regressions provide tests of the predictive power of the various models.

4. Evidence of monthly risk premia seasonality

4.1. Systematic risk premia

Average values of the estimated coefficients of regression (1) are reported in table 2. Over the entire testing period (from January 1971 to December 1983) the relationship between realized returns and systematic risk is, on average, significantly negative. This result is consistent with the evidence reported by HM (1982). They found a significantly negative relationship over the period December 1976 to November 1980 (the reported slope coefficient in their table 1 is equal to -0.0076 with a t-statistic of -1.87).

But the month-to-month average values of the estimated systematic risk premia reveal another picture. January is the only month of the year during which the risk premium is significantly positive. It is equal to 1.49 percent or 17.52 percent on an annual basis, the largest of all months (in absolute value). If we exclude the month of January from the data the negative relationship between returns and systematic risk is even more pronounced mostly as the result of the contribution of August and September during which the systematic risk premium is equal to -2.71 percent or -16.26 percent on an annual basis.

There is no definitive explanation of this phenomenon. The positive January effect may be tax-induced (Corhay, Hawawini and Michel (1987)) and possibly related to the trading activity of institutional investors. We have no explanation of the negative "late summer" effect.

In order to test the hypothesis of equal month-to-month average intercept and slope coefficients of the two parameters model (regression (1)) we run the following dummy-variable regression:

$$\gamma_{kt} = a_1 + \sum_{J=2}^{12} a_j D_j + e_{kt}$$

where k=0 is the intercept and k=1 is the slope coefficient. The variable

TABLE 2

Average values of the Fama and MacBeth estimates of the intercept (γ_0) and slope (γ_1) coefficients of the two-parameter model[a]:

$$R_{pt} = \gamma_{0t} + \gamma_{1t} \cdot \beta_{p,t-1} + \mu_{p\,t}$$

Average over	$\bar{\gamma}_0$ (Intercept)	$\bar{\gamma}_1$ (beta)	Sample size
All months	0.0120 [b] (4.72)	-0.0028 [b] (-1.89)	156
All months except January	0.0104 [b] (3.97)	-0.0044 [b] (-2.96)	143
JANUARY	0.0296 [b] (3.20)	0.0149 [b] (2.66)	13
FEBRUARY	0.0234 [b] (3.18)	-0.0027 (-0.68)	13
MARCH	0.0117 (1.69)	-0.0075 (-1.44)	13
APRIL	0.0255 [b] (2.60)	-0.0043 (-1.32)	13
MAY	-0.0024 (-0.31)	0.0033 (0.73)	13
JUNE	0.0201 [b] (2.72)	-0.0085 (-1.65)	13
JULY	0.0171 [b] (2.49)	-0.0005 (-0.10)	13
AUGUST	0.0160 (1.59)	-0.0128 [b] (-2.17)	13
SEPTEMBER	-0.0064 (-0.68)	-0.0143 [b] (-3.00)	13
OCTOBER	 (1.58)	-0.0049 (-1.62)	13
NOVEMBER	-0.0061 (-0.77)	0.0004 (0.10)	13
DECEMBER	0.0132 (1.32)	0.0031 (0.43)	

a. estimated with monthly data and the equally-weighted index from January 1971 to December 1983.

b. t statistics are in parentheses below average values. Framed coefficients are statistically significant at the 0.05 level

D_2 to D_{12} are dummy variables representing the months of the year from February to December. The coefficient a_1 is a measure of average γ_k in January while the coefficients a_2 through a_{12} are a measure of the difference between average γ_k in February to December and average γ_k in January. If the average systematic risk premium in January is the same as the average risk premium during month j, the estimate of a_j will not be statistically different from zero. Turning to table 3 we see that the estimated coefficients a_j are all negative from February to December. This means that γ_0 and γ_1 are smaller during February to December than during January although not significantly so for all eleven months. In particular, the average systematic risk premium (γ_1) in May and December is not significantly smaller than in January.

4.2. Seasonality in the risk premia of the four-factor return-generating model

The average estimated coefficients of the four-factor regression model are reported in table 4. When all months are considered, only unsystematic risk is priced in the market. Excluding January from the data does not modify this result which is not consistent with the CAPM. The month-to-month risk premia indicate, again, that the relationship between returns and systematic risk is only significant in January but it appears to be concave rather than linear. Also, note that the negative systematic risk premia in the late summer months (August and September) reported in table 2 are now replaced by a positive unsystematic risk premia. This result may be explained by the fact that systematic risk and unsystematic risk are negatively related: securities with low betas tend to have above average level of unsystematic risk. Clearly, in August and September the unsystematic-risk effect prevails when both systematic and unsystematic risks are in the pricing equation (regression (3)).

5. Evidence of a size effect and its relationship to seasonality

The characteristics of the five size-portfolios ranked by decreasing

TABLE 3

Test of the hypothesis of equal month-to-month average intercept (γ_0) and slope (γ_1) coefficients of the two-parameter model using the dummy-variable regression[a]:

$$\gamma_{kt} = a_1 + \sum_{j=2}^{12} a_j D_j + e_{kt}$$

Month of the year	SEASONALITY IN INTERCEPT	SEASONALITY IN SLOPE	Month of the year	SEASONALITY IN INTERCEPT	SEASONALITY IN SLOPE	SAMPLE SIZE
JANUARY	0.0296[b]	0.0149[b]	JULY	-0.0126	-0.0154[b]	156
	(3.53)	(3.02)		(-1.06)	(-2.21)	
FEBRUARY	-0.0062	-0.0176[b]	AUGUST	-0.0136	-0.0278[b]	156
	(-0.52)	(-2.52)		(-1.14)	(-3.97)	
MARCH	-0.0179	-0.0224[b]	SEPTEMBER	-0.0232[b]	-0.0292[b]	156
	(-1.51)	(-3.20)		(-1.96)	(-4.17)	
APRIL	-0.0041	-0.0193[b]	OCTOBER	-0.0407[b]	-0.0198[b]	156
	(-0.35)	(-2.76)		(-3.42)	(-2.83)	
MAY	-0.0320[b]	-0.0116	NOVEMBER	-0.0357[b]	-0.0145[b]	156
	(-2.70)	(-1.66)		(-3.01)	(-2.07)	
JUNE	-0.0095	-0.0234[b]	DECEMBER	-0.0165	-0.0118	156
	(-0.80)	(-3.35)		(-1.39)	(-1.69)	
F-Test	2.357	2.584	F-Test	2.357	2.584	
Probability	0.010	0.005	Probability	0.010	0.005	

a. k=0 (intercept) and 1 (slope) respectively. The variable D2 through D12 are dummy variables representing the months of the year from February to December. The coefficient a_1 is a measure of average γ_k in January while the coefficients a_2 through a_{12} are a measure of the difference between average γ_k in February to December and average γ_k in January. The t-statistics are in parentheses.

b. Significant at the 0.05 level

TABLE 4

Average values of the Fama and MacBeth estimates of the coefficients of the four-parameter model[a]:

$$R_{pt} = \gamma'_{0t} + \gamma'_{1t}\cdot\beta_{p,t-1} + \gamma_{2t}\cdot\beta^2_{p,t-1} + \gamma_{3t}\cdot SE_{p,t-1} + \mu'_{p\,t}$$

Average over	$\bar{\gamma}'_0$ (Intercept)	$\bar{\gamma}'_1$ (beta)	$\bar{\gamma}_2$ (beta)^2	$\bar{\gamma}_3$ (Unsyst.risk)	Sample size
All months	0.0050 (1.30)	-0.0021 (-0.55)	-0.0011 (-0.74)	**0.1502** (2.84)[b]	156
All months except January	0.0045 (1.13)	-0.0051 (-1.33)	-0.0005 (-0.31)	**0.1381** (2.65)[b]	143
JANUARY	0.0107 (0.69)	**0.0134** (2.44)[b]	**-0.0077** (-2.02)[b]	0.2830 (1.01)	13
FEBRUARY	0.0170 (1.56)	0.0063 (0.48)	-0.0063 (-1.39)	0.1321 (0.87)	13
MARCH	0.0054 (0.39)	-0.0235 (-1.54)	0.0082 (1.29)	0.1726 (1.30)	13
APRIL	**0.0282** (2.44)[b]	-0.0091 (-0.97)	0.0024 (0.56)	-0.0039 (-0.03)	13
MAY	-0.0009 (-0.08)	0.0158 (1.22)	-0.0053 (-1.16)	-0.0682 (-0.53)	13
JUNE	**0.0294** (2.65)[b]	-0.0198 (-1.77)	0.0026 (0.59)	-0.0551 (-0.39)	13
JULY	0.0069 (0.66)	-0.0078 (-0.92)	0.0041 (1.01)	0.1961 (1.14)	13
AUGUST	-0.0119 (-0.95)	-0.0116 (-1.18)	-0.0053 (-1.24)	**0.5945** (2.30)[b]	13
SEPTEMBER	-0.0054 (-0.39)	-0.0210 (-1.53)	-0.0001 (-0.02)	**0.3063** (2.00)[b]	13
OCTOBER	**-0.0278** (-2.05)[b]	-0.0000 (-0.00)	-0.0020 (-0.29)	0.2514 (1.39)	13
NOVEMBER	-0.0138 (-0.88)	0.0058 (0.40)	-0.0004 (-0.07)	0.1194 (0.59)	13
DECEMBER	0.0226 (1.47)	0.0088 (0.61)	-0.0032 (-0.60)	-0.1265 (-0.82)	13

a. estimated with monthly data and the equally-weighted index from January 1971 to December 1983.

b. t statistics are in parentheses below average values. Framed coefficients are statistically significant at the 0.05 level market value are reported in table 5. The largest portfolio which includes about 22 percent of the stocks in the sample represents 86 percent of the total market capitalization whereas the smallest portfolio with the same number of stocks represents less than one half of one percent of the total market capitalization. Note that the five portfolios have roughly the same betas (approximately equal to one).

All months considered, the largest portfolio earned an average monthly return of 0.65 percent and the smallest earned 1.17 percent. The differential return between the smallest and the largest portfolios is not, however, statistically significant. There are only four months of the year during which some of the portfolio returns were significantly different from zero: these are January, August, September and December. During the first three, the smallest portfolio outperformed the largest but during December we have a reverse size effect: the largest portfolio outperforms the smallest but the differential return is not statistically significant.

Another way to look at the size effect is to examine the average values of the estimated slope coefficients (the size premium) of regression (3) reported in table 6. There is a significantly negative relationship between returns and size over the entire sample period. But the negative size effect is particularly pronounced in the months of January, July, August and September. In December we have a positive size effect. This positive December size effect which precedes the negative January size effect is consistent with any explanation of the size effect which predicts the sale of small firms during December and their subsequent repurchase during January. Selling pressure will lower the return of small firms vis-à-vis the return of large firms during December and buying pressure will raise the return of small firms vis-à-vis the return of large firms during January. Consequently, small firms will underperform large firms during December and outperform their during January.

Recall that the five size-portfolios have been divided into four subportfolios according to their level of systematic risk. The characteristics of the four subportfolios are reported in table 7 for the largest and the smallest portfolio. Note that within each size-portfolio there is a clear positive relationship between average returns and systematic risk.

TABLE 5

Characteristics of five portfolios ranked by decreasing market capitalization measured in thousands of Belgian francs at the end of December. Values in the table are average over a 13-year period from January 1971 to December 1983.

PORTFOLIO SIZE			RISK	AVERAGE MONTHLY RETURNS				
IN THOUSANDS B.F.	PERCENT	No. STOCKS	(BETA)	ALL YEAR	JANUARY	AUGUST	SEPTEMBER	DECEMBER
6,586,917	86.05%	37	0.98	0.65% [a] (2.41)	3.04% [a] (3.23)	-0.60% (0.85)	-1.51% [a] (1.89)	2.72% [a] (2.11)
687,388	8.99%	32	1.13	0.62% [a] (2.33)	4.57% [a] (4.13)	-0.19% (0.15)	-2.15% [a] (2.75)	1.66% (1.50)
247,057	3.22%	32	1.02	0.93% [a] (3.69)	4.90% [a] (4.81)	0.61% (0.78)	-0.42% (0.52)	1.86% (1.76)
99,180	1.29%	32	0.93	0.87% [a] (3.87)	3.69% [a] (4.09)	0.93% (1.20)	-1.07% (1.43)	0.76% (0.85)
34,454	0.44%	37	1.01	1.17% [a] (4.65)	5.35% [a] (4.65)	1.88% [a] (1.92)	0.31% (0.84)	1.31% (1.28)
Differential return between smallest and largest portfolios (t-statistic in parentheses)				0.52% (1.41)	2.31% [a] (1.95)	2.48% [a] (2.05)	1.81% [a] (2.05)	-1.41% (0.89)

a. t statistics are in parentheses below average values. Framed coefficients are statistically significant at the 0.05 level.

TABLE 6

Average values of the estimated intercept and slope coefficients of the regression

$$R_{pt} = \gamma''_{0t} + \gamma_{4t}\left[\frac{Vp - Vm}{Vm}\right]_{t-1} + \mu''_{p\,t}$$

Where Vp and Vm are the market capitalization of portfolio and the market, respectively[a].

Average over	$\bar{\gamma}''_o$ (Intercept)	$\bar{\gamma}_4$ (Relative size)	Sample size
All months	0.0091[b] (3.54)	-0.0007[b] (-2.05)	156
All months except January	0.0058[b] (2.38)	-0.0006 (-1.65)	143
JANUARY	0.0444[b] (4.18)	-0.0019[b] (-1.96)	13
FEBRUARY	0.0205 (2.73)	-0.0016 (-1.51)	13
MARCH	0.0042 (0.51)	-0.0008 (-0.69)	13
APRIL	0.0212[b] (2.74)	0.0007 (0.52)	13
MAY	0.0009 (0.14)	-0.0004 (-0.64)	13
JUNE	0.0115[b] (2.02)	0.0001 (0.14)	13
JULY	0.0164[b] (2.63)	-0.0014[b] (-2.47)	13
AUGUST	0.0027[b] (0.34)	-0.0042[b] (-3.42)	13
SEPTEMBER	-0.0083 (-0.98)	-0.0031[b] (-4.20)	13
OCTOBER	-0.0160[b] (-2.54)	-0.0014 (-1.47)	13
NOVEMBER	-0.0055 (-0.73)	0.0017 (0.86)	13
DECEMBER	0.0167 (1.50)	0.0036[b] (2.17)	13

a. estimated with monthly data and the equally-weighted index from January 1971 to December 1983.

b. t statistics are in parentheses below average values. Framed coefficients are statistically significant at the 0.05 level.

TABLE 7

Characteristics of the largest and smallest size portfolios which have been partioned into four subportfolios ranked by decreasing magnitude of their beta coefficient. Values in the table are average over a 13-year period from January 1971 to December 1983.

PORTFOLIO SIZE (Thousands BF)	SUBPORTFOLIOS RANKED BY BETAS			AVERAGE MONTHLY RETURNS				
	BETA	No STOCKS	SIZE	ALL YEAR	JANUARY	AUGUST	SEPTEMBER	DECEMBER
	1.75	13	5,984,648	0.82% [a]	6.11% [a]	-0.79	-2.42% [a]	3.49%
				(2.01)	(3.61)	(0.71)	(2.04)	(1.56)
LARGEST	1.11	8	6,048,503	0.77% [a]	3.36% [a]	-0.53	-1.59%	2.54%
(6,586,917)				(2.60)	3.18)	(0.63)	(1.67)	(1.73)
(see table 5)	0.79	8	8,278,489	0.38%	2.12% [a]	-0.89	-1.65% [a]	3.21% [a]
				(1.55)	(3.00)	1.13)	(2.92)	(2.87)
	0.28	8	6,036,027	0.61% [a]	0.58% [a]	-0.17	-0.39	1.65% [a]
				(3.47)	(0.86)	(0.36)	(0.60)	3.07)
	2.42	13	33,462	2.15% [a]	10.31% [a]	4.83% [a]	-0.85%	5.04% [a]
				(3.52)	(3.99)	(1.99)	(0.45)	(1.98)
SMALLEST	1.19	8	37,368	0.96% [a]	5.77% [a]	1.28%	-1.52%	1.01%
(34,454)				(2.85)	(3.77)	(1.31)	(1.31)	(0.88)
(see table 5)	0.64	8	34,185	0.75% [a]	3.58% [a]	0.58%	-0.24%	-0.35
				(2.98)	(3.26)	(0.59)	(0.26)	(0.41)
	-0.20	8	32,800	0.81% [a]	1.74% [a]	0.82%	1.39%	-0.43
				(4.25)	(2.87)	(1.01)	(1.84)	(0.90)

a. t statistics are in parentheses below average values. Framed coefficients are statistically significant at the 0.05 level.

This is true when all months are considered together as well as in January, August, September and December. A clear pattern emerges: (1) the smallest portfolio generally outperforms the largest portfolio, particularly during January; and (2) within in a size portfolio, high beta subportfolios outperform low beta portfolios, particularly during January. Hence the highest return is earned during January by the subportfolio with the smallest size and the highest beta: 10.31 percent which represents an annualized rate of return of 124 percent.

6. Seasonality, size and equity pricing

What is the relationship between common stock returns and risk when size and seasonality are taken into account? The answer to this question can be found by examining the average estimated coefficients of regressions (8) and (9) which are reported in table 8 and table 9, respectively.

Consider first regression (8) where risk is only systematic (beta). Over the entire sample period there is a negative size effect and no significant risk effect. This means that market value (size) is, on average, a better predictor of stock returns than systematic risk, a conclusion that is inconsistent with equity pricing according to the CAPM. Turning to the results for regression (9) in table 9 over the entire sample period we can see that when unsystematic risk is taken into consideration, it is the only significant variable in the pricing equation, a result which is again inconsistent with equity pricing according to the CAPM.

How does seasonality affect the results reported above? The answer is found in the month-to-month average estimated regression coefficients given in tables 8 and 9. January is the only month of the year during which the systematic risk premium is significantly positive with no premium earned for bearing unsystematic risk. One may conclude that equity pricing is consistent with the CAPM during January but unfortunately the relationship is <u>not</u> linear and a significant size effect is present during January. These two characteristics are not consistent with the CAPM. The CAPM must be rejected even during January despite the positive systematic risk premium and the absence of an unsystematic risk premium.

TABLE 8

Average values of the estimated intercept and slope coefficients of the regression :

$$R_{pt} = \gamma^S_{0t} + \gamma^S_{1t}\beta_{p,t-1} + \gamma^S_{4t}\cdot\left[\frac{Vp - Vm}{Vm}\right]_{t-1} + \mu^S_{p\,t}$$

Where Vp and Vm are the market capitalization of portfolio p and the market, respectively[a].

Average over	$\bar{\gamma}^S_o$ (Intercept)	$\bar{\gamma}^S_1$ (beta)	$\bar{\gamma}^*_4$ (relative size)	Sample size
All months	0.0110 [b] (4.45)	-0.0020 (-1.30)	-0.0008 [b] (-2.30)	156
All months except January	0.0096 [b] (3.73)	-0.0037 [b] (-2.48)	-0.0007 [b] (-1.86)	143
JANUARY	0.0272 [b] (3.22)	0.0172 [b] (3.05)	-0.0022 [b] (-1.95)	13
FEBRUARY	0.0213 [b] (3.83)	-0.0007 (-0.13)	-0.0022 (-1.56)	13
MARCH	0.0099 (1.42)	-0.0058 (-1.16)	-0.0010 (-0.86)	13
APRIL	0.0242 [b] (2.34)	-0.0030 (-0.79)	0.0006 (0.43)	13
MAY	-0.0023 (-0.29)	0.0032 (0.67)	-0.0003 (-0.39)	13
JUNE	0.0205 [b] (2.76)	-0.0089 (-1.64)	-0.0001 (-0.16)	13
JULY	0.0156 [b] (2.35)	0.0007 (0.16)	-0.0015 [b] (-2.76)	13
AUGUST	0.0135 (1.47)	-0.0107 [b] (-2.22)	-0.0041 [b] (-3.53)	13
SEPTEMBER	0.0046 (0.51)	-0.0128 [b] (-2.45)	-0.0032 [b] (-4.11)	13
OCTOBER	-0.0119 (-1.69)	-0.0041 (-1.33)	-0.0012 (-1.26)	13
NOVEMBER	-0.0070 (-0.86)	0.0015 (0.34)	0.0013 (0.68)	13
DECEMBER	0.0168 (1.66)	-0.0002 (-0.03)	0.0037 [b] (2.41)	13

a. estimated with monthly data and the equally-weighted index from January 1971 to December 1983.

b. t statistics are in parentheses below average values. Framed coefficients are statistically significant at the 0.05 level.

TABLE 9

Average values of the estimated intercept and slope of the regression :

$$R_{pt} = \gamma^*_{0t} + \gamma^*_{1t}\beta_{p,t-1} + \gamma^*_{2t}\beta^2_{p,t-1} + \gamma^*_{3t}\, SE_{p,t-1} + \gamma^*_{4t}\left[\frac{Vp - Vm}{Vm}\right]_{t-1} + \mu^*_{p\,t}$$

Where Vp and Vm are the market capitalization of portfolio p and the market, respectively[a].

Average over	$\bar{\gamma}^*_0$ (Intercept)	$\bar{\gamma}^*_1$ (beta)	$\bar{\gamma}^*_2$ $(beta)^2$	$\bar{\gamma}^*_3$ (Unsyst. risk)	$\bar{\gamma}^*_4$ (size)	Sample size
All months	0.0045 (1.18)	-0.0014 (-0.37)	-0.0010 (-0.65)	**0.1390** **(2.59)** [b]	-0.0003 (-0.93)	156
All months except January	0.0037 (0.93)	-0.0047 (-1.23)	-0.0004 (-0.24)	**0.1374** **(2.60)** [b]	-0.0002 (-0.48)	143
JANUARY	0.0138 (0.89)	**0.0353** **(2.81)** [b]	**-0.0076** **(-1.99)** [b]	0.1569 (0.54)	**-0.0021** **(-1.90)** [b]	13
FEBRUARY	0.0144 (1.62)	0.0105 (0.65)	-0.0065 (-1.34)	0.1031 (0.76)	-0.0017 (-0.97)	13
MARCH	0.0024 (0.20)	-0.0206 (-1.34)	0.0070 (1.10)	**0.2028** **(2.01)** [b]	0.0001 (0.11)	13
APRIL	**0.0249** **(2.19)** [b]	-0.0120 (-1.25)	0.0037 (0.82)	0.0722 (0.52)	0.0007 (0.52)	13
MAY	0.0032 (0.26)	0.0188 (1.53)	-0.0059 (-1.32)	-0.1727 (-1.16)	**-0.0017** **(-3.41)** [b]	13
JUNE	**0.0277** **(2.35)** [b]	-0.0207 (-1.76)	0.0031 (0.70)	-0.0404 (-0.24)	0.0001 (0.10)	13
JULY	0.0082 (0.68)	-0.0060 (-0.68)	0.0042 (0.96)	0.1208 (0.52)	-0.0011 (-0.88)	13
AUGUST	-0.0094 (-0.78)	-0.0079 (-0.84)	-0.0058 (-1.37)	**0.4880** **(1.88)** [b]	**-0.0018** **(-2.96)** [b]	13
SEPTEMBER	-0.0028 (-0.21)	-0.0160 (-1.24)	-0.0009 (-0.19)	0.2097 (1.36)	**-0.0021** **(-2.56)** [b]	13
OCTOBER	**-0.0257** **(-1.95)** [b]	-0.0010 (-0.07)	-0.0017 (-0.24)	0.2128 (1.24)	-0.0004 (-0.41)	13
NOVEMBER	-0.0190 (-1.23)	0.0027 (0.20)	0.0003 (0.04)	0.2282 (1.15)	0.0021 (1.11)	13
DECEMBER	0.0163 (1.03)	0.0003 (0.03)	-0.0016 (-0.30)	0.0865 (0.52)	**0.0037** **(2.43)** [b]	13

a. estimated with monthly data and the equally-weighted index from January 1971 to December 1983.

b. t statistics are in parentheses below average values. Framed coefficients are statistically significant at the 0.05 level.

Finally, note that during August and September we have a significant negative size effect and that during December we have a positive size effect even after controlling for both systematic and unsystematic risks.

7. Conclusion

The purpose of this paper was to re-examine the pricing of common stocks on the Belgian Stock Exchange in light of two related phenomena recently reported in the literature: the size effect and risk premia seasonality. We have shown that if these two phenomena are ignored we cannot reject the hypothesis that the behavior of common stock prices conform to the CAPM. However, once size and seasonality are accounted for in the stochastic process that generates returns, the hypothesis that the CAPM describes (and explains) the pricing of common stocks must be rejected, even during the month of January despite the presence of a positive systematic risk premium and the absence of an unsystematic risk premium during that month.

References

1. BANZ, R. "The Relationship Between Return and Market Value of Common Stocks", Journal of Financial Economics, 9 (March 1981), 3-18.

2. BLACK, F. "Capital Market Equilibrium with Restricted Borrowing", Journal of Business, 45 (July 1972), 445-455.

3. CORHAY, A., G. HAWAWINI and P. MICHEL "Seasonality in the Risk-Return Relationship: Some International Evidence", Journal of Finance, 42 (March 1987a), 49-68.

4. CORHAY, A., G. HAWAWINI and P. MICHEL "The Pricing of Equity on the London Stock Exchange: Seasonality and Size Premium" in Stock Market Anomalies, edited by E. Dimson, Cambridge University Press (1987b).

5. FAMA, E. Foundations of Finance, Basic Books: New York (1976).

6. FAMA, E. and J. MACBETH "Risk, Return and Equilibrium: Empirical Tests", Journal of Political Economy, 81 (May/June 1973), 607-636.

7. GULTEKIN, M.N. and N.B. GULTEKIN "Stock Market Seasonality: International Evidence", Journal of Financial Economics, 12 (December 1983) 469-482.

8. HAWAWINI, G. European Equity Markets: Price Behavior and Efficiency, Salomon Brothers Center for the Study of Financial Institutions, Graduate School of Business Administration, New York University, Monograph 4/5 (1984).

9. HAWAWINI, G. and P. MICHEL "The Pricing or Risky Assets on the Belgian Stock Market" Journal of Banking and Finance, 6 (June 1982), 161-178.

10. KEIM, D. "Size-Related Anomalies and Stock Return Seasonality: Further Empirical Evidence", Journal of Financial Economics, 12 (June 1983), 13-32.

11. ROLL, R. "Vas ist das? The Turn-of-the-Year Effect and the Return Premia of Small Firms", Journal of Portfolio Management, 9 (Winter 1963), 18-28.

12. ROZEFF, M. and W. KINNEY "Capital Market Seasonality: The Case of Stock Returns", Journal of Financial Economics, 3 (October 1976), 379-402.

13. SHARPE, W. "A Simplified Model for Portfolio Analysis", Management Science, 9 (January 1963), 277-293.

14. SHARPE, W. "Capital Asset Prices: A Theory of Market Equilibrium under Conditions of Risk", Journal of Finance, 19 (September 1964), 425-442.

15. TINIC, S. and R. WEST "Risk and Return: January Versus the Rest of the Year", Journal of Financial Economics, 13 (December 1984), 561-574.

16. TINIC, S. and R. WEST "Risk, Return, and Equilibrium: A Revisit", Journal of Political Economy, 94 (February 1986), 126-147

MARKET SIZE, PE RATIOS, DIVIDEND YIELD AND SHARE PRICES: THE UK EVIDENCE

Mario Levis

School of Management
University of Bath
Claverton Down
Bath BA2 7AY
England

KEYWORDS: DIVIDEND YIELD; LONDON STOCK EXCHANGE; PE RATIO; SHARE PRICES; SIZE EFFECT; STOCK MARKET ANOMALIES

ABSTRACT

This paper reports evidence documenting the presence of a number of irregularities in stock price behaviour of firms on the London Stock Exchange. The size effect not only is not the sole anomaly but is not even the most dominant one. Specifically, investment strategies based on dividend yield, PE ratios and share prices appear as profitable , if not more, as a strategy concentrating on firm size. Although there is a large degree of interdependency between all four effects, it is still apparent that the dividend yield and PE ratios subsume the size and share price effects.

NATO ASI Series, Vol. F54
A Reappraisal of the Efficiency of Financial Markets
Edited by Rui M.C. Guimaraes et al.

1. Introduction

The volume of empirical evidence that followed Banz's (1981) and Reinganum's (1981) seminal papers has firmly established the existence of a market size anomaly in stock price behaviour. In the process of searching for explanations for this phenomenon a number of other 'irregularities' have surfaced. The discovery of the January effect, for example, provided further valuable insight into the size anomaly but in effect added to rather than resolved the puzzle. Furthermore, it seems that investment strategies based on earnings or dividend yields have earned, over sufficiently long time periods, positive and significant abnormal returns. The presence of such anomalies is not confined to the US market alone.[1] Evidence of the size effect for other markets has been less forthcoming, but the results of Brown, Kleidon and Marsh (1983) for the Australian market, Berges, McConnell and Schlarbaum (1984) for Canada, Nakamura and Tarada (1984) for the Tokyo Stock Exchange and Levis (1985) for the London Stock Exchange (LSE) point to a similar size anomaly in these markets as well. With regard to the dividend and earnings yield effects the evidence for other than the US market is still scarce.

The main question surrounding these findings is whether such additional anomalies are independent of or related to market size. The evidence on this issue is rather controversial. While Reinganum (1981) argues that the size effect subsumes the PE effect, Basu (1983) asserts quite the opposite -i.e. size related anomalies disappear when one controls for the PE effect. Cook and Rozeff's (1984) investigation of this discrepancy added to the controversy by concluding that both views are misguided; their work suggests that "both effects (at least) are at work" (p. 464). Peavy and Goodman (1983) introduced an additional dimension to the analysis; they argue that the PE effect may in fact be an industry effect, since firms in the same industry tend to have similar PE multiples. When, however, a direct comparison between PE and firm size is undertaken, Goodman, Peavy and Cox (1986) conclude that size usually serves as a proxy for the PE effect.

---

1. See for example Gultekin and Gultekin (1983).

The relation between dividend yields and stock returns has also received close scrutiny in the academic literature. For example, the studies of Litzenberger and Ramaswamy (1979), Blume (1980), Gordon and Bradford (1980), Miller and Scholes (1982) and Elton, Gruber and Rentzler (1983) point to a positive and significant relation between dividend yield and returns but disagree about the underlying sources of this relation; while some attribute it to the disparity in the tax rates for dividend yields and capital gains, others maintain that yield related effects are due to information bias. Keim's (1985) evidence provides an alternative view; it indicates a strong interaction between dividend yield and firm size which suggests that the positive dividend yield-return relation is a direct result of the concentration of smaller firms in certain high dividend yield categories.

As the common factor between the three variables - market size, PE multiples and dividend yields - is the share price, it is not inconceivable that these three effects may be attributed to some underlying relationship between share price and stock returns. The evidence of Blume and Husic (1973), Stoll and Whaley (1983) and Blume and Stambaugh (1983) points to a negative relation between share prices and stock returns.

It appears that one of the main sources of the continuing controversy regarding the relative importance of the four documented anomalies is the fact that they have been investigated separately using different data sets and various methodologies. This paper provides a systematic examination of the stock price behaviour of firms on the LSE in search for evidence regarding the presence and possible interrelations of the market size, dividend yield, PE multiple and share price effects. Such an analysis is crucial not only because it provides for the first time a comprehensive evaluation of all four anomalies using a unique set of data under a uniform methodology, but also because it offers the opportunity to contrast the US stock price behaviour irregularities with that of one of the largest capital markets. If indeed it emerges that such phenomena are "market specific", it would imply that application of conclusions drawn from one market to the other is unwarranted and even misleading.

Nevertheless, the implications in terms of investment strategy and academic research have been already universally adopted.[2]

Section 2 describes the data and methodology used in this study. Section 3 examines the properties of the portfolios generated under the four ranking procedures, while sections 4 and 5 provide a detailed analysis of the four anomalies under investigation and their potential interactions respectively. Finally, the main conclusions of this study and its implications are outlined in the section 6.

2. The Data and Methodology

A. Data and portfolio formation procedures

The data used in this study are from the London Share Price Database (LSPD) monthly returns file and source file. The latter provides the data required to estimate market value, PE multiples, dividend yields and share prices, while the former contains monthly rates of return, inclusive of dividends and capital gains. Market value of the firm is defined as the market price at the calendar year-end T (T=1955, 1956,...,1983), times the number of shares outstanding. The dividend yield is measured by the ratio of the dividends paid during the twelve months period of a calendar year to the market price of common stock at the end of this year. Earnings per share are estimated as the twelve months earnings divided by the number of shares outstanding at the calendar year-end; this estimate over the share price at the end of the same year determines the PE ratio.[3]

In the first instance, a single classificatory procedure is used to construct portfolios for each of the four attributes under investigation. At the end of each calendar year T firms are

---

2. Dimson and Marsh (1986), for example, have made a strong case for the small size effect to be incorporated into the estimation of abnormal returns in event studies.

3. This is the definition used by Reinganum (1981), Basu (1983) and Cook and Rozeff (1984). In case of firms with a calendar fiscal year-end this definition of dividend yield and PE ratio may incorporate a look-ahead bias. (See Banz and Breen (1986) and following note). Ball's (1978) evidence, however, indicates that the likely effects of experimental bias are not sufficient to explain the magnitude of the PE anomaly.

ranked separately in ascending order according to market value, dividend yield, PE ratio and share price. Portfolio returns are then computed for the 12-month period commencing the following April, by combining returns of individual firms using equal weights.[4] The ranking and portfolio formation procedures for each of the four attributes were repeated 29 times to cover the period April 1956 to March 1985. To qualify for inclusion in a given calendar year, a firm need only possess data for the particular ranking procedure at the end of this year and a valid rate of return for April of the following year. Every year firms enter or leave the sample due to mergers or bankruptcies. Thus, no survival bias requirements are imposed on the sample. Given the ambivalent interpretation of negative earnings and following the practice of previous studies, a firm was dropped from the sample in any year in which it had negative earnings. A preliminary analysis of the data indicated substantial differences in data availability when earnings-per-share (eps) were considered. While, for example, the ranking procedures for market value, dividend yield and share price resulted in very similar sample sizes, ranging from 1150 firms in the beginning of seventies to 2300 in mid-70's, the PE procedure resulted in a sample ranging from 770 to 1920 firms.[5] The differences in the sample size would be unimportant for the purposes of this study if the missing eps

---

4. Starting the calculation of portfolio returns in the following April minimises the potential bias of accumulating returns over a three-month period, at the beginning of each year, when the dividends and earnings assumed known in the dividend yield and PE calculations are in fact unknown. This is the method used by Basu (1983) and Cook and Rozeff (1984). To test, however, for the extent of this bias the whole analysis was repeated for portfolios running from January instead of April.

5. For the period January 1956 to December 1974 the sample of companies on the LSPD returns file is somewhat biased towards larger firms. From January 1975 onwards the database has been extended to cover all listed shares on the London Stock Exchange (see Smithers (1986)). Thus, the small firm effect reported in this study may be understated during the former period. On the other hand, it is worth noting that the increase in the size of the sample on January 1975 did not result to any significant change in the monthly rates of return of the various market size portfolios.

data was occurring randomly across the quintiles of the four attributes. Since this was not the case, a direct comparison of the various effects utilising different sample sizes would be misleading; on the other hand, the adoption of a unified sample which could satisfy all four criteria in terms of data availability would result in an even greater reduction of the data set with undesirable consequences. Thus, the whole analysis is repeated using two data sets. The full sample is utilised when the market size, dividend yield and share price (or any combination of them) are used as the ranking procedures. On the other hand, where the PE ratio is involved, on its own or in combination with any of the other attributes, a reduced sample is used. Both sets of results are presented when comparisons among ranking procedures are in order. A simple MV1 notation is used to identify the smaller size portfolio, based on the full sample, while MV1! denotes the same portfolio based on the reduced sample.

To control for the interaction effects between the four attributes, combined portfolios are constructed. Both within-groups only and within-groups plus randomisation methods are used. According to the former, all firms in either the full or reduced sample were ranked first by a chosen criterion and quintiles are formed. Then within each quintile firms are reranked on a second variable and quintiles are formed within each of the original quintiles; twenty-five portfolios are formed for each combination of two attributes. The process was repeated 25 times to generate portfolios within each of the four characteristics used in this study as a primary variable and the remaining three as secondary grouping; to cover all possible combinations of attributes 300 (5x5x3x4) portfolios were generated. Within groups portfolios were created by ranking, for example, first on size and next on dividend yield, PE, and share price. The within-groups method has been used by Basu (1983), Banz (1981) and tested by Cook and Rozeff (1984).

The within-groups plus randomisation method was also used by Basu (1983) and Cook and Rozeff (1984). The randomisation method follows from the within-groups method described above; the 25 portfolios generated for each combination of pairs are combined to form the randomised portfolios. Market size portfolios, for example, are constructed by randomising separately with respect to dividend yield, PE multiple and share price. The MV1*DV portfolio, for example, includes securities of the first market size quintile but is drawn from the entire set of dividend yield classes; thus it can be viewed as being randomised with respect to dividend yield. In a similar manner, portfolio DV1*MV contains firms of the lowest dividend yield but includes firms from all market size classes -i.e. randomised with respect to firm size. To cover all pairs of combinations of the four ranking procedures used in this study, 12 randomisation procedures were required, resulting in sixty randomised portfolios.[6]

B. Risk adjustment issues

Abnormal returns (u_{pt}) are estimated by subtracting from the actual portfolio return (R_{pt}) the returns predicted by the model used, given the market return (R_{mt}), the risk free rate (R_{ft}) and the parameter estimates (b_t). Two main models were employed in this study:

$$u_{pt} = (R_{pt} - R_{ft}) - (R_{mt} - R_{ft}) \quad (1)$$

$$u_{pt} = (R_{pt} - R_{ft}) - b_p(R_{mt} - R_{ft}) \quad (2)$$

Model (1) can be regarded as a limiting case of model (2), the simple CAPM framework, whereby all betas are assumed to be unity and the abnormal return is estimated by subtracting the market from the portfolio return. Model (2) involves a two-stage estimation procedure. The first stage consists of the estimation of the respective beta coefficients. A sixty month base period is used for this purpose; the first base period is April 1956 to March 1961. In the second stage the base period beta estimates are used to obtain abnormal returns for a subsequent holdout period. Holdout periods run for twelve months at a time beginning

---

6. All within-groups only and within-groups plus randomisation portfolios that include the PE ratio either as a primary or secondary ranking variable are based on the reduced sample. All other portfolios utilise the full set of data available.

in April following the base year (April 1961 in the first instance) and running through March of the following year. Betas are updated annually by rolling over the base period twelve months at a time. Thus, the last base period is April 1979 to March 1984, while the last holdout period is April 1984 to March 1985. The total number of months in the holdout period is 288.

Marsh (1979) concluded that the results are remarkably robust to the precise variant of the single factor Market Model and to the estimates of beta. They are, however, very sensitive to the choice of portfolio weighting scheme, so that quite different abnormal returns were obtained when equally rather than market value weighted indices were employed. Accordingly, abnormal returns in this study are estimated using a specially constructed equally weighted index consisting of all securities on the London Stock Exchange. Furthermore, given the well-documented problems of thin trading evident with UK data, abnormal returns based on model (2) but using the Dimson (1979) Aggregated Coefficients (AC) method for beta estimates were also estimated for all portfolios. Thus, model (2) takes the form:

$$u_{pt} = (R_{pt} - R_{ft}) - \sum_{k=-1}^{+5} b_{pk}(R_{m,t+k} - R_{f,t+k}) \qquad (3)$$

Following Dimson, aggregated beta coefficients are estimated using five lagged and one leading market variable. [7]

3. The Properties of the Four Portfolio Ranking Procedures

A. Rates of return

Table I shows the monthly average raw rates of return for the quintiles generated by each of the four single ranking procedures over the period April 1961 to March 1985. Each panel also shows the standard deviation of the portfolio (column 2), the mean return per unit of standard deviation (column 4) and the difference between this amount and the corresponding values for the FTA value weighted and an equally weighted index, are shown in columns 5 and 6 respectively. These results are directly comparable with the evidence reported in US studies.

---

7. Experimentation with a different lag structure indicated that AC beta estimates are robust around the number of lagging and leading variables adopted in this study.

A survey of the results in part 1 of the table, the full sample, indicates that consistent with other markets, a firm size effect is also evident in the UK data. A direct comparison of the relative magnitude of the size effect across other capital markets is difficult because of differing time periods and research design. However, the bulk of the US evidence points to the presence of a higher size premium than the 5.1 per cent per annum (0.42 per cent per month) observed for the LSE.[8] The UK size effect is also markedly lower than the premium reported by Brown, Kleidon and Marsh (1983) for the Australian market, Berges, McConnell and Schlarbaum (1984) for Canada (about 9 per cent per annum) and Nakamura and Tarada (1984) for the Tokyo Stock Exchange (10.7 per cent per annum). Panel B of the same table confirms the existence of a positive relation between dividend yield and returns. The difference between the two extreme yield portfolios is equal to 10.0 per cent per annum, a premium higher than that reported by Keim (1983) for NYSE firms. The share price ranking procedure in panel C exhibits a pattern of raw average monthly returns remarkably similar to the one found for market size. Estimates of the PE effect are shown in part 2 of the table. For comparative purposes, equivalent estimates for the other three ranking procedures, based on the reduced sample, are presented as well. First, it is worth noting the differences due to the sample size on the portfolio returns reviewed in part 1 of the table. The exclusion of firms with negative earnings, in conjunction with the missing data, resulted in an increase of the monthly returns of the first quintile across all three ranking procedures. Thus, based on the reduced sample, the market size effect reaches a level of 7.7 per cent per annum over the period April 1961 to March 1985, a premium comparable to the 9.5 per cent premium reported by Basu (1983) for NYSE firms. Panel G documents a negative relation between the

---

8. A decile instead of a quintile classification augment the size premium markedly. The average monthly return for the smaller size decile is equal 1.63 per cent per month producing a size premium of 8.6 per cent per annum. Thus in contrast to the US evidence does not appear to be a linear relationship between market size and stock returns across all size portfolios.

Table I

Monthly Rates of Return and Other Summary Statistics for the Full and Reduced Sample in the Period April 1961 to March 1985

	Mean (1)	SD (2)	(1)/(2) (3)	(3)-FTA (4)	(3)-EQUAL (5)
PART 1: FULL SAMPLE					
A. Market Value					
MV1	1.32	3.85	0.343	0.174	0.127
MV2	1.19	4.60	0.259	0.090	0.043
MV3	1.00	5.26	0.190	0.021	-0.026
MV4	0.94	5.76	0.163	-0.006	-0.053
MV5	0.90	6.32	0.142	-0.027	-0.074
B. Dividend Yield					
DV1	0.74	5.22	0.142	-0.027	-0.074
DV2	0.80	5.30	0.151	-0.018	-0.065
DV3	1.03	5.16	0.200	0.031	-0.016
DV4	1.20	4.90	0.245	0.076	0.029
DV5	1.57	4.59	0.342	0.173	0.126
C. Share Price					
PR1	1.33	4.67	0.285	0.116	0.069
PR2	1.20	4.96	0.242	0.073	0.026
PR3	1.01	5.23	0.193	0.024	-0.023
PR4	0.93	5.26	0.177	0.008	-0.039
PR5	0.91	5.14	0.177	0.008	-0.039

PART 2: REDUCED SAMPLE

D. Market Value					
MV1!	1.51	3.72	0.406	0.237	0.190
MV2!	1.16	4.47	0.259	0.090	0.043
MV3!	1.05	5.30	0.198	0.029	-0.018
MV4!	0.98	5.94	0.165	-0.004	-0.051
MV5!	0.87	6.32	0.138	-0.031	-0.078
E. Dividend Yield					
DV1!	0.77	5.51	0.140	-0.029	-0.076
DV2!	0.91	5.29	0.172	0.003	-0.044
DV3!	1.08	5.05	0.214	0.045	-0.002
DV4!	1.23	4.84	0.254	0.085	0.038
DV5!	1.55	4.54	0.341	0.172	0.125
F. Share Price					
PR1!	1.47	4.58	0.321	0.152	0.105
PR2!	1.20	5.06	0.237	0.068	0.021
PR3!	1.00	5.13	0.195	0.026	-0.021
PR4!	0.95	5.30	0.179	0.010	-0.037
PR5!	0.92	5.20	0.177	0.008	-0.039
G. PE ratio					
PE1!	1.48	4.75	0.311	0.142	0.095
PE2!	1.19	5.01	0.237	0.068	0.021
PE3!	1.05	5.03	0.209	0.040	-0.007
PE4!	0.95	5.14	0.185	0.016	-0.031
PE5!	0.90	5.24	0.172	0.003	-0.044
H. Market Indices					
FTA Value Weighted	1.04	6.14	0.169		
Equally Weighted	1.05	4.87	0.216		

Period April 1961 to March 1985, 288 observations.

PE ratio and rates of return. The average PE effect of 7.0 per cent per annum is similar to the effect reported by Basu (1977) (1983) and Reinganum (1981). In short, the monthly average returns of the portfolios based on the four ranking procedures indicate that during the period April 1961 to March 1985, an investment strategy based on dividend yields would have outperformed a PE ratio strategy by 2.40 per cent per annum and a market size and a share price strategy by 1.68 and 2.76 per cent per annum respectively.[9]

Even more interesting, however, are the results shown in column 3 of this table regarding the variability of the portfolios of the various ranking procedures. While the total risk of the five dividend yield, PE and share price portfolios are almost identical, the market size portfolios are strikingly different both to modern portfolio theory and intuition i.e. the higher returns of the smaller portfolios appear to be associated with lower levels of total risk. As a consequence, the mean return per unit of variability of the smaller market size quintile is more than twice the size of its largest counterpart, while the UK scaled size premium is 1.8 times higher than its US equivalent. There is little doubt that the low variability of stock returns of the smaller firms' portfolios is at least partially, attributable to infrequent trading.[10] The returns per unit of variability for the PE portfolios exhibit a similar pattern to those found for US data but are consistently about 50 per cent higher than the estimates reported by Basu (1983). Similar conclusions are drawn by comparing the abnormal returns

---

9. A comparison of these estimates with the equivalent results based on the alternative portfolio construction procedures mentioned in note 3, instantly reveals that the look-ahead bias problem is relevant to the UK data as well. While the rates of return for market size and share price portfolios remain essentially unchanged the dividend yield and PE effects could be biased upwards by as much as 2.8 per cent per annum over the period under consideration.

10. Roll (1981) has shown that infrequent trading causes both covariance and variance terms to be downwards biased, while Dimson and Marsh (1983) reported a correlation coefficient of 0.81 between trading frequency and market capitalisation for the London Stock Exchange.

(in terms of total risk) earned by the smallest size portfolio (MV1) for both the equally and value-weighted market indices. It is also interesting to note that while the market value (MV) and share price (PR) portfolios earn similar rates of return, hinting at the possibility of one acting as a proxy for the other, their respective variances are markedly different; in fact, the standard deviation estimates for all five share price portfolios are essentially the same. On this evidence alone it would appear that market size and share price are not perfectly substitutable ranking procedures. This issue is further explored in the following sections.

B. Autocorrelations and beta coefficients

The first five autocorrelations coefficients for each of the portfolios of the four different ranking procedures, the OLS as well as the AC beta estimates are given in Table II. A significant feature relative to the statistics of US monthly returns is the high first-order serial correlation ranging from 0.16 to 0.43 for the market value ranking procedure and the significantly higher order correlations observed for the two smaller portfolios. It is also important to note the invariably significant first order serial correlations observed for each of the portfolios by all four ranking procedures. This discrepancy with the US data is consistent with the view that the problem of thin trading is more severe in the British market than in the US. In spite of the strong indication of the existence of thin trading the OLS beta estimates are rather surprising: the beta coefficients range from 0.7 for smaller size portfolio to 1.21 for MV5; furthermore, the beta estimates for all portfolios of the three other ranking procedures are essentially equal to unity. It is also worth noticing that the odd disparity between beta estimates would be markedly amplified if a value weighted index was used as the market portfolio. When account of thin trading is taken by using the Aggregated Coefficients method suggested by Dimson (1979), using five lagged and one leading market coefficient, the smaller firms still do not emerge as riskier than their larger counterparts. In fact, our results indicate that all AC beta estimates are not different from unity.

Table II

OLS, Aggregated Beta Coefficients and Autocorrelations of Rates of Return

	Betas		Autocorrelations				
	OLS	AC	r1	r2	r3	r4	r5
A. Market Value							
MV1	0.70	0.96	.43	.25	.24	.09	.08
MV2	0.92	1.02	.34	.14	.19	.01	-.07
MV3	1.06	1.07	.29	.07	.13	.00	-.10
MV4	1.15	1.04	.27	.03	.09	.00	-.13
MV5	1.21	0.92	.16	-.07	.11	.00	-.15
B. Dividend Yield							
DV1	1.01	1.06	.31	.09	.12	.01	-.05
DV2	1.06	0.98	.26	-.01	.15	.00	-.13
DV3	1.03	0.98	.27	-.03	.13	.01	-.12
DV4	1.01	1.01	.30	.07	.12	.00	-.09
DV5	0.95	0.99	.30	.09	.17	-.01	-.11
C. PE ratio							
PE1	0.98	1.04	.30	.11	.13	-.02	-.10
PE2	1.03	1.00	.29	.05	.13	.12	-.12
PE3	1.04	0.99	.27	.03	.15	.03	-.11
PE4	0.99	0.99	.28	.04	.15	.04	-.08
PE5	1.04	0.94	.26	-.02	.09	.02	-.13
D. Share Price							
PR1	0.94	1.04	.31	.16	.16	-.02	-.07
PR2	1.02	1.02	.28	.07	.15	-.01	-.09
PR3	1.05	1.02	.28	.05	.14	.00	-.12
PR4	1.06	1.00	.28	.02	.14	.02	-.11
PR5	0.99	0.94	.28	.09	.12	.01	-.11
FTA Value Weighted Index			.13	-.09	.13	-.04	-.14
Equally weighted Index			.29	.06	.14	.00	-.09

OLS and AC Betas are estimated using an Equally Weighted Index. The AC beta is estimated using five lagged and one leading market coefficient.

This evidence is obviously in sharp contrast with the US findings but not entirely surprising for the UK framework. Although no formal tests of the risk-return relationship have been carried out on UK data, there is considerable scattered evidence in a number of studies hinting at some marked deviations from the CAPM framework. Dimson's (1979) tables 7 and 8, for example, show that even when betas are adjusted by the AC method for thin trading, smaller firms appear to be associated with lower betas; the betas of the 20 per cent lowest beta estimates do not exceed 0.9, even when more terms are added to the regression. Marsh's (1979) study of UK rights issues concludes that all of the large positive abnormal returns were small companies. Furthermore, Dimson and Marsh (1983) using the Trade-to-Trade method for beta estimation still point to the same paradox -i.e. smaller firms have lower betas than their larger counterparts and the riskiness of smaller firms is not stationary over time. More recently Corhay, Hawawini and Michel (1987) concluded that April "is the only month of the year during which the relationship between average portfolio returns and systematic risk is significantly positive on the LSE" (p.67).

4. Risk-Return Relations for the Four Effects

Table III presents three different types of abnormal returns using the estimates of models (1), (2) and (3). The results for each one of the ranking procedures, for both the complete and reduced sample, are shown in separate panels. Panel A, for example, shows the abnormal returns based on each of the three risk adjustment models estimates for the five non-randomised market size portfolios and portfolios randomised for dividend yield, share price and PE ratio. A single notation -i.e. MV, DV, PE, and PR refers to non-randomised portfolios; randomised portfolios are labelled with a double code; the smallest market size portfolio, for example, randomised by dividend yield is labelled as MV1*DV. The second part of the code always refers to the randomisation procedure in operation. The t-values test the hypothesis that the individual portfolio abnormal return is equal to zero, while the Hotelling T^2-statistic and the corresponding F-values test the hypothesis that the abnormal return vector for

Table III

Excess Returns, based on three Models, for Straight and Randomised Portfolios

A. Market Value

	Model (2)			Model (3)			Model (1)		
	u_p	$t(u_p)$	T^2 $F(u_p)$	u_p	$t(u_p)$	T^2 $F(u_p)$	u_p	$t(u_p)$	T^2 $F(u_p)$
MV1	0.452	3.74	.11	0.330	2.04	.07	0.253	1.77	.04
MV2	0.196	2.94	6.21	0.163	1.92	4.15	0.135	1.91	2.24
MV3	-0.084	-2.03		-0.111	-2.50		-0.061	-1.40	
MV4	-0.200	-3.58		-0.161	-2.18		-0.128	-1.86	
MV5	-0.296	-2.34		-0.182	-1.08		-0.164	-1.21	
MV1*DV	0.416	4.17	.10	0.333	2.45	.08	0.250	1.90	.04
MV2*DV	0.045	0.69	5.82	-0.014	-0.17	4.68	-0.011	-0.17	2.20*
MV3*DV	-0.096	-2.43		-0.086	-2.17		-0.078	-1.88	
MV4*DV	-0.173	-3.40		-0.148	-2.15		-0.090	-1.32	
MV5*DV	-0.211	-1.90		-0.103	-0.70		-0.091	-0.76	
MV1*PR	0.329	3.38	.08	0.222	1.70	.04	0.153	1.09	.03
MV2*PR	0.158	2.67	4.34	0.110	1.51	2.39	0.106	1.74	1.50*
MV3*PR	-0.092	-2.35		-0.081	-2.05		-0.067	-1.56	
MV4*PR	-0.142	-2.65		-0.093	-1.32		-0.056	-0.79	
MV5*PR	-0.225	-2.13		-0.126	-0.94		-0.112	-0.97	
MV1!	0.607	5.65	.18	0.508	3.28	.11	0.441	3.15	.08
MV2!	0.153	2.30	10.08	0.093	1.12	6.00	0.090	1.23	4.51
MV3!	-0.050	-1.12		-0.056	-1.16		-0.021	-0.44	
MV4!	-0.190	-2.83		-0.133	-1.47		-0.095	-1.13	
MV5!	-0.328	-2.45		-0.213	-1.22		-0.197	-1.41	
MV1*PE!	0.528	5.08	.17	0.422	2.89	.13	0.368	2.73	.11
MV2*PE!	0.085	1.41	9.98	0.024	0.33	7.24	0.025	0.37	6.20
MV3*PE!	-0.077	-1.71		-0.074	-1.58		-0.049	-1.03	
MV4*PE!	-0.083	-1.23		-0.027	-0.29		0.011	0.14	
MV5*PE!	-0.258	-2.13		-0.143	-0.91		-0.134	-1.04	

B. Dividend Yield

	Model (2)			Model (3)			Model (1)		
	u_p	$t(u_p)$	T^2 $F(u_p)$	u_p	$t(u_p)$	T^2 $F(u_p)$	u_p	$t(u_p)$	T^2 $F(u_p)$
DV1	-0.330	-4.65	.24	-0.341	-4.30	.23	-0.330	-4.72	.20
DV2	-0.299	-4.99	13.46	-0.302	-3.90	12.86	-0.269	-4.45	11.36
DV3	-0.058	-1.40		-0.051	-1.09		-0.046	-1.12	
DV4	0.131	3.25		0.129	2.92		0.128	3.21	
DV5	0.537	7.30		0.547	6.79		0.498	6.50	
DV1*MV	-0.346	-5.64	.19	-0.357	-5.60	.19	-0.338	-5.59	.19
DV2*MV	-0.180	-4.47	10.56	-0.197	-4.73	10.61	-0.183	-4.54	10.93
DV3*MV	0.001	0.03		-0.005	-0.14		-0.006	-0.18	
DV4*MV	0.154	4.20		0.159	4.09		0.151	4.15	
DV5*MV	0.371	6.39		0.400	6.52		0.377	6.74	
DV1*PR	-0.359	-6.32	.24	-0.368	-6.00	.21	-0.351	-6.29	.20
DV2*PR	-0.242	-5.69	13.39	-0.241	-5.12	11.94	-0.220	-4.91	11.27
DV3*PR	-0.065	-1.77		-0.061	-1.60		0.058	-1.61	
DV4*PR	0.166	4.45		0.176	4.41		0.158	4.28	
DV5*PR	0.436	7.05		0.440	6.82		0.408	6.31	
DV1!	-0.344	-5.03	.18	-0.345	-4.34	.15	-0.302	-4.18	.13
DV2!	-0.196	-3.36	10.16	-0.182	-2.56	8.31	-0.163	-2.79	7.62
DV3!	0.003	0.08		0.000	0.00		0.003	0.08	
DV4!	0.166	3.36		0.164	2.98		0.154	3.21	
DV5!	0.515	6.55		0.520	5.85		0.479	5.74	
DV1*PE!	-0.215	-4.02	.16	-0.216	-3.62	.14	-0.183	-3.28	.11
DV2*PE!	-0.158	-2.96	9.34	-0.148	-2.35	7.95	-0.132	-2.38	6.32
DV3*PE!	0.004	0.08		0.025	0.52		0.021	0.45	
DV4*PE!	0.094	2.22		0.092	2.10		0.088	2.12	
DV5*PE!	0.416	6.10		0.400	5.58		0.374	4.92	

C. PE Ratio

	Model (2)			Model (3)			Model (1)		
	u_p	$t(u_p)$	T^2 / $F(u_p)$	u_p	$t(u_p)$	T^2 / $F(u_p)$	u_p	$t(u_p)$	T^2 / $F(u_p)$
PE1!	0.422	5.55	.12	0.440	5.60	.12	0.411	5.52	.12
PE2!	0.125	2.55	6.98	0.132	2.52	7.13	0.121	2.49	7.06
PE3!	-0.018	-0.42		0.005	0.12		-0.017	-0.41	
PE4!	-0.141	-2.56		-0.155	-2.41		-0.118	-2.15	
PE5!	-0.192	-2.39		-0.221	-2.58		-0.176	-2.21	
PE1*MV!	0.263	4.40	.07	0.278	4.63	.08	0.282	4.96	.09
PE2*MV!	0.098	1.96	4.23	0.118	2.29	4.42	0.101	2.02	5.25
PE3*MV!	0.007	0.16		0.024	0.55		0.007	0.17	
PE4*MV!	-0.065	-1.53		-0.070	-1.56		-0.063	-1.49	
PE5*MV!	-0.109	-1.55		-0.151	-2.12		-0.110	-1.57	
PE1*DV!	0.217	3.92	.07	0.213	3.79	.06	0.210	3.81	.07
PE2*DV!	0.027	0.51	4.11	0.062	1.18	3.26	0.062	1.17	3.88
PE3*DV!	-0.046	-1.02		-0.031	-0.66		-0.043	-0.94	
PE4*DV!	-0.037	-0.80		-0.035	-0.78		-0.039	-0.88	
PE5*DV!	-0.016	-0.26		-0.050	-0.79		-0.015	-0.24	
PE1*PR!	0.346	5.41	.11	0.350	5.33	.10	0.335	5.28	.11
PE2*PR!	0.079	1.47	6.13	0.095	1.71	5.93	0.090	1.70	6.05
PE3*PR!	-0.042	-0.95		-0.023	-0.50		-0.042	-0.95	
PE4*PR!	-0.095	-2.02		-0.103	-2.14		-0.085	-1.85	
PE5*PR!	-0.135	-1.82		-0.157	-2.04		-0.123	-1.68	

D. Price

	Model (2)			Model (3)			Model (1)		
	u_p	$t(u_p)$	T^2 / $F(u_p)$	u_p	$t(u_p)$	T^2 / $F(u_p)$	u_p	$t(u_p)$	T^2 / $F(u_p)$
PR1	0.335	3.43	.08	0.314	2.42	.05	0.261	2.60	.04
PR2	0.136	2.68	4.46	0.125	2.19	2.59	0.123	2.44	2.47
PR3	-0.089	-2.30		-0.078	-1.81		-0.059	-1.43	
PR4	-0.175	-3.53		-0.154	-2.47		-0.138	-2.72	
PR5	-0.177	-2.41		-0.176	-1.88		-0.162	-2.25	
PR1*MV	0.140	2.10	.05	0.176	2.47	.05	0.152	2.28	.04
PR2*MV	-0.011	-0.25	2.83	0.024	0.49	2.75	0.026	0.51	2.35
PR3*MV	-0.032	-0.85		-0.037	-0.93		-0.008	-0.21	
PR4*MV	-0.032	-0.84		-0.033	-0.84		-0.038	-0.98	
PR5*MV	-0.023	-0.43		-0.090	-1.41		-0.098	-1.36	
PR1*DV	0.278	3.36	.09	0.271	2.54	.07	0.212	2.55	.05
PR2*DV	0.044	1.02	5.33	0.026	0.56	4.20	0.048	1.10	2.96
PR3*DV	-0.132	-3.63		-0.114	-2.85		-0.103	-2.71	
PR4*DV	-0.172	-3.92		-0.174	-3.56		-0.140	-3.07	
PR5*DV	-0.071	-1.16		-0.049	-0.64		-0.065	-1.10	
PR1!	0.455	5.30	.13	0.431	3.94	.09	0.396	4.39	.10
PR2!	0.128	2.65	7.32	0.120	2.30	5.07	0.128	2.70	5.62
PR3!	-0.096	-2.05		-0.091	-1.79		-0.077	-1.65	
PR4!	-0.163	-2.87		-0.133	-1.90		-0.119	-2.04	
PR5!	-0.172	-2.29		-0.165	-1.72		-0.153	-2.07	
PR1*PE!	0.393	4.88	.11	0.356	3.61	.08	0.331	4.03	.08
PR2*PE!	0.054	1.11	6.52	0.046	0.96	4.36	0.063	1.34	4.81
PR3*PE!	-0.046	-1.10		-0.041	-0.95		-0.027	-0.63	
PR4*PE!	-0.163	-3.09		-0.124	-1.98		-0.124	-2.38	
PR5*PE	-0.086	-1.21		-0.074	-0.87		-0.067	-0.98	

Based on monthly data for the period April 1961 to March 1985.
F-values not significant at the 5% level are noted with a '*'.

Notation: u_p - abnormal portfolio return

$t(u_p)$ - t-statistic for u_p

T^2 - Hotelling T^2-statistic

$F(u_p)$ - F-value for T^2-statistic

a particular ranking procedure, MV1 to MV5 for example, is equal to zero.

Consistent with the pattern of beta estimates shown in Table II, risk adjustment models (2) and (3) produce market size premiums markedly higher than model (1) estimates. Thus, the market size effect not only is not eliminated or reduced but is indeed increased when a CAPM risk adjustment is applied. On the other hand, given the beta estimates, it is not surprising that the abnormal returns of the dividend yield, PE and share price portfolios are remarkably robust to the particular type of model employed for risk adjustment purposes.

An examination of the non-randomised portfolios across the four panels suggests the presence of significant abnormal returns for all four ranking procedures for both the full and reduced samples. It is apparent from the F-values, however, that the size effect is not the most pronounced anomaly on the LSE in comparison to the dividend yield and PE irregularities. The dividend yield ranking procedure, for example, yields a risk-adjusted premium, based on model 1, of 0.83 per cent per month for the full sample, which is almost twice the amount of the 0.42 per cent premium observed for market size effect. Randomising the market size portfolios to account for dividend yield differences has a definite, albeit marginal, impact on the vector of abnormal returns; as portfolios MV2*DV to MV5*DV become virtually identical, any remaining indications of a size effect are entirely attributable to the persistent strength of the MV1*DV portfolio. On the other hand, applying a market randomisation to the dividend yield portfolios (DV1*MV to DV5*MV in panel B) has no material impact on either the strength or configuration of the already documented dividend yield effect.

The reduced sample estimates in panels A and C provide the evidence for comparing the size versus the PE effects. The F-values for both non-randomised sets of portfolios indicate abnormal returns significantly different from zero and almost identical premiums. Moreover, controlling the market size portfolios for PE differences or the equivalent PE set for size differences does not alter the essence of these results in any substantive way. On this basis, the results of this study suggest that both effects were present on the LSE for the period under consideration. This conclusion is in line with Cook and Rozzeff's (1984) results but is in contrast to both Basu's (1983) and Reinganum's (1981) findings, which support the superiority of either a PE or a size effect respectively. It is also interesting to note that the magnitude of the PE effect is markedly reduced when controlling for dividend yield differences. The appropriate F-value, in panel C - model 1, is reduced from 7.06 to 3.88 while the PE premium, the abnormal return difference between portfolios PE1*DV! and PE5*DV!, is reduced to 0.23 per cent per month from the 0.59 per cent equivalent premium present between portfolios PE1! and PE5!. These results provide further support to the emerging overall dominance of the dividend yield effect.

With respect to the share price ranking procedure, it is immediately apparent from the relevant non-randomised portfolios in panels A and D that the size and price effects are virtually identical both in terms of premiums and consistency. The noticeable relative prominence evident in the risk-adjusted returns (models 2 and 3) of market size portfolios is entirely due to the uncharacteristic nature of their beta coefficients reported in the previous section. Panel D indicates that the share price effect appears to be resilient to both the market size and dividend yield randomisation procedures; the vectors of abnormal returns of the share price portfolios randomised for market size and dividend yield are still significantly different from zero in spite of the reduction of the relevant premiums. This evidence is in direct contrast to the configuration of market size portfolio returns observed in panel A. These results lead one to infer that an investment strategy based on the share price as the sole security selection criterion is better suited for the investor interested in long term consistent performance but reluctant to restrict his individual holdings to shares that conform to narrow boundaries in terms of market size and dividend yields.

In short, the findings presented in this section are consistent with the hypothesis that the dividend yield and PE ratio have a significant impact on the risk-adjusted returns of

UK firms and are largely independent from each other and other confounding effects. The market size anomaly resembles in many respects the share price effect but ceases to be pervasive when such portfolios are controlled for the differences in dividend yield and PE effects.

5. Interaction Between the Four Effects

The evidence in the previous section confirms the presence of a significant dividend yield, PE effects and to a lesser extent a market size and share price effect as well during the period April 1961 to March 1985. This evidence, however, is not sufficient on its own to indicate whether these effects are homogeneous across each of the particular quintiles of the four ranking procedures. Thus, the issue investigated in this section is to what extent the individual effects depended on the particular quintile of the portfolio formation procedure in operation. If, for example, the dividend yield and the firm size effect are independent of each other, one would expect the abnormal return to be enhanced by adhering to a high dividend yield small size investment strategy. On the other hand, if the two effects are highly interrelated, then an additive return possibility would not exist, since one effect would merely serve as a proxy for the other.

Table IV presents the abnormal returns using model (1) for all pairs of primary and secondary portfolio groupings. Each of the four panels (A to D) refers to one of the ranking procedures as the primary grouping variable and the other three as the secondary. As the emphasis in this section is on the search for anomalies within the same quintile of the primary ranking variable, only the results based on the full sample are presented (portfolios involving the PE ratio as a primary or secondary variable are based on the estimates derived from the reduced sample). Thus, accurate comparisons of abnormal returns can only be made across the quintiles of the same primary variable and not across quintiles of different primary ranking procedures, since the reduced sample was found to have a material impact on the excess return estimates. Due to space considerations, only the estimates based on model (1) are presented in this paper; given the specific nature of the beta coefficients, discussed in section III, estimates of abnormal returns based on models (2) and (3) do not alter the substance of the results presented in this section.[11]

The findings of the previous section indicated that the size and PE effects appear to work independently from each other. Closer investigation of the evidence in panels A and C, however, reveals that the aggregate results in Table III obscure some of the subtleties involved in the interaction between market size and PE effects. Examination of the five market size portfolios in panel A indicates that the PE effect is firmly established within the smallest market size portfolio. The F-values for all other portfolios are not significant or very marginally so at the 5% level. Panel C points to a very similar picture with regard to the nature of the size effect -i.e. the size effect is mainly concentrated within the smallest PE quintile; within higher PE portfolios its presence is at best marginal. In that sense it seems that there is very little to distinguish between the relative overall power of the two effects, although in terms of consistency the size effect could be regarded as marginally superior.

The relation between market size and dividend yield effects is rather more complicated. A comparison with the estimates in Table III, panel A, confirms that a combination of small size and high dividend yield generates portfolios earning consistently higher abnormal returns than the equivalent aggregate market size portfolios. The F-values in Table IV, panel A, point to the presence of a dividend yield effect at each level of market size; this effect, however, gradually declines as one moves from portfolio MV1 to MV5 but remains significant at the 5% level. Moreover, the dividend yield premium (the difference between the smallest and largest dividend yield quintile within each market size portfolio in panel A of the same table) is never lower than 0.5 per cent per month and increases gradually from dividend yield quintile 1 to 5. This evidence, in conjunction

---

11. Detailed results based on models (2) and (3) are available from the author on request.

Table IV

Excess Returns of Various Combination Portfolios
Based on Model (1)

A. Market Value as Primary Group

		u_p	$t(u_p)$	T^2 $F(u_p)$	u_p	$t(u_p)$	T^2 $F(u_p)$	u_p	$t(u_p)$	T^2 $F(u_p)$
		Dividend Yield			PE Ratio			Share Price		
MV1	1	0.011	0.04	.14	0.839	4.40	.08	0.564	2.50	.03
	2	-0.242	-1.36	8.14	0.406	2.38	4.38	0.328	1.85	1.96*
	3	0.136	0.87		0.480	2.85		0.168	0.99	
	4	0.446	2.62		0.208	1.33		0.202	1.19	
	5	0.884	4.87		0.272	1.41		0.002	0.01	
MV2	1	-0.474	-3.58	.15	0.339	3.01	.04	0.211	1.52	.02
	2	0.020	0.19	8.29	0.186	1.59	2.34	0.215	1.91	1.17*
	3	0.235	2.40		-0.016	-0.14		0.148	1.51	
	4	0.303	3.14		0.079	0.72		0.048	0.46	
	5	0.505	3.97		-0.136	-0.95		0.053	0.40	
MV3	1	-0.398	-3.67	.09	0.150	1.44	.04	0.010	0.09	.02
	2	-0.277	-3.10	5.39	0.125	1.37	2.06*	-0.060	-0.57	0.89*
	3	-0.036	-0.47		-0.008	-0.09		-0.026	-0.27	
	4	0.095	1.10		-0.202	-2.11		-0.057	-0.70	
	5	0.274	2.74		-0.170	-1.52		-0.172	-1.72	
MV4	1	-0.399	-3.36	.06	0.038	0.32	.02	0.033	0.29	.03
	2	-0.211	-2.08	3.17	-0.004	-0.04	0.91*	-0.190	-1.73	1.52*
	3	-0.157	-1.75		-0.155	-1.42		-0.195	-1.91	
	4	-0.036	-0.38		-0.163	-1.46		-0.151	-1.67	
	5	0.151	1.50		-0.192	-1.28		-0.138	-1.53	
MV5	1	-0.432	-2.60	.05	0.047	0.30	.04	-0.056	-0.36	.02
	2	-0.206	-1.36	2.67	-0.210	-1.39	2.34*	-0.163	-1.04	1.17*
	3	-0.209	-1.35		-0.265	-1.72		-0.134	-0.89	
	4	-0.053	-0.38		-0.239	-1.56		-0.234	-1.72	
	5	0.068	0.49		-0.322	-1.70		-0.235	-1.57	

B. Dividend Yield as Primary Group

		Market Value			PE ratio			Share Price		
		u_p	$t(u_p)$	T^2 $F(u_p)$	u_p	$t(u_p)$	T^2 $F(u_p)$	u_p	$t(u_p)$	T^2 $F(u_p)$
DV1	1	0.023	0.09	.10	-0.037	-0.33	.06	0.086	0.04	.16
	2	-0.426	-2.50	6.02	-0.319	-3.12	3.73	-0.340	-2.03	8.97
	3	-0.424	-3.31		-0.353	-3.09		-0.306	-2.61	
	4	-0.432	-3.30		-0.374	-2.98		-0.587	-5.61	
	5	-0.389	-2.32		-0.426	-2.88		-0.475	-3.82	
DV2	1	-0.114	-0.90	.14	-0.009	-0.98	.03	-0.219	-2.24	.09
	2	-0.370	-4.34	7.76	-0.173	-1.93	1.84*	-0.261	-2.79	4.92
	3	-0.369	-3.81		-0.219	-2.24		-0.361	-3.55	
	4	-0.170	-1.28		-0.218	-2.08		-0.241	-2.24	
	5	-0.325	-1.90		-0.194	-1.42		-0.265	-2.53	
DV3	1	0.198	1.46	.02	0.030	0.31	.01	0.013	0.12	.02
	2	-0.131	-1.47	1.29*	0.002	0.02	0.35*	0.000	0.00	1.11*
	3	-0.034	-0.45		0.001	0.01		-0.163	-2.05	
	4	-0.106	-1.03		-0.084	-0.92		-0.128	-1.56	
	5	-0.156	-1.07		0.069	0.69		-0.061	-0.74	
DV4	1	0.290	1.86	.06	0.333	3.06	.05	0.340	2.90	.09
	2	0.263	2.73	3.31	0.245	2.53	3.08	0.252	2.75	5.04
	3	0.054	0.70		0.057	0.69		-0.096	-1.25	
	4	-0.044	-0.47		0.082	0.95		0.039	0.52	
	5	0.075	0.61		0.054	0.50		0.112	1.52	
DV5	1	0.853	4.56	.20	0.722	4.25	.14	0.839	5.54	.17
	2	0.606	4.67	11.5	0.555	4.25	7.64	0.587	5.36	9.48
	3	0.384	3.13		0.299	2.33		0.411	3.99	
	4	0.303	3.08		0.399	3.38		0.216	2.27	
	5	0.341	3.08		0.419	3.06		0.363	3.83	

C. PE ratio as Primary Group

		u_p	$t(u_p)$	T^2 / $F(u_p)$	u_p	$t(u_p)$	T^2 / $F(u_p)$	u_p	$t(u_p)$	T^2 / $F(u_p)$
		Market Value			Dividend Yield			Share Price		
PE1	1	0.901	4.41	.13	0.182	1.69	.13	0.912	5.59	.14
	2	0.476	3.42	7.44	0.174	1.70	7.40	0.431	3.38	8.21
	3	0.243	2.10		0.392	3.56		0.422	3.83	
	4	0.262	2.29		0.419	3.41		0.099	0.99	
	5	0.173	1.30		0.842	5.68		0.182	1.76	
PE2	1	0.158	0.92	.03	-0.178	-1.90	.06	0.265	2.04	.03
	2	0.145	1.26	1.42*	0.062	0.65	3.12	0.161	1.54	1.53*
	3	0.128	1.26		0.159	1.82		0.036	0.38	
	4	0.163	1.52		0.220	2.28		0.001	0.01	
	5	0.011	0.07		0.323	2.57		0.076	0.89	
PE3	1	0.413	2.78	.05	-0.232	-2.30	.04	0.189	1.54	.03
	2	-0.109	-1.00	2.97	-0.185	-2.05	2.05*	0.040	0.41	1.74*
	3	-0.127	-1.37		-0.046	-0.50		-0.125	-1.44	
	4	-0.083	-0.73		-0.041	-0.51		-0.233	-2.53	
	5	-0.182	-1.23		0.235	2.01		-0.103	-1.01	
PE4	1	0.254	1.43	.06	-0.345	-3.20	.06	0.289	2.16	.05
	2	-0.109	-1.10	3.19	-0.316	-2.89	3.30	-0.079	-0.85	2.85
	3	-0.305	-3.06		-0.096	-0.89		-0.299	-3.22	
	4	-0.109	-0.82		-0.075	-0.89		-0.247	-2.21	
	5	-0.322	-1.98		0.310	2.32		-0.224	-1.93	
PE5	1	0.112	0.62	.04	-0.344	-2.58	.04	0.002	0.01	.03
	2	-0.278	-2.30	2.35	-0.397	-3.02	2.57	-0.236	-2.06	1.43*
	3	-0.185	-1.58		-0.303	-2.38		-0.170	-1.37	
	4	-0.178	-1.14		-0.081	-0.69		-0.242	-1.88	
	5	-0.349	-1.92		0.163	1.44		-0.269	-2.21	

D. Share Price as Primary Group

		u_p	$t(u_p)$	T^2	u_p	$t(u_p)$	T^2	u_p	$t(u_p)$	T^2
				$F(u_p)$			$F(u_p)$			$F(u_p)$
		Market Value			Dividend Yield			PE Ratio		
PR1	1	0.693	2.71	.05	0.057	0.26	.16	0.760	4.79	.11
	2	0.394	2.39	2.87	-0.292	-1.88	11.2	0.522	3.53	6.21
	3	-0.012	-0.08		-0.001	-0.01		0.383	3.05	
	4	0.174	1.34		0.562	4.73		0.189	1.51	
	5	0.054	0.41		0.834	5.86		0.124	0.74	
PR2	1	0.193	1.10	.03	-0.378	-3.10	.12	0.441	3.71	.06
	2	0.238	2.07	1.48*	0.035	0.43	6.80	0.172	1.73	3.29
	3	0.178	1.76		0.114	1.31		0.014	0.13	
	4	0.020	0.19		0.235	2.49		0.083	0.89	
	5	-0.014	-0.11		0.498	4.48		-0.068	-0.65	
PR3	1	-0.086	-0.60	.03	-0.349	3.69	.06	0.117	1.16	.02
	2	0.111	1.27	1.79*	-0.187	-2.12	3.24	-0.053	-0.54	1.27*
	3	-0.130	-1.34		-0.068	-0.93		-0.160	-1.80	
	4	-0.151	-1.38		0.035	0.44		-0.143	-1.56	
	5	-0.040	-0.26		0.194	2.21		-0.144	-1.13	
PR4	1	-0.011	-0.07	.05	-0.581	-5.34	.12	0.300	3.06	.08
	2	-0.019	-0.22	2.69	-0.274	-2.88	6.92	-0.179	-1.99	4.54
	3	-0.290	-3.23		-0.177	-2.09		-0.261	-2.70	
	4	-0.129	-1.09		-0.003	-0.04		-0.210	-2.18	
	5	-0.243	-1.47		0.275	3.30		-0.246	-1.75	
PR5	1	-0.020	-0.15	.03	-0.505	-4.03	.10	0.058	0.60	.04
	2	-0.195	-2.13	1.86*	-0.382	-3.34	5.91	-0.011	-0.12	2.45
	3	-0.081	-0.85		-0.160	-1.65		-0.185	-1.72	
	4	-0.193	-1.45		-0.040	-0.50		-0.346	-2.98	
	5	-0.320	-1.84		0.238	2.97		-0.280	-2.23	

Based on monthly data for the period April 1961 to March 1985.
F-values not significant at the 5% level are noted with a '*'.

Notation: u_p - abnormal portfolio return based on model (1)

$t(u_p)$ - t-statistic for u_p

T^2 - Hotelling T^2-statistic

$F(u_p)$ - F-value for T^2-statistic

with the results of the previous section, leave little doubt about the pervasive nature and persistence of the dividend yield effect. On the other hand, closer investigation of the results in panel B casts further doubts on the efficacy of the size effect. First, observe the inconsistent pattern of F-values across the five dividend yield portfolios; the size effect appears not to be entirely independent of the level of dividend yield; its presence is clearly firmer within the highest dividend yield quintile. Second, the pattern of abnormal returns for size portfolios within quintiles DIV1 to DIV3 does not provide unambiguous evidence in support of a size effect since there is very little to distinguish between the abnormal returns of market size portfolios 2 to 4. Keim (1985) conjectured that the excess return of dividend yield portfolios reflects the contents of these portfolios in terms of market size firms -i.e. a large proportion of smaller firms are concentrated in the high dividend yield categories. To further investigate the validity of this conjecture for UK data, the average dividend yield of each market size quintile was computed as well as the composition of these portfolios in terms of dividend yields. The analysis supports Keim's hypothesis. The mean dividend yield of the smaller portfolio is 8.0 per cent in contrast to the 4.6 per cent dividend yield of its larger counterpart. Furthermore, the smaller market size portfolios contained a disproportionately larger proportion of high dividend yield firms, while a high concentration of low to medium yield stocks was evident in larger size portfolios.[12] Although the emerging picture is remarkably similar to the US evidence -i.e. high concentration of smaller (larger) firms within the higher (lower) dividend yield groups, on balance the weight of evidence does not support the notion that the dividend yield is simply a surrogate for market size.

A direct comparison between the dividend yield and PE effects in Table III shows that both effects are at work independently. Controlling one for the confounding effects of the other does not alter the essence of the observed irregularities.

---

12. For further details on average dividend yields and portfolio composition see Levis (1987).

At the same time, it is also clear that the PE effect is markedly reduced when full account is taken of the differences in dividend yields across the five PE portfolios. The results in Table IV, panels B and C, confirm this conclusion. Observe, for example, the PE premiums across each of the five dividend yield portfolios; the largest such premium is evident within the lowest dividend yield quintile, namely 0.39 per cent per month. Panel C, however, indicates the dividend yield effect produces premiums consistently superior. The largest premium for quintile PE1 was 0.66 per cent while the lowest, quintile PE3, was 0.47 per cent per month. Thus, there is little doubt that these effects are to a certain extent interrelated, but the dividend yield can be still be confidently regarded as the dominant one.

A survey of panels A to D confirms the overall striking resemblance between the size and price effects mentioned in the previous section. Both exhibit very similar premiums and F-values across the four panels. Moreover, a direct comparison between the two provides further support for the notion that there is a strong interaction between the two. The price effect, for example, is virtually non-existent within individual market size portfolios. On the other hand, the presence of a size effect is apparent within the lowest price quintile only. Further support for this interaction between market size and share price can also be obtained from an analysis of the mean share price of each market size quintile and the share price composition of these quintiles. The average share price of the firms included in the smaller market size portfolio was equal to 51 pence (in 1984 prices) while that of the largest was four times higher. Furthermore, about 57 per cent of the population of firms included in the smaller size portfolio were firms belonging to the lowest share price quintile. On the other hand, 46 per cent of those in the larger market size group were also members of the highest share price group.

6. Conclusions

The empirical evidence reported in this paper indicates that at least during the April 1961 to March 1985 time period the LSE exhibited a number of irregularities in stock price behaviour.

The well documented size effect appears to be only one of them. Investment strategies based on dividend yields, PE multiples and share prices seem to be at least as profitable, if not more, as strategies based on market size. Furthermore, the size effect is not entirely independent of the other three portfolio formation procedures. The significant market size effect, for example, is markedly reduced when control over the differences in dividend yield is exercised. Any further size effects are attributed entirely to the uncharacteristic nature of beta coefficients observed for smaller size portfolios. The implied risk-return relation is not altered even when a Dimson type beta estimate is applied. Closer examination reveals that the market size effect is not consistent across all dividend yields, PE or share price quintiles. It is also worth noting that from the configuration of abnormal returns across the various portfolio formation procedures it is often hard to distinguish between the size and share price effects. This evidence lends further credence to the view that these two variables are either proxies for each other or both are just proxies for more fundamental determinants of expected returns for common stocks. The dividend yield or the PE multiple for example, appear as possible candidates for such a proxy. Their individual effects are still maintained even when control for their reciprocal differences is exercised, in spite the fact that neither one is consistent at every single level of the other.

In short, the weight of the evidence presented in this paper raises questions about the strength of firm size as an independent determinant of the stock returns generating process. Its strong dependence with the other firm attributes suggest that it cannot be viewed as either an independent anomaly or as a profitable investment strategy in its own right. In that sense, the results also have implications for various types of event studies. If one is to control for factors other than risk, then the dividend yield and PE multiple differences might be more appropriate factors. Such adjustments are particularly important for the LSE in view of the fact that the direction of the risk-return relation is still rather ambiguous.

References

Ball, R., 1978, Anomalies in Relationships Between Securities' Yields and Yield-Surrogates, Journal of Financial Economics 6, June, 103-126.

Banz, R.W., 1979, The Relationship Between Return and Market Value of Common Stocks, Journal of Financial Economics 9, March, 3-18.

Banz, R.W. and W.J. Breen, 1986, Sample Dependent Results Using Accounting and Market Data: Some Evidence, Journal of Finance 41, September,779-794.

Basu, S., 1977, Investment Performance of Common Stocks in Relation to their Price-Earnings Ratios: A Test of the Efficient Market Hypothesis, Journal of Finance 32, June, 663-682.

Basu, S., 1983, The Relationship Between Earnings' Yields, Market Value and the Returns for NYSE Stocks: Further Evidence, Journal of Financial Economics 12, June, 129-156.

Berges, A., J.J. McConnell and G.G. Schlarbaum, 1984, The Turn-of -the-Year in Canada, Journal of Finance 39, March, 185-192.

Blume, M., 1980, Stock Returns and Dividend Yields: Some More Evidence, Review of Economics and Statistics 62, November, 567-577.

Blume, M. and F. Husic, 1973, Price, Beta and Exchange Listing, Journal of Finance 28, May, 283-299.

Blume, M. and R. Stambaugh, 1983, Biases in Computed Returns: An Application to the Size Effect, Journal of Financial Economics 12, November, 387-404.

Brown, P., A. Kleidon and T. Marsh, 1983, New Evidence on the Nature of Size-Related Anomalies in Stock Prices, Journal of Financial Economics 12, June, 33-56.

Cook, J. and M.S. Rozeff, 1984, Size and Earnings/Price Ratio Anomalies: One Effect or Two?, Journal of Financial and Quantitative Analysis 19, December, 449-466.

Corhay, A., G. Hawawini and P. Michel, 1987, Seasonality in the Risk-Return Relationship: Some International Evidence, Journal of Finance 42, March, 49-68.

Dimson, E., 1979, Risk Measurement When Shares are Subject to Infrequent Trading, Journal of Financial Economics 7, June, 197-226.

Dimson, E. and P. Marsh, 1983, The Stability of UK Risk Measures and the Problem of Thin Trading, Journal of Finance 38, June, 753-783.

Dimson, E. and P. Marsh, 1986, Event Study Methodologies and the Size Effect: The Case of UK Press Recommendations, Journal of Financial Economics 17, 113-143.

Elton, E., M. Gruber and J. Rentzler, 1983, A Simple Examination of the Empirical Relationship Between Dividend Yields and Deviations from the CAPM, Journal of Banking and Finance 7, March, 135-146.

Gordon, R.H. and D. F. Bradford, 1980, Taxation and the Stock Market Valuation on Capital Gains and Dividends: Theory and Empirical Results, Journal of Public Economics 14, 109-136.

Gultekin, M.F. and N.B. Gultekin, 1983, Stock Market Seasonality: International Evidence, Journal of Financial Economics 12, December, 469-482.

Goodman, D.A., J.W. Peavy and E.L. Cox, 1986, The Interaction of Firm Size and Price-Earnings Ratio on Portfolio Performance, Financial Analyst Journal, January-February, 9-12.

Keim, D., 1983, Size Related Anomalies and Stock Return Seasonality: Further Empirical Evidence, Journal of Financial Economics 12, June,13-32.

Keim, D., 1985, Dividend Yields and Stock Returns, Journal of Financial Economics 14, 473-489.

Levis, M., 1985, Are Small Firms Big Performers?, The Investment Analyst 76, April, 21-26.

Levis, M., 1987, An Exploratory Investigation into the Small Size Effect, Manuscript (University of Bath 1987).

Marsh, P., 1979, Equity Rights Issues and the Efficiency of the UK Stock Market, Journal of Finance 34, September, 839-62.

Litzenberger, R.H. and K. Ramaswamy, 1979, The Effect of Personal Taxes and Dividends on Capital Asset Prices: Theory and Empirical Evidence, Journal of Financial Economics 7, June, 163-95.

Miller, M. and M. Scholes, 1982, Dividend and Taxes: Some Empirical Evidence, Journal of Political Economy 90, 1118-1141.

Nakamura, T. and N. Tarada, 1984, The Size Effect and Seasonality in Japanese Stock Returns, Manuscript, (Nomura Research Institute).

Peavy, J.W. and D. A. Goodman, 1983, Industry-Relative Price-Earnings Ratios as Indicators of Investment Returns, Financial Analyst Journal, July-August.

Reinganum, M., 1981, Misspecification of Capital Asset Pricing: Empirical Anomalies Based on Earnings' Yields and Market Values, Journal of Financial Economics 9, March, 19-46.

Reinganum, M., 1983, The Anomalous Stock Market Behaviour of Small Firms in January. Empirical Tests for Tax-Loss Selling Effects, Journal of Financial Economics 12, June, 89-104.

Roll, R., 1981, A Possible Explanation of the Small Firm Effect, Journal of Finance 36, September, 879-888.

Smithers, J., 1986, London Share Price Data Base, London Business School, September.

Stoll, H.R. and R.E. Whaley, 1983, Transaction Costs and the Small Firm Effect, Journal of Financial Economics 12, 57-78.

Comments on Mario Levis "Market Size, PE Ratios, Dividend Yield and Share Prices: Their Impact on Common Stock Returns

by Angelien G.Z. Kemna

In this paper an excellent overview is given on previous (mostly American) studies on the impact of market size, PE ratios, dividend yield and share prices. The author concentrates on documenting the presence of irregularities in stock price behaviour on the London market. From the different studies it is clear that using more detailed data can lead to different results. It is therefore remarkable that the author only uses monthly data, instead of weekly or daily data. This fact can cause differences in the values of the β's found by the author. Especially in case of the small firms, very uncharacteristic β's are found. This may be due to the limited data used and my suggestion is to look at the differences in results using more detailed data, or provide us with tests on the stabilility of the β's over time. Another explanation for the small firms may be found in the so called 'neglected firm effect' indicating no stable relation with any market index. It might be the case that for these firms the CAPM is not a good theory, because the pricing is based more on the supply side of the economy, or what market participants think this firms' prospects are. It seems therefore that the author should provide better evidence for his results, by showing that the results are not caused by jumping β's over time.

Besides the problem of the stability of the β's, which is a more general problem, the author is somewhat unclear about the lagged model he uses. As can be seen by the outcomes (the β for the CAPM and the adjusted β hardly differ), it seems that the lagged model is only useful for daily data, because trading in small stocks might not take place every day. Further, it is the question what implications significant lagged β's have for the CAPM. And finally, the author does not mention the estimation method used for the lagged model.

NATO ASI Series, Vol. F54
A Reappraisal of the Efficiency of Financial Markets
Edited by Rui M. C. Guimaraes et al.

CANADIAN CALENDAR ANOMALIES
AND THE CAPITAL ASSET PRICING MODEL

Charles Bram Cadsby
Department of Economics
University of Guelph
Guelph, Ontario N1G 2W1
Canada

KEYWORDS/ABSTRACT: seasonal anomalies / calendar anomalies / Canadian stock markets / Toronto Stock Exchange / January Effect / Weekend Effect / Monday Effect /Capital Asset Pricing Model

The CAPM is examined using daily Canadian stock returns. There is no January Effect but there are Turn-Of-The-Year, Turn-Of-The-Month, October and Monday Effects. For each calendar effect on stock returns, there is a corresponding effect on the risk-return relationship. Thus, calendar effects on a given portfolio are proportional to the level of market risk associated with it.

I should like to acknowledge the careful and skilled research assistance of Sydney Allan. Thanks are also due to Murray Frank and Francis Tapon for many hours of conversations about calendar effects on the stock market and to D. Fraser and other participants in the NATO Advanced Research Workshop for useful comments on an earlier draft of this paper.

NATO ASI Series, Vol. F54
A Reappraisal of the Efficiency of Financial Markets
Edited by Rui M. C. Guimaraes et al.

1. Introduction

Some puzzling empirical facts about the relationship between the stock market and the calendar have recently been uncovered. First, average monthly returns for an equally weighted index of all firms listed on the New York Stock Exchange are significantly higher in January than during the rest of the year (Rozeff and Kinney, 1976). This phenomenon is especially pronounced for small firms that have done poorly during the previous year (Reinganum, 1983) and is particularly apparent during the first five trading days of January (Keim, 1983). Gultekin and Gultekin (1983) document a similar January seasonality on CIP value weighted indices for Canada and other industrialized countries, using monthly data from January, 1959 to November, 1979. This result is corroborated by Berges, McConnell and Schlarbaum (1984), who use monthly data from January 1950 to December 1980 on 391 companies listed on the Toronto and Montreal stock exchanges.

Second, average daily returns for the S&P 500 index are negative on Monday, positive on other days and highest on Wednesday and Friday over a number of different time periods when returns are measured from daily close to daily close (Cross, 1973; French, 1980). A similar pattern of returns is observed for the Dow Jones Industrial Average (DJIA). The overall negative effect between Friday close and Monday close for the DJIA occurred on Monday itself during the 1960's but moved backward to the period between Friday close and Monday opening by the late 1970's (Rogalski, 1984; Smirlock and Starks, 1986). During January, average returns on the S&P 500 and on the DJIA from Friday close to Monday close are positive (Rogalski, 1984). Average daily returns on the Toronto Stock Exchange 300 Index from January 2, 1976 to November 30, 1983 are also negative on Monday and positive on other days. They are highest on Wednesday, Thursday and Friday (Jaffe and Westerfield, 1985). Jaffe and Westerfield (1985) find similar results for several other countries.

Third, average returns during the month of October on an equally weighted index of New York Stock Exchange daily returns from 1963 through 1985 are significantly less than returns in other months, the so-called

Mark Twain effect (Cadsby 1988).[1]

Fourth, average returns for the DJIA are positive for the four day period which includes the last and first three days of the month but negative for the period which includes all remaining days (Lakonishok and Smidt, 1987).[2]

Perhaps even more puzzling is the relationship between the calendar and empirical tests of the Capital Asset Pricing Model. Using a large sample of New York Stock Exchange monthly data, Tinic and West (1984) find that the risk-return relationship described by the two-factor CAPM exists only during January and not during the other eleven months of the year. Furthermore, Tinic and West (1986) show that, even when the two-parameter CAPM is extended to permit specific risk as well as nonlinearities in the relationship between market risk and return to play a role in asset pricing, important seasonal anomalies remain in the NYSE data. Monthly Toronto Stock Exchange data yield similar results for the two-parameter case (Cadsby and Tapon, 1987; Tinic and Barone-Adesi, 1987). Corhay, Hawawini, and Michel (1987) find similar but not identical seasonalities in a number of European countries.

Cadsby (1988) uses daily CRSP data from January, 1963 to December, 1985 to examine further the risk-return relationship in the context of the CAPM. In contrast to Tinic and West (1984), Cadsby (1988) finds that the CAPM risk premium is significant both during January and during the rest of the year. However, the turn-of-the-year period running from December 24 to January 28 exhibits a significant risk premium while the rest of the year does not. The CAPM does exhibit a significant risk premium both from December 24 to January 28 and during the rest of the year when Monday data are eliminated from the sample. Thus, the Tinic and West (1984) result appears to arise solely from the behavior of stock prices on Mondays from January 29 to December 23.

Cadsby (1988) also shows that other calendar anomalies on stock market returns have corresponding effects on the CAPM risk-return

---

[1]The relevant quotation comes from Mark Twain's classic novel, <u>Pudd'nhead Wilson</u>, and reads as follows: (Twain, 1981, p.75): "October. This is one of the peculiarly dangerous months to speculate in stocks in. The others are July, January, September, April, November, May, March, June, December, August, and February."

[2]Other anomalies include holiday effects and intraday effects. A full discussion is contained in Thaler (1987a) and Thaler (1987b).

relationship. For example, the CAPM risk premium is significant around the turn of the month but not significant during the rest of the year, even when that part of January not at the turn of the month is included in the data for the rest of the year. The CAPM risk premium is significant on Wednesdays, Thursdays and Fridays but not on the low return days of Monday and Tuesday. Finally, the risk premium is significantly negative in October and significantly different from the risk premium in every other month.

The purpose of this paper is to explore the robustness of the results in Cadsby (1988) by systematically examining the CAPM using a recently developed daily data base of Canadian stock returns. There are a number of motivations for this exercise. First, the CAPM has generally been tested using monthly data while the Arbitrage Pricing Theory has more often been subjected to tests using daily data. It seems reasonable to expose these two theories to the same data set. Second, use of daily data allows us to compare calendar anomalies on stock returns based on periods of less than a month with the risk-return relationship over similar periods.

The paper is organized as follows. The second section deals with the data and methodology used to estimate the CAPM. The third section discusses the results and compares calendar effects on rates of return with calendar effects on the risk-return relationship. The fourth section of the paper looks briefly at calendar effects in the context of the four-parameter model originally estimated by Fama and MacBeth (1973) and later Tinic and West (1986) as a further check on the validity of the CAPM. Some conclusions are drawn in the fifth section.

2. Data and Methodology

The data for this study are taken from the TSE/Western Daily Rates of Return and Daily Index Files which contain information on all securities listed on the Toronto Stock Exchange as well as a small number of securities listed on the Vancouver or Montreal Exchanges. The necessary requirements for inclusion in the study are that a common stock exhibit no more than 30 days of missing returns per year for the period of four years needed to form portfolios and calculate portfolio betas.[3] The data base runs from January 2, 1975 to December 31, 1987. However, the years 1975 and 1976 contain a great deal of missing data. Therefore, January 2, 1977 is used as the start date for this project. The number of stocks included in the study ranges between 208 and 507 depending upon the years under consideration. An equally weighted index of all securities in the data base is used to represent the market rate of return.

The methodology used in this paper is similar to that employed in the classic study of the CAPM using monthly U.S. data by Fama and MacBeth (1973) and a similar study using monthly Canadian data by Calvet and Lefoll (1985). Stocks are divided into portfolios based on the size of the stock's beta estimated over a two year portfolio formation period. Betas are estimated by performing an OLS regression on Equation (1) for each stock, initially using data from January 2, 1977 to December 31, 1978 inclusive.

$$R_{it} = \alpha_i + \beta_i RME_t + u_{it} \quad (1)$$

where i = $1, \ldots N$
t = $1, \ldots T$
R_{it} = return on asset i in period t
RME_t = return on the market portfolio in period t as proxied by an equally weighted index
u_{it} = a zero mean, spherical random disturbance term

These estimates are used to rank the stocks by decreasing order of estimated beta, $\hat{\beta}_i$, and to divide them into 15 portfolios according to rank. The middle 13 portfolios each contain int(N/15) stocks where int(N/15) is the largest integer equal to or less than N/15. If N is even, the first and last portfolios are each assigned int(N/15) + 0.5[N-15int(N/15)] stocks. If N is odd, the high $\hat{\beta}_i$ portfolio is assigned the extra stock.

Note that the betas estimated from the 1977-78 data are used only to form portfolios. Stocks are divided into portfolios because estimates of portfolio betas ($\hat{\beta}_{pt}$) are more precise than estimates of betas on individual securities. The portfolios are formed by rank ordering of the

---

[3]The portfolio formation and estimation procedure is described below. The TSE/Western data base has only recently been made publicly available. A careful check for outliers among the security returns revealed some obvious errors in the case of a small number of stocks. These stocks were eliminated from the analysis.

betas to ensure that a wide range of portfolio betas is obtained (Fama and MacBeth, 1973).

Portfolio betas for use on January 2, 1981 are calculated by averaging betas reestimated for individual securities within each of the 15 portfolios using data from January 2, 1979 to December 31, 1980. Only stocks for which returns are reported on January 2, 1981 are used to calculate portfolio betas for that day. This averaging procedure is repeated for each day of 1981 to take account of delisted securities or securities for which returns are missing.

In order to calculate portfolio betas for 1982, the start date is moved up one year and the process of portfolio formation and portfolio estimation is repeated using data from 1978 to 1981. Similar updates are made until the portfolio betas are obtained for each day from January 2, 1981 to December 31, 1987. Finally, following Calvet and Lefoll (1985), the portfolio formation and estimation processes are repeated working backwards to produce portfolio betas for each day from January 2, 1977 to December 31, 1980.

Daily portfolio returns (R_{pt}) are calculated as arithmetic averages of returns within each portfolio. The daily portfolio returns and the portfolio betas are then used to estimate a zero-beta rate of return ($\hat{\gamma}_0$) and a market risk premium ($\hat{\gamma}_1$) for each day from January 2, 1977 to December 31, 1987 inclusive using Equation (2).

$$R_{pt} = \gamma_{0t} + \gamma_{1t}\hat{\beta}_{pt-1} + u_{pt} \tag{2}$$

where p = 1, . . . 15. Averages of these estimates over various time periods are reported below.

3. Results of the Two-Parameter Case

Table 1 reports the average rate of return on the equally weighted index and on the average values of $\hat{\gamma}_0$ and $\hat{\gamma}_1$ for all months together and for each month individually. Table 2 reports the same information for all days in all months excluding each month in turn. The first thing to notice is that the average rate of return, $\bar{\hat{\gamma}}_0$, and $\bar{\hat{\gamma}}_1$ are all positive and significant when averaged over all days between January 2, 1977 and December 31, 1987. This is consistent with previous results. However, in contrast to previous studies, there is little evidence of a January Effect on either returns or on the risk-return relationship. January was not a bad month to be in the stock market. However, December, August, and

TABLE 1

AVERAGE RATE OF RETURN ON THE EQUALLY WEIGHTED INDEX AND AVERAGE VALUES OF THE INTERCEPT AND SLOPE COEFFICIENTS OF THE TWO-PARAMETER MODEL, BY MONTH, ESTIMATED WITH DAILY DATA FROM JANUARY 2, 1977 TO DECEMBER 31, 1987.[a]

Averaged over all days in	Avg rate of return on market index	Avg. Intercept Coefficient ($\bar{\hat{\gamma}}_0$)	Avg. Slope Coefficient ($\bar{\hat{\gamma}}_1$)	Sample Size
All months	0.00172 (b) (12.44544)	0.00063 (b) (5.55794)	0.00042 (b) (2.27269)	2773
January	0.00257 (b) (5.15961)	0.00086 (b) (2.29756)	0.00108 (b) (1.67908)	233
February	0.00117 (b) (3.17372)	0.00070 (b) (1.75467)	-0.00042 (-0.71306)	222
March	0.00192 (b) (3.68464)	0.00078 (b) (2.13778)	0.00072 (0.94806)	241
April	0.00173 (b) (6.16315)	0.00089 (b) (2.39565)	0.00017 (0.28609)	227
May	0.00203 (b) (6.29888)	0.00073 (b) (2.21266)	0.00031 (0.66871)	232
June	0.00135 (b) (4.20644)	0.00042 (1.25646)	0.00056 (1.18182)	236
July	0.00155 (b) (4.38793)	0.00038 (1.05868)	0.00059 (1.19703)	233
August	0.00261 (b) (7.31812)	0.00070 (b) (1.97829)	0.00152 (b) (3.02109)	232
September	0.00064 (1.35993)	-0.00009 (-0.24147)	0.00003 (0.04351)	225
October	-0.00030 (-0.32058)	-0.00048 (-0.78370)	-0.00124 (-1.12625)	233
November	0.00258 (b) (6.21647)	0.00113 (b) (2.97598)	0.00124 (b) (1.91404)	235
December	0.00270 (b) (5.89343)	0.00159 (b) (4.05922)	0.00042 (0.77147)	224

[a] The t statistics are presented in parentheses.

[b] Significant at the 5 percent level using one-tailed test.

TABLE 2

AVERAGE RATE OF RETURN ON THE EQUALLY WEIGHTED INDEX AND AVERAGE VALUES OF THE INTERCEPT AND SLOPE COEFFICIENTS OF THE TWO-PARAMETER MODEL, FOR INDICATED ELEVEN MONTH PERIODS, ESTIMATED WITH DAILY DATA FROM JANUARY 2, 1977 TO DECEMBER 31, 1987.[a]

Averaged over all days in all months excluding	Avg rate of return on market index	Avg. Intercept Coefficient $(\bar{\hat{\gamma}}_0)$	Avg. Slope Coefficient $(\bar{\hat{\gamma}}_1)$	Sample Size
January	0.00164 (b) (11.42272)	0.00061 (b) (5.12164)	0.00036 (b) (1.86395)	2540
February	0.00176 (b) (12.04730)	0.00063 (b) (5.27690)	0.00050 (b) (2.53601)	2551
March	0.00170 (b) (11.89308)	0.00062 (b) (5.16552)	0.00039 (b) (2.07047)	2532
April	0.00171 (b) (11.57817)	0.00061 (b) (5.10391)	0.00045 (b) (2.27507)	2546
May	0.00169 (b) (11.43398)	0.00062 (b) (5.17564)	0.00043 (b) (2.18104)	2541
June	0.00175 (b) (11.84832)	0.00065 (b) (5.41562)	0.00041 (b) (2.06398)	2537
July	0.00173 (b) (11.77674)	0.00066 (b) (5.47199)	0.00041 (b) (2.05702)	2540
August	0.00163 (b) (11.13135)	0.00063 (b) (5.22163)	0.00032 (1.63057)	2541
September	0.00181 (b) (12.57145)	0.00070 (b) (5.83719)	0.00046 (b) (2.34994)	2548
October	0.00190 (b) (15.50161)	0.00074 (b) (6.64077)	0.00057 (b) (3.26583)	2540
November	0.00164 (b) (11.23576)	0.00059 (b) (4.91755)	0.00035 (b) (1.78626)	2538
December	0.00163 (b) (11.28425)	0.00055 (b) (4.61812)	0.00042 (b) (2.15083)	2549

(a) The t statistics are presented in parentheses.

(b) Significant at the 5 percent level using one-tailed test.

November each produced higher returns than January on average. The risk-return relationship is significant in January as well as in August and November. However, it is also significant when calculated using all months excluding January. The only month that exhibits a result comparable to that found in Tinic and West (1984) for January is August in that excluding August from the data causes the $\hat{\gamma}_1$ to lose significance. The earlier studies which found evidence of a January seasonality in Canada used data primarily from the 1960's and 1970's (Gultekin and Gultekin, 1983; Berges, McConnell, and Schlarbaum, 1984). It appears that the January Effect has now virtually disappeared from Canada, perhaps in response to the publicity it has received.

Further evidence of the diminished significance of the January Effect may be obtained by running dummy variable regressions of the following form:

$$RME = \Phi_1 + \Sigma_{i=2}^{12} \Phi_i D_i + e_t \quad (3)$$

$$\hat{\gamma}_{jt} = \Phi_1 + \Sigma_{i=2}^{12} \Phi_i D_i + e_{jt} \quad (4)$$

where j = 0, 1. The intercept term represents January and D_2 through D_{12} are dummy variables representing the other months of the year from February through December. The results of this regression are reported in Table 3. Four months earn significantly lower returns than January. However, the risk premium is significantly lower than in January only in October. This result stands in marked contrast to that reported in Tinic and West (1984) for the United States and in Cadsby and Tapon (1987) for Canada.

Table 1 also indicates the presence of a Mark Twain Effect in Canada in that October is the month in which RME and $\bar{\gamma}_1$ are lowest. Dummy variable regressions not reported here in detail indicate that RME was significantly higher in every month of the year but September and that $\hat{\gamma}_1$ was significantly higher in eight of the remaining eleven months of the year.[4]

Average rates of return and average values of $\hat{\gamma}_0$ and $\hat{\gamma}_1$ were also calculated by week and by day of the year. These results are not reported

---

[4]Detailed results are available from the author upon request. When data from the crash year of 1987 were removed from the analysis, RME was still lowest in October but significantly lower in the case of only six months. $\hat{\gamma}_1$ was no longer lowest in October. No other results reported in this paper were qualitatively different when 1987 was removed.

TABLE 3

DIFFERENCES IN RETURNS ON THE EQUALLY WEIGHTED INDEX (RME), $\hat{\gamma}_0$ AND $\hat{\gamma}_1$, BY MONTH, WITH JANUARY AS THE INTERCEPT AND A DUMMY VARIABLE FOR EACH OTHER MONTH.[a]

Variable	RME	($\hat{\gamma}_0$)	($\hat{\gamma}_1$)
Φ_1	0.00257 (b) (5.441)	0.00086 (b) (2.197)	0.00108 (b) (1.691)
Φ_2	-0.00141 (b) (-2.708)	-0.00016 (-0.293)	-0.00150 (-1.638)
Φ_3	-0.00065 (-0.980)	-0.00008 (-0.143)	-0.00036 (-0.404)
Φ_4	-0.00084 (-1.250)	0.00003 (0.046)	-0.00092 (-1.006)
Φ_5	-0.00054 (-0.812)	-0.00013 (-0.239)	-0.00077 (-0.854)
Φ_6	-0.00123 (b) (-1.842)	-0.00044 (-0.792)	-0.00052 (-0.575)
Φ_7	-0.00103 (-1.536)	-0.00048 (-0.872)	-0.00049 (-0.543)
Φ_8	0.00004 (0.056)	-0.00016 (-0.284)	0.00044 (0.484)
Φ_9	-0.00193 (b) (-2.865)	-0.00095 (b) (-1.702)	-0.00106 (-1.156)
Φ_{10}	-0.00288 (b) (-4.30)	-0.00134 (b) (-2.420)	-0.00232 (b) (-2.561)
Φ_{11}	0.00001 (0.016)	0.00027 (0.488)	0.00016 (0.176)
Φ_{12}	0.00013 (0.191)	0.00073 (1.294)	-0.00066 (-0.724)

(a) The estimated equations are:
$RME = \Phi_1 + \Sigma_{i=2}^{12} \Phi_i D_i + e_t$ and $\hat{\gamma}_{jt} = \Phi_1 + \Sigma_{i=2}^{12} \Phi_i D_i + e_{jt}$ with j=0,1 respectively. D_2 through D_{12} are dummy variables representing the months of the year from February to December. The t statistics are presented in parentheses.

(b) Significant at the 5 percent level using one-tailed test.

in detail here in order to economize on space.[5] They are interesting primarily in that they suggest the presence of a Turn-Of-The-Year Effect during the 13 days from December 21 to January 5. For example, the weekly results show that $\bar{\hat{\gamma}}_1$ is significantly positive in nine weeks out of 52. Only 3 of these weeks are adjacent, namely the last two weeks of December and the first week of January. The daily results show that $\bar{\hat{\gamma}}_1$ is significantly positive on five of the 13 days between December 21 and January 5. In contrast, $\bar{\hat{\gamma}}_1$ is significantly positive on no other days in December, just one other day in January, and just 16 days throughout the rest of the year.

The presence of a Turn-Of-The-Year Effect is established by the results reported in Tables 4 and 5. Table 4 shows that the average value of the CAPM risk premium is significantly positive during the turn of the year but not during the rest of the year. Table 5 reports dummy variable regressions on equations analogous to Equations (3) and (4) in which the turn of the year is the intercept and each other month or part month is represented by a dummy variable. Notice that both average RME and $\bar{\hat{\gamma}}_1$ are significantly lower than during the turn of the year in every other month, including those parts of December and January not covered by the turn-of-the-year period. The apparent movement of the Turn-Of-The-Year Effect backwards in time from January, as reported in earlier studies, to the period between December 21 and January 5 may reflect the presence of a slow learning process resulting from the apparently gradual discovery and attempt to exploit this empirical regularity.

Table 6 reports the average rate of return on the equally weighted index and the average value of $\hat{\gamma}_0$ and $\hat{\gamma}_1$ by day of the week. As in Jaffe and Westerfield (1985), average RME is lowest on Mondays, low on Tuesdays, and highest on Wednesdays, Thursdays, and Fridays. The relatively low measured RME on Tuesdays could be the result of measurement error owing to thin trading causing some part of the well-known weekend effect to be diffused over Tuesdays (Theobald and Price, 1984).[6]

The results in Table 6 also indicate that there is a significantly positive CAPM risk premium on Wednesdays, Thursdays, and Fridays but not on Mondays or Tuesdays. In fact, if the t statistics attached to $\bar{\hat{\gamma}}_1$ for

---

[5]They are available upon request from the author.

[6]Theobald and Price (1984) show that thin trading tends to cause measurement error which may mask calendar effects in the data.

TABLE 4

AVERAGE RATE OF RETURN ON THE EQUALLY WEIGHTED INDEX AND AVERAGE VALUES OF THE INTERCEPT AND SLOPE COEFFICIENTS OF THE TWO-PARAMETER MODEL, FOR TURN OF THE YEAR (DEC 21 TO JAN 5) VERSUS REST OF THE YEAR, ESTIMATED WITH DAILY DATA FROM JANUARY 2, 1977 TO DECEMBER 31, 1987.[a]

Averaged over all days from	Avg rate of return on market index	Avg. Intercept Coefficient ($\bar{\hat{\gamma}}_0$)	Avg. Slope Coefficient ($\bar{\hat{\gamma}}_1$)	Sample Size
Dec 21 to Jan 5	0.00639 (b) (9.45742)	0.00147 (b) (2.33935)	0.00390 (b) (4.96394)	96
Jan 6 to Dec 20	0.00155 (b) (11.08407)	0.00060 (b) (5.20803)	0.00030 (1.56621)	2677

(a) The t statistics are presented in parentheses.

(b) Significant at the 5 percent level using one-tailed test.

TABLE 5

DIFFERENCES IN RETURNS ON THE EQUALLY WEIGHTED INDEX (RME), $\hat{\gamma}_0$ AND $\hat{\gamma}_1$, WITH THE TURN OF THE YEAR (DEC 21 TO JAN 5) AS THE INTERCEPT AND A DUMMY VARIABLE FOR EACH OTHER MONTH OR PART MONTH.[a]

Variable	RME	$(\hat{\gamma}_0)$	$(\hat{\gamma}_1)$
Φ_0	0.00639 (b) (8.726)	0.00147 (b) (2.403)	0.00390 (b) (3.919)
Φ_1	-0.00396 (b) (-4.461)	-0.00033 (-0.451)	-0.00320 (b) (-2.651)
Φ_2	-0.00522 (b) (-5.959)	-0.00077 (-1.054)	-0.00432 (b) (-3.626)
Φ_3	-0.00446 (b) (-5.157)	-0.00069 (-0.948)	-0.00318 (b) (-2.702)
Φ_4	-0.00466 (b) (-5.331)	-0.00058 (-0.797)	-0.00374 (b) (-3.145)
Φ_5	-0.00436 (b) (-5.006)	-0.00074 (-1.018)	-0.00359 (b) (-3.034)
Φ_6	-0.00504 (b) (-5.807)	-0.00105 (-1.442)	-0.00334 (b) (-2.826)
Φ_7	-0.00484 (b) (-5.565)	-0.00109 (-1.501)	-0.00331 (b) (-2.798)
Φ_8	-0.00378 (b) (-4.338)	-0.00077 (-1.053)	-0.00238 (b) (-2.010)
Φ_9	-0.00575 (b) (-6.573)	-0.00156 (b) (-2.136)	-0.00388 (b) (-3.258)
Φ_{10}	-0.00669 (b) (-7.691)	-0.00195 (b) (-2.648)	-0.00514 (b) (-4.343)
Φ_{11}	-0.00380 (b) (-4.337)	-0.00034 (-0.465)	-0.00266 (b) (-2.250)
Φ_{12}	-0.00577 (b) (-6.211)	-0.00030 (-0.385)	-0.00499 (b) (-3.947)

(a) The estimated equations are:

$RME = \Phi_0 + \Sigma_{i=1}^{12} \Phi_i D_i + e_t$ and $\hat{\gamma}_{jt} = \Phi_0 + \Sigma_{i=1}^{12} \Phi_i D_i + e_{jt}$ with j=0,1 respectively. D_1 is a dummy variable representing the days from Jan 6 to Jan 31, D_2 through D_{11} are dummy variables representing February through November and D_{12} is a dummy variable representing the days from Dec 1 to Dec 20. The t statistics are presented in parentheses.

(b) Significant at the 5 percent level using one-tailed test.

TABLE 6

AVERAGE RATE OF RETURN ON THE EQUALLY WEIGHTED INDEX AND AVERAGE VALUES OF THE INTERCEPT AND SLOPE COEFFICIENTS OF THE TWO-PARAMETER MODEL, BY DAY OF THE WEEK, ESTIMATED WITH DAILY DATA FROM JANUARY 2, 1977 TO DECEMBER 31, 1987.[a]

Averaged over all	Avg rate of return on market index	Avg. Intercept Coefficient ($\bar{\hat{\gamma}}_0$)	Avg. Slope Coefficient ($\bar{\hat{\gamma}}_1$)	Sample Size
Mondays	0.00024 (0.67655)	0.00014 (0.52030)	-0.00119 (-2.66348)	517
Tuesdays	0.00053 (b) (1.70662)	0.00091 (b) (3.57170)	-0.00095 (-2.18941)	566
Wednesdays	0.00222 (b) (6.89239)	0.00080 (b) (3.02886)	0.00091 (b) (2.21497)	568
Thursdays	0.00220 (b) (7.87360)	0.00080 (b) (3.50590)	0.00097 (b) (2.52672)	568
Fridays	0.00329 (b) (13.09433)	0.00047 (b) (1.87903)	0.00227 (b) (5.93362)	554
Mondays and Tuesdays	0.00039 (b) (1.66286)	0.00055 (b) (2.89594)	-0.00107 (-3.42148)	1083
All days excl. Monday	0.00205 (b) (13.93333)	0.00075 (b) (5.97744)	0.00079 (b) (3.89874)	2256
All days excl. Mon and Tues	0.00257 (b) (15.47766)	0.00069 (b) (4.82813)	0.00138 (b) (6.05054)	1690

(a) The t statistics are presented in parentheses.

(b) Significant at the 5 percent level using one-tailed test.

Mondays and Tuesdays are regarded as testing the null hypothesis against the two-tailed alternative that $\hat{\gamma}_1 \neq 0$, the risk premium for these days may be viewed as negatively significant. Thus, the CAPM appears to work as predicted only during the latter part of the week. Table 7 reports the results of dummy variable regressions similar to Equations (3) and (4) with Monday as the intercept and a dummy variable for each other day. They indicate that the average return on the equally weighted index and $\bar{\hat{\gamma}}_1$ are significantly higher on Wednesdays, Thursdays, and Fridays than on Mondays. These results are similar to those found by Cadsby (1988) for the United States.

Table 8 looks at the interrelationship between Turn-Of-The-Year and Day-Of-The-Week Effects. The risk premium is positive and significant on Tuesdays to Fridays at the turn of the year, on Mondays at the turn of the year, and on Tuesdays to Fridays during the rest of the year although the actual estimate of the value of the risk premium looks very different for each of these three periods. On the other hand, the risk premium for Mondays during the rest of the year is negative and the t statistic quite large in absolute value. It was reported in Tinic and West (1984) for the U.S. and in Cadsby and Tapon (1985) for Canada that a CAPM with a positive risk premium appeared to exist only during January. It is reported above that removing a 13 day period around the turn of the year causes the CAPM risk premium to lose statistical significance. However, the results in Table 8 suggest that the underlying reason for this result in the Canadian case is the peculiar behavior of stock prices on Mondays between January 6 and December 20. This result is similar to that found by Cadsby (1988) for the United States.

Lakonishok and Smidt (1987) found that over a 90 year period returns on the DJIA were positive around the turn of the month, defined as the last and first three trading days of the month, but negative during the rest of the year. Tables 9 and 10 indicate a less dramatic Turn-Of-The-Month Effect for Canadian stocks over the last ten years. Although the equally weighted index earns positive returns both at the turn of the month and during the rest of the year, the dummy variable regression reported in Table 10 indicates that returns are significantly lower during the rest of the year. Once again, the calendar effect on returns makes itself felt in the results on the risk-return relationship. Table 9 indicates that the risk premium is significantly positive during the turn-of-the-month period but not during the rest of the year. The dummy

TABLE 7

DIFFERENCES IN RETURNS ON THE EQUALLY WEIGHTED INDEX (RME), $\hat{\gamma}_0$ AND $\hat{\gamma}_1$, BY DAY OF THE WEEK, WITH MONDAY AS THE INTERCEPT AND A DUMMY VARIBLE FOR EACH OTHER DAY.[a]

Variable	RME	$(\hat{\gamma}_0)$	$(\hat{\gamma}_1)$
Φ_1	0.00024 (0.768)	0.00014 (0.547)	-0.00119 (-2.795)
Φ_2	0.00028 (0.649)	0.00077 (b) (2.101)	0.00024 (0.411)
Φ_3	0.00198 (b) (4.535)	0.00065 (b) (1.787)	0.00211 (b) (3.571)
Φ_4	0.00196 (b) (4.494)	0.00065 (b) (1.784)	0.00217 (b) (3.667)
Φ_5	0.00305 (b) (6.947)	0.00033 (0.896)	0.00346 (b) (5.828)

(a) The estimated equations are:
$RME = \Phi_1 + \Sigma_{i=2}^{5} \Phi_i D_i + e_t$ and $\hat{\gamma}_{jt} = \Phi_1 + \Sigma_{i=2}^{5} \Phi_i D_i + e_{jt}$ with j=0,1 respectively. D_2 through D_5 are dummy variables representing the days of the week from Tuesday through Friday. The t statistics are presented in parentheses.

(b) Significant at the 5 percent level using one-tailed test.

TABLE 8

AVERAGE RATE OF RETURN ON THE EQUALLY WEIGHTED INDEX AND AVERAGE VALUES OF THE INTERCEPT AND SLOPE COEFFICIENTS OF THE TWO-PARAMETER MODEL, BY TURN OF THE YEAR (DEC 21 TO JAN 5) AND PART OF THE WEEK, ESTIMATED WITH DAILY DATA FROM JANUARY 2, 1977 TO DECEMBER 31, 1987.[a]

Averaged over all	Avg rate of return on market index	Avg. Intercept Coefficient ($\bar{\hat{\gamma}}_0$)	Avg. Slope Coefficient ($\bar{\hat{\gamma}}_1$)	Sample Size
Tues to Fri at turn of year	0.00667 (b) (8.67858)	0.00156 (b) (2.29669)	0.00415 (b) (4.63396)	79
Mondays at turn of year	0.00508 (b) (3.79983)	0.00103 (0.62530)	0.00274 (b) (1.75821)	17
Tues to Fri for rest of year	0.00189 (b) (12.66074)	0.00072 (b) (5.64295)	0.00067 (b) (3.22913)	2177
Mondays for rest of year	0.00008 (0.21308)	0.00011 (0.40594)	-0.00133 (-2.88993)	500

(a) The t statistics are presented in parentheses.

(b) Significant at the 5 percent level using one-tailed test.

TABLE 9

AVERAGE RATE OF RETURN ON THE EQUALLY WEIGHTED INDEX AND AVERAGE VALUES OF THE INTERCEPT AND SLOPE COEFFICIENTS OF THE TWO-PARAMETER MODEL, BY TURN OF THE MONTH (LAST AND FIRST THREE TRADING DAYS OF EACH MONTH) VERSUS ALL OTHER DAYS IN THE YEAR, ESTIMATED WITH DAILY DATA FROM JANUARY 2, 1977 TO DECEMBER 31, 1987.[(a)]

Averaged over all days in	Avg rate of return on market index	Avg. Intercept Coefficient ($\bar{\hat{\gamma}}_0$)	Avg. Slope Coefficient ($\bar{\hat{\gamma}}_1$)	Sample Size
Turn of month	0.00271 (b) (10.34151)	0.00083 (b) (3.13766)	0.00143 (b) (3.59489)	528
Rest of year	0.00148 (b) (9.35887)	0.00059 (b) (4.64981)	0.00019 (0.88541)	2245

(a) The t statistics are presented in parentheses.

(b) Significant at the 5 percent level using one-tailed test.

TABLE 10

DIFFERENCES IN RETURNS ON THE EQUALLY WEIGHTED INDEX (RME), $\hat{\gamma}_0$ AND $\hat{\gamma}_1$, WITH THE TURN OF THE MONTH (LAST AND FIRST THREE TRADING DAYS OF EACH MONTH) AS INTERCEPT AND ALL OTHER DAYS IN THE YEAR REPRESENTED BY A SINGLE DUMMY VARIABLE.[(a)]

Variable	RME	($\hat{\gamma}_0$)	($\hat{\gamma}_1$)
Φ_1	0.00271 (b) (8.510)	0.00083 (b) (3.177)	0.00143 (b) (3.361)
Φ_2	-0.00123 (b) (-3.500)	-0.00024 (-0.0853)	-0.00125 (b) (-2.633)

(a) The estimated equations are:

$RME = \Phi_1 + \Phi_2 D_2 + e_t$ and $\hat{\gamma}_{jt} = \Phi_1 + \Phi_2 D_i + e_{jt}$ with j=0,1

respectively. D_1 represents all days falling at the turn of the month (last day and first 3 trading days of each month) and D_2 represents all other days in the year. The t statistics are presented in parentheses.

(b) Significant at the 5 percent level using one-tailed test.

variable regression results reported in Table 10 show that the risk premium is significantly lower during the rest of the year than at the turn of the month.

Table 11 reports on the interrelationship between Turn-Of-The-Month and Day-Of-The-Week Effects. The CAPM risk premium is positive and significant from Tuesdays to Fridays both at the turn of the month and during the rest of the year, though both returns and the risk premium are higher during the turn-of-the-month period. The risk premium on Mondays at the turn of the month is negative and would be significant if the alternative to the null hypothesis were interpreted as $\bar{\hat{\gamma}}_1 \neq 0$. Thus, the lack of empirical corroboration for a CAPM with a positive risk premium during the non-turn-of-the-month period is due, as in the non-turn-of-the-year case, primarily to the behavior of stock returns on Mondays during the period in question.

The results reported so far have indicated that both the turn of the year and the turn of the month were relatively good times to be in the Canadian stock markets between 1977 and 1987. During these periods, returns were high and risk was rewarded. Table 12 presents a comparison between the turn of the month, the turn of the year and the rest of the year in a dummy variable framework. The last trading day of December and the first three trading days of January are considered part of the turn of the year but are excluded from the turn-of-the-month data for this purpose. The results show that both returns and the estimated risk premium are significantly higher at the turn of the year than at the turn of the month. Both returns and the estimated risk premium are significantly lower during the rest of the year than at the turn of the month with the last day of December and the first three days of January excluded. These results are similar but not identical to those reported in Cadsby (1988) for the United States.

The results reported in this paper for Canada and in Cadsby (1988) for the United States do not explain calendar effects on stock market returns. However, they do allow the initially startling results of Tinic and West (1984), which suggested that a positive risk premium exists only in January, to be seen in some perspective. There are many ways of partitioning the days of the year. However they are partitioned, days during which the stock market did well also exhibit a significant return to risk in this study. A crude indicator of the relationship between the level of returns and the estimated risk premium is the Pearson correlation

TABLE 11

AVERAGE RATE OF RETURN ON THE EQUALLY WEIGHTED INDEX AND AVERAGE VALUES OF THE INTERCEPT AND SLOPE COEFFICIENTS OF THE TWO-PARAMETER MODEL, BY TURN OF THE MONTH (LAST AND FIRST 3 TRADING DAYS OF EACH MONTH) AND PART OF THE WEEK, ESTIMATED WITH DAILY DATA FROM JANUARY 2, 1977 TO DECEMBER 31, 1987.[a]

Averaged over all days in	Avg rate of return on market index	Avg. Intercept Coefficient $(\bar{\hat{\gamma}}_0)$	Avg. Slope Coefficient $(\bar{\hat{\gamma}}_1)$	Sample Size
Tues to Fri at turn of month	0.00298 (b) (10.52221)	0.00080 (b) (2.80313)	0.00183 (b) (4.24236)	435
Mondays at turn of month	0.00146 (b) (2.18288)	0.00096 (1.40287)	-0.00042 (-0.41357)	93
Tues to Fri for rest of year	0.00183 (b) (10.83015)	0.00073 (b) (5.28108)	0.00055 (b) (2.37777)	1821
Mondays for rest of year	-0.00002 (-0.05797)	-0.00004 (-0.11578)	-0.00136 (-2.72911)	424

(a) The t statistics are presented in parentheses.

(b) Significant at the 5 percent level using one-tailed test.

TABLE 12

DIFFERENCES IN RETURNS ON THE EQUALLY WEIGHTED INDEX (RME), $\hat{\gamma}_0$ AND $\hat{\gamma}_1$, WITH THE TURN OF THE MONTH (LAST DAY AND FIRST 3 TRADING DAYS OF EACH MONTH EXCLUDING DEC 31 TO JAN 3) AS THE INTERCEPT, ONE DUMMY VARIABLE FOR THE TURN OF THE YEAR (DEC 21 TO JAN 5) AND A THIRD DUMMY VARIABLE FOR ALL OTHER DAYS IN THE YEAR.[a]

Variable	RME	$(\hat{\gamma}_0)$	$(\hat{\gamma}_1)$
Φ_1	0.00250 (b) (7.673)	0.00073 (b) (2.703)	0.00135 (b) (3.054)
Φ_2	0.00389 (b) (4.845)	0.00074 (1.099)	0.00256 (b) (2.345)
Φ_3	-0.00116 (b) (3.224)	-0.00016 (-0.531)	-0.00129 (b) (-2.632)

(a) The estimated equations are:
$RME = \Phi_1 + \Phi_2 D_2 + \Phi_3 D_3 + e_t$ and $\hat{\gamma}_{jt} = \Phi_1 + \Phi_2 D_2 + \Phi_3 D_3 + e_{jt}$ with $j=0,1$ respectively. D_1 represents the turn of the month (last and first three trading days of each month excluding Dec 31 to Jan 3), D_2 represents the turn of the year (Dec 21 to Jan 5) and D_3 represents all other days in the year. The t statistics are presented in parentheses.

(b) Significant at the 5 percent level using a one-tailed test for Φ_1 and Φ_3 and a two-tailed test for Φ_2.

coefficient between the two which is equal to 0.71. In contrast, the correlation between RME and $\hat{\gamma}_0$ is equal to only 0.19. This should not be surprising. High beta portfolios should do exceptionally well when the market does well, exceptionally poorly when the market does poorly, and not much differently than the market when market returns are close to zero. The real puzzle is not that the estimated CAPM risk premium is significant only during periods when the stock market does well, of which January in the United States over the Tinic and West (1984) estimation period is but one example. On the contrary, the puzzle and the challenge to the notion of market efficiency is posed by the various calendar effects on the returns themselves.

4. The Four-Parameter Case

Both Fama and MacBeth (1973) and Tinic and West (1986) estimate the four-parameter model in Equation (5) below as a further test of the CAPM.

$$R_{pt} = \gamma_{0t} + \gamma_{1t}\hat{\beta}_{pt-1} + \gamma_{2t}\hat{\beta}^2_{pt-1} + \gamma_{3t}S(\epsilon_{pt-1}) + w_{pt} \tag{5}$$

where $\hat{\beta}^2_{pt-1}$ is the average of the squares of the individual $\hat{\beta}_i$ coefficients and $S(\epsilon_{pt-1})$ is the average of the individual specific risk coefficients of securities in portfolio p, calculated over the portfolio estimation period.[7] Fama and MacBeth (1973) argue that the two-parameter CAPM predicts that the average values of neither $\hat{\gamma}_2$ nor $\hat{\gamma}_3$ should be significantly different from zero and get this result when averages are calculated across their entire data set. The results of Tinic and West (1986) vary according to subperiod. However, in general, the average value of $\hat{\gamma}_3$ alone is significant in January while the average values of $\hat{\gamma}_1$ and sometimes $\hat{\gamma}_2$ are significant during the rest of the year. Cadsby and Tapon (1987) estimate the four-parameter model for Canada using monthly data and find that nothing is significant, either in January or during the rest of the year.

Table 13 reports results for Canada using daily data from January 2, 1977 to December 31, 1987 which indicate that nothing is significant when the period is considered as a whole. However, when January is taken alone, the specific risk coefficient, $\bar{\hat{\gamma}}_3$, becomes significant, as in

---

[7]Tinic and West (1986) also look at a five-parameter model which includes firm size as an explanatory variable. Unfortunately, data on firm size were not available to the author.

TABLE 13

AVERAGE VALUES OF THE COEFFICIENTS OF THE FOUR-PARAMETER MODEL ESTIMATED WITH DAILY DATA FROM JANUARY 2, 1977 TO DECEMBER 31, 1987.[a]

Averaged over all	$(\bar{\hat{\gamma}}_0)$	$(\bar{\hat{\gamma}}_1)$	$(\bar{\hat{\gamma}}_2)$	$(\bar{\hat{\gamma}}_3)$	Sample Size
Days in year	0.00015 (0.34064)	0.00004 (0.07481)	0.00014 (0.60838)	0.02682 (1.22181)	2773
Days in January	-0.00269 (-1.783)	0.00264 (1.48275)	-0.00139 (-1.6621)	0.14191 (b) (1.95684)	233
Days in Feb to Dec	0.00041 (0.87599)	-0.00020 (-0.41023)	0.00028 (1.16946)	0.01626 (0.70654)	2540
Days between Dec 21 - Jan 5	-0.00176 (-0.69393)	0.00265 (1.03519)	-0.00116 (-1.0274)	0.22615 (b) (1.82208)	96
Days between Jan 6 - Dec 20	0.00022 (0.48454)	-0.00006 (-0.11966)	0.00019 (0.79230)	0.01967 (0.88248)	2677
Days over last and 1st 3 trade days of each month	-0.0008 (-0.7987)	0.0002 (0.1746)	-0.0001 (-0.1167)	0.1126 (b) (2.3007)	528
Days except last and 1st 3 trade days of each month	0.0004 (0.7557)	-0.0000 (-0.0029)	0.0002 (0.7413)	0.0066 (0.2705)	2245
Mondays	0.00227 (b) (2.18036)	-0.00447 (-3.6782)	0.00158 (b) (2.59733)	-0.04553 (-0.89191)	517
Tuesdays to Fridays	-0.00033 (-0.65912)	0.00107 (b) (2.07967)	-0.00019 (-0.76025)	0.04340 (b) (1.78575)	2256

(a) The t statistics are presented in parentheses.

(b) Significant at the 5 percent level using a one-tailed test for $\bar{\hat{\gamma}}_0$, $\bar{\hat{\gamma}}_1$ and $\bar{\hat{\gamma}}_3$ and a two-tailed test for $\bar{\hat{\gamma}}_2$.

Tinic and West (1986). In contrast to Tinic and West (1986), nothing is significant from February through December. When the turn of the year is compared with the rest of the year, the results look very similar to those just described for January versus February through December. The same is true when the turn of the month is compared with the rest of the year. Mondays are extracted and compared with the rest of the week in the same table. As in the two-parameter case, $\hat{\gamma}_1$ is significantly negative on Mondays; the parameter representing a non-linear response to beta, $\hat{\gamma}_2$, is significantly positive. The rest of the week exhibits significantly positive risk premiums attached to both market and specific risk. This result is similar to the results reported by Tinic and West (1986) for their entire sample period based on monthly data.

Table 14 reports the results of dummy variable regressions similar to Equations (3) and (4) in which Monday is the intercept and a dummy is defined for each other day of the week. The premium on market risk, $\bar{\hat{\gamma}}_1$, is significantly higher on every other day of the week than on Mondays. $\bar{\hat{\gamma}}_2$, on the other hand, is significantly lower on Tuesdays, Wednesdays, and Fridays than on Mondays. $\bar{\hat{\gamma}}_3$ is significantly higher on Wednesdays and Fridays.

Finally, Table 15 looks at the interrelationship between the turn of the year and the day of the week in the context of the four-parameter model. When Monday is excluded, the results look very much like the calendar effects found by Tinic and West (1986) for January versus the rest of the year. From Tuesday to Friday at the turn of the year, $\bar{\hat{\gamma}}_3$ is positive and significant. However, from Tuesday to Friday during the rest of the year, $\bar{\hat{\gamma}}_1$ alone is significant. Thus, if both the anomalously high average returns at the turn of the year and the anomalously low average returns at the beginning of the week are removed from the data, the prediction of the CAPM that only market risk should matter is corroborated. The strong Monday or Weekend Effect in the Canadian data during the rest of the year appears to be responsible for the fact that neither $\bar{\hat{\gamma}}_1$ nor $\bar{\hat{\gamma}}_3$ appear significant when all days during the rest of the year are considered together.

5. Conclusion

The most important new results contained in this paper include the following. First, in contrast to studies using monthly data from an

TABLE 14

DIFFERENCES IN VALUES OF $\hat{\gamma}_0$, $\hat{\gamma}_1$, $\hat{\gamma}_2$ and $\hat{\gamma}_3$, BY DAY OF THE WEEK, WITH MONDAY AS THE INTERCEPT AND A DUMMY VARIABLE FOR EACH OTHER DAY OF THE WEEK.[a]

Variable	($\hat{\gamma}_0$)	($\hat{\gamma}_1$)	($\hat{\gamma}_2$)	($\hat{\gamma}_3$)
Φ_1	0.00227 (b) (2.169)	-0.00447 (b) (-4.059)	0.00158 (b) (2.946)	-0.04553 (-0.897)
Φ_2	-0.00194 (-1.346)	0.00474 (b) (3.111)	-0.00197 (b) (-2.654)	0.03264 (0.465)
Φ_3	-0.00357 (b) (-2.475)	0.00592 (b) (3.889)	-0.00216 (b) (-2.907)	0.16170 (b) (2.305)
Φ_4	-0.00125 (-0.836)	0.00556 (b) (3.652)	-0.00120 (-1.618)	-0.00051 (-0.007)
Φ_5	-0.00364 (b) (-2.507)	0.00594 (b) (3.880)	-0.00175 (b) (-2.348)	0.16352 (b) (2.317)

(a) The estimated equations are:

$RME = \Phi_1 + \Sigma_{i=2}^{5} \Phi_i D_i + e_t$ and $\hat{\gamma}_{jt} = \Phi_1 + \Sigma_{i=2}^{5} \Phi_i D_i + e_{jt}$ with j=0,1,2,3 respectively. D_1 represents Mondays and D_2 through D_5 represent each of the other days in the week. The t statistics are presented in parentheses.

(b) Significant at the 5 percent level using two-tailed test.

TABLE 15

AVERAGE VALUES OF THE COEFFICIENTS OF THE FOUR-PARAMETER MODEL, BY TURN OF THE YEAR (DEC 21 TO JAN 5) AND PART OF THE WEEK, ESTIMATED WITH DAILY DATA FROM JANUARY 2, 1977 TO DECEMBER 31, 1987.[(a)]

Averaged over all	$(\bar{\hat{\gamma}}_0)$	$(\bar{\hat{\gamma}}_1)$	$(\bar{\hat{\gamma}}_2)$	$(\bar{\hat{\gamma}}_3)$	Sample Size
Tues-Fri at turn of year	-0.00253 (-0.87922)	0.00315 (1.12393)	-0.00134 (-1.1102)	0.28382 (b) (2.00391)	79
Mondays at turn of year	0.00182 (0.35249)	0.00033 (0.05093)	-0.00029 (-0.09452)	-0.04184 (-0.17586)	17
Tues-Fri in rest of year	-0.00025 (-0.49240)	0.00099 (b) (1.89969)	-0.00015 (-0.57921)	0.03467 (1.40716)	2177
Mondays in rest if year	0.00228 (b) (2.14994)	-0.00464 (-3.7428)	0.00164 (b) (2.64754)	-0.04566 (-0.87467)	500

(a) The t statistics are presented in parentheses.

(b) Significant at the 5 percent level using a one-tailed test for $\bar{\hat{\gamma}}_0$, $\bar{\hat{\gamma}}_1$, and $\bar{\hat{\gamma}}_3$ and a two-tailed test for $\bar{\hat{\gamma}}_2$.

earlier time period, there is little evidence of a January Effect on stock returns from 1977 to 1987 in Canada. Second, there is a Turn-Of-The-Year Effect on stock returns, where the turn of the year runs from December 21 to January 5. Third, there is a Turn-Of-The-Month Effect on stock returns in Canada similar to the one recently found by Lakonishok and Smidt (1987) for the United States. Fourth, there is a Mark Twain Effect on stock returns which are significantly lower in October than in other months. Fifth, as in the U.S. case discussed by Cadsby (1988), for each calendar effect on stock returns there is a corresponding calendar effect on the risk-return relationship. In particular, estimates of the CAPM risk premium are positive and significant during periods such as the turn of the year, the turn of the month, and the latter part of the week in which stock returns do particularly well. The Tinic and West (1984) result is but one example of this phenomenon. Sixth, when Mondays are removed from the data the estimated CAPM risk premium is positive and significant even over non-turn-of-the-year or non-turn-of-the-month periods. Seventh, when Mondays are removed from the data, there are calendar effects on the parameters of the four-parameter model which look much like those reported by Tinic and West (1986). The CAPM works as predicted from Tuesdays to Fridays from January 6 to December 20.

Calendar effects on the risk-return relationship appear to be closely related to calendar effects on measured stock returns themselves in Canada.[8] Thus, the importance of the calendar to an individual stock or portfolio appears to be directly related to the level of market risk associated with that stock or portfolio.

---

[8]Corhay, Hawawini and Michel (1987) appear to find some evidence to the contrary in the cases of the United Kingdom, France, and Belgium.

References

Berges, A., J.J. McConnell and G.G. Schlarbaum, 1984, The Turn-of-the-Year in Canada, Journal of Finance 39, 185-92.

Cadsby, C.B., 1988, The CAPM and the Calendar: A Systematic Treatment of Empirical Anomalies, University of Guelph Discussion Paper 1988-9.

Cadsby, C.B. and F. Tapon, 1987, Risk and Return on the Toronto Stock Exchange: January versus the Rest of the Year, University of Guelph Discussion Paper 1987-1.

Calvet, A.L. and J. Lefoll, 1985, Risk and Return on the Canadian Capital Markets: Estimation and Sensitivity Analysis, University of Ottawa Working Paper 1985-36.

Corhay, A., G. Hawawini and P. Michel, 1987, Seasonality in the Risk-Return Relationship: Some International Evidence, Journal of Finance 42, 49-68.

Cross, F., 1973, The Behavior of Stock Prices on Fridays and Mondays, Financial Analysts Journal, November-December, 67-69.

Fama, E., and J. MacBeth, 1973, Risk, Return and Equilibrium: Empirical Tests, Journal of Political Economy 38, 607-636.

French, K., 1980, Stock Returns and the Weekend Effect, Journal of Financial Economics 8, 55-69.

Gultekin, M.N. and N.B.Gultekin, 1983, Stock Market Seasonality: International Evidence, Journal of Financial Economics 12, 469-81.

Jaffe,J. and R. Westerfield, 1985, The Week-end Effect in Common Stock Returns: The International Evidence, Journal of Finance 40, 433-54.

Keim, D.B., 1983, Size Related Anomalies and Stock Return Seasonality: Further Empirical Evidence, Journal of Financial Economics 12, 13-22.

Lakonishok, J. and S. Smidt, 1987, Are Seasonal Anomalies Real? A Ninety-Year Perspective, Cornell University Working Paper.

Reinganum, M.R., 1983, The Anomalous Stock Market Behavior of Small Firms in January: Empirical Tests for Tax-loss Selling Effects, Journal of Financial Economics 12, 89-104.

Rogalski, R., 1984, New Findings Regarding Day-of-the-Week Returns Over Trading and Non-Trading Periods: A Note, Journal of Finance 34, 1603-14.

Rozeff, M.S. and W.R. Kinney, Jr., 1976, Capital Market Seasonality: The Case of Stock Returns, Journal of Financial Economics 3, 379-402.

Smirlock, M. and L. Starks, 1986, Day of the Week and Intraday Effects in Stock Returns, Journal of Financial Economics 17, 197-210.

Thaler, R.H., 1987a, The January Effect, Journal of Economic Perspectives 1, Summer, 197-201.

Thaler, R.H., 1987b, Seasonal Movements in Security Prices II: Weekend, Holiday, Turn of the Month, and Intraday Effects, Journal of Economic Perspectives 1, Fall, 169-177.

Tinic, S.M. and G. Barone-Adesi, 1987, Stock Return Seasonality and the Tests of Asset Pricing Models: Canadian Evidence, in: E. Dimson, ed., Stock Market Anomalies (Cambridge University Press, Cambridge, U.K.) 130-146.

Tinic, S.M. and R.R. West, 1984, Risk and Return: January vs. the Rest of the Year, Journal of Financial Economics 13, 561-74.

Tinic, S.M. and R.R. West, 1986, Risk, Return, and Equilibrium: A Revisit, Journal of Political Economy 94, 126-147.

Theobald, M. and V. Price, 1984, Seasonality Estimation in Thin Markets, Journal of Finance 39, 377-392.

Twain, M., 1981, Pudd'nhead Wilson (Bantam Books, Toronto)

Comments on C.B. Cadsby's "Canadian Calendar Anomalies and the Capital Asset Pricing Model"
by Donald R. Fraser

Financial economists have devoted a great deal of effort in recent years to the investigation of a number of interrelated empirical regularities or anomalies as they are sometimes called. These anomalies include day-of-the week or weekend effects, turn-of-the-year effects, the January effect, month-of-the year effects, turn-of-the-month effects, size effects, earnings-price ratio effects, and other such empirical regularities. Indeed, with the availability of intra-day data, it is now possible to investigate these anomalies in considerably more detail, so that we may have in the future the lunch-time effect, the tea-time effect, and the coffee break effect.

The existence of these empirical regularities is important for at least two reasons. First that such anomalies should persist over some period of time allowing the possibility of attaining excess risk adjusted returns casts doubt on the degree of market efficiency. Second, the existence of these anomalies raises questions about the ability of asset pricing models to accurately explain returns on financial assets. Such questions go to the very heart of the finance discipline.

Most of the plethora of studies that have investigated these market anomalies have been thorough and meticulous efforts to extract empirical regularities from a set of stock price data. Although one may quibble with some of the particular approaches (the measurement of returns for example) on balance the research is of high quality. Yet, on balance also, the research suffers from a lack of firm grounding in economic and financial theory. Although some researchers have sought to provide a theoretical foundation for their empirical work, in other cases the studies represent more of a fishing expedition; the line between valid empirical research and data dredging is sometimes a rather narrow one. In so many cases, the reader searches in vain for a testable hypothesis that is grounded in the behavior of risk averse investors.

This paper falls well within the framework of the existing, extensive literature on market anomalies. To a considerable degree, the strengths of that literature are the strengths of professor Cadsby's paper, but also the weaknesses of that literature are the weaknesses of the paper. The study uses a new and up-to-date data base on Canadian stocks (one that extends through the October, 1987 market crash and includes daily observations). The research is carefully done and explores virtually every question about

NATO ASI Series, Vol. F54
A Reappraisal of the Efficiency of Financial Markets
Edited by Rui M.C. Guimaraes et al.

these empirical regularities as they relate to Canadian equities. Yet there is little in the way of explanation of the results, either in a rigorous fashion or by intuition.

Professor Cadsby finds little evidence of a January effect on stock returns from 1977 to 1987 in Canada. Although this is inconsistent with previous research in Canadian equities and with the bulk of research on U.S. equities, it is entirely consistent with the notion of an adaptive market adjusting to opportunities to realize excess returns. Indeed, Pearce (1987) found that, for U.S. equities, the January effect has been reduced over time and that from 1976 to 1985 (a period very similar to that used in Cadsby's paper) there was no statistically significant January effect.

Professor Cadsby finds that returns in October are significantly lower than in other months for Canadian equities (even excluding the October 1987 crash). This is an interesting result and certainly conforms to recent experiences as well as to the 1929 crash. Yet this result may be due to the interrelationship of the size and seasonality factors. For example, Keim (1983) shows that a size discount existed for U.S. equities in October in the 1963-1979 period (and a size premium existed for January). The potential interaction of size and seasonality factors further suggests the desirability of a value weighted index as a supplement to the equally weighted index used in this study. Use of an equally weighted index produces a small firm bias. Pearce (1987) has recently shown substantially different results in exploring seasonality patterns with the use of value weighted than with equally weighted indexes.

My final comment relates back to my concern about the insufficient grounding of much of the literature on market anomalies in economic and financial theory. Given the fundamental empirical nature of the research, it would be desirable to place more emphasis on the time-series stationarity of these relationships. At a minimum, this suggests that professor Cadsby might consider dividing his study into one or more subperiods. Perhaps more innovatively, he might consider alternative statistical techniques not generally used in this literature to explore the stationarity of the relationships.

References

Keim, D., 1983, Size-Related Anomalies and Stock Return Seasonality, Journal of Financial Economics, 12, 23-32.

Pearce, D., 1987, Challenges to the Concept of Stock Market Efficiency, Federal Reserve Bank Of Kansas City Economic Review, 16-33.

AN INVESTIGATION OF DAILY SEASONALITY IN THE GREEK EQUITY MARKET

Leda Condoyanni
Doctoral Student
Department of Accounting and Finance
University of Lancaster
Lancaster LA1 4YX, U.K.

Stuart McLeay
TSB Professor of Treasury
University College of North Wales
Gwynedd LL57 2DG, U.K.

John O'Hanlon
Lecturer in Accounting and Finance
Department of Accounting and Finance
University of Lancaster
Lancaster LA1 4YX, U.K.

KEYWORDS/ABSTRACT : Day of week effect/ Seasonality/ Equity markets/ Athens Stock Exchange/Student's Distribution.

Using regression, a non-parametric test and an alternative parametric technique, this paper tests for a day of the week effect in the returns of shares quoted on the Athens Stock Exchange. Patterns are similar to those observed in other countries' markets in that returns tend to be low early in the week and high on Friday. Settlement factors probably account for part of the Greek day of the week effect but do not fully explain it.

ACKNOWLEDGEMENT : We are grateful to S.G. Warburg Securities for financial support for the creation of a database of Greek share returns.

NATO ASI Series, Vol. F54
A Reappraisal of the Efficiency of Financial Markets
Edited by Rui M. C. Guimaraes et al.

Jensen (1978) defines a market as being "weak form" efficient if it is impossible to make economic profits by trading solely on the basis of information contained in the past price history of the market. The existence of a predictable component in a return series would suggest the availability of profitable trading rules based on analyses of past price series and would thus constitute evidence against the "weak form" of the efficient markets hypothesis. The discovery in recent years of seasonal patterns in daily share price changes in the U.S. and other markets thus represents a challenge to this hypothesis. Using indices constructed from daily share price data collected from the Athens Stock Exchange (ASE), this paper seeks to establish whether the daily seasonal anomalies observed elsewhere are also present in the Greek market.

The paper is structured as follows. Daily seasonal patterns observed in other equity markets are reviewed in Section 1. Section 2 provides some institutional background information on the ASE and briefly considers previous studies of market efficiency in that market. Section 3 describes the data collection and validation procedures. Section 4 describes the tests carried out and reports the results of those tests.

1. Daily Seasonality in other Equity Markets

1.1 The U.S. market

A number of U.S. researchers (e.g. Cross (1973), French (1980), Gibbons and Hess (1981), Lakonishok and Levi (1982), Keim and Stambaugh (1984), Rogalski (1984), Harris (1986) and Keim (1987)) have tested for the day of the week effect in the U.S. equity market and have usually rejected the hypothesis that the mean stock return is equal for all days of the week. U.S. researchers have usually found an abnormally low, sometimes negative, mean return for Friday close - Monday close and a relatively high mean return for Thursday close - Friday close. Keim and Stambaugh (1984) also report that, for the period during which the New York Stock Exchange traded on Saturday, the mean return on Saturday tended to be the highest of the week. Rogalski (1984) reported that the negative weekend return accrued during the period Friday close - Monday open.

Evidence presented by Gibbons and Hess (1981), Lakonishok and Levi (1982), Dyl and Martin (1985) and Keim and Stambaugh (1984) indicated that differences in the length of the settlement period did not fully account for the observed differences in daily mean returns in the U.S. market. French (1980) tested the hypothesis that the observed "weekend effect" would disappear if one assumed that returns were generated in calendar time rather than in trading time. His division of the weekend return by three did not eliminate the weekend effect. The trading time/calendar time question was also investigated by Fama (1965) who observed that, if returns were generated in calendar time, the variance of weekend returns would be approximately three times the variance of within week returns. His finding that the weekend variance was 1.22 times greater than the within week return variance suggested that the weekend was marginally longer in information absorption terms than the other days of the week but nowhere near three times longer. Results reported by French (1980), Gibbons and Hess (1981) and Keim and Stambaugh (1984) confirm that the variance of U.S. weekend returns tends to be between 1.10 and 1.50 times the size of the within week variance. U.S. results thus appear to support the trading time rather than the calendar time hypothesis.

Analyses by Keim and Stambaugh (1984), Rogalski (1984) and Keim (1987) of size based U.S. portfolios have produced evidence of an inverse relationship between firm size and strength of daily seasonality, a particularly striking feature being the inverse relationship between firm size and the magnitude of the Friday return. This relationship between size and Friday return can also be detected in the Gibbons and Hess (1981) study which reported the results of seasonality tests on equally and value weighted indices.

Keim and Stambaugh (1984) find that systematic measurement error does not explain the weekend effect in the U.S.. Penman (1987) presents evidence of a daily seasonal in U.S. market reaction to earnings announcements which suggests the possibility that poor earnings announcements are delayed until the weekend and that the market then reacts mechanically to them, thus contributing to the low weekend return.

1.2 Non-U.S. markets

Jaffe and Westerfield (1985) tested for daily seasonality in the Japanese, Canadian, U.K. and Australian market indices and Condoyanni, O'Hanlon and Ward (1987) analysed these markets plus Singapore and France. In most cases the hypothesis of equality of mean return across the week was rejected by these studies.

Both studies found that most non-U.S. markets had a low mean weekend return and that those markets for which closing indices were compiled before the U.S. market opened had a negative mean Tuesday return. There was evidence to suggest that the "Tuesday effect" in Far Eastern and European markets was partially caused by those markets following the poor overnight performance of (Monday) Wall Street. Condoyanni, O'Hanlon and Ward also reported that, as in the case of the U.S. studies, the variance of weekend returns in the non-U.S. markets was always marginally greater than the within week variance of returns for those markets.

In figure 1 a diagrammatic representation of the 1980-1986 mean daily returns on 9 national market indices (France, West Germany, U.K., Australia, Hong Kong, Japan, Singapore, Canada, U.S.) is reproduced from O'Hanlon and Papaspirou (1988). This shows that most major world equity markets perform poorly early in the week and perform well late in the week. There appears to be a worldwide "early in the week" effect.

FIG 1:MEAN RETURNS BY DAY OF WEEK -9 COUNTRIES,1980-86

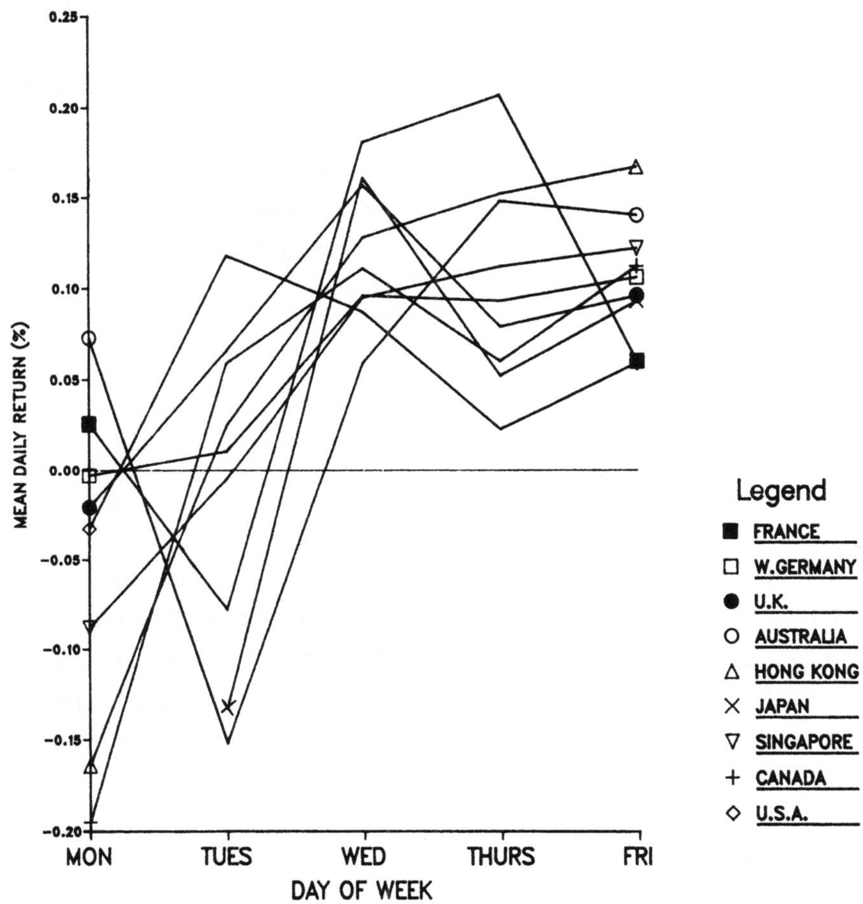

Reproduced from O'Hanlon and Papaspirou (1988).

The Japanese stock exchange usually trades on Saturday but the data source used for the O'Hanlon and Papaspirou study did not permit the Saturday and Monday returns to be split. Hence, the Japanese "Monday" return has been eliminated from this graph.

Studies by Theobald and Price (1984) and Choy and O'Hanlon (1988, forthcoming) confirm the low mean weekend return in the U.K. market and show that this mean weekend return would be even lower if one were to adjust for the significant level of distortion induced by settlement procedures on the London Stock Exchange. An analysis by Santesmases (1986) of Spanish data found no day of the week effect in the Spanish market. A study of the German market by Frantzmann (1987) confirms the existence of a low Monday and Tuesday mean return in that market which conforms with the patterns observed in other markets in which the closing indices are compiled before Wall Street opens.

2. The Greek Market

2.1 Institutional background

In this section of the paper we provide some information on the institutional background to share trading on the Athens Stock Exchange and we focus in particular on factors which appear to have contributed to differences between mean share returns on different days of the week in other markets. We also consider the way in which the recorded closing prices are arrived at.

2.1.1 Trading hours

Trading on the ASE occurs between 10.00a.m. and 12.00 midday. The market thus closes before Wall Street opens. Any Wall Street generated behaviour is thus likely to be reflected on the day after Wall Street trades rather than on the same day.

2.1.2. Settlement Procedures

On the Greek stock market, transactions may either be for cash or on account. Cash transactions must be settled on the working day after execution and account transactions are settled on the settlement day following the transaction. Settlement days are the 1st and 16th day of the month (or next working day). For account transactions there is thus no systematic difference between the settlement period allowed for transactions occurring on different days of the week. However, for cash transactions there is a difference of two days between the settlement period for Friday transactions and the settlement period for transactions occurring on other days. This is likely to cause the observed Friday return to be higher than would otherwise be the case and for the observed Monday return to be lower. Unfortunately, we have no data on the relative volume of cash and account transactions and cannot therefore make a reliable estimate of the probable effect of this factor. However, ASE staff inform us that a significant majority of transactions are for cash. Therefore we would expect the observed mean returns to be affected in some way by this factor.

2.1.3 Closing prices

Trading on the ASE is by open outcry. During trading, the price board shows the latest transaction price and/or the latest bid or ask price. For each day, the closing daily price in the series which was collected from the ASE was the latest of the last bid price quoted, the last ask price quoted and the last transaction price. Therefore some of the closing prices in our series do not represent transaction prices. In this connection we noted that, in some cases, changes occurred in a quoted share price on a day on which no trade in the share occurred. The existence of this problem was one of the reasons for our adoption of a traded value weighting method in one of the return series used in our empirical tests.

2.1.4 Dividends

In Greece dividends are subject to income tax whereas Capital Gains on share trading are not subject to tax. It is therefore possible that shares will command a tax generated premium on the ex-dividend day. In markets where ex-div days cluster on one day of the week (e.g. London where, for institutional reasons, they almost always fall on Monday) the ex-div day premium might contribute to daily differences in the mean return. In Greece, however, there is no institutionally generated clustering of ex-div days on any day of the week and it is therefore unlikely that ex-div day premiums contribute to differences in the mean returns for different days of the week.

2.2 Previous efficiency studies on the Greek market

We are aware of two recent empirical studies of share price behaviour on the ASE. Papaioannou (1983) analysed daily return data on 25 ASE stocks, including both actively and thinly traded issues, for the period 1970-1975 and observed that all but one of the stocks exhibited high autocorrelation. Bletsas and Tebbutt (1984) used serial correlation analysis, spectral analysis and regression to test for randomness in the monthly returns on a number of sector based indices. They concluded that their results did not support the hypothesis that the Greek market was weak form efficient.

3. Data

3.1 Sample selection and data collection

This study uses daily returns for the period 1st January 1978 to 31st December 1986 for 28 Greek shares quoted on the ASE. The study thus includes about one quarter of the average number of shares quoted on the ASE at any one time during that period. The data consists of closing daily share prices, daily trading volumes, and information on the number of shares in issue, dividend payments, stock splits, consolidations and rights issues. The prime sources for this information were manuscript records maintained by the statistical department of the ASE. Some of the data also appeared in the Stock Exchange Year Book and the Stock Exchange Annual Statistical Bulletin. In those cases in which the same data was available from two separate ASE sources, the sources were compared and discrepancies were investigated in consultation with ASE staff.

In order to identify potential errors in the company share price series, all proportional daily price changes in excess of 30% were investigated. Also we investigated all cases in which a proportional price change with an absolute value of greater than 10% was followed by a proportional price change of opposite sign with an absolute value of greater than 10%.

The sample of shares chosen for the study consisted of all shares which appeared for at least three years in the annual list of the most frequently traded shares published in the Annual Statistical Bulletin. The names of

Table 1

	COMPANY NAME	SECTOR	NUMBER OF DAYS TRADED (Maximum possible:2245)
1	General Bank of Greece	Banks	1449
2	National Bank of Greece	Banks	2238
3	Bank of Greece	Banks	2099
4	Commercial Bank of Greece	Banks	1816
5	Ergobank S.A.	Banks	2077
6	Bank of Crete S.A. (Introduced 18.12.78)	Banks	1330 (out of 2002)
7	National Mortgage Bank	Banks	1816
8	Ionian and Popular Bank of Greece	Banks	1123
9	Bank of Macedonia - Thrace (Introduced 27.8.80)	Banks	1415 (out of 1585)
10	Credit Bank	Banks	1790
11	'Ethniki' General Insurance Company	Insurance and Investment	937
12	Hellenic Investment Company S.A.	Insurance and Investment	1374
13	Ergo Investment S.A.	Insurance and Investment	1374
14	'ETMA' Rayon Manufacturing Co.	Textiles	995
15	Piraiki - Patraiki Cotton Industry S.A.	Textiles	1145
16	Chemical Products and Fertilizers Co.	Chemical Products	1391
17	A.G. Petzetakis S.A.	Chemical Products	1240
18	'Heracles' General Cement Co. S.A.	Building Materials	2019
19	'Titan' Cement Co. S.A.	Building Materials	1852
20	'Halkis' Cement Co. S.A.	Building Materials	1707
21	Financial Corporation - Mines	Metallurgical - Mines	220
22	Aluminium de Grece S.A.	Metallurgical - Mines	951
23	Viochalko - Copper Co.	Metallurgical - Mines	147
24	M.E.T.K.A.	Metallurgical - Mines	1320
25	Andrew P. Cambas - Wines and Spirits Co.	Food - Spirits	695
26	Lampsa Hotel Co.	Hotels	626
27	'Athinea' S.A.	Miscellaneous	1388
28	'Vioter' S.A.	Miscellaneous	1294

the companies included in the sample together with their industrial sector and the number of days (out of a total of 2245) on which the shares were traded in the period are given in Table 1.

In addition to the ASE market data, a series of daily logarithmic price relatives for the Dow Jones Industrial index was compiled from DATASTREAM for the period 1978 to 1986.

3.2 Return Series

For each of the twenty eight companies in the sample, a daily logarithmic return series was computed as follows :

$$R_t = \ln \frac{P_t + D_t}{P_{t-1}} \tag{1}$$

Appropriate adjustments were made for stock splits, consolidation and rights issues on the basis of the manuscript and published information obtained from the ASE. The exchange was closed for 102 days during our sample period. In each case the zero return for these days was replaced by a missing value indicator in our data set.

Three sets of differently weighted portfolio return series were then computed from the twenty-eight companies' returns:

i) An equally weighted series

ii) A market value weighted series computed as follows :

$$VWR_t = \frac{\sum_{j=1}^{j=28} R_{jt} P_{jt} N_{jt}}{\sum_{j-1}^{j=28} P_{jt} N_{jt}} \tag{2}$$

where

VWR_t = The value weighted portfolio return for day t

R_{jt} = The return for share j on day t

P_{jt} = The share price of share j on day t

N_{jt} = The number of shares in issue for share j on day t

iii) A series weighted by the value of each share traded on day t :

$$TVWR_t = \frac{\sum_{j=1}^{j=28} R_{jt} P_{jt} T_{jt}}{\sum_{j=1}^{j=28} P_{jt} T_{jt}} \qquad (3)$$

where

$TVWR_t$ = The traded value weighted portfolio return for day t

R_{jt} = The return for share j on day t

P_{jt} = The share price of share j on day t

T_{jt} = The number of units of share j traded on day t

This weighting scheme which reduces the effect of price changes which coincide with low, or zero, trading volume will cause the return series to reflect the behaviour of large and frequently traded issues.

4. Tests and Results

4.1 Regression Analysis

For each return series we used the following regression model :

$$R_t = \sum_{i=1}^{i=5} B_i D_{it} + e_t \tag{4}$$

where

R_t	=	the return on day t
D1	=	a dummy variable taking the value 1 for a Monday and zero otherwise
D2-5	=	Dummy variables for Tuesday to Friday

The parameter estimates (mean returns) and t statistics from these regressions together with descriptive statistics are presented in Table 2. The regressions were also run in an amended form with four dummy variables plus an intercept term. The F statistics from these regressions enable us to test the hypothesis of equality of daily mean returns and these are also reported in Table 2.

A summary of the autocorrelation coefficients at lags up to five for each of the three Greek return series is presented in Table 3 together with (i) the first order autocorrelation conditional on the day of the week and (ii) the correlation with the previous day price relative of the Dow Jones Industrial Average conditional on the day of the week. The return series, particularly the equally weighted series, have a high level of autocorrelation at lag 1. The equally weighted series also has an order 2 autocorrelation coefficient of .18.

Consequently we repeated the dummy variable regressions on the residuals computed from running an autoregressive model of order p where p = 2 in the case of the equally weighted series and p = 1 in the case of the other two series.

4.2 Discussion of regression results

Unsurprisingly, in view of the fact that our sample contains some relatively thinly traded shares (see Table 1) the equally weighted return series exhibits a high degree of autocorrelation at lag 1 and evidence of autocorrelation at lag 2. In the market value weighted and trade value weighted series the lag 2 autocorrelation disappears and the lag 1 autocorrelation diminishes significantly, particularly in the latter series. However, the first order autocorrelation coefficient remains significantly different from zero in both of these series.

The daily seasonal patterns reported in tables 2 and 4 are similar to those observed in other non-U.S. markets. The return series results reported in Table 2 show a high Friday return and relatively low Tuesday and Wednesday returns. Unusually there is a significantly positive Monday mean return in two of the return series. The hypothesis of equality of mean returns is rejected in each case. The high Monday return disappears when the residuals are tested for seasonality, as shown in Table 4. In fact the most striking difference between the patterns reported in Tables 2 and 4 is this disappearance of the significantly positive Monday return . We also note that our non-parametric and alternative parametric tests (see 4.3 and 4.4 below) do not indicate a high Monday return.

The F statistics reported both in Table 2 and 4, fall as one moves from the equally weighted, through the market value weighted to the trade value weighted series. This suggests that daily seasonality is stronger in small thinly traded issues than in large frequently traded issues. This pattern is similar to that found by researchers of the U.S. market.

Table 2

Descriptive Statistics and Regression Results : Greek Share Price Returns Series (A)

	Monday	Tuesday	Wednesday	Thursday	Friday	All Days	F Stat(B)
	Equally weighted return series						
Mean	.078	-.010	-.056	.003	.139	.030	
Standard Dev.	.645	.611	.552	.603	.570	.600	
Kurtosis	9.20	17.71	2.40	16.53	7.57	11.46	
Skewness	1.86	1.86	0.14	-0.94	1.32	0.89	
N	424	455	460	458	448	2245	
t statistics (C)	2.68**	-.031	-1.94	0.11	4.92***		7.38***
	Market value weighted return series						
Mean	0.070	-.058	-.073	.041	.160	.028	
Standard Dev.	.905	.817	.768	.874	.703	.819	
Kurtosis	7.45	13.33	3.55	19.24	7.57	11.39	
Skewness	0.77	1.16	-0.60	0.15	1.02	0.48	
N	424	455	460	458	448	2245	
t statistics (C)	1.77	-1.47	-1.88	1.06	4.16***		6.17***
	Return series weighted by value traded						
Mean	.102	.000	-.015	.080	.187	.070	
Standard Dev.	1.151	1.048	1.002	1.114	0.937	1.053	
Kurtosis	8.55	13.40	12.16	15.80	16.12	13.03	
Skewness	0.72	-0.94	1.07	0.18	-1.19	-0.11	
N	424	455	460	458	448	2245	
t statistics (C)	1.99*	0.00	-0.28	1.62	3.76***		2.72*

* Significant at 5% level
** Significant at 1% level
*** Significant at 0.1% level

(A) The mean return information is expressed in fractions of a percentage point.

(B) These F Statistics correspond to the regression of the returns against 4 dummy variables, an intercept term being estimated. In each case the number of degrees of freedom in the numerator and denominator are 4 and 2240 respectively.

(C) From regression (see equation (4)).

Table 3

Correlation Analysis

Autocorrelation of Greek share return series 1978-1986			Autocorrelation conditional on day of week			Correlation with price relatives of Dow Jones index conditional on day of week		
Equally weighted return series								
Lag 1	:	.50	Fri-Mon	:	.04	Fri (DJ) - Mon	:	.09
Lag 2	:	.18	Mon-Tues	:	.04	Mon (DJ) - Tues	:	.04
Lag 3	:	.05	Tues-Wed	:	.36	Tues (DJ) - Wed	:	.00
Lag 4	:	.02	Wed-Thurs	:	.57	Wed (DJ) - Thurs	:	.05
Lag 5	:	.00	Thurs-Fri	:	.55	Thurs (DJ) - Fri	:	-.05
Market value weighted return series								
Lag 1	:	.37	Fri-Mon	:	.00	Fri (DJ) - Mon	:	.10
Lag 2	:	.01	Mon-Tues	:	.01	Mon (DJ) - Tues	:	.08
Lag 3	:	-.07	Tues-Wed	:	.25	Tues (DJ) - Wed	:	.03
Lag 4	:	-.05	Wed-Thurs	:	.40	Wed (DJ) - Thurs	:	.10
Lag 5	:	-.03	Thurs-Fri	:	.36	Thurs (DJ) - Fri	:	-.03
Return series weighted by value traded								
Lag 1	:	.28	Fri-Mon	:	.03	Fri (DJ) - Mon	:	.09
Lag 2	:	.03	Mon-Tues	:	.05	Mon (DJ) - Tues	:	.05
Lag 3	:	.02	Tues-Wed	:	.18	Tues (DJ) - Wed	:	.02
Lag 4	:	.01	Wed-Thurs	:	.26	Wed (DJ) - Thurs	:	.07
Lag 5	:	.01	Thurs-Fri	:	.24	Thurs (DJ) - Fri	:	.02

Table 4

Regression Results : Test for seasonality in residuals of autoregression of Greek return series (A)

	Monday	Tuesday	Wednesday	Thursday	Friday	F Stat(B)
Equally weighted return series						
Mean	-.006	-.052	-.059	.017	.120	
t statistics	-0.23	-2.13*	-2.46*	0.72	4.92***	8.82***
Market value weighted return series						
Mean	.006	-.096	-.069	.051	.135	
t statistics	0.15	-2.69**	-1.94	1.42	3.77***	6.80***
Return series weighted by value traded						
Mean	.009	-.071	-.064	.036	.123	
t statistic	0.19	-1.51	-1.36	0.76	2.57*	2.81*

* Significant at 5% level
** Significant at 1% level
*** Significant at 0.1% level

(A) In the case of the equally weighted return series these are the residuals of AR(2). In the other two cases they are the residuals of AR(1).

(B) These F Statistics correspond to the regression of the returns against 4 dummy variables, an intercept term being estimated. In each case the numbers of degrees of freedom in the numerator and denominator are 4 and 2240 respectively.

It is interesting to note that the relationship between weekend return variance and within week return variance in the Greek market is similar to that observed by Fama (1965), Keim and Stambaugh (1984) and Condoyanni, O'Hanlon and Ward (1987) in the U.S. and other markets. For each return series the weekend variance is marginally higher than the variance of each of the other four trading days. The ratios of weekend variance to average within week variance are 1.22, 1.30 and 1.26 for the equally weighted, market value weighted and traded value weighted series respectively. There thus seems to be little evidence to suggest that share returns are generated in calendar time rather than trading time.

There is little evidence to suggest that the observed seasonal patterns are due to the market following the previous day's Wall Street performance. The coefficients of correlation between the Greek market and the previous day's Dow Jones index reported in Table 3 are low and never exceed 0.10.

Finally, we note that the skewness and kurtosis coefficients are in some cases high, as were those observed in a number of non-U.S. markets by Jaffe and Westerfield (1985). These statistics suggest that the assumption of normality may be violated and that our tests need to be supplemlented by inferential procedures which do not rely on such assumptions. The results of our supplementary analysis are presented below.

4.3 Non-parametric tests

In Table 5 we present the results of the application of the non-parametric Kruskal-Wallis test to each of the three return series. This technique uses the rankings of the observations to test the null hypothesis that the mean return for each day is equal to the mean return for every other day. If the null hypothesis is true, the Kruskal-Wallis statistic follows approximately a chi-square distribution with k-1 degrees of freedom where k equals the number of samples (in this case 5).

The patterns are similar to those observed in the regression results. In each case the hypothesis of equality of means is rejected The smallest test statistic is observed in the case of the traded value weighted series, which conforms with the regression finding that the strength of the observed seasonality is at its lowest for this series. The highest average ranking

Table 5

Results of Kruskal-Wallis Tests

Day	Average rank for day less overall average rank (=1123.0)	K.W. statistic
Equally weighted return series		
Monday	19.7	
Tuesday	-61.8	
Wednesday	-93.2	
Thursday	- 5.2	
Friday	145.2	36.57***
Market value weighted return series		
Monday	8.4	
Tuesday	-94.2	
Wednesday	-80.5	
Thursday	30.2	
Friday	139.4	38.50***
Return series weighted by value traded		
Monday	-2.9	
Tuesday	-53.0	
Wednesday	-73.6	
Thursday	21.7	
Friday	109.9	22.37***

*** Significant at 0.1% level

by far is always for Friday, with Tuesday and Wednesday always having the lowest average ranking. The most striking difference between the regression and Kruskal-Wallis results is that there is little evidence of a high Monday return in the non-parametric analysis. This suggests that the positive Monday effect observed in the regression results may have been due to a small number of outliers.

4.4 Alternative parametric tests

In tables 6 and 7, we present the results of a likelihood analysis where it is assumed that the returns may be approximated by a t-distribution. Whilst a number of distributions have been suggested as models of security price returns, there has been little use of these theoretical functions as a basis for drawing inferences in seasonality research. Indeed, in some cases, the potential for inference is severely limited by cumbersome parameterisation of generalised models, as demonstrated by McDonald (1987).

In the case of t, the pertinent properties were discussed by Praetz (1972) and Blattberg and Gonedes (1974) and a solution to the maximum likelihood estimates (MLEs) was given by McLeay (1986). Essentially, t, is a three parameter location-scale-kurtosis model where the third parameter v acts as an index of tail behaviour and offers an infinite variance model where $v < 2$. For our data, MLEs of v were obtained by maximising concentrated log likelihoods over a 0.1 (0.1) 6.0 grid of values of the 'degrees of freedom' parameter v, the location and scale parameters being estimated at each of the fractional values of v using the algorithm given in the Appendix.

For the equally weighted series, the most plausible values of v exceeded 2, but for the market value weighted series and the traded value weighted series, the MLEs were about 2. Furthermore, the limits of the 1% plausibility region (where $L(\hat{\theta}v,\hat{\sigma}v,v)/L(\hat{\theta},\hat{\sigma},\hat{v})=.01$) are for a range of relatively low values of v as shown in Table 6. This demonstrates clearly the pertinence of a model for our data which allows for considerable density in the tails.

For each of the three return series, estimates of $\hat{\theta}$ were obtained for fits of the t_2 model to returns for each of the five days, and compared with the regression means. These results are given in Table 7 along with the maximum

Table 6

Maximum Likelihood Estimation of v

	Monday	Tuesday	Wednesday	Thursday	Friday
Equally Weighted Series	2.3	2.8	3.5	3.1	2.6
Market Value Weighted Series	2.1	2.1	2.6	2.0	2.3
Traded Value Weighted Series	1.9	2.0	2.1	1.7	2.1

Limiting plausible values of v (1% likelihood regions)

	Monday	Tuesday	Wednesday	Thursday	Friday
Equally Weighted Series	1.5/3.8	1.8/4.7	2.1/6.0*	1.9/5.3	1.6/4.4
Market Value Weighted Series	1.4/3.3	1.4/3.4	1.6/4.5	1.3/3.0	1.5/3.8
Traded Value Weighted Series	1.3/3.1	1.3/3.1	1.4/3.2	1.1/2.5	1.4/3.3

* Estimates for fractional values of v were not continued beyond 6.0 but, using integers, it was found that $L(v=6) > L(v=7)$

Table 7

	Regression parameter estimates	θ (v=2)	$\hat{\theta}$ (v=$\hat{v}$)	Plausible region of θ
Equally Weighted Series				
Monday	.078**	-.0170	-.0133	-.0239/ .0013
Tuesday	-.010	-.0589	-.0530	-.0608/-.0448
Wednesday	-.056	-.0697	-.0657	-.0693/-.0626
Thursday	.003	.0025	-.0017	-.0034/ .0031
Friday	.139***	.0786	.0821	.0762/ .0910
Market Value Weighted Series				
Monday	.070	.0130	.0136	.0079/ .0192
Tuesday	-.058	-.0541	-.0545	-.0522/-.0582
Wednesday	-.073	-.0441	-.0472	-.0407/-.0512
Thursday	.041	.0467	.0467	.0480/ .0460
Friday	.160***	.1193	.1210	.1158/ .1269
Traded Value Weighted Series				
Monday	.102*	.0139	.0122	.0002/ .0288
Tuesday	.000	-.0216	-.0216	-.0228/-.0179
Wednesday	-.015	-.0332	-.0331	-.0347/-.0324
Thursday	.080	.0548	.0534	.0509/ .0575
Friday	.187***	.1137	.1161	.0952/ .1366

*	Significant at 5% level
**	Significant at 1% level
***	Significant at 0.1 level

Figure 2

Plausibility Regions for Characteristic Values of Stock Returns Conditional on Day of the Week

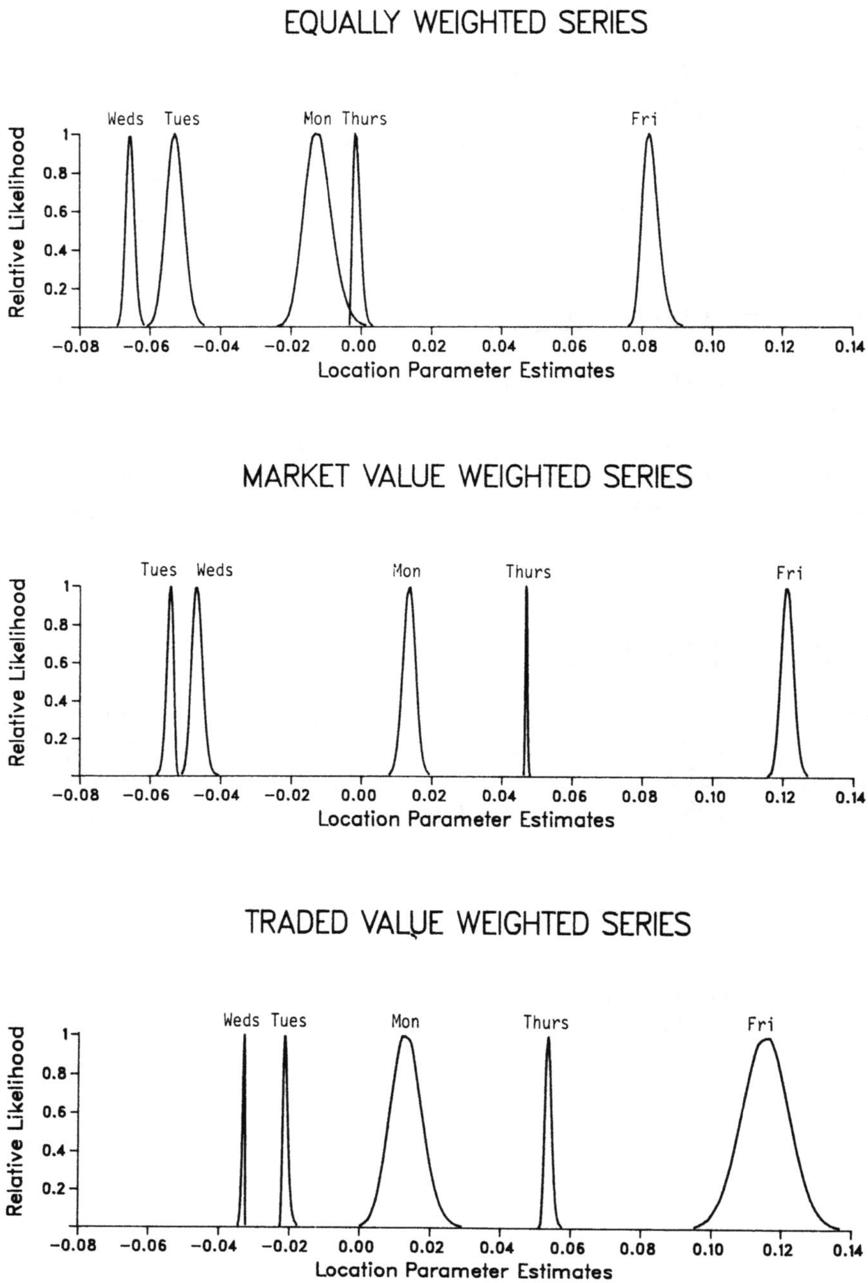

likelihood estimates of θ where $v = \hat{v}$. Although the estimates differ from the regression estimates as a result of the lower weight that is attached to extreme observations in the returns series, our earlier observations concerning positive Friday returns are confirmed in the light of this alternative statistical model. However, it is worth noting that the characteristic value of Monday returns is close to zero for each of the three series.

The results of an analysis of the plausible regions of θ are also reported in Table 7. The parameter of scale σ and the degrees of freedom parameter v were not fixed as nuisance parameters for this test but were allowed to vary, thus providing extreme estimates of the plausibility limits of θ. Likelihood functions were interpolated from the grid and are presented in Figure 2. In effect, these likelihood profiles have been constructed by plotting values of θ over the range of relative likelihoods from RL=.01 to RL=1, and can be interpreted as representations of the plausibility intervals of the (weighted) mean return. The main inferences that can be drawn here are that the characteristic value of returns is relatively high at the end of the week, and negative on Tuesdays and Wednesdays.

4.5 A note on the Settlement Effect

The high Friday returns observed in our tests suggest that the day of the week effect in Greece may be due to the settlement factor which might be expected to increase the observed Friday return and reduce the observed Monday return (see paragraph 2.1.2). The relatively low Friday-Monday autocorrelation also suggest this. To investigate this possibility we calculated the magnitude of the difference between the Friday mean return and the average of the Tuesday, Wednesday and Thursday return and compared this difference with our estimate of the effect of the settlement induced distortion. The latter was computed as two days' interest based on mid-rates quoted for commercial bank operations in Greece during the period. In estimating this effect we assumed that all transactions were "cash" rather than "account" transactions and it is therefore probable that we overestimated the effect of the settlement distortion. Our examination of the regression results indicated that the difference in the mean returns was, depending on the return series, between 1.9 and 2.3 times greater than the (probably excessive) estimate of settlement distortion. Examination of the maximum likelihood estimates of the location parameters computed in our alternative parametric tests indicated that the ratio of return difference to settlement distortion ranged from 1.4 to 1.7. Settlement factors may thus provide a partial explanation of the high Friday return. However, we note the absence of a corresponding abnormally low Monday return which one would expect to observe if settlement factors alone were responsible for the high Friday return.

5. Conclusions

In this paper we have tested for daily return seasonality in the ASE using regression analysis, a non-parametric test and a parametric technique which does not assume normality. The daily seasonal patterns appear similar to those observed elsewhere in the world. Returns appear to be low early in the week and high later in the week, particularly on Friday. It is likely that part of the high Friday return can be explained by settlement factors but this is not a complete explanation. The patterns observed may be indicative of weak form inefficiency in the Greek market but it is unlikely that the magnitude of the daily return differences would be such as to permit the profitable use of mechanical trading rules. Furthermore, the results of the regression analysis suggest that the observed seasonality may be stronger in small relatively thinly traded issues than in larger more frequently traded issues.

Appendix

The density function of standard t with v degrees of freedom is

$$f(t_v) = \left[v^{\frac{1}{2}} B(\tfrac{1}{2},\tfrac{1}{2}v) \left(1 + \frac{t^2}{v}\right)^{(v+1)/2} \right]^{-1}$$

where Beta (B) is indexed on the degrees of freedom parameter, v.

As $v \to \infty$, the distribution of t will tend to the standard Normal density with $\lim f(t_v) = 2\pi^{-\frac{1}{2}} e^{-\frac{1}{2}t^2}$. Thus, the Normal ($t_\infty$) is the limiting case and has the least tail density. When v = 1, the function again simplifies and t_1 has a Cauchy distribution, where $f(t_1) = [\pi(1 + t^2)]^{-1}$.

For a variable y, with location parameter θ and scale parameter σ, the likelihood function for a sample size n from the t-distribution is given by :

$$L = \prod_{i=1}^{n} \left[\frac{1}{\sigma} \frac{1}{\sqrt{v}} \frac{1}{B(\frac{1}{2},\frac{1}{2}v)} \frac{1}{\left(1 + \frac{1}{v}\left(\frac{y_i - \theta}{\sigma}\right)^2\right)^{(v+1)/2}} \right] \qquad (1)$$

As it is easier to maximise log L than L, it helps to re-express equation (1) as the log likelihood function :

$$\log L = -n\log\sigma - \frac{n}{2} \log v - n\log B(\tfrac{1}{2},\tfrac{1}{2}v) - \frac{v+1}{2} \sum_{i=1}^{n} \log\left(1 + \frac{1}{v}\left(\frac{y_i - \theta}{\sigma}\right)^2\right) \qquad (2)$$

For any fixed value of v, the most plausible estimates of θ_v and σ_v will be obtained when log L is maximised. Accordingly, the likelihood equations are partial derivatives, first with respect to the parameter of location, θ

$$\frac{\partial \log L}{\partial \theta} = \frac{v+1}{2} \sum_{i=1}^{n} \frac{\frac{2}{\sigma v}\left(\frac{y_i-\theta}{\sigma}\right)}{1+\frac{1}{v}\left(\frac{y_i-\theta}{\sigma}\right)^2} = 0 \tag{3}$$

and, second, with respect to σ^2

$$\frac{\partial \log L}{\partial \sigma^2} = \frac{-n}{2\sigma^2} + \frac{v+1}{2} \sum_{i=1}^{n} \frac{\frac{1}{v\sigma^2}\left(\frac{y_i-\theta}{\sigma}\right)^2}{1+\frac{1}{v}\left(\frac{y_i-\theta}{\sigma}\right)^2} = 0 \tag{4}$$

For numerical solution, a weight may be set which, at the jth iteration, will be

$$w_{i(j)} = \frac{1}{1+\frac{1}{v}\left(\frac{y_i-\theta_{(j-1)}}{\sigma_{(j-1)}}\right)^2} \tag{5}$$

Therefore, for any one t-density, an iterative solution to the maximum likelihood estimates of parameters of location and scale will be given by :

$$\theta_{(j)} = \frac{\Sigma y_i w_{i(j)}}{\Sigma w_{i(j)}} \tag{6}$$

and

$$\sigma^2_{(j)} = \frac{v+1}{vn} \sum_{i=1}^{n} w_{i_{(j)}} (y_i - \theta_{(j)})^2 \tag{7}$$

Note that the weight given in equation (5) is the kernel of the probability function.

For any one value of the degrees of freedom parameter v, convergence to $\hat{\theta}_v$ and $\hat{\sigma}_v$ will be achieved with the algorithm given by equations (5), (6) and (7). Thus, for a fixed degree of freedom, the concentrated likelihood will reach its maximum at $L(\hat{\theta}_v, \hat{\sigma}_v)$. It follows that the likelihood function given in equation (1) will reach its maximum value at $L(\hat{\theta},\hat{\sigma},\hat{v})$ where $\hat{v}$ is the maximum likelihood estimate of the degrees of freedom parameter. Alternatively, the best supported combination of all three parameters may be found by repeated solution of equation (2) over a three-dimensional array in θ, σ and v. Maximisation of the array will identify $t_{\hat{v}}$ (the most plausible t-distribution for the data) and its maximum likelihood estimates of location and scale, $\hat{\theta}$ and $\hat{\sigma}$. Furthermore, the ratio of likelihoods RL = $L(\theta,\sigma,v)/L(\hat{\theta},\hat{\sigma},\hat{v})$ will indicate the relative likelihood of any particular combination of parameter values and, consequently, inferences about the plausibility of parameter values may be based on a direct likelihood ratio test.

References

Blattberg, R.C., and N.J. Gonedes, 1974, "A Comparison of the Stable and Student Distribution as Statistical Models for Stock Prices", Journal of Business, 47, pp. 244-280.

Bletsas, A.D., and S.G. Tebbutt, 1984 "Efficiency of the Greek Stock Market : An Empirical Investigation", in G.A. Hawawini and P.A. Michel, eds., European Equity Markets : Risk Return and Efficiency (Garland Publishing Inc., New York and London) pp.335-365.

Choy, A. and J. O'Hanlon ,1988, (forthcoming) "Day of the Week Effects in the U.K. Equity Market : A Cross Sectional Analysis" Journal of Business Finance and Accounting, forthcoming.

Condoyanni, L., J. O'Hanlon and C.W.R. Ward ,1987, "Day of the Week Effects on Stock Returns : International Evidence", Journal of Business Finance and Accounting 14, pp.159-174.

Cross, F. ,1973, "The Behaviour of Stock Prices on Fridays and Mondays", Financial Analysts Journal, pp.67-69.

Dyl, E.A. and S.A. Martin ,1985, "Weekend Effects on Stock Returns : A Comment" Journal of Finance, 40, pp.347-352.

Fama, E.F.,1965, "The Behaviour of Stock Market Prices", Journal of Business, 38, pp.34-105.

Frantzmann, H.J., 1987, "Return and Pricing Seasonalities in the German Stock Market", presented at the meeting of the European Finance Association, Madrid, August 1987.

French, K.R., 1980, "Stock Returns and the Weekend Effect", Journal of Financial Economics, 8, pp.55-69.

Gibbons, M.R. and P. Hess, 1981, "Day of the Week Effects and Asset Returns", Journal of Business, 54, 579-596.

Harris, L., 1986, "A Transaction Data Study of Weekly and Intradaily Patterns in Stock Returns", Journal of Financial Economics, 16, pp.99-117.

Jaffe, J. and R. Westerfield ,1985, "The Week-end Effect in Common Stock Returns : The International Evidence" Journal of Finance, 40, pp.433-454.

Jensen, M. ,1978, "Some anomalous evidence regarding market efficiency" Journal of Financial Economics, 6, pp.95-101.

Keim, D. ,1987, "Daily returns and size related premiums : one more time" Journal of Portfolio Management, Winter 1987, pp.41-47.

Keim, D. and R. Stambaugh ,1984, "A further investigation of the day of the week effect in stock returns", Journal of Finance, 39, pp.819-840.

Lakonishok, J. and M. Levi ,1982, "Weekend effects on stock returns : A note", Journal of Finance, 37, pp.883-889.

McDonald, J.B., 1987, "A General Distribution for Describing Security Price Returns", Journal of Business, 60, pp. 401-424.

McLeay, S.J., 1986, "Student's t and the Distribution of Financial Ratios", Journal of Business Finance and Accounting, 12, pp. 209-222.

O'Hanlon, J. and P. Papaspirou ,1988, "The daily behaviour of national equity markets : Seasonal patterns and inter-relationships", forthcoming Investment Analyst, July 1988.

Papaioannou, G. ,1983, "Thinness and short run price dependence in the Athens Stock Exchange", Greek Economic Review, 1983, pp.315-333.

Penman, S. ,1987, "The distribution of earnings news over time and seasonalities in aggregate stock returns", Journal of Financial Economics, 18, pp.199-228.

Praetz, P.D., 1972, "The Distribution of Share Price Changes", Journal of Business, 45, pp.49-55.

Rogalski, R. ,1984, "New findings regarding day of the week returns over trading and non-trading periods", Journal of Finance, 39, pp.1603-1614.

Santesmases, M. ,1986, "An investigation of the Spanish stock market seasonalities, Journal of Business Finance and Accounting, 13, 267-276.

Theobald, M. and V. Price ,1984, "Seasonality estimation in thin markets", Journal of Finance, 39, 377-392.

Comments on Condoyanni, O'Hanlon and McLeay

"An Investigation of Daily Seasonality in the Greek Equity Market"

by Donald B. Keim

This paper examines stock returns on the Athens Stock Exchange (ASE) for evidence of the daily pattern in returns that has been documented for numerous other exchanges. Using both parametric and non-parametric tests, the authors find a day-of-the-week pattern similar to that documented previously for European, Japanese and Australian exchanges -- to wit, stock returns tend to be low in the beginning of the week and highest on Friday. Also, consistent with other results for Japan and Australia, Monday returns are positive, perhaps because the ASE closes on Monday before the NYSE opens.

Results like these are now so familiar that if the same patterns didn't emerge in new data, we would consider the findings anomalous. Nevertheless, I find this paper interesting and useful since verification of prior research with new data is important. The authors have done an admirable job of both creating from scratch a new data file and presenting the results of their empirical investigation. If there is a major deficiency in the paper, it is the lack of any serious attempt to test hypotheses relating to explanations for these daily patterns. The authors expend considerable econometric effort to demonstrate the existence of a daily pattern that is obvious from inter-occular inspection. This effort may have received a bigger payoff had it been spent on trying to explain the daily pattern. At this stage, further documentation is helpful, but explanation should be the main goal. Of course that is a lot to ask; and I certainly don't want to diminish the contribution of this paper for failing to accomplish what no one else in this literature has been able to do. The authors do direct some discussion to the possibility of settlement

NATO ASI Series, Vol. F54
A Reappraisal of the Efficiency of Financial Markets
Edited by Rui M. C. Guimaraes et al.

factors accounting for a high Friday - low Monday pattern, but this seems a bit misdirected since that pattern is not evident in the Greek data (Tuesday's return is lowest). I would have thought that measurment error in prices would have been a more natural avenue to pursue, given the thinness of trading and (likely) high bid-ask spreads in this market.

I would like to briefly make some additional detailed comments regarding the data and generality of the results. The authors have done a very careful job of constructing their data file. Unfortunately, they are dealing with a small number of stocks (28) over a very short time period (9 years), which makes generalizations quite difficult. If these 28 stocks represent the bulk of the market both in market value and trading volume, then things aren't so bad. However, comparisons to the U.S. or other European markets over this same 9-year period would be helpful. Biases always creep into empirical work, and this paper is no exception. I worry that the sample of 28 firms used here is heavily tilted towards banks and financial institutions (55% of the daily observations belong to these firms) and that the 3-year survival requirement may be a problem.

Finally, thinness of trading on the ASE prompted the authors to construct several alternative aggregate return measures. The intra-week patterns aren't very sensitive to the construction of the index, but the distribution statistics estimated over all days (Table 2) seem to be dependent on the method of index construction. My priors would have suggested that the value-weighted and the value-traded indexes would have been more similar, but the results show that the equal- and the value-weighted indexes were more similar. The value-traded index has a substantially higher mean and standard deviation. Apparently, market values don't differ very much across firms on the ASE and the more actively traded stocks have considerably different return distributions. Examination of the individual stock returns for both day-of-the-week patterns and for overall return distribution differences would be informative.

RANDOM WALKS AND ANOMALIES ON THE COPENHAGEN STOCK EXCHANGE IN THE 1890´S

L. Peter Jennergren
Stockholm School of Economics
Box 6501
S-11383 Stockholm, Sweden

Bjarne G. Sörensen
Odense University
Campusvej 55
DK-5230 Odense M, Denmark

Keywords / Abstract: random walk / weak-form efficiency / autocorrelations / runs / anomalies / week-day effect / month effect / ex-day effect

Using daily price data for 25 stocks for the period 1890 - 1900, we investigate price formation on the Copenhagen Stock Exchange. The usual random walk tests are reported on. After that, we give results of some anomalies tests, concerning week-day, month-of-the-year, and ex-day effects. We find deviations from the random walk hypothesis of about the same magnitude as have been found for the Scandinavian stock markets in more recent times. As for anomalies, there is very weak evidence of a Monday effect, a rather strong January effect, and a slightly smaller than expected price fall on ex-dividend days.

1. Introduction

There has been trading in stocks for as long as there have been corporations. Until the 19th century, this trading went on in a rather unorganized fashion, whereever merchants met, for instance in public houses (pubs). However, eventually it became necessary to provide a more formal institutional set-up. Several of the stock exhanges which exist today were founded in the 19th century, for instance the ones in Brussels (1801), London (1802), New York (1817), and Tokyo (1878).

This development also took place in Denmark. Copenhagen is an old trading town, and trading in stocks can be traced back

NATO ASI Series, Vol. F54
A Reappraisal of the Efficiency of Financial Markets
Edited by Rui M. C. Guimaraes et al.

to the 17th century. Daily trading on the Copenhagen Stock Exchange started in 1823. Around 1840 an auction system of trading was introduced, actually the same system which is used even today (an electronic system is now gradually introduced, in 1988). The number of shares quoted on the Copenhagen Stock Exchange was very small until the end of the 19th century, though. Industrialization started in Denmark around 1870, and a number of corporations became listed on the Copenhagen Stock Exchange as a consequence. From around 1880, a stock market, as we think of it today, may be said to exist in Denmark.

A vast number of empirical studies of stock markets all over the world have been undertaken in the last 25 years. These studies have given deep insights into financial markets. The functioning of present-day markets is discussed using concepts such as market efficiency and anomalies, and these concepts are related to specific institutional aspects of the various stock exchanges. An interesting research issue in this connection is whether the evidence of efficiency and anomalies which we know from present-day markets can also be detected in stock market data from earlier times. We are now seeing an increasing number of empirical investigations using older stock market data. This article belongs to that line of research, since our data set consists of daily price quotes for 25 Danish stocks for the period 1890 - 1900.

In the next section, we mention some facts about the Copenhagen Stock Exchange in the 1890's and about our data set. After that, in Section 3, we give results of market efficiency tests. We are only concerned with <u>weak efficiency</u>, which is related to the question whether or not quoted stock market prices reflect previous price movements. In particular, we use two conventional random walk tests and compare the results with findings from several investigations of present-day stock markets in Scandinavia. This section draws upon an earlier paper by ourselves (Jennergren and Sörensen 1986).

Sections 4 - 7 are concerned with market anomalies. This is a designation for certain puzzling patterns in stock market price formation which have been discovered in recent years, including abnormal returns on particular week days and months.

As an introduction to that topic, Section 4 mentions some aspects of the income tax system in Denmark in the 1890´s, since tax effects have sometimes been suggested as explanations for anomalies. Section 5 investigates the week-day effect, and Section 6 the month effect. Section 7 deals with the ex-day effect, that is whether or not quoted prices fall as expected on days when the stocks go ex-dividend.

Section 8 contains concluding remarks.

2. The Copenhagen Stock Exchange in the 1890´s, and our Data

In the last century, as well as today, only certified brokers were allowed to trade on the Copenhagen Stock Exchange. In the 1890´s, there were 52 such brokers. The Exchange was open six days a week (i. e., including Saturdays). Trading was by auction, as already mentioned. The Exchange convened at 1:30 p.m. and closed around 3:00 p.m.

The daily auction was conducted by a leader, who called out the stocks in a specified order. For each stock, the brokers signaled their offers to buy and sell. A transaction was carried out whenever there were matching buy and sell offers. All transactions concerned a given block size, normally 2000 Crowns in nominal value. When there were no more matches between buy and sell offers, the auction leader moved on to the next stock. All transactions had to be settled in cash, before 12:00 noon on the following week day (i. e., Saturday transactions had to be paid for before noon the following Monday).

Most of the stocks were quoted in percent of their nominal values. The smallest price change permitted was 0.25%. The prices which were recorded, then as well as now, were transaction prices, bid prices, and ask prices. Transaction prices are prices at which transactions actually take place. Bid prices are the highest buy offer prices remaining after all matching buy and sell offers have been eliminated. Ask prices are the lowest sell offer prices remaining at that point. If the gap between buy and sell prices was more than 2 percentage points, no bid price was quoted that day. The prices were written down in a large record book, one for each year. The data for this investigation have been copied from those record books.

In the 1890´s, there were around 40 - 45 stocks listed on the Copenhagen Stock Exchange (actually, on the "main" Exchange; some additional 30 stocks were traded in supplementary trading sessions on Wednesdays). The volume of actual transactions on the Exchange was rather limited. However, the prices quoted also served as guidelines for transactions which took place outside the Exchange.

For our investigation, we have collected daily price quotes for 25 stocks during the 11 years 1890 - 1900. During this period, the Stock Exchange was open 3335 days and closed 108 days due to holidays during Mondays through Saturdays. The price data are bid prices, with transaction prices substituted in a few cases where the latter are available but not the former. The alternative, using transaction prices only, would not have been feasible, since there were rather few transactions on the whole during that time period, as just mentioned. Moreover, bid prices, then as well as today, have always been considered in Denmark as "the official" price quotes and the ones which most fairly reflect real stock values. Even using bid prices, there are gaps in the price series, though. Actually, only one stock of the 25 in our sample was quoted every single day out of the 3335 during the period 1890 - 1900.

Our criteria for including a particular stock in the sample of 25 were, in the first place, that it should have been listed on the Exchange during the period 1890 - 1900, or at least during most of that period. Secondly, it should have been quoted reasonably often, in order to avoid too many gaps in the price series. The 25 stocks which are included in our investigation are certainly among the most important Danish ones from that period. As for the breakdown into industries, there are 7 banks, 6 shipping lines, 11 manufacturing firms, and one tramway company.

In addition to the price quotes, our data set includes information about dividends and rights issues. Several of the tests to be discussed in what follows refer to rates of return from holding stocks from one day to the next. The <u>rate of return from holding stock i from day t-1 to day t</u> is

$$R_{it} = [\ln(P_{it} + D_{it} + T_{it}) - \ln(P_{i,t-1})]x100,$$

where

R_{it}	rate of return on stock i between days t-1 and t,
P_{it}	price of stock i on day t,
D_{it}	amount of dividends paid after day t-1 up to and including day t,
T_{it}	value of rights for new issues occurring after day t-1 up to and including day t,
$P_{i,t-1}$	price of stock i on day t-1.

The value of a right is computed in accordance with the usual formula in finance text books; see, e. g., Brealey and Myers 1984, p. 310. The rate of return R_{it} will sometimes be referred to as "log price difference" in what follows.

3. Random Walk Tests: Autocorrelations and Runs

In this section, we give results from two simple random walk tests. According to the <u>random walk hypotehsis</u>, successive stock price changes are independent and identically distributed random variables. This hypothesis is now recognized to be a special case of weak market efficiency (cf. Fama 1970). Weak market efficiency is actually all that we can hope to test in the case of the Danish stock market in the 1890´s. Semistrong efficiency, whether or not current stock prices accurately reflect all public information, cannot be investigated, since we do not know the precise dates when specific events took place or particular items of information became public. For instance, we cannot really say whether the Danish stock market in the 1890´s accurately reflected the information in annual earnings announcements, since we cannot establish the dates when those announcements were made. Strong efficiency, whether private or privileged information as well is accurately reflected in the prices of stocks, is of course very hard to test in any case, regardless of the time period under consideration.

The two random walk tests are autocorrelations and runs. These tests are very well known and have been applied to a multitude of stock markets all over the world. Hence we may merely refer to the classical article by Fama (1965) for definitions and formulas.

Using daily data, we have derived a series of log price differences for each stock in our sample. For each such series, we have computed autocorrelation coefficients for various lags. Table 1 gives the average (i. e., averaged over the 25 stocks in the sample) autocorrelation coefficient for daily data, lag 1, for our investigation, as well as for a number of other studies of present-day stock markets in Scandinavia. When using daily data, we have simply ignored gaps due to missing price quotes (the same procedure has usually been used in the other studies cited in Table 1 as well). We have also derived another series of log price differences for each stock, by taking weekly data (i. e., the first price observation in each week). In this case, i. e., using weekly data, we have filled in gaps by substituting for each missing weekly observation the previous week´s price. Table 1 also gives the average autocorrelation coefficient for weekly data, lag 1.

Apparently, the Danish stock market in the 1890´s is rather similar to the Scandinavian markets in more recent periods. There is no evidence of the 1890´s being less efficient, as measured by deviations from randomness (i. e., deviations from autocorrelations equal to zero), than more recent periods. There is a difference, though, in that the individual autocorrelation coefficients for daily data and lag 1 are sometimes negative (13 cases out of 25). In the other investigations of Scandinavian stock markets in recent periods, the corresponding individual coefficients are almost all positive. For longer lags, the individual autocorrelations on the Copenhagen Exchange in the 1890´s are usually rather small.

Using the same series of daily and weekly log price differences, we have computed standardized runs test variables

Table 1. Autocorrelations for the Danish Stock Market in the 1890´s and for Scandinavian Markets in More Recent Periods (Lag = 1)

Country	Period	Number of stocks	Mean auto-correlation	Mean absolute autocorrelation	Source
<u>1. Daily data</u>					
Denmark	1890-1900	25	-0.011	0.089	a
Denmark	1973-1975	15	0.166	0.166	b
Finland	1970-1981	11	0.233		c
Finland	1977-1981	60	0.1514		c
Norway	1967-1971	15	0.068	0.083	d
Sweden	1967-1971	30	0.102	0.109	d
Sweden	1978-1984	49	0.081	0.0827	e
<u>2. Weekly data</u>					
Denmark	1890-1900	25	-0.027	0.062	a
Denmark	1975-1985	15	-0.144	0.148	a

Sources:
a Jennergren and Sörensen 1986
b Sörensen 1982, p. 3.11
c Berglund et al. 1983
d Jennergren and Korsvold 1975
e Claesson 1986, p. 66

(standardized deviations from expected number of runs), for each of the 25 stocks in the sample. Average results are given in Table 2, together with similar results from more recent times. Once more, we note that the Danish stock market in the 1890´s appears to be similar to Scandinavian markets more recently. Using daily data, all individual standardized deviations from expected number of runs are negative, as is generally the case in the other Scandinavian studies. The

Table 2. Standardized Deviations from Expected Number of Runs for the Danish Stock Market in the 1890´s and for Scandinavian Markets in More Recent Periods

Country	Period	Number of stocks	Mean stand. deviation	Mean absolute stand. deviation	Source
1. Daily data					
Denmark	1890-1900	25	-6.915	6.915	a
Denmark	1973-1975	15	-5.05	5.05	f
Finland	1970-1981	11	-6.5	6.5	c
Finland	1977-1981	60	-2.7		c
Norway	1967-1971	15	-4.69	4.69	d
Sweden	1967-1971	30	-4.64	4.64	d
2. Weekly data					
Denmark	1890-1900	25	-1.265	1.506	a
Denmark	1975-1985	15	-6.013	6.013	a

Sources:

a Jennergren and Sörensen 1986

c Berglund et al. 1983

d Jennergren and Korsvold 1975

f Jennergren and Toft-Nielsen 1977

average standardized deviation for the Danish stocks in the 1890´s is somewhat higher in absolute value than the other averages in Table 2 for daily data. On the other hand, the corresponding standardized deviation for weekly data is relatively small in absolute value.

It may also be mentioned that the empirical distributions of log price differences for our data set, daily as well as weekly, exhibit the same leptokurtic tendency which has been found in many studies of present-day stock markets, including the Scandinavian ones. That is, those distributions have too many observations near the mean and too fat tails and hence are not normal.

To sum up, the autocorrelation and runs tests of our data from the Copenhagen Stock Exchange in the 1890´s have indicated the same types of consistent deviations from randomness as the ones which have been found in many other investigations of small stock markets using more recent data. In general, one would have to conclude that there does not seem to be any fundamental difference between the Danish stock market in the period 1890 - 1900 and its latter-day Scandinavian counterparts.

4. Taxes on Dividends and Capital Gains in Denmark in the 1890´s

Before turning to our next topic, anomalies, we mention a few words about the Danish tax system in the 1890´s. It was rather different from today´s system. There were direct taxes both to the state and to the municipalities (towns and cities). There was only one direct state tax, levied on real estate. There were two direct municipal taxes, imposed on real estate and income. The only kind of tax which is relevant for the present investigation is thus the municipal tax on income, which included dividends and capital gains.

The income tax assessment was different from one municipality to another. In the towns, it was based mainly on subjective estimates of the economic situation of each citizen. In the cities, there were formal procedures based on income tax statements, somewhat like the procedure in use in Denmark today. In Copenhagen, in particular, there was an established tax authority. The income tax in that city was regulated by a national law from 1861. In that law, it was stipulated that all interest and dividend income from bonds, shares of stock, and other financial instruments was subject to income tax. The same also applied to capital gains from selling shares of stock and other securities. Capital losses were not deductible, except for brokers and other individuals dealing with financial instruments.

In a very informative article about the income tax in

Copenhagen written by a local tax inspector, it is stated that capital gains were often realized through buying and selling a share of stock in the same year; capital gains of this type were rarely included in the income tax assessments (Jensen 1890, p. 487). It would thus appear that tax cheating was a known phenomenon already in the 1890's.

Assessed incomes were taxed at a very low rate. In Copenhagen, that rate was around 3% in the 1890's. In some other cities and towns, it was somewhat higher (betweeen 4% and 10%). In addition, it must have been very easy to cheat in one's income tax statements. For these reasons, we surmise that tax considerations were of rather minor importance in connection with stock investments on the Copenhagen Stock Exchange in the 1890's.

5. The Week-Day Effect

In this section and the subsequent one, we investigate anomalies related to specific days and months. For that purpose, we use an index for the Danish stock market in the 1890's and check that index for unusual returns. Our index has been constructed as follows: The first day in the series is Thursday, January 2, 1890. The index for that day is 100. The last day is Monday, December 31, 1900. For a given stock i, the rate of return from holding that stock from some day t-1 when it was quoted to the subsequent day t when it was also quoted is R_{it}, as defined in section 2. Let C_{it} be the nominal amount of equity capital in company i on day t. The rate of return on the stock market as a whole on day t is then

$$R_{Mt} = (\Sigma R_{it} x P_{it} x C_{it})/(\Sigma P_{it} x C_{it}),$$

where the summations are over those stocks which were quoted that day t (also remember that the price quotes P_{it} are in percent of the nominal values, as mentioned in Section 2). The market rate of return R_{Mt} is hence a weighted average of the individual stock rates of return. It is defined to be zero for week days when the Exchange was closed. Let I_t be the index value for some day t. I_{t+1} is then computed as

$$I_{t+1} = I_t x[1+(R_{Mt}/100)].$$

That is, we use our sample of the 25 most important stocks on the Copenhagen Stock Exchange to construct an index for that stock market. The index fluctuates around 100 during 1890 - 1893. After that, it rises rather steadily to around 165 at the end of 1900. In our earlier paper (Jennergren and Sörensen 1986), we discuss in some detail our index and how it reflects various Danish and international political and economic developments.

Now consider the week-day effect on the Copenhagen Stock Exchange in the 1890's. We have computed the rate of return on our index between all adjacent days t and t+1 when the Stock Exchange was open, as follows:

$$[\ln(I_{t+1}) - \ln(I_t)]x100.$$

All pairs of adjacent days when the Exchange was closed on day t+1 or day t (or both), due to holidays falling on Monday through Saturday, have been deleted. Table 3 exhibits the average returns, for the different week days.

Table 3 displays results for the total period 1890 - 1900 and for the two subperiods 1890 - 1892 and 1893 - 1900. The reason for this division into subperiods is that the index is fairly stable around the level 100 for the first three years, and rises after that, as already mentioned. In that fashion, we can see whether there are differences in returns for the various week days depending on general market conditions.

The week-day effect has attracted a fair amount of attention in the recent literature. For the US, it has been shown that Monday returns are the smallest on the average (actually negative; cf. Smirlock and Starks 1986 for one recent paper which also contains references to earlier contributions). For other stock markets, there may be similar Tuesday effects (for instance, Japan and Australia; cf. Jaffe and Westerfield 1985). In her investigation of the Swedish stock market in the period 1978 - 1984, Kerstin Claesson also found a Tuesday effect (Claesson 1986, pp. 117-128). That is, Tuesday had the

Table 3. Return on the Index for the Danish Stock Market in the 1890´s, for Different Week Days

Day	Number of observations	Mean return	Standard deviation
1. 1890 - 1900			
Monday	538	0.00878	0.15120
Tuesday	536	0.01366	0.13048
Wednesday	559	0.01236	0.14934
Thursday	543	0.02121	0.14734
Friday	532	0.02707	0.12638
Saturday	540	0.01160	0.13373
All days	3248	0.01574	0.14033
F ratio, 5 and 3242 degrees of freedom: 1.3061			
2. 1890 - 1892			
Monday	148	-0.01172	0.19450
Tuesday	148	0.00180	0.14635
Wednesday	154	0.00365	0.18045
Thursday	147	-0.01218	0.13533
Friday	143	0.03732	0.12867
Saturday	147	0.00613	0.15316
All days	887	0.00399	0.15936
F ratio, 5 and 881 degrees of freedom: 1.8597			
3. 1893 - 1900			
Monday	390	0.01656	0.13023
Tuesday	388	0.01819	0.12359
Wednesday	405	0.01567	0.13551
Thursday	396	0.03361	0.14967
Friday	389	0.02330	0.12532
Saturday	393	0.01365	0.12563
All days	2361	0.02016	0.13221
F ratio, 5 and 2355 degrees of freedom: 1.2225			

smallest mean return (negative; the other week days had positive mean returns).

In our case, it is seen in Table 3 that the rate of return on Mondays is the smallest, although positive, for the entire period 1890 - 1900. For the two subperiods, however, other week days have smaller mean returns. The differences between the week days are not significant at the 5% level.

Thus, our data contain only very weak evidence of a possible Monday effect. If one accepts that effect, then the question is why. The most obvious explanation relates to the rules for paying for transactions. As mentioned earlier, all transactions on the Copenhagen Exchange had to be settled before noon the following week day. This means that an individual purchasing shares on a Saturday had one extra day of interest before settling on Monday morning. This would result in slightly higher Saturday prices, which would show up as a higher mean return on Saturdays and a lower mean return on Mondays. This pattern, however, is not exhibited in Table 3: Monday as well as Saturday mean returns are comparatively low, both for the entire period 1890 - 1900 and the two subperiods.

6. The Month Effect

The month effect refers to higher mean returns from holding stocks in certain months than in others. In particular, many investigations have documented higher mean returns for the month of January. The most common explanation for this January effect is tax considerations. That is, investors wish to reduce taxes by realizing capital losses at the end of the year, thereby depressing stock prices in December. Things return to normal at the beginning of the following year, leading to excessive returns in January. This explanation is part of finance industry folk lore, also in Denmark, as evidenced for instance by an article in the business daily Börsen of Dec. 3, 1987, entitled "Manufacturing Industry Shares Should be Bought in December".

The January effect is well established by now, but the empirical evidence as regards the tax explanation of that effect is somewhat mixed. For instance, one recent study of the London Stock Exchange (Reinganum and Shapiro 1987) provides some support, since there was no unusual mean January return prior to the introduction of capital gains taxation in 1965; but this changed after that year. Another recent study of the Toronto Stock Exchange (Tinic et al. 1987) finds turn-of-the-year effects both prior to and after the introduction of capital gains taxation in Canada in 1972. Yet another recent study (Jones et al. 1987) finds a greater than average January return on the New York Stock Exchange both before and after the 1917 tax act, which apparently marked the beginning of effective income taxes in the US. The Jones et al. study draws on data series starting in 1871 and is hence one of the empirical investigations using older stock market data alluded to in the introduction to this article.

We have computed average returns on our index for each month of the year (averaged over the years 1890 - 1900). Results are displayed in Table 4. The return on the index for any one month has been calculated by considering the first and last week days in the month on which the Stock Exchange was open. It is seen that the January mean return is the largest one, followed by December. The hypothesis that all months have the same mean return can be rejected at the 2.5% significance level.

The fact that December has the second highest mean return indicates that the January effect may actually start already at the end of December, as suggested by Roll (1983), among others. That is, the January effect may really be a turn-of-the-year effect. In order to investigate this possibility, one may consider "displaced" months. This is done in the second part of Table 4: Each month is taken to begin on the 17th of the previous month. That is, January begins on December 17 and ends on January 16, and so on. This type of displacement apparently accentuates the month effect. The hypothesis that all months have the same mean return can now be rejected at the 1% level.

In order to see the turn-of-the-year effect more clearly, one may examine the development of the index around January 1. For each year 1890 to 1899, we normalize the index to be 100 on

Table 4. Return on the Index for the Danish Stock Market in the 1890's, for Different Months

Month	Number of observations	Mean return	Standard deviation
1. Calendar months			
January	11	1.08944	1.05228
February	11	0.11126	1.03702
March	11	0.05016	1.12975
April	11	0.71028	0.70219
May	11	0.02814	0.83074
June	11	0.77478	0.66242
July	11	0.12848	0.34459
August	11	-0.01345	1.28874
September	11	0.24790	0.76504
October	11	-0.14719	0.86536
November	11	0.51574	1.29360
December	11	1.06806	0.82973
All months	132	0.38030	1.02612
F ratio, 11 and 120 degrees of freedom: 2.1477			
2. Each month starting on the 17th of the previous month			
January	10	1.45957	1.20516
February	11	0.28475	0.81888
March	11	-0.35414	0.99609
April	11	0.49155	1.06975
May	11	0.06890	1.06153
June	11	0.63477	0.35505
July	11	0.28071	0.65132
August	11	-0.03283	0.96262
September	11	0.28971	0.99605
October	11	0.03970	0.96919
November	11	-0.00635	0.77422
December	11	0.80789	0.89129
All months	131	0.32173	1.02182
F ratio, 11 and 119 degrees of freedom: 2.5579			

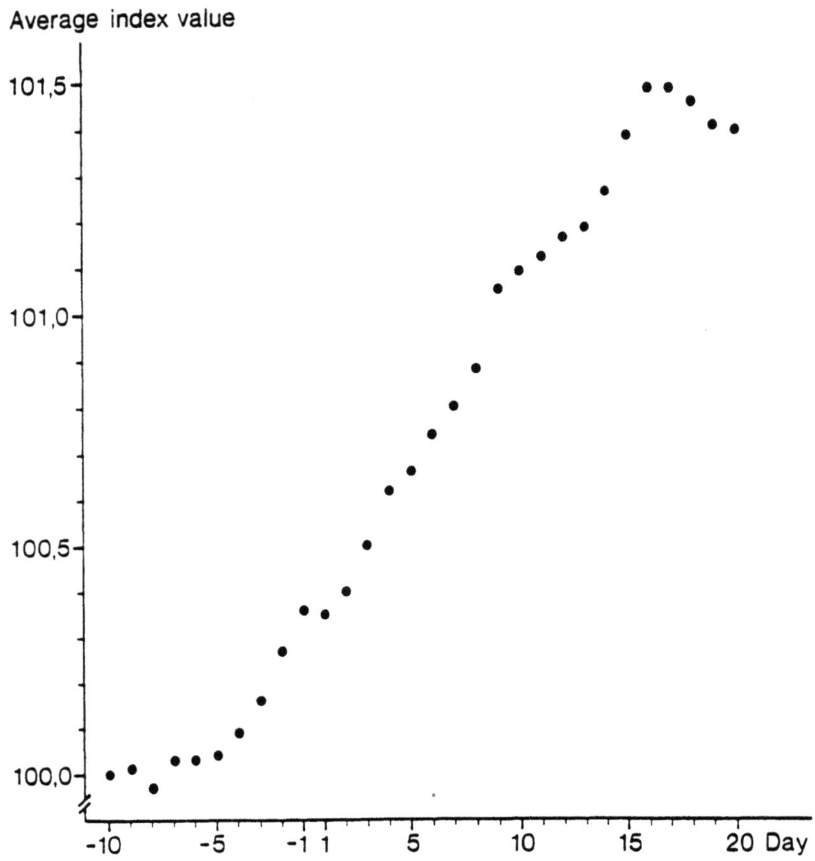

Figure 1. Index Development Around the Turn of the Year

the 10th last week day of December and then compute the index for the 29 following week days. For each turn of the year 1890-91, 1891-92 ... 1899-1900, this procedure gives an index series for days labeled -10, -9, -8 ... -2, -1, 1, 2 ... 18, 19, 20 (where the index value for day -10 is 100, as already indicated). The negative labels thus denote week days in December, the positive labels week days in January. We then average these index series, i. e., over turns of the year 1890-

91, 1891-92 ... 1899-1900. The result is displayed in Figure 1. It is clear from that figure that the index starts to rise during the four last week days of December. This rise continues for about 15 days in January.

Hence there is a rather strong January effect (or perhaps more precisely, a turn-of-the-year effect) on the Danish stock market in the 1890´s. As in other cases where such effects have been found, one wonders about possible explanations. Tax considerations cannot be the reason, since taxes were rather insignificant and since tax cheating was probably very easy. More importantly, the tax rules did not allow deductions for capital losses in selling securities, as already mentioned in Section 4. Hence, there was no reason for investors to sell shares in December in order to realize capital losses.

We have no other explanation but note merely that the Danish stock market in the 1890´s provides yet another example of a January effect which cannot be explained by tax considerations.

Another type of month effect has been reported by Ariel (1987): Using CRSP stock indices for 1963 - 1981, he found positive daily returns for the first half of calendar months but zero daily returns for the last half. Our data contain no evidence of this type of effect.

7. The Ex-Day Effect

Finally, consider the ex-day effect. The question is hence whether stock prices fall as expected on days when the shares are traded without dividend or new issue rights. We consider only ex-dividend days, since the number of new issues in our data set is very small. The number of dividends, on the other hand, is 264. In what follows, we will be interested only in returns between days t-1 and t, where t is the ex-dividend day and t-1 the week day immediately preceding the ex-dividend day. That is, we ignore those dividends where there was no price quote of the stock in question on the ex-dividend day or the previous week day. We also ignore dividends where the Stock Exchange was closed on the week day preceding the ex-dividend day. This eliminates 76 dividends. Out of the remaining 188, there are 20 instances of two different stocks having the same ex-dividend day, and 2 instances of three different stocks with the same ex-dividend day. Following Barclay 1987, we pool the stocks that go ex-dividend on the same day and treat each daily portfolio as a single observation. There are thus 164 observations altogether.

Now let p_B be the quoted price of a stock (or portfolio) on the day before the ex-dividend day, and let p_A be the price on the ex-dividend day. For each of our 164 observations, we compute $(p_B-p_A)/D$, where D is the dividend amount. This is the price-change-to-dividend ratio (cf. also Lakonishok and Vermaelen 1983 for a discussion of a somewhat different ratio measure). We also compute $[\ln(p_A+D)-\ln(p_B)]x100$, which is the ex-dividend day return. We then average these two quantities over the number of observations, i. e., 164. Table 5 contains results. For comparison, Table 5 also includes similar results from Barclay 1987 (p. 36) for the New York Stock Exchange for the period 1900 - 1910 (578 observations).

In these computations, we have not adjusted for general market movements, for the reason that the average daily return was very small in Denmark during 1890 - 1900 (cf. Table 3, above). The NYSE results in Table 5 also do not include adjustments for market movements. The t value for ex-dividend day return concerns the hypothesis of zero return.

As discussed by Elton and Gruber (1970), the price-change-to-dividend ratio should equal $(1-T_o)/(1-T_c)$, where T_o is the tax rate on ordinary income and T_c on capital gains. Otherwise, profitable arbitrage would be possible. In our case, we have argued that there was no effective taxation, since cheating must have been easy. This implies that T_o and T_c are zero, and hence that $(1-T_o)/(1-T_c)$ is equal to unity. The t value for the price-change-to-dividend ratio relates to the hypothesis of that ratio being equal to unity. Apparently, that hypothesis cannot be rejected.

However, an alternative interpretation of the tax situation in Denmark in the 1890´s is that ordinary income, including dividends, was honestly reported, but not capital

Table 5. Price-Change-to-Dividend Ratio and Ex-Dividend Day Return for Denmark 1890 - 1900 and New York Stock Exchange 1900 - 1910

Quantity	Mean	Standard deviation	t value
1. Denmark 1890 - 1900			
Price-change-to-div. ratio	0.9373	0.7073	-1.1356
Ex-dividend day return	0.1966	2.1848	1.1524
2. NYSE 1900 - 1910			
Price-change-to-div. ratio	0.959	1.280	-0.77
Ex-dividend day return	0.019	1.903	0.24

gains (this seems to be what tax inspector F. Jensen is saying in his article cited earlier). If so, T_c would be zero but not T_o. T_o would fall somewhere between 3% and 10%, depending on the town or city, as already mentioned in Section 4. If one assumes a value of T_o equal to 6%, then the observed mean price-change-to-dividend ratio corresponds rather precisely to the value predicted by Elton and Gruber. But this is only speculation on our part. Perhaps it is best to say that we have found evidence of slightly smaller price falls than expected on ex-dividend days.

8. Conclusion

In this article, we have only touched upon a rather limited range of aspects of price formation in the Danish stock market in the 1890's. Many more tests could have been undertaken, and several additional phenomena could have been looked into. However, given that our data set is somewhat limited, it would perhaps be less than meaningful to proceed much further. Take for instance the small-firm effect. This is another anomaly, meaning that the risk-adjusted return on small firms is greater than that of large ones on the average. We did not investigate this effect because almost all the firms in our sample would have to be classified as small. Even so, one could perhaps divide the 25 stocks into small and "less small". But that would place all the less frequently quoted stocks, and hence most of the gaps in the data series, in the small firm category.

As mentioned in the introduction, it is interesting to study financial markets in earlier time periods. One reason is, of course, that it broadens the range of institutional settings for empirical work. Effects or phenomena which are persistent across the range of settings, i. e., occur also in earlier periods, may thus be identified as intrinsic to financial markets in general. On the other hand, phenomena which can be observed today but cannot be detected in historical data could be due to recent institutional factors. That is, one may hope to gain insights into financial markets in general by studying such markets in earlier time periods. In conclusion, we summarize briefly the insights which have been provided by this investigation.

The results of the random walk tests in Section 3 fit rather well into an emerging picture of small stock markets. The random walk hypothesis originally met with some acceptance as a description of very large stock markets, such as the US one. It has now become clear that it is not an entirely satisfactory hypothesis for smaller stock markets. The present study provides yet another confirmation of a rather pervasive pattern of deviations from randomness in small markets, a pattern which can be found not only in present-day Scandinavia but also in small markets elsewhere (see e. g., Cooper 1982).

With respect to anomalies, the results are only partially clear. The ideal result of an investigation of an anomaly in some earlier period is a clean yes or no -- the effect either did or did not exist, thus pointing to anomalies which are intrinsic to financial markets in general, or alternatively are caused by recent institutional innovations, as already mentioned. In our case, there are indications of Monday and ex-dividend day effects. However, the evidence is really rather weak, so one cannot say much about those effects. On the other hand, the effect identified by Ariel (1987), positive daily returns for the first half of calendar months but zero returns for the second half, cannot be detected in our data set. Hence, this effect may be peculiar to the market that he investigated. Finally, and this is the most significant result in our paper, there is a rather strong turn-of-the-year effect. Since that effect is not due to taxes, our investigation lends additional support to the proposition that the January effect must be related to factors other than tax considerations.

References

Ariel, R. A., 1987, A Monthly Effect in Stock Returns, Journal of Financial Economics 18: 161-174.

Barclay, M. J., 1987, Dividends, Taxes, and Common Stock Prices, Journal of Financial Economics 19: 31-44.

Berglund, T., B. Wahlroos, and A. Örnmark, 1983, The Weak-Form Efficiency of the Finnish and Scandinavian Stock Exchanges, Scandinavian Journal of Economics 85: 521-530.

Brealey, R. and S. Myers, 1984, Principles of Corporate Finance, 2nd edition (McGraw-Hill, New York).

Claesson, K., 1986, Effektiviteten på Stockholms Fondbörs (doctoral dissertation, Stockholm School of Economics).

Cooper, J. C. B., 1982, World Stock Markets: Some Random Walk Tests, Applied Economics 14: 515-531.

Elton, E. J. and M. J. Gruber, 1970, Marginal Stockholder Tax Rates and the Clientele Effect, Review of Economics and Statistics 52: 68-74.

Fama, E. F., 1965, The Behavior of Stock Market Prices, Journal of Business 38: 34-105.

Fama, E. F., 1970, Efficient Capital Markets: A Review of Theory and Empirical Work, Journal of Finance 25: 383-417.

Jaffe, J. and R. Westerfield, 1985, The Week-End Effect in Common Stock Returns: The International Evidence, Journal of Finance 40: 433-454.

Jennergren, L. P. and P. E. Korsvold, 1975, The Non-Random Character of Norwegian and Swedish Stock Market Prices, in: E. J. Elton and M. J. Gruber, eds., International Capital Markets (North-Holland, Amsterdam) 37-54.

Jennergren, L. P. and B. G. Sörensen, 1986, Price Formation in the Danish Stock Market in the 1890's, fortcoming in Scandinavian Economic History Review.

Jennergren, L. P. and P. Toft-Nielsen, 1977, An Investigation of Random Walks in the Danish Stock Market, Nationalökonomisk Tidsskrift 115: 254-269.

Jensen, F., 1890, Indkomstskatten i Köbenhavn, Nationalökonomisk Tidsskrift 28: 442-504.

Jones, C. P., D. K. Pearce, and J. W. Wilson, 1987, Can Tax-Loss Selling Explain the January Effect? A Note, Journal of Finance 42: 453-461.

Lakonishok, J. and T. Vermaelen, 1983, Tax Reform and Ex-Dividend Day Behavior, Journal of Finance 38: 1157-1179.

Reinganum, M. R. and A. C. Shapiro, 1987, Taxes and Stock Return Seasonality: Evidence from the London Stock Exchange, Journal of Business 60: 281-295.

Roll, R., 1983, Vas ist das? The Turn-of-the-Year Effect and the Return Premia of Small Firms, Journal of Portfolio Management 9 (Winter): 18-28.

Smirlock, M. and L. Starks, 1986, Day-of-the-Week and Intraday Effects in Stock Returns, Journal of Financial Economics 17: 197-210.

Sörensen, B. G., 1982, En empirisk analyse af det danske aktie-markeds effektivitet (doctoral dissertation, Odense University).

Tinic, S. M., G. Barone-Adesi, and R. R. West, 1987, Seasonality in Canadian Stock Prices: A Test of the "Tax-Loss-Selling" Hypothesis, Journal of Financial and Quantitative Analysis 22: 51-63.

Comments on L P Jennergren and B Sorensen "Random Walks and Anomalies on the Copenhagen Stock Exchange in the 1890's"

by Peter F Pope

This is an interesting paper and I was immediately impressed by the dedication and perseverance that must have been necessary to collect and code the daily data for the 25 firms over the 11 year period. Briefly, I will restrict my comments to three main areas: (1) the role of this type of study; (2) the quality of the data; and (3) the tests of weak form efficiency.

The authors state that their motivation for studying data almost 100 years old is their interest to discover whether results on efficiency and anomalies obtained from more recent (and typically U.S.) data are to be found for the earlier period. Historical studies and studies of contemporaneous data from different (non-U.S.) markets have a potential role to play in increasing our confidence in the robustness of known results, if they are replicated and assuming that the characteristics of the markets/regimes are comparable. Studies such as this can also potentially improve our understanding of the causes of results that might puzzle us, such as market anomalies, if there is variation in possible explanatory factors across studies, e.g. tax in this study.

Generally it would appear that the characteristics of the nineteenth century market were broadly in line with the modern day equivalent, apart from the tax system. However, it would be interesting to have some data on the depth of the market because it seems likely that this would have been very different in the 1890's. Indeed we are told that there were few transactions, thus causing the authors to rely on bid quotes. The returns series did not consequently reflect realisable returns on a round trip transaction, but of course this point also applies to most studies using more recent data based on (say) middle market prices. It could also be argued that since the quoted prices frequently did not induce transactions they were not a good measure of "value". However, there was no real alternative available to the authors.

The weak form efficiency tests take the form of standard tests of the random walk hypothesis. The authors point out that this is only a special case of weak form efficiency. A point that is frequently

NATO ASI Series, Vol. F54
A Reappraisal of the Efficiency of Financial Markets
Edited by Rui M. C. Guimaraes et al.

overlooked in discussions of market efficiency is that rejection of a random walk is not necessarily inconsistent with an efficient market which in general would require only that the market is a fair game. Turning to the results, the autocorrelation tests, whilst on average zero, apparently have 12 out of 25 negative. Could this be the result of spurious autocorrelation induced by the use of bid quotes? Also, significantly fewer runs were observed than expected and this could be due to the occurrence of several relatively long no-change runs which would be symptomatic of a thin market. The evidence of leptokurtic returns would also seem to be consistent with a high frequency of zero returns in a thin market.

Turning to the results on the day-of-the-week, the evidence is not very conclusive although there does seem to be some suggestion that Monday returns were lower. It would be interesting to know if the results are sensitive to the choice of index weighting scheme. Also, in general it seems that more light might be shed on this and other anomalies by analysing data on individual stocks and seeking explanations of variations in the magnitude of the anomaly effect.

The most striking results are for the turn-of-the-year effect. Assuming that returns have been properly measured then the pattern found in late December/early January is generally consistent with recent findings. However, it would be interesting to know whether similar patterns of returns can be found for other 19 day periods in the sample and also whether there is any evidence of abnormal volume around the turn-of-the-year.

January Skewness, Another Enigma?

by

Phelim P. Boyle
School of Accountancy
and Department of Statistics and
Actuarial Science
University of Waterloo
Waterloo, Ontario, Canada
N2L 3G1
(519) 885-1211 ext. 6513

William M. Taylor
School of Management
Boston University,
704 Commonwealth Avenue
Boston, MA 02215
U.S.A.
(617) 353-5714

KEYWORDS/ABSTRACT: skewness/January anomaly/arbitrage pricing theory

This paper examines the behaviour of the skewness of the returns on individual stocks and portfolios of stocks. Individual stocks have generally positive skewness. Grouping stocks into portfolios reduces this skewness. However, the skewness of equally weighted portfolios shows a markedly different pattern in January. In January, the portfolio skewness is significantly positive. A one factor APT model is used to interpret our empirical findings. Stock returns are assumed to be generated by two skewed factors. The systematic skewness of a stock is related to the skewness of the common factor while the unique factor is responsible for most of the skewness of an individual stock. We find that the skewness of the common factor changes dramatically in January. It is generally small or negative throughout the year but is strongly positive in January. We comment on the significance of this result.

Professor Boyle is grateful to the Social Sciences and Humanities Research Council of Canada and the Centre for Accounting Research and Education of the University of Waterloo for research support. The authors thank Duane Kennedy and Anthony Atkinson for helpful comments.

NATO ASI Series, Vol. F54
A Reappraisal of the Efficiency of Financial Markets
Edited by Rui M. C. Guimaraes et al.

1. INTRODUCTION

Several papers in the finance literature have examined the skewness of common stock returns. Topics covered include: the behaviour of the skewness of individual stocks and portfolios, the persistence of skewness over time of stocks and portfolios, the impact of skewness on optimal portfolio selection and the development of asset pricing models to include the third moment.

Simkowitz and Beedles (1978) examined the skewness of monthly returns for individual stocks and portfolios over the period 1945-1965. They found that the skewness of individual stocks was positive and that as stocks were combined into portfolios, the skewness of the portfolio return diminished and eventually became negative.

Roll and Ross (1980) provided empirical details of the skewness of daily returns and monthly returns of 1260 individual stocks for the time period 1962-1972. For daily returns, the average skewness was .681 and over 96% of the individual stocks had positive skewness over this time interval. The corresponding figures for monthly return skewness were .654 and 90%. Singleton and Wingender (1986) have recently examined the persistence of skewness over time for the 20-year period 1961-1980. These authors used monthly, semi-annual and annual returns in their tests. They also found that positive skewness was prevalent among individual stock returns.

Conine and Tamarkin (1981) explored the implications of investor preference for positive skewness on optimal portfolio size. Given a preference for positive skewness there is a tendency not to diversify as fully as one would in the absence of that preference. Several papers have examined asset pricing models which incorporate third order moments. Such papers include those by Kraus and Litzenberger (1976) and Barone-Adesi (1985).

In addition to these studies which have investigated the skewness of returns, the seasonality of common stock returns has received considerable attention. Studies by Rozeff and Kinney (1976), Gultekin and Gultekin (1983), and others have generally found that on average, January returns are significantly higher than the returns for other months. Banz (1981) and Reinganum (1981) have found abnormally high returns in small market value firms, and Keim (1983) has related this to the first few trading days of January.

Seasonality in risk premiums has been found by Rozeff and Kinney (1976), Keim (1980), and Tinic and West (1984) in a CAPM framework. January appears to be the only month in which there is a consistently positive and statistically significant expected return-risk relationship.

More recently, Cho and Taylor (1987) and Gultekin and Gultekin (1985) have examined daily stock returns within the framework of the APT. Cho and Taylor (1987) examined the seasonal stability of the factor structure of daily returns and found some significant differences among calendar months in the estimated number of return generating factors. A January effect and a small firm effect in returns were also found.

The above studies provide some interesting descriptions of stock returns and a diminution of skewness when portfolios are formed. However, none of these studies examined skewness on a calendar month basis. They implicitly assume that the return distributions are stationary across calendar months.

On the other hand, the seasonality studies have examined average returns and CAPM and APT risk premiums by calendar month. Significant differences across calendar months, particularly for January, have been found in these studies.

In view of this contrast between these two groups of studies, we believe it is useful to investigate the nature of skewness in stock returns on a calendar month basis. The Miller and Scholes (1972) argument that skewness can create dependence between the sample mean and sample standard deviation, and thus bias the significance of the stock's own variance as an explanatory factor in return regressions adds to the need for an investigation into the seasonality of skewness.

Hence, the present paper examines certain aspects of the skewness of returns of individual stocks and portfolios. We find, as did previous researchers, that while individual returns are generally positively skewed, this skewness diminishes as stocks are grouped into portfolios. However, in January, the skewness of equally weighted portfolios in particular is significantly positive. This result can be interpreted within the framework of a one factor APT model where both the common factor and the unique factor exhibit skewness. The January effect can be interpreted as a change in the skewness of the common factor during this month.

This paper is organized as follows. In Section 2, we develop expressions for the skewness of individual securities and portfolios in the context of a single factor APT model. Section 3 analyzes the skewness attributes of daily returns for samples of individual stocks and portfolios. We find strong evidence of a systematic skewness in the common factor even though the return distribution does not appear to be stationary. The systematic skewness is strongly positive in January in all samples of equally weighted portfolios. Section 4 examines the seasonality of skewness in daily

CRSP (Centre for Research in Security Prices) equally and value weighted indexed and in the daily S&P 500 index. Section 5 considers the seasonality of skewness in monthly CRSP equally and value weighted indexes. The final section of the paper comments on these results and indicates their potential relevance for additional research.

2. SKEWNESS OF INDIVIDUAL STOCKS AND PORTFOLIOS OF STOCKS

In this section, we use a simple one factor APT model to develop expressions for skewness of individual stocks and portfolios of stocks.

Assume that the return on security i, r_i is generated by a one factor APT model:

$$r_i = E(r_i) + \beta_i f + \epsilon_i \tag{1}$$

where f is the mean zero common factor and ϵ_i is the mean zero unique factor.

Assume that f and ϵ_i are independently distributed and the ϵ_i and ϵ_j are independently distributed for all i = j. It is convenient to subtract out the mean expected return and use

$$y_i = r_i - E(r_i).$$

Given the independence assumption, the moments are as follows:

$$E(y^2_i) = \beta^2_i E(f^2) + E(\epsilon^2_i)$$

$$E(y^3_i) = \beta^3_i E(f^3) + E(\epsilon^3_i)$$

$$E(f^2) = Var(f)$$

and $$E(\epsilon_i^2) = Var(\epsilon_i).$$

Further, the skewness coefficients are

$$Skew(\gamma) = \frac{E(\gamma^3)}{[\ var(\gamma)]^{1.5}}.$$

where γ represents either f, or ε_i: , or y_i .

The skewness of y_i can be expressed as a function of the skewness of f and the skewness of ε_i

$$Skew(y_i) = \frac{\beta_i^3 E(f^3) + E(\varepsilon_i^3)}{[\beta_i^2\ var(\varepsilon_i)]^{1.5}}$$

If we let $var(\varepsilon_i) = var(f)\lambda_i^2$ then we can write;

$$Skew(y_i) = \phi_i^3\ skew(f) + \omega_i^3\ skew(\varepsilon_i), \qquad (2)$$

where

$$\phi_i^3 [1 + \lambda_i^2 \beta_i^{-2}]^{1.5} = 1 ,$$

and

$$\omega_i^3 [1 + \lambda_i^{-2} \beta_i^2]^{1.5} = 1 ,$$

It is a straightforward empirical matter to obtain estimates of λ_i and β_i and thus ϕ_i and ω_i. Hence, if we know the skewness of f we can estimate the skewness of y_i from the data and thus infer the skewness of ε_i.

To obtain the skewness of f, let us consider the skewness of an equally weighted portfolio of N securities. We have;

$$\frac{1}{N}\sum_{i=1}^{N} y_i = E[\frac{1}{N}\sum_{i=1}^{N} [\beta_i f + \varepsilon_i]]^3$$

$$= E[\beta_p f + \varepsilon_p]^3$$

where β_p and ε_p have the obvious definition. Given our independence assumptions the third central moment becomes:

$$\beta_p^3 E(f^3) + E(\varepsilon_p^3).$$

Further, the portfolio variance is

$$\beta^2_p \text{var } f + \text{var}(\epsilon_p).$$

Thus, the portfolio skewness, skew(p) is given by

$$\frac{\beta^3_p E(f^3) + E(\epsilon_p{}^3)}{[\beta^2_p \text{var}(f) + \text{var}(\epsilon_p)]^{1.5}} \tag{3}$$

As N becomes large, the terms involving ϵ_p tend to zero so that the portfolio skewness approaches

$$\text{skew}(f)$$

We therefore expect that for medium sized diversified portfolios ($N \geq 30$) that the portfolio skewness will be a reasonable approximation for the skewness of f.

3. SEASONAL SKEWNESS IN DAILY RETURNS

We first examine the seasonality of skewness in samples of individual common stocks. Then we form equally weighted portfolios of 30 stocks and evaluate the seasonality of the diversifiability of skewness.

The basic data set consists of 340 individual common stock returns from the Centre for Research in Security Prices (CRSP) Daily Returns File. Daily data for the 11 year period from January 2, 1973 to December 30, 1983 was used in the study. To be included in the sample each stock was listed on both the first and last days of the trading period and had no more than fifteen missing observations in the entire period. Details of the sample selection procedure and further information on the stocks included are given in the Cho and Taylor (1987) paper. The characteristics of this sample base enable one to examine the characteristics of individual stocks (and portfolios) along the dimensions of industry group and also by firm size. For our analysis, it is also convenient to use diversified portfolios of stocks and the sample lends itself readily to this purpose as well. While we analyzed the data in different ways, the main results reported here relate to our most interesting finding. This has to do with the seasonal pattern of the reduction in skewness when stocks are grouped into portfolios. That is, there is a seasonal pattern in the diversifiability of skewness in equally weighted portfolios.

The broad details of the portfolio groupings developed by Cho and Taylor (1987) and used in this paper are displayed in Table 1. The six industry samples are labelled as I_1 through I_6. The firm size samples are denoted by M_1 through to M_5 while R_1, R_2 and R_3 represent stratified random samples that correspond to well diversified portfolios.

Table 1 **Details of Cho-Taylor Samples**

Sample Label	Brief Description		Number of Stocks
I_1	Foods		30
I_2	Machineries		30
I_3	Electronics		30
I_4	Utilities		30
I_5	Retail		30
I_6	Financial Institutions		30
M_1	Market Value $,000,000's	1.4-36	30
M_2		36-122	30
M_3		122-281	30
M_4		282-688	30
M_5		694-18,214	30
R_1	Random across industries and size		30
R_2	Random across industries and size		30
R_3	Random across industries and size		30

It should be pointed out that not all of the fourteen portfolios are independent. However, there is no duplication of companies within the three major subgroups. Thus, the six industry portfolios consist of 180 different stocks. The five size portfolios consist of 150 different stocks and the three diversified portfolios consist of 90 different stocks.

Table 2 gives summary details of the skewness of the individual stock returns for each of the fourteen portfolios. Note that these skewness computations correspond to the entire 11 year period. For example, in the case of the 30 stocks in I_1, the average skewness of the individual stocks in this group was .526 while the smallest skewness for this group was -.250.[1]

It is also interesting to note that of the 14 samples the average skewness is highest in the sample of 30 small market value of equity companies. Further, within the five size samples, the average skewness declines as market value increases from M_1 to M_4.[2]

The overall impression from Table 2 is that the skewness of the large majority of individual stocks is positive. This finding is in accord with the earlier empirical studies of the skewness of the individual stocks.

In order to examine the impact of portfolio formation on the skewness, we turn to Table 3. Table 3 displays the skewness of the returns for equally weighted portfolios over the entire 11 year period. As previous researchers have discovered, the skewness tends to be diversified away by the formation of portfolios. In some cases, the portfolio skewness is negative. Simkowitz and Beedles (1978) used monthly return data to examine the impact of diversification on skewness and found an even more pronounced effect. In other words, the skewness of their portfolios was lower than ours while the skewness of individual stocks was similar.

---

[1] The sampling distribution of skewness is not known, so it is difficult to measure significant differences. This was noted by Roll and Ross (1980) who infer that the differences in skewness in their sample appear to be too large to be due to chance alone and suggest that population skewness differs across assets. In this study, we use Pearson's criterion that skewness of magnitude $> .3$ is significant.

[2] While we do not have a direct test, these differences between size samples might be related to the small firm results found by previous authors including Keim (1983), Cho and Taylor (1987), Huberman and Kandel (1985) and Huberman, Kandel and Karolyi (1987).

Table 2 **Skewness Characteristics of Individual Stock Returns for Entire Period 1973-1983. Daily Return Data**

Sample	Average Skewness of Stocks in Sample	Number Positive	Smallest	Largest
I_1	.526	28	- .250	2.236
I_2	.587	28	-1.815	3.061
I_3	.576	29	-0.012	1.415
I_4	.234	25	-5.515	1.557
I_5	.472	30	.101	1.966
I_6	.589	28	- .266	2.102
M_1	.792	29	- .109	2.102
M_2	.592	27	- .242	1.883
M_3	.420	30	.012	1.032
M_4	.351	28	- .121	0.981
M_5	.433	28	- .039	5.038
R_1	.460	28	- .250	1.032
R_2	.600	28	- .109	3.061
R_3	.593	29	- .097	2.102

Table 3 **Portfolio Skewness; Daily Data, (Period 1973-1983)**

Sample	Skewness	Sample	Skewness
I_1	- .113	M_1	- .136
I_2	- .056	M_2	.065
I_3	.085	M_3	- .101
I_4	.906	M_4	.112
I_5	.008	M_5	.394
I_6	.246		
		R_1	- .080
		R_2	.162
		R_3	- .002

Comparing the average skewness in Table 2 with the corresponding portfolio skewness in Table 3, the high positive M_1 average skewness of .792 has been diversified away to - .136, while the positive skewness remains in the largest market value sample, M_5.[3] Thus, there is apparently a difference across firm size in the diversifiability of skewness in equally weighted portfolios. There is apparently more systematic skewness in the high market value sample (both in absolute magnitude and as a percent of average skewness).[4]

If there is a systematic (skewed) common factor in the generation of security returns, then our analysis in Section 2 indicates that the skewness of portfolios should tend to the skewness of this factor. Even if the return distribution is non-stationary, and there is evidence to suggest this is the case, the skewness of different portfolios should be correlated. We explored this by computing the correlation of the skewness between pairs of portfolios for our three major subsets of portfolios. For each portfolio, we computed the skewness of the portfolio return using daily data for each calendar year. Thus, for example, in the case of R_1, we had eleven skewness numbers for each of the years 1973 through 1983. In the same way, there were eleven corresponding numbers for portfolio R_2. The correlation between these two sets of eleven numbers is given in Table 4 as .95. The correlations between the skewness of the diversified portfolios are all very high as one would expect. Table 4 is consistent with the presence of a systematic skewed common factor in the generation of security returns.

---

[3] Note from Table 2 that the M_5 sample contains one significant outlier with skewness equal to 5.038. This observation could affect some of our conclusions concerning the diversifiability of skewness with respect to firm size.

[4] Cho and Taylor (1987), for purposes of comparison, found more return generating factors in the large size sample (10) than in the smallest size sample (5) when daily returns were pooled over all months. The results in Tables 2 and 3 are consistent with the idea that systematic skewness and the number of factors found in a multivariate normal maximum likelihood factor analysis are positively related. However, skewness may provide only a partial explanation of the differences found by Cho and Taylor.

Table 4 **Correlation Matrices for Skewness of Portfolio Returns Skewness Computed Each Year Using Daily Data**

Portfolio	I_1	I_2	I_3	I_4	I_5	I_6
I_1	1.00	.83	.76	.70	.78	.91
I_2	.83	1.00	.83	.67	.94	.92
I_3	.76	.83	1.00	.75	.93	.79
I_4	.70	.67	.75	1.00	.72	.76
I_5	.78	.94	.93	.72	1.00	.90
I_6	.91	.92	.79	.76	.90	1.00

Portfolio	M_1	M_2	M_3	M_4	M_5
M_1	1.00	.91	.89	.83	.53
M_2	.91	1.00	.84	.86	.59
M_3	.89	.84	1.00	.86	.67
M_4	.83	.86	.86	1.00	.68
M_5	.53	.59	.67	.68	1.00

Portfolio	R_1	R_2	R_3
R_1	1.00	.95	.91
R_2	.95	1.00	.95
R_3	.91	.95	1.00

Our most interesting results relate to the seasonal pattern of the skewness of individual stocks and the skewness of portfolios of stocks. The main point of this paper is that January is also exceptional as far as the skewness of portfolios is concerned. For the entire period, the formation of portfolios significantly reduces skewness. However, in January, skewness is not diversified away by the formation of equally weighted portfolios. This effect is illustrated by the figures in Table 5.

This table presents the skewness of the returns on the individual portfolios where the time intervals consist of the individual calendar months linked together. Tests for seasonality confirm that January is distinctly different from the other eleven months. The portfolio skewness in January is strongly positive whereas the portfolio skewness tends to be reduced through the process of diversification in the remaining calendar months. This phenomenon is clearly evident from an inspection of Table 5. If we use the Pearson categorization (see Singleton and Wingender (1986)) and classify distributions with skewness of .3 or greater as having positive skewness, all of the fourteen portfolios had positively skewed returns in January. The number of non-

January panels in Table 5 is 154 = 11 x 14 and of these only 23 or 14.9% have positive skewness (skewness above .3).[5]

Table 5 **Skewness of Portfolios by Calendar Months for the Period 1973-1983; Daily Return Data**

Month	J	F	M	A	M	J	J	A	S	O	N	D
Portfolio												
I_1	.6	0.0	-.5	0.0	-.2	.2	.2	-.1	-.1	-.6	-.4	-.1
I_2	.8	.2	-.4	.1	-.1	-.1	.1	.1	-.3	-.3	-.6	-.2
I_3	.3	.2	.2	.7	-.1	.1	-.2	.1	0.0	-.2	.2	-.2
I_4	2.2	-.1	-.6	.4	-.6	.6	-.1	.6	.3	1.5	0.0	1.0
I_5	1.0	0.0	-.2	0.0	-.6	-.1	0.0	.2	-.1	-.3	-.4	0.0
I_6	.9	.1	0.0	.4	-.1	0.0	.7	.7	-.1	-.2	.4	0.0
M_1	.3	.2	-1.2	0.0	-.2	.2	.2	0.0	-.2	-.7	.2	-.1
M_2	.8	.2	- .3	.4	-.2	.1	0.0	0.0	-.2	-.7	-.2	.6
M_3	.5	.2	- .3	.2	-.2	.1	.5	.2	-.2	-.3	-.7	-.4
M_4	1.3	.5	.1	-.1	.3	-.1	.2	.3	-.1	.1	-.6	-.5
M_5	.7	.2	.2	.2	.2	0.0	.1	1.2	.1	.9	.2	.1
R_1	.4	.4	- .3	.1	-.4	-.1	0.0	.4	-.3	-.4	0.0	-.2
R_2	1.0	0.0	- .1	.4	-.3	.6	.2	.3	0.0	-.2	-.2	-.2
R_3	.9	-.2	- .5	0.0	-.1	-.1	-.1	.3	-.1	-.5	0.0	0.0
Average	.8	.1	- .3	.2	-.2	.1	.1	.3	-.1	-.1	-.1	0.0

4. SEASONAL SKEWNESS OF DAILY INDEX RETURNS

We now turn to an examination of the seasonality of skewness in stock market indexes. The indexes are the daily return series for the equally and value weighted CRSP indexes and the S&P 500 index, for the period from January 2, 1973 to December 30, 1983.[6] The broad diversification these indexes represent provides further evidence

---

5 To arrive at these numbers, the original figures for skewness were used rather than the rounded figures in Table 5.

6 Similar patterns of results were obtained for the longer series of daily returns from January, 1963 through December, 1985. The shorter series results are reported here for consistency with the daily return period available for the samples analyzed in Section 3.

on the seasonality of the diversifiability of skewness.

The results are shown in Table 6. As in the equally weighted portfolios of Table 5, the CRSP equally weighted index exhibits high positive skewness in January.

Table 6 **Daily Stock Index Return Skewness, Mean, and Variance by Calendar Month-January 2, 1973 to December 30, 1983.**

Month	J	F	M	A	M	J	J	A	S	O	N	D
						Skewness						
Equally Weighted (EW)*	.71	-.1	-1.0	-.1	-.8	-.4	.1	.08	-.4	-.8	-.2	-.1
Value Weighted (VW)*	.06	-.2	- .2	.3	.02	-.02	.3	.7	.06	.5	.08	-.1
S&P 500	.05	-.2	- .2	.4	.1	.07	.3	.8	.2	.6	.2	0.0
Number of Observations	234	210	242	227	232	236	231	244	225	243	223	233
						Mean (x 1,000)						
EW	3.7	.4	1.0	1.0	.5	1.1	.9	.1	.1	-.1	1.2	.3
VW	.9	-.2	.3	.8	.2	.8	-.1	.2	-.3	.6	1.0	.2
S&P 500	.7	-.5	.2	.8	-.3	.7	-.3	-.1	-.5	.6	.6	.1
						Variance (x 10,000)						
EW	1.1	.5	.8	.4	.5	.4	.6	.6	.7	1.0	.9	.8
VW	.9	.7	.8	.6	.6	.5	.7	.8	1.0	1.2	1.1	.8
S&P 500	.9	.7	.8	.7	.6	.6	.7	.9	1.0	1.3	1.2	.9

*EW and VW are, respectively, the Centre for Research in Security Prices (CRSP) equally weighted and value weighted daily index returns.

This is not true for the value weighted CRSP and S&P 500 indexes. This is consistent with systematic skewness, particularly in January, being associated with a factor representing a size effect since the smaller market value firms have proportionately more weight in the equally weighted index.[7]

The result is contrary to the finding in earlier studies that positive skewness is diversified away when portfolios are formed. This conclusion must now be modified to add that: positive skewness is diversified away except in January for equally weighted portfolios. These results suggest that asset pricing models should accommodate that seasonality in the diversifiability of skewness in daily returns.

The statistics in Table 6 can be used to compute Spearman rank correlation coefficients between the skewness and mean, and between the magnitude of skewness and variance for the three indexes. These correlation coefficients are contained in Table 7. These positive rank correlations are consistent with those of Roll and Ross (19).[8]

Table 7 **Spearman Rank Correlation Coefficients of Skewness with Mean and Variance for the Daily Return Indexes from Table 6**

	Mean	Variance*
EW	.31	.45
VW	.25	.28
S&P 500	.18	.24

* variance is correlated with the magnitude of skewness.

The results of Keim (1983), which show that more than fifty percent of the daily return January firm "size effect" is attributable to high returns during the first week of trading, suggest a further examination of the results in Table 6. If we omit the

[7] Huberman and Kandel (1985) developed a return model based on three size indexes. The pattern of skewness in Table 6 is implicit in the size effects they report, but the importance of this pattern to the differences among the size groups remains to be determined.

[8] The asymptotic distribution of $\sqrt{n-1}$ x Spearman's coefficient is N(0,1) under the null hypothesis of independence. With n=12, this gives a rough approximate critical value against a two-sided hypothesis of 0.5 at the 10 percent level of significance. See, e.g. Hettmansperger (1984). p. 220.

first five trading days of January, the January skewness in the equally weighted CRSP index is reduced to 0.09. Indeed, if we only eliminate the first contiguous trading days of January each year, the January skewness becomes -.11 for the daily returns. This is consistent with the prevalence of high daily returns being sufficiently pronounced at the beginning of January to affect the skewness of the equally weighted index in January. The association of this occurrence with the equally weighted index rather than the value weighted index is consistent with this effect being associated with firm size.

5. SEASONAL SKEWNESS OF MONTHLY INDEX RETURNS

In view of the seasonality in the diversifiability of skewness which we have found for the daily returns of equally weighted portfolios, a re-examination of the skewness in monthly return indexes is in order. In this section, the CRSP NYSE-AMEX equally weighted and value weighted monthly index returns from January 1973 through December 1983 provide the data.

Table 8 shows the skewness of the monthly returns by calendar month. Although each statistic is based on only 11 observations, we see that the highest positive skewness occurs in January for the equally weighted index. The skewness values have a wide range from -1.9 to 1.0.

Table 8 **Skewness of Monthly CRSP Index Returns by Calendar Month, January 1973 to December 1983.**

Month	J	F	M	A	M	J	J	A	S	O	N	D
EW	1.0	.5	-1.2	- .6	-.2	-0.0	1.0	.2	-.2	-.7	-1.9	.5
VW	.6	.3	-1.4	-0.0	.6	- .2	.1	.5	-1.0	.4	-1.2	.5

If we pool all 132 months as previous studies have done, the skewness is 0.5 for the equally weighted index and 0.2 for the value weighted index. In Simkowitz and Breedles (1978) more than 92 percent of the monthly return raw skewness was diversified away in portfolios of only five stocks. Here, significant systematic skewness remains in the CRSP equally weighted index.[9]

[9] Singleton and Wingender (1986) investigated the persistence of systematic skewness of monthly returns in equally weighted 5 and 20 stock portfolios during the period 1960-1980. They did not find evidence that portfolio skewness was persistent.

6. SUMMARY AND CONCLUSIONS

The main result of this paper is that the skewness of the returns on individual stocks can be diversified away by the formation of equally weighted portfolios in all months except January. This provides another striking demonstration that January is different. In this section, we will give some reflections on this result and relate it to previous and contemporary literature. We will also indicate some possible implications of this result that may be of interest.

Rozeff and Kinney (1976), Roll (1983) and Keim (1983) have documented that U.S. stock market returns are on an average higher in January than during the remaining eleven months of the year. Keim (1983) and others have related the January effect to the firm size effect. The systematic skewness which we have found in January in the equally weighted portfolios and indexes is consistent with a relationship between systematic skewness and an underlying factor associated with the size effect.

Tinic and West (1984), (1986) found the presence of a January seasonal in the coefficients of the estimated relationship between average portfolio returns and systemic risk. In fact, Tinic and West conclude that the positive relationship between risk and return appears to exist only in January. Interestingly enough, earlier work by Beedles (1979) and McEnally (1974) discovered a positive correlation between skewness and beta. These findings are consistent with our results.

One way of interpreting our results is suggested by the theoretical framework developed in the second section. If security returns are generated by a one factor model where the common factor is not assumed to be stationary and is not assumed to be normal then the empirical results indicate a structural change in this factor during January. In essence, the common factor exhibits strong positive skewness in January (related to the first trading days of January) whereas its skewness is much less in the rest of the year and in some months may be negative. Such an interpretation is not inconsistent with earlier research findings on skewness. However, it highlights one aspect of the January seasonality that does not seem to have been explicitly addressed in the literature. There is a seasonality to the diversifiability of skewness in equally weighted portfolios. The fact that equally weighted portfolio skewness is strongly positive in January illustrates another aspect of the January seasonality that has been

---

If we divide our CRSP index period into the first and last five years, the equally weighted index skewness is 1.3 and -.6, respectively. There are, then, short periods in which the positive skewness does not appear.

discovered in other studies of security returns.

A lack of persistence of skewness as found by Singleton and Wingender (1986) would limit the usefulness of ex post skewness in stock portfolio planning. However, while there is variation in skewness from one five-year period to the next, the longer periods support a positive systematic skewness in January. Much the same pattern has been discovered for the so-called size effect which is not present in all years. This is consistent with a stochastic, rather than deterministic, seasonality in systematic skewness.

Our results may be suggestive in the context of empirical testing of the APT. Virtually all of the empirical tests to date assume that security returns are generated by a multinormal distribution. Thus, the most usual procedure involves the use of factor analysis which restricts attention to the variance-covariance matrix of the return distribution. Our results indicate that the skewness of the common factor exhibits distinctly different behaviour in January. It is difficult to see how this difference can be accommodated within the framework of traditional common factor analysis since the conventional approach does not utilize moments higher than the second. This suggests that the use of a procedure to extract common factors which utilizes third order moments and third order cross products may be fruitful approach. Such a procedure has been developed by Mooijaart (1985). The authors are currently working on the application of Mooijaart's procedure to empirical testing of the APT.

There may be additional advantages to the inclusion of skewness in the empirical tests of APT. The conventional approach to factor analysis produces factor loadings that are not unique. This arbitrariness of the factor loadings causes significant problems in the execution and interpretation of meaningful tests. The factor loading indeterminacy is intimately related to the normality assumption. It can be shown that if the normality assumption is dispensed with the factor loadings can be identified uniquely. This is an exciting prospect. However, the non-stationarity of the factor structure will continue to pose difficulties.

Another area where our results may be of interest relates to the pricing of options on market indexes. Such options have gained enormous popularity in recent years. If a Black-Scholes pricing formula which assumes lognormality and stationarity is used, our research indicates that this model is unlikely to be in accord with the actual return distribution of portfolio returns. In particular, the distributional characteristics of the January returns are quite different from those of the other months and it would not be surprising if option market prices recognized this difference. It might be of interest to explore the implications of this seasonality using empirical data.

To summarize, this paper has documented evidence of a difference in the January skewness of portfolios. We interpret this in terms of seasonal behaviour of a systematic common factor affecting security returns. Some implications of this finding for contemporary research issues in finance were suggested.

REFERENCES

Banz, R., (1981), "The Relationship Between Return and Market Value of Common Stocks, "Journal of Financial Economics, 9, pp. 3-18.

Barone-Adesi, G.,(1985), "Arbitrage Equilibrium with Skewed Asset Returns," Journal of Financial and Quantitative Analysis, 20, No. 3. pp. 299-314.

Beedles, W.L., (1979), "Return, Dispersion and Skewness: Synthesis and Investment Strategy," Journal of Financial Research, 2, pp. 71-80.

Cho, D.C. and W.M. Taylor, (1987), "The Seasonal Stability of the Factor Structure of Stock Returns," Journal of Finance, 42, No.5, pp. 1195-1211.

Conine, T.E. Jr. and M.J. Tamarkin, (1981), "On Diversification Given Asymmetry in Returns," Journal of Finance, 36, pp. 1143-1155.

Gultekin, M.N. and N.B. Gultekin, (1983), "Stock Market Seasonality: International Evidence," Journal of Financial Economics, 12, pp. 469-481.

Gultekin, M.N. and N.B. Gultekin, (1985), "Stock Return Anomalies and the Asset Pricing Tests," Working Paper, The Wharton School, University of Pennsylvania.

Hettmansperger, T.P., (1984), Statistical Inference Based on Ranks, New York: J. Wiley & Sons Inc.

Huberman, G. and S. Kandel, (1985), "A Sized Based Stock Returns Model," Working Paper, University of Chicago.

Huberman, G., S. Kandel and G.A. Karolyi, (1987), "Size and Industry Related Covariations of Stock Returns", Working Paper, University of Chicago.

Keim, D., (1983), "Size-Related Anomalies and Stock Market Seasonality: Further Empirical Evidence," Journal of Financial Economics, 12, pp. 13-22.

Keim, D., (1980), "Asset Pricing Anomalies and Capital Market Seasonality: Empirical Evidence," Unpublished Manuscript, University of Chicago.

Kraus, A. and R.H. Litzenberger, (1976), "Skewness Preference and the Valuation of Risk Assets," Journal of Finance, 31, pp. 1085-1100.

McEnally, R.W., (1974), "A Note on the Return Behaviour of High Risk Common Stocks,"_ Journal of Finance, 29, pp. 199-202.

Miller, M.H. and M. Scholes, (1972), "Rates of Return in Relation to Risk: A Re-examination of Some Recent Findings," in M.C. Jensen, ed., Studies in the Theory of Capital Markets, pp. 47-78, New York: Praeger.

Mooijaart, A., (1985), "Factor Analysis with Non-Normal Variables," Psychometrika, Vol. 50, No. 3, pp. 323-342.

Reinganum, M.R., (1981), "Misspecification of Capital Asset Pricing: Empirical Anomalies Based on Earnings Yields and Market Values." Journal of Financial Economics, 9, pp. 19-46.

Roll, R., (1983),"The Turn-of-the-Year Effect and the Return Premia of Small Firms." Journal of Portfolio Management, 9, pp. 18-28.

Roll, R. and S.A. Ross, (1980), "An Empirical Investigation of the Arbitrage Pricing Theory." Journal of Finance, Vol. 35, No. 5, pp. 1073-1103.

Rozeff, M. and W. Kinney, (1976), "Capital Market Seasonality: The Case of Stock Returns."Journal of Financial Economics, 3, pp. 379-402.

Simkowitz, M.A. and W.L. Beedles, (1978), "Diversification in a Three-Moment World." Journal of Financial and Quantitative Analysis, Vol. 21, No. 3, pp. 927-941.

Singleton, J.C. and J. Wingender, (1986), "Skewness Persistence in Common Stock Returns." Journal of Financial and Quantitative Analysis, Vol. 21, No. 3, pp. 335-341.

Tinic, S. and R. West, (1984), "Risk and Return: January Versus and the Rest of the Year." Journal of Financial Economics, 13.

Tinic, S. and R. West, (1986), "Risk Return and Equilibrium: A Revisit." Journal of Political Economy, 94, pp. 126-147.

FORECASTING PRICE TRENDS AT THE LISBON STOCK EXCHANGE [1]

Nuno Crato [2]
Universidade dos Açores / Universidade Técnica de Lisboa,
Instituto Superior de Economia

Álvaro Assis Lopes
Universidade Técnica de Lisboa, Instituto Superior Técnico
Av. Rovisco Pais, 1000 Lisboa, Portugal

ABSTRACT: *The behaviour of stock price series at Lisbon stock exchange is not compatible with the main implications of the efficient–market hypothesis: the analysis of some main securities traded at Lisbon between 1985 and 1987 show strong autocorrelations and visible trends; applying filter rules similar to that of Alexander it is possible to achieve superior rates of return; a structural model with a trend and a cyclical component achieves a good forecasting perfomance.*

KEYWORDS: *efficient–market hypothesis / filter tests / price cycles / price trends / stock prices forecasting / structural models / trade rules.*

1. Introduction

The main purpose of this paper is to present the recent evolution of the Lisbon stock exchange and show how its behaviour is incompatible with the main implications of the efficient–market hypothesis.

The paper is organized as follows: (1) A brief history of the Lisbon stock exchange is outlined and some economic fundamentals of its natural "inefficiency" are singled out. (2) Some implications of the efficient–market hypothesis are faced with empirical evidence. First, **the memory of the stock prices** series is discussed and **strong trends** are detected. Second, the possibility of achieving **superior rates of return** over a relatively long period is demonstrated. Some **filter rules**,

---

[1] We appreciate the comments of participants at the research workshop. We particularly thank S. Ekern and R.J. Sweeney for their valuable comments and suggestions, as well as the assistance of A. Egídio in the final computations.

[2] Address: Av. Sacadura Cabral, 5, 5ºE, 1000 Lisboa, Portugal.

NATO ASI Series, Vol. F54
A Reappraisal of the Efficiency of Financial Markets
Edited by Rui M.C. Guimaraes et al.

based on the existence of trends, are applied showing the possibility of a further increase on the profits. (3) Particular attention is paid to a very simple structural model which, during some recognizable periods, has a good forecasting performance. (4) The last section summarizes the main conclusions.

2. Ups and downs of the Lisbon stock exchange

In 1985 Portuguese stock markets began a spectacular rise. Until the end of 1987 this rise maintained a strong rate, attracting all kind of investors and speculators.

At Lisbon, the official market increased the volume of transactions by 793 per cent from 1985 to 1986. In the first nine months of 1987 this volume became ten times superior to that of all the precedent year.

At the same time, the most reliable price index — that of Banco Totta & Açores — reported an increase of more than 2 times from December 1985 to December 1986 and about 11 times since December 1985 to September 87 (table 1).

Table 1
BTA STOCK PRICE INDEX (last day of the month)
March 1977 = 100

	1984	1985	1986	1987	
JAN	180.9	239.5	835.2	1556.0	
FEB	218.9	243.5	824.5	1646.0	
MAR	205.6	257.1	932.5	1989.1	
APR	206.2	281.6	911.6	2467.3	
MAY	207.1	322.5	876.1	2782.6	
JUN	196.4	345.1	904.3	2533.1	
JUL	189.0	389.2	953.5	2968.2	
AGO	193.3	447.9	977.0	3879.8	
SEP	195.7	505.3	1108.3	6489.1	
OCT	208.5	548.5	1158.1	4855.6	
NOV	246.7	534.1	1146.3	3873.0	
DEC	249.7	566.4	1202.0	3481.1	(1)

Source: Banco Totta & Açores (1) Dec.11

For those who were aware of the economic and political evolution of the country a strong developement of the stock market was predictable although anyone could foretell such a spectacular rise.

As a matter of fact the stock market, just before the revolution of April 1974, showed a strong movement and remained almost inactive during the next few years. The liberalization of financial markets slowly became a reality after the beginning of the 80's, and surely became a need after the visible integration in the EEC, that finally took place at 1986. These structural changes in the Portuguese economic system should lead to other important changes in the financial markets.

However, some particular reasons should exist to explain the abnormal rise of the Portuguese stock markets.

The recovery of the european financial markets in the 80's is certainly an important factor, although not a decisive one. What seems to be of utmost importance is the unbalance between demand and supply of financial assets, wich occurred after the gradual liberalization of Portuguese financial markets.The demand for alternative investment has been a reality since the fall of nominal interest rates, that began at the end of 1984. Moreover, the real interest rates had never been really attractive, as they were very low (1–4 per cent) if not negative. Portuguese people, looking for alternative applications for their savings, suddenly realized that stock prices were continuously moving up. At the some time, most corporations began a rush for public issues, which became a quick and profitable way of financing.

In a context of lack of alternative financial applications, with Portuguese financial markets still dominated by tight rules, this movement created an euphoria on stock markets, benefiting small investors, shareholders and corporations. The movement was self–sustained and belief was spread that demand would continue growing faster then supply.

In this situation stock prices became almost a fiction. As a matter of fact, they were independent on firm returns. Public issues, priced systematically at a value higher that book–value plus goodwill, were easily sold (Barreto, 1987).

Until the end of 1987 public authorities seemed unable to call the market to a stabilization point and some actions probably have had perverse effects. It is worthwhile to refer to a controversy rule that, in a normal situation, would prevent the prices to play an informative role and that, in this context, probably delayed the normal evolution of stock prices. It is the so-called "five per cent rule", which prevents, daily, a movement of the prices superior to + - 5 per cent. The rule appeared on March 1986 and it was effective until mid 1987. It explains some systematic patterns of stock prices.

Finally, on October 1987, the prime–minister, on a television speech, seriously warned small investors. The speech led to the inevitable crash. Within a month, the stock price index fell to half its previous value.

3. Memory of stock prices and trends in the market

In order to study the memory of stock prices three series will be analysed from January 1986 to November 10, 1987. The first time series is the stock price index published by Banco Totta & Açores — BTA. The second one represents the stock prices of MARCONI Co., which securities are responsible for 20 per cent of the last year transactions at Lisbon stock exchange. The third one is the security prices of another "blue–chip", the CISF, one of the Portuguese most important financial corporations. The series represents transaction prices.

The figures below show the evolution of the three series.

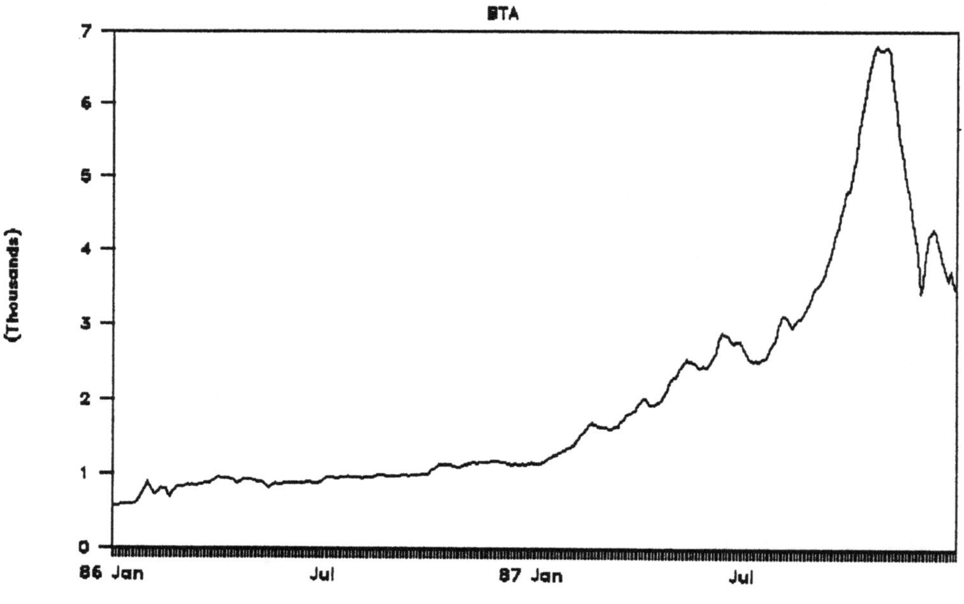

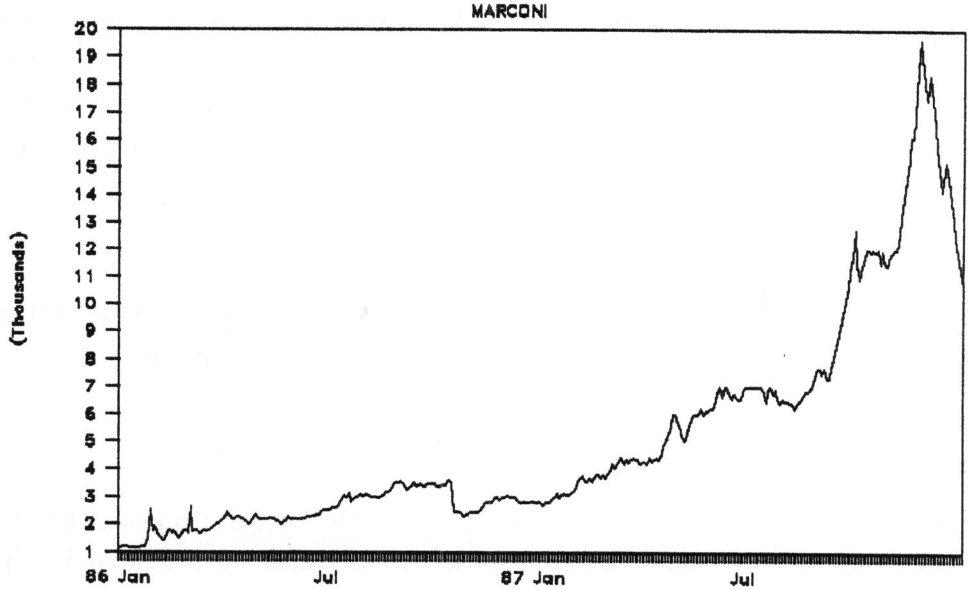
MARCONI
(Thousands)
20
19
18
17
16
15
14
13
12
11
10
9
8
7
6
5
4
3
2
1
86 Jan
Jul
87 Jan
Jul

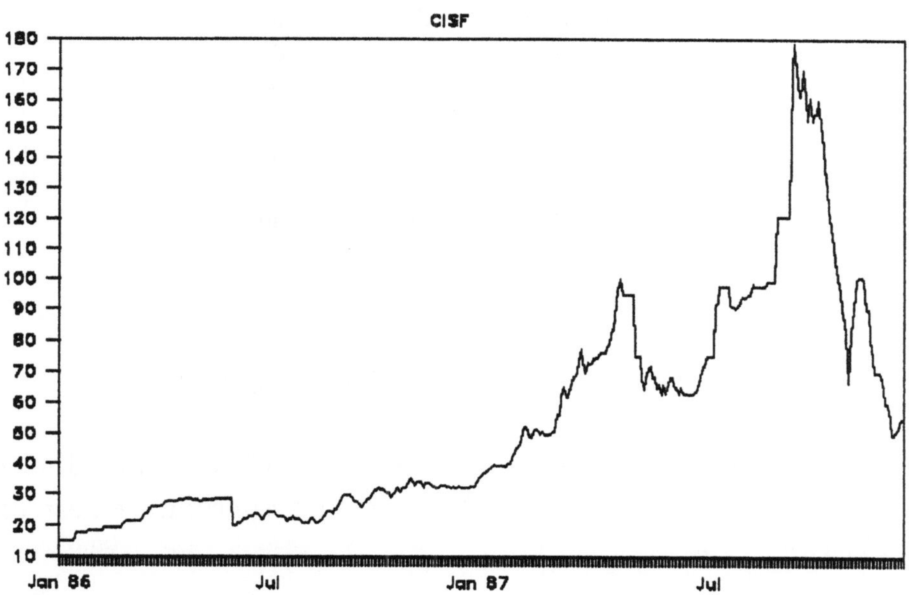
CISF
180
170
160
150
140
130
120
110
100
90
80
70
60
50
40
30
20
10
Jan 86
Jul
Jan 87
Jul

To study the nature of the series it is necessary to pretransform them and study the series of the returns. Representing by $\{z_t\}$ the series of stock index values or the price of stock transactions, the returns, ignoring dividends, can be defined as the first differences of logarithms:

$$x_t = \log z_t - \log z_{t-1} \tag{1}$$

According to Taylor (1986), the random walk hypothesis compatible with efficient–market assumption can be formulated as follows

$$H_0: \; EX_t = EX_{t+\tau}, \; Cov(X_t, X_{t+\tau}) = 0, \; \forall_{t,\tau} \tag{2}$$

To test the randomness of the return series the correlation coefficients, at lags one to ten, were calculated and their values are shown in the following table:

Table 2
AUTOCORRELATION COEFFICIENTS OF RETURN SERIES

	BTA	MARCONI(1)	CISF
r_1	.62*	.20*	.11*
r_2	.34*	.04	.02
r_3	.14*	.05	.05
r_4	.08	.07	.09
r_5	.13	.03	.01
r_6	.20*	.03	.01
r_7	.22*	.08	.07
r_8	.15*	.05	.09
r_9	−.02	−.06	−.03
r_{10}	−.07	−.06	−.01

(1) From March 1986 to November 10, 1987

The significant coefficients, at 5 per cent level, are pointed out with a star – *. But, as Taylor (1986) noted, it is appropriate here to test the statistic

$$Q_k = n \sum_{\tau=1}^{k} r_\tau^2 \tag{3}$$

Knowing that $n(R_1^2 + \cdots + R_k^2) \sim \chi_k^2$ if the independence of the coefficients is assumed, H_0 is rejected at a 5 per cent level for the first two series, as $Q_{10} > 18.31$: BTA $Q_{10} = 238.89$; MARCONI $Q_{10} = 20.32$; CISF$Q_{10} = 13.65$.

The most striking aspect is the strong autocorrelation presented at BTA series, as if the random fluctuations in the individual stock prices were compensated, generating a collective evolution with a visible trend.

Another interesting aspect is the negative value of autocorrelations of lag 9. At Lisbon stock exchange there are four trading days each week. The values suggest a cycle in the series that will be discussed at a next section of this paper.

Finally, it should be noted that the strong movement presented in the series during the first two months of 1986 can disturb the analysis of the subsequent period. Marconi security prices showed a very random behaviour in that period, with a negative autocorrelation at lag one. So, the values of these two months have been regarded as outlier observations.

4. The achievement of superior rates of return

Another well known consequence of the efficient-market hypothesis is the impossibility of the achievement of superior rates of return.

A direct inspection of the behaviour of the series is sufficient to see that the investment on the securities had provided high returns during a relatively long period. Random investments, which roughly correspond to returns given by BTA index, generated, from the beginning of 1986 to November of 1987 a profit of 584 per cent!

Applying simple filter rules to the stock series returns can still be increased. Ignoring trade cost — not a particularly misleading simplification given the high returns involved — such filter rules can give an idea of the increased profits that some particular investors, or speculators, could get.

The first filter rule here applied is that of selling stocks the day next to the one in which the prices fall down more than g per cent, and to buy stocks the day after the one in which prices increase more than g per cent. It is a simplified version of the Alexander filter rule (1961).

The results are shown in the next table, for different values of g. Each value in the table represents the total amount hold at the end of the period due to an unitary investment.

Table 3
ALEXANDER FILTER (1 day)

g	BTA	MARCONI	CISF
$1.0E-12$	16.405	9.231	11.810
.0005	16.093	9.231	11.810
.0010	15.761	9.231	11.810
.0050	16.614	9.776	10.276
.0100	13.211	7.343	10.005
.0150	12.524	7.429	9.520
.0200	12.191	7.188	8.021
.0300	11.233	8.718	8.908
.0400	11.396	7.229	7.057
.0500	7.510	3.334	4.651
.1000	6.841	1.010	1.592
.5000	6.841	9.330	5.477

The results of a buy–and–hold policy are equivalent to those obtained with $g = 50$ per cent. Results are singled out in next table.

Table 4
TOTAL AMOUNT HELD AT NOVEMBER 10, 1987
DUE TO A UNITARY INVESTIMENT AT JANUARY 2, 1986
WITH BUY–AND–HOLD POLICY

BTA	MARCONI	CISF
6.841	9.330	5.477

The increased profits of diversified investments is apparent in the results obtained with BTA index. No filter rule could lead to profits lower then those got with a buy–and–hold policy. Naturally, this fact derives from the highly autocorrelated index series.

It is also interesting to notice how the profits decrease with the value of g, as it can be seen at the next figure.

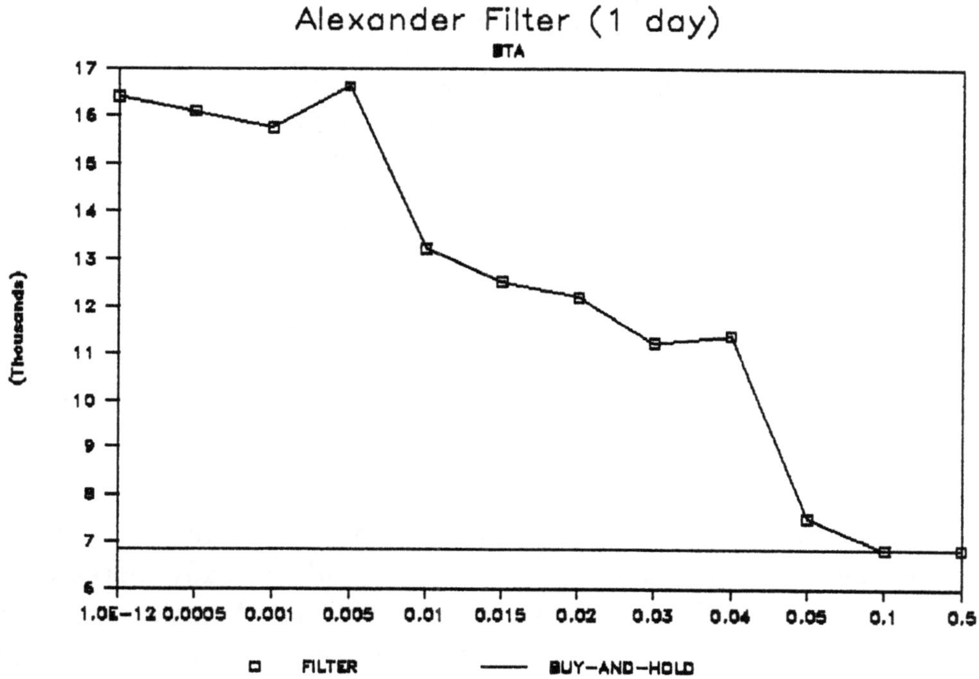

With individual investments the results are not so conclusive. The filter trade rule, applied to Marconi securities, is almost unable to increase the profits. The same rule, applied to CISF securities, can provide returns that double those obtained with no trade rule. Within the range $0 < g < .01$ the value of the profits does not change very much.

There is, of course, a strong limitation on this trade rule, since it needs a quick and on line system to control daily trades. Only financial institutions could profit from that device.

Another trade rule here studied is the one of selling and buying according to the increase or decrease in the prices during the previous two weeks. It is also a filter that derives directly from the assumption on the existence of trends. The results of the simulations are presented in the next table. The trade decisions are taken according to the total evolution of the prices during 8 trading days — the two weeks before the day of the decision.

Table 5
ALEXANDER FILTER (8 days)

g	BTA	MARCONI	CISF
.0005	14.916	30.638	20.798
.0010	14.916	30.638	20.798
.0050	14.574	28.887	20.383
.0100	13.833	27.144	20.450
.0150	14.266	26.560	19.998
.0200	14.058	22.674	19.440
.0300	14.781	18.938	18.375
.0400	13.526	20.748	17.707
.0500	12.892	20.150	16.639
.1000	7.955	16.171	16.916
.5000	6.718	8.868	5.477

The results are even more convicing then those obtained on a one day trading rule basis. First, the profits are substantially increased in all series. Second, this eight days trading rule is based on the possibility of detecting short term movements in the prices more accurately than analyzing consecutive changes.

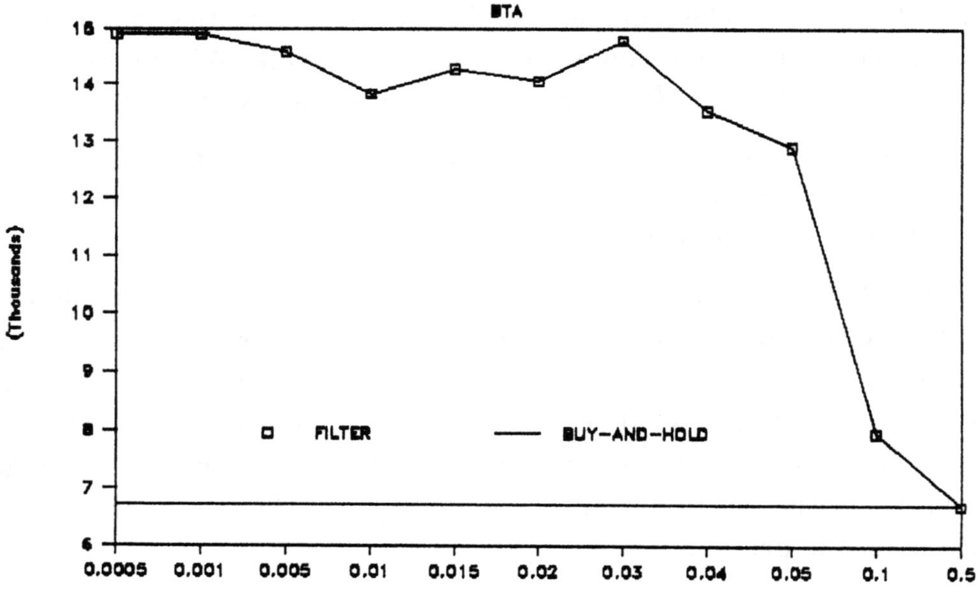

Alexander Filter (8 days)

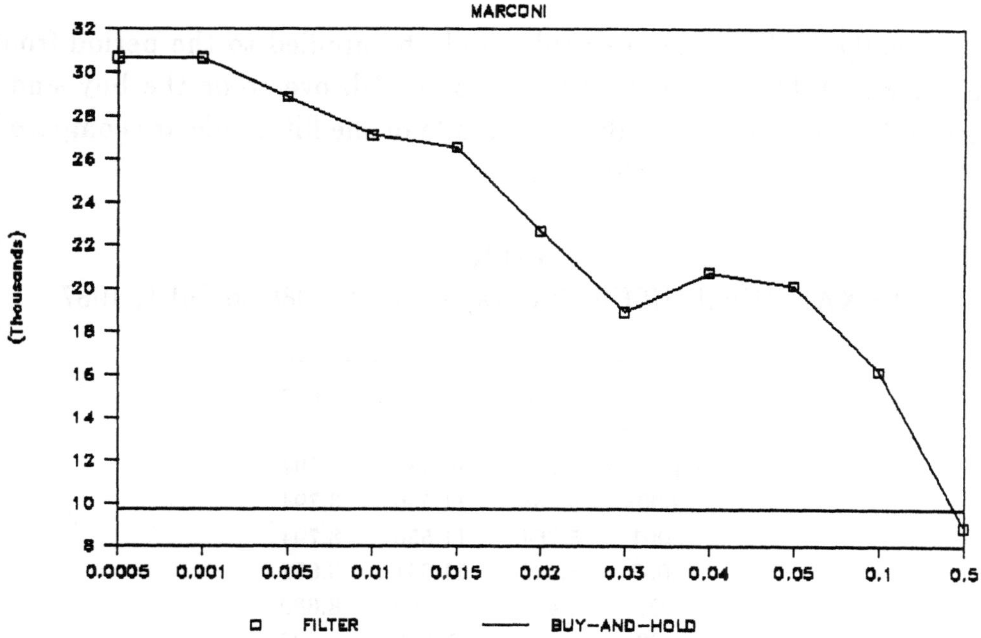

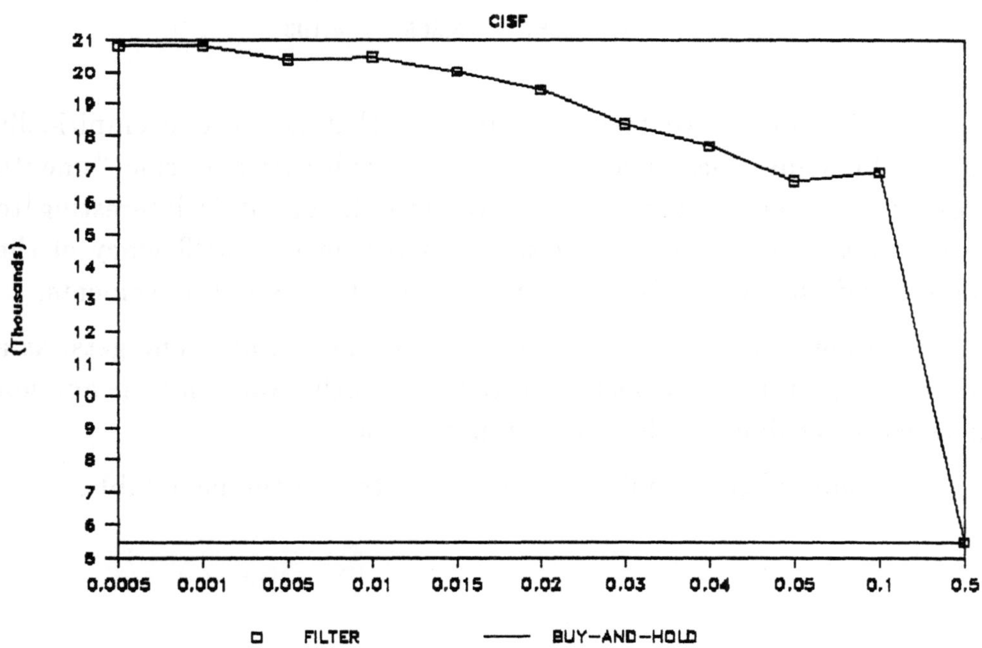

It could be argued that the increased profits are due to the behaviour of the series in the second semester of 1987, where a peak is easily detected. As a mather of fact, a buy–and–hold policy would bear the substantial decrease in prices after October 14, 1987.

Actually, if the same filter rule would be applied to the period from January 2, 1986 to July 1, 1987 it would still overcome the buy–and–hold policy. On the next table the results of the filter rule are compared with those of buy–and–hold policy.

Table 6

ALEXANDER FILTER (8 days) – Jan 2, 1986 to Jul 1, 1987

g	BTA	MARCONI	CISF
$1.E-12$	5.708	10.983	8.794
.0005	5.764	11.556	8.794
.001	5.764	11.556	8.794
.005	5.632	11.031	8.652
.01	5.415	10.386	8.680
.02	5.526	9.004	8.527
.03	5.810	7.636	8.149
.05	5.290	8.407	7.418
.1	3.317	7.124	7.184
.5	4.387	5.565	4.193
$B-H$	4.387	5.565	4.193

It is whorthwhile to test another filter that is the one empirically applied by some small investors. We shall call this new rule "smooth Portuguese filter", a famous cigarette brand, and it is interesting to notice that it corresponds to a strong belief on the inefficiency of the market and on the provisional characters of the upward movements.

According to that rule one sells stock at the moment one gets, as a profit, the quantity previously invested — in such a way that the amount invested never doubles the original investment.

The results of the simulations are presented on the next table.

Table 7
PORTUGUESE SMOOTH FILTER

g	BTA	MARCONI	CISF
.0005	4.986	6.211	5.434
.0010	4.986	6.211	5.434
.0050	4.908	6.133	5.438
.0100	4.831	12.029	5.473
.0150	4.876	6.085	5.411
.0200	4.846	5.694	5.371
.0300	4.954	5.500	5.592
.0400	4.849	5.658	5.402
.0500	4.687	5.649	5.290
.1000	4.038	5.241	5.564
.5000	3.867	4.705	3.731

The results are again stable over a large range of the parameter g. This filter rule is obviously not a rational one and its results are modest when compared with those obtained by Alexander filters. In any way, they show the possibility of obtaining superior rates of return reducing the risk to a low level.

5. Forecasting trends in prices

Assuming that return series do not follow the random pattern defined at (3), wich is compatible with the efficient–market hypothesis, it is natural to study the forecasting perfomance of a model that includes a trend to explain the behaviour of stock prices.

Let $\{z_t\}$ be the original series. A linear structural model can be applied to the series $\{y_t\}$ defined by

$$y_t = log z_t \tag{4}$$

The structural model adopted is the one of Theil and Goldberg (1964) with a level μ_t and a trend β_t following a random walk:

$$\begin{aligned} y_t &= \mu_t + u_t \\ \mu_t &= \mu_{t-1} + \beta_{t-1} + v_t \\ \beta_{t-1} &= \beta_{t-2} + w_{t-1} \end{aligned} \tag{5}$$

$Eu_t = Ev_t = Ew_t = 0$ for all t; $Eu_tu_\tau = Ev_tv_\tau = Ew_tw_\tau = 0$ and $Eu_tv_t = Eu_tw_t = Ev_tw_t = 0$ for all t and τ.

This model can be presented in state space form with the transition equation and measurement equation as follows:

$$\begin{bmatrix} \mu_t \\ \beta_t \end{bmatrix} = \begin{bmatrix} 1 & 1 \\ 0 & 1 \end{bmatrix} \begin{bmatrix} \mu_{t-1} \\ \beta_{t-1} \end{bmatrix} + \begin{bmatrix} v_t \\ w_t \end{bmatrix} \tag{6}$$

$$Y_t = \begin{bmatrix} 1 & 0 \end{bmatrix} \begin{bmatrix} \mu_t \\ \beta_t \end{bmatrix} + u_t$$

With the Kalman filter algorithm the model was applied to MARCONI series. The parameter estimation and the one step ahead prediction have been accomplished with the SSM package (from the London School of Economics).

As result of the calculations, significant level and trend parameters were found, (steady state at period 48):

PARAMETER	COEFICIENT (lastperiod)	S.ERROR
LEVEL	9.6775	.0248
TREND	.0139	.0070

$R^2 = .994$ for the one step ahead prediction

At the same time a model with a cyclical component had been fitted, now to the series $\{Z_t\}$. The component Γ is added to the transition equation allowing

$$\mu_t = \mu_{t-1} + \beta_{t-1} + \Gamma_{t-1} + u_t \tag{7}$$

and its own transition is given by

$$\begin{bmatrix} \Gamma_t \\ \Gamma_t^* \end{bmatrix} = \delta \begin{bmatrix} \cos\theta & \sin\theta \\ -\sin\theta & \cos\theta \end{bmatrix} \begin{bmatrix} \Gamma_{t-1} \\ \Gamma_{t-1}^* \end{bmatrix} + \begin{bmatrix} \epsilon_t \\ \epsilon_t^* \end{bmatrix} \tag{8}$$

where ϵ_t^* and ϵ_t are uncorrelated zero mean disturbance terms and Γ^* appears by construction (cf. Harvey, 1984).

The interesting thing is that a significant cyclical component has been found and a period of 20 days has been identified. The same component is confirmed with the seasonal ARIMA model:

$$\underset{(.060)}{(1+.176B^{18}).Z_t} = \underset{(14.678)}{44.100} + (\underset{(.059)}{1+.161B} + \underset{(.060)}{.107B^2} + \underset{(.060)}{.146B^3}).\epsilon_t \qquad (9)$$

The reason for the existence of this cyclical component is not evident but the results seem to be conclusive. The most striking aspect is that the period corresponds to 19–20 trading days, roughly a month. Perhaps the regularity of monthly proceedings of financial institutions could be an explanation, but it seems that the investments from personal savings, made just after salary payments, are responsible for this cycle in stock prices.

6. Conclusions

The stock market here analyzed is particularly disturbing since it maintained, during two years, unusual upward movements in prices. Nevertheless it is interesting to compare its behaviour with standard implications (cf. Brealey and Myers, 1984) of the efficient market hypothesis.

The time series of stock prices show strong autocorrelations. These autocorrelations could be exploited applying filter rules similar to that of Alexander. Some trading rules were simulated and the more profitable ones were those relying on the existance of medium term trends.

A structural forecasting model was fitted to price series with Kalman filter algorithm. The model seems to be particularly able to adapt itself to changes in price movements and can be used with little historical information. That attractive feature seems to be useful to time series showing a turbulent behaviour. With the state space model a cyclical component in price series was detected and Box–Jenkins seasonal ARIMA confirmed its existence.

REFERENCES

Alexander, S.S., 1961, Price movements in speculative markets: trends or random walks, Industrial Management Review 2, 7–26.

Barreto, I., 1987, Acções: o Jogo do Investimento (Texto Editora, Lisboa)

Brealey, R. and Myers, S., 1984, Principles of Corporate Finance (McGraw–Hill)

Harvey, A.C., 1984, Trends and cycles in macroeconomic time series, LSE Discussion Paper A–45

Praetz, P.D., 1976, Rates of return on filter tests, The Journal of Finance XXXI N.1, 71–75

Taylor, S.J., 1986, Modelling Financial Time Series (John Wiley & Sons, Chichester)

Theil, H. and Wage, S., 1964, Some observations on adaptive forecasting, Management Science 6, 324–43.

Comments on Nuno Crato and Alvaro Assis Lopes "The Lisbon Stock Exchange: A Particularly Disturbing Market"

by Steinar Ekern

Without going into more recent time-related or size-related anomalies, the authors use somewhat classic approaches to checking for inefficiency of the Lisbon Stock Exchange. Their data set is restricted to 3 time series of daily prices, i.e., one stock index and two individual stocks. Information on the construction of the index and on the type of prices were lacking in the paper as presented, which also contained apparent inconsistencies between tables and verbal comments.

The autocorrelation analysis showing significant correlations for several days might have been supplemented with run tests. If so, I guess the authors would have reported conspicuously long runs of positive price increases not found elsewhere in the literature. In their filter analysis they use simplified versions rather than the more conventional filter rule versions. Quite surprisingly, they show that, for the stock index, any filter causing trades will yield a higher final wealth than the more risky buy and hold policy. Thus they get both a higher expected return and a smaller risk using the filters. So the Portuguese may both eat their cake and keep it as well.

In the final forecasting part of the paper, relevant parameters for the return series for one particular individual stock are estimated, first by a Kalman filter approach and then by an ARIMA model. A good fitting power for a given sample does not necessarily imply corresponding superior forecasting performance for out of sample data. Unfortunately, no measure of the forecasting accuracy, like bias, MAD, or RMSE, are presented. Furthermore, it would have been interesting to know whether a more simple alternative, like standard Holt-Winters exponential smoothing, would yield approximately as good forecasts as those obtained by more complex schemes. Also, if cyclical movements are a major concern, then spectral analysis might be tried out.

The Jennergren and Sorensen paper presented at this conference demonstrated how efficient the Copenhagen stock exchange was in the 1890's. Hence it is a puzzle how the Lisbon stock exchange in the 1980's may be inefficient to such an extent. The authors may be kept busy for years updating the developing efficiency of the Lisbon market following the integration into the EEC.

NATO ASI Series, Vol. F54
A Reappraisal of the Efficiency of Financial Markets
Edited by Rui M. C. Guimaraes et al.

The Market for Initial Public Offerings.
An analysis of the Amsterdam Stock Exchange (1982-1987).

Roberto E. Wessels

Erasmus University Rotterdam
P.O.Box 1738
3000 DR ROTTERDAM
The Netherlands

Keywords/Abstract Initial Public Offerings / Methods of issuing new stock / Market efficiency.

The Amsterdam Stock Exchange permits initial public offerings to be made in various ways. The price adjustment following the introduction is analysed and the differences between methods tested. Although one method in particular seems to produce severe underpricing and thus is a source of potential excess returns for investors, we could not find evidence that investors are able to predict which issues are likely to be underpriced. The paper concludes that the market appears to function quite efficiently even though the question why some firms should choose to underprice their shares remains unanswered.

NATO ASI Series, Vol. F54
A Reappraisal of the Efficiency of Financial Markets
Edited by Rui M. C. Guimaraes et al.

1. Introduction[1]

The initial return on the shares of firms going public is often unusually high. This high return however, is only a very short-run phenomenon and is in general not sustained in the aftermarket. In the literature[2], this phenomenon known as as the underpricing of initial public offerings (IPOs).

A number of interesting questions can be posed with respect to the underpricing phenomenon. First, is it the case that what is recorded as underpricing in turn implies that investors can expect to earn excess returns when they subscribe to initial public offerings? Do investors really receive windfall gains? Second, do firms which go public suffer opportunity losses? In other words, is the cost of raising capital higher than necessary?

These questions seek answers to different aspects of market efficiency. The first question is addressed to the problem of market efficiency from the point of view of the investor; the second question looks at the problem of underpricing from the point of view of the firm. Despite a great deal of folklore, as well as serious research in this area, the problem of why initial public offerings are underpriced remains yet another of the many unsolved puzzles in the literature of finance[3].

In this paper we examine an institutional environment in which firms seeking to make an IPO, have a choice by which method the initial or offering price will be determined. The evidence presented in this paper suggests that the incidence of underpricing very much depends on the method used to determine the offering price. Different methods produce different degrees of underpricing. As the degree of underpricing in each method is different, one cannot but help wonder why in a competitive market, the pricing methods which produce the most underpricing, should survive. Perhaps even more puzzling is that in our sample, the method associated with the largest degree of underpricing is the one used in about half of the IPOs in the sample.

The rest of the paper is organised as follows. In the next two sections we first describe the institutional characteristics of the Amsterdam equity market and then the methods by which shares can be offered in an IPO. In section 4, the sample data is described. Then, in section 5, the returns on initial public offerings, classified according to a number of different criteria, are analysed. In section 6, we pose the question investors can predict which stocks are most likely to be underpriced. In a sense, this is a test of the efficiency of the market for initial public offerings. Our results tend to support the notion that this market is efficient. The results of the paper are summarized in section 7.

2. Initial public offerings on the Amsterdam Stock Exchange.

In the Netherlands there are two equity markets on which firms can make an IPO. The largest and most important is the Amsterdam Stock Exchange. This is a market run by the professional association of security dealers in the Netherlands. The other market is an over-the-counter market operated by two small banks. These two markets are generally referred to as the official and the unofficial or parallel market.

In 1982, the Amsterdam Stock Exchange created a second tier (essentially a market for small firms) with less stringent listing requirements. This second tier of the official market became known, confusingly, as the official parallel market since the initially listed shares were originally traded in the unofficial or parallel market. In the paper we shall refer to the two tiers of the Amsterdam Stock Exchange as the official market and the parallel market respectively, and to the unofficial market as the OTC market.

Before a firm can make an IPO it must first obtain permission from the Ministry of Finance to have its shares listed on an exchange. In the case that the shares are listed on the Amsterdam Stock Exchange, the professional association acts as the regulatory agent for the Ministry. For a listing on the OTC market, the request is reviewed directly by the Ministry.

The request for a listing must be made on the basis of a 'notice of introduction', whose contents are subject to detailed regulation. If the request for listing is made because the firm wishes to simultaneously launch an IPO, the 'notice of introduction' serves as the prospectus for the offering and additional requirements must be met.

In order to obtain a listing two main requirements must be met. First, the issuing firm must meet certain informational criteria such as providing its annual accounts over the past three years, specifying to what uses the proceeds of the offering will be put and disclosing the shareholdings of the management and board of directors. Second, external certification or bonding of the information revealed in the notice must be provided. The firm's annual accounts must be certified by a chartered public accountant and the prospectus must be submitted to the Stock Exchange by a member of the association, i.e. a stockbroker or bank who therefore sponsors the request.

Unfortunately, the notice does not reveal what contractual arrangements have been concluded between the issuing firm and the member of the Stock Exchange signing the prospectus. In particular, one cannot determine from the notice whether an IPO has been underwritten (in the case of a rights offer, whether there is a stand-by agreement), whether the offer is made on a best-efforts basis, or whether the member is simply acting as a collecting agent with no further distribution or marketing effort on its part.

The main differences in the stringency of the requirements between the official market and the parallel market are the minimum size of the issue (parallel market: 2.5 million guilders; official market: 30 million guilders), and the percentage of shares outstanding for which listing must be requested. For the official market the requirement is 100%; for the parallel market it is only 10%

3. Setting the offering price.

A very interesting feature of the Amsterdam equity markets is that IPOs can be made in a variety of ways. Firms going public on the Amsterdam Stock Exchange have a choice - at least in principle - by which method their shares will be offered for sale to the public. There are no regulations similar to those in the United States or France specifying how the price of the offer must be determined[4].

However, only three methods have been used: the fixed price offer, the rights offer and the offer by tender.

The fixed price offer is very similar to the one commonly used in the U.S. The notice-cum-prospectus states the number of shares being offered for sale and the price per share. Investors can then submit bids for the number of shares they wish to take up at the stated price. There is no posting of a bond or prepayment involved. Payment for the shares is made after the allocation of the bids is announced and trading starts. In fact, investors can easily sell any allocated shares on the first day of trade and only settle the difference between the offering price and the price at which the shares are sold. The Stock Exchange does not have any rules on how oversubscribed issues are to be allocated other than the general principle that the allocation must be done systematically. However, it is not clear what this latter term implies in practice.

In an offer by tender the issuing firm sollicits bids (combinations of price and quantity) for a given number of shares. According to the rules of the Stock Exchange, the bids must be allocated competitively, that is to say, without using price discrimination. This method resembles a sealed-bid competitive auction (see Harris and Raviv, 1981) and is very similar to the one used for initial public offerings on the Paris Bourse (see McDonald and Jacquillat, 1974).

Finally, in a rights offer, the issuing firm offers to sell to holders of a designated right a share at a fixed price. The right must be acquired from existing shareholders. An initial public offering made through a rights offer can be thought of as a two-stage procedure. First, about two weeks prior to the offering date, a market is made in the rights. Investors interested in subscribing to the offer then have the opportunity to acquire the appropriate number of rights by placing orders with specialists on the floor of the exchange. At the same time, existing shareholders can place selling orders with the specialists. In the second stage, the holders of the rights can exercise their option to buy new or existing shares, as the case may be, at a price which is fixed in advance.

In the literature, the rights offer is generally discussed as a method of selling new shares in so-called primary distributions. Our sample however, also contains has some cases in which an initial public offerings of existing shares (secondary distributions) was made through a rights offer. Although it might seem strange why this procedure is adopted to sell existing shares, it should be recognized that it provides a way for shareholders to receive the market price of the shares before the shares are listed on the exchange and a market price has been observed. Of course, the same result could be achieved if shareholders could first "test the water" by offering only a small proportion of the shares they wished to sell, and then sold the rest after having observed a market price. The problem is that as the shares are not listed, this cannot be done without evading the regulations. A way to get around this constraint would be to create a grey market (i.e. in which transactions take place on the condition that the securities are actually issued), prior to the offering.

The three methods of determining the offering price have different implications for the allocation of subscriptions to IPOs. With a fixed price offering, if the offering price is set too low, there will be oversubscription and the price on the first day of trade will rise over the offering price. If the price is set too high, there will be excess supply and the price on the first day of trade will decrease with respect to the offering price. For some strange reason, in the parlance of the market, these two situations are characterized as showing that the IPO was "successful" (i.e. when the price increases) or "unsuccessful" (i.e. when the price decreases). From the perspective of the firm making the IPO, it must however be doubted whether the success or failure of the offering would be judged on quite the same criteria.

This then leads us to the observation that IPOs made by either the rights or tender method can be undersubscribed, but not oversubscribed. In other words, the problem of an excess demand for shares which is so often observed with fixed price offerings, is not present if the offering is made through a tender or through a rights issue. From the perspective of the firm, the two methods are therefore to be preferred to fixed price offerings. Given that we observe firms choosing to make the IPO by the fixed price method notwithstanding this choice, we are left with the question what determines the choice.

Thus in addition to trying to explain why it is so commonly observed that fixed price offers are systematically priced below the price in the aftermarket, there is also the need for an explanation of what determines the method by which the offering price is set. A fixed price issue, in and by itself, must also have some intrinsic value, at least to those firms who choose not to avoid the underpricing phenomenon by availing themselves of the rights or tender method.

Although the answer to this question lies outside of the scope of this paper, an analysis of a sample of firm going public under the three regimes for determing the offering price can perhaps help to shed some light on the nature of the problem. But first the sample data will be described in the next section.

4. The sample data.

In the U.S. the great majority of the initial public offerings are made on the over-the-counter market (see Ibbotson, 1975). The significance of the Amsterdam over-the-counter market is however quite limited. In the recent past, the great majority of the initial public offerings have been made on one of the two tiers of the Amsterdam Stock Exchange, i.e. either on the official market or on the parallel market. The number of offerings on the over-the-counter market have been very small. In addition, reliable price data is difficult to obtain so that we have not included any offerings from this market in our sample.

The sampling period is from when trading started on the parallel market (January 28, 1982), up to October 9, 1987. During this period, a total of 122 previously unlisted shares were offered for sale on the official and the parallel market. Five criteria were used to select which offerings would be included in the sample:

1. The initial offering comprised only common stock. A total of five issues were excluded because the offering was a combination of stock and some other financial instrument such as warrants, or convertible debt;

2. At the time of offering, the shares were not listed on a local or a foreign exchange. Only two offerings were excluded because the shares were already listed abroad (London Stock Exchange). In addition, 18 offerings were excluded because they previously were traded on the Amsterdam OTC market.

3. The issuing firm was not a mutual fund. About one third (47) of the all the offerings during the sample period were initial offerings of mutual fund stock.

4. The IPO was made by either the fixed price method, the tender method or the rights method. Three offerings were excluded because they did not meet this requirement. In these three cases, there was no public offering to speak of. Rather, the Stock Exchange allowed the shares to be temporarily listed. In one case, the listing was later withdrawn due to insufficient trading interest. In order for shares to be listed in this way, the Stock Exchange must be given proof of substantial previous volume of unofficial trade, i.e. trades on the OTC market.

5. After listing, the shares were not subject to thin trading. In order to be included in the sample, the shares had to have a record of at least thirty price quotations in the forty trading days subsequent to the offering. Only one offering was dropped from the sample due to this requirement.

In total, 46 initial public offerings (out of 122) satisfied the above five criteria. Descriptive statistics of these initial public offerings, disaggregated by market of listing, type of distribution and method of offering are provided in Tables 1.1 and 1.2.

First, Table 1.1 provides a breakdown of the size of the firms making the IPO; Table 1.2. provides a breakdown of the relative size of the initial public offerings, where relative size is defined as the amount raised by the IPO divided by the market value of the issuing firms' equity.

Initial public offerings on the parallel market outnumber offerings on the official market in the sample by almost 2 to 1. By this measure, the parallel market therefore seems to have been successful in facilitating the access of small firms to the public equity market.

By method of issue, the sample contains 19 fixed price offerings, 20 offerings made through a rights issue and only 7 offerings by means of the tender method. There is no obvious reason why the tender method should not have been used more frequently. However, in private communication, several investment bankers expressed the opinion that "the market thinks it's too complicated".

In Tables 1.1. and 1.2 the offerings in the sample are divided into three categories: primary, secondary and combined distributions. Primary distributions are defined to comprise offerings involving only new shares; secondary distributions involve offerings of existing shares and combined distributions are offerings of a package of both new and existing shares.

This disaggregation by type of distribution provides some insights into why firms were taken public. In general there are two motives for taking a firm public. First, the existing shareholders may wish to diversify their portfolios by reducing their interest in the firm. Existing shares are then sold to a group of new shareholders, i.e. a secondary distribution. The second motive is that the firm needs to raise new capital for investment purposes and has decided to increase its equity capital by offering to sell new shares, i.e. a primary distribution.

The difference between primary and secondary offerings is that in secondary offerings the number of shares outstanding is not affected by the offering and that the proceeds of the IPO go entirely to the existing shareholders. Primary distributions increase the number of shares outstanding and the proceeds go mainly to the firm[5].

Table 1.1: Size of the issuing firm disaggregated by market, type of distribution and method of issue. (Size is measured as the post-offering market value of the common stock, in units of 10 million guilders.)

	Market					
Distribution	Parallel			Official		
	N	Mean	S.e.	N	Mean	S.e.
Primary						
Rights	2	2.120	0.955	.		
Fixed	1	1.977	.	.		
Total	3	2.072	0.553	.		
Secondary						
Rights	6	6.703	2.171	2	6.625	0.425
Tender	1	1.575	.	.		
Fixed	3	3.741	0.971	4	19.812	6.268
Total	10	5.302	1.414	6	15.416	4.843
Combined						
Rights	5	7.580	1.883	5	15.591	5.834
Tender	5	9.257	1.688	1	13.454	.
Fixed	7	3.877	0.596	4	18.807	10.630
Total	17	6.548	0.929	10	16.664	4.797
Aggregate						
Rights	13	6.335	1.286	7	13.029	4.353
Tender	6	7.977	1.881	1	13.454	.
Fixed	11	3.667	0.465	8	19.310	5.716
Total	30	5.685	0.735	16	16.196	3.404

Table 1.2: Relative size of IPOs disaggregated by market, type of distribution and method of issue. (Relative size is the ratio of the number of shares in the IPO to the number of shares outstanding after the IPO.

	Market					
Distribution	Parallel			Official		
	N	Mean	S.e.	N	Mean	S.e.
Primary						
Rights	2	0.262	0.138	.		
Fixed	1	0.598	.	.		
Total	3	0.374	0.138	.		
Secondary						
Rights	6	0.215	0.072	2	0.487	0.155
Tender	1	0.155	.			
Fixed	3	0.685	0.132	4	0.535	0.117
Total	10	0.350	0.091	6	0.519	0.085
Combined						
Rights	5	0.255	0.042	5	0.434	0.067
Tender	5	0.365	0.099	1	0.505	.
Fixed	7	0.342	0.033	4	0.411	0.052
Total	17	0.323	0.034	10	0.431	0.038
Aggregate						
Rights	13	0.237	0.039	7	0.449	0.058
Tender	6	0.330	0.088	1	0.505	.
Fixed	11	0.459	0.062	8	0.473	0.064
Total	30	0.337	0.037	16	0.464	0.039

As the sample includes only 3 purely primary offerings as opposed to 16 secondary offerings, it is clear that the most important motive for taking a firm public is the desire of existing shareholders to diversify their portfolios rather than the need to raise new capital to finance investments.

Although from Table 1.1 it is apparent the size of the firms listed on the parallel market is much smaller of the firms listed on the official market, both the composition and the relative size of the package offered in the two markets - see Table 1.2 - appear to be very similar. However, the initial public offerings made on the official market are relatively larger, comprising a larger amount of the firm's equity, than initial public offerings made on the parallel market. This means that the original shareholders involved in initial public offerings on the official market retain a smaller proportion of the shares in their firms compared to shareholders launching their firms on the parallel market. In Leland and Pyle (1977), the share retained by the owner-entrepreneur acts as a signal to the market of the firm's true value. The larger the share retained, the more valuable the firm is perceived to be.

More evidence on the motives for taking firms public is given in Table 2. There, I have tabulated the ratio of new shares to the total number of shares included in the IPO, disaggregated by market and by method of issue. What emerges clearly from this table is that in taking a firm public, portfolio or diversification motives are much more important than the raising of new investment capital . On average, slightly less than one third of an IPO comprises new equity capital, the rest is existing shares. This finding holds both across markets and methods of offering.

These figures contrast with the composition of initial public offerings in the U.S. market (see Stanley and Block, 1980, p. 35 and Asquith and Mullins, 1986, p. 67), in which issues of new shares are predominant. They also contrast with comparable data for the French market (see McDonald and Jacquillat, 1974 and Jacquillat et al, 1978) where by law, only initial secondary distributions are permitted, i.e. a firm must be listed before it can make an offering of new shares.

5. Price adjustments on IPOs.

In the literature, one of the most puzzling aspects of IPOs is the observed large price adjustments between the offering price and the

Table 2: Proportion of primary distributions in IPOs disaggregated by market and method of issue.

Method of Issue	Market					
	Parallel			Official		
	N	Mean	S.e.	N	Mean	S.e.
Rights	13	0.312	0.105	7	0.226	0.080
Tender	6	0.212	0.086	1	0.309	.
Fixed	11	0.304	0.104	8	0.211	0.095
Total	30	0.289	0.060	16	0.224	0.057

Table 3.1: Price adjustment of IPOs. Method of issue: rights.

Price adjustment from:	Market			
	Parallel (N=13)		Official (N=7)	
	Mean (%)	t-stat	Mean (%)	t-stat
Offering price to Day 1	-1.752	-1.126	-0.745	-0.576
Day 1 to Day 2	-0.132	-0.371	-0.088	-0.204
Day 1 to Day 3	-0.627	-1.541	-0.601	-0.725
Day 1 to Day 4	-0.623	-0.860	-1.170	-1.150
Day 1 to Day 5	-1.023	-1.112	-0.581	-0.484
Day 1 to Day 10	-1.647	-1.191	0.381	0.124
Day 1 to Day 20	-3.461	-2.398	0.214	0.064
Day 1 to Day 30	-2.827	-1.023	1.172	0.313
Day 1 to Day 40	-2.571	-0.999	0.457	0.096

Table 3.2: Price adjustment of IPOs. Method of issue: tender.

	Market			
Price adjustment from:	Parallel (N=6)		Official (N=1)	
	Mean (%)	t-stat	Mean (%)	t-stat
Offering price to Day 1	4.450	2.681	0.963	.
Day 1 to Day 2	1.266	4.523	0.637	.
Day 1 to Day 3	2.206	1.764	0.954	.
Day 1 to Day 4	2.550	1.726	-0.641	.
Day 1 to Day 5	1.926	0.963	-0.320	.
Day 1 to Day 10	-0.868	-0.388	-0.641	.
Day 1 to Day 20	-1.457	-0.344	1.270	.
Day 1 to Day 30	-0.291	-0.086	-2.918	.
Day 1 to Day 40	4.360	1.446	-3.247	.

Table 3.3: Price adjustment of IPOs. Method of issue: fixed price.

	Market			
Price adjustment of:	Parallel (N=11)		Official (N=8)	
	Mean (%)	t-stat	Mean (%)	t-stat
Offering price to Day1	19.500	2.853	2.471	1.128
Day 1 to Day 2	0.143	0.119	-0.029	-0.050
Day 1 to Day 3	-0.883	-0.656	-0.359	-0.424
Day 1 to Day 4	-1.475	-0.743	-0.694	-0.969
Day 1 to Day 5	-1.054	-0.327	-0.987	-1.135
Day 1 to Day 10	2.232	0.504	-2.182	-2.741
Day 1 to Day 20	1.009	0.358	-2.386	-1.181
Day 1 to Day 30	0.514	0.172	-4.189	-1.294
Day 1 to Day 40	1.044	0.280	-4.647	-0.985

subsequent market price. In this section we examine the daily return performance of shares after they have been introduced on the Amsterdam Stock Exchange.

In our description of the data we pointed out that in the sample the offering or initial price could be determined by one of three methods of issue: fixed price, rights or tender. In addition, the introduction to the Stock Exchange could be made either on the official market or on the parallel market. We therefore can observe the price adjustment across two dimensions: method of issue and market. This division will prove useful when we examine the question whether IPOs are always underpriced, or whether the underpricing depends on the method of issue and/or the market being used for the introduction.

Cumulated daily returns for the three methods of issue over a forty day period are presented[6] in Figures 1, 2 and 3.

The returns are calculated as follows. For each IPO in the sample we calculate the daily return as the relative price adjustment from the opening price to the closing price. For the first day, the return is calculated as the relative price adjustment from the offering price[7] to the closing price on the first day of trade. The daily returns are then ordered by day of trade following the introduction and averaged across IPOs. Thus, for example, the entry for Day 1 can be thought of as the gross return on an equally weighted portfolio of shares all of which have been traded for one day on the exchange.

Two striking results emerge from these figures. First, only fixed price issues on the parallel market seem to conform to situation described in the literature as underpricing: a large return on the day that the shares first start trading and very little thereafter.

The second result of interest is that the same fixed price method produces a much smaller degree of underpricing on the official market than is observed in the parallel market. Although the firms issuing on the official market are much larger and therefore different from the firms issuing on the parallel market, it would seem as though the underpricing witnessed in the parallel market cannot be explained solely in terms of the method used to determine the offering price.

In order examine these results more closely we have calculated the degree of price adjustment from the offering price to the close of the first day of trading, and then from the first closing price to Day(i) where i=2,40. These results are presented in Tables 3.1, 3.2 and 3.3.

Figure 1: Cumulative daily returns of IPOs
Method of issue: tender

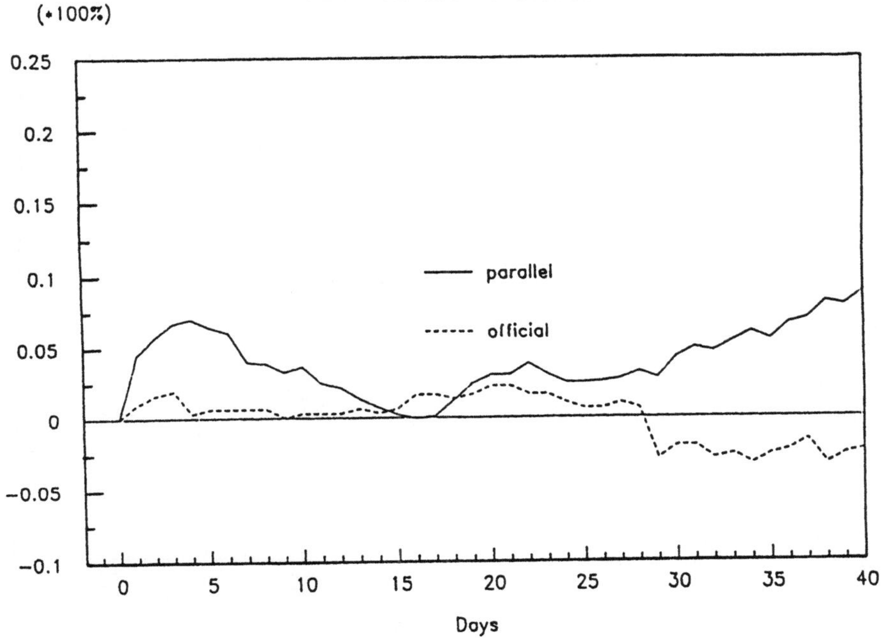

Figure 2: Cumulative daily returns of IPOs
Method of issue: rights

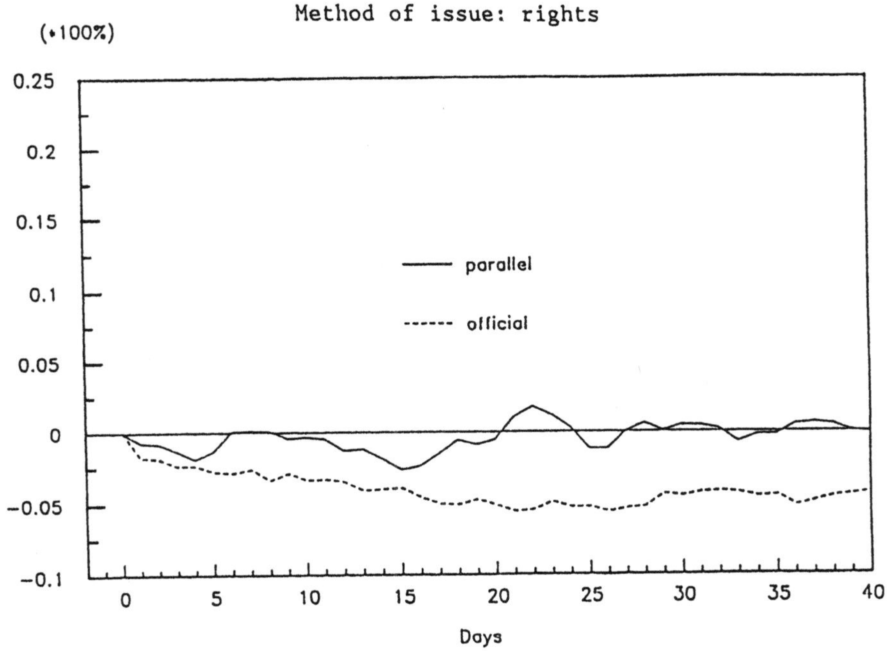

Figure 3: Cumulative daily returns of IPOs

Method of issue: fixed

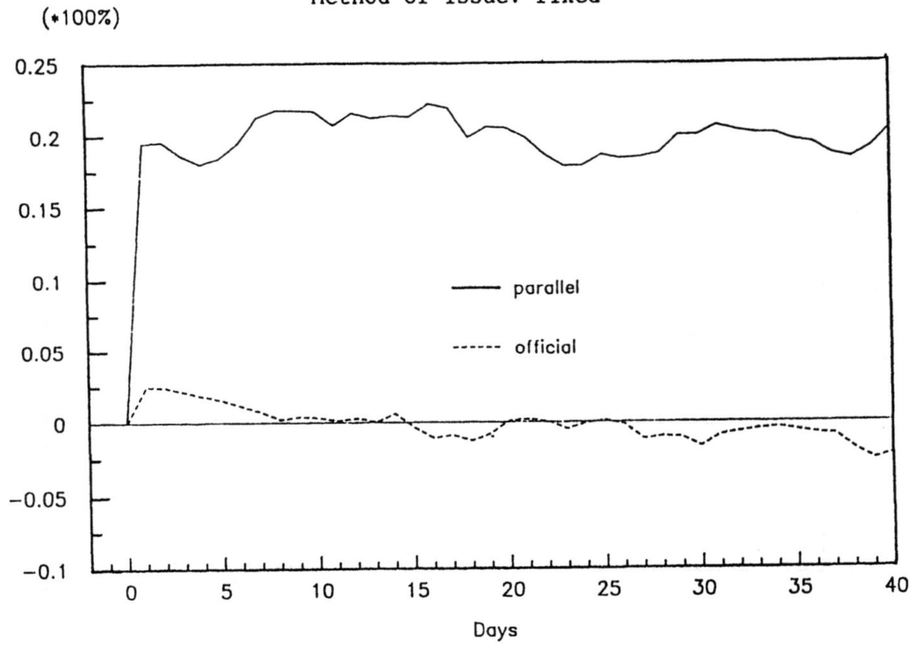

What emerges from these tables is that if we abstract from the return earned by investors buying at the offering price and selling at the closing price of the first day, that the return on an IPO after 40 trading days is essentially zero. Thus only on the first day of trade does any significant price pattern emerge.

It should be pointed out that although the price adjustments are not corrected for market movements or some other measure of risk, the order of magnitude of the price adjustment on the first day of trade precludes that such a correction would account for the observed return. In this case, correcting for risk or adjusting for market movements would introduce unnecessary noise into the data without providing any benefits.

It must be stressed that by the nature of the process being examined, that a comparison of first-day returns by method of initial pricing is but a statistical construct. In particular, the first day returns for the fixed price and tender methods implied by the observed price adjustments do not represent the expected return to an investor subscribing to shares issued by either of these methods.

In order to derive the expected return we would have to multiply the mean return by the probability that the investor is allotted the shares he subscribes to. Given that these introductions are often oversubscribed, this probability is small (see Rock, 1986).

For rights issues however, the mean return on the first trading day does equal the expected return since is there is no oversubscription problem and thus an investor receives the full number of shares he has a "right" to.

In Table 4 we present summary statistics for the price adjustment on the first trading day disaggregated by market of introduction and method of issue. From this table it is again apparent that there are wide differences between the price adjustments across markets, and across methods of issue.

These differences are also tested more formally. In Table 5 we present results for a series of Kruskal-Wallis nonparametric tests on the differences between the relative price adjusment on the the first day of trade by markets and methods of issue. We shall denote this adjustment by DAY1 return, noting that strictly speaking it is not a return in the usual sense of the word.

Table 4: Distribution characteristics of initial returns in percent per day, disaggregated by market and method of issue.

Method of issue	Market: Parallel	Market: Official
Rights:		
Mean	-1.752	-0.745
Median	0.0	-0.480
Std	5.612	3.424
Max	7.095	3.704
Min	-13.482	-6.788
N obs (N neg)	13 (6)	7 (4)
Tenders:		
Mean	4.450	0.963
Median	4.20	0.090
Std	4.066	.
Max	11.488	0.963
Min	0.307	0.963
N obs (N neg)	6 (0)	1 (0)
Fixed:		
Mean	19.500	2.471
Median	7.232	1.238
Std	22.668	6.194
Max	62.415	12.921
Min	-0.729	-5.557
N obs (N neg)	11 (1)	8 (4)
Total:		
Mean	7.281	0.969
Std	16.969	5.017
Max	62.415	12.921
Min	-13.482	-6.788
N obs (N neg)	30 (7)	16 (8)

The first test is a test of the proposition that the DAY1 return is equal for the three methods of issue. As indicated by the chi-square statistic of 10.8 (2) this proposition can be rejected. Thus the test confirms that the three methods of setting the initial price produce significantly different DAY1 returns.

The second test looks at the differences in DAY1 returns between markets. The statistic implies a rejection of different DAY1 returns in the two markets.

The third and fourth test repeat the first two tests but add a second level of classification. The third test examines whether the DAY1 returns for the three methods are equal within each market. This is found not be the case in the parallel market. Thus differences in the DAY1 return associated with the different methods of offering are only discernable in the data pertaining to the parallel market. Finally, the fourth test looks at which methods of issue have different DAY1 returns in the two markets. This is found to be the case only for the fixed price method. Thus tests 3 and 4 indicate that only the DAY1 returns of fixed price issues on the parallel market are different from the all the other categories of DAY1 returns we have examined.

One possible explanation of the large price adjustment on the first day of trade is that the market gets carried away in its enthusiasm for the new issue and in fact "overshoots" the equilibrium price. For this to be the case, the adjustment on days following the first day, should be negative.

But as we have already seen in Tables 3.1, 3.2 and 3.3. the amount of price adjustment after the first day of trade is negligible. Thus, not only is there no evidence of a negative correction of the first closing price, but there is also no evidence that the closing price on the first day of trade is not the equilibrium price.

To summarize, the picture that emerges from the sample data is the following. First, when shares are introduced on the Amsterdam Stock Exchange, there is a significantly positive DAY1 effect. On average, on the first day of trade, the relative difference between opening and closing prices prices is 5.1%; this implies that on average, shares, are offered at a 4.8% discount over the closing price on the first day of trade. For a firm offering to sell 10 million guilders worth of shares, these numbers imply that in addition to the (substantial) out-of-pocket expenses costs incurred by going public, an additional 500.000 guilders is "left on the table" by the initial public offering[8]. What is interesting however, is that there is considerable variation in this number depending on the method chosen to make the IPO with.

Second, examination of the price adjustment following the introduction, fails to reveal that the market price established on the first day of trade is not the equilibrium price. The market for IPOs thus appears to be efficient in the semi-strong form.

Third, if the method of issue is not taken into account, there are no differences between the two markets markets in the degree of price adjustment on the first day of trade. Thus we find no support for the notion that the market for new issues is segmented.

The price adjustment however varies significantly according to the method by which the initial price of the IPO is established. Fixed price issues have a large price adjustment; in rights issues we find no price adjustment. In terms of differences in the degree of underpricing, it appears that differences between methods are much more pronounced in the parallel market and that in particular the fixed price method can be associated with large differences in the degree of price adjustment following an IPO.

6. Can underpriced offerings be predicted?

In this section we ask the question whether factors other than the method of initial pricing contribute to the observed price adjustment. In particular whether the large price adjustment observed in fixed price IPOs is a predictable event.

The hypothesis we therefore wish to test is whether the degree of underpricing is predictable, allowing investors to identify issues for which there will be excess demand on the first day of trading. This is similar to asking whether investors can avoid the problem of winner's curse: receiving a full allotment when an issue is revealed ex post to have been overpriced and being rationed when the issue is underpriced. (see Ritter, 1984a). This again is a test of the efficiency of the market. If the market for initial offerings is efficient we would expect investors to be unable to avoid the problem of winner's curse by predicting on the basis of available information whether an offer will be oversubscribed (which implies that the DAY1 return will be positive) or not.

In this section we report on the outcome of performing a regression analysis on a dummy variable for each fixed price IPO in the sample, which takes the value of one if the DAY1 return for that IPO was positive, and equals zero otherwise.

Potentially, there are many variables which could convey information on underpricing. For instance, an investor could consider whether the offering price is consistent with the stock's undiversifiable risk. For unseasoned stock however, it is difficult to derive a measure of this risk, given that the stock has no track record[9]. We therefore rely on a crude measure of risk, namely the logarithm of the market value of equity (LSIZE), to proxy for risk. The well-known small-firm effect is another reason for including size as a proxy for risk. To be a consistent signal of systematic underpricing one would expect that the larger the firm the more information available and the less probable that the issue will be underpriced. Thus, in the regression, the coefficient of LSIZE variable is expected to be negative.

The variable LSIZE equals the log of the product of the total number of shares times the closing price of the shares on the first day of trade.

A related variable is the market on which the offering takes place. Smaller offerings which are perhaps perceived to be more risky are made on the parallel market, while larger offers are made on the official market. To examine whether the market of introduction makes any difference we included a dummy variable, MARKET, which equals one if the offering was made on the official market and equals zero otherwise.

A second factor which could affect the valuation of the offering is the stake retained by the insiders after the company goes public. We denote this variable by INSIDER. The larger the stake retained the more valuable the stock will be perceived to be by outsiders. This result is due to a model by Leland and Pyle (1977) which has been empirically tested by Ritter (1984b). The variable INSIDER equals the ratio of the total number of shares to be distributed, divided by the total number of shares outstanding. One minus this variable then measures the stake retained by the firm's insiders after the firm goes public.

Finally, from the large literature that has investigated the effects of different "events" on stock valuation we know that when firms announce primary offerings of shares, stock prices decline (e.g. Asquith and Mullins, 1986). Thus the larger the proportion of primary or new shares

Table 5: Kruskal-Wallis tests of differences of DAY1 returns by methods of issue and markets.

Classification of DAY1	Chi-square	(d.f)
returns by:		
1) Method of issue:	10.8*	(2)
2) Market of introduction:	1.9	(1)
3) Method and market:		
-official	1.0	(2)
-parallel	10.5*	(2)
4) Market and method:		
-rights	0.0	(1)
-tender	0.3	(1)
-fixed	3.6**	(1)

*) significant at the 5% level;

**) significant at the 10% level.

Table 6. Logit estimation of the probability of oversubscription (fixed price issues).

Variable	Parameter Estimate [1)]	Standard Error	T for H0: Parameter=0
INTERCEP	7.08	7.78	0.91
INSIDER	-2.20	1.55	-1.41
PRIMARY	0.39	1.65	-0.00
LSIZE	-0.00	0.44	-0.00
MARKET	-0.46	0.81	-0.57

Chi-square = 17.291 (d.o.f. 14)

1) In the estimation procedure, 5 was added to the intercept and the logit was divided by two.

in the offering, the smaller the DAY1 effect will be and thus the smaller the probability that the offer will be oversubscribed. In another study on IPOs, Logue (1973) also finds evidence that the proportion of the primary offering in the offering has a negative effect on the stocks' initial performance. In the regression the variable measuring the proportion of primary shares in the total offering is denoted by PRIMARY. This variable is defined as the number of new shares being issued divided by the total number of shares being offered (i.e. primary plus secondary offering).

In order to test the predictive value of these variables on the underpricing phenomenon we estimated a logit model which attempts to measure the probability that a given fixed price issue will be underpriced. Thus we are only concerned with estimating on the basis of ex ante information which issues will end up having a positive DAY1 return. If this prediction turns out to yield significant results, then the winnner's curse problem is less severe than is generally assumed.

In Table 6 we present the estimated coefficients of this model. As can be seen, all of the estimated coefficients have relatively large standard errors and are thus statistically indistinguishable from zero. On the basis of this equation, an investor would not be able to predict better than by flipping a true coin, which issues are likely to be oversubscribed (i.e.underpriced). Therefore, the hypothesis that the market for initial public offerings is efficient cannot be rejected.

What we can, however, reject is the hypothesis that the market of introduction plays a role in determining excess demand for fixed price offerings, since the estimated coefficient of MARKET is found not to have any incremental predictive power. This means that the unconditional expectation that an issue will be oversubscribed if it is introduced on the official market is not different from the same expectation for the parallel market. Apparently, the factors which lead the authorities of the Amsterdam Stock Exchange to segment the listed stocks into two markets are not perceived by investors to be relevant for their pricing decisions. Put slightly differently, investors do not demand differential premia for the fact shares are introduced on different markets.

7. Summary.

The data sampled in this study indicates that the most likely source of abnormally large price adjustments on the day a firm's shares starts trading on the stock exchange, is the method used to initially price the shares. Investors who succesfully subscribe to shares introduced at a fixed price can expect to get a substantially higher return than if the offering is performed by either the tender method or through a rights issue. This return increases significantly if the investor can succesfully subscribe to shares being introduced on the parallel market.

However, none of the other variables with which we attempted to predict whether there would be excess demand for an an offering proved to provide the investor with an incremental ability to predict underpricing. The market for initial public offerings therefore, seems to be quite efficient even though the puzzle why shares are initially underpriced still remains.

The results presented here provide some contrast with earlier studies in the literature. First, fixed price issues (and the resulting underpricing phenomenon) can be observed even when firms could avoid the problem by using alternative methods for its initial public offering. Second, the degree of underpricing and the size of the firm seem to be closely related as evidenced by the difference in the adjustment of prices between the official and the parallel market. These results would therefore suggest that the underpricing phenomenon is related to the services which underwriters can provide to small firms and which are paid for by means of a discount on the value of the issue. Why this payment is made in the form of a discount and not by means of a fee, is likely to be related to some form of risk-sharing arrangement designed to bond the underwriters' services to the firm.

Footnotes.

1. An earlier version of this paper was presented at the meeting of the European Finance Association, Madrid 1987. Research assistance by Marga van Winsen and Jan-Willem van Oostveen as well as comments by Elroy Dimson, Marius Jonkhart and Mario Levis are hereby gratefully acknowledged.

2. There are several studies documenting this phenomenon in different countries. For the U.S. see inter alia Ibbotson 1975 and Ritter 1984a. For France, see McDonald and Jacquillat 1974. For the United Kingdom, see Davis and Yeoman 1976. For a study of Malysia, Hong Kong and Singapore, see Dawson 1987a. Theoretical work in this area has only started to appear quite recently in the literature. See Baron 1982, Hansen and Pinkerton 1982, Heinkel and Schwartz 1986 and Rock 1986. Finally, the reader is referred to the the excellent review article by Smith 1986.

3. This particular problem is listed as number 6 in Brealey and Myers' compendium, 1984, p.783-788.

4. For a description of the U.S. regulations, see Chalk and Peavy, 1986. The French system is described in McDonald and Jacquillat, 1974.

5. Mainly, but not entirely, since if the offering is done through a rights issue, the proceeds are split between the firm and the existing shareholders.

6. For rights issues the offer price was constructed as the price at which the right could be exercised plus the closing price for the right on the first day the right traded on the exchange.

7. See Dawson 1987b for an alternative method of calculating the opportunity loss when shares are underpriced.

8. Ibbotson (1975) has solved this problem. Application of his method, however, requires that the size of the sample be much larger than the one available here.

List of references.

Asquith,P. and D.Mullins. 1986. Equity Issues and Offering Dilution. Journal of Financial Economics 15, 61-89.

Baron,D.P. 1982. A Model of the Demand for Investment Banking Advising and Distribution Services for New Issues. Journal of Finance 37, 955-976.

Brealey,R. and S.Myers. 1984. Principles of Corporate Finance. New York:McGraw-Hill.

Davis,E.W. and K.A.Yeomans. 1976. Market Discount on New Issues of Equity, The Influence of Firm Size, Method and Market Volatility. Journal of Business Finance and Accounting 3, 27-43.

Dawson,S.M. 1987a. Secondary Market Performance of Initial Public Offers, Hong Kong, Singapore,and Malaysia: 1978-1984. Journal of Business Finance & Accounting 14, 63-76.

Dawson,S.M. 1987b. Initial Public Offer Underpricing: The Issuer's View - A Note. Journal of Finance 42, 159-162.

Hansen,R.S. and J.M.Pinkerton. 1982. Direct Equity Financing: A resolution of a paradox. Journal of Finance 37, 651-665.

Harris,M. and A.Raviv. 1981. Allocation Mechanisms and the Design of Auctions. Econometrica 49, 1477-1499.

Ibbotson,R.G. 1975. Price Performance of Common Stock New Issues. Journal of Financial Economics 2, 235-272.

Ibbotson,R.G. and J.F.Jaffe. 1975. Hot Issue Markets. Journal of Finance 30, 1027-1042.

Leland,H.E. and D.H.Pyle 1977. Informational Asymmetries, Financial Structure and Financial Intermediaries. Journal of Finance 32, 371-387.

McDonald,J.G. and B.C.Jacquillat. 1974. Pricing of Initial Equity Issues: The French Sealed-Bid Auctions. Journal of Business 47, 37-47.

Ritter,J.R. 1984a. The Hot Issue Market of 1980. Journal of Business 57, 215-240.

Ritter,J.R. 1984b. Signaling and the Valuation of Unseasoned New Issues: A Comment. Journal of Finance 39, 1231-1237.

Rock,K. 1986. Why New Issues are Underpriced. Journal of Financial Economics 15. 187-212.

Smith,C.W. 1986. Investment Banking and the Capital Acquisition Process. Journal of Financial Economics 15, 3-29.

FRENCH NEW ISSUES, UNDERPRICING AND ALTERNATIVE METHODS OF DISTRIBUTION

Bruno Husson
Centre HEC-ISA
1, rue de la Libération
78350 Jouy en Josas

Bertrand Jacquillat
Université Paris Dauphine
Place du Ml de Lattre de Tassigny
75775 Paris cedex 16

The authors thank Bernard Mirat for help in providing the data and his encouragements and Gilles Brechet for computer assistance

NATO ASI Series, Vol. F54
A Reappraisal of the Efficiency of Financial Markets
Edited by Rui M. C. Guimaraes et al.

1. INTRODUCTION

Since February 1983, France has experienced a new section on its equity market known as *"Second Marché"* which followed the creation of the London Unlisted Securities Market. The objective of the promoters of the *"Second Marché"* was to accomodate medium sized companies with a capital market of their own which could help them fulfill their financial needs and development. Compared with the official market *"Cote Officielle"*, the rules of the *"Second Marché"* for initial public equity offerings (IPO's thereafter) are indeed much looser.

This aspect of the deregulation of the French capital markets has had a profound influence on the number of companies seeking listing. Whereas before 1983, only 2 to 10 with an average of 7 companies went public every year in France, from 1983 to 1987, more than 200 French companies have become public on the *"Second Marché"*.

Both the existence of an underpricing phenomenon for new issues - on the US market as well as on the French and other capital markets - and the existence of different investment banking contracts between the issuing firm and its investment banker have been indeed well documented in the literature.

The purpose of this paper is threefold :

- Evaluate the degree of underpricing of French IPO's on the *"Second Marché"* and to compare it with previous results obtained on initial public offerings on the *"Cote Officielle"*, by Mc Donald and Jacquillat (1974) and Jacquillat, Mc Donald and Rolfo (1978, JMDR thereafter).

- Link the general underpricing of French unseasoned equity issues with the different methods of distribution chosen by the companies going public and their investment bankers.

-Estimate the influence of different marketing arrangements between the initial shareholders and the investment bankers on the risk and the excess returns of IPO'S : the firm commitment and the best efforts contract.

The paper is organized as follows. Section 2 presents the offering methods and the nature of the alternative forms of underwriting contracts which are used for IPO's on the *"Second Marché"*. Section 3 describes the sample and the empirical methodologies used to compute the post offering abnormal returns ; section 4 presents the results and section 5 some concluding remarks.

2. OFFERING METHODS AND ALTERNATIVE FORMS OF UNDERWRITING CONTRACTS

2.1. Offering methods

Basically, IPO's can be done in France by one of three possible methods : the "mise en vente", the "procédure ordinaire" and the "offre publique de vente". Hereafter, we present the basic caracteristics of each of them.

The *"mise en vente"* procedure

The *"mise en vente"* procedure represents a modified version of the competitive auction as evidenced by Mc Donald and Jacquillat (1974). It proceeds in two stages as far as the pricing of the securities to be offered is concerned. About six months prior to the offering date, the advising investment banker meet with the company's directors and work out a minimum price (*prix d'offre*) with the research department of the bank.

Several days before the offering, this minimum price acceptable to the company is announced. The issue is not underwritten, as the issuing stockholders bear in principle the price risk as well as the very small risk that the issue cannot be sold at the minimum price. The day before the auction, the banks and the brokers gather the bids, specifying price and quantity for individuals and institutional investors and transmit them to the *"Société des Bourses Françaises"* (the governing body of the Paris Bourse -the SBF thereafter) which centralizes and processes the bids. The bids are ranked by price on a computer printout and this confidential list is used by a committee of company directors, their bankers and officials of the SBF in setting the offering price (*cours d'introduction*) on the morning of the allocation.

The day of the offering, the committee which meets to set up the offering price disposes of a computer printout where all the market orders are listed and uses it as an indication of the market sentiment and interest in the offering. It enforces a ban on market orders in the auction and rejects a portion of the highest bids, designated as "disguised market orders". In setting the offering price, the committee appears to treat the schedule of bids as a useful but upward-biased reflection of the true quantities demanded for the stock. It allocates the shares on a prorata basis so as to exhaust the issue at an offering price below that they feel will be the equilibrium price in the aftermarket.

Up to now and with two exceptions, the quantity of shares demanded by the public has exceeded the quantity of shares offered, and many times by a vast amount. It is not quite clear what the committee would decide in the exceptional case where the numbers of shares demanded fell short of the quantity offered. The most recent case where such circumstances happened was in 1972, when Banque Hervert asked for official listing on the Paris bourse. The only written rule for official listing enforced by the French equivalent of the SEC , the *Commission des Opérations de Bourse* (COB thereafter) is that the initial shareholders sell at least 25% of the total number of shares. In this case the demand was around 15% of total shares offered by the initial shareholders. The initial shareholders asked the COB the permission to go through and that the company be listed notwithstanding the fact that the 25% rule was broken. The permission was granted by the COB. In the days following the offering, Banque Hervert exhibited a strong negative abnormal return .

In that case one can make the hypothesis that only uninformed investors applied for shares and that they got a negative return because of the permission granted by the COB for the listing to go through, thus breaking its own rule. If it were to be strictly enforced, and the issue was undersubscribed, all the shares offered would be given back to the initial shareholders. Thus, this rule would represent a put option similar to the one existing in the best efforts underwriting contract.

The "offre publique de vente"

The "*offre publique de vente*" procedure (OPV hereafter) is a tender offer made by the shareholders to the investing public. Shareholders who initiate this procedure propose a fixed quantity of shares at a fixed price. Whereas in the "*mise en vente*", there is uncertainty both about the price which will be paid and about the quantity of shares received, in the OPV there is uncertainty only as far as the quantity of shares which will be received is concerned. The technical committee in charge of the IPO's at the Paris bourse makes a proportional reduction of orders if the quantity of shares demanded is higher than the quantity of shares offered.

In order to use this method of sale, additional constraints are imposed. IPO's through OPV can be used only if the number of shares offered represent at least 10% of total outstanding shares and 5 millions francs or 5% of total outstanding shares and 10 millions F (about 2 millions USD at present exchange rates).

Within the OPV category, one has to make two additional distinctions: the non nominative versus the nominative OPV, and the direct versus indirect OPV.

In a nominative tender offer, everyone who places a buy order must be clearly identified by name and adress, whereas the non nominative tender offer is anonymous. The nominative OPV bears higher administrative costs ; its objective is to consider only one application form per buyer. This distinction will not be carried further in this paper since only two IPO'S have been pursued this way.

As shown later, the OPV is often used when one of the two other procedures have failed because of a large disequilibrium between shares offered and demanded. In this case it is called an "indirect OPV".

The "procédure ordinaire"

The "*procédure ordinaire*" is the closest procedure to a competitive auction. Contrary to the two procedures precidingly exposed, it can only be used if the original shareholders have sold their shares prior to the IPO to investment bankers and brokerage houses. Also subscribers are allowed to pass "market orders". The financial intermediaries take care of the technicalities of all the IPO procedure under the control of the Bourse authorities. In concrete terms, if the investment bankers are faced with too strong a disequilibrium between demand and supply of shares, it can raised the offering price and ask the bidders to renew their orders -if they wish to do so- at the new offering price. This process continues this way on and on until an equilibrium is reached. The underwriting syndicate has always the possibility to switch procedure and adopt the "indirect OPV".

2.2. Underwriting contracts

The "*Second Marché*" has innovated in several respects. By allowing initial shareholders to put up a maximum of only 10 % of total capital instead of 25 % for the "*Cote Officielle*", the promoters of the "*Second Marché*" have undoubtly taken the most single important deregulatory measure which has boosted initial public offerings.

By allowing medium-sized firms to become public with so little capital being sold to outside investors, the promoters of the "*Second Marché*" feared that its success would be possibly impaired by the lack of liquidity in the secondary market. Therefore, they officially insisted that "liquidity contracts" be passed between the issuing firms and their investment bankers and brokers, whereby the latter would provide the former with liquidity services in the after-market. Although these contracts are confidential, we have had access to some of them and discussions with Paris Bourse officials and members of the French banking association have given us a good understanding of the economics of such contracts. Most but not all of newly listed firms on the "*Second Marché*" have contracted with their investment bankers for such "liquidity services".

The "*Second Marché*" has also innovated as far as underwriting contracts employed in IPO'S are concerned. Several possibilities have been extended.

Two alternative forms of underwriting contracts are typically employed in initial public offerings, as described by Smith (1986). The first is a firm commitment underwriting agreement under which the underwriter agrees to purchase the whole issue from the firm at a particular price for resale to the public. The second is a best efforts underwriting agreement under which the underwriter acts only as a marketing agent for the firm. The underwriter does not agree to purchase the issue at a predetermined price, but sells the security and takes a predetermined spread, with the firm taking the residual.

Until 1983 where all initial public offerings went through the "*mise en vente*" procedure on the "*Cote Officielle*", only the second arrangement was allowed : the agents acting on a best efforts basis. Since 1983, an IPO on a firm commitment basis is allowed. Although a firm commitment contract can be coupled with any offering methods, informal discussions with Bourse authorities show that such marketing agreements have been coupled only with the "*procédure ordinaire*" offering method.

In section 4, we discuss the returns for IPO'S in light both of the offering methods and the underwriting agreements.

3. SAMPLE AND EMPIRICAL METHODOLOGY

3.1. Sample

The "*Second Marché*" opened in February 1983. With a few exceptions for the listing of foreign corporations on the Paris Bourse, almost all IPO'S took place on the "*Second Marché*".

Table 1 presents a breakdown year by year and by procedure of all IPO'S on the "*Second Marché*" up to the end of 1986

(TABLE 1)

Sample of IPO's on the "*Second Marché*"
1983-1986

	1983	1984	1985	1986	1983-86
Procédure ordinaire	9 60%	2 8.0%	1 2.2%	2 4.3%	14 10.7%
Mise en vente	1 6.7%	7 28.0%	23 51.1%	16 34.8%	47 35.9%
OPV	3 20.0%	6 24.0%	6 8.5%	9 19.6%	24 18.3%
Indirect OPV	2 13.3%	10 40.0%	15 33.3%	19 41.3%	46 35.1%
TOTAL	15 100.0%	25 100.0%	45 100.0%	46 100.0%	131 100.0%

Several remarks are in order :

- The sample is composed of all IPO'S on the "*Second Marché*", 131 companies, over the total period 1983-1986. Close to 100 companies have come on the "*Second Marché*" in 1987. They have not been taken into account in this study because of the empirical methodology used as explained thereafter.

- The breakdown by procedure shows that each of them has been used with a strong preference by corporations for the "*mise en vente*" and the necessity for them in 35.1 % of cases to adopt the "indirect OPV".

- The "*procédure ordinaire*" has had a mitigated success. It represents the closest to the underwriting procedure used in the US. The "*mise en vente*" which was the only procedure for IPO'S prior to the opening of the "*Second Marché*" dominates the other procedures after 1984.

3.2. Methodology

The empirical methodology used in this study is the one used in the so-called event studies. Its purpose is to measure the wealth effect of a given event by computing the abnormal performance of the participating firms around the event date.

In this study, the event date, designed hereafter by day 0, is defined as the day when the shares of the company going public are bought by outside investors. Therefore, depending on the type of issuing procedure used, the event date may differ from the day when the procedure began. For example, this is the case when the "indirect OPV" technique is used after another procedure has failed.

For every firm in the sample, abnormal daily returns are computed for each day of a period denoted event period and extending from the event day to 120 trading days after day 0. Abnormal returns are defined as follows.

$$AR_{i,t} = R_{i,t} - K_{i,t}$$

where $AR_{i,t}$: abnormal return of firm i on day t
$R_{i,t}$: observed return of firm i on day t
$K_{i,t}$: for a given valuation model, predicted return of firm i on day t.

Three valuation models have been considered, corresponding to three alternative adjustment methods commonly used in the event study literature.

The Mean adjusted return.

In this approach, first developed in Masulis (1980a and 1980b), $K_{i,t}$ is constant over time and estimated by averaging the observed return over a time period called comparison period. In this study, a comparison period extending from day + 121 to day +170 is used :

$$K_{i,t} = K_i = \frac{1}{50} \sum_{t=121}^{170} R_{i,t}$$

The Market adjusted return

In this methodology, $K_{i,t}$ is the observed return of a market index on the same period :

$$K_{i,t} = R_{m,t}$$

where $R_{m,t}$ is the return of a given market index on day t.

The Risk adjusted return

The underlying valuation model of this third methodology is the Market Model which specifies the following linear relationship between security i returns and returns on a market portfolio :

$$R_{i,t} = \alpha_i + \beta_i R_{m,t} + \varepsilon_{i,t}$$

where :

β_i = cov $(R_{i,t} ; R_{m,t}) / \mathrm{Var}\,(R_{m,t})$

α_i = expected value of $(R_i - \beta_i R_m)$

$\varepsilon_{i,t}$ = model error term of security i over day t, with expected return equal to zero, constant variance and cov $(\varepsilon_i ; \varepsilon_j) = 0$ for $i \neq j$.

Therefore, $K_{i,t}$ is defined as :

$$K_{i,t} = \hat{\alpha}_i + \hat{\beta}_i R_{mt}$$

where $\hat{\alpha}_i$ and $\hat{\beta}_i$ are the parameters estimates of the Market Model

In this study, these estimates have been computed using the same 50 days comparison period presented in the first adjustment approach.

After an adjustment method has been chosen and daily abnormal returns computed over the event period for each firm in the sample, the next step is to compute daily average abnormal returns by aggregating over all securities :

$$AAR_t = \frac{I}{N} \sum_{i=1}^{N} AR_{i,t}$$

where AAR_t is the average abnormal return on day t and N the sample size.

Summing the AAR's over a given period allows then to obtain a cumulative average abnormal return which measures the average wealth effect of the event over that period :

$$CAAR_{t_1,t_2} = \sum_{t=t_1}^{t_2} AAR_t$$

where t_1 and t_2 are the boundaries of the period considered.

Finally, in order to examine whether the average abnormal return over a given day t is significantly different from zero, t-statistics are performed as follows :

$$t = AAR_t/\sigma\,(AAR_t)$$

where $\sigma(AAR_t)$ denotes the estimated standard deviation of AAR_t[1].

In fact, two different t-statistics are performed, depending on whether the standard deviation considered is a time series or a cross-sectionnal estimate. In the first case, $\sigma(AAR_t)$ is computed using the average abnormal returns of the comparison period that was previously defined :

---

1 . When testing the statistical significance of cumulative abnormal returns, the t-statistic is given by : $t= [\ CAAR_{t_1,t_2}/p] \ / \ [\ s\ (AAR_t)/\sqrt{p}]$ where $p = t_1 - t_2 + 1$ represents the number of days over which the average abnormal returns are cumulated.

$$\sigma(AAR_t) = \left[\frac{1}{49} \sum_{t=121}^{170} (AAR_t - \overline{AAR})^2 \right]^{1/2}$$

$$\text{where} \quad \overline{AAR} = \frac{1}{50} \sum_{t=121}^{170} AAA_t$$

In the cross sectionnal case, σ (AR_t) is defined as :

$$\sigma(AAR_t) = \left[\frac{1}{N-1} \sum_{i=1}^{N} (AR_{i,t} - AAR_t)^2 \right]^{1/2}$$

4. RESULTS

Empirical results investigate three different phenomena. They first measure the degree of underpricing of French initial public offerings on the "*Second Marché*" and its comparison with previous results obtained by Mc Donald and Jacquillat (1974)and JMDR (1978) on the "Cote-Officielle". Second, they investigate the possible link between the underpricing phenomenon and the different methods of distribution chosen by the companies going public and their investment bankers. Third, empirical results evaluate the influence of different marketing arrangements -firm commitment and best efforts contract- between the initial shareholders and the investment bankers on the risk and the excess return of IPO's.

4.1. The under pricing phenomenon

Examination of the return behavior of IPO's from day 0 to 120 days after seasoning indicates that the average issue is offered at a significant discount from the price expected in the after-market as indicated on Table 2.

These results are consistent with previous results obtained by Mc Donald and Jacquillat (1974) and JMDR (1978) on all initial public offerings at the "*Cote Officielle*" on the Paris Bourse. In the first study, the average discount for a population of companies was 4.8% for the first week of seasoning. The discount in the second study where the population was significantly larger was 15 % for a six months seasoning period.

Whichever the empirical approach used, the cumulative average abnormal return is close to 4% for the 120 days event

TABLE 2

Return behaviour of IPO's in
the after market on the "Second Marché"
1983 -1986

Distribution method (sample size)	Procédure ordinaire 14	Mise en vente 47	0PV 24	Indirect OPV 46	Total 131
Non adjusted return	4.5%* (1.90;1)	4.0%** (3.41;1)	18.1%** (2.11;3)	18.3%** (2.27;3)	10.4%* 1.89;2
Mean ajusted return	4.4%* (1.77;1)	3.9%** (3.12;1)	12.1%** (2.34;2)	17.8%** (2.11;3)	4.2%** (2.41;1)
Market Adjusted retur	4.2%* (1.84;1)	3.9%** (2.81;1)	11.4%** (2.14;2)	17.4%** (2.09;3)	4.0%** (2.12;1)
Risk Adjusted return	4.4%* (1.74;1)	3.9%** (3.08;1)	11.8%** (2.28;2)	17.5%** (2.05;3)	4.1%** (2.27;1)

Each cumulative average abnormal return in percentage terms is followed underneath by a pair of numbers in parentheses. The first number ratio of the Cumulative Average Abnormal Return (CAAR except for the non adjusted return computation where iT is simply the cumulative average return) to the cross sectionnally computed standard deviation : $t = \frac{CAAR}{\sigma CAAR}$. The second number is the number of days during which the cumulative average abnormal returns are statistically signifiant, at the 5% (**) OR 10% (*) level.

period (statistically significant at the 5% level). The average non adjusted return over the same period is 10.4 %, (statiscally significant at the 10% level).[1]

Observation of the breakdown of results by procedure call for additional remarks :

- Returns and excess returns are far higher for OPV and "indirect OPV" than for the two other procedures. Whereas the excess return for the OPV and the "indirect OPV" is in the neighborhood of 12% and 17 % respectively, it is in the 4 % to 4.5 % range for the "*mise en vente*" and the "*procédure ordinaire*" respectively. The differences are statistically significant at the 1% level whichever the adjustment method used. Recall that the Mc Donald Jacquillat and the JMDR studies applied to the "*mise en vente*" procedure exclusively. Therefore results obtained for IPO'S with the same procedure both for the *"Cote Officielle"* in the 1969-1976 period and on the "*Second Marché*" for the 1983 - 1986 period are totally consistent.

- The already mentioned studies for IPO'S on the *"Cote Officielle"* showed that over 50 % of the excess return during the first week of seasoning was obtained at the end of the second day of trading. The second number in parentheses in Table 2 indicates the number of days during which the cimulative excess return is statiscally signifiant at the 5 % level. With the same "*mise en vente*" procedure on the *"Second Marché"*, 100 % of the adjustment takes place during one first trading day. This tends to confirm a greater efficiency of the Paris Bourse during the recent period compared with fifteen years ago.

- Whenever the adjustment takes place beyond the first trading day - this is the case for the OPV and "indirect OPV" procedures - Table 3 indicates the day by day breakdown of the realization of the excess return. Over all it takes place over the first trading day. It takes four and six days for the OPV and the "indirect OPV". [2]

---

1 . Abnormal return are far higher for a sample of 48 companies which made secondary offerings within one year following the initial offering : 19.3% for the total sample and respectively 10.7% (procédure ordinaire), 14.9% (mise en vente) and 24.0% (OPV).

2 . Note that this adjustment period is not necessarily an indication of market inefficiency. Stock market authorities impose price limits on the daily variations of share prices as it exists on Futures markets. The size of these price limits is subject to their discretion. They can go as high as 10%. If the price rises or falls beyond the price limit, no trading takes places and a new price is quoted without transaction taking place price. This new price is the closing price for the day.

(TABLE 3)
Distribution of the statistically signifiant
abnormal return in the after market

Number of days after day 0 price	Procedure ordinaire	Mise en vente	OPV	Indirect OPV	Total Sample
1	100%	100%	21%	26%	100%
2	-	-	45%	44%	
3	-	-	34%	31%	-
TOTAL	100%	100%	100%	100%	100%

4.2. The underpricing phenomenon and the different methods of distribution

The large difference in returns between the two sets of procedures - the "*procedure ordinaire*" and the "*mise en vente*" on the one hand - and the OPV on the other hand needs an explanation.

As it has been pointed out by Rock (1986) and Beatty and Ritter (1986), in an offering, there is uncertainty about the market clearing price. If the offer price is set at its expected market-clearing price, uninformed investors systematically earn below abnormal returns ; if an issue is underpriced, informed investors as well as uninformed investors submit bids and as a result the issue is rationed. On the other hand, if the offer price is set too high compared with its after-market equilibrium price, informed investors are less likely to submit bids and the issue is more likely to be undersubscribed. Hence, uninformed investors systematically receive more of overpriced issues and less of underpriced issues. Uninformed investors anticipate this adverse selection problem. Therefore they will only bid if the offer price is below their expected after-market price by a sufficient amount to compensate for their losses on overpriced issues. This implies that the average underpricing is greater for issues with greater uncertainty.

Baron (1982) analyzes an optimal contract between a firm and its investment banker who is better informed about the market demand for the firm's securities than is the firm. Since the firm must compensate the investment banker for providing advice and for marketing the securities, the optimal offer price is a decreasing function of the uncertainty about the market demand for the issue. Reciprocally, the value of delegation to the underwriter is an increasing function of uncertainty.

While the two hypotheses focus on two different informational asymetry problems - between informed and uninformed potential securityholders on the one hand and between the issuing firm and its investment banker on the other hand - the two yield similar implications about the underpricing phenomenon : issues with greater uncertainty command a lower offer price, all other things being equal, and thus a higher discount.

The information problem between informed and uninformed potential security holders, as well as the information and contracting problems between the issuing firm and its investment banker influence also the choice between the two possible underwriting contracts : firm commitment and best efforts contracts.

Ritter (1985) has argued that in a best efforts contract, if the issue is overpriced and the issue sale falls short of the minimum specified in the underwriting contract, the offer is cancelled and the losses to uninformed investors are reduced. Structuring the contract in this manner reduces the problem faced by uninformed potential security holders, and thus reduces the discount necessary to induce them to bid.

Mandelker and Raviv (1977), Baron (1979, 1982) and Baron and Holmstrom (1980) hypothesize that there is uncertainty among the capital market participants about the market-clearing price for the securities. Furthermore, their models focus on the conflict of interest between the issuing firm and its underwriter.

They derive optimal investment banking contracts for new issues based on the uncertainty associated with the issue and the degree of risk aversion of the issuer and the investment banker. More specifically, in their analyses a firm commitment is more likely to be optimal, the more risk-adverse the issuer, the less risk-adverse the investment banker, the less the uncertainty about the market clearing security price, the less the assymetry in information between the issuer and the investment banker and the more observable the investment banker's effort.

Therefore, both lines of analysis suggest that best efforts contracts are more likely, the greater the uncertainty in the after-market issue price. The firm underwriting agreement will be chosen when the uncertainty about the after-market clearing price is relatively small.

Two proxies have been used in the literature to test this phenomenon. The first proxy for ex-ante uncertainty is the inverse of the gross proceeds raised in an offering. This captures the empirical regularity that smaller offerings are more speculative, on average, than larger offerings, as documented by Ritter (1984) for new issues. The second proxy for ex-ante uncertainty is simply the after-market standard deviation of returns.

Table 4 presents the result using the second proxy : the standard deviation of daily abnormal returns over the 21 to 120 days period of seasoning and the following 121 to 170 days period of seasoning for each issuing method.

As it has been suggested , best effort contracts become relatively more attractive when more uncertainty prevails about after-market prices. Firm commitment contracts have been used exclusively with the "*procédure ordinaire*". Table 4 shows clearly that ex-post uncertainty measured with the standard deviation of returns during both after-market periods is significantly lower than average (1.55% and 1.58% vs 1.71% and 1.97% respectively). It is significantly lower for "*procedure ordinaire*" than for the "Indirect OPV" and the "*mise en vente*".

Standard deviations tend to increase in the 50 days period beyond the 21-121 days period of seasoning. It remains to be seen if such a jump is due to the existence of the above mentioned "liquidity contracts" between the initial shareholders and the investment bankers and brokers which is peculiar to the "*Second*

Marché". This is one of the areas of ongoing research on this subject.

(TABLE 4)

Standard Deviation (%) of daily returns

	N	Event period (21;120)		Event period (121;170)		Difference
		μ_1	σ_1	μ_2	σ_2	$\mu_1 - \mu_2$
Procédure ordinaire	14	1.55	.26	1.58	.45	.03 (.22)
Mise en vente	47	1.70* (1.52)	.48	2.05* (1.62)	.58	.35* (3.19)
OPV	24	1.60	.63	1.49	.53	.11 (.66)
Indirect OPV	46	1.82** (2.7)	.55	1.97** (2.6)	.62	.15 (1.23)
Total	131	1.71	.52	1.97	.62	.28* (3.96)

N is the number of issues

μ_i and σ_i (i=1,2) represents the sample standard deviation of observed daily returns and the standard deviation of it respectively with the statistical significance (inparentheses) of the difference of the standard deviation of observed daily returns of each of the issuing procedure with the standard deviation of the observed daily returns for the "procédure ordinaire".

$\mu_1 - \mu_2$ gives the difference in means between the two sample periods with its statistical significance in parentheses.

one star (*) indicates a 10% confidence level significance and two stars(**) a 5% confidence level.

5 . CONCLUDING REMARKS AND FURTHER RESEARCH

As a consequence of the opening of the *"Second Marché"* in February 1983 by the French Bourse authorities, a large quantity of medium sized companies have become public.

This paper has examined the excess returns in the after-market of all IPO'S between 1983 and 1986 both in light of the principal offering methods which companies use to go public - the "*procédure ordinaire*", the "*mise en vente*" and the OPV procedures - and of the underwriting arrangements between the initial shareholders of the company going public and their investment bankers - on a firm commitment basis or on a best efforts basis.

Preliminary results are the following : Excess returns of IPO'S appear in the after-market whichever the empirical methodology used to measure abnormal performance. Excess returns show quite rapidly - one to three days - depending on the offering method. Excess returns seem to be larger for offering methods which use predominantly a marketing arrangement on a best efforts basis and lower when they are done on a firm commitment basis.

Further research should examine how beneficial is the "stabilization" activity of the underwriters based on a "liquidity contract" who typically trade in the secondary market after a security offering, and also investigate some other institutional details which are peculiar to the *"Second Marché"*.

BIBLIOGRAPHY

BARON D., The Incentive Problem and the Design of Investment Banking Contracts, Journal of Banking and Finance, 3, 1979.

BARON D., "A Model of the Demand for Investment Banking Advising and Distribution Services for New Issues", Journal of Finance, 1982.

BARON D. and B. HOLSTROM, "The Investment Banking Contract for New Issues under Asymetric Information : Delegation and the Incentive Problem", Journal of Finance, 35, 1980.

BEATTY R. et J. RITTER, "Investment Banking, Reputation, and the Underpricing of Initial Public Offerings", Journal of Financial Economics,15, 1986.

JACQUILLAT B., J. G. Mc DONALD et ROLFO, "French Auctions of Common Stock Issues, 1966 - 1974, Journal of Banking and Finance, 2, 1978.

Mc DONALD J. et B. JACQUILLAT, "Pricing of Initial Equity Issues : the French Sealed Bid Auction", Journal of Business, 47, 1974.

MANDELKER G. and A. RAVIV, "Investment Banking : an Economic Analysis of Optimal Underwriting Contracts", Journal of Finance, 32, 1977.

MASULIS R., "The effects of Capital Structure Change on Security Prices : A Study of Exchange Offers", Journal of Financial Economics, Vol 8, 1980 a.

MASULIS R., "Stock Repurchase by Tender Offer : An Analysis of the Causes of Common Stock Price Changes", Journal of Finance, Vol 35, 1980b.

RITTER J., "The "Hot Issue" Market of 1980", Journal of Business, 57, 1984.

RITTER J., "The Choice Between Firm Commitment and Best Effort Contracts", Unpublished Manuscript, 1985, University of Pennsylvania.

ROCK K., "Why New Issues are Underpricing", Journal of Financial Economics, Vol. 15, 1986.

SMITH W, Jr., "Investment Banking and the Capital Acquisition Process", Journal of Financial Economics, Vol. 15, 1986

GOING PUBLIC IN THE F.R.G.

Helmut UHLIR
University of Giessen, Faculty of Economics
Licher Straße 74, D-6300 Giessen, FRG

KEYWORDS: initial public equity offerings, the German IPO market, going public, initial returns, underpricing, information asymmetry, stagging strategy, primary market efficiency, after-market efficiency.

ABSTRACT

After several decades of stagnation a considerable increase in initial public equity offerings (IPOs) has taken place starting in 1983. Observed mean initial return exceeds 20%. The underwriting market is not very competitive and new issues are only offered on a firm commitment basis. Two indirect tests of Rock's model are performed supporting his basic ideas. It is argued that investment banks underpriced too much in the past: there is indication that abnormal returns could have been earned applying a stagging strategy. Return behaviour in the early secondary market is in line with efficient market theory. In the long run, however, there is evidence of a persistent negative trend in cumulative portfolio returns.

1. Introduction

During the sixties and seventies every year more stocks were delisted than initially offered to the public. The number of German stocks quoted continuously declined to a level of about 450 (1982/83). Then a remarkable change occured. In the following five years the number of listed companies - either common stocks or preferred stocks - rose to far more than 500. The remarkable increase can mainly be attributed to approximately 90 initial public equity offerings (IPOs) taken place during this period of time. This figure, when related to the number of already listed companies, is considerable large and underlines the importance of 'going public' for German equity markets.

NATO ASI Series, Vol. F54
A Reappraisal of the Efficiency of Financial Markets
Edited by Rui M. C. Guimaraes et al.

The main purpose of the study is to find out to what extent German IPO markets can be considered efficient. Two major lines of research are intended: (1) To evaluate primary market efficiency initial returns and the underpricing phenomenon are analyzed. (2) Price behaviour in the aftermarket is studied in order to test for secondary market efficiency. Throughout the paper we use the standard definition of market efficiency referring to the semistrong version. More specifically prices should be set reflecting all publicly available information on IPOs such that average excess returns will not be significantly different from zero.

The paper is organized as follows. Section 2 gives a brief description of the data and sample composition and tells how returns are calculated. Section 3 deals with the primary IPO market. Starting with a breakdown of distributional features initial returns are analyzed across time and IPOs. Information asymmetry is addressed to explain the level of underpricing. Finally the profitability of a simple investment strategy is discussed. Section 4 extends the analysis of new issue price behaviour to secondary market trading. Excess portfolio returns are under study to detect whether price adjustments will continue after initial prices are set.

2. Sample design and methodology

The study includes all new equity listings reported between 1977 and 1987. 106 companies were identified from various data sources during this period. But not all of those issues can be viewed as IPOs. Only issues which are offered to the public associated with an initial listing are admitted. Four firms were initially listed but did not offer new equity. Shares of three companies emerging from spin-offs/carve-outs got listed but were not offered to the public. Finally two companies solely changed the market segment, so neither initial listing occurred nor new equity was offered. Altogether 9 companies did not conform to the selection criteria above.

As a result a total of 97 IPOs remains (sample A)[1].

Six companies went public in the late 1987 and got involved in the period immediately after the 'Black Monday'. Unfortunately price data for individual stocks and the market index were not reported for the same point in time - i.e. such leads and lags might distort adjusted returns (see also footnote 12). For that reason in a few cases a sample is used where those IPOs are removed (sample B (N=91)). When studying price behaviour in the long run the sample size must be reduced to 70 IPOs in order to be able to observe aftermarket returns up to 12 months (sample C (N=70)).

As mentioned in section 1 empirical evidence should be provided on the efficiency of unseasoned new equity issues. This is claimed for both the primary market (initial returns) and for the price performance in the secondary market. Therefore excess return calculation is needed. Obviously a return can only be considered 'abnormal' if corrected for the expected return of an investment of equal risk.

For all IPOs percentage return is defined as excess return:

$$ER_{it} = R_{it} - E(R_{it}) \qquad (1)$$

where R_{it} is the return for IPO i, that is

$$R_{it} = (P_{it} - P_{io})/P_{io} \qquad (2)$$

where: P_{io} is the observed price at t_o

P_{it} is the observed price at time t

If initial returns are calculated t_o is the offer date, P_{io} is the fixed offering price and P_{it} is the price on the first trading day[2].

and $E(R_{it})$ is the expected return on issue i.

---

[1]The list of companies and the dates of initial trading can be obtained by request from the author.

[2]Since only very few issues started trading on a continuous basis - i.e. opening prices and closing prices were reported - P_{it} for all IPOs are 'Einheitskurse' (official market clearing prices on day t).

Usually the expected return is defined within the standard CAPM-framework. Since there exists no return history for IPOs to estimate systematic risk a beta of unity is assumed for all issues; in doing so we get the following simple equation:

$$ER_{it} = R_{it} - R_{mt} \qquad (3)$$

where R_{mt} is the return on the market portfolio proxied by the return on the 'Index des Statistischen Bundesamtes' -i.e.

$$R_{mt} = (I_t - I_o)/I_o \qquad (4)$$

where I_t and I_o are the corresponding index levels[3].

The average excess return for a sample of IPOs for time period t (e.g. the mean initial return) is:

$$ER_t = \frac{1}{N} \sum_{i=1}^{N} ER_{it} \qquad (5)$$

where N is the number of issues in the sample.

The cumulative excess return for each issue i is cumputed as follows:

$$CER_{iT} = \{ \prod_{t=1}^{T} (1+ER_{it}) \} - 1 \qquad (6)$$

where T is the number of periods (days, months) depending on the interval under study. Given CER_{iT} the average cumulative excess return for a sample of IPOs is:

$$CER_T = \frac{1}{N} \sum_{i=1}^{N} CER_{iT} \qquad (7)$$

In all cases our null hypothesis (H_o) states, that mean excess returns computed as in (5) or (7) are zero. T-statistics are calculated in the usual manner. If t-values are not reported in tables and if H_o is rejected on a 1% (5%) level of significance figures are marked with **(*).

---

[3]Neither index-figures nor R_{it} are controlled for dividends, if any. No dividend payments occured in the short run, so initial return calculations and the early aftermarket performance cannot be affected at all.

3. Underpricing of initial public equity offerings

3.1. First evidence on initial returns

On average IPOs are generating significantly high excess returns during the period immediately following their issuance, especially on the first trading day. This effect as well as the prevalence of positive initial returns in the aftermarket has been well documented by numerous empirical studies. Early research on unseasoned new equity issues was dominated by studies on US-markets. Now price behaviour of IPOs is also analyzed outside the U.S. even for relatively small and thin markets mostly confirming the tenor of previous findings. (For a fine summary see Dawson (1987)).

As described in section 2 initial returns are defined as percentage changes between offering prices to first trading prices adjusted for general market movements. On average there are two weeks between the offering date and the first trading day in the secondary market[4]. Computing mean returns for different samples concerning size and composition no substantial differences occured whether market-value weighted returns or equally weighted returns are used. As it is more convenient to work with the latter further analysis is based on equally weighted return data (equations (5) and (7)).

For German IPOs (sample A) a highly significant mean initial return of 21,5% is observed. Table 1a (column 2) gives evidence on the distributional features of initial returns. The distribution is strongly skewed caused by IPOs with extraordinary high initial returns. As a consequence the median (10,1%) might be a more reliable measure of average return. For instance, looking at the lower quartil we can learn that 25% of all IPOs have initial returns which are less than about 3%, but no issue experienced a substantial negative initial return.

---

[4]There might be some 'grey trading' during this period distorting initial returns somehow.

Table 1a

Distributional features of initial returns: data from German IPOs (sample A) compared with recent data from U.K.[a] and Sweden[b]

	U.K.	F.R.G.	Sweden
Mean	6.9	21.5	40.5
(t-value)	(3.3)	(6.4)	(4.7)
Std.dev.	15.3	33.0	63.8
Max.	70.1	197.3	360.0
Quartil 3	12.2	27.5	N.A.
Median	6.8	10.1	22.0
Quartil 1	-3.0	3.3	N.A.
Min.	-22.3	-2.7	-16.0
No.of issues	54	97	55

a) Levis (1987,p.19); IPOs 1986.
b) De Ridder (1986,p.155); IPOs 1983-1985.

If German sample statistics are compared with recent evidence on the IPO markets in the U.K. and Sweden (see columns 1 and 3 of table 1a) two inferences might be drawn: Firstly average initial returns seem to be the higher the smaller is the capitalization and/or trading volume of equity markets. Secondly return distributions in the U.K. and Sweden are also skewed but obviously show a greater portion of negative initial returns, that is overpriced issues. Taking a closer look at the negative tail of the distribution of German IPOs solely one out of 97 IPOs had an opening price in the secondary market which was lower than the offering price. After being adjusted for market movements we find only eight issues experiencing negative initial returns which are hardly below zero having a group mean of -1,2% (see table 1b last column).

More specifically all issues turned out to be underpriced and no issue was in fact overpriced. This is the most striking feature of the observed distribution, particularly if compared with evidence of other IPO markets (table 1b). One third of all issues in the U.K. was 'unsuccessful' on average and overpriced by 7%. Jog and Riding (1987) report a fraction of 37% for overpriced issues whereas only 8% of all German issues belong to this group.

Table 1b

Initial returns of underpriced and overpriced issues: German IPOs versus U.K. IPOs[a)]

	underpriced		overpriced	
	U.K.	F.R.G.	U.K.	F.R.G.
Mean	13.8	23.6	-7.1	-1.2
(t-value)	(6.0)	(6.6)	(-5.3)	(4.2)
Std.dev.	13.7	33.7	5.7	0.8
Fraction of total issues	66.7%	91.8%	33.3%	8.2%

a) Levis (1987,p.19,table 1 part B and C)

Now we are left with two unanswered questions: (1) Why should IPOs be underpriced on average? Some clarification will be given in chapter 3.3.1. (2) If an investment in German IPOs will promise a non-negative abnormal return and such a distribution will turn out to be stable over time investing in IPOs would be a profitable game. Whether a stagging-strategy on IPOs would have been systematically succesful in the past is briefly discussed in chapter 3.3.3.

3.2. The behaviour of initial returns over time

3.2.1. The 'learning effect'-hypothesis

Approximately up to 1983 more companies have been removed from quotation than became listed. Between 1977 and 1982 only one or two companies went public every year. In the following years a great change could be observed. At the same time as stock markets began to boom 'going public' suddenly was of general interest and IPOs became an exciting topic among the investment community.

At that early stage pricing of unseasoned equity was a very uncommon task for investment bankers and investors as well. Relatively unknown companies with high investment risk (i.e.

electronics, software-houses) were offered to the public. The extremely small capitalization of early IPOs led to enormous oversubscription and this, at least partially, has led to exceptionally high initial returns. This experience was of a self-generating kind and increased the speculative demand for further IPOs. In this context it should be mentioned that the German underwriting market is not very competitive. More specifically it is dominated by one bank[5]. But competition among underwriters begins to grow: starting with 2 in 1983, 11 competitors can be observed in the IPO market in 1987. As time passes one can imagine that all parties involved in the pricing process are learning how to price IPOs more accurately.

Assuming such a learning process for the period 1983-1987 the sample was structured as follows: all issues taken place between 1977 and 1982 were treated as a separate group (N=9) and the remaining companies (N=88) were ranked by their listing date. Then the ranked IPOs were divided into four equally sized groups (table 2).

Table 2

Average initial returns for different periods of time
(t-values in parentheses)

Period		mean		min.	max.
1977-1982		8.79	(4.28)	2.22	18.95
1983 - 1987	Quart. 1	40.67	(3.40)	-2.35	197.24
	Quart. 2	21.60	(4.35)	1.17	84.02
	Quart. 3	20.45	(5.03)	0.69	60.72
	Quart. 4	8.50	(4.01)	-2.74	30.24

The results shown in table 2 seem to be in line with the hypothesis mentioned above. Starting with a 'normal' market during 1977-1982 - mean initial return is about 9% - we are

[5]Between 1983 and 1987 about 50% of all IPOs and 67% of the new equity capital raised was managed by this underwriter.

moving through a rather booming, possibly overshooting market, reaching an early peak with approximately 40%. After that a period of consolidation at a level of about 20% can be observed. Finally mean initial return is coming back down to the previous level. Interpretations can only be thought very tentative because one must admit that several yet unrevealed factors may have an impact on the level of initial returns.

3.2.2. The 'hot market'-hypothesis

To avoid misunderstanding we clearly should distinguish between 'hot issue'-markets and 'hot'-markets. Hot issue-markets simply are defined as IPO markets in which observed initial returns are clearly above average (Ibbotson and Jaffe (1975), Ritter (1984)). The existence of hot (cold) issue markets can already be seen from table 2. On the other hand a hot (cold) market is a description of the 'mood' of the entire stock market. In this context 'hot' and 'cold' is similar to what is meant by a bull and a bear market period (see also Klein and Rosenfeld (1987)).

What we are doing now is to relate the level of initial returns to the general 'mood' of the stock market. For hot markets it is claimed both that there is an excessive demand for IPOs driving prices up and that investors are willing to accept more risk as usual. In cold markets the reverse should be the case. To investigate in that matter we must discribe the market cycle more operationally. A hot market is defined as a longer period - let us say half a year or more - of clearly above average market returns associated with high trading activity and high volatility. Cold markets are characterized by poor performance (zero or negative market returns), low transaction volume and moderate volatility. One should be aware that any definition of that type remains somehow arbitrary.

Especially the periods 1977-1981 and 1987 have been cold markets while 1985 turned out as a typical hot market. If the hypothesis holds mean initial returns during hot markets should be significantly different from those during cold markets. Average initial returns associated with hot and with cold markets are shown in table 3.

Table 3

Average initial returns during hot and cold stock markets
(t-values in parentheses)

Period	No. of issues	Designated as 'cold' market		'hot' market		min.	max.
1977-1981	8	9.11	(3.98)			2.22	18.95
1982-1983	12			53.30	(2.59)	-2.35	197.24
1984	21	17.25	(4.45)			-0.53	64.13
1985-1986	37			23.26	(6.40)	0.69	84.02
1987	19	8.00	(3.39)			-2.74	30.24
Mean cold a)	48	12.23	(5.89)			-2.74	64.13
Mean hot a)	49			30.62	(5.08)	-2.35	197.24

a) T-test for H_0: mean return on both markets is equal
t-statistic = 2,84**

Results are quite impressive. Looking at hot (cold) markets as a group mean initial returns are significantly above (below) the total sample mean. Even if taken period by period average initial returns in cold markets are dominated by those in hot markets.

To summarize there obviously exist distinct return patterns. Two competing hypotheses are on hand to explain why the level of underpricing varies over time: the 'learning effect'-hypothesis and the 'hot market'-hypothesis.

3.3. Underpricing and primary market efficiency

Early work on IPOs could not explain the somehow startling findings about initial returns. Ibbotson (1975) termed the phenomenon a 'mystery'. In the meantime several ad-hoc arguments are mentioned but none of them is really convincing, for instance Ritter (1983) mentioned three alternative hypotheses to explain underpricing: the 'Institutional Lag'-

hypothesis, the 'Speculative Bubble'-hypothesis and the 'Monopsony Power'-hypothesis. Furthermore empirical studies present determinants of underpricing like issue size, use of funds, line of business, flotation methods,offering prices, listing requirements etc. Usually regression analysis is applied but the explanatory power of such models in terms of R^2 is very low. Evidence for the German IPO market is in line with those poor results. Among others, especially the issue size and the market segment in which initial listing has taken place were tested but none of these variables turned out to be relevant.

3.3.1. Why IPOs should be underpriced

More recently it is claimed that IPOs will be intentionally underpriced by investment bankers [6]. The first explanation which has an appealing theoretical underpinning can be attributed to Rock (1986). The approach which is based on the assumption of information asymmetry among investors is now well understood and accepted in the literature.

The main argument depends on the existence of a group of investors whose information is superior to that of other investors including the IPO candidate and its investment bank[7]. If unseasoned equity is priced in the early secondary market at its expected value 'informed' investors crowd out the 'uninformed' investors in case good issues are offered and they withdraw from the market in case bad issues are offered.

Good issues will be associated with excess demand and new shares must be rationed. On the other hand bad issues will not be oversubscribed in general. Now if uninformed investors begin to find out that they will receive (nearly) no allocation of subscribed shares of underpriced issues due to severe rationing brought on by informed demand and (nearly) all of the overpriced issues, then they are not willing to partici-

---

[6] e.g. the monopsony power-hypothesis states that underwriters intentionally underprice IPOs and earn profits by allocating shares mainly to favoured clients.

[7] For a thorough discussion of this argument see Rock (1986,p.190).

pate in the IPO market until prices fall enough to be compensated for the 'bias' in allocation. As a consequence issuers must offer their shares at a discount otherwise there is no guarantee that uninformed investors will purchase the IPO.

The institutional framework in Germany is in line with Rock's model. The new issuer market is no auction market but a market for 'firm commitment offerings'. That means that the issuer and its investment bank agree on a prefixed price and quantity of new shares offered to the public. Once price and quantity are set, no further adjustments are allowed (e.g. there are no green-shoe options). In case of oversubscription shares have to be rationed.

Following Rock's hypothesis there should be a positive relation between the level of underpricing and the amount of oversubscription or rationing. Unfortunately the actual amount of rationing cannot be directly observed for German IPOs. Investment banks are quite reluctant to publish the precise oversubscription ratios or how they definitely allot shares to individual investors. Testing Rock's model indirectly two different approaches are presented in the following chapters.

3.3.2. The relation between expected underpricing and ex ante uncertainty

Issuers are clearly uncertain about the true market value of unseasoned new equity. If they were not they would not face any risk placing all shares and consequently would not need underwriters. Despite the greater expertise of investment banks some uncertainty about the true price of an IPO in the aftermarket still remains. It is plausible that underwriters intentionally underprice IPOs in relation to the degree of that type of uncertainty. Therefore we follow the arguments of Beatty and Ritter (1986,p.216) who hypothesize: 'the greater is the ex ante uncertainty about the value of an issue, the greater is the expected underpricing'.

However, the above variables cannot be observed directly or measured ex ante, so we have to figure out some surrogates. In case of the expected underpricing the observed initial return is taken as a proxy. In order to measure the ex ante uncertainty of the true aftermarket value the early secondary market variability of returns may serve as a surrogate.

The basic idea using aftermarket return variability is as follows: the greater the uncertainty about the true aftermarket value the longer it will take participants in the market to establish the 'correct' price in the secondary market. This should effect trading such that early prices are subject to substantial correction activities in either direction which in turn leads to greater return volatility. As a measure for that variability the standard deviation of secondary market returns is used. Immediately after the first trading day the following 19 days are taken to calculate standard deviation of daily returns.

Testing for the above hypothesis OLS regression techniques are applied. Using underpricing (UP)[8] as the dependent variable and the standard deviation of early secondary market returns (σ_i) as the explanatory variable we get the results reported in table 4.

Table 4

Regression statistics for the model: $UP_i = a+b_i\sigma_i + \varepsilon$

Sample (No.of observations)	a	b	R²	F-value
Sample A (97)	-0.016 (0.114)	-6.195 (0.815)	0.378	57.8
Sample B (91)	-0.004 (0.107)	-7.359 (0.827)	0.471	79.2
Sample B hot markets (49)	-0.015 (0.132)	-6.832 (1.255)	0.387	29.6
Sample B cold markets (42)	0.031 (0.068)	-10.534 (1.430)	0.576	54.3

F-statistics are significant on a 0.1% level

[8]Underpricing is defined as: $UP_i=[(P_{io}-P_{it})/P_{it}]-[(I_o-I_t)/I_t]$

Coefficients of the explanatory variable indicate that IPOs with a high standard deviation of daily aftermarket returns show also a substantially high level of underpricing. In other words there exists a significantly positive relationship between ex ante uncertainty about the true aftermarket value and expected underpricing of IPOs[9]. It is worth noting that regression results are quite uniform across different sample compositions. Even if considering hot and cold markets separately general findings remain unchanged. Empirical evidence, however, underlines the relevance of Rock's hypothesis also for the German IPO market.

Finally R^2 which turned out to be surprisingly high in all cases should be interpreted. Normally such a result would be reported as a desirable feature because it gives evidence on the explanatory power of the regression. Following Beatty and Ritter (1986,p.223), R^2 has to be very low. They argue that there should be only a positive relation between ex ante uncertainty and expected underpricing. That means, it must remain difficult for investors to predict the actual initial return on a single individual IPO even though the average initial return of a large sample can be predicted with reasonable accuracy. On the contrary a high R^2 implies that the actual underpricing (initial return) of an IPO is predictable to a great extent. In our context this argument, however, overlooks the fact that the explanatory variable cannot be observed in advance.

3.3.3. On the profitability of a stagging strategy

If information asymmetry prevails in the IPO market than it is convincingly argued that new issues have to be underpriced in order to compensate uninformed investors for the allocation bias. Moreover from Rock's hypothesis described in

---

[9] It should be noted that we are testing for a joint hypothesis: (1) there is a positive relation between ex ante uncertainty and mean initial returns and (2) secondary market standard deviation of return is an adequate proxy for ex ante uncertainty.

chapter 3.3.1. follows: 'If the model is correct, weighting the (initial) returns by the probabilities of obtaining an allocation should leave the uninformed investor earning the riskless rate' (Rock (1986,p.205)). Since there are only a few days between subscription of shares and initial trading interest cost can be ignored. With other words: in equilibrium 'effective' underpricing should be zero on average. What we essentially observe is 'nominal' underpricing which has to be controlled for the 'winner's curse effect (see Levis (1987)). Given the individual subscription ratios it would be possible to test whether observed nominal underpricing has the appropriate level. If the effective underpricing is significantly different from zero the efficient market hypothesis cannot be accepted.

Utilizing precise data on the actual allocation details of oversubscribed new issues in the U.K. market De Ridder (1986, p.190f.) and Levis (1987) performed direct tests on Rock's model by running a stagging strategy. Such an investment rule can easily be established: buy an IPO at the offering price and sell it immediately on the first trading day in the aftermarket. (The main problem uninformed investors are faced with is that they neither know in advance how an individual IPO will be oversubscribed nor do they know how they will be individually rationed by investment banks.) Their results suggest that after controlling for rationing and interest cost uninformed investors do not earn a gain.

As mentioned earlier underwriters are reluctant to disclose either precise figures on oversubscription ratios or how individual IPOs are rationed among investors. As a consequence we cannot run a conclusive test on the profitability of a stagging strategy. Instead we can do some simple modelling on the environment of such a strategy in order to figure out whether a stagging on IPOs should probably have rendered a substantial gain. Let us assume the following:

- stags neither know the amount of initial return nor the oversubscription ratio and the actual allotment of shares for an individual IPO in advance.

- the distribution of past initial returns (see table 1a) is used and stags will be rationed according to Rock's model - i.e. issues with high initial returns will be highly oversubscribed and IPOs with (low) or zero initial returns are assumed to be (nearly) fully alloted.
- application forms must be accompanied by payments for the full amount of shares requested. Multiple applications for the same issue by a single investor are not allowed.

There is evidence that German IPOs are heavily oversubscribed on average. From casual information we know that rationing down to 5% or even less is not unusual. In the absence of precise data several levels of rationing and different schemes of allocation are applied. Given the average initial return of 21.5% for sample A running a stagging strategy would have left investors with adjusted raw returns of significant amount even if assuming an extremely high degree of rationing[10].

In contrast to evidence found for the U.K. stagging on German IPOs probably would have been a profitable strategy. Since such a strategy would have been successful without the ability to effectively identify 'good' and 'bad' issues this suggests: (1) the efficient market hypothesis for the primary IPO market has to be rejected and (2) nominal underpricing turned out to be too high on average.

4. Secondary market efficiency

Previous empirical research on IPOs considering secondary market price behaviour reaches a general consensus that the market quickly adjusts for underpricing in early trading. Investors who purchased new equity in the aftermarkets would not have earned excess returns on average over at least the first few months. There are, however, several remarkable exceptions and also difficulties in comparing the results. An excellent overview is given in Dawson (1987,p.66).

---

[10]Mean gross returns turned out to be in a range between 8.6% and 3.6%. Since broker fees are charged only for transactions in the aftermarket substantial profits would have remained on average.

4.1. Price behaviour in the aftermarkets

There are substantial differences between the pricing process in the primary market (= initial pricing) and the pricing in the secondary market. Initial returns are a result of the prefixed offering price and quantity set by the issuer and its advisors and the market's initial valuation of the shares. In the secondary market, in contrast, there are no price rigidities. Once trading begins the market is free to establish its own value for the shares. In chapter 4.2. empirical evidence concerning the price behaviour either in the short run (1 month) and in the long run (1 year) is reported. There are several reasons to make this distinction although any specification of 'short' and 'long' is somehow arbitrary.

Firstly when IPOs open for trading the market must incorporate a large amount of information about the newly listed securities. Though investors do have access to a large quantity of new information there remains a lack of 'history' on reported data (e.g. accounting data). In any case there is presumably a lower information level and therefore a greater uncertainty about the value of an IPO at the early stage of pricing in the aftermarket. Uncertainty of that type should diminish in the long run.

Secondly in early aftermarket trading IPOs might initially be overvalued in a surge of optimism led by investor enthusiasm about the underpricing of the issue and the number of times the issue is oversubscribed. In addition, investors unable to obtain shares in the initial offer will seek to purchase them in the secondary market and this will add to the demand for the new shares. As a result investors overestimate the return potential and/or underestimate the risk characteristics of new issues. Subsequently, as investors evaluate informations more accurately and less emotionally they revise their former expectations and prices will 'normalize'.

Lastly, issuer and/or underwriters might pursue the policy to enforce the disclosure of positive informations they have when setting the offering price and during the early aftermarket. As a result the later aftermarket is characterized by a series of more unfavourable news announcements which where not anticipated by investors.

Since in an efficient market the initial market price will fully reflect available information - that is anticipating favourable and unfavourable news as well - we should expect that prices for new issues will establish very quickly. Any pricing errors will be randomly distributed and therefore no profitable trading rules can be derived from them. New issues purchased in the secondary market can then be viewed by investors as equivalent to other securities with differences in expected returns being primarily explained by differences in risk. In other words prices in the secondary market will not be significantly different from prices when trading begins.

4.2. Empirical evidence

4.2.1. Return behaviour in the short run

In this chapter the price performance of the early aftermarket is studied. From the 19 days following the initial trading day, returns are calculated[11] to determine whether underpricing continues to occur beyond the first market clearing. If the early aftermarket is efficient one would not expect daily aftermarket returns to be significantly different from zero. Otherwise investors would have had the opportunity to establish a profitable investment strategy.

Results are shown in table 5. After the first trading day (mean initial return of sample A: 21.5%) daily returns in the secondary market are small on average, have alternating signs and are generally not significantly different from zero. Only one out of 19 trading days has a mean return with an associated t-statistic exceeding 1.66 (= 10% level of significance).

---

[11]Raw return data is used as a proxy for excess returns. This procedure can be justified because daily returns are relatively small on average and evenly spread over hot and cold markets in our sample. Positive and negative market price trends are expected to compensate across time and across IPOs.

Moreover mean daily returns became rapidly less disperse and also less skewed. Taking the cumulative average return over the entire period - which is approximately equivalent to the aftermarket performance of the first month - a nonsignificant minus 0.9% can be observed.

It should be mentioned, however, that six issues included in sample A just started their early secondary market trading as the period after the 'Black Monday' turned down prices tremendously. No wonder that the aftermarket performance of those IPOs was severely influenced. The cumulative mean return for this group is negative and show a much higher variability even if controlled for general market movements [12]. By excluding those IPOs - that is forming sample B (see table 5, column 5) -

Table 5

Average daily returns ER_t (day 1 through day 19) and average cumulative daily returns CER_T in the aftermarket

Day	Sample A: All issues		Sample A: lower half	Sample A: upper half	Sample B	Sample C
	ER_t	CER_t	CER_T	CER_T	CER_T	CER_T
1	0.12	0.12	0.49	-0.25	0.23	0.20
2	0.36	0.53	0.72	0.34	0.79	0.85
3	-0.40	0.12	0.12	0.11	0.47	0.24
4	-0.24	-0.10	-0.15	-0.06	0.31	0.08
5	-0.23	-0.31	-0.54	-0.08	0.19	-0.12
6	-0.51	-0.83	-1.16	-0.51	-0.21	-0.48
7	0.05	-0.81	-1.24	-0.39	-0.17	-0.45
8	-0.27	-1.00	-1.38	-0.64	-0.35	-0.89
9	0.03	-0.98	-1.70*	-0.27	-0.17	-0.75
10	0.16	-0.72	-1.95*	0.49	0.20	-0.25
11	-0.17	-0.75	-2.54*	1.01	0.38	0.16
12	0.34	-0.37	-2.65**	1.86	0.77	0.60
13	0.05	-0.25	-2.38**	1.84	0.95	0.95
14	0.52	0.74	-2.33*	3.75	2.10	2.21
15	-0.48	-0.36	-2.69*	1.91	0.98	0.74
16	-0.05	-0.38	-2.99*	2.17	1.05	0.61
17	-0.02	-0.38	-3.13*	2.32	1.05	0.55
18	-0.24	-0.65	-3.07*	1.72	0.94	0.38
19	-0.11	-0.86	-3.20*	1.44	0.76	0.04

[12] In this context severe measurement problems emerged because reported market indices could not 'synchronized' with reported prices of IPOs. Since market trends often changed intradaily unbiased controlling for market movements was not possible.

the expected 'bias' is supposed to be removed. This turns out to be true but does not alter previous conclusions. Mean daily returns remain relatively small, are of different sign and again not significantly different from zero. The performance over the whole period changes now to a non significant positive return of 0.8%.

Ranking IPOs (sample A) by their amount of initial return and dividing the entire sample into two equally sized groups for the first time there appears some slight indication of price trend in the early secondary market. Issues with above average initial returns are showing mean cumulative returns which are persistently negative starting with the forth trading day. Cumulative portfolio returns became statistically significant for the second half of the observed period summing up to -3.2%. This figure is about 2.3% lower than the overall mean. As a consequence the mean initial return for this group (3.4%) was washed away completely. On the other hand IPOs with above average initial returns (group mean: 39.1%) end up with a small but insignificant gain of 1.4%. Empirical evidence shows that the observed deviations from zero portfolio returns are only spurious. Moreover if samples B and C are considered no significant price trends can be detected in case subsamples are formed.

To summarize heavy price adjustments do occur only on the first trading day that is in the primary market. Daily portfolio returns in the aftermarket up to one month do not exhibit significant deviations from zero excess returns. Consequently initial returns once established in the primary market remain unchanged in the aftermarket. Insofar the efficiency of the early secondary market cannot be rejected.

4.2.2. Return behaviour in the long run

As reported in section 2 an investigation of the long run performance required a reduction of the original sample size. 27 IPOs of sample A have to be removed in order to achieve sufficient return data up to one year after initial pricing

(= sample C). For this sample a mean initial return of 26.1% was observed[13].

Taking the entire sample inspection of the monthly average returns (table 6, first column) reveals no spectacular price

Table 6

Average monthly returns ER_t (month 1 through month 12) and average cumulative monthly returns CER_T in the aftermarket (sample C).

Month	All issues ER_t	All issues CER_T	lower half CER_T	upper half CER_T	upper quartil ER_t	upper quartil CER_T
1	-0.49	-0.49	-0.08	-0.89	-1.56	-1.56
2	0.68	-0.03	0.02	-0.08	-0.66	-3.12
3	-0.16	-0.20	-0.09	-0.30	-2.53	-6.36
4	0.61	0.25	0.89	-0.39	-1.22	-9.14*
5	-1.71*	-1.61	0.23	-3.44	-4.92*	-14.82**
6	0.15	-1.82	0.14	-3.78	1.87	-14.30*
7	-0.16	-2.17	-0.66	-3.68	-0.80	-15.73*
8	0.44	-1.57	-0.18	-2.95	-2.20	-18.08**
9	-0.03	-1.31	0.44	-3.06	-1.61	-19.36**
10	-1.20	-2.69	-0.73	-4.65	-1.85	-22.12**
11	-1.69	-4.43	-0.14	-8.73	-6.15	-27.53**
12	-2.75**	-7.41	-2.33	-12.49	-3.89**	-30.85**
0-12	-	14.56*	3.24	25.89*	-	19.47

behaviour during the first 9 months after initial quotation (with one exception in the fifth month showing a significant negative return of 1.7%). In the last quarter of the year monthly portfolio returns became substantially negative and escalate to a significant minus 2.8% in month 12. Cumulative portfolio returns increased to a final score of -7.4%, thus reducing the average initial return from previous 26% down to approximately 15%.

---

[13]The higher mean is mainly explained by the fact that the majority of the removed IPOs went public during a 'cold' market. Since no other structural deviations between both samples can be detected (see also table 5 last column) previous findings in chapter 4.2.1. need not be corrected for that specific reason.

Let us turn now to a more detailed investigation. It will be similar in structure to the research on secondary market performance in the short run. IPOs are ranked by their amount of initial return and subgroups of different size are formed. Results are also reported in table 6 (columns 3 to 6). Splitting the entire sample into two equally sized strata previous evidence becomes more pronounced now for the group with relatively high initial returns. Cumulative portfolio returns turn out to be persistent quite earlier and are of remarkable amount. They are summing up to a final score of -12.5% at the end of the observation period. IPOs belonging to the group having low initial returns show only a moderate negative price behaviour. Monthly mean returns remain in a relatively close range. Unfortunately figures are not statistically significant at an acceptable level (i.e. at least at a 10%-level of significance).

Finally if considering the upper quartil - that is the group with the highest initial returns (mean: 72.3%) negative portfolio returns increase dramatically. Monthly mean returns are negative in 11 out of 12 months. Cumulative monthly returns turn out to be very high starting with a significant minus 9% in the forth month. Negative return performance is persistent and highly significant up to month 12 reaching a cumulative result of approximately -31% for that portfolio. This in turn means that initial returns earned in the primary market are substantially reduced on average: they fell from about 70% to a level of 20% at the end of the first year's aftermarket trading.

To summarize there is remarkable evidence that portfolio excess returns are different from zero. More specifically the observed return trends clearly are negative, thus reducing initial returns substantially. Given the observation period of one year's secondary market trading the efficient market hypothesis must be rejected.

Now it is not an easy task to explain such a return pattern. Presumably investors are too overoptimistic about the future prospects of IPOs in general, even over a longer period of time. This might be due to the fact that issuer and/or investment banks concentrate positive announcements on IPOs at the offering date and during the early aftermarket period, e.g. optimistic statements concerning dividend payments are made or they even will deliberately withhold 'negative' information. Altogether, promises given probably are positively biased. As time passes real facts will come about and force investors to revise down former valuations.

Secondary market trends, like the observed ones, may also shed further light on the initial price differential between the offering price and the first market price. A decline in secondary market prices, for example, will indicate that initial price rises were overstated and underpricing by investment bankers was not as large as it appeared.

5. Summary

Initial returns in the primary market are found to be approximately 20% across time and across issues. The observed distribution is heavily skewed and has a median of 10%. Closer inspection reveals remarkable patterns. In contrast to empirical evidence on other IPO markets nearly no issue turned out to be really overpriced. The level of underpricing seems to be too high and issuers may have lost money on the table. This was probably due to the specific institutional environment. But the primary IPO market is signalling structural changes since 1987. Competition among underwriters has increased and investment banks / investors have 'learned their lesson' towards more efficient underpricing: mean initial returns are significantly lower now and 40% of individual IPOs are 'unsuccessful' issues.

In general German IPOs are offered on a firm commitment basis. All but a few issues have been heavily oversubscribed. Since there are no precise data available how new shares are rationed and allocated to investors Rock's hypothesis could be only tested in an indirect way. (1) A rather strong relation was found between the degree of underpricing and the ex ante uncertainty about the true secondary market value of IPOs, thus supporting the basic idea of Rock. (2) If nominal underpricing is controlled for rationing no investor should earn more than the riskless rate - i.e. effective underpricing has to be equal to the risk-free rate. Though no conclusive test on the profitability of a stagging strategy could have been worked out there is indication that substantial abnormal returns possibly could have been earned even if controlled for heavy rationing and transaction costs.

Now let us turn to the findings on secondary market efficiency. If we consider price behaviour in the short run, that means observating daily returns during the first month of aftermarket trading, the efficient market hypothesis cannot be rejected: price adjustments do occur only on the first trading day as it should be. Portfolio returns of the first month were not significantly different from zero.

In the long run (one year) price performance shows a quite different picture. Cumulative portfolio returns become significantly negative at the end of the observation period. Moreover taking portfolios of IPOs which are initially underpriced above average a substantial and persistent negative return performance can be observed. This trend becomes significant already four months after initial pricing. Clearly such a return pattern does not conform to the efficient market hypothesis. But conclusions should be drawn very cautiously at least for two reasons: firstly return data might be obscured in the absence of an appropriate risk adjustment procedure and secondly sample size is relatively small.

References

Asquith, P. and D. Mullins, 1986. Equity issues and offering dilution. Journal of Financial Economics 15, 61-89.

Baron, D.P. and B. Holmström, 1980. The investment banking contract for new issues under asymmetric information: Delegation and the incentive problem. Journal of Finance 35, 1115-1138.

Beatty, R.P. and J.R. Ritter, 1986. Investment banking, reputation, and the underpricing of initial public offerings. Journal of Financial Economics 15, 213-232.

Booth, J.R. and R.L. Smith,III, 1986. Capital raising, underwriting and the certification hypothesis. Journal of Financial Economics 15, 261-281.

Chalk, A.J. and J.W. Peavy, III, 1987. Initial public offerings: Daily returns, offering types and the price effect. Financial Analysts Journal Sept.-Oct., 65-69.

Dawson, S.M., 1987. Secondary stock market performance of initial public offers, Hong Kong, Singapore and Malaysia: 1978-1984. Journal of Business Finance & Accounting 14, 65-76.

De Ridder, A., 1986. Access to the Stock Market - An empirical study of the efficiency of the British and the Swedish primary markets (The federation of Swedish Industries, Stockholm).

Dimson, E. and P. Marsh, 1986. Event study methodologies and the size effect. Journal of Financial Economics 17, 113-142.

Ibbotson,R.G.,1975. Price performance of common stock new issues. Journal of Financial Economics 2, 235-272.

Ibbotson, R.G. and J.F. Jaffe, 1975. 'Hot issue' markets. Journal of Finance 30, 1027-1042.

Jog, V. and A.Riding, 1987. Underpricing in Canadian IPOs. Financial Analysts Journal Nov.-Dec., 48-55.

Klein, A. and J. Rosenfeld, 1987. The influence of market conditions on event-study residuals. Journal of Financial and Quantitative Analysis 22, 345-351.

Levis, M., 1987. Are new issues really underpriced? Some empirical evidence from the London Stock Exchange (paper presented at the EFA-conference, Madrid, Sept. 1987).

Myers, St.C. and N.S. Majluf, 1984. Corporate financing and investment decisions when firms have information that investors do not have. Journal of Financial Economics 13, 187-221.

Parsons, J. and A. Raviv, 1985. Underpricing of seasoned issues. Journal of Financial Economics 14, 377-397.

Ritter, J.R., 1984. The 'hot issue' market of 1980. Journal of Business 57, 215-240.

Rock, K., 1986. Why new issues are underpriced. Journal of Financial Economics 15, 187-212.

Smith, C., 1977. Alternative methods for raising capital: Rights versus underwritten offerings. Journal of Financial Economics 5, 273-307.

Smith, C., 1986. Investment banking and the capital acquisition process. Journal of Financial Economics 15, 3-29.

TRADING RULES AROUND REPURCHASE TENDER OFFERS

Josef Lakonishok
University of Illinois at Urbana Champaign
1206 South Sixth Street
Champaign, IL 61280, U.S.A.

Theo Vermaelen
INSEAD
Boulevard de Constance
F-77300 Fontainebleau, France

Keywords / Abstract : Stock Repurchase / Tender Offer / Market Efficiency / Signalling / Arbitrage / Insider Trading

This paper reports a new anomaly in finance: buying shares before the expiration date of a repurchase tender offer and tendering to the firm produces returns of more than 9% per week, on average. It is also found that repurchasing companies beat the value weighted index with 10 per cent per year in the two years after the repurchase. However, the fact that we can't beat the equally weighted market index suggests that we have "rediscovered" the size effect.

1. Introduction

A firm can buy back its own stock in two ways: either through an open market purchase where small quantities are purchased over a prolonged period of time, or through a repurchase tender offer where a firm offers to buy back a large fraction of its shares at a premium above the market price. Our discussion will focus on the second procedure: repurchase through tender offer.

NATO ASI Series, Vol. F54
A Reappraisal of the Efficiency of Financial Markets
Edited by Rui M. C. Guimaraes et al.

Repurchase tender offers have become a more common event in recent years. E.g., while in the 18 year period from 1962 until 1979, 146 NYSE-AMEX firms made repurchase offers, (or 8 per year), more than 100 firms have made such offers in the period 1980-1986. At the same time the event has created a large number of research questions:

1. What happens with stock prices around the announcement ?

2. Why do prices change as a result of the announcement ?

3. Is the market efficient in the strong or semi-strong sense ?

Using data before 1978, Dann (1981), Massulis (1980) and Vermaelen (1981) have reported significant price increases of around 15% after repurchase tender offer announcements. Typically, firms offer premia of around 22% for 15% of their shares.

While everyone seems to agree that repurchase increases market values, disagreement exists about the reason for the value increase. In effect, a repurchase tender offer can be considered as a capital structure change, as an instrument to reduce free cash-flow and therefore agency cost, as an alternative to pay a dividend, and as an information signal. Hence, there is no shortage of financial theories and models to "explain" why a repurchase should benefit shareholders. The capital structure view would argue that, to the extent the repurchase is debt financed, the firm will benefit from increased corporate tax shields. It may also argue that the repurchase transfers wealth from bond holders because it makes their claims more risky.

The free-cash flow theory would argue that the repurchase is a way to get rid of excess cash which would otherwise be wasted by managers in negative net present value projects. The view that a repurchase is essentially a change in dividend policy states that shareholders saved taxes this way in the old days when dividends were taxed higher than capital gains. The market value change just reflects the present value of the personal tax savings incorporated in the market price.

Typical for all the explanations above is the presumption that repurchase tender offers affect real corporate or personal cash flows and therefore create value. The final alternative explanation, the signaling hypothesis, argues that repurchases only affect the perceived cash flows. Even if the repurchase would not have taken place, shareholders would have realised the abnormal returns eventually when the information that the repurchase is supposed to announce is revealed publicly (thru earnings reports, etc.). In other words, the signalling hypothesis argues that the firm repurchases shares when it is undervalued. Note that the hypothesis does not necessarily imply that firms repurchase in order to reveal this information. E.g. it may well happen that managers want to prevent a takeover bid thru a repurchase because, if they don't tender during the repurchase offer, their control over the firm will be increased. However, if the management does not tender and holds a lot of shares of the firm, it will bear a significant cost if it pays a premium for its own stock, unless it is undervalued (see Vermaelen (1984)). Thus the market will indirectly infer from the repurchase something about managerial expectations about future cash flows.

After examining the capital structure, dividend policy and signalling hypothesis, Dann (1981) and Vermaelen (1981) conclude that the signalling hypothesis is the predominant explanation for the value increase at least in the period 1962-1978.

While the signalling hypothesis seems plausible, it raises a number of issues. For example, it is found that tendering shareholders receive, on average, premia of 23%, while the abnormal return to non-tendering shareholders is equal to only 13%. Tendering shareholders are much better off than non-tendering shareholders, which include the management, which, on average owns 17% of the stock. If the signalling hypothesis is true, why do managers agree to reduce their own wealth in order to reveal information early ? One explanation, which deserves further investigation is that the market does not fully realise the cost to the management and underestimates the positive news. This implies that buying stocks after repurchase tender offers should produce abnormal returns, and the abnormal returns should be related to the by the market perceived signalling cost.

Hence, the results of past research suggest one particular trading strategy: buying shares after the expiration day of repurchase tender offers and holding the shares for several years (i.e. until the "true" value of the firm is revealed thru earnings reports, etc.).

A second test of semi-strong form efficiency is suggested by the fact that repurchase tender offers provide opportunities for risk arbitrage. In an efficient market, market prices during the tender period should be set in such a way that investors are indifferent between selling their shares in the market place or tendering to the firm. As will be shown below, this requires that the market makes unbiased assessments of the fraction of shares purchased by the management, the fraction tendered by the shareholders and the price after the expiration of the offer. One way to test for efficiency is to buy shares before the expiration date and tender them to the company, whenever the market price is "significantly" below the tender price. Such a strategy should not provide any "abnormal" returns.

Thus, the main purpose of this paper is to examine whether it is possible to obtain "abnormal" returns from trading after repurchase tender offer announcements. Two types of trading strategies are considered: buying shares before the expiration date and tendering them to the company. The second strategy simply involves buying after the expiration date and holding the shares for several years afterwards. As will be shown below, the return of the first strategy depends on how successful the market is in predicting the fraction of shares tendered, the fraction purchased by the company and the price prevailing after the expiration date. The second strategy will be successful if the market systematically underestimates the "correct" value change of the firm. Hence, the aim of this paper is to provide some straightforward tests of market efficiency.

The preliminary findings of this paper are that (1) the first trading rule generates statistically and economically significant profits (2) the second trading rule allows one to "beat the market" if the market is the Value Weighted Index. If one uses the Equally Weighted Index, the abnormal performance disappears. Thus, it looks like we have rediscovered the "small firm" effect.

This paper is organised as follows. In the next section we discuss our data base. In section three we present our first trading rule with some preliminary results. In section four, the second trading rule is presented. Section five provides a summary and suggestions for further research.

2. Data

The data base consists of the announcement and expiration dates, the terms (fraction sought, tender price) and outcome (fraction tendered, fraction purchased) of all 251 repurchase tender offers which occurred between 1962 and 1986 by firms traded on the AMEX and NYSE. The first set of date covers 131 observations between 1962 and 1977 and is adapted from Vermaelen (1981). Data for 1978 and 1979 were taken from the Wall Street Journal Index which started summarizing repurchase announcements in 1978. From 1980 on we had access to all the 13-e4 filings and the filing date. We used the filing date to trace back the repurchase announcement and other relevant data in the Wall Street Journal Index. If no announcement was found, a questionnaire was sent to the corporation. For the firms that did not reply, we searched the Wall Street Journal Index until we found an announcement (advertisement) of the event. Data on stock prices and returns were taken from the daily return and master file from the Center for Research in Security Prices of the University of Chicago.

3. Trading rules around the expiration date

3.1 Methodology

A first trading rule consists of buying shares before the original expiration date and tendering to the firm. In order to compute the gains from such a strategy, it is important to keep in mind the rules governing the repurchase tender mechanism. If the offer is undersubscribed (i.e., the fraction of shares tendered, F_T, is less than the fraction of shares sought) the firm will repurchase all shares tendered. This is true, even when the offer is extended and becomes overestimated later on.

If the offer is oversubscribed, the firm will either buy back all the shares tendered, or allocate pro-rata so that each shareholder can sell a fraction F_p/F_T of his shares to the company (where F_p is the fraction purchased). Thus, the profit from buying a stock at a price P_B during the tender period and tendering it to the firm is equal to $P_T - P_B$ if the offer is undersubscribed at the first expiration date and equal to:

$$P_T \frac{F_p}{F_T} + (1 - \frac{F_p}{P_E}) P_E - P_b$$

if the offer is oversubscribed at the first expiration date, where P_E is the price after the expiration day. In cases where $P_T < P_B$, no trading was undertaken.

Different trading strategies (corresponding to different value of P_B and P_E) were tried out. Vermaelen (1981) presents a similar trading rule, but looks at the total sample. In this paper we only analyse a sub-sample where the market price is at least 3% below the tender price. He also uses ex-post information, because this trading rule is tested around the final expiration date.

3.2 Results

Our preliminary investigations indicate that, on average, the trading rule produces returns of 9.6%, with a median of 5.8%. In at least 95% of the cases, the returns are positive (for more details, see Lakonishok and Vermaelen (1988)).

The effect does not appear to be arbitraged away in recent years. If anything, the results have been stronger is the eighties: on average the trading strategy generated returns of 11.26%, and in all 46 cases where the tender price was at least 3% above the market price, the returns were positive. Interestingly, the returns became larger the higher the underpricing (i.e. the more the market price stays below the tender price). Thus, an investor can increase the return or its investment by concentrating on cases where the market price is signficantly above the tender price. Of course, the number of investment opportunities declines if one concentrates on deep-discount offers. For example, there are 110 cases where the market price was at least 3% below the tender price but only 77 cases where the market price was at least 5% below the tender price.

3.3 Normal vs abnormal returns

To what extent are these returns "abnormal" returns ? After all, any test of market efficiency is always a joint test of efficiency and a model of market equilibrium. However, considering the very short holding period (1 week) and the low risk of the strategy, it seems that the norma, expected return is all but negligable.

With regard to the risk of the strategy, it should be pointed out that, for undersubscribed offers, the strategy is riskless and in oversubscribed offers companies generaly buy back 80% of all the shares tendered so that only a small fraction of the investment is risky.

What about transactions costs ? Tendering is a costless activity. Thus, only a one-way transaction cost has to be paid when purchasing stocks. In addition, when the non-repurchased shares are sold, an additional transaction cost has to be paid (on less than 20% of the investment). Hence, the trading rule is clearly profitable after transaction costs.

Such large returns seem an implausible risk premium, in spite of all the uncertainty the traders have to bear: what will be the outcome of the tender offer, i.e. how many shares will be tendered ? What will the company do: allocate pro-rata or buy up all the shares tendered ? What is the information content of the offer ? Hence we conclude that an opportunity for abnormal profits existed in the sample period.

4. Trading rules after the expiration date

Previous research (Dann (1981), Masulis (1980) and Vermaelen (1981)) reports that repurchase tender premia exceed abnormal returns to non-tendering shareholders by almost 10%. Or, tendering shareholders are significantly better off than non-tendering shareholders. If the value charge is an information signal, then the insiders-managers in the corporation (who don't tender) incur a significant signalling cost (see Vermaelen (1984)). Consequently, there has to be some other managerial incentive to counter-balance these costs, e.g., deterring a raider, we could argue that the market does not fully realise "how good" the signal is, so that the "apparent" cost (as estimated by the market around the announcement) is below the the true cost. This implies that buying stocks after the expiration of the offer and holding them for several years (until the "true" value of information becomes available) should produce positive abnormal returns.

4.1 Computing abnormal returns

Computing abnormal returns requires specifying a model of market equilibrium which specifies "normal" returns. Typically, the market model is employed, i.e., expected returns are equal to

$$E\ (R_{it}/R_{mt}) = \alpha_i + \beta_t\ R_{mt}$$

where α_i and β_i are estimated in an (estimation) period. The choice of the appropriate estimation period is crucial if the event is preceded (or followed, if post announcement dates are included) by abnormal returns. E.g., if repurchase tender offers are preceded by negative "abnormal" returns, α_i will be underestimated, so that subsequent "abnormal" returns are overestimated.

An alternative methodology involves simply subtracting the return of a broadly defined market index from the return of the security.

In this paper we focus on the last method and employ two indices: the equally weighted CRSP index and the value weighted CRSP index.

Hence, we define the excess return for security i in day t as:

$$e_{it} = R_{it} - R_{vt} \quad \text{(value weighted index)}$$

or as

$$e_{it} = R_{it} - R_{et} \quad \text{(equally weighted index)}$$

Average abnormal returns and cumulative average abnormal returns are computed over all the firms in the sample, are computed from 5 days before the announcement until 500 days after. In the table below we assume that 20 trading days is equivalent to a "monthly" return, so that our test period consists of 24 "months" after the announcement date.

In each case, we examine the total observation period (1962-1986), the first sub-period (1962-1979) and the second sub-period.

4.2 Results

The results using the value weighted index as a benchmark are reported in Table 1. The announcement return is equal to 14.56 per cent. The announcement has a more positive effect before 1980 (15.73%) than after 1980 (11.54%), in spite of the fact that, on average, the premia and fraction purchased are similar in both periods. In the first sub-period firms repurchase, on average, 16.7% of their shares at an average premium of 22.9%. The corresponding numbers in the second sub-period are 19% and 20%, respectively.

Table 1 **AVERAGE (AR) AND CUMULATIVE (CAR) AVERAGE ABNORMAL RETURNS FROM THE ANNOUNCEMENT MONTHS UNTIL 24 MONTHS AFTER THE REPURCHASE, RELATIVE TO A VALUE-WEIGHTED INDEX (TOTAL SAMPLE)**

MONTH	N	AR	t	CAR
+ 0	251	14.09	14.56	14.09
+ 1	250	0.05	0.10	14.15
2	249	- 0.94	- 1.47	13.20
3	246	0.26	0.48	13.46
4	246	0.37	0.45	13.83
5	245	1.14	1.48	14.97
6	245	- 0.36	- 0.62	14.61
7	245	0.31	0.44	14.92
8	244	1.49	2.11	16.40
9	244	- 0.00	- 0.00	16.40
10	243	1.61	2.22	18.02
11	243	1.08	1.75	19.09
12	243	1.22	1.80	20.32
13	243	0.69	1.16	21.00
14	238	1.57	2.30	22.57
15	237	0.20	0.30	22.77
16	234	1.25	1.73	24.02
17	233	0.68	1.06	24.70
18	231	1.72	2.48	26.42
19	223	0.94	1.22	27.36
20	222	1.71	1.89	29.06
21	218	2.17	2.07	31.23
22	216	1.95	2.38	33.18
23	214	1.18	1.60	34.37
24	211	0.97	1.31	35.33

A number of explanations can be proposed for this difference. First, because repurchases have become more popular in general, they are less "unexpected" than in the past. Second, managerial incentives to signal may actually have increased in recent periods. Vermaelen (1984) finds evidence that firms tend to make repurchase tender offers when there is a lot of takeover activity. This suggests that firms may want to signal in order to prevent being taken over at a too "low" stock price. Hence, the merger and takeover wave of the eighties may have encouraged managers to offer large premia for the company's shares, even if these offers entailed a reduction in their personal wealth. Finally, the repurchase tender offer may have been a less convincing signal today than in the past, because the typical firm is larger and is less controlled by insiders. Hence lower insider holdings mean lower costs of "false" signalling and therefore lower credibility.

Table 1 shows that that from 2 months after the announcement until 24 months after the announcement, repurchasing stocks experienced an abnormal return of 22.13%. Table 2, however, shows that this result is very sensitive to the choice of the market index. When returns are compared with an equally weighted index, the "abnormal" performance in the post expiration period all but disappears.

The difference in results can be experienced by the "size effect" (for a similar explanation of abnormal performance after broker recommendations, see Dimson and Marsh (1986)): a value weighted index will mainly reflect the performance of the largest firms. As small firms have historically outperformed large firms (see Banz (1981)), and the repurchasing firms tend to be smaller (at least in the earlier period, see Vermaelen (1981)), the post-announcement performance merely reflects the "small firm" effect.

Table 2 AVERAGE (AR) AND CUMULATIVE AVERAGE (CAR) ABNORMAL RETURNS FROM THE ANNOUNCEMENT MONTH UNTIL 24 MONTHS AFTER THE REPURCHASE, RELATIVE TO AN EQUALLY WEIGHTED INDEX (TOTAL SAMPLE)

MONTH	N	AR	t	CAR
0	251	13.92	14.92	13.92
1	250	- 0.72	- 1.30	13.20
2	249	- 1.86	- 2.94	11.34
3	246	- 0.52	- 0.97	10.83
4	246	- 0.87	- 1.11	9.95
5	245	0.72	0.93	10.66
6	245	- 0.86	- 1.60	9.81
7	245	- 0.34	- 0.50	9.47
8	244	0.51	0.79	9.98
9	244	- 0.83	- 1.31	9.13
10	243	0.43	0.63	9.58
11	243	- 0.07	- 0.12	9.52
12	243	0.64	0.99	10.16
13	243	0.12	0.21	10.28
14	238	0.36	0.56	10.63
15	237	- 0.83	- 1.28	9.86
16	234	0.47	0.65	10.27
17	233	- 0.44	- 0.69	9.83
18	231	1.00	1.52	10.83
19	223	- 0.29	- 0.40	10.54
20	222	0.54	0.66	11.08
21	218	1.10	1.08	12.19
22	216	0.53	0.66	12.71
23	214	- 0.13	- 0.18	12.58
24	211	0.07	0.01	12.59

5. Summary

This paper presents a new anomaly: by buying shares before the first expiration date of a repurchase tender offer and tendering them to the firm, we obtain a return, on average, of 9%, a value too large to qualify as a "normal" rate of return over a 3-day period. Thus, the market seems to underestimate the value increase resulting from the repurchase offer, or the fraction of shares purchased. For longer, two-year holding periods it appears that buying a portfolio of repurchasing companies allows one to beat the value weighted market index with more than 10% per cent per year. However, the fact that you can't beat the equally weighted index suggests that the "abnormal" performance reflects the small firm effect.

Further research is necessary to investigate whether it is possible to improve our trading performance by developing more specific models about the behavior of shareholders around tender offers. This would enable us to refine our trading strategy by incorporating forecasts about the outcome of tender offers and the repurchase decisions by managers.

REFERENCES

Banz, Rolf, 1981, The Relationship between return and market value of common stock, Journal of Financial Economics, 9, 3-18

Dann, Larry, 1981, Common stock repurchases: an anlysis of returns to bondholders and stockholders, Journal of Financial Economics, 9, 115-138

Dimson, Elroy and Paul Marsh, 1986, Event study methodologies and the size effect: the case of UK press recommendations, Journal of Financial Economics, 17, 113-143

Lakonishok, Josef and Theo Vermaelen, 1988, "Anomalous Price Behavior around Repurchase Tender Offers", manuscript, INSEAD.

Masulis, Ron, 1980, Stock Repurchase by tender offer: an analysis of common stock price changes, Journal of Finance, 35, 305-318

Vermaelen, Theo, 1981, Common Stock Repurchases and Market Signalling, Journal of Finance Economics, 9, 139-183

Vermaelen, Theo, 1984, Repurchase tender offers, signalling and managerial incentives, Journal of Financial and Quantitative Analysis, 19, 163-181

PRICE-CONDITIONAL VECTOR AUTOREGRESSIONS AND THEORIES OF STOCK PRICE DETERMINATION[1]

Robert J. Shiller
Cowles Foundation
Yale University
Box 2125 Yale Station
New Haven CT 06520
U. S. A.

KEYWORDS/ABSTRACT: stock market/stock prices/share prices/dividends/earnings/volatility/ratio/forecasts/expectations/efficient markets/vector autoregression/price conditional/cointegrated model

The time series properties of price, dividend and earnings series for the aggregate stock market, as well as of interest rate series, are compared with an efficient markets model. For this purpose, price-conditional vector autoregressions, i. e., vector autoregressions that put price per share in the information set, are particularly useful. An interpretation of results with such vector autoregressions is that prices overreact to current dividends.

---

[1] This research was supported by the U. S. National Science Foundation.

NATO ASI Series, Vol. F54
A Reappraisal of the Efficiency of Financial Markets
Edited by Rui M. C. Guimaraes et al.

1. Introduction

Are the movements through time in stock prices justified by information about fundamentals? The theory of efficient markets would imply that they must be so justifiable, yet it has seemed to many observers that it is unlikely that the price movements are a rational response to anything. About a decade ago LeRoy and Porter (1981) and I (1979, 1981a, b) presented some statistical analysis that was interpreted as implying stock prices are too volatile to be explained in terms of such fundamentals.

Since then, there has appeared a lot of econometric work in the literature that has tried to find out whether stock prices indeed show such excess volatility. The original work of LeRoy and Porter and myself was strongly criticized (see for example Flavin (1983), Kleidon (1986), and Marsh and Merton (1986)) and also found some new supporters (see for example Mankiw, Romer and Shapiro (1985), Summers (1986), and West (1987b)). Other evidence that is suggestive of excess volatility in financial markets has also appeared (DeBondt and Thaler (1985), Fama and French (1987a,b), Flood Hodrick and Kaplan (1986), Poterba and Summers (1987), and Cutler, Poterba and Summers (1987)). The debate has shed light on the validity of efficient markets models that goes beyond the issue of the alleged excess volatility in financial markets. This debate has been surveyed recently by Gilles and Leroy (1987) and West (1987). Both concluded that there is indeed evidence that the volatility of stock prices cannot be readily accommodated in terms of the efficient markets model.

In this paper, I will present my own current view of the volatility debate with special attention to a recent contribution to this literature that John Campbell and I made (1987a,b,d). This contribution is an application of vector-autoregressive time-series models that incorporate a variable related to price in the vector. Here I will call these price-conditional vector autoregressive models. The variable that is related to price is either a difference between the dividend and a constant times price or is a log dividend-price ratio. Such models are an outgrowth of the recent econometric literature on co-integrated econometric models (Granger and Engle (1987)). These price-conditional vector autoregressions allow us to deal effectively both with the nonstationarity problem that had been an issue with earlier research and with the possibility that market participants may observe relevant information variables not observed by the econometrician. With such price-conditional vector autoregressions we can estimate what the dividend-price ratio _should_ be if markets are efficient, and compare this with the actual dividend-price ratio. Moreover, with such price-conditional vector autoregressions we can compute what the return or change in stock price should be if markets are efficient, and compare this with actual returns or change in stock price.

2. Definition of Market Efficiency

In the form used here, the theory of efficient markets states that the excess one-period return of a stock or other risky asset over some one-period interest rate is unforecastable. This means that, in terms of expected return, there is no good or bad time to buy stocks. It means that one can never predict that the stock market at some time will do well or poorly relative to an alternative investment at the interest rate. Of course, there are other notions of market efficiency, besides the one used here. In some other definitions, the risk premium between stocks and debt moves through time: even though excess returns are forecastable there is no change through time in the relative attractiveness of stocks versus investments at the interest rate, since the market becomes more or less risky through time. Market efficiency by these other definitions has been studied elsewhere (see for example Campbell and Shiller (1987a) and Poterba and Summers (1987)). These alternative definitions of market efficiency are used far less commonly than the one used here. The definition of market efficiency adopted here is the "conventional wisdom" story that is usually alluded to when efficient markets are described, and merits careful study.

We will let P_t denote the price per share of a stock (or other risky asset) at time period t and D_t the dividend paid per share at time t. The (one-period) return on the stock is given by $R_t = (P_{t+1} - P_t + D_t)/P_t$. It is the total capital gain $(P_{t+1} - P_t)$ plus dividend earned D_t as a proportion of the initial investment P_t. If r_t is the one-period interest rate at time t, then the excess return is $R_t - r_t$, and the efficient markets theory is that:

$$(1) \qquad E_t(R_t - r_t) = C$$

where C is a constant. E_t denotes mathematical expectation conditional on all available information.

If both P_t and r_t are in the information set at time t, then (1) implies, subject to a terminal condition ruling out infinite bubbles, that P_t is the expected present value discounted by $r_{t+j} + C$, j = 0, 1, 2, . . . of future dividends D_{t+j}, j = 0, 1, 2, ... Thus, the same definition of market efficiency that we have already adopted can be restated as that price is determined by fundamentals, where fundamentals are dividends appropriately discounted.

The theory that price is representable as the expected present value of future dividends is, if it is right, a powerful one. It says that nothing that is not reflected directly either in dividends or interest rates can ever have any effect on stock prices. Specifically, there are not fashions or fads in financial markets, no changes in investor optimism or pessimism except as warranted by optimal forecasts of interest rates or dividends, no bear or bull markets. Moreover, the efficient markets model also restricts the way information about future dividends or interest rates affects price. Thus, for example, we have the Modigliani-Miller proposition that the dividend policy of the firm has no effect on value.

3. A Linearized Model

The return R_t is not linear in price and the present value formula is not linear in interest rates. It helps, therefore, to linearize the expression for excess return, so that we can write linearized excess return and linearized present value in terms of a single set of variables. Following Campbell and Shiller (1987b) we will write the linearized return in terms of the change in log dividend $\Delta d_t = d_t - d_{t-1}$ and the log dividend-price ratio $\delta_t = d_{t-1} - p_t$.[2] In this paper, lower-case letters denote natural logs of the upper-case counterparts. The linearized return ξ_t, a linear approximation around $\Delta d_t = g$ and $\delta_t = \delta$ to the log of $1 + R_t$, is given by:

$$(2) \qquad \xi_t = \delta_t - \rho\delta_{t+1} + \Delta d_t + k$$

where $\rho = 1/(1+\exp(\delta))$ and $k = \ln(1+\exp(\delta)) - \delta\exp(\delta)/(1+\exp(\delta))$. The quality of this approximation is discussed in Campbell and Shiller (1987b).

If we assume that equation (1) applies to ξ_t, i. e., that $E_t(\xi_t - r_t) = C$, and if we impose a terminal condition that rules out infinite bubbles, then it follows that the log dividend-price ratio δ_t should equal δ'_t where δ'_t is defined by:

$$(3) \qquad \delta'_t = E_t\delta^*_t$$

[2] The log dividend-price ratio is written in terms of the lagged dividend rather than the current dividend, because with the data set used here the current dividend is not available as of the time the current price is quoted. P_t is January price, and D_t is dividend totalled for the year. Thus, our definition accords with the common definition of the dividend-price ratio.

and where δ_t^*, the 'perfect foresight' or 'ex-post rational' log dividend-price ratio is defined by:

$$(4) \qquad \delta_t^* = \sum_{j=0}^{\infty} \rho^j (r_{t+j} - \Delta d_{t+j}) + k/(1-\rho)$$

Equations (3) and (4) are the basic relations to be used in this paper, and so they bear scrutiny. By (4) the perfect-foresight dividend price ratio δ_t^* (or the dividend-price ratio that would obtain by the linearized efficient markets model if investors could foretell the future perfectly) is a sort of present value of future 'growth adjusted interest rates", equal to $r_{t+j} - \Delta d_{t+j}$ j = 1, 2, ... By (3) the actual log dividend-price ratio at time t, δ_t, is the optimal forecast with all information available at time t of δ_t^*.

Interpretation of the model implicit in (3) and (4) may be helped by considering some special cases. If r_t is the nominal interest rate and if dividends change only due to price inflation (so that real dividends are constant through time) then the growth-adjusted real interest rate $r_t - \Delta d_t$ is a one-period real interest rate.[3] The log dividend-price ratio δ_t, a weighted average of expected future one-period real interest rates, then is, by (3) and (4) together, a sort of long-term real interest rate. On the other hand, if dividends change through time for reasons other than inflation, so that real dividends are not constant through time, then the growth-adjusted real interest rate has a different interpretation. It may be regarded as a sort of measure of how much information about proportional changes in future dividends should be discounted in arriving at today's price, a measure that takes into account both interest rates and the level of dividends in the future.

Equations (3) and (4) may also be described as a sort of dynamic 'Gordon model', after the familiar model that Myron Gordon (1962) deduced in the context of a growth model. The Gordon model asserted that the dividend-price ratio equals the discount rate minus the growth rate of dividends. The Gordon model did not describe how the dividend-price ratio should change through time if there are predictable fluctuations in either interest rates or growth rates of dividends. Equations (3) and (4) make just such predictions, and thus

---

[3]The theory here assumes that r_t is measured at the beginning of time period t, while the dividend d_t is paid at the end of time period t, though in fact dividends are not all paid at that one time.

extend the Gordon model beyond the growth model context. The quality of the approximation implicit in (3) and (4) is studied in Campbell and Shiller (1987b).

4. Two Special Cases of the Model

Two special cases of the model (3) and (4) will be considered here. In the constant real rate (CRR) model, r_t is a real interest rate that is constant through time and p_t and d_t are measured in real terms, that is, are corrected for inflation. For applications below we will subtract from the log price and dividend the log consumer price index, to arrive at real series. In this version of the model, no interest rate data are used at all. In the varying real return (VRR) model, r_t is taken to be the nominal one-year commercial paper rate (plus a constant, a 'risk premium' that we can ignore in our analysis) In the VRR model p_t and d_t are measured in nominal terms. The two models, the CRR and the VRR models, are consistent if the real treasury bill rate is constant through time, for in that case the treasury bill rate is achieving the same deflation of nominal values as does the price index. Of course, the real treasury bill rate has not been constant through time and has (with the possible exception of the time period 1953-71 studied by Fama (1975)) shown predictable movements (see for example Huizinga and Mishkin (1986)). The two versions of the model thus cannot both be right, but the difference between them may also not be important in the sense that changes in p_t are so big as to swamp out r_t in determining excess returns.

Other special cases of the efficient markets model were studied in Campbell and Shiller (1987a, d): a consumption-based asset pricing model in which the discount factor was inferred from marginal rates of substitution in consumption, and a time varying volatility model in which rates of discount were related to the observed volatility of financial markets. There is likely to be an element of truth to both of these models, but neither of these simple special cases considered in isolation seemed to be supported by the data. A hybrid of all these models may be useful, but is beyond the scope of this paper; I therefore disregard the consumption-based and time-varying-volatility model here.

5. A Preliminary Look at the Data

Prices track dividends through time. Figure (1) shows a plot of the log real price p_t and log real dividend d_t series that are the underlying data for the CRR version of the model for the U. S. for the years 1871 to 1986 (see Appendix for sources of data). The plot shows that the two series are actually

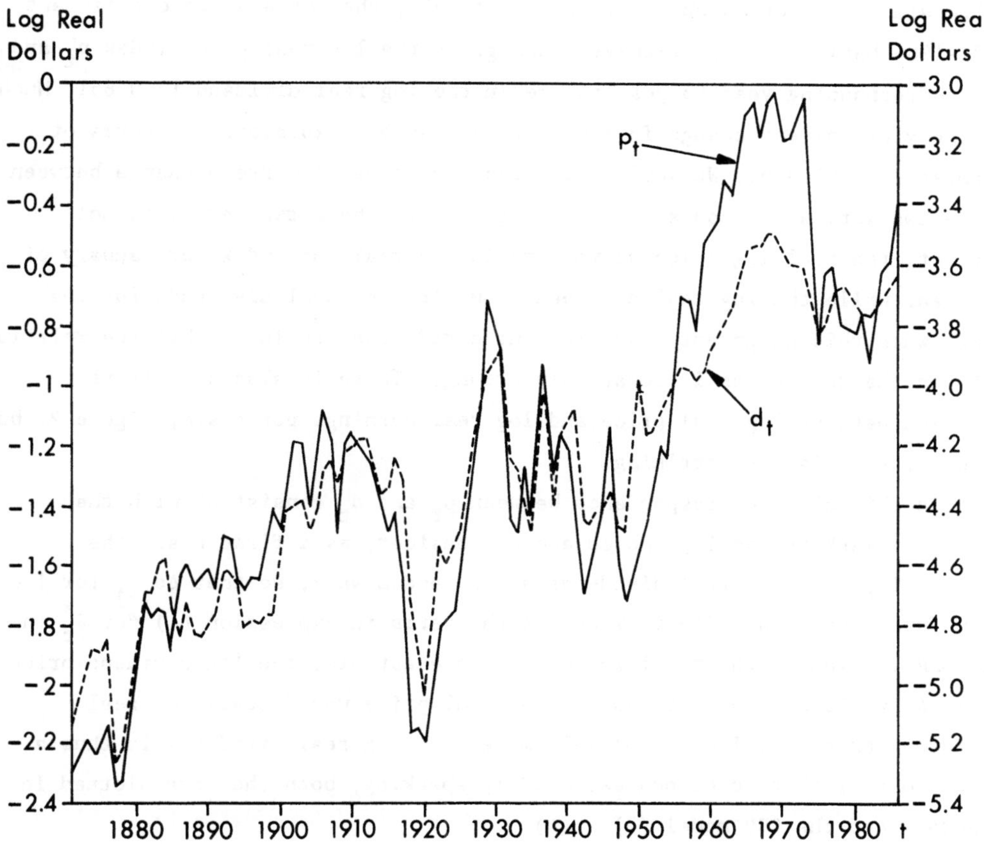

Figure 1. Real price and real dividends. The solid line is p_t, the log real Standard and Poor Composite Stock Price Index for January. The dashed line is d_t, the log real dividend per share, adjusted to index, total for year. Both series are deflated using the producer price index. See appendix for source of data.

quite similar in broad outline. Quantitatively, the correlation coefficient 1871-1986 between the year-to-year change in the log real price index p_t and the corresponding year-to-year change in the log real dividend is 0.651. Much of the year-to-year change in stock prices can be 'explained' in terms of changes in dividends. We would not expect too close a correspondence between these two series, of course, since alignment of these two series is not perfect: the real log price shown here is the real log index for January of the year while the log real dividend shown is the total dividends for the year. When this alignment issue is considered, one concludes that the relation between the two series is remarkably strong.[4] There is also a positive relation between log real price and log real earnings per share, figure 2, but this relation is less striking.

Is this close correspondence between p_t and d_t consistent with the efficient markets model proposed above? Consider, as a first pass, the possibility that log real dividends are a random walk, so that Δd_{t+j} for $j \geq 0$ is unforecastable at time t. Then all the terms in expression (4) for δ_t^* in the CRR version of the model would be unforecastable, the log dividend-price ratio δ_t would be constant, and so log real price would track log real dividend perfectly. The random-walk model for log real dividends is thus a story to tell that accommodates, crudely speaking, both the data plotted in Figure 1 and the CRR model (3) - (4).

We should not jump too quickly at the conclusion that the random walk story for log real dividends coupled with the efficient markets model is a good story, even as a crude approximation, to tell about the actual data. First, we can reject the random walk model for this log real dividend series based on a Dickey-Fuller test, Shiller (1981b)[5] or a test along lines developed by Phillips (1986), see Perron (1986). Second, prices and dividends, while highly correlated, do show separate movements, i. e., the log dividend-price ratio is not constant. While these separate movements may look small in the plot of the century-long series, over shorter time intervals the separate movements look rather important.

Before embarking on a discussion of whether these variations in the log

---

[4]The decision was made to study here point-sampled prices and unit-averaged dividends because a. the model (3-4) uses point-sampled price, and b. annual averaged dividends are all that are available for the full sample used here.

[5]See, however, the discussion in Kleidon (1986).

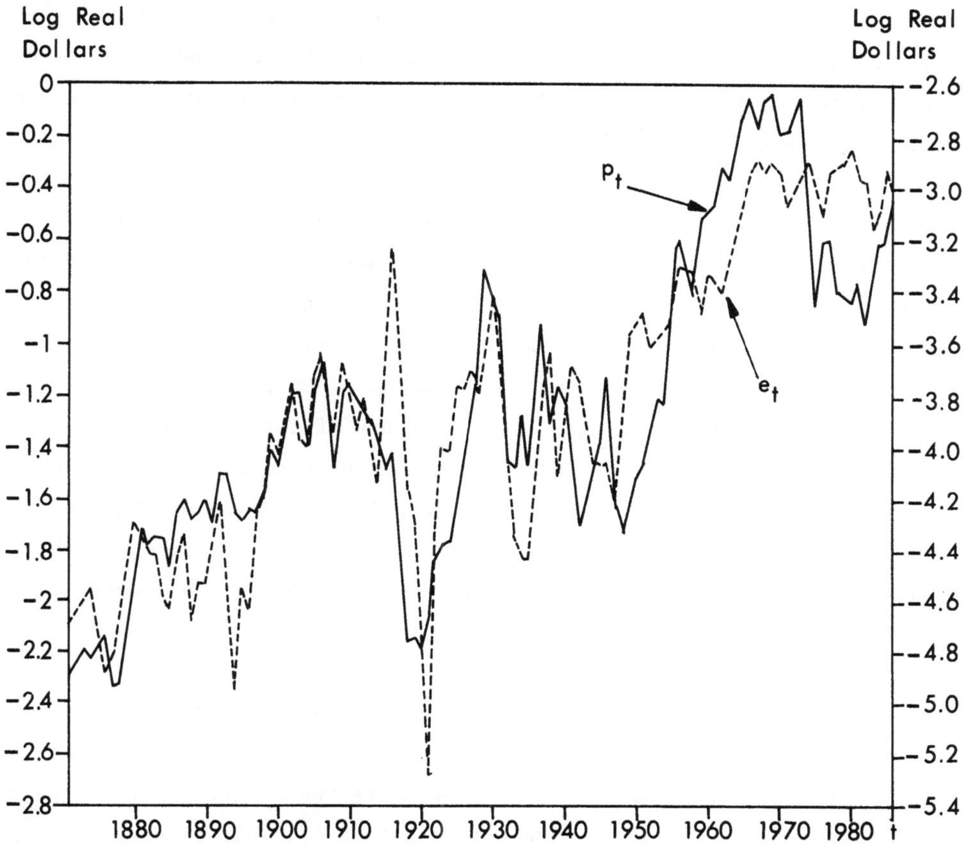

Figure 2. Real price and real earnings. The solid line is p_t, the log real Standard and Poor Composite Stock Price Index for January. The dashed line is e_t, the log real earnings per share, adjusted to index, total for year. Both series are deflated using the producer price index. See appendix for source of data.

dividend-price ratio can be reconciled with the efficient markets model, let us consider an alternative interpretation of the strong correlation we have observed between p_t and d_t. Dividends are, of course, determined by managers of firms. Is it possible that firms are setting dividends so as to make dividends close to price? The direction of causality would then run from price to dividend, rather than dividend to price as was supposed above. This interpretation of the correlation between dividends and prices was urged by Marsh and Merton (1987). They claimed that the dividends are set by managers in consideration of the 'permanent earnings' of the firm, the long-run or average earnings to be expected over coming decades. Current earnings may be a poor measure of permanent earnings. If markets are efficient, then, they argued, price per share ought to correlate highly with permanent earnings. Thus, there is an implied correlation between price and dividend. The Marsh Merton model is discussed in Campbell and Shiller (1987c). We conclude that while it is likely that there is an element of truth to their argument, the evidence they gave for this view was rather weak.

6. Perfect Foresight Dividend-Price Ratios

The most direct way to evaluate the efficient markets model in equations (3) and (4) is just to compare δ_t with δ^*_t. The model says that δ_t is the optimal forecast at time t of δ^*_t. If we plot these two series together, we can compare them and see if δ_t looks like a forecast of δ^*_t. This is done in figure (3) for the CRR model and figure (4) for the VRR model (see Appendix for description of data used to generate these series). The discount rate ρ was taken to be .936, which is more or less consistent with observed dividend-price ratios. Of course, we do not know the growth-adjusted interest rates after 1986, which enter into the infinite summation in (4), and so some assumption has to be made about these. The assumption was made here that growth-adjusted interest rates after 1986 are such as to make the 1987 value of δ^*_t coincide with the 1987 value of δ_t. The values of δ^*_t near the end of our sample are thus heavily influenced by this arbitrary terminal condition. However, the values of δ^*_t plotted a couple decades or more before the end of the sample are likely to be a good measure of actual δ^*_t.

In looking at figures 3 and 4, one sees very little relation between the two series. But of course, one should be careful in judging the model adversely from this evidence alone. The efficient markets model (3) and (4) does not assert that δ_t is a good forecast of δ^*_t, only that it is the best possible forecast of δ_t.

On the other hand, it is still possible to see evidence, from the looking

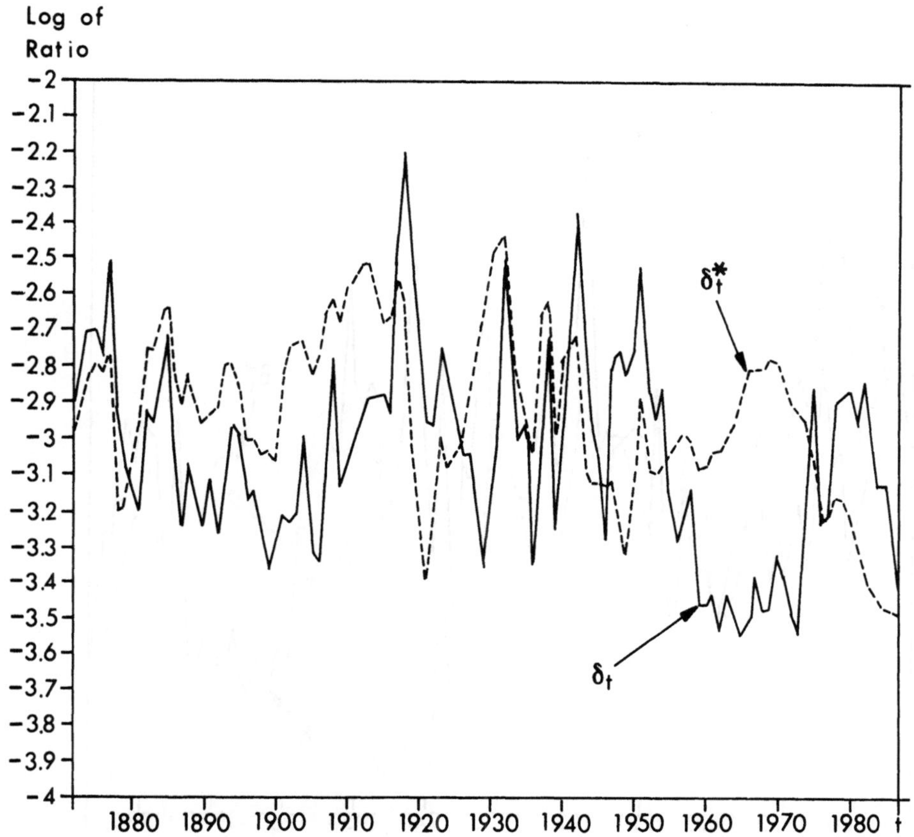

Figure 3. Dividend price ratios δ_t and δ^*_t, CRR version of the model. The solid line is δ_t, equal to $d_{t-1} - p_t$ where d_t and p_t are as shown in figure 1. The dashed line is the perfect foresight dividend-price ratio, computed from expression 3 in the text where d_t is measured in real terms and r is a constant, equal to ln(1+r) where r is the average real return over the sample.

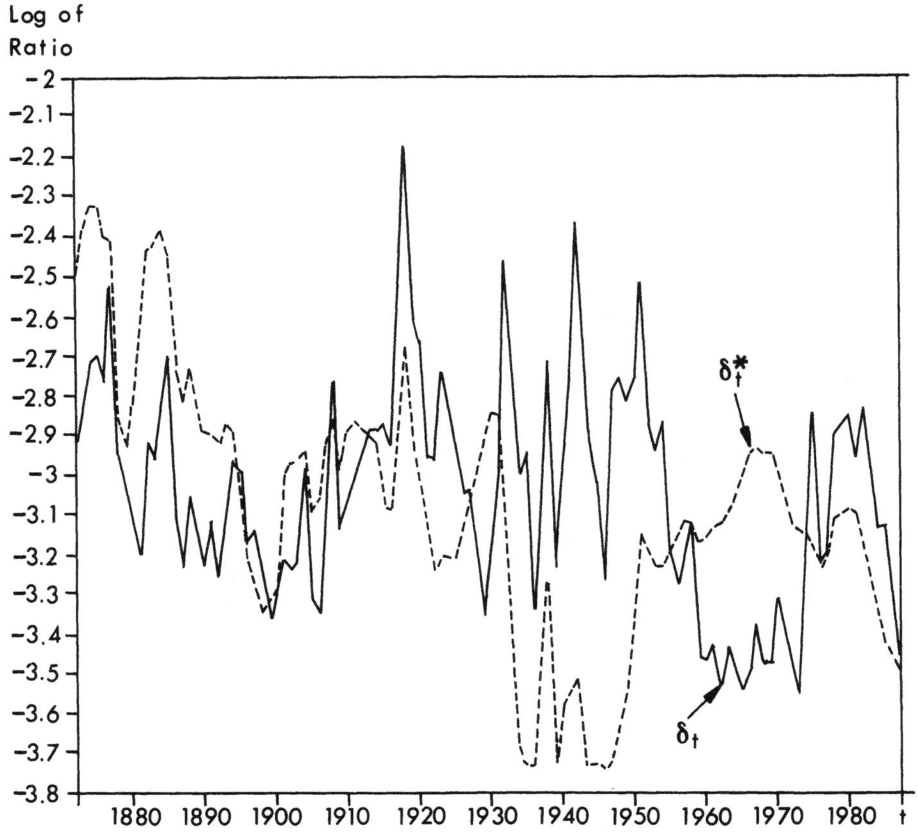

Figure 4. Dividend price ratios δ_t and δ^*_t, VRR version of the model. The solid line is δ_t, equal to $d_{t-1} - p_t$ where d_t and p_t are as shown in figure 1. The dashed line is the perfect foresight dividend-price ratio, computed from expression 3 in the text where d_t is measured in nominal terms and r_t is the one-year interest rate plus a constant, so that the sample mean of r_t equals the sample average $\ln(1+R_t)$ where R_t is the nominal return on the Standard and Poor index.

at the figure alone, that the model (3) and (4) is very wrong. This evidence comes from the fact that the forecast δ_t is about as volatile as the variable forecasted, δ_t^*, and has very low correlation with it. Now this is inconsistent with the efficient markets model; it follows from (3) and (4) and definitions that:

$$(5) \qquad \sigma(\delta_t) = \text{corr}(\delta_t, \delta_t^*)\sigma(\delta_t^*)$$

where σ denotes standard deviation and corr denotes correlation coefficient. Equation 5 says that δ_t can be as volatile as δ_t^* only if it is highly correlated with it. Given the negligible correlation between δ_t and δ_t^*, the standard deviation of δ_t is too high. There appears to be excess volatility of the dividend-price ratio. In other words, the ratio moves around a great deal and forecasts very little.

This impression can be quantified by just regressing δ_t^* onto δ_t and a constant. If the efficient markets model is true then (except for sampling error) the coefficient of δ_t should be 1.00. For the CRR model (using the data in Figure 3) the regression coefficient for δ_t is estimated to be 0.145 and the R squared 0.029. For the VRR model (using the data in Figure 4) the regression coefficient is estimated to be 0.166 and the R squared 0.019.[6] These coefficient values are so close to zero as to be somewhat affected by the terminal condition used to compute δ_t^*. For slightly different terminal condition, the regression coefficient of δ_t with the VRR model is negative.[7]

It appears from this evidence that the efficient markets model just doesn't square with the data. However, what we have shown does not constitute a formal hypothesis test that would allow us to compute significance levels. The t-statistics in the simple regressions of δ_t^* onto δ_t are not valid because of serially correlated residuals. Testing the efficient markets hypothesis more formally requires setting up a maintained hypothesis about the stochastic properties of the time series, which we have not yet discussed in this paper.

Comparisons of estimated perfect foresight series with forecasts of them,

---

[6]The bad correlation is not due to the approximation error in the linearization that gave rise to (3) and (4). In fact, if present values are computed without the linearization, the correlation between δ_t and δ_t^* is no better, Shiller (1987d).

[7]There is also a negative correlation between the dividend-price ratio and the ex-post rational (VRR) dividend-price ratio computed in levels (not logs) without the linearization (4), see Shiller (1987).

as in Figures 3 and 4 here, were part of the original argument (LeRoy and Porter (1981), Shiller (1979, 1981a, b) that stock prices appear to be too volatile to accord with efficient markets theories. These comparisons have also come into a lot of criticism, notably Flavin (1983), Kleidon (1986), and Marsh and Merton (1986). One component of their criticism was related to the possibility that the series might be nonstationary, or, failing that, at least have a very strong low-frequency component. That criticism is much less apt with regard to the ratios plotted here than with the levels that LeRoy and Porter and I used in our earlier papers, since the ratios appear stationary and show much less of a low frequency component. Another component of their criticism had to do with possible misinterpretations that readers might make who look at plots like those shown in figures 3 and 4. The theory in (3) and (4) does not imply that the short-run wiggles in the two series should correspond. In a sense, with $\rho = .936$, the weighted average implicit in (4) extends over a couple decades. The number of relatively independent observations we have of δ_t^* is not likely to be more than a half dozen.[8]

I think that it is still fair to say from looking at figures 3 and 4 alone, and taking full account of the criticism that has been made of such methods of evaluating market efficiency, that the evidence just does not appear to support the efficient markets model. Whether we can statistically reject the model is another matter, to which we now turn.

7. Price-Conditional Vector Autoregressions

Let us suppose, following Campbell and Shiller (1987a, b) that the zero-mean n-element ($n \geq 2$) vector time series z_t includes the variable δ_t minus its mean as its first element, the variable $r_{t-1} - \Delta d_{t-1}$ minus its mean as its second element, and includes possibly other variables. Let us also suppose that z_t has a first-order autoregressive representation:

$$(6) \qquad z_t = Az_{t-1} + v_t$$

where A is an $n \times n$ matrix of coefficients and v_t is a serially uncorrelated noise term. The vector z_t may also include as other variables δ_{t-j} and $r_{t-j-1} - \Delta d_{t-j-1}$ $j \geq 1$. In that case, we may have in effect a vector autoregression of order higher than one written in its companion form (see Sargent (1979)).

[8] I pointed out in my first paper on the subject of volatility in financial markets (1979) that we should not expect the short-run movements in the perfect foresight series to resemble the corresponding movements in the variable that forecasts this series.

Because δ_t is itself a sort of detrended log price - detrended by the current log dividend - we call (6) a price-conditional vector autoregression.

The optimal forecast at time t of z_{t+k} $k \geq 0$ is just $A^k z_t$. Let e_1 be the n-element row vector whose first element is 1 and whose remaining elements are zero, and let e_2 be the n-element row vector whose second element is 1 and whose remaining elements are zero. Then $e_1 z_t = \delta_t$ minus its mean, and $E_t(r_{t+j} - \Delta d_{t+j})$ minus its mean equals $e_2 A^{j+1} z_t$. Substituting into (4) and evaluating the summation, we find that the efficient markets model implies that δ_t should equal δ'_t where the latter is defined by:

$$\text{(7)} \qquad \delta'_t = e_2 A(I-\rho A)^{-1} z_t + (k-\mu)/(1-\rho).$$

Note that since δ_t is in the information set z_t, the relation (7) should hold even if market participants use other information, not included in the vector z_t, to forecast. In effect, since the optimal forecast δ_t is itself included in the information set that we use for econometric analysis, we do not need to take account of other information variables.

Note that since δ_t (demeaned) equals $e_1 z_t$ the restriction that $\delta_t = \delta'_t$ can also be written as that $e_1 = e_2 A(I-\rho A)^{-1}$, or, multiplying both sides of this equation by $(I-\rho A)$, that $e_1(I-\rho A) = e_2 A$. This sort of restriction is possible only because the vector autoregression included the variable δ_t, which as was noted is a transformed price. Testing the latter restriction by conventional methods amounts to merely regressing the linearized excess return onto z_t and testing for the significance of coefficients. Such regression tests, which Campbell and Shiller (1987a, b) found often reject market efficient at conventional significance levels, are hardly innovative. What is more interesting is the way the model fails, as shown by the divergence between δ'_t and δ_t.

Another comparison that is enlightening is that between ξ_t and ξ'_t, where the latter is defined by $\xi'_t = \delta'_t - \rho\delta'_{t+1} + \Delta d_t + k$. Since the efficient markets model implies that $\delta_t = \delta'_t$, the model must also imply that $\xi_t = \xi'_t$. We can actually estimate what the return at time t <u>should</u> be under the assumption of efficient markets. We have here another comparison that relies on the price-conditional vector autoregression. If δ_t were not included in the vector z_t, then we could not say that δ_t should by the efficient markets model equal δ'_t, and thus could not say that ξ_t should equal ξ'_t.

Yet another comparison worth noting is that between p_t and p'_t, where the latter is defined by $p'_t = d_{t-1} - \delta'_t$. Since the efficient markets model implies that $\delta_t = \delta'_t$, the model must also imply that $p_t = p'_t$. As with δ'_t and ξ'_t, we can estimate (since δ_t is in the vector autoregression) what the log price should be under the assumption of efficient markets.

Campbell and I found that a price-conditional vector autoregression that forecasts present values very well has only three elements: the first element of z_t is δ_t, the second is $r_{t-1} - \Delta d_{t-1}$, and the third is a sort of log earnings-price ratio ϵ_t^{30}, equal to a thirty-year moving average $e_t^{30} = \Sigma(i=1,30)e_{t-i}/30$ of log real earnings e_t minus the current log real price p_t. The last variable was introduced as a measure of fundamental value relative to price. Earnings-price ratios are often used to gauge fundamental value relative to price. Using a moving average of earnings in the ratio, rather than the latest earnings as is customary, is done to smooth out the short-run fluctuations in earnings. Such smoothing has long been advocated (see for example Graham and Dodd (1934)), although we extended the averaging period further than is usual.

When the CRR model was estimated with this vector (Campbell and Shiller (1987b)) we found a striking result: the correlation coefficient between δ_t and δ'_t was virtually zero, at 0.131. Thus, dividend-price ratios are essentially uncorrelated with what they should be, given the present value model. The standard deviation of ξ'_t was only .277 times that of ξ_t. Thus, actual excess returns are much more volatile than they should be, by a factor of nearly four. This all looks very bad for the efficient markets model.

We did find, however, one result that offers a thread of encouragement for the efficient markets model. The correlation coefficient between actual returns ξ_t and theoretical returns ξ'_t was quite high, at 0.908. To understand this result, it helps to look at the derived formula for p'_t, using equation 7 above and the definition of δ'_t. This formula was estimated to be $p'_t = .761e_t^{30} + 0.261p_t + 0.068d_{t-1} - .090d_{t-2}$, plus a constant. Essentially, p'_t is a weighted average of e_t^{30} and p_t with three quarters of the weight on e_t^{30} and one quarter of the weight on p_t. In other words, the moving average of earnings is given much more weight as a forecaster of the present value of future dividends than is the price. Since e_t^{30} is smoothed, it shows very little short-run fluctuations, and so almost all short-run movements in p'_t are due to log price p_t. Since returns are essentially the change in log price, we thus find a high correlation between ξ_t and ξ'_t, yet find that the former has a standard deviation about four times as high as the latter.

The results with the VRR model were found to be very similar, though the departures from the present value model were somewhat less dramatic. The formula for p'_t was estimated to be $p'_t = .638e^{30}_t + 0.288p_t + .074d_{t-1} + 0.041(r_{t-1} - \Delta d_{t-1})$, which again puts most of the weight on e^{30}_t. The correlation between δ_t and δ'_t was 0.246. The standard deviation of ξ'_t was 0.478 times that of ξ_t, and the correlation between the two was 0.727.

8. Prices Overreact to Dividends

We have seen that prices appear to move too much to accord with present value models. We saw above that a plot of real price and real dividends shows them to be moving together on a more or less one-to-one basis. This means that prices overreact to dividends.

However, it is an oversimplification to say that prices overreact to current dividends. To quantify better how they do react, it is worthwhile doing some data analysis.

The year-to-year changes in dividends feed into price on a more or less one-to-one basis, but price shows substantial noise apparently unrelated to dividends. When, using the data in Figure 1, the January-to-January change in the log real price index p_t is regressed 1871-1986 on a constant and the contemporaneous change in log real dividends d_t the slope coefficient is 0.877, and not significantly different from 1.00 (at the 5% level). (See Table 1) The R^2 in this regression is higher than one might have expected, at 0.424.

Another way of quantifying the relation between price and dividend is to regress with the data shown in Figure 1 real log price p_t on real log dividend and a constant and time. In such a regression the coefficient of d_t is 1.452, suggesting that prices move more than in proportion to dividends, and that the dividend-price ratio is negatively correlated with deviations of dividend from trend. Why is the coefficient so much different from the aforementioned regression, where the coefficient of the change in dividend was less than one? The answer is that the low-frequency or longer run movements in dividends are reflected in price on a more than one-to-one basis, while the higher frequency movements in dividends are reflected on a one-to-one basis. Looking at the data, there are two dramatic long swings in which prices rose substantially more than dividends: the bull market of the 1920's and the bull market of the 1950's and early 1960's.

The differing relation between price and dividend at different frequencies can be assessed by regressing the level of log real price p_t onto the level of log real dividends d_t with a band-spectrum regression that deletes all cycles with a wavelength greater than or equal to five years. Such a regression reveals the short-run (cycles less than five years) relation between p_t and d_t. The coefficient of log real dividends in such a regression is 1.051, not much different from 1.00. This means that the short-run wiggles in dividends are reflected on a more-or-less one-to-one basis in price, or, equivalently, that there isn't much of a relation between the short-run wiggles in the dividend-price ratio and the dividend itself.

This essentially one-to-one correspondence between price and dividend is an overreaction of price to dividend in the sense that the optimal forecast of the present value of future dividends does not react so much to dividends. It does not follow, of course, that people are literally reacting to dividends in setting price: both dividends and price could be responding to another variable.

9. A Summing Up: The Status of the Efficient Markets Models

It was found using comparisons in time series plots of the dividend-price ratio along with the perfect foresight dividend price ratio that the former does not look much like the optimal forecast of the latter, and that dividend-price ratios seem to show substantial volatility unrelated to the predictions of the efficient markets model. Dividend-price ratios just behave noisily, without regard for future dividends or interest rates. This conclusion is supported by the evidence with the price-conditional vector autoregressive methods.

The results with the price-conditional vector autoregressive models imply also that returns on stock prices appear to be about two to four times as volatile as they should be given the efficient markets model.

The conclusion here is that price overreacts to current dividends. By the present value models prices should not look as they do in figure 1, moving on a roughly one-to-one basis with dividends. It appears that they should move with dividends, but in an sharply attenuated manner. Price might also be described as overreacting to current earnings. The correlation between price and earnings is lower than that between price and dividend, but since earnings are less likely to respond (through firms' decisions) to price, it might even be better to characterize price as responding to earnings.

That there is an apparent correlation between returns and theoretical returns on an annual basis is not evidence that there is much correlation with daily returns. Daily price changes may be largely noise unrelated to changing forecasts of the present value of dividends. The results described here concern annual data only. It is also possible that introducing another information variable into the analysis will make the correlation between actual return ξ_t and theoretical return ξ'_t fall dramatically.

Appendix: Data Sources

All data used in this paper are the same as used in Campbell and Shiller (1987a, b, d). The (nominal) stock price index is the Standard and Poor Composite Index for January of each year. The (nominal) dividend series is the total dividends per share for the year adjusted to index. The nominal earnings series for 1926 to 1986 is from Standard and Poor Statistical Service: earnings per share adjusted to index, composite, four quarter total, fourth quarter. Before 1926, our nominal earnings is series R-1 (Cowles (1939) pages 404-5) times the annual average Standard and Poor Composite Index for the year.

The commodity price index that was used to deflate the nominal series is the producer price index is the BLS series (formerly wholesale price index) for January starting in 1900, annual average before 1900. The nominal interest rate series was computed as the total return to investing for six months in January at the January 4-6 month prime commercial paper rate (six month starting January 1980) and for another six months at the July 4-6 month prime commercial paper rate (six month starting July 1980).

The accuracy of some of these data are discussed in Campbell and Shiller (1987d) and Wilson and Jones (1987).

References

Campbell, J. Y. and R. J. Shiller, 1987, "Cointegration and Tests of Present Value Models", Journal of Political Economy 95, 1062-1088. (a)

Campbell, J. Y., and R. J. Shiller, 1987, "The Dividend-Price Ratio and Expectations of Future Dividends and Discount Factors," unpublished paper, Princeton University and Yale University. (b)

Campbell, J. Y., and R. J. Shiller, 1987, "Interpreting Cointegrated Models," reproduced, Princeton University and Yale University. (c)

Campbell, J. Y., and R. J. Shiller, 1987, "Stock Prices, Earnings and Expected Dividends," reproduced, Princeton University and Yale University. (d)

Cowles 3rd, A., and Associates, 1939, Common-Stock Indexes, Second Edition, Principia Press, Bloomington Indiana.

Cutler, D. M., J. M. Poterba, and L. H. Summers, 1987, "What Moves Stock Prices?" reproduced, M. I. T. and Harvard University.

DeBondt, W., and R. Thaler, 1985, "Does the Stock Market Overreact?" Journal of Finance, 60, 793-805, July 1985.

Fama. E. F., 1975, "Short-Term Interest Rates as Predictors of Inflation," American Economic Review 67, 269-82.

Fama, E. F. and K. R. French, 1987, "Permanent and Temporary Components of Stock Prices", forthcoming Journal of Political Economy. (a)

Fama, E, F. and K. R. French, 1987, "Dividend Yields and Expected Stock Returns", unpublished paper, University of Chicago. (b)

Flavin, M., 1983, "Excess Volatility in the Financial Markets: A Reassessment of the Empirical Evidence," Journal of Political Economy 91, 929-56.

Flood, R. P., R. J. Hodrick and P. Kaplan, 1986, "An Evaluation of Recent Evidence on Stock Market Bubbles", NBER Working Paper No. 1971 (Cambridge, MA).

Gilles, C. and S. F. LeRoy, 1987,"The Variance-Bounds Tests: A Critical Survey", unpublished paper, University of California Santa Barbara.

Graham, B., and D. L. Dodd, 1934, Security Analysis, First Edition, McGraw Hill, New York.

Granger, C. W. J., and R. F. Engle, 1987, "Cointegration and Error Correction: Representation, Estimation and Testing," Econometrica 55, 251-76.

Huizinga, J., and F. S. Mishkin, 1986, "Monetary Policy Regime Shifts and the Unusual Behavior of Real Interest Rates," Carnegie-Rochester Conference Series on Public Policy 24, 231-74.

Kleidon, A. W., 1986, "Variance Bounds Tests and Stock Price Valuation Models", Journal of Political Economy 94, 953-1001.

LeRoy, S. F. and R. D. Porter, 1981, "Stock Price Volatility: Tests Based on Implied Variance Bounds", Econometrica 49, 97-113.

Mankiw, N. G., D. Romer, and M. D. Shapiro, 1985, "An Unbiased Reexamination of Stock Market Volatility," Journal of Finance 40, 677-87.

Marsh, T. A. and R. C. Merton, 1986, "Dividend Variability and Variance Bounds Tests for the Rationality of Stock Market Prices", American Economic Review 76:483-498, June 1986.

Marsh, T. A. and R. C. Merton, 1987, "Dividend Behavior for the Aggregate Stock Market", Journal of Business 60, 1-40.

Perron, Pierre, 1986, "Trends and Random Walks in Macroeconomic Time Series: Further Evidence from a New Approach," Departement de sciences economiques et C.R.D.E., Universite de Montreal.

Phillips, P. C. B., 1986, "Towards a Unified Asymptotic Theory for Autoregression," Cowles Foundation Discussion Paper #781, Yale University.

Poterba, J. M. and L. H. Summers, 1987, "Mean Reversion in Stock Prices: Evidence and Implications", unpublished paper, Harvard University.

Sargent, T. J., 1979, "A Note on the Estimation of the Rational Expectations Model of the Term Structure," Journal of Monetary Economics, 5, 133-43.

Shiller, R. J., 1981, "Do Stock Prices Move Too Much to be Justified by Subsequent Changes in Dividends?", American Economic Review 71, 421-436.

Shiller, R. J., 1984, "Stock Prices and Social Dynamics", Brookings Papers on Economic Activity 2, 457-498.

Shiller, R. J., 1981, "The Use of Volatility Measures in Assessing Market Efficiency," Journal of Finance 36, 291-304.

Shiller, R. J., 1979, "The Volatility of Long-Term Interest Rates and Expectations Models of the Term Structure," Journal of Political Economy 87, 1190-1219.

Shiller, R. J., 1987, "The Volatility of Stock Market Prices," Science 235, 33-7.

Summers, L. H., 1986, "Does the Stock Market Rationally Reflect Fundamental Values?", Journal of Finance 41:591-601, July 1986.

West, K. D., 1987, "Bubbles, Fads and Stock Price Volatility Tests: A Partial Evaluation," reproduced, Princeton University. (a)

West, K. D., 1987, "Dividend Innovations and Stock Price Volatility", forthcoming Econometrica. (b)

Wilson, J. W., and C. P. Jones, 1987, "A Comparison of Annual Common Stock Returns: 1871-1925 with 1926-85," Journal of Business, 60.

Comments on R J Shiller: "Price-conditional Vector Autoregressions and Theories of stock price determination"

by George Bulkley

This paper embodies two important recent contributions by Campbell and Shiller to the methodology of volatility tests. The first is the generalisation of the Gordon (1962) model of the dividend price ratio to allow for predictable fluctuations in future interest rates or dividend growth rates. Interest rates, and dividend growth rates are then modelled as a Vector Autoregression (VAR). The second contribution is the idea that current equity prices should be included in the VAR model to pick up information available to the market, but not to the econometrician. This latter idea will doubtless find widespread application in many other areas where VAR models are applied in financial markets.

Using this VAR model Shiller demonstrates that the time series of the actual dividend price ratio bears no resemblance to that which would be implied if agents forecasted using the VAR estimated by Shiller. Also actual excess returns are approximately four times more volatile than excess returns which would have resulted had Shiller's estimated VAR been used for forecasting. That is the market's forecasts do not appear to be minimum variance forecasts, which rational expectations would require.

I believe that the status of these results as evidence in the efficient markets debate turns on the precise definition of efficient markets which is chosen. Following Fama (1970) one definition of efficient markets is that prices behave as if (a) there were no transactions costs, (b) all available information is costlessly available to all market participants, and (c) all know, and agree upon, the true model of the variable to be forecast. If we interpret the VAR estimated by Shiller as the true model, then (c) justifies

NATO ASI Series, Vol. F54
A Reappraisal of the Efficiency of Financial Markets
Edited by Rui M. C. Guimaraes et al.

Shiller's identification of forecasts from his VAR as rational expectations forecasts as each date within the sample period. Hence Shiller's paper constitutes important evidence against efficient markets on this definition. However another definition of efficient markets, due to Jensen (1978), makes weaker assumptions about agents information than this, as Bulkley and Tonks discuss elsewhere in this volume. Jensen defines efficient markets as those where agents could not have constructed a profitable trading rule, based on current information. This implies that agents forecast not using the true model, but only an estimated model. In this case it is not possible to identify forecasts obtained from a VAR estimated over the whole sample, with those made within the sample when a smaller data set would have doubtless resulted in different estimated coefficients of the VAR. Indeed at earlier dates within the sample different explanatory variables might have appeared appropriate.

This may play some part in explaining the divergence between actual price dividend ratios and those implied by Shiller's VAR. It also provides an explanation of why actual excess returns are more volatile than those implied by the VAR estimated in this paper. In practice model "errors" are an additional source of forecast error, as agents in practice have to forecast out of sample, in contrast to Shiller's forecasts which are calculated from a VAR estimated over the whole data set.

Fama, E.F., 1970, Efficient capital markets; a review of theory and empirical work, Journal of Finance 25, 383-417

Jensen, M.C., 1978, Some anomalous evidence regarding market efficiency, Journal of Financial Economics, 6, 95-101

IS THE UK EQUITY MARKET CONSISTENT WITH THE "EFFICIENT MARKETS" MODEL?

George Bulkley
Department of Economics
University of Exeter
Rennes Drive
Exeter EX4 4RJ

Ian Tonks
Department of Accounting and Finance
London School of Economics
Houghton Street
London WC2A 2AE

Keywords / equity prices / excess volatility / trading rules / equity premium / efficient markets / rational expectations

There is now considerable evidence that stock prices are excessively volatile, compared with rational expectations/efficient markets prices. In this paper we argue that volatility tests address a particularly strong definition of efficient markets. We test the UK equity market against Jensen's weaker definition of market efficiency. We investigate whether a profitable trading rule can be found using synthetic stock price data from the UK 1919-1985, generated by Monte Carlo methods from the model of stock prices estimated over this period.

1. Introduction

In recent years tests of the rational expectations/efficient markets hypothesis have fallen into two classes: regression based tests and excess volatility tests. Regression based tests examine whether forecasts implicit in market prices are unbiased and efficient forecasts of the present discounted value of future returns. (See for example Modigliani and Cohn (1979), Cohn and Lessard (1981).) Excess volatility tests involve calculating an upper limit to the volatility which rational expectations prices should exhibit over time and examining whether or not actual prices are more volatile than this bound (LeRoy and Porter (1980), Shiller (1981a), Kleidon (1986) Campbell and Shiller (1987)).

Shiller (1981b) argues that these two approaches are not just "different", but rather are complementary in that volatility tests may have more

NATO ASI Series, Vol. F54
A Reappraisal of the Efficiency of Financial Markets
Edited by Rui M. C. Guimaraes et al.

power in certain areas of the parameter space, or be more robust with respect to some kinds of data problems, for example misaligned data.

In order to interpret the results of such tests, which typically imply rejection of the rational expectations/efficient markets model, it is useful to emphasise, following Friedman (1979), that the rational expectations hypothesis in the tradition of Muth (1961) can usefully be broken down into two distinct components:

"(a) The general assumption that economic agents use efficiently whatever information is available and (b) A specific assumption identifying the available set of information."

Friedman (1979) p25

In particular, assumption (b) takes the form

"the information which is available to agents is sufficient to permit them to form expectations characterised by conditional subjective distributions of outcomes that are equivalent to the conditional objective distribution of outcomes indicated by the relevant economic theory".

Friedman (1979) p25

Assumption (a) then is essentially a behavioural hypothesis, whereas assumption (b) concerns the technology of the economy: the production of information.

Friedman emphasises that regression based tests are joint tests of these two components of the rational expectations hypothesis. If assumption (a) is maintained, but (b) is relaxed so that for example agents have to learn about the structure of the true model, then regression tests may reject the RE hypothesis. Friedman shows that if agents use an estimated model, not the true model, to generate forecasts, even if they have obtained the estimated model using optimal learning by a least squares method, the data will not in general exhibit the required independence between forecast errors and information known at the date of the forecast.

Although Friedman was writing about RE in the context of macro-economic models, exactly the same issues arise in equity markets. The same distinction between the behavioural assumption ((a) above) and the technology assumption ((b) above) is necessary to an interpretation of the excess volatility results.

The upper bound in the volatility tests, when either a stationary or non-stationary model of dividends is adopted, always assumes that agents know throughout the whole period the true parameters of the assumed model of dividends. As Friedman goes on to emphasise, again in the context of macro-economic models, there are two reasons why agents may not use the true model. Firstly, incorrect specification of the underlying model: for example incorrect functional form or wrong specification of explanatory variables. Secondly even if agents are using the correct specification of the model, in finite data sets estimated coefficients will not converge completely to the true model. Both of these problems are ruled out in the calculation of the volatility of rational expectations prices, where uncertainty/forecast errors for dividends are solely due to the errors/innovations in a given "true" model: uncertainty about the model itself is not allowed for. For example Shiller writes "uncertainty about future dividends is measured by the sample standard deviation of real dividends around their long term exponential growth path". (Shiller, 1981, p 434). It is additional uncertainty about this long run exponential growth path <u>itself</u> which may account for the observed volatility af actual prices.

The excess volatility tests are a joint test of three hypotheses:

(i) the model of equity prices as the discounted present value of expected future dividends.

(ii) the assumption that agents process all information they receive efficiently.

(iii) the assumption that agents know the true model which generates expected future dividends, whatever this is taken to be in any particular paper.

We believe that an interesting question which merits separate testing is the validity of the behavioural component of the rational expectations hypothesis, (ii), in conjunction with (i). In particular, this means that in any tests, regardless of the model of dividend growth assumed, whether stationary or non-stationary, agents' expectations of dividends should be obtained using an estimated model, not the true model, and that only data currently available at the time of the forecast are used to estimate the parameters of this model.

It is not clear how to amend conventional volatility tests so that the upper bound for rational expectations prices takes into account volatility due to revised model parameters within the sample. Therefore we take a different approach, which is a direct application of a definition of efficient markets of Jensen (1978) who stated:

"a market is efficient with respect to information set $_t$ if it is impossible to make economic profits by trading on the basis of $_t$ By economic profits we mean the risk adjusted rate of return, net of all costs."

Jensen (1978) p96

Shiller (1981(a)) recognises that volatility tests address a different definition of efficient markets to that of Jensen, for he emphasises that his results do not logically imply a profitable trading rule, although they are suggestive of one.

"...if real stock prices are "too volatile" as it is defined here, then there may well be a sort of real profit opportunity. Time variation in expected real interest rates does not itself imply that any trading rule dominates a buy and hold strategy, but really large variations in expected returns might seem to suggest that such a trading rule exists."

Shiller (1981(a)) p423

We proceed by directly testing the UK equity market against Jensen's definition of efficiency - could agents, who had formed rational expectations and accepted (i) above as the correct long term model, have constructed a trading rule which exploited excess fluctuations in the stock market and so yielded greater profits than a simple buy and hold policy. We emphasise that any trading rule must be strictly conditioned on only currently available information - in particular the model of dividend growth or discount rate must be estimated from only that data available at the date of any transactions. A necessary condition, which is not sufficient, (as we explain below), for the existence of a profitable trading rule is evidence that actual prices are not set equal to the expected present discounted value of dividends, where that expectation is strictly conditional only on currently available information. If there were in fact no unexploited profit opportunities available to agents who subscribed to the efficient markets model, then efficient markets on this definition should not be rejected, regardless of the violation of variance bounds which were calculated ex poste, using throughout the period a model of dividends, estimated over the whole data set, or a single unchanging discount rate.

Rather than rejecting the assumption of rational expectations in conjunction with model (i), West (1988) interprets his excess volatility results as evidence against the model where asset values equal the expected present value of dividends. Instead he believes it "suggests the possibility that the volatility is due either to rational bubbles (eg Blanchard and Watson (1982)) or nearly rational "fads" (eg Summers (1986)), whose profit opportunities (if any) are difficult to detect".

We would argue that this rejection of efficient markets is premature. First it must be shown that agents who worked with the conventional efficient market model, where asset values equal the discounted present value of future dividends, could have, on average, successfully identified profitable opportunities within the data set in which excess volatility was demonstrated.

A considerable literature in the late 1960s examined the question of whether there existed a profitable trading rule. After the initial work of Alexander (1961), who claimed to uncover such a profitable rule, a consensus emerged in later work that, after allowing for transactions costs, no systematic trading rule could consistently beat a simple "buy and hold" strategy. See Fama and Blume (1966) for a survey of this evidence. However trading rules studied in this literature were filter rules based on short term price movements of individual securities, even though these rules were sometimes applied over long periods. For example Alexander studied a filter rule, where x is the filter: if the daily closing price of a particular security moves up by at least x per cent buy and hold the security until its price moves down at least x per cent from a subsequent high, at which time simultaneously sell and go short.

The trading rule implied by the excess volatility literature is of a very different form to these rules. It suggests buying, and holding a broad based market portfolio, whenever the stock market index is low relative to its mean, and holding until it is high relative to its mean. It is essentially a long run rule, with an average period of five years between transactions. Rules of this structure, which exploited the long run stationarity of the data, were not studied in the earlier literature. A rule of this form also avoids three problems which plagued short term filter rules. Firstly transactions costs are now of a second order of significance, given the infrequency of trades. Secondly, since securities or bonds are always held, the question of how to measure earnings at times when no profitable opportunities are present does not arise. Thirdly since the holding period is always at least one year, it is straightforward to include the appropriate dividends in earnings, whereas this caused considerable data problems with short term trading rules.

In the next section we describe our rule, and the results of applying it to synthetic UK data 1918-1986, using Monte Carlo methods on a model of UK stock prices estimated over the period 1918-1985.

2. A trading rule

The trading rule which we examine in this section is based on the assumption that the true model which generates dividends is stationary, after detrending. See Poterba and Summers (1987) for recent evidence in support of this assumption on the US equity market. We test the null hypothesis that UK real stock prices follow a nonstationary process using the tests provided by

Fuller (1976) and Dickey and Fuller (1979). The simplest test is to model the movement in the logarithm of stock prices as a first order autoregressive process, and under the null hypothesis that the process is nonstationary test for a unit root. Letting P denote the log of real trended stock prices, the following equation was estimated, where the terms in brackets denote standard errors.

$$P_t = \underset{(0.216)}{0.632} + \underset{(0.071)}{0.795}P_{t-1} \qquad R^2 = 0.66 \quad n = 67 \quad DW = 1.83$$

To test whether the coefficient on the lagged dependent variable was significantly different from unity, we used two tests. Firstly we calculated the t-statistic of -2.894 and compared it with the ten per cent critical value of -2.60 for a sample size, n = 50, from Fuller (1976). Secondly we computed the Dickey-Fuller Statistic, n(0.795-1) = -13.7, and compared this with the 10 per cent critical value of -10.7. In both cases we were able to reject the null hypothesis of nonstationarity of the data.

Thus we make the same assumption about the model of aggregate dividends as Shiller (1981a) and LeRoy and Porter (1980) - that dividends follow an exponential growth process - i.e. detrended dividends are stationary. If stock prices, P_t, are the present discounted value of expected future dividends, D^e_τ, and the real risk adjusted rate of interest, r, is assumed constant, then this implies that stock prices also follow an exponential growth process, g, in the long run. That is, in discrete time:

$$P_t = \sum_{\tau=t}^{\infty} \frac{D^e{}_\tau}{(1+r)^{\tau-t}} \tag{1}$$

$$D_t = D_0(1+g)^t + v_t \tag{2}$$

where D_0 are dividends payable in the base year.
Assume for ease of exposition that v_t is i.i.d. Then rational expectations implies E(v) = 0. Substituting (2) into (1), assuming rational expectations

implies:

$$P_t = \frac{D_0(1+g)^t\ (1+r)}{r - g} \qquad (3)$$

Equation (1) is the well known efficient markets model, equation (2) the assumed model of dividends, and equation (3) follows from the rational expectations assumption, in the sense of both parts (a) and (b) above, i.e. agents know the true model of dividends. The assumption that v_t was i.i.d. resulted in the absence of all fluctuations in P_t around the exponential growth. In general serial correlation in v_t will imply deviations in P_t from its long run trend. Equation (3) makes it clear that the efficient markets equity price depends on three parameters, D_0, r, g, none of which are known a priori. P_t will follow an exponential growth path, and we assume agents directly
estimate (3) from data on past prices.

Thus at each date t within the sample (1929-1985), agents first have to estimate equation (3) over the sub period (1919 - t) i.e. they estimate:

$$\log P_\tau = \alpha + \beta\tau + u_\tau \qquad (4)$$

The fitted value from equation (4) is then taken to be the best available forecast, based on current information, of the efficient markets price. The object of the trading rule is to try to exploit the fluctuations around this efficient markets price which are implied by the excess volatility results.

The rule we consider is appropriate to a trader who starts in 1929 with £100. We examine whether, by attempting to buy low and sell high, an agent could do better than simply buying and holding a representative market portfolio. We have to make a judgement about what assets are held when equities are not chosen. Fixed interest securities are the closest substitute for equities, having low transactions and information costs. We could have considered gilts but they should on average have a very similar yield, and it would have made computations slightly more complicated, because of their fluctuating capital value. In Bulkley and Tonks (1987) we report that such a trading rule yields a rate of return of 1.61% above the yield on buying and holding the "market portfolio" over the period 1929-1985. This market portfolio was that used in the de Zoete and Wedd annual Equity Price Index, which consists of thirty "blue chip" stocks, over the period 1918-1985. We start the individual with £100 in December 1929, and each year, in December he has to choose whether to hold bonds or equities for the following twelve months. Thus he compares the fitted value from equation (4), estimated on current data, to actual prices, and buys equities if prices are k% below trend, and continues holding until such time as they rise k% above trend, when they are sold, and bonds are purchased. The value for k is actually chosen by an iterative search procedure, as that value which would, ex poste, have been optimal to have used over the period 1919 to that decision year. In this way the trading rule conforms strictly to the requirement that it is to be based only on current information. When holding the stock market portfolio the investor receives the dividend payment due on that portfolio each period. When holding bonds the investor receives the safe 1 year rate of interest. All returns are reinvested.

The problem with this result, that a trading rule does yield an excess return, is that one cannot report relevant confidence intervals. It is not clear how to obtain confidence intervals analytically, and so here we extend our earlier work by reporting Monte Carlo simulation exercises, based on the actual UK stock price series 1919-85. We generate data from the equation estimated over the whole period.

$$\log P_t = 2.8 + 0.0057\ \text{time} + u_t$$
$$u_t = 0.81\, u_{t-1} + \epsilon_t \qquad \text{where } \epsilon_t \ \ N(0, 0.229)$$

Using these estimated parameters, we obtained 100 runs of synthetic data, 1919-85. For each run we then applied the trading rule and the buy and hold strategies, and compared the respective end of period pay-offs. Table I reports the results, where on 49% of the runs the buy and hold strategy beat the trading rule.

Table I

One hundred runs from a Monte Carlo study of
Returns from a Trading Rule versus
buying and holding a market portfolio
Wealth in real pounds in 1985, as a result of investing £100 in 1929

Trading Rule	Buy and Hold Strategy	Trading Rule	Buy and Hold Strategy
7,091	2,495	4,344	2,001
26,075	5,494	4,070	1,538
2,941	2,202	2,961	2,199
4,372	1,039	6,999	4,001
15,596	13,893	1,227	5,201
3,756	1,378	8,307	9,590
2,083	5,733	6,291	2,245
1,642	3,872	3,902	9,023
33,879	5,460	2,787	1,991
3,504	7,181	3,956	7,163
19,686	1,924	1,675	10,929
3,192	3,079	10,667	4,043
3,942	7,159	6,225	22,589
4,315	1,055	12,421	2,212
2,605	6,157	5,161	6,297
8,377	3,775	2,973	6,686
3,308	1,509	740	1,915
2,869	11,270	14,023	3,826
10,038	3,336	2,925	4,164
8,364	6,914	2,680	14,680
9,981	4,844	1,953	1,759
6,473	1,973	13,800	21,906
10,957	31,557	594	7,833
3,258	6,296	5,089	3,045
8,650	3,089	2,123	6,007
3,185	6,989	10,812	7,823
10,427	2,487	512	1,133
5,175	2,931	1,943	12,990
4,226	3,876	4,870	12,517
1,128	2,179	6,233	6,954
1,727	15,718	1,563	4,733
28,825	24,191	3,442	8,243
1,882	11,603	2,502	15,559
14,082	11,414	1,078	4,526
4,603	5,913	1,377	4,941
2,757	6,834	2,123	4,305
3,319	2,417	3,213	3,364
1,115	2,156	7,214	3,787
6,142	10,978	1,836	5,078
2,588	5,485	4,070	7,620
8,247	14,593	994	724
21,262	17,923	6,576	7,137
4,154	4,877	5,476	2,498
2,610	6,152	10,457	4,250
8,947	7,755	4,596	3,708
4,384	8,013	5,478	1,575
6,211	5,504	5,835	23,734
398	2,224	6,837	1,444
1,685	9,506	7,183	5,356
12,954	5,755	11,538	14,198
		8,750	5,026

If indeed there is no profitable trading rule, then in terms of the components (a) and (b) of the rational expectations hypothesis discussed above, this would suggest that it is imperfect information about the true model which explains the excess volatility results. The behavioural hypothesis that there exists a pool of agents who form rational expectations of future dividends, given available information, and use the model summarised in (1) cannot be rejected if there was no more profitable strategy available to such agents than to simply hold the market portfolio through its upswings and downswings. Indeed this is exactly Jensen's (1978) definition of efficient markets which we reproduced above. The essential reasoning behind this definition is that prices respond to expressed excess demands. If prices were not so low/high relative to trend that there were unexploited profits available to agents who formed rational expectations and accepted model (1), then there was no economic force available to damp the observed volatility.

Although prices did not diverge sufficiently far from efficient markets values to allow excess profit opportunities, it remains true that stock prices seem to move in ways that cannot be explained by the efficient markets model. However it is widely accepted in finance that some traders will be "noise" traders or "liquidity" traders. If their excess demands are significant there will be price shocks in response to these noise traders. The standard argument however is that providing there exists a pool of rational expectations/efficient market traders these will quickly move to exploit any resulting profit opportunities and so quickly (instantaneously) return prices to efficient market valuations. It is the activities of marginal traders, with rational expectations, who discipline the market, despite the existence of intra marginal noise traders. The failure to find a profitable trading rule thus suggests that prices are not driven by noise traders so far outside a corridor around the efficient markets price that the rational expectations traders can profitably intervene to damp the volatility.

Given the scale of the excess volatility reported in some tests, it may be considered surprising that the corridor within which profitable opportunities cannot be identified is so wide. We turn now to a discussion of why identification of profitable trading opportunities is so difficult in practice.

We have considered bonds as the alternative to equities on the grounds that transactions and information costs an other types of assets are likely to be so high as to preclude them from serving as short or medium term substitutes for equities. However the average real return on equities over the period 1918-1985 was 7.1% whereas the real return on bonds was 0.03%. A similar gap between yields on equities and bonds has been noted also in the US market, and has been referred to as the "equity premium puzzle".

In order for a trading rule to make profits, it is necessary that when equity prices are above trend, the expected yield on bonds must exceed that on equities. The implication of this excessive yield gap is that when equities are overpriced they must be expected to return to trend values very quickly. In fact the yield gap of 7.07% implies that if equities are overpriced by 28.28% it must be expected that they will return to the underlying trend within four years if bonds are to appear to be a higher yielding investment. In the UK data the average period to return to trend was approximatly four years. (Since we only have annual data this figure cannot be calculated accurately.) The equity premium thus implies that the magnitude of the volatility must be looked at in conjunction with the long cycles of stock prices about their trend values, shown in Figure I, before profitable opportunities cannot be deduced.

With this equity premia in mind we turn to a discussion of exactly what went wrong in those simulation exercises where the trading rule performance was inferior to the buy and hold policy. The first, and probably most substantial, problem was that estimation of the coefficients of equation (4) produced estimates that were significantly different, especially in the early years, from the true model. There is very strong serial correlation in the deviation of actual prices from trend. Thus in the simulated data there is superimposed on the underlying exponential growth trend another time trend which is the decay of each new disturbance. Thus for example a large positive shock to prices at the beginning of the constructed data set, followed by its gradual decay, resulted in a significant negative growth rate being estimated over the first decade. Actual synthetic prices then did not fall sufficiently far below estimated trend to result in a decision to buy equities for perhaps

Figure 1

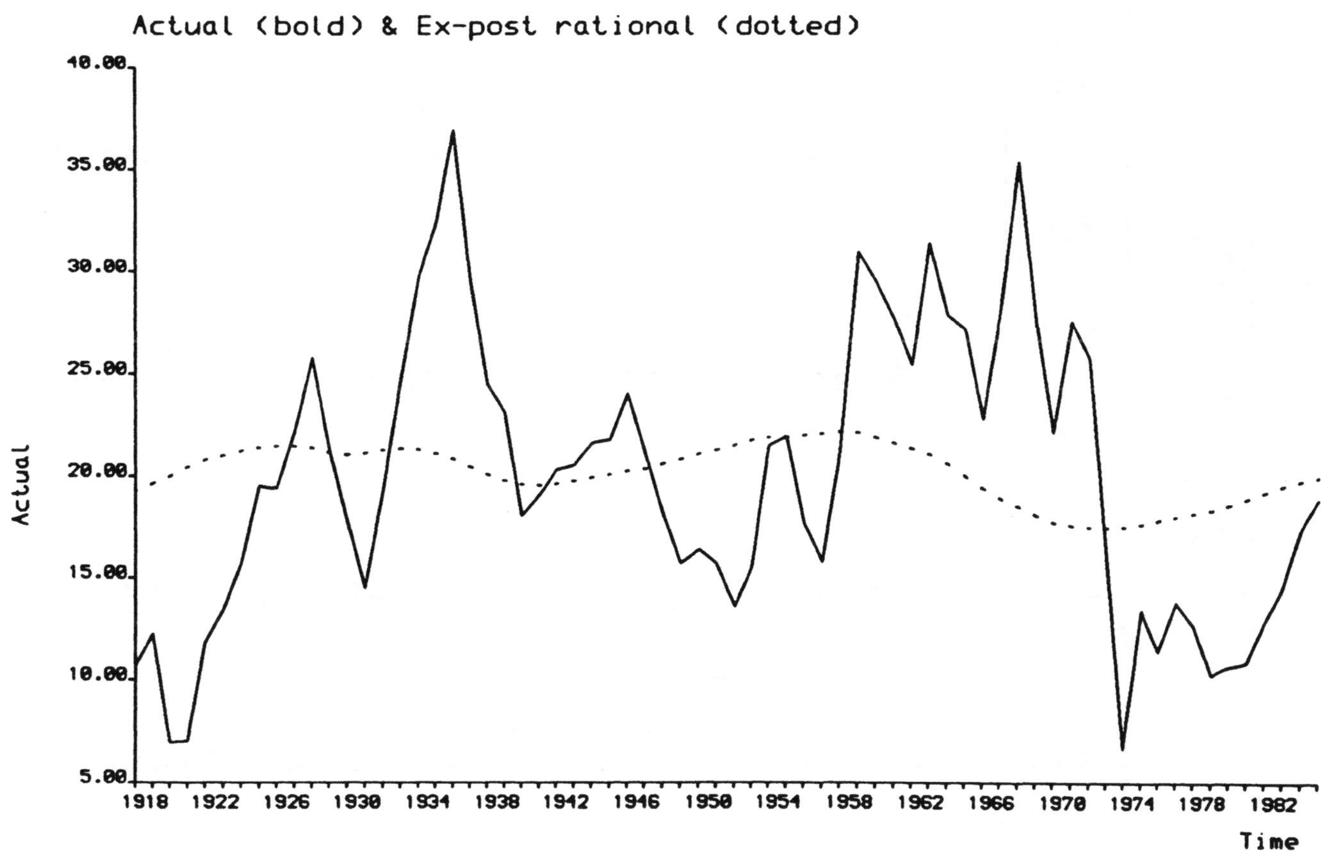

Actual (bold) & Ex-post rational (dotted)
40.00
35.00
30.00
25.00
20.00
15.00
10.00
5.00
Actual
1918
1922
1926
1930
1934
1938
1942
1946
1950
1954
1958
1962
1966
1970
1974
1978
1982
Time

Table 2

An example of a particular simulation where the Trading Rule performed badly compared to Buy and Hold

Dec 31	Monte Carlo price	Wealth under Buy and Hold	Wealth under Optimal Trading rule	Holding Shares (S) or Bonds (B)	Estimated slope coefficient
1929	9.49	100	100	B	-0.054
1930	11.89	138	101	B	-0.043
1931	19.87	245	101	B	-0.020
1932	13.74	185	102	B	-0.014
1933	14.31	209	102	B	-0.009
1934	10.48	171	103	B	-0.011
1935	8.02	151	104	B	-0.018
1936	9.87	210	144	S	-0.018
1937	11.78	276	189	S	-0.016
1938	10.97	286	190	B	-0.015
1939	9.90	291	192	B	-0.016
1940	11.87	538	193	B	-0.014
1941	12.52	446	194	B	-0.012
1942	10.15	406	195	B	-0.012
1943	8.68	396	196	B	-0.013
1944	8.23	432	198	B	-0.015
1945	8.91	532	244	S	-0.015
1946	14.08	916	419	S	-0.012
1947	14.79	1042	422	B	-0.009
1948	18.14	1365	424	B	-0.006
1949	17.20	1387	427	B	-0.003
1950	17.37	1501	429	B	-0.001
1951	27.44	2477	432	B	-0.003
1952	25.40	2405	435	B	0.006
1953	32.87	3229	437	B	0.010
1954	28.32	2903	440	B	0.012
1955	31.16	3322	442	B	0.015
1956	37.45	4124	445	B	0.018
1957	40.66	4614	448	B	0.020
1958	25.85	3073	451	B	0.021
1959	25.35	3161	453	B	0.021
1960	27.95	3639	456	B	0.022
1961	20.49	2828	459	B	0.022
1962	20.73	3033	492	S	0.022
1963	22.79	3514	570	S	0.021
1964	19.58	3210	521	S	0.020
1965	18.16	3181	516	S	0.019
1966	14.72	2794	453	S	0.018
1967	21.42	4300	698	S	0.018
1968	16.20	3500	568	S	0.017

1969	24.89	5646	916	S	0.017
1970	18.40	4455	723	S	0.016
1971	12.64	3359	545	S	0.015
1942	13.51	3919	636	S	0.014
1973	14.76	4640	753	S	0.013
1974	16.55	5591	907	S	0.013
1975	16.91	6127	994	S	0.012
1976	14.41	5670	920	S	0.011
1977	18.66	7872	1277	S	0.011
1978	19.09	8527	1384	S	0.011
1979	11.54	5705	926	S	0.010
1980	11.83	6463	1049	S	0.009
1981	13.51	8055	1307	S	0.008
1982	13.63	8863	1438	S	0.008
1983	16.52	11543	1873	S	0.007
1984	20.97	15515	2517	S	0.007
1985	14.44	11604	1882	S	0.007

another decade, bonds being held in the meantime. The magnitude of the equity premium then meant a large initial real loss. Generally the runs where buy and hold dominated the trading rule were those where the underlying growth rate of dividends had been wrongly estimated so that bonds were held when in fact equities were not overpriced, so annual real relative losses of 7% per annum were being incurred. Table II reports the details of one simulation exercise where the trading rule performed particlarly badly compared to the buy and hold strategy. For those readers who study the evolution of wealth under buy and hold we should emphasise that the dividend per share paid each year was the average dividend over the whole sample period. The reason we chose to apply Monte Carlo techniques only to the price series, and not to the dividend series, was that the excess volatility applies to stock prices in relation to the relatively smooth dividend series. This implies that when stock prices are low, the dividend is relatively large as a percentage return, and conversely when prices are high. Of course, there are always many ways to perform a Monte Carlo study, and thus our results must be regarded as a first attempt.

3. Conclusions

The rational expectations assumption is at the heart of any definition of efficient markets. Since there are, as we emphasised above, two logically distinct components to the rational expectations hypothesis, it is not surprising that this has resulted in different definitions of efficient markets emerging in the literature. We have reported the inability to reject efficiency on Jensen's definition which emphasises a behavioural interpretation. We constructed a trading rule which corresponded to the behaviour of an individual who formed rational expectations and accepted the model of prices as the present value of dividends, and a stationary model of dividends themselves. Although with hindsight prices appear excessively volatile, nevertheless constrained to use only current information to estimate the mean of the stationary model of dividends it proved impossible at the time on average to identify profitably deviations of price from this model.

On the other hand Fama (1970, p 389) stated that sufficient conditions for efficient markets were "(i) There are no transactions costs in trading securities (ii) All available information is costlessly available to all market participants, and (iii) All agree on the implications of current information for the current price and distribution of future prices of each security."

These are sufficient conditions because they need not in fact hold, providing actual prices behave as if they hold. This definition invokes both parts of the rational expectations hypothesis described above, and clearly requires agents to form expectations as if they knew the true model of dividends. The excess volatility results are powerful evidence against this definition of efficient markets. We would argue that both definitions of efficiency are potentially useful and worthy of test, and that which is preferred must depend upon the particular problem at hand.

REFERENCES

Alexander, S.S., 1961, Price movements in speculative markets: trends or random walks, Industrial Management Review, May, 7-26

Blanchard, O., and M. Watson, 1982, Bubbles, rational expectations and Financial markets, NBER Working Paper No 945

Bulkley, I.G. and I Tonks, 1987, Are UK stock prices excessively volatile?, London School of Economics Financial Markets Working Paper, November.

Campbell, J.Y. and R.J. Shiller, 1987, Cointegration and tests of present value models, Journal of Political Economy 95, 1062-1088

Cohn, R.A. and D.R.Lessard, 1981, The effect of inflation on stock prices: international evidence, Journal of Finance, May, 277-290

Dickey, D.A., and W.A. Fuller, 1979, Distribution of the estimators for autoregressive time series with a unit root, Journal of the American Statistical Association, 74, 427-431

Fama, E.F., 1970, Efficient capital markets; a review of theory and empirical work, Journal of Finance 25, 383-417

Fama, E.F., and M.E. Blume, 1966, Filter rules and stock market trading, Journal of Business, 226-241

Flavin, M., 1983, Excess volatility in the financial markets: a reassessment of the empirical evidence, Journal of Political Economy 91, 929-56

Friedman, B.M., 1979, Optimal expectations of the extrme information assumptions of 'Rational Expectations' macromodels, Journal of Monetary Economics, v, 23-41

Fuller, W.A., 1976, Introduction to statistical time series, (New York, John Wiley)

Jensen, M.C., 1978, Some anomalous evidence regarding market efficiency, Journal of Financial Economics, 6, 95-101

Kleidon, A.W., 1986, Variance bounds tests and stock price valuation models, Journal of Political Economy 94, 953-1001

LeRoy S.F. and R.D. Porter, 1980, Stock price volatility: tests based on implied variance bounds, Econometrica 49, 97-113

Modigliani, F., and R.A. Cohn, 1979, Inflation, rational valuation, and the market, Financial Analysts Journal, March/April, 24-44

Muth, J.F., 1961, Rational Expectations and the theory of price movements, Econometrica, 29, 315-335

Poterba, J.M., and L.H. Summers, 1987, Mean reversion in stock prices: evidence and implications, NBER Working Paper, November

Shiller, R.J., 1981a, Do stock prices move too much to be justified by subsequent changes in dividends?, American Economic Review 71, 421-436

Shiller, R.J., 1981b, The use of volatility measures in assessing market efficiency, Journal of Finance 36, 291-304

Summers, L.H., 1986, Does the stock market rationally reflect fundamental values?, Journal of Finance, 41, 591-600

West, K.D., 1988, Dividend innovations and stock price volatility, Econometrica, vol 56, 1, 37-62

Are UK Stock Prices Excessively Volatile: A Comment

by Charles Bram Cadsby

George Bulkley and Ian Tonks make three related but distinct points in this paper. First, they apply the variance bounds test developed by Shiller (1981) to UK stock market data. Their results are similar to those obtained by Shiller (1981) for the US. Actual stock prices are excessively volatile relative to ex post rational prices.

Second, they develop a new test which retains the assumption that dividends are generated by a long-run exponential growth process but which relaxes Shiller's implicit assumption that agents know the true parameters of this process. The new test assumes instead that agents estimate these parameters and hence the expected value of the perfect foresight price at each moment in time, making optimal use of all information available to them at the moment in question. The fundamental idea as well as its empirical implementation is virtually identical to the notion of statistical-rational expectations, developed and implemented by Friedman (1979) in a somewhat different context. Bulkley and Tonks find that UK stock prices no longer appear excessively volatile when subjected to their new test.

Third, the authors show that agents using only information available at the time of estimation to forecast perfect foresight prices could have used those estimates to construct a profitable trading rule. They argue that the possibility of constructing such a rule indicates that UK stock prices were excessively volatile after all.

Their replication of Shiller's test on UK data is of some but limited interest because this test has been convincingly criticized by Flavin (1983), Kleidon (1986), Marsh and Merton (1986) and by the authors themselves. Their new excess volatility test may be an improvement over Shiller (1981) but appears to be rendered somewhat superfluous by the recent development of a volatility test which depends neither upon the stationarity of detrended dividends nor upon the ability to calculate expectations of the perfect foresight price (West, 1988). It would certainly be useful to perform West's volatility test on UK data, especially in light of the different conclusions about excess volatility that arise out of the various methodologies applied in this paper.

On the other hand, the authors' apparently successful trading rule is very interesting and serves to refocus attention on a number of important

NATO ASI Series, Vol. F54
A Reappraisal of the Efficiency of Financial Markets
Edited by Rui M. C. Guimaraes et al.

issues. In this connection, it is useful to recall the remarks made by Shiller (1981) when introducing the notion of excess volatility into the literature:

> Much of the literature on efficient markets concerns the investigation of nominal "profit opportunities" (variously defined) and whether transactions costs prohibit their exploitation. Of course, if real stock prices are "too volatile" as it is defined here, then there may well be a sort of real profit opportunity. Time variation in expected real interest rates does not itself imply that any trading rule dominates a buy and hold strategy, but really large variations in expected returns might seem to suggest that such a trading rule exists. This paper is concerned, however, instead with a more interesting (from an economic standpoint) question: what accounts for movements in real stock prices and can they be explained by new information about subsequent real dividends? If the model fails due to excessive volatility, then we will have seen a new characterization of how the simple model fails. The characterization is not equivalent to other characterizations of its failure, such as that one-period holding returns are forecastable, or that stocks have not been good inflation hedges recently.

Bulkley and Tonks appear to have brought the discussion of excess volatility full circle by suggesting that it is implicit in their trading rule. Shiller (1981) did not spell out the precise relationship between excess volatility and the existence of a profitable trading rule, though he does seem to argue that neither one implies the other. Bulkley and Tonks find a special kind of trading rule which seems intuitively to suggest excess volatility. However, the precise relationship between the two is never spelled out analytically. The Bulkley and Tonks results suggest that this may be an important task to undertake. Any such analysis should consider whether the existence of a profitable trading rule, making use of optimally estimated perfect foresight prices, can provide a clue as to the source of any excess volatility that may exist. (See West, 1988, p. 44-45.)

It is unlikely that anyone has actually made money following a strategy similar to the one suggested by Bulkley and Tonks. Although their strategy appears to yield impressive results, one wonders just how costly it would have been to implement. The authors argue that transactions cost would have had to be in the neighbourhood of 12.5% in order to erase the excess profits from their strategy. They correctly point out that brokerage and related fees could not have been that high since the investor would have traded on only seven separate occasions between 1929 to 1985. However, one wonders about the costs of developing the Bulkley and Tonks strategy as well as the costs of using available information to produce optimal predictions of perfect foresight prices in the days before computers and calculators were commonly available.

In summary, Bulkley and Tonks have raised some important issues and presented them forcefully in their paper on excess volatility in the UK. Their trading rule appears impressive and interesting from an economic standpoint. However, the precise relationship between the existence of such a trading rule and the notion of excess volatility remains to be worked out.

References

Flavin, M., 1983, Excess Volatility in the Financial Markets: a Reassessment of the Empirical Evidence, Journal of Political Economy 91, 929-956.

Friedman, B., 1979, Optimal Expections and the Extreme Information Assumptions of 'Rational Expectations' Macromodels, Journal of Monetary Economics 5, 23-41.

Kleidon, A.W., 1986, Variance Bounds Tests and Stock Price Valuation Models, Journal of Political Economy 94, 953-1001.

Marsh, T. and R.C. Merton, 1986, Divided Variability and Variance Bounds Tests for the Rationality of Stock Market Prices, American Economic Review, 483-498.

Shiller, R.J., 1981, Do Stock Prices Move Too Much to be Justified by Subsequent Changes in Dividends?, American Economic Review 71, 421-436.

West, K.D., 1988, Dividend Innovations and Stock Price Volatility, Econometrica 56, No. 1, 37-62.

Rational Expectations and Perfect Foresight Prices

by

G.C. Uselton and D.R. Fraser
Texas A&M University
Department of Finance
College Station, Texas 77843
U.S.A.

Keywords: perfect foresight prices / market efficiency / noise / price volatility / rational expectations / dividend valuation model

Abstract: Shiller's notion of perfect foresight prices is adapted to a crossectional study of 400 firms. Distribution-free statistics, which are unencumbered by the restrictive assumptions underlying parametric methods such as those used in the "implied variance bounds" literature, are used to test hypotheses concerning market efficiency. Market prices of equities are shown, for the period studied, to have been distributed above and below the corresponding perfect foresight prices; and some support is found for the claim that contemporaneous information was not fully impounded in all market prices.

NATO ASI Series, Vol. F54
A Reappraisal of the Efficiency of Financial Markets
Edited by Rui M. C. Guimaraes et al.

RATIONAL EXPECTATIONS AND PERFECT FORESIGHT PRICES

In a perfectly efficient market observed prices would be identical with true values. In an efficient market with a stochastic component prices would be noisy estimates of true values and would be randomly distributed above and below the true values. Given such a distribution, regardless of its variance, one could argue that the market in question was efficient. A test for market efficiency so defined requires none of the usual assumptions of parametric statistics.[1]

I. Market Prices, Perfect Foresight Values, and Noise

Black (1986) argues that the price of any security comprises two components: the true value of the security and a noise component (any deviation from the true value):

$$P(t) = V(t) + N(t) \tag{1}$$

where $P(t)$ = the price of a stock at time t,

$V(t)$ = the true value of the stock,

and $N(t)$ = the noise component.[2]

Although we cannot know how far away today's price is from a security's true value, we can determine approximately the differences between security prices and their corresponding perfect foresight values at some time in the remote past. This knowledge proceeds directly from the dividend valuation model:

$$V(t) = \sum_{k=1}^{n} \theta^k CF(t+k) \tag{2}$$

where $CF(t)$ = cash flow in period t,

$\theta = 1/(1+r)$, a discount factor,

r = appropriate discount rate,

and n = number of periods.

---

[1] Elton and Gruber (1984) present a clear discussion of the efficient markets hypothesis, its various forms, the debate concerning the degree of efficiency, and the tests for efficiency.

[2] As an alternative to the inclusion of a noise component, Michener (1981) attributes "...the sensitivity of asset prices to current dividends to the diminishing marginal utility of consumption" in a general equilibrium model, an argument which is similar to that presented in Grossman and Shiller (1981).

The value, V(t), is equivalent to Schiller's (1981a) "perfect foresight or ex-post rational price."

LeRoy and Porter (1981) pointed out that their tests based upon implied variance bounds utilized aggregate data whereas their theory applied to individual firms. This study focuses upon individual firm data. Observe the price of a specific firm's stock at some time (t) in the past. Calculate the value at time t of the stream of dividends paid by the firm over the next twenty years plus the market price at time t+20 of a share of the firm's stock discounted to time t. The calculated value at time t was the approximate[3] value, V(t), of the stock at that time. The difference between the observed market price and the calculated value (both at time t) is the noise component, N(t), of equation (1) above.

For the value calculation described above, the appropriate discount rate, r, is the interest rate (at t) on (20-year) U. S. Government bonds. The dividend stream, the inflation rate, and the selling price after twenty years are known with certainty, hence, the risk-free rate for a bond of the same maturity as implied by the twenty-year present value calculation. This real value calculation will be used as a basis for estimating the dispersion of prices about the perfect foresight values.[4]

The S&P 500, a list of stocks composed of 40 Utilities, 40 Financials, 20 Transportations, and 400 Industrials, is frequently used as a proxy for "the market." For each firm from these four subsets of the S&P 500 stocks, values were calculated as explained. Standard & Poor's Corporation's Compustat Tapes were used.

Some of the firms included in the S&P 500 in 1984 were not included in 1965. The four subsets actually used comprised 29 Utilities, 26 Financials, 16 Transportations, and 332 Industrials. Value estimates were made for the end of 1965 so that the 1965 lagging earnings could be used later in the earnings-based value estimates.

---

[3]This value estimate is only approximate because the final cash flow includes the market price at the end of the series. The larger the discount rate, the less important is the influence of this "noisy" approximation of the value of the stock 20 years from the valuation date.

[4]If the discount rate used is insufficient to compensate investors for the capital losses due to inflation over the period in question, the calculated values will overstate the true values. The value calculations for this study have been adjusted for inflation.

II. Noisy Estimates

If stock prices are noisy estimates of the true values of stocks, the dispersion of market prices about the true values can be estimated for 1 January 1966. Because of the differences in magnitudes of prices of securities, this study examines the distribution of the magnitudes of the ratios of perfect foresight values to market prices (V/P). If the ratio of value to price, V/P, were unity, a stock would have been correctly priced by the market. If the V/P ratio were greater (less) than unity, the market would have been underpricing (overpricing) the security. Stocks with V/P ratios greater than two or less than one-half would have been inefficiently priced by Black's (1986) criteria, i.e., the range of efficiency would be:

$$1/2 \leq V/P \leq 2. \tag{3}$$

A value/price ratio was calculated for each firm in each subset of the sample. The results are summarized in Table 1.

Table 1. Numbers and Percentages of Stocks Priced "Efficiently"

	Grossly Underpriced		Efficient Market Range		Grossly Overpriced		
	V/P > 2		2 > V/P > 0.5		V/P < 0.5		
	%	#	%	#	%	#	TOTAL FIRMS
Utilities	6.3	2	87.5	28	6.3	2	32
Financials	3.9	1	73.1	19	23.1	6	26
Transports	43.8	7	43.8	7	12.5	2	16
Industrials	0.6	2	44.9	149	54.5	181	332

Note: If V/P > 2, P < 0.5V and if V/P < 0.5, P > 2V.

Of the 32 utility companies in the sample almost 90 percent fell within the range defined as "efficient." That the market prices closely approximated the calculated true values is not surprising. Consider the facts. (1) Utility stocks were (in 1965) generally considered to be conservative, low-risk investments. (In fact, Uselton, Kolari, and Fraser (1986) showed that the increased risk of utility shares following Three

Mile Island was ephemeral.) (2) Investors in utility stocks are usually interested in the income from dividends. (3) Forecasts of utility stock dividends have been more reliable than most economic forecasts.

The prices of stocks in the Financials group were within the "efficient" range more than 73 percent of the time. Six firms (23 percent of its members) were priced at more than twice their true values (perhaps a reflection of the bull market in progress at the time)[5], and only 3.9 percent were grossly underpriced.

Only in the case of the Transports did the market fail to price more than 90 percent of the firms above one-half their true values. Of the 16 Transports seven were priced in the "range of efficiency," seven were grossly underpriced (less than one-half true value), and two were grossly overpriced (more than twice true value).

The sample from the S&P 400 Industrials contained 332 stocks. More than fifty percent (181) were grossly overpriced, but only two (less than one percent) were grossly underpriced. Almost 45 percent (149) were priced in the efficient range.

This evidence of substantial spreads between value and price over a large sample of firms is similar to that adduced by Schiller (1981a), LeRoy and Porter(1981), and Singleton (1980). The present study, however, because of the nonparametric tests applied to crossectional data for individual firms, is not subject to Flavin's (1983) criticism of the three referenced papers to the effect that the reported excessive volatility of security prices was only statistical aberration. Kleidon (1986) noted that earlier tests of stock price rationality based upon variance bounds relied upon "...the assumption of stationarity and ergodic processes for prices and dividends." The present study makes no assumption of ergodicity or stationarity.

---

[5]The notion that prices on average will be higher than the corresponding true values during bull markets (and lower during bear markets) was evaluated for the utilities group only, that group being the one which most nearly approximated the conditions for efficiency specified by Black. The ratios of true value to market price were calculated for each utility company at the market high in December 1968 and at the market low in December 1974. At the 1968 market high no prices were less than one-half the corresponding values whereas two stocks had prices higher than twice the corresponding values. At the 1974 market low no firms had prices greater than twice their values but 13 had prices which were less than one-half their perfect foresight values. The median value/price ratio for 1968 was 0.699; the same measure for 1974 was 2.097. Apparently the market overprices the shares of utility firms in bull markets and underprices them in bear markets.

If the bull market that was in progress in the mid-sixties was responsible for the overpricing observed, must one conclude that markets are inefficient? If periods in which more than ten percent of the stocks are overpriced or underpriced by the established criteria occur less than ten percent of the time, the financial markets could be considered "efficient" under the definition suggested by Black (1986).

Are market prices "noisy estimates" of true values? For the utilities group the answer, based upon the value calculations described, is "Yes." The 26 Financials did not meet the criteria; but, with only six of 26 stocks grossly overpriced during a bull market, the cyclic skewing was mild. Similarly, the distribution of Industrials prices, given the bull market, may have been only a temporary aberration. The ratio of perfect foresight values to market prices of stocks may tend to be normally distributed with means of unity but skewed upward or downward during bull or bear markets. The market cycle does not, however, explain the large proportion of grossly undervalued stocks in the Transports group in 1966.

III. Perfect Foresight and the Earnings Capitalization Rate

If a market is to be considered "efficient," the market prices of securities must reflect all available information. It would be impossible consistently to improve upon price as an estimate of true value by utilizing published information (such as a firm's earnings history).

A firm's earnings per share over the past year multiplied by a suitable capitalization rate can be used to produce an estimate of the firm's value per share. However, only to the extent that noise traders ignore earnings records in planning their trading strategies, will these estimates provide a better approximation of the stocks' true values than will the market prices themselves. (Black, 1986)

"Suitable" earnings capitalization rates were determined for this study, given that twenty years of future dividends and prices were known with certainty, by choosing for each industry represented in the S&P 500 a multiplier that produced an estimated value-to-price ratio whose mean was equal to that of the perfect foresight value-to-price ratio. Two separate rankings for each of the four subsets of the S&P 500 were produced, one based upon the perfect foresight value to price ratios, the other based upon the value to price ratios generated by the capitalization rates. Each set of ratios was arranged in decending order (most underpriced to most overpriced). Well-known nonparametric tests were used to evaluate the null hypothesis: the variables (the two sets of ranks) are unrelated. The results are summarized in Table 2.

Table 2. Rank Correlation Coefficients

	Spearman	t	Kendall	z	N
Utilities	0.646	4.634*	0.460	3.697*	32
Financials	0.422	2.277**	0.299	2.138*	26
Transports	-0.068	-0.254	-0.067	-0.360	16
Industrials	0.495	10.342*	0.360	9.793*	332

* Significant at the 0.01 level.
** Significant at the 0.05 level.

The two rankings for each of the Utilities, Financials, and Industrials are positively correlated and the correlations are significant. The rankings of the Transportations show low negative but insignificant correlation. The null hypothesis is rejected for the former three and accepted for the latter. The rankings are related for the Utilities, Financials, and Industrials and are unrelated for the Transportations. These findings of significant positive correlations between the rankings according to perfect foresight value and the estimates based upon earnings lend strong support to the notion that noise traders fail to take full advantage of the information contained in the recent earnings records of firms.

IV. Stock Selection by Capitalization Ratio

Should investors, on the basis of the evidence presented, establish a single criterion for choosing stocks for a portfolio? Would equal dollar amounts invested in the most underpriced stocks, as identified by the earnings capitalization method, produce a portfolio with a perfect foresight value in excess of the amount invested?

Four portfolios were produced, one for each of the four groups comprising the S&P 500. The value/price ratios generated by the earnings capitalization method described were ranked in descending order (from the most underpriced to the most overpriced). Equal dollar amounts were "invested" in each of the first twenty stocks (or in those stocks with a value estimate/market price ratio greater than unity if there were fewer than twenty). The amounts invested in each of the four portfolios were compared with the perfect foresight values of the portfolios. The results are presented in Table 3.

Table 3. Earnings-Based Value Estimates

Components S&P 500	Number of Stocks Purchased	Investment Outlay	Perfect Foresight Value of Portfolio
Utilities	18	$18.00	$22.96
Financials	16	16.00	19.57
Transports	14	14.00	32.29
Industrials	8	8.00	8.94
Totals	56	$56.00	$83.76

Only 18 of the 32 Utilities had estimated value-to-price ratios greater than one; so, in accordance with the stated rule, only $18 was invested in utility stocks. This $18 investment had a perfect foresight value of $22.96. The portfolio of Utilities was purchased at a 22% discount from value; or, from another perspective, the portfolio purchased for $18 had a 28% appreciation potential. (These figures neglect transactions costs.)

The Financials portfolio contained 16 stocks, a total outlay of $16. Its value was $19.57. The portfolio of 16 stocks was bought at an 18% discount; or, alternatively, had a 22% appreciation potential.

Ironically, the biggest gains were in the transportation stocks where no significant correlation between the rankings of the perfect foresight values and the earnings capitalization estimates was found. According to the earnings-based estimates, 14 of the 16 stocks in this subgroup were priced below value. The $14 investment had a perfect foresight value of $32.29. This portfolio was purchased at a 57% discount with an appreciation potential of 130%. Of the 14 transportation stocks selected by the earnings-based value estimates, nine had perfect foresight values greater than their prices. Eleven of the 16 stocks were priced below their perfect foresight values and the capitalization factor identified nine of those eleven. The earnings-based value estimates identified the undervalued securities even though the rank order correlation statistic was not significant.

The industrials group was subdivided on the basis of SIC numbers into fourteen subgroups and a separate capitalization ratio estimated for each.[6] The simulated investment experiment was then replicated fourteen times, applying the same criteria for investing in a given firm as before. The use of fourteen capitalization ratios, one for each subgroup, selected only eight stocks from the industrials group. The $8.00 investment had a perfect foresight value of $8.94. The portfolio of Industrials was purchased at a discount of eleven percent; or, alternatively, it had an appreciation potential of about twelve percent.

Overall the earnings-based valuation procedure worked well. The investment outlay of $56.00 (one-dollar invested in each of 56 stocks) had a true value of $83.76. The combined portfolios would have been purchased at a discount of 33% and would have had an appreciation potential of 50%. Apparently earnings did (in 1965) contain information in addition to that impounded in the market prices.

V. The Volatilities of Price and Value

Kleidon (1986b) showed time series plots of (perfect foresight) values to be much smoother than those of the corresponding market prices "...even if crossectional variance bounds are satisfied." If the prices of all securities tend to vary randomly above and below their perfect foresight values, then one should be able to infer something about the degree of correlation between the true values and the random components in the corresponding prices. Recall equation (1):

$$P(t) = V(t) + N(t) \qquad (1)$$

---

[6]If the Industrials group, comprising 332 heterogeneous stocks, had been treated as if it were homogeneous, the experiment would have selected the twenty most underpriced stocks according to the earnings-based valuation method. The $20 investment would have had a true value of only $19.16. Attempting to identify a capitalization factor that is "appropriate" for all 332 stocks in the sample from the S&P 400 Industrials is unrealistic, given the heterogeneity of this sample, hence the subdividing.

From a well-known statistical theorem[7]

$$\sigma_P^2 = \sigma_V^2 + \sigma_N^2 + 2\rho_{VN}\sigma_V\sigma_N. \quad (4)$$

If the value component of price is relatively stable and price varies above and below value, then

$$\sigma_P^2 \geq \sigma_V^2, \quad (5)$$

and solving for ρ_{VN}:

$$\rho_{VN} \geq -(1/2)(\sigma_N/\sigma_V). \quad (6)$$

The ratio of the standard deviation of the noise component to that of the true value cannot exceed two since the correlation coefficient cannot be less than negative unity.

The calculations which have been made in this study have generated value estimates at a moment in time. The resulting series of crossectional variance calculations yields explicit information concerning the correlations between the value series and the noise series. Furthermore, they support the assumption concerning the relative magnitudes of the variances of the price and value series, i.e., the variance of market prices exceeds that of perfect foresight values. These estimates of correlation are presented in Table 4.[8]

Table 4. The Degree of Correlation between Value and Noise

Subgroup	ρ_{VN}
Utilities	-0.138
Financials	-0.270
Transports	-0.056
Industrials	-0.690

For the Utilities, Financials, and Transports the correlations between the value and the noise series were negative but greater than -1/2, a result consistent with the assumption that $\sigma_V = \sigma_N$. For the industrials

[7]Shiller (1981a) notes that if P(t) is an optimal forecast of V(t), then P(t) and N(t) must be uncorrelated. The calculated values, V(t), are not forecasts but perfect foresight values about which the market prices are presumed to vary, hence no assumption is made concerning the correlation of V(t) and the noise component, N(t).

[8]Before calculating the variances of the market prices and perfect foresight values the series were "normalized" so that their means were unity. This procedure was used to eliminate the distortions due to differences in magnitudes of the original numbers. (These calculations are, of course, not nonparametric.)

the correlation was less than -1/2 (-0.68) which suggests a slightly higher variance in the noise series realtive to the true value series.

VI. Summary

For the purposes of this study market prices have been divided into two components: perfect foresight values and noise. By the criteria established financial markets do appear to have been imperfect (in January 1966). A firm's earnings history apparently added some information to that contained in prices (on 1/1/66). Noise does seem to complicate the process of choosing undervalued stocks (especially if a simple one-criterion rule is being used). And finally, the relative volatilities of prices and values that are implied by the theory were supported by the data.

REFERENCES

Black, F., 1986, Noise, Journal of Finance 41, 529-542.

Elton, E. J. and M. J. Gruber, 1984, Modern Portfolio Theory and Investment Analysis (2d ed., John Wiley & Sons, New York) 394ff.

Flavin, M. A. 1983, Excess Volatility in the Financial Markets: A Reassessment of the Empirical Evidence, Journal of Political Economy 91 (No. 6), 929-956.

Grossman, S. J. and R. J. Shiller, 1981, The Determinants of the Variability of Stock Market Prices, American Economic Review 71, 222-227.

Kleidon, A. W., 1986a, Bias in Small Sample Tests of Stock Price Rationality, Journal of Business 59 (No. 2), 237-261.

______, 1986b, Variance Bounds Tests and Stock Price Valuation Models, Journal of Political Economy 94 (NO. 5), 953-1001.

LeRoy, S. F. and R. D. Porter, 1981, The Present-Value Relation: Tests Based on Implied Variance Bounds, Econometrica 49, 555-574.

Michener, R. W., 1982, Variance Bounds in a Simple Model of Asset Pricing, Journal of Political Economy 90, 166-175.

Pierce, D. K., 1987, Challenges to the Concept of Stock Market Efficiency, Federal Reserve Bank of Kansas City, Economic Review 90, 16-33.

Shiller, R. J., 1981a, Do Stock Prices Move Too Much to be Justified by Subsequent Changes in Dividends? American Economic Review 71, 421-436.

______, 1981b, The Uses of Volatility Measures in Assessing Market Efficiency, Journal of Finance 36, 291-311.

Singleton, K., 1980, Expectations Models of the Term Structure and Implied Variance Bounds, Journal of Political Economy 88, 1159-1176.

Uselton, G. C., J. W. Kolari, and D. R. Fraser, 1986, Long-Term Trends in the Riskiness of Electric Utility Shares, Journal of Business Finance & Accounting 13, 453-459.

A RE-EXAMINATION OF EXCESS RATIONAL PRICE APPROXIMATIONS AND EXCESS VOLATILITY IN THE STOCK MARKET

Gary S. Shea
Department of Finance
609 Business Administration Building
University Park, PA 16802
USA

KEYWORDS / ABSTRACT : Bootstrapping / Cointegration / Error Correction / Excess Volatility / Stock Prices / Vector Autoregression

Excess volatility tests have resulted in apparent rejections of the present-value relation when ex–post price approximations are employed. These approximations are based upon a sample terminal condition for prices, are necessarily heteroskedastic time series, and do not result in statistics with readily calculable standard errors. Volatility statistics do not always have positive expected value, as previously believed, and in a bootstrapped cointegration model do not reject the present-value relation in small samples. Approximations based upon a 'rolling' terminal condition result in volatility statistics which have calculable standard errors, but even these standard errors are inadequate.

NATO ASI Series, Vol. F54
A Reappraisal of the Efficiency of Financial Markets
Edited by Rui M. C. Guimaraes et al.

1. Introduction

This paper shows that the statistical reliability of some excess-volatility tests of the present-value relation is profoundly affected by the very approximations to ex–post rational stock prices that appear in some of the more recent literature. The problems posed are a mixture of incorrect design and interpretation of test statistics. We shall look at an exemplary application of ex–post price approximations in the present-value literature, the excess-volatility tests developed by Mankiw, Romer, and Shapiro (1985). We develop ex-post price approximations that depend upon a 'rolling' terminal price, that are as justified as the approximations currently appearing in the literature, but which result in test statistics with readily calculable standard errors. Finally, we perform bootstrap simulations of a model, developed by Campbell and Shiller (1987), which imposes the cointegration constraints implied by the present-value model of stock price determination. The simulations show the extent of the problems in the Mankiw, Romer, and Shapiro (1985) procedures and the small sample reliability of statistics based upon ex-post price approximations.

2. The Mankiw, Romer, and Shapiro Statistics

Mankiw, Romer, and Shapiro (1985, hereafter referred to as MRS) developed tests for excess-volatility in the stock market which exploit the presumed variance–covariance stationarity of the differences between actual prices, ex–post rational prices, and a naive forecast price conditioned upon at least a part of the information set which is available to the market. The advantages claimed for the MRS test statistics were unbiasedness and positive expected values in a wide range of circumstances under the null hypothesis of no excess volatility. We deal here with the problems of test statistic design and interpretation which are posed by ex-post rational prices and their approximations. For one, such approximations depend upon a fixed terminal condition for sample prices and because of this measures of the accuracy of MRS test statistics, such as standard errors, are practically unobtainable; the MRS methodology yields only point estimates of statistics of interest. Later, we develop statistics based upon a moving terminal condition for sample prices have distinct advantages over those presented by MRS in that they, first, take account of sample variation in terminal stock prices and, second, allow asymptotic standard errors to be calculated. Evidence of excess volatility in these new statistics is scarce.

A simple rational expectations hypothesis (hereafter referred to as the null hypothesis) of stock price determination would suggest that prices are linked to expected future dividends by the following mechanism.

$$P_t = \sum_{i=0}^{\infty} \gamma^{i+1} E(D_{t+i} | \Phi_t) . \tag{1}$$

γ is the constant discount factor and E is the expectations operator. The symbol Φ_t will denote the relevant set of information upon which market expectations at time t are conditioned. With perfect foresight, a typical investor would pay an ex–post rational price for the stock, P_t^*, where

$$P_t^* = \sum_{i=0}^{\infty} \gamma^{i+1} D_{t+i} . \tag{2}$$

An approximate measure for that price was defined by MRS as

$$P^*_{t|T} = \sum_{i=0}^{T-t-1} \gamma^{i+1} D_{t+i} + \gamma^{T-t} P_T , \tag{3}$$

where T is the terminal date of the investment and where $P^*_{t|T}$ denotes that this is an actual ex–post rational price only if P_T is equal to the actual ex–post rational price at time T, P^*_T. Finally, MRS defined a "naive" price, P^0_t, as

$$P^0_t = \sum_{i=0}^{\infty} \gamma^{i+1} D_{t-1} = [\gamma/(1-\gamma)] D_{t-1} . \tag{4}$$

They then go on to assert that $P^*_{t|T}-P^0_t$, $P^*_{t|T}-P_t$, and $P_t-P^0_t$ are all jointly distributed as variance–covariance stationary time series. Under the null hypothesis,

$$E(P^*_{t|T}-P^0_t)^2 = E(P^*_{t|T}-P_t)^2 + E(P_t-P^0_t)^2 , \tag{5}$$

and from this they obtained the inequalities

$$E(P^*_{t|T}-P^0_t)^2 \geq E(P^*_{t|T}-P_t)^2 , \tag{6}$$

and

$$E(P^*_{t|T}-P^0_t)^2 \geq E(P_t-P^0_t)^2 . \tag{7}$$

MRS define a test statistic $S_{1|T}$ as $\frac{1}{T}\sum_{t=1}^{T}(P^*_{t|T}-P^0_t)^2 - \frac{1}{T}\sum_{t=1}^{T}(P^*_{t|T}-P_t)^2$ and the statistic $S_{2|T}$ as $\frac{1}{T}\sum_{t=1}^{T}(P^*_{t|T}-P^0_t)^2 - \frac{1}{T}\sum_{t=1}^{T}(P_t-P^0_t)^2$. It was shown that both statistics have positive expected values; $E(S_{1|T})$ equals $\frac{1}{T}\sum_{t=1}^{T} E(P_t-P_t^o)^2$ and $E(S_{2|T})$ equals $\frac{1}{T}\sum_{t=1}^{T} E(P^*_{t|T}-P_t)^2$. They found that for most cases of discount rates (r, so that $\gamma = 1/(1+r)$) between 0.04 and 0.10 the inequalities (6) and (7) were violated. That is, they found that sample test statistics were usually negative, but no standard errors were given.

3. Conditional and Unconditional Statistics

Although the MRS ex-post rational prices are not the actual ex–post rational prices, it was hoped that they would be adequate approximations to actual P^*_t. The relationship between the distribution of $P^*_{t|T}$ and that of P^*_t was not investigated, however. From equations (2) and (3) it is clear that

$$P^*_t = \sum_{i=0}^{T-t-1} \gamma^{i+1} D_{t+i} + \gamma^{T-t} P^*_T \text{, and therefore,} \tag{8}$$

$$P^*_t = P^*_{t|T} + \gamma^{T-t}[P^*_T-P_T] \ . \tag{9}$$

$P^*_{t|T}$ differs from actual P^*_t by the discounted difference between P^*_T and P_T and $P^*_T-P_T$ can be thought of as a forecast error for dividends subsequent to period T. Although we find that the statistics based upon P^*_t are different from the MRS statistics, the fact remains that MRS statistics still could be useful if we could properly anticipate their expected value and if their standard errors could be calculated. In this section we investigate the relationship between P_t^* and $P_{t|T}^*$ and the statistics based upon them.

The annual price and dividend series used by Campbell and Shiller (1987) updated to the period from 1871 through 1986 are used in this paper. The data are slightly revised from that used by MRS. The $P_{t|T}^*$ series was calculated conditional upon a holding-period terminal date, T, which in the MRS study was chosen to be 1983, but in this study will be 1986. These differences in data and procedures from those used by MRS will have no material effect upon results or conclusions of this paper, however. It is pertinent to their experiments that in previous studies T was chosen to be 1983 and not 1982 nor 1942, nor any other date for that matter. There were actually 113 possible choices for T between 1871 and 1983, inclusive. Since the $P_{t|T}^*$ series calculated by MRS was sampled from a very large population of available $P_{t|T}^*$'s, can we say that sample $P_{t|T}^*$ based upon only T = 1983 or 1986 are fairly representative data with which to test inequalities (6) and (7)? This hardly seems likely in light of the considerable sample variation we have observed in $P_{t|T}^*$ series for different terminal dates.[1]

The finite sample distributions of the volatility statistics can also be linked to their population distributions. We note that from Equations (3) and (4) that

$$P_{t|T}^* - P_t = (P_t^* - P_t) - \gamma^{T-t}(P_T^* - P_T) \text{ and} \tag{10}$$

$$P_{t|T}^* - P_t^o = (P_t^* - P_t^o) - \gamma^{T-t}(P_T^* - P_T)\,. \tag{11}$$

From Equation (10) we have

[1]Indeed, we found that by repeating the MRS procedures for each of the available 113 T, MRS would have generally reported results favorable to the null hypothesis in cases of T prior to the mid-1960's.

$$E(P^*_{t|T}-P_t)^2 = E(P^*_t-P_t)^2 + \gamma^{2(T-t)}E(P^*_T-P_T)^2$$
$$-\,2\gamma^{T-t}E\Big[(P^*_t-P_t)(P^*_T-P_T)\Big]\,. \tag{12}$$

Equation (12) can be simplified. Under the null hypothesis, $P^*_t-P_t$ and $P^*_T-P_T$ will be stationary and ergodic time series and it will follow that $E(P^*_t-P_t)^2$ will equal $E(P^*_T-P_T)^2$, which we can denote as Ψ_0. Likewise we can denote $E\Big[(P^*_t-P_t)(P^*_T-P_T)\Big]$ as Ψ_{T-t}. Let Π be a forecast error operator so that $\Pi(D_{t+i}|\Phi_t)$ equals $D_{t+i} - E(D_{t+i}|\Phi_t)$. Since we assume dividends come from a discrete, linear multivariate stochastic nonstationary model of dividends and its n–1 leading indicators, the dividend forecast errors will have a compact stochastic characterization which we denote $\Pi(D_{t+i}|\Phi_t) = \delta_i(B)'\epsilon_{t+i}$. $\delta_i(B)'$ equals $\Big[\delta_0' + \delta_1'B + \delta_2'B^2 + \cdots + \delta_i'B^i\Big]$ with δ_i' being a 1×n row vector of impulse-response weights for dividends. It follows that under the null hypothesis,

$$P^*_t-P_t = \sum_{i=0}^{\infty} \gamma^{i+1}\Pi(D_{t+i}|\Phi_t) = \gamma\delta_0'\epsilon_t + \gamma^2\Big[\delta_0'\epsilon_{t+1}+\delta_1'\epsilon_t\Big] + \cdots$$
$$+\gamma^{T-t}\Big[\delta_0'\epsilon_{T-1}+\delta_1'\epsilon_{T-2}+\cdots+\delta_{T-t-1}'\epsilon_t\Big]+\gamma^{T-t+1}\Big[\delta_0'\epsilon_T+\delta_1'\epsilon_{T-1}+\cdots+\delta_{T-t}'\epsilon_t\Big]+\cdots. \tag{13}$$

By defining a 1×n row vector $a_j' = \sum_{k=j}^{\infty} \gamma^{k-j}\delta_k'$ (see LeRoy and Porter's Equation (5)), Equation (13) reduces to

$$P^*_t-P_t = a_0'\sum_{i=0}^{\infty}\gamma^{i+1}\epsilon_{t+i} = a_0'\left[\sum_{i=0}^{T-t-1}\gamma^{i+1}\epsilon_{t+i}+\gamma^{T-t}\sum_{i=0}^{\infty}\gamma^{i+1}\epsilon_{T+i}\right]. \tag{14}$$

We note that $\Psi_0 = \frac{\gamma^2}{1-\gamma^2} a_0' \Sigma\, a_0$ where Σ is $E(\epsilon_t \epsilon_t')$. More interestingly, we see that, with the help of Equation (14),

$$\Psi_{T-t} = E\left[(P_t^*-P_t)(P_T^*-P_T)\right] = \frac{\gamma^{T-t+2}}{1-\gamma^2} a_0' \Sigma\, a_0 = \gamma^{T-t} \Psi_0 \,. \tag{15}$$

The MRS assumption that $P_t^*-P_t$, $P_t^*-P_t^o$, and $P_t-P_t^o$ each have finite variance does not require a stationary multivariate model for dividends such as that used by LeRoy and Porter in their Equation (2). Clearly, however, we must assume that the quantity $a_0' \Sigma a_0$ is finite so that meaningful estimates of MRS test statistics can be constructed.

Equation (10) can now be simplified to

$$E(P_{t|T}^*-P_t)^2 = \left[1-\gamma^{2(T-t)}\right] E(P_t^*-P_t)^2 \,. \tag{16}$$

Similarly, the unconditional expectation of $(P_{t|T}^*-P_t^o)^2$ is expressed,

$$E(P_{t|T}^*-P_t^o)^2 = E(P_t^*-P_t^o)^2 - \gamma^{2(T-t)} E(P_t^*-P_t)^2 \,, \tag{17}$$

which depends upon the fact that population $E\left[(P_t-P_t^o)(P_T^*-P_T)\right] = 0$.

Thus we see that the MRS test statistics are distinct from their population counterparts, S_1 and S_2. The MRS test statistics are related to population test statistics as,

$$S_{1|T} = S_1 - \frac{2(P_T^*-P_T)}{T} \sum_{t=1}^{T} \gamma^{T-t} (P_t-P_t^o), \text{ and} \tag{18}$$

$$S_{2|T} = S_2 + \frac{(P_T^*-P_T)^2}{T}\sum_{t=1}^{T}\gamma^{2(T-t)} - \frac{2(P_T^*-P_T)}{T}\sum_{t=1}^{T}\gamma^{T-t}(P_t^*-P_t^o). \quad (19)$$

The fact $E[(P_T^*-P_T)(P_t-P_t^o)]=0$ in the population assures us that $E(S_{1|T})=E(S_1)$ which also equals $E(P_t-P_t^o)^2$, as demonstrated by MRS. From Equations (19) and (15), we see that population

$$E(S_{2|T}) = E(S_2) - \frac{1}{T}\frac{\gamma^{2T}}{1-\gamma^2}\Psi_0$$

$$= \Psi_0\left[1 - \frac{1}{T}\frac{\gamma^{2T}}{1-\gamma^2}\right].$$

Not surprisingly, only the conditional distributions (for $P_T^*=P_T$) of MRS test statistics could possibly correspond to the distributions of the population test statistics. In general, calculated MRS test statistics $S_{1|T}$ and $S_{2|T}$ will have a complex relationship with population S_1 and S_2 which will be dependent upon γ and T–t. $S_{1|T}$ and $S_{2|T}$ are asymptotically equivalent to S_1 and S_2, but we have no practical means of assessing the finite sample reliability of these statistics. MRS did not address this question and, hence, while their empirical results seem to refute the null hypothesis, we cannot tell whether they significantly do so. There is a second problem which concerns the fact that the MRS statistics are functions of γ as well as T. Although MRS presented results calculated for different γ, a reasonable theory for estimating γ and the impact of possible sample variation in γ under the null hypothesis were not examined. In the next section we rely upon cointegration equilibrium theory to address both of these problems.

We cannot be assured that sample means of any of these statistics have the usually assumed positive expected values in finite samples. Why such assumptions are unwarranted has been extensively analyzed by Kleidon (1986a,b); we summarize his results here and discuss their implications for our own study. Basically, an ex-post rational price series will, by definition, be sampled from a distribution determined by the path of all past and future dividends. Actual stock prices, however, are determined only by expected future dividends. In finite samples, therefore, each time series will respectively have been sampled from a distribution which is by necessity conditioned upon a different information set. This is significant since the variance-bounds inequalities such as those given by LeRoy and Porter (1981), Shiller (1981, 1987), and Mankiw, Romer, and Shapiro (1985) all require that dividends, prices, ex-post rational prices be sampled from distributions conditioned upon the same information set. What Kleidon has shown, with a particularly simple theoretical model, is that in certain circumstances the sample variance of ex–post rational prices will be less than that of actual prices by construction as a function of the predictability of dividends, the discount rate, and sample size. The finite sample simulations of Kleidon's model show that there can be substantial smoothing of ex-post rational prices relative to actual stock prices even in samples of size 1000, leading to mistaken rejection of the present-value relation in 80% of his simulations. Extending Kleidon's insights to our research, we can make the following observations. In finite samples, $E(S_{1|T})$ and $E(S_{2|T})$ will not necessarily be positive. While these statistics are positive in expected value in population, in a finite sample $P^*_{t|T}$ may be sufficiently smooth relative to P_t so that the relative sample variances of $P^*_{t|T}-P^o_t$ and $P^*_{t|T}-P_t$ will result in $S_{1|T}$ and $S_{2|T}$ with negative expected values. In Section 5 we propose a means of simulating the sampling distributions of test statistics by which we can assess the extent of this problem.

4. Alternative Statistics and their Asymptotic Standard Errors

Consider the spread variables $x_t(j) = P^*_{t|t+j} - P^o_t$, $y_t(j) = P^*_{t|t+j} - P_t$, and $z_t = P_t - P^o_t$. These are very similar to the variables that MRS used to construct $S_{1|T}$ and $S_{2|T}$, except that the ex–post rational price approximations are now based upon a constant distance between t and the terminal date t+j. We might call these 'rolling' ex–post prices, and note that, by inspection of Equations (10) and (11) $P^*_{t|t+j} - P_t$ and $P^*_{t|t+j} - P^o_t$ are not functions of t and represent ergodic time series as long as $P^*_t - P^o_t$ and $P^*_t - P_t$ are ergodic. Let 'overbar' denote a sample mean such as $\overline{y^2_t(j)} = \frac{1}{T-j} \sum_{t=1}^{T-j} (P^*_{t|t+j} - P_t)^2$ and let T now denote the length of the price and dividend series. Some test statistic alternatives to the MRS statistics can be expressed as

$$S^a_1(j) = \overline{x^2_t(j)} - \overline{y^2_t(j)}, \tag{20}$$

and

$$S^a_2(j) = \overline{x^2_t(j)} - \overline{z^2_t(j)}\,. \tag{21}$$

j denotes the fixed distance between the t+j and t in the rolling ex–post price approximations. The distributions of $S^a_1(j)$ and $S^a_2(j)$ are also related to the population statistics' distributions and the cointegration model parameters. $E(S^a_1(j)) = E(S_1)$ which equals $E(P_t - P^o_t)^2 > 0$ and $E(S^a_2(j)) = E(P^*_{t|t+j} - P_t)^2$ which, in turn, equals $\gamma^2 a_0' \Sigma a_0 \left[\frac{1-\gamma^{j+1}}{1-\gamma^2} \right] > 0$ for $\gamma < 1$.

Since $P^*_t - P^o_t$ and $P^*_t - P_t$ are, under MRS's assumptions, variance–covariance stationary and nondeterministic time series, $P^*_{t|t+j} - P^o_t$ and $P^*_{t|t+j} - P_t$ are also nondeterministic and stationary series. Indeed, $P^*_{t|t+j}-P^o_t$, $P^*_{t|t+j}-P_t$, and $P_t-P^o_t$ will have a joint, stationary moving average representation of the form

$$\begin{bmatrix} P^*_{t|t+j}-P^o_t \\ P^*_{t|t+j}-P_t \\ P_t-P^o_t \end{bmatrix} \equiv C(B)\times\epsilon_t ,$$

where C(B) is a 3×n matrix of polynomials in B and the forward shift operator, F.[2] In these circumstances Singleton (1980) (using arguments advanced by Anderson (1971)) showed that variables such as $\overline{x^2_t(j)}$, $\overline{y^2_t(j)}$, and $\overline{z^2_t(j)}$ (which equals $\frac{1}{T-j}\sum_{t=1}^{T-j}(P_t-P^o_t)^2$) are all asymptotically multivariate normal and are unbiased estimators of $E(P^*_{t|t+j}-P^o_t)^2$, $E(P^*_{t|t+j}-P_t)^2$, and $E(P^*_t-P^o_t)^2$ respectively. More important, he further showed that the variance–covariance matrix for these estimates is expressed as,

$$\operatorname{var}\begin{bmatrix} \overline{x^2_t(j)} \\ \overline{y^2_t(j)} \\ \overline{z^2_t(j)} \end{bmatrix} = \frac{4\Pi}{T-j}\begin{bmatrix} \Upsilon_{x(j),x(j)} & \Upsilon_{x(j),y(j)} & \Upsilon_{x(j),z} \\ \Upsilon_{y(j),x(j)} & \Upsilon_{y(j),y(j)} & \Upsilon_{y(j),z} \\ \Upsilon_{z,x(j)} & \Upsilon_{z,y(j)} & \Upsilon_{z,z} \end{bmatrix}, \qquad (22)$$

where $\Upsilon_{x(j),x(j)}$, for example, is the cumulated squared spectral density of $x_t(j)$ over all frequencies and $\Upsilon_{x(j),y(j)}$ is the cumulated squared cospectrum plus the cumulated squared quadrature spectrum of $x_t(j)$ and $y_t(j)$ over all frequencies. All these results imply that the asymptotic standard errors of $S^a_1(j)$ and $S^a_2(j)$ are readily calculable using Equation (22) and sample spectral estimates for $P^*_{t|t+j}-P^o_t$, $P^*_{t|t+j}-P_t$, and $P_t-P^o_t$.

---

[2]In the next section a fuller description and justification of C(B) is given in light of the cointegration restrictions implied by the present-value relation. n stands for the number of leading indicators for dividends.

5. A Cointegration Model of Dividends and Prices

To gain some sense as to the repeated sampling behavior of our alternative statistics and to assess the small sample reliability of the asymptotic standard errors, we require a model which is consistent with the null hypothesis and the stochastic character of prices and dividends as originally assumed by MRS. A model has been conveniently provided by Campbell and Shiller (1987) and is a cointegration, or error-correction, model of the type described by Engle and Granger (1987). It was demonstrated that the present–value relation will imply that prices and dividends are cointegrated of order 1,1 or, as it is usually denoted, C(1,1), when prices and dividends themselves require differencing to achieve stationarity. Since the constant discount rate applied to the present–value relation can be consistently estimated by several means and then be incorporated into the error–correction form of the model, we not only have a theoretically justified means of obtaining estimates of the discount rate, but we also are provided with a measure of the sample variability of discount rate estimates which, in the data we use, might be considerable and thus greatly affect the reliability of test statistics.

Campbell and Shiller (1987) have shown that Equation (1) along with the assumption that both dividends and prices require differencing to render them stationary imply a cointegration model for dividends and prices. The error-correction form of the model amounts to a restricted VAR on $[\Delta D_{t-1,} SL_t]'$, where SL_t is equal to $P_t - \theta D_{t-1}$. θ is the coefficient of proportionality between dividends and prices so that SL_t is a stationary time series. ΔD_{t-1} appears in the vector instead of ΔD_t since the timing of dividends and prices in our data is not contemporaneous. Dividends are actually paid within the period t, and so we assume that the market, at the start of period t, knows only dividends as of period t–1. Campbell and Shiller show that SL_t is a leading indicator of ΔD_{t-1} and, therefore, a moving–average representation of their cointegration model forms a basis (like Equation (2) in LeRoy and Porter (1981)) for construction of excess-volatility statistics. We may parenthetically note that Campbell and Shiller's cointegration model has distinct advantages as a simulation model when compared to the autoregressive model for dividends and prices employed by Kleidon (1986a,b). There is, first, the obvious advantage in that it is an empirical model. It also flexibly models the joint dynamics of dividends and prices while simultaneously making them obey the cointegration constraint implied by the present-value relation. It is a more general model in that expected dividends are conditioned by past prices as well as past dividends whereas in the Kleidon model expected dividends are, by construction, conditioned on past dividends alone. Most important for our purposes, however, is that it allows us to simulate the impact on inference of uncertainty about the appropriate value of the discount rate.

Now, let us say the moving-average representation of our cointegration model is

$$\begin{bmatrix} \Delta D_{t-1} \\ SL_t \end{bmatrix} = D(B)\times\epsilon_t\ , \tag{23}$$

where D(B) is a matrix of polynomials in the backshift operator B. The question of interest to us is whether the system put forward in the text,

$$\begin{bmatrix} x_t(j) \\ y_t(j) \\ z_t \end{bmatrix} = C(B)\times\epsilon_t \tag{24}$$

describes a system of stationary variables and is linked to this cointegration model. It is rather easy to show that C(B) is the result of applying a stationary filter to D(B). First, z_t is stationary since it is simply the spread variable, SL_t, itself; $P_t - P_t^o$ equals $P_t - \frac{\gamma}{1-\gamma} D_{t-1} = P_t - \theta D_{t-1} = SL_t$. Secondly, $y_t(j)$ must also be a stationary variable since it is nothing but a finite sum of j forecast errors for dividends. Thirdly, $x_t(j)$ must be a stationary variable because it is simply a linear combination of $y_t(j)$ and z_t.

The precise relation between C(B) and D(B) is a bit more complex to express. Define

$$D(B) = \begin{bmatrix} \eta_0' + \eta_1' B + \eta_2' B^2 + \cdots \\ \lambda_0' + \lambda_1' B + \lambda_2' B^2 + \cdots \end{bmatrix}, \tag{25}$$

where η_i and λ_i are the appropriate 2x1 vectors of moving average coefficients. Let us define a 'push' operator (call it P, to distinguish it from the forward shift operator, F) which operates on i of η_i and λ_i so that $P\eta_i = \eta_{i+1}$. It can be shown that C(B) equals A(B) D(B) where

$$A(B) = \begin{bmatrix} \frac{\gamma}{1-\gamma} \frac{1\text{-}PB}{(1-\gamma P)(1-\gamma F)} & -1 \\ \frac{\gamma}{1-\gamma} \frac{1\text{-}PB}{(1-\gamma P)(1-\gamma F)} & 0 \\ 0 & 1 \end{bmatrix}. \tag{26}$$

Since the system $C(B)\times\epsilon_t$ describes a stationary process, the spectral technique embodied in Equation (12) for the estimating the asymptotic variances of $\overline{x_t^2(j)}$, $\overline{y_t^2(j)}$, and $\overline{z_t^2(j)}$ is therefore appropriate.

The first step in estimating the model is to obtain a cointegration vector. We have employed three means to obtain an estimate of the cointegration vector,

$[-\theta, 1]'$.[3] θ is interpreted as the coefficient of proportionality between dividends and prices so that a spread variable, such as $P_t-\theta D_t$, is a stationary time series. Conditional upon a cointegration vector estimated by one of the three methods, we estimated a restricted VAR on $[\Delta D_{t-1}, SL_t]'$, where SL_t is the spread variable, $P_t-\theta D_{t-1}$. This model is repeatedly simulated to obtain prices, dividends and ex–post rational price time series.

The nonparametric bootstrap method is used to simulate the cointegration model of dividends and prices. The nonparametric bootstrap depends upon the repeated sampling of estimated residuals with replacement and these estimated residuals are then used to simulate the restricted VAR. The simulations will also provide an empirical demonstration of the wrong–variance measure problem and we shall see that, indeed, the expected values of the MRS statistics and our alternative statistics are not always positive in finite samples.

Table 1 presents sample estimates and bootstrapped values for the factor of proportionality, θ, and MRS statistics. The most remarkable results from this table are the uniformly negative simulated values for $S_{1|T}$ which closely correspond to the negative sample values found by MRS themselves. So it is clear that the finite sample reliability of estimating the positive expected <u>population</u> values for $S_{1|T}$ is truly quite limited in the ways anticipated by Kleidon; in the cointegration model we have a model which is simultaneously consistent with the present-value relation, but which persistently gives up negative simulated $S_{1|T}$'s in finite samples and apparently in even quite large samples. We note that the bootstrapped standard deviations are also quite large so that it appears that our simulated values for $S_{1|T}$ and $S_{2|T}$ and their standard

---

[3] Refer to Table 1B in Campbell and Shiller (1987). These three methods are respectively i) the cointegration regression, ii) the error-correction regression, and iii) the calculation of the sample mean return. Simulations based upon the third method were usually unstable and we do not report results based upon it and report results instead based upon the first two methods only.

Table 1. Bootstrapped Cointegration Vectors and MRS Statistics

	Cointegration Vector Determination			
	Method 1		Method 2	
θ and Discount Rates	θ	r	θ	r
Sample (N=116)	30.5	3.3%	34.5	2.9%
Bootstrap				
(N=116)	29.5	3.4%	57.5	1.7%
	(3.4)	(.4%)	(89.6)	(3.0%)
(N=600)	30.3	3.3%	35.7	2.8%
	(0.5)	(.1%)	(1.4)	(.1%)
(N=1200)	30.4	3.3%	35.0	2.9%
	(0.2)	(.02%)	(0.6)	(.05%)

	Cointegration Vector Determination			
	Method 1		Method 2	
MRS Statistics	$S_{1\|T}$	$S_{2\|T}$	$S_{1\|T}$	$S_{2\|T}$
Sample (N=116)	−460.5	−0.7	−669.5	−103.9
Bootstrap				
(N=116)	−188.2	630.5	−484.0	452.1
	(479.1)	(803.1)	(606.5)	(682.3)
(N=600)	−377.4	866.9	−788.3	688.9
	(227.9)	(452.2)	(360.6)	(429.4)
(N=1200)	−378.8	875.0	−836.4	753.8
	(131.4)	(293.3)	(241.0)	(325.8)

NOTE: Values listed under 'Bootstrap' are the mean of 100 simulations. The standard deviation of the bootstrapped statistic appears in parentheses below. The sample terminal date is 1986. The terminal date for the construction of the simulated MRS statistics corresponds to the final observation in the sample. For example, T=1200 for bootstrap simulations of size 1200. N indicates the sample size or the number of simulated prices and dividends. Following Campbell and Shiller (1987), the simulating restricted VAR's were of length 2.

errors easily capture the sample values. The result suggests that MRS–like statistics might have very large standard errors and may not be accurate even in cases when they are constructed and interpreted correctly. We shall make some observations on this matter when we look at Table 2's results. We also see that the two methods of obtaining the cointegration vector have somewhat different finite sample behavior with Method 1 results converging more rapidly to stable estimates of θ as a function of sample size than do Method 2 results.

Now that we see that MRS statistics can have positive or negative expected values in finite samples depending upon whether we are speaking of $S_{1|T}$ or $S_{2|T}$ and depending upon sample size, we might expect that similar observations might be made of the alternative statistics developed in Section 4. Simulated standard deviations of MRS statistics seem to be quite large and perhaps all MRS–like statistics might not be very accurate in finite samples. The question of the finite sample reliability of these standard errors thus arises and we again use the bootstrap to answer it. In Table 2 we present bootstrapped alternative statistics, their estimated asymptotic standard errors, and their bootstrapped standard deviations. As in Table 1, we see that the simulated expected values of the test statistics are not always positive as they would be in the population. While simulated $S_2^a(j)$ are entirely positive, simulated $S_1^a(j)$ is positive or negative on average as a function of j and sample size. By calculating a large number of impulse response weights for the estimated cointegration model, we can approximate the quantity $a_0' \Sigma a_0$ and thereby calculate approximations to the population expected values for $S_1^a(j)$ and $S_2^a(j)$. These respective expected values are $E(P_t-P_t^o)^2$ and $\gamma^2 a_0' \Sigma a_0 \left[\frac{1-\gamma^{j+1}}{1-\gamma^2} \right]$. Since we get different estimates of γ, a_0', and Σ with each of the different methods for obtaining the cointegration vector, we present their respective values for each method. Population $E(P_t-P_t^o)^2$ based upon model parameters under Method 1 and Method 2 are respectively, 135.2 and 122.5. Population $E(S_2^a(j))$ for

Table 2. Bootstrapped Alternative Statistics

	Sample (N=116)				Bootstrap (N=116)			
	Method 1		Method 2		Method 1		Method 2	
Leads (j)	$S_1^a(j)$	$S_2^a(j)$	$S_1^a(j)$	$S_2^a(j)$	$S_1^a(j)$	$S_2^a(j)$	$S_1^a(j)$	$S_2^a(j)$
1	202.5	5.0	381.2	-6.2	260.4	25.1	391.6	7.7
	(25.2)	(10.5)	(27.7)	(11.7)	(39.8)	(14.1)	(31.6)	(13.3)
					[141.1]	[25.0]	[159.4]	[24.7]
2	154.4	4.0	320.1	-16.6	247.6	53.2	363.5	20.3
	(29.2)	(20.6)	(32.6)	(22.9)	(46.8)	(28.4)	(37.9)	(26.5)
					[150.5]	[49.4]	[168.6]	[49.1]
5	74.7	33.4	208.3	-3.5	201.8	122.0	271.9	46.8
	(38.4)	(50.4)	(49.7)	(57.2)	(66.5)	(71.2)	(56.1)	(66.4)
					[182.7]	[118.5]	[200.1]	[109.4]
10	-69.6	110.8	14.8	66.7	131.3	232.9	127.9	95.2
	(52.9)	(85.0)	(51.2)	(99.8)	(88.6)	(128.7)	(76.2)	(120.6)
					[245.3]	[235.8]	[259.6]	[194.9]
50	-337.0	-12.1	-532.9	-112.7	-212.0	685.8	-571.5	410.8
	(24.4)	(25.0)	(32.7)	(33.9)	(94.2)	(162.1)	(83.7)	(147.2)
					[524.8]	[1062.2]	[650.5]	[808.4]
90	-287.1	106.7	-496.8	123.0	-318.3	683.3	-693.1	594.0
	(5.0)	(4.4)	(6.4)	(5.5)	(55.5)	(67.1)	(59.5)	(77.7)
					[678.6]	[1122.8]	[895.8]	[1306.9]

(contd.)

Table 2. Bootstrapped Alternative Statistics (contd.)

	Bootstrap (N=600)				Bootstrap (N=1200)			
	Method 1		Method 2		Method 1		Method 2	
Leads (j)	$S_1^a(j)$	$S_2^a(j)$	$S_1^a(j)$	$S_2^a(j)$	$S_1^a(j)$	$S_2^a(j)$	$S_1^a(j)$	$S_2^a(j)$
1	233.8	23.9	409.8	8.4	235.0	24.4	411.2	7.9
	(22.4)	(6.6)	(19.5)	(6.4)	(16.7)	(4.7)	(14.8)	(4.7)
	[63.2]	[12.0]	[66.0]	[11.8]	[48.5]	[7.5]	[44.5]	[7.6]
2	220.6	50.4	381.8	22.5	222.1	51.3	382.5	21.4
	(26.3)	(13.4)	(23.2)	(13.1)	(19.6)	(9.7)	(17.5)	(9.5)
	[68.7]	[23.6]	[73.1]	[22.6]	[52.0]	[15.3]	[48.6]	[14.9]
5	169.9	114.5	292.7	51.3	173.3	116.9	291.2	49.9
	(37.3)	(35.4)	(33.9)	(34.7)	(27.8)	(25.8)	(25.6)	(26.4)
	[84.9]	[53.7]	[95.5]	[49.8]	[61.4]	[31.9]	[61.0]	[32.8]
10	86.4	220.3	149.2	106.9	92.1	222.6	144.2	107.5
	(51.1)	(72.0)	(47.6)	(71.6)	(38.4)	(53.5)	(36.2)	(53.4)
	[107.1]	[94.7]	[135.2]	[87.0]	[72.7]	[53.7]	[86.4]	[60.1]
50	-284.8	304.7	-523.4	504.1	-261.7	700.2	-553.0	515.4
	(77.6)	(178.4)	(76.4)	(197.7)	(60.9)	(150.3)	(59.6)	(162.0)
	[197.5]	[328.1]	[317.9]	[298.6]	[114.7]	[204.1]	[195.0]	[216.0]
90	-388.0	833.6	-736.7	667.6	-358.9	841.2	-780.2	692.7
	(78.2)	(179.6)	(78.4)	(205.3)	(62.6)	(159.1)	(61.8)	(172.7)
	[231.3]	[448.7]	[377.5]	[422.4]	[125.2]	[306.7]	[230.5]	[306.8]

NOTE: The statistics in the columns labelled 'Bootstrap' are the means of the simulated statistics over 100 bootstrap replications. The figures in the parentheses below each statistic are the asymptotic standard errors. The figures in the brackets are the standard deviations of the simulated statistics.

Method 1 and for j = 1, 2, 5, 10, 50, and 90 respectively are 46.6, 90.3, 205.7, 354.7, 716.4, and 740.1 and for Method 2 the same values are 46.4, 90.3, 207.8, 364.1, 788.6, and 825.2. We further note that the asymptotic standard errors are in most cases too small relative to the 'actual' simulated standard deviations of the test statistics, although there appears to be a substantial convergence in these two means of obtaining standard errors as sample size grows.[4] It is nevertheless clear that in samples of sizes we would realistically be expected to encounter, the asymptotic standard errors tend to be too small.

The bootstrap method of obtaining standard errors is the apparently viable alternative to calculating the asymptotic standard errors in small samples. Although we need to have a theoretically justified estimation model (such as the cointegration model here) to perform the bootstrap, it is no more burdensome in a programming sense to use the bootstrap than it is to calculate standard errors using spectral techniques. The bootstrapped test statistics and their standard deviations (for N=116) also easily capture most of the sample estimates of the test statistics, which suggests that our sample test statistics, be they positive or negative, are well explained by a cointegration model of dividends and prices in which the present-value relation is imposed as a constraint.

We have seen that MRS statistics are constructed from ex-post rational price approximations which are in themselves heteroskedastic as a function of time. This would make the statistics difficult enough to use if there were not also the fact that we have no firm expectation for what the sign of these statistics should have except in the population as a whole. We have surmounted these problems in several steps. First we

---

[4]This is consistent with the results in Table 1 in which the simulated standard errors around the discount rate are very small in large samples, but in small samples are quite large. The asymptotic standard errors around $S_1^a(j)$ and $S_2^a(j)$ are conditional upon fixed and known discount rates and so will probably understate the true standard errors in small samples.

constructed rolling price approximations which would result in statistics for which standard errors could be easily calculated. We then presented a simulation model for the present–value relation with which we could study two phenomena: i) the finite sample reliability of our new methods for calculating volatility statistic standard errors, and ii) the finite sample behavior of the average test statistic itself. In Tables 1 and 2 we found that simulated volatility test statistics ($S_{1|T}$ and $S_1^a(j)$ in particular) actually have negative expected values in finite samples contrary to the analysis that has appeared in the previous literature. Although our new price approximations do not give us statistics whose asymptotic standard errors can be relied upon in finite samples, we have seen that, by the bootstrap standard errors instead, the present-value relation is easily satisfied by sample volatility statistics. A bootstrap simulation model, perhaps of the cointegration type, is possibly the method of choice for producing standard errors and for checking the finite sample behavior of statistics that cannot be understood via analytical means.

5. Conclusions

In this paper we investigated the consequences of ex-post rational price approximations for the empirical reliability of the present-value relation. Since researchers who have used these approximations have almost uniformly rejected that relation and investigators who have eschewed their use, such as LeRoy and Porter (1981), have found mixed evidence for and against the present-value relation, it occurred to us that the approximations themselves might be unduly increasing the probability of rejection of an empirically valid hypothesis.

We have shown that the commonly used price approximations cannot be the stationary time series they are often presumed to be by investigators. In the case of some proposed volatility statistics, we saw that the use of the usual ex-post price approximations would complicate the construction of measures for their accuracy. This fact was not appreciated perhaps because no attempt to construct standard errors and the like had been made. We proposed some alternative ex-post rational price approximations which would result in volatility statistics for which standard errors could be easily constructed. In simulations it appeared that the asymptotic standard errors (which were conditioned upon perfect certainty concerning the discount rate) were a bit too small to be useful even in samples of fairly large size. The same simulations also revealed that the expected values of the volatility statistics were not uniformly positive as had been previously believed, but could be positive or negative as a function of sample size and the ex-post price approximations employed. Volatility statistics were sampled from distributions that have a very different relation to the null hypothesis than that possessed by their population distributions. A bootstrap model was used to simulate the expected value and the standards errors of our test statistics. Since our sample volatility statistics look very much like the bootstrapped statistics produced by a present-value model, we conclude that previous rejections of the hypothesis was the result of misinterpreting the sample statistics and partly the result of reliance upon inadequate ex-post rational price approximations. The previous literature has understated the empirical reliability of the present-value relation, not because it is revealed truth, but because the data approximations employed and misinterpreted test statistics have led to false and overly confident rejections of the relation.

ACKNOWLEDGMENTS

I would like to thank those persons whose comments on a earlier version of the paper helped improve it to its present form, although they cannot be held responsible for any of its remaining shortcomings. Participants at the European Finance Association meetings, Western Finance Association meetings, the Department of Finance at Penn State University, and the Board of Governors of the Federal Reserve System were all helpful. Helpful comments have also been personally conveyed by Stephen LeRoy, David Peel and Robert Shiller. Robert Shiller kindly provided the revised data which were employed by Campbell and Shiller (1987).

REFERENCES

Anderson, T.W., 1971, The Statistical analysis of time series, (John Wiley & Sons, New York).

Campbell, J.Y. and Shiller, R.J., 1987, Cointegration and tests of present value models, Journal of Political Economy 95, 1062–1088.

Engle, R.F. and Granger, C.W.J., 1987, Co-integration and error correction: representation, estimation and testing, Econometrica 55, 251-276.

Kleidon, A.W., 1986a, Bias in small sample tests of stock price rationality, Journal of Business 59, 237–261.

____________, 1986b, Variance bounds tests and stock price valuation models, Journal of Political Economy 94, 953–1001.

LeRoy, S.F. and Porter, R.D., 1981, The Present-Value relation: tests based on implied variance bounds, Econometrica 49, 555–574.

Mankiw, N.G., Romer, D., and Shapiro, M.D., 1985, An Unbiased reexamination of stock market volatility, Journal of Finance 40, 677–87.

Shiller, R.J., 1981, Do stock prices move too much to be justified by subsequent changes in dividends? American Economic Review 71, 421–436.

____________, 1987, The Volatility of stock market prices, Science 235, 3337.

Singleton, K.J., 1980, Expectations models of the term structure and implied variance bounds, Journal of Political Economy 88, 1159–76.

Comments on Gary Shea "Ex-Post Rational Price Approximations and the Empirical Reliability of the Present Value Relation

by Robert J. Shiller

The finite sample properties of the variance bounds tests are crucial for the validity of test results. It is important to know whether variance irregularities can often be violated just by chance even if markets are efficient. Others have explored using Monte Carlo methods the finite sample properties of such tests before: Marjorie Flavin, Allan Kleidon, Joe Mattey and Richard Meese, and Louis Scott, among others. Gary Shea has done his Monte Carlo work in a way that would appear to be more satisfactory than those who came before him. Shea has used an estimated cointegrated vector autoregressive model for his simulations, and he uses bootstrap methods that eliminate the need to assume that error terms are drawn from the normal distribution.

Shea has chosen to emphasize here the volatility tests of N. Gregory Markiw, David Romer and Matthew Shapiro (MRS). It should first be pointed out that these tests, while they are variance inequality tests, are not really good tests for the kind of excess volatility I and Stephen LeRoy and Richard Porter claimed to find with U.S. data. The S_1 statistic tests whether P^o (dividend divided by a discount factor) is a better forecast of P^* (ex-post rational price) than is price itself. Since dividends are about as volatile as prices (see figure 1 in my paper in this volume) it is not at all clear that excess volatility of stock prices per se should imply that dividends are a better forecast than prices. The other test statistic S_2 might be a test of excess volatility if P^o were a smooth time series, but since P^o is a scaled dividend here its not at all clear that excess volatility per se implies that the test statistic S_2 should be negative. The test statistics S_1 and S_2 are nonetheless useful as tests of the simple efficient markets hypothesis against a different alternative from the one I have had in mind.

Shea makes a "speculation" that expected values of S_1 and S_2 may be negative under certain circumstances even if the model is true. His bootstrap methods appear to support this speculation for S_1. Since D and P move roughly proportionally in the data, I would expect them to do so in the simulations too. Perhaps if D simulates to be a little smoother than P,

NATO ASI Series, Vol. F54
A Reappraisal of the Efficiency of Financial Markets
Edited by Rui M. C. Guimaraes et al.

then D may be a better forecast of P^* than is P in small samples, due to considerations emphasized earlier by Kleidon.

The statistic S_2 is (Table 3) still positive in expected value in his simulations, but its standard error is so large that the test results reported by Mankiw, Romer and Shapiro would not be significant.

I am a little surprised that S_2 has such a large standard error in his simulation, and would like to check his simulations before I conclude that it's right. I am also surprised at the standard deviations of the slope coefficients in a regression of SL^* on SL with 116 observations, the number of observations John Campbell and I used in our paper. It should be pointed out, however, that regressions of SL^* on SL were not the centerpiece of that paper.

The alternative statistics Shea proposes, $S_1^a(j)$ and $S_2^a(j)$ are apparently not much better for j moderately large than the MRS statistics in terms of average expected value. S_1 still produces negative expected $S_1^a(j)$ for moderate j. I think his alternative statistics should not be used for very low or very high j. For j very small, the test statistics don't get at the kind of alternative hypothesis we probably want to look at. For j very large, his test method throws away too much data to be useful.

THE ITALIAN STOCK MARKET: EFFICIENCY AND PRICE FORMATION

Giovanni Verga
Universita' degli Studi di Parma
via Kennedy
Parma, Italy

Keywords / Abstract: stock price formation / dividends / Italian stock market / long term equilibrium / short term fluctuations / extrapolators / co-integration / error correction representation / efficiency / risk

Using annual, quarterly and monthly data we investigate price formation in Italian stock market. We find that there is a strong long term connection between prices and dividends, however some short term abnormal fluctuations ("bubbles"), probably due to "naive" extrapolators, do exist. A model consistent with these short and long term market characteristics has been estimated by means of co-integration techniques. After reporting some tests on weak efficiency, a comparison between efficiency and our model is considered. It turns out that upward price movements are partially predictable, but they are connected to abnormal levels of risk

1. Introduction

Italian stock prices seem to fluctuate widely around a sort of long term equilibrium determined by dividends. Since this phenomenon is not sufficiently considered in the existing models of the Italian market, (see Barone and Cristini [1981], Mortara [1976], Vaciago and Verga [1987]), this paper tries to evaluate a new model consistent with its long and short term

NATO ASI Series, Vol. F54
A Reappraisal of the Efficiency of Financial Markets
Edited by Rui M. C. Guimaraes et al.

characteristics. In section 2 some characteristics of the Italian stock market prices that will suggest the model introduced in section 3 are presented. This model is estimated by using co-integration techniques. Since it appears that such fluctuations are mainly due to the behaviour of naive extrapolators entering the market after a sufficiently prolonged increase in prices, the resulting problem of efficiency is briefly considered in section 4. The result is that the risk implicit in the stock market is higher during the upward movement of the process, so that the risk-averse speculator requires a higher rate of return which prevents the market from reaching its equilibrium value immediately. In any case, it is very difficult to discover the exact turning points, and moreover the usual "trading rules" fail to give extra-profits.

2. Some characteristics of the Italian Stock Exchange

Before presenting our model of stock price determination and the econometric results, it may be useful to give some information about Italian stock market behaviour [1] Figures 1 and 2 show the log of nominal and real stock price and dividend indices respectively, along with the income deflator, for the period 1913-1987 (annual data) [2]. They show a strong

----

1 An analysis on dimension and other characteristics of Italian Stock Exchange can be found in IRS [1988].

2 All data are from Bank of Italy source, apart from price deflator (ISCO-ISTAT), and MIB stock price index (Comitato Agenti di Cambio). Annual and quarterly data are average values, monthly data are end of period values. The periods under consideration are 1914-1987 for annual data, 1960.1-1987.4 for quarterly data, 1975.01-1987.12 for monthly data. For computational reasons, however, some observations are lost in our estimation procedures. For what concerns annual data, the nominal rate of return is the long-term public bonds one, and

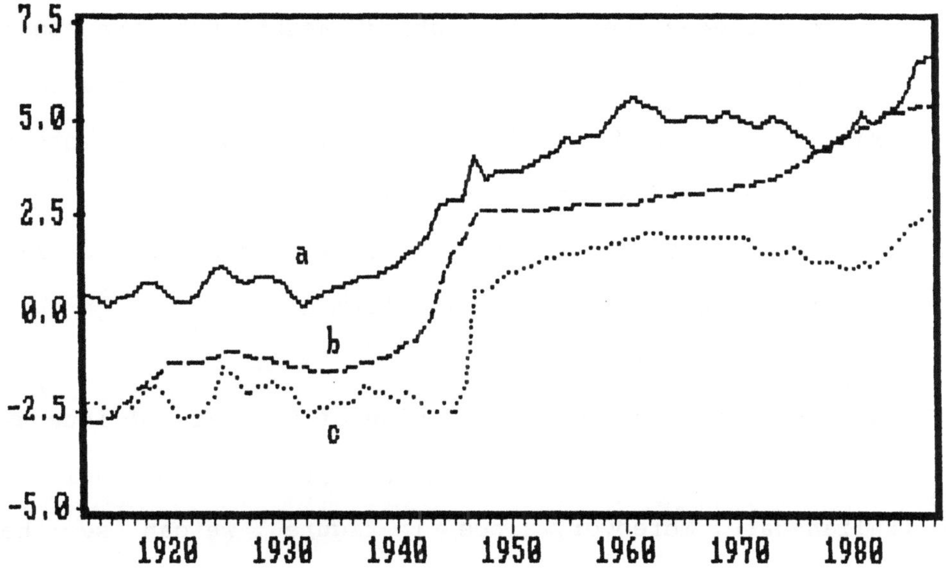

FIGURE 1. Logs of stock price (a) and dividend (c) indices, and income price deflator (b), (1913-1987, annual data)

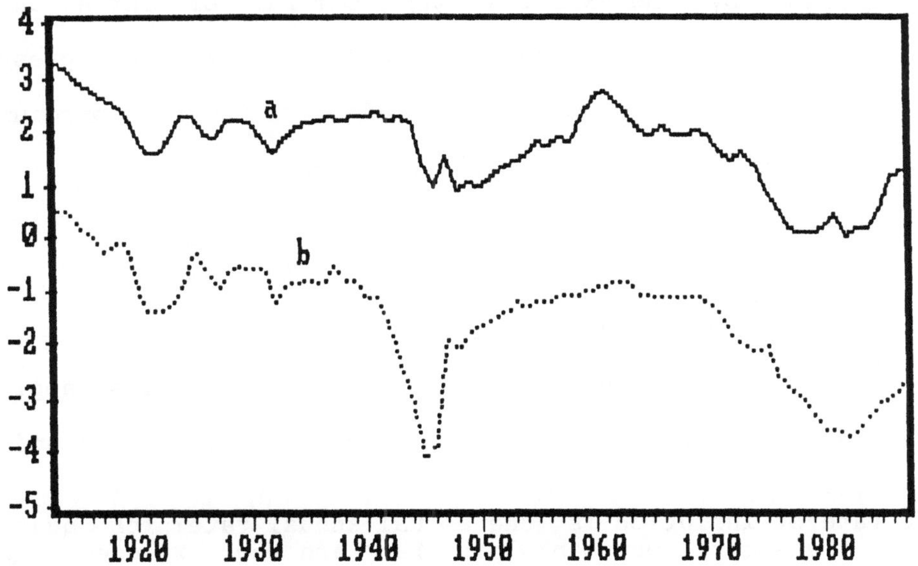

FIGURE 2. Logs of real stock price (a) and real dividend (b) indices (1913-1987, annual data)

correlation between the two variables, apart from the period 1941-47 characterized by a fall in profits during the Second World War, and by a particularly low level of real interest rates in the hyperinflation period which started in 1943.

It appears therefore that, at least as a first approximation, the usual equilibrium formula,

1) $A = D^e / (R + g^e + s)$

linking stock prices A, expected dividends D^e, rate of interest R, expected dividend growth g^e, and risk-premium s may hold in the Italian case. Moreover, since in figure 1 we can see there exists a strong connection between the nominal dividends index and the income deflator, while at the same time figure 2 shows only a small downward trend in real dividends, it is possible to identify the long term growth in nominal dividends as mainly determined by the expected long term rate of inflation p^e, (plus a small negative constant). We can therefore express g^e in (1) by p^e plus a constant to be added to the risk premium:

2) $A = D^e / (R - p^e + s + const) = D^e / (r^e + s')$

or, approximately,

2') $\log(A) = \log(D^e) + a + b\, r^e \quad , \quad (b < 0)$

(where r is the real rate of interest)

The considerations given for the annual data also apply to the quarterly data of the period 1960-1987 (figs. 3 and 4).

----

the rate of inflation is the actual annual rate; for quarterly data, the short term bank loan rate and the expected 6-months rate of inflation (processed by the Bank of Italy) have been applied; for monthly data, the treasury bills rate along with the actual 6-months ahead annual inflation rate have been used. This particular choice is due to the availability of data. Remember that in Italy long terms bonds have not been issued since 1978-79; moreover, the relevant interest rate at present is the treasury bills rate, but these assets were first issued only in 1976. The dividends index is based on the last officially announced values.

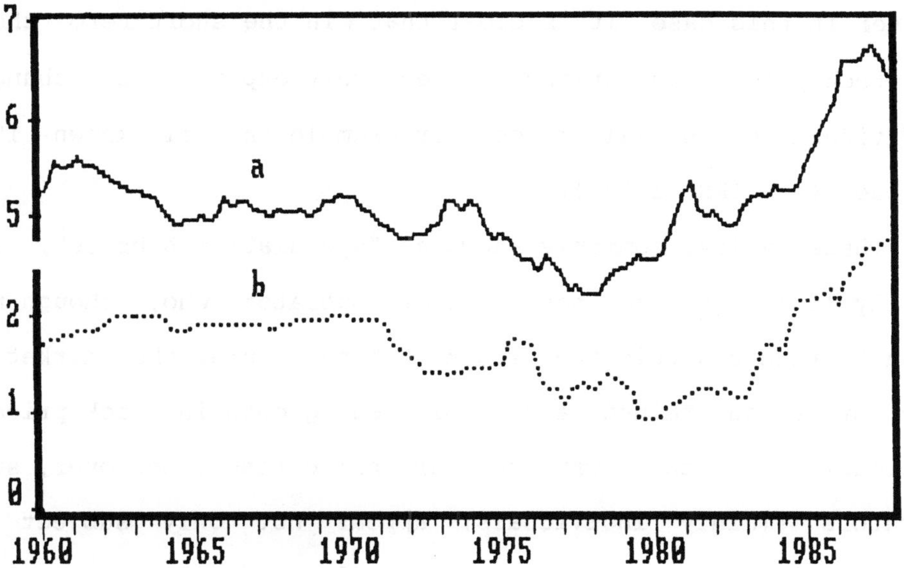

FIGURE 3. Logs of stock price (a) and dividend (b) indices (1960.1-1987.4, quarterly data)

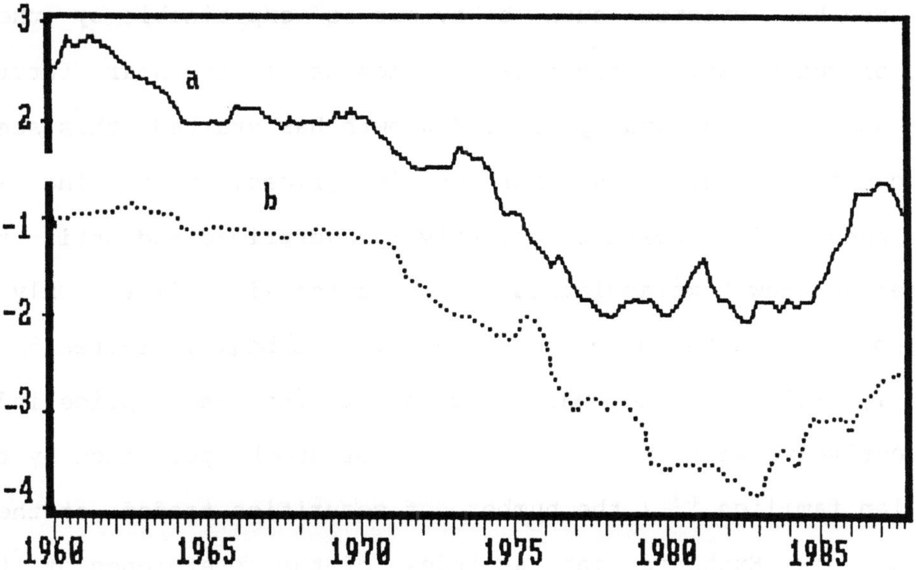

FIGURE 4. Logs of real stock price (a) and real dividend (b) indices (1960.1-1987.4, quarterly data)

However in this case it is clear that in the short term there are stock price fluctuations not entirely explained by changes in dividends or in real rates (for example the well-known 1981 episode) (see IRS [1988]).

These cycles, commonly known as "speculative bubbles", are usually linked to the behaviour of operators who, though not "usual" traders within the stock exchange, enter the market in case of a substained and prolonged growth in stock prices, determining in this way further price rises. Moreover, such operators (mainly individuals) appear not only subject to extrapolative expectations, but also display asymmetric behaviour in bullish and bearish periods. While entering the market relatively quickly in the first instance, they are slower in selling their securities and leaving the market after a price decrease has started: such behaviour is explainable by their hope of recuperating their capital losses in the near future. Once a significant and prolonged growth has started this seems to cause a continuous increase in prices; this increase continues until stocks are excessively overpriced and until the number of new "extrapolators" has reached its limit. Only at this point does the opposite price movement begin. Figures 5, 6 and 7, relating the past growth of the share price index respectively with the net number of stocks purchased by the Italian families [3] the number of securities traded at the Milan Stock Exchange, and an index of the preference of the public between stock and bond mutual funds [4] seem actually

----

[3] Obtained as the ratio of the value of stocks purchased by Italian families to the corresponding stock index. Since Italian mutual funds became operating only recently (end 1984), a series including also the number of stocks purchased by the funds has

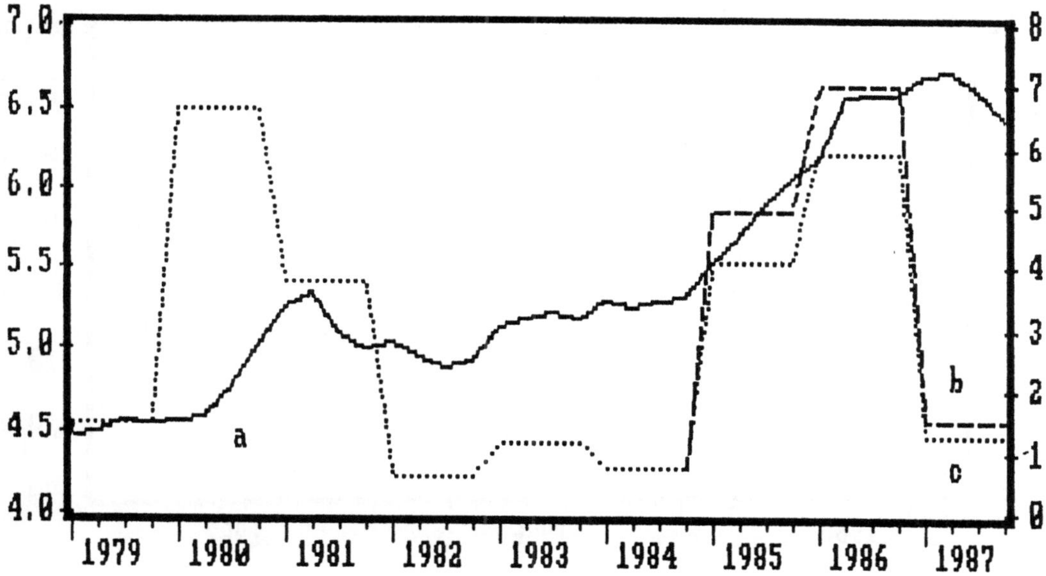

FIGURE 5. Log of stock price index (a), net number of stocks purchased by the Italian families (c) , and (b) = (a) + stocks purchased by mutual funds (1979.1 1987.4, quarterly and annual data)

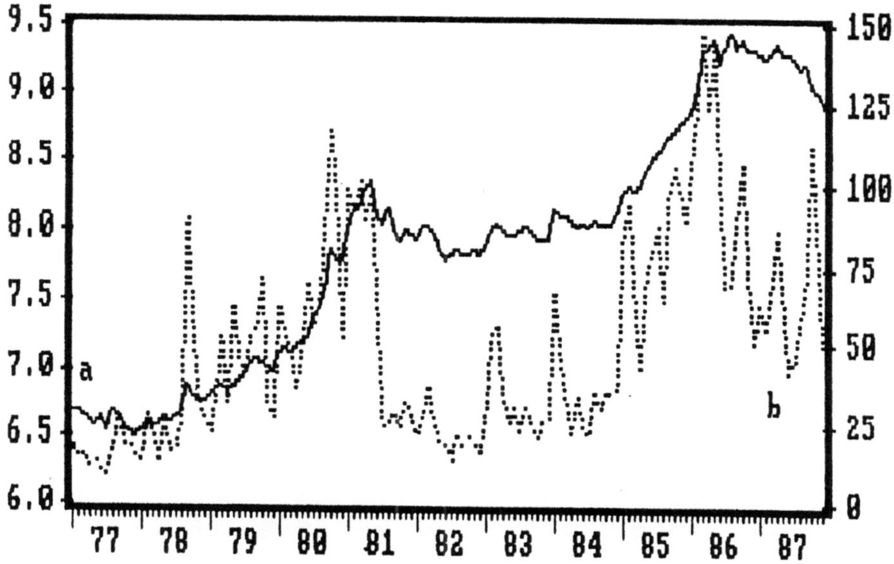

FIGURE 6. Log of stock price index (a), and mumber of securities traded at the Milan Stock Exchange (b) (1975.01 1987.12, monthly data)

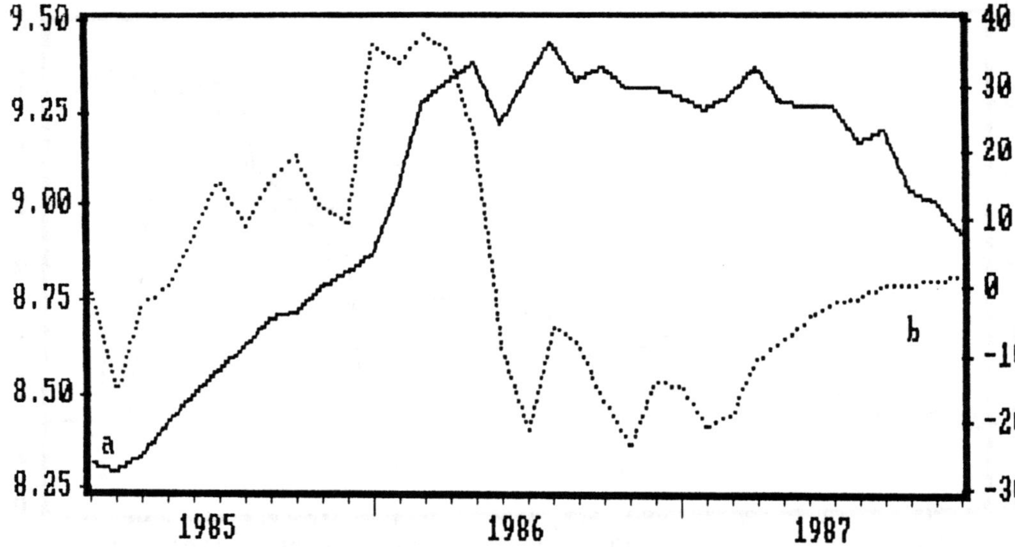

FIGURE 7. Log of stock price index (a), and index of the preference of the public between stock and bond mutual funds (b) (1985.02-1987.12, monthly data)

to confirm the hypothesis of such behaviour, at least in the case of some investors. It is also clear from figure 8 and 9 that price volatility (measured by the SE of the daily changes in the log of the stock price during each month), and the risk percived by the market (measured by the premium on the "dont" option contracts) [5] are higher than normal during such speculative market upward movements.

3. The model

In deciding which model best represents the Italian stock market, and in selecting the most appropriate econometric procedure, it is useful to consider the characteristics of the market itself seen in the previous paragraph. First of all, the model must be able to describe the short term fluctuations but at the same time in the long term it must be consistent with the equilibrium equation (1). On the other hand, the econometric technique must be able not only to take into acount all these problems, but also to deal with the variables under consideration, which at a first sight seem strongly autocorrelated. In particular, the logs of stock prices and dividends seem to follow a random walk. Since this might be a case of cointegration, our preference is for the two steps Granger-Engle estimation procedure (see Engle and Yoo [1987],

----

been elaborated.

[4] First differences in the ratio of net families' investment in stock and "balanced" mutual funds to net total families' investment in mutual funds.

[5] Ratio of the "dont" value to its corresponding stock price. The "dont" value is the price of the option carrying the claim to purchase after some days a given ammount of stocks, at a predetermined price. Its value is high when stock prices are volatile.

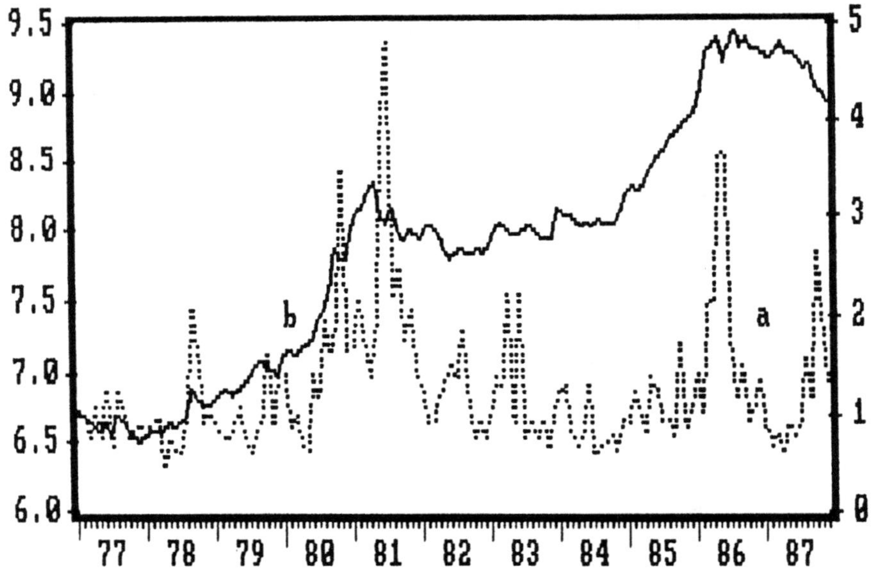

FIGURE 8. Log of stock price index (a), and stock price volatility (b) (1977.01 1987.12, monthly data)

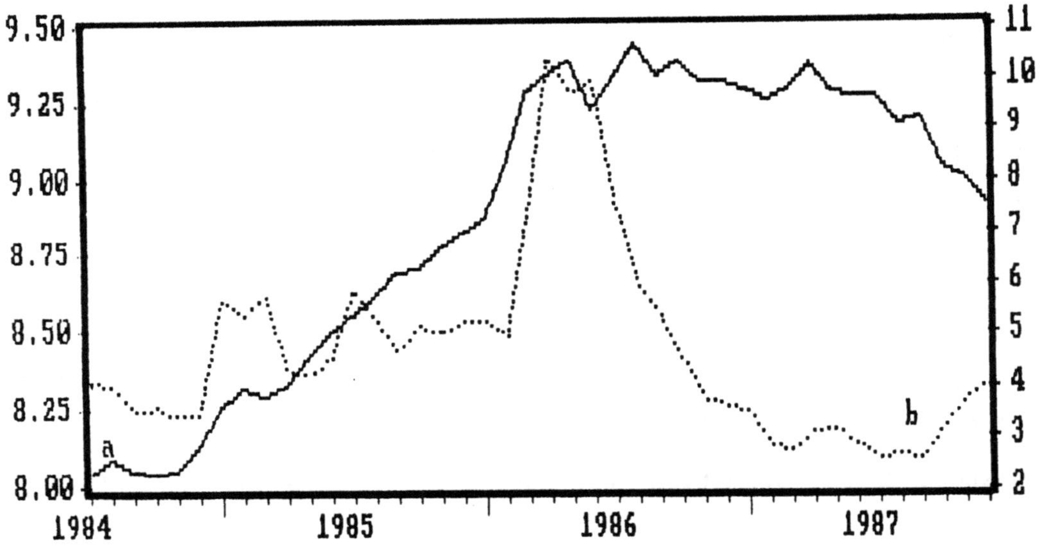

FIGURE 9. Log of stock price index (a), and premium on the "dont" option contracts (b) (1984.07-1987.12, monthly data)

Engle and Granger [1987], Granger and Engle [1985],) which leads to error correction representation.

In building our model, we start from the hypothesis that there are three main groups of operators: the fundamentalists, the "naive" extrapolators (or "unusual traders") and the risk-adverse speculators (see Shiller [1984]) .

Fundamentalists are supposed to estimate the intrinsic stock value $\log(A^e_{Ft})$ from some model of the type eq. (2'), and to sell securities when the actual price exceeds this value, causing by this way a potential price movement like:

3) $h_F[(\log(A^e_{Ft}) - \log(A_t)]$.

The second group of agents has extrapolative expectations, and behaves as described in section 2. Their actions generate a price variation of the type

4) $d \log(A_{t+1}) = \varphi(L)\, d \log(A_t)$,

where $\varphi(L)$ is asymmetric, in the sense that "naive" extrapolators enters the market massively after a prolonged positive price increase.

Risk-adverse speculators are able to predict price changes to some extent from other groups' behaviour, but they know that when a strong upward movement in prices occurs, risk is higher than usual. In such circumstances they require a higher expected rate of return on stocks r^e_S , and they purchase (or sell) securities up to the point the price level $\log(A_t)$ is such that

5) $r^e = \log A^e_{St} - \log A_t = d \log(A^e_{St}) = h_F [\log(A^e_{Ft}$
$- \log(\log A_t)] + \varphi(L)\, d \log(A_t)$

By supposing that A^e_{Ft} can be explained as a combination of lagged values of the explanatory variables in eq. 2', and that its changes depend on the innovations in the same variables, this model can be written in the error correction form:

6) $d \log (A_t) = \alpha Z_{t-1} + \beta_1 d \log(D) + \beta_2(L) d r,$

where Z are the residuals of the long term equilibrium formula (2') obtained by substituting the actual values of the variables for their expectations.

Eq. (6) is the reduced form model we have estimated, and our main results are presented in the following pages.

First of all we checked that the variables were of the same order of integration. The evidence on the presence of unit roots in all our data is given in tables 1, reporting the CDRDW (Durbin-Watson statistics), DF (Dickey-Fuller) and/or ADF (Augmented DF) tests for annual and quarterly data respectively, which show that the hypothesis of I(1) integrated variables are acceptable (for the tests used in this paper see Engle and Yoo [1987], Engle and Granger [1987]).

After that, the long term equations of the type eq. 2' (parameters of the cointegrated vector) have been estimated, and the residual Z(t) submitted to the AF or ADF tests for cointegration (see table 2). The main result is a one-to-one equilibrium connection between the log of nominal stock price and the log of nominal dividend. However, if the nominal dividend is split into the income deflator and the real dividend, the equilibrium elasticity between the stock price index and the deflator appears to be one, while the real dividend has an elasticity less than one, especially with annual data. The real rate of interest has a negative effect on the stock market. Since the coefficient of the income deflator is one, we re-estimated our function in real terms: the results are

	levels		first differences	
annual data	CRDW	DF	CRDW	DF
	(1914-1986)			
log(A)	.02	-.27	1.64	-7.00
log(D)	.04	-.82	1.68	-7.16
Log(P)	.01	-.57	.47	-3.12
log(A/P)	.12	-1.92	1.48	-6.32
log(D/P)	.13	-1.71	1.57	-6.79
r	.44	-2.92	1.29	-5.65

	levels			first differences	
quarterly data	CRDW	DF	ADF	CRDW	DF
	(1962.1-1987.3)				
log(A)	.04	.47	-1.54	1.25	-8.50
log(D)	.05	.31	-.50	1.37	-7.32
log(P)	.00	1.41	-.64	.68	-4.53
log(A/P)	.02	-1.89	-1.55	1.18	-6.48
log(D/P)	.01	-1.32	-1.29	1.31	-7.09
r	.14	-1.88	-2.53	1.38	-7.37

TABLE 1 TESTS FOR UNIT ROOTS
(See Engle and Granger [1987] pp.269-270, and Engle and Yoo [1987] pp.157-158)

dependent variable	independent variables				R^2	DW	DF	ADF
annual data	const	log(P)	log(D/P)	r/100				
		(1914-1986)						
log(A)	2.69 (34.47)	1.00 (43.11)	.70 (11.82)	-1.14 (-6.40)	.98	.69	-3.65	
log(A/P)	2.70 (41.41)	-	.70 (18.95)	-1.15 (-7.62)	.83	.70	-3.68°	
quarterly data								
		(1962.1-1986.4)						
log(A)	3.00 (19.54)	1.05 (15.87)	.83* (16.51)	-3.38 (-4.06)	.74	.35	-3.03	-3.63°
log(A/P)	3.10 (53.40)	-	.80* (29.85)	-3.06 (-4.31)	.93	.33	-2.90	-3.45°

TABLE 2 COINTEGRATION EQUATIONS

(* log(D/P) is taken at t+4 ; °co-integration is accepted at least at the 5 per cent level) similar, and the tests seem to favour the hypothesis that our variables constitute a cointegrated vector. It must be stressed, however, that the results are stronger when using annual data.[6]

The corresponding short term equations (final models) are shown in table 3, and were obtained in the second step of the Granger-Engle method. They were derived from the addition of the error correction representation to the equilibrium equations, and by dropping the non-significant parameters [7]. When using quarterly data, in order to capture the unfrequent traders' behaviour ("naive" extrapolators), a dummy variable POS2 (defined as the sum of the last two quarterly changes in the log of stock prices if both are positive, and zero otherwise) has been introduced among the regressors [8] The high level of Student's t associated with this variable shows that in periods of prolonged price increases there is actually a tendency in the market to reinforce upward movement in price.

----

6 An inspection to quarterly data reveals that the real expected rate of return has been constant since 1980, but the dividend price ratio seems to decrease. This might be a consequence of the less than one-to-one elasticity of stock prices to real dividends. A possible alternative explaination is that the public debt expansion has caused a sort of crowding-in phenomenon in favour of the stock market. However, inclusion of the public debt/income ratio (or the financial assets/income ratio), among the regressors does not improve the results.

7 Since this is an explanation model and not a forecasting one, also future "lags" in variables should be introduced in the r. h. s. of the equations. They represent the influence that expectations on future values have on present stock prices. Our results show that investors can predict some future variables, in particular dividends, at least to some extent.

8 This variables should be interpreted as the empirical counterpart of the condition "sufficiently prolonged growths in prices" (see also IRS [1988]. Also variables corresponding to continuous positive price increases on 3, 4, and 5 quarters were considered, however POS2 gave the best results.

annual data

(1914-1986)

$$d\,\log(A) = \underset{(1.10)}{.23} \; \underset{(-2.59)}{-.21}\, Z_{t-1} \; \underset{(-6.22)}{-.91}\, dr/100 \; \underset{(7.58)}{+.44}\, d\,\log(D/P) \; +$$

$$\underset{(2.62)}{+.18}\, d\,\log(D/P)_{t+1} \; \underset{(5.22)}{+.68}\, d\,\log(P)_{t+1} \; \underset{(2.11)}{+.16}\, d\,\log(A)_{t-1}$$

$R^2 = .63$, DW = 1.78

quarterly data

(1962.1 1986.4)

$$d\,\log(A) = \underset{(-1.5)}{-.02} \; \underset{(-4.35)}{-.19}\, Z_{t-1} \; \underset{(-2.47)}{-1.61}\, d\,r/100 \; \underset{(5.42)}{+.43}\, POS2$$

$R^2 = .27$, DW = 1.87

TABLE 3: FINAL EQUATIONS
(corresponding to table 2 second eqs.)

4. Market efficiency and our model

Among the various definitionsof efficiency applied to the stock market, two are particularly common in economic literature. The first is related to the possibility of obtaining extra-profits by the appropriate use of available information. The hypothesis of efficiency is that the market elaborates this information so rapidly that it is already incorporated in the prices and cannot therefore been used to "beat" the market (see for example Fama [1970]). The second consists in assessing whether the usual equivalence between the actual value of the dividend stream and the stock price is acceptable under a variance bound test (see Shiller [1981a and 1981b], Giannasca and Macchiati [1986]).

The studies on the Italian stock exchange refer mainly to the first definition of efficiency, and in particular to the so-called weak and semistrong cases [9] even though some analysis of strong efficiency does exist (see Cristini [1978], Hawawini [1984],). In particular, a recent paper has stressed that there is no evidence that mutual funds have "beaten" the market by using "private" information (see Bruni, Pototschnig and Zingales [1988]).

These analyses (see Biffignandi and Stefani [1981], Cristini [1978], Giannasca and Macchiati [1986], Hawawini [1984], Moorkerje [1987], Romei [1987], Vaciago and Verga [1987], Verga [1984], Zambruno [1984]) generally favour the acceptance of the hypotheses, and tables 4 and 5 present new evidence. The autocorrelogram coefficients of price changes are

----

9 The causality Granger's test is usually applied in semi-

	monthly data		daily data	
lags	ac	pc	ac	pc
1	.154	.154	.202	.202
1	-.032	-.057	-.048	-.093
3	.153	.171	.047	.080
4	.062	.007	.046	.015
5	.110	.123	-.016	-.021
6	.194	.145	-.004	.007
7	.132	.093	-.006	-.014
8	-.048	-.097	-.007	-.001
9	-.065	-.093	.032	.035
10	-.024	-.075	.048	.034
11	.069	.056	.005	-.007
12	.046	.000	-.003	.000

TABLE 4 AUTOCORRELATION AND PARTIAL AUTOCORRELATION COEFFICIENTSOF LOG CHANGES IN STOCK PRICE INDEX (period 1975-1987)
(SE of correlations: monthly = .083, daily = .017)

STRATEGY (initial sum = 1000)	BUY AND HOLD	ALEXANDER FILTERS 5%	10%	20%	25 MA.
N. of transactions	2	126	50	20	224
Days in the market (%)	100	55.0	59.9	59.4	53.3
Final capital (not considering transaction costs, dividens, and returnes gained when out the stock market)	7560	7695	10155	6448	13880
Minus transaction costs	7454	3175	7147	6603	2878
Plus interests gained when out the stock market (*)	7454 7454	5347 4424	11383 9610	8975 7561	4941 4060
plus dividends(*)	9679 8988	6018 4814	12648 10362	9986 8161	5586 4432
Actual total annual yield (*)	19.1 18.4	14.8 12.4	21.5 19.7	19.4 17.5	14.1 12.1

TABLE 5: COMPARISON BETWEEN BUY AND HOLD AND TRADING RULES (period: 1975-1987, return when out the market = bank deposit rate of return; (*) data are net of taxes; first number=families, second number=other investors; data are only approximated)

very small although some are significant, suggesting that it is very difficult to forecast future prices by using a simple linear combination of past changes. Also the usual trading rules (Alexander's filters and moving average rules [10] fail to beat the buy-and-hold strategy once transaction costs are considered (see also Fama [1966 and 1970]).

All this seems to be in contrast with our statements about the "speculative bubbles", which to some degree are predictable in advance, and contradicts the ability of our model to explain the stock index changes.

As we observed previously, however, it is reasonable to suppose that during such 'bubbles' the stock market risk increases so that the risk-adverse speculator does not bring the market to its "normal" equilibrium level because he requires a high risk premium and therefore a high return.

In order to demonstrate this, we considered the end of the month stock market data from 1976 to 1987 [11]. After constructing the variable POS2 for every month, we compared it to the index growth for the next three months. It appears that a positive correlation exists but at the same time the price variability and the premium on the "dont" option contracts are particularly high, supporting the conclusion that the market in such periods requires a higher risk premium than usual (table 6). This can also explain the failure of trading rules to give

----

strong efficiency studies for Italian stock market.

10 In Italy the so-called 25 days moving average rule is usually strongly recommended. It states that one should be in the market when the price is over its 25 past days average value, out otherwise.

11 The MIB was substituted for the Bank of Italy stock price index because end of period data are required in this analysis, but Bank of Italy provides only average values. MIB has been first introduced in 1975.

Dep. variable	const	POS2	$\bar{R}^2$	period
1. price index growth ($\log A_{t+3}-\log A_t$)	.02 (1.40)	.59 (4.51)	.10	1976.09-87.09
2. abs. value of eq. 1 residuals	.09 (10.20)	.27 (3.15)	.06	" "
3. price volatility	1.05 (20.54)	3.24 (7.25)	.28	" "
4. "dont" premium	3.53 (15.70)	12.83 (8.36)	.64	1984.06-87.09

TABLE 6: POS2, NEXT THREE MONTHS PRICE INDEX GROWTH, AND RISK (monthly data, dependent variables are three months average values; for definitions see text)

1. $\log(A_{t+3})-\log(A_t) = \underset{(.02)}{.00} \; \underset{(-3.61)}{-.11} Z_t \; \underset{(3.44)}{+.25} (\log(D_{t+12}) - \log(D_t)) \; \underset{(-2.88)}{-.77} r_{t+3}/100 \; \underset{(5.22)}{+.68}$ POS2 ; $\bar{R}^2 = .23$

2. $\text{abs}(u) = \underset{(10.44)}{.08} \; \underset{(2.79)}{.25} e$

3. $\text{abs}(u) = \underset{(10.81)}{.08} \; \underset{(3.29)}{.24} \text{POS2}_t$

4. $\log(A_{t+3})-\log(A_t) = \underset{(1.76)}{.03} \; \underset{(-3.10)}{-.10} Z_t \; \underset{(-2.03)}{-.60} r_t/100 + \underset{(4.95)}{+.69}$ POS2 ; $\bar{R}^2 = .18$

TABLE 7: THREE MONTHS STOCK PRICE GROWTH ESTIMATIONS AND RESIDUALS VARIABILITY (final equations; monthly data, period 1976.09-87.09; u = eq.1 residuals, e = eq.1 estimated values; Z_t is the equilibrium equation residual obtained by regressing $\log A_t$ on $\log D_t$)

extra-profits: even if the turning points are correctly identified, the prices are so irregular and so many movements in and out the market are made at the wrong moment that the transaction costs absorb any potential gain.

We derived the same results by applying the more sophisticated model (6) to the monthly data (see table 7) in order to have three months period ahead forecasts [12] the periods for which the model predicts an increase in the price are associated with abnormal volatility in the forecasting error (measured by the absolute value between the estimation and the future values).

5. Conclusion

In this paper we have presented a new model for the Italian Stock market which has been empirically estimated by using annual, quarterly and monthly data. It seems that the strong link between the stock index and the usual explanatory variables is confirmed, but that at the same time there are wide fluctuations, probably due to the behaviour of naive extrapolators. Some market movements are partially predictable, but the difficulty in identifying the "true" turning points, the costs of transactions and the abnormal stock market risk associated with the periods of the upward movement of the price

----

12 In this model, dividends are determined on the base of Bank of Italy data. The real rate of return that fitted our equations best was the six months real rate of return on treasury bills; however it is not included in the equilibrium equation since it was not found significant. The first final equation of the table represents the best result, while the second includes only data actually available at time t among the regressors: in the second case too the error Z improves the estimation and POS2 is highly significant.

make it difficult for a risk-adverse speculator to gain extraprofits. The possibility of forecasting some future price movements does not imply inefficiency if it is to compensate the higher risk premium required by market operators.

REFERENCES

Barone, E. and Cristini, G., 1981, Corsi delle azioni e dividendi attesi: verifica empirica per un campione di societa` italiane, in: Contributi alla ricerca economica, n.9 (Banca d'Italia, Roma) 7-62.

Biffignandi, S. and Stefani, S., 1981, Modelli statistici per l'analisi dei prezzi e dei volumi azionari, Analisi moderna delle serie economiche, (F. Angeli, Milano).

Bruni, F., Pototschnig A. and Zingales, L., 1988, Diversificazione di portafoglio, specializzazione tra fondi comuni di investimento ed efficacia nella gestione del risparmio, Diritto ed Economia, 1, 179-220.

Cristini, G., 1978, I rendimenti delle azioni e l'efficienza della borsa, in: Contributi alla ricerca economica n.8 (Banca d'Italia, Roma) 113-162.

Engle, R.F. and Yoo, B.S., 1987, Forecasting and testing in co-integrated systems, Journal of Econometrics, 35, 143-159.

Engle, R. and Granger, W.J., 1987, Co-integration and error correction representation, estimation and testing, Econometrica, 2, 251-276.

Fama, E.F. and Blume, M., 1966, Filter rules and stock market trading profits, Journal of Business, 1, 226-241.

Fama, E.F., 1970, Efficient capital markets: a review of theory and empirical work, Journal of Finance, 25, 383-417.

Giannasca, C. and Macchiati, A., 1986, Considerazioni sull' efficienza del mercato azionario italiano, (paper presented at the Convegno dell'Industria, Milano).

Granger, C.W., 1969, Investigating causal relations by econometric models and cross spectral methods, Econometrica, 37, 424-438.

Granger, C.W. and Engle, R.F., 1985, Dynamic model specification with equilibrium constraints: cointegration and error correction, (paper presented at the World Congress of the Econometric Society, Boston).

Hawawini, G., 1984, European equity markets: price behaviour and efficiency, (Salomon Bros. Center for the study of financial Institution, New York).

IRS, 1988, Rapporto sul mercato azionario, (Edizioni del Sole 24 Ore, Milano-Varese)

Moorkerjee, R., 1987, Monetary policy and the informational efficiency of the stock market: the evidence from many countries, Applied Economics, 19, 1521-1532.

Mortara, C.A., 1976, Moneta e corsi azionari in Italia, Bancaria, 5, 463-474.

Romei. P., 1987, La verifica dell'efficienza debole del mercato azionario italiano: l'analisi fondamentale e tecnica, (unpublished dissertation, Universita` Cattolica, Milano).

Shiller, R.J., 1981a, Do stock prices move too much to be justified by subsequent changes in dividends?, American Economic Review, 7, 421-436.

Shiller, R. J., 1981b, The use of volatility measures in assessing market efficiency, Journal of Finance, 36, 291-304.

Shiller, R.J. , 1984, Stock prices and social dynamics, Brooking Papers on Economic Activity, 2, 457-498.

Vaciago, G. and Verga, G., 1987, Mercato azionario e meccanismi di trasmissione della politica monetaria, in: Ricerche quantitative e basi statistiche per la politica economica (Banca d'Italia, Roma), 795-1010.

Verga, G., 1984, Il mercato azionario: teoria e verifica empirica, (CUSL-UC, Milano).

Zambruno, G., 1984, On the efficiency of the Italian stock market, reprinted in G. Hawawini and P. Michel, eds; European equity market: return, risk and equilibrium, (Garland Publishing Company, New York and London).

THE IMPACT OF EMH LOGIC IN PRACTICE

Simon M Keane
Department of Accounting and Finance
Glasgow University
67 Southpark Ave
Glasgow G44 3DF
UK

ABSTRACT

The paper considers the implications of the efficient market literature for practitioners in the investment, corporate finance and financial reporting areas. An "efficient market perspective", substantially consistent with the recent anomalous evidence, is identified, and four axioms of financial practice are reviewed within such a framework.

KEYWORDS

Efficient market theory and the problem of proof; efficient market perspective; impact of EMH on financial practice.

NATO ASI Series, Vol. F54
A Reappraisal of the Efficiency of Financial Markets
Edited by Rui M. C. Guimaraes et al.

THE IMPACT OF EMH LOGIC IN PRACTICE

The market efficiency debate is about more than simply assessing the market's capacity to process different information sets. It is about the validity of a belief system which not only determines an investor's fundamental investment strategy but touches upon the basic assumptions and perspectives of every market-related financial institution. The extent of its impact in practice, however, depends on the degree of recognition accorded to the evidence and on the interpretation of its logic by relevant decision-makers. The purpose of this paper is to consider the significance of EMH in practice and the potential consequences of failing to recognise its implications.

Two factors inhibit a wider recognition of EMH logic. First, there is a tendency to assume that as long as the verdict on the issue remains "not proven", practitioners are justified in deferring their recognition of EMH as an operational concept. Secondly, there is a common belief that wider knowledge of EMH might adversely affect the market's efficiency, on the assumption that for sufficient information-processing activity to be sustained, a significant number of investors must remain unaware of, or at least sceptical of, the evidence.

The EMH Perspective

There are two issues, therefore, whether the evidence for EMH deserves to be taken seriously by market participants, and, if so, whether it is beneficial for its logic to exert an influence on their behaviour. Both issues can be attributed in part to a tendency to view the debate in simple true-or-false terms - to view the market as "efficient or inefficient". In addition, because of the weight of practitioner opinion in favour of the latter, and because of the novelty of the efficient market proposition, the assumption is that the market is inefficient until proven otherwise beyond all reasonable doubt.

Two observations, however, need to be made. First a

stronger verdict than "not proven" can never be reached as long as it is possible to argue that more powerful statistical tools in the future might unearth previously unrecognised market inefficiencies. It is therefore essential to stress that the market's efficiency does not need to be proved or its pricing mechanism fully understood for EMH to have important economic policy implications. The avoidable risks and transaction costs of any active investment strategy associated with the conventional belief system imply that it makes economic sense for most investors to behave as if the market is efficient until proof to the contrary is forthcoming. The logical premise for any investor entering the equity market is to accept the market as a single risky investment opportunity rather than to seek out any subset of the market as a special opportunity unless the evidence convincingly demonstrates the existence of inefficient pricing within that subset.

Secondly, any inefficiency shown to exist must be material and exploitable before the logic of EMH can be disregarded. It is misleading to characterize the EMH debate in simple dichotomous terms of true or false. Efficiency, like intelligence, is a matter of degree which, as indicated in Table 1, ranges from perfect efficiency to outright inefficiency. The relevant debate is not between the two extremes - a world where no investor, including the expert analyst, can earn even moderate excess returns, and a world where superior investment performance is accessible to any investor who diligently applies his mind to the task. Rather, it is about whether the market pricing mechanism is sufficiently unreliable for the ordinary investor to be able realistically to use publicly available information, personally or through the agency of a professional adviser, to identify significantly mispriced securities. Although the precise degree to which the market is efficient is a matter of dispute, the collective empirical evidence rejects a degree of inefficiency significantly to the right of point 2 on the efficiency scale. Anomalies such as the size, day-of-the-week and time-of-the-year and other seasonal effects, and issues such as those raised by Shiller (1981) Summers (1986) and Grossman and Stiglitz (1980) suggest a degree of irrationality in

TABLE 1

1	2	3	4
Perfectly efficient	Operationally efficient	Moderately inefficient	Grossly inefficient
No superior returns even to experts	Inefficiencies perceptible only to a few experts but nonstransmittible to others	Inefficiencies perceptible to "qualified" analysts and transmittible to lay investors	Inefficiencies apparent even to informed lay investors

DEGREES OF MARKET EFFICIENCY

market price behaviour, but, given the magnitude of the phenomena, they indicate a locus on the efficiency spectrum to the right of point 1 with little support for assuming a position significantly beyond point 2.

Within the framework of such an efficiency scale, it is possible, therefore, to distil from the evidence an "EMH perspective", a core belief system which has sufficient support from the accumulated empirical evidence to have compelling relevance to practitioners and policy-makers in various decision areas. The core elements of such a belief system can be summarised as follows: 1) the market is a speedy and relatively reliable interpreter of fundamental economic data, 2) with the exception of insider trading, superior investment performance appears to be confined substantially to economic rents earned by a relatively small number of highly skilled information-processors, 3) it is futile for most investors and other market observers to look behind security prices on the basis of their personal interpretation of publicly available information.

The dependency of market efficiency on investor scepticism

The belief that greater recognition of EMH might militate against the market's continuing efficiency stems from the assumption that a significant proportion of the investment community must be fooled into routinely pursuing mispriced securities for the necessary information-processing activity of the market to be maintained. However, although such an assumption is incontestable in terms of degree 1 efficiency, it is possible for degree 2 efficiency to exist without any investors being fooled or being ignorant of the fact. There is no empirical support for believing that it requires more than a relatively small number of professional analysts earning modest rewards for their efforts to prevent significant security mispricing, whilst the majority of investors pursue a substantially passive investment strategy. It is reasonable to assume that one of the attributes of an efficient market is that it can accommodate sufficient price deviation from fundamental economic value to provide a modest reward mechanism for skilled information processors, but insufficient to make it worthwhile for the majority of investors to look behind security prices. It may be possible for all investors to recognize this attribute without diminishing the market's information-processing capability.

In addition, the costs of ignorance are potentially more pervasive and farreaching than any possible benefits, and the risk that widespread awareness of the market's efficiency might undermine the security pricing mechanism appears relatively insignificant when weighed against such costs. The next section considers some of these costs.

EMH in practice

The market's efficiency in interpreting economic events has potential relevance in at least four major decision areas, corporate financial practice, economic policy-making, investment strategy and corporate financial reporting. It is proposed to examine an 'axiom of practice' in each of these areas to illustrate the potential cost of failing to recognize the market's efficiency, an axiom of practice being defined as a principle widely recognised by practitioners and having immediate intuitive appeal.

i) THE WEALTH MAXIMISATION RULE

Axiom: 'Any company which actively pursues a wealth-maximising objective can reasonably expect periodically to generate an increase in the market value of its shares'.

Although corporate finance theory is firmly rooted in an EMH perspective, curiously its cornerstone of wealth-maximisation appears invariably to be interpreted by text-book writers within an inefficient market framework. The superiority of the NPV criterion is conventionally defended on the grounds that it measures the increase in the firm's value consequent on a project's acceptance, and, where supported by adequate financial disclosure, measures in turn the expected corresponding increase in share price.

Accordingly, setting aside price increases resulting from inflation, earnings retentions and normal volatility, the share price history of a company under a wealth-maximising regime is conventionally perceived (curve A in Figure 1) as a series of stepped accretions over the life of the company. It is assumed that any shareholder who buys into the series can expect on average to earn abnormal returns as each accretion occurs. Similarly, by implication all ex post measures of security returns will reflect the average internal rates of return earned on the underlying projects rather than the ex ante required returns on the shares.

Such a scenario is inconsistent with the fundamental principle of market efficiency that all securities are substantially zero NPV investments, and posits at best a myopically efficient market which reacts only to events as they occur and fails to anticipate them. A truly efficient market, however, will take cognizance of all future excess-return opportunites in the real product market by discounting in the share price each company's estimated collective stream of future wealth accretions (Findlay and Williams, 1979). At flotation, therefore, the shares of every firm with a reasonable prospect of generating positive NPVs in the future will be valued accordingly. Thereafter, the share price will increase only in recognition of the gradual proximity of each new generation of excess-return projects (curve B). The actual announcement by the company of a positive NPV project will be associated with a share price reaction (increase or decrease) only to the extent that the NPV exceeds or falls short of the market's expectation. The upward-sloping direction of the curve reflects the projected increasing dividend stream arising from the excess returns earned as each new NPV phase is implemented. It must be stressed, however, that this increase in share value is a component of the normal rate of return on the share and does not represent an increase in shareholder wealth in an incremental sense. In an efficient market, all other share price movements represent revisions by the market of its unbiased estimates of the future.

To illustrate this, assume a firm's cost of capital is k, but, given its expected share of future positive NPV projects, the firm is estimated to earn an average return of (k + w) on its formation capital C. If the company matches its dividend payout to actual earnings, and earns a return of k on C until the first positive NPV project is intitiated, then in period 1 the dividend yield on the flotation value of the equity $C(k + w)/k$ will be

$$\frac{Ck}{C(k+w)/k} = \frac{k^2}{k + w}$$

For the shareholder to achieve the normal rate of return k the share price can be expected during the period to increase in percentage terms by

$$\frac{Cw}{C(k+w)/k} = \frac{wk}{k + w}$$

This increase, however, is not in any sense incremental wealth to the shareholders. It is in effect an implicit form of earnings retention in the sense of a nondistribution of the returns resulting from the increase in value induced by the

FIGURE 1

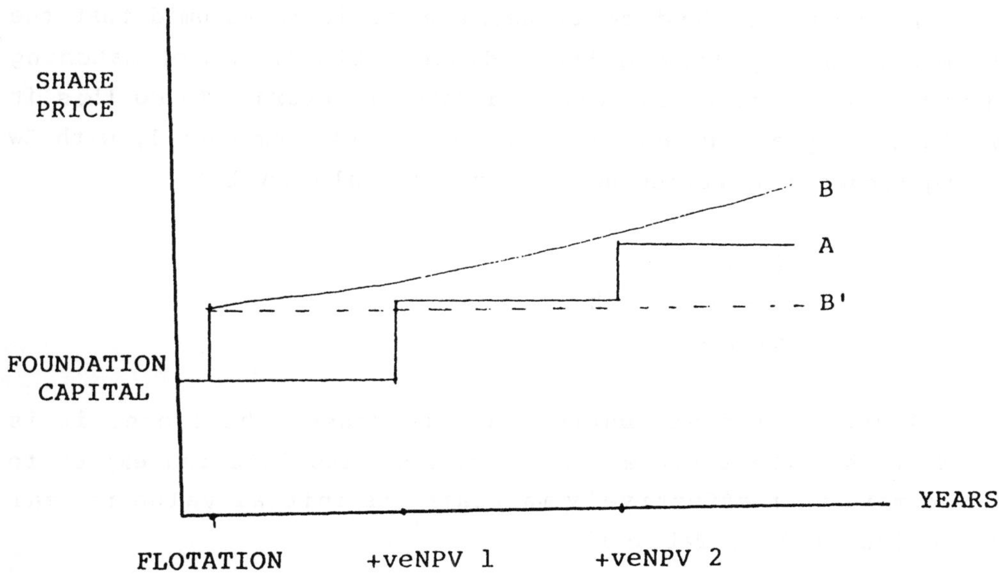

Alternative interpretations of stock price behaviour of average wealth-maximising company in the absence of inflation, earnings retention and random volatility - Conventional (A), EMH with distribution of realised earnings (B), and EMH with full distribution of expected average earnings (B').

approach of future increases in dividends.

The point can best be illustrated if it is assumed that the firm pursues a policy of "full distribution", i.e. of matching dividend yield to k, the required rate of return. To do this it would now pay a constant dividend of (k + w) from year 1, with Cw being financed by borrowing. The yield would now be

$$\frac{C(k+w)}{C(k+w)/k} = k$$

Given full distribution in this sense, therefore, it is evident that the average firm throughout its life can expect to do no more than effectively maintain its initial value in real terms (curve B' in Table 1).

It follows that, if the market is semi-strong efficient to any reasonable degree, the concept of wealth maximisation cannot be interpreted in the traditional sense of adding to the firm's market value when wealth-creating projects are undertaken. Firms should certainly strive to increase the share price when the opportunity presents itself, but, if the market's estimates of the future are unbiased, they cannot expect on average to do any more than fulfil the expectations captured in the post-flotation price. The primary beneficiaries of the wealth-maximising process are the founder shareholders. Thereafter, investors face zero NPV investments from their shares notwithstanding the existence of an ongoing and successful positive NPV programme by the companies underlying their securities. This effect has important practical implications if not understood by financial managers in that, when share prices fail to react to a NPV announcement, rather than this being recognised as evidence of the market's farsightedness, it may be interpreted it as an inability by the market to take the long-term view inherent in NPV measurement, thus giving support to the use of short-term capital budgeting criteria such as Payback. In addition, there may be significant financial reporting implications where the effectiveness of the financial reporting system is judged by the impact on share prices of disclosures relating to the firm's "wealth creating" decisions.

ii) INVESTMENT STRATEGY AND THE ROLE OF THE INTERMEDIARY.

Axiom: 'The discount on investment trust shares can be eliminated only by altering investors' perception of the attractiveness of investment companies, or by liquidating the company's assets.'

The appropriate investment strategy indicated by EMH for nonprofessional investors is the combination of a well-diversified portfolio with borrowing or lending according to risk preferences. Because of transaction costs in establishing and maintaining an international portfolio, pooling of resources via an intermediary is likely to be beneficial for most investors with limited investment capital. In addition, higher interest charges on loans transacted at an individual level suggest that borrowing is also more beneficial through an intermediary for investors seeking a higher than average risk-return exposure. Therefore, given the opportunity for any investor with lower risk-return preferences to adjust his lending position as necessary, it follows that the optimal investment vehicle for most investors is likely to be a closed-end levered investment company. This is particularly true where, as in the UK, no international index fund exists. Unlike mutual funds, the shares of an actively managed investment company will be discounted by an efficient market to price away all future expected active-strategy costs, effectively converting the fund into its passive equivalent. However badly managed the fund, the shares of the trust can on average be expected to yield the return appropriate to a passive portfolio of the same risk class.

Although, in practice, investment trust shares can be observed on average to stand at a significant discount to their net asset values, this can be attributed to a combination of factors, including taxation idiosyncracies, asset valuation discrepancies and management costs. The precise interpretation of the discount, therefore, is a matter of debate. A widespread belief, however, is that an important contributing factor is a consistent failure by the market to recognize the inherent advantages of investment trusts rather than a discounting of the inherent disadvantages. The behaviour of the Investment Trust Association has reinforced this perception by emphasising in its promotion literature that the discount provides access to the underlying assets on favourable terms, and by engaging the services of a public relations officer to correct the market's "misperception" of the value of investment trusts.

The existence of a discount, therefore, implies one of three possibilities depending on how rational the market is perceived to be, a) the need for management to revise its investment strategy by minimising its future active strategy costs, b) the need to persuade the market about the true value of its existing strategy, or c) the desirability of liquidating (or unitising) the fund. If the market is recognised as efficient it is possible that only the first policy is necessary or desirable. Although it remains a matter of speculation to what extent the discount would be reduced by the adoption of a passive investment strategy, the evidence in favour of index funding suggests the likelihood of a significant reduction if the first policy were adopted. In the light of the efforts of the Investment Trust Association, the second policy can be assumed to be futile. Unfortunately, an increasing number of investment trusts have elected for the third policy, a phenomenon which has been paralleled in the US. In summary, failure by financial institutions to recognize the extent of the market's efficiency may in the long run extinguish the optimal investment vehicle available to investors.

iii) THE INFORMATION CONTENT OF MARKET PRICES

Axiom: 'A sharp adjustment in share price levels such as that of October 1987 is likely to be driven by market sentiment rather than by economic fundamentals.'

In addition to responding efficiently to the economic signals it receives, an efficient market will at times emit signals about the economic environment which have significant information content. These signals, however, will have little behavioural impact if market participants do not recognize the market's interpretative powers. Problems of moral hazard arise if decision-makers dismiss significant price movements as idiosyncratic quirks of the market, or if they incorrectly interpret the price movements as creating opportunities or impediments which affect their decision choices.

These issues were poignantly illustrated by reactions to the October crash of 1987. The Financial Times stated that "share price falls of 20% in a day make a mockery of academic claims that stock markets are efficient" (24 October, 1987). In sympathy with this view, some commentators interpreted the fall as an overdue correction to an overheated market, and others as a herd reaction to a combination of computerised trading and irrational panic. Now it is clear that a rational market will on occasions have to revise drastically its probability profile of future economic circumstances such that a sudden fall in prices, even of 20% in one day, cannot in itself be assumed to indicate market irrationality, but few observers were willing at the time to acknowledge the possibility that the 1987 price decline was a rational reassessment of economic fundamentals. Certainly the rationality of individual market reactions cannnot readily be proved, any more than their irrationality, but when viewed in the context of the cumulative research findings testifying the interpretative power of the market relative to that of individual observers, it is reasonable to assume that, even when the market's behaviour is perplexing, its signals deserve to be taken seriously.

Other commentators, in contrast, attached unwarranted significance to the price fall, interpreting it as signalling immediate consequences for the cost of equity capital. For example, the chairman of the UK stock exchange noted on 4th November 1987, that a fall of that magnitude "not only increases the cost of new risk capital, it virtually closes down the supply." The logic of this view is not clear, but it appears to arise from the belief that the market's economic judgment has temporarily ceased to be rational. It is, of course, logical for any firm which perceives its shares to be materially mispriced to consider delaying or accelerating its investment plans in the hope of raising capital on more favourable terms. Therefore, given management's comparative informational advantage over the company's future prospects, such behaviour is at times consistent with recognition of the market's semi-strong efficiency. Equally, however, lack of trust in the market's capacity to interpret publicly available economic data can act as a barrier to profitable investment. Although an increase in the cost of equity is likely to cause a decline in equity values, the reverse does not necessarily hold. Bond yields in fact declined immediately after the October fall, and if there was a rise in the cost of equity it could only have been due to an increase in the risk premium. However, there is no compelling reason to assume that a price decline per se is associated with an increase in perceived risk.

One explanation for this assumption of a link between share price levels and equity costs is the belief, as articulated by the Financial Times above, that a sudden decline in values is intrinsically inconsistent with efficient pricing - the notion that security prices could not be 20% different on successive days and be efficiently priced on both days. Therefore, with such a fall in prices, the implication is that equities have departed from their fundamental economic values. Accordingly, although the required return on equity capital may be acknowledged not to have changed directly with the fall in prices, it could be logically assumed that raising new capital before a correction takes place would present an opportunity to new shareholders to acquire a disproportionate share of the existing cake. From this perspective, it would appear rational for firms to defer their capital raising plans or to raise the cut-off rate for new investments to compensate for such opportunity costs.

In summary, given that an efficient market by definition is forward-looking and perceptive in its judgment of economic fundamentals, economic policy-makers who fail to recognize its efficiency are denying themselves an important source of insight.

iv) CORPORATE FINANCIAL REPORTING PRACTICES

Axiom: 'All shareholders should be treated equally in respect of the company's financial disclosure output'.

The conventional corporate financial reporting system is based on the premise that financial disclosure should be directed primarily to the company's shareholders to inform their buy-hold-sell decisions. Three principles are assumed to be central to this process: a) information should be disseminated to all shareholders simultaneously, b) financial reports should be multi-purpose and the information released primarily through the medium of standardised income and financial position statements, and c) the content should be comprehensible to the reasonably informed layman.

It would seem that these principles lose much of their relevance if the ordinary shareholder is unable systematically to use the information to make superior buy-hold-sell decisions. Since even an efficient market, however, needs information to perform its security-pricing function, it seems unlikely that a reporting system based on the above principles is relevant to its needs.

Although little is actually known about the process by which information is impounded into share prices, the implication of the research findings is that prices behave as if they are set by sophisticated information-processors. There are no grounds for believing that the process depends for its effectiveness on the information-disclosure system being inhibited to meet the needs of unsophisticated users. The significance of the efficient market perspective for financial reporting is that the market ceases to be just another user of conventional periodic financial statements, but that its information needs are fundamentally different from those of other users. Whereas, for an inefficient market, and for most other external financial reporting uses, the accountant's role is a quasi-valuational one of transforming raw financial numbers into decision-output measures suitable for contracting purposes (eg for dividend decisions or profit-sharing schemes etc), his role vis-a-vis an efficient market is primarily to procure the timely disclosure of relevant decision-input data for the market to fulfil its expert valuational function. The ordinary shareholder's need is not for information for personal use to seek out mispriced securities, but for the efficient release of data to the market's professional information processors to narrow the gap between the semi-strong and strong values of securities.

To achieve this goal, it can be assumed that the ideal financial reporting system an efficient market should have certain characteristics: i) it should be free from the structural constraints imposed by the conventional income and financial position models, ie the content should be essentially unprocessed, forward-oriented, and probabilistic. ii) it should be focussed on unsystematic data, i.e. events over which the firm has a comparative advantage relative to the market's alternative information sources, iii) it should be a continuous output rather than periodic iv) it should be separate from systems intended for stewardship reporting and other contracting purposes.

In summary, failure to recognize the market's capacity to process information efficiently is likely to operate as a potential barrier to effective disclosure, and help sustain the conditions which facilitate successful insider trading.

The implications of the efficient market perspective, of course, extend beyond these four axioms and beyond these four financial decision areas. There are, for example, equally important implications for corporate take-over policies, bankruptcy decisions, the formulation of advertising standards for investment advisory firms, and for the courts in judging prudent investment management. It has not, however, been the purpose of the paper to review these implications exhaustively, but to demonstrate that, although an efficient market perspective has for some time arguably deserved to be accepted as an economic fact of life, there are important areas of financial practice and theory where its influence and logic have so far failed to have any significant impact.

SUMMARY AND CONCLUSION

Although the precise degree to which the securities market is efficient is, and is likely to remain, a matter of uncertainty, that it is efficient is beyond dispute. The popular myth of a market driven as much by psychological whim as by economic logic, where prices can be observed to drift at times capriciously from their fundamental values, offering rich pickings to any investor with reasonable insight or flair, is wholly inconsistent with the evidence. The weight of the evidence indicates that superior performance is out of reach for all but a few professional specialists, and even then only to a modest extent. In effect, the market is marginally inefficient for some investors but unassailably efficient for most.

EMH, therefore, can no longer be set aside as a potentially important theory awaiting verification. The accumulated research, even with its anomalies and imperfect statistical tools, has established beyond reasonable doubt the empirical validity of an "efficient market perspective", a minimum set of propositions which have important and immediate consequences for all relevant areas of financial practice. The essence of this perspective is that for most purposes market prices can be trusted implicitly, and that failure to do so can have serious practical implications. These implications are sufficiently far-reaching to underscore the need for the perspective to be disseminated to a much wider audience. The widely held notion that the stock market depends for its efficiency on its participants remaining ignorant or sceptical of the evidence has little logical, ethical or empirical justification.

REFERENCES

Findlay, M and E Williams, "Owners' Surplus, the Marginal Efficiency of Capital and Market Equilibrium", Journal of Business Finance and Accounting, (Spring 1979).

Grossman, S and J Stiglitz, "On the Impossibility of Informationally Efficient Markets," American Economic Review, (June, 1980)

Keane, S, Stock Market Efficiency, Philip Allan, 1983.

Shiller, R, "Do Stock Prices Move too much to be justified by Subsequent Changes in Dividends?" American Economic Review (June 1981).

Summers, L "Does the Stock Market Rationally Reflect Fundamental Values?" Journal of Finance, (July 1986).

Comments on Simon M. Keane
"The Impact of EMH Logic in Practice"
by Helmut Uhlir

Growing out of the random-walk hypothesis the EMH conceptionally was initiated by Fama and rapidly became a well recognized framework how information may be processed in highly competitive security markets.During the seventies a lot of empirical research was done and evidence clearly turned out in favour of the EMH. As a consequence the EMH became widely accepted, at least by academicians. The acceptance by practitioners, e.g.investment advisors and corporate financial managers was relatively poor. Although deficiences in testing methods and statistical tools as well as recent evidence on a variety of 'anomalies' could not really undermine the belief in the 'efficient market perspective' this scenario probably will not alter the existing attitude of practitioners.

Keane, undoubtedly an ardent advocat of the EMH,claims that the existence of efficient security markets has important consequences for many decision areas in practice. In order to demonstrate the potential relevance of EMH in each of four selected areas a typical 'axiom of practice' is chosen. On two of them I would like to make some comments. Let me start with the wealth maximisation rule and the NPV concept.

If evidence tells us that security markets are semi-strong efficient wealth maximisation clearly cannot be interpreted in the sense of adding to the company's market value when wealth increasing projects are undertaken. Theoretically there is not much to argue I suppose. Far less from being clear are the consequences in practice especially to financial managers who have to find out profitable investment projects. Besides that Keane does not specify the costs of failing to recognize this impact of the EMH.

We may blame textbook writers for not precisely describing the underlying scenarios when explaining how to use capital budget acceptance rules. (In this context one must be careful not to confound the conditions of perfect capital markets with those of the EMH.) But we should be very reluctant to blame

NATO ASI Series, Vol. F54
A Reappraisal of the Efficiency of Financial Markets
Edited by Rui M. C. Guimaraes et al.

practitioners in treating the decision processes of financial managers andshareholders mainly as an unrelated issue. First of all it is not an easy task to determine the appropriate discount rate,i.e.the acceptable rate for a given risk class. Secondly the market of physical assets and product markets may be inefficient even for competitive industries. Thirdly only a small proportion of existing companies is listed and will be frequently traded, hence security market efficiency may have little relevance to them. Lastly,if portfolio aspects are considered financial managers can ignore individual risk-return preferences of their shareholders (and should therefore obey the wealth maximisation rule!)only in case security markets are efficient.

Traditional corporate financial statements and reporting systems still rest on the premise that financial disclosure is predominately addressed to shareholders. Moreover it is claimed that the released information can be profitably contribute to their buy-hold-sell decisions. From a huge body of empirical research we know that the informational content of disclosed data is relatively low because relevant information obviously will be revealed earlier in the market and will be disseminated through other channels. To summarize conventional financial reporting produces redundant information which is only of limited value to shareholders even if unsophisticated laymen are considered. Given the accumulated evidence on this matter there is no justification to make costly efforts to extend or improve existing reporting systems as long as there will be no structural change.

I would generally agree upon the features of an ideal reporting system outlined by Keane released to professional information processors "to narrow the gap between the semi-strong and strong value of securities". Such a reporting system has primarily the goal to impede profitable insider trading and would contribute to achieve a higher level of efficiency. Whether this will be a desirable state of the world,i.e.in a cost-benefit sense unfortunately is not discussed. Since we do not know how semi-strong values deviate from (unobservable) strong values the above question remains unanswered.

THE EFFICIENCY OF THE CHICAGO BOARD OF TRADE FUTURES AND FUTURES OPTIONS MARKETS

P.J. Catania
Chicago Board of Trade
LaSalle at Jackson
Chicago, IL 60604
USA.

KEYWORDS/ABSTRACT: stocks/futures/options/market crash

Important areas for futures research are reviewed against the background of the international market crashes of October 1987.

As an industry practitioner my aim is to attempt to stimulate further research that I believe to be critical to the continued success of the futures and futures options industry. The theme of this conference is "The Efficiency of World Financial Markets". The events of October 19, 1987 certainly tested the efficiency as well as the capacity, performance, and financial integrity of all world financial markets. Subsequent to the events of last October, the futures industry in the United States has increasingly come under attack and has been cited as the cause of the collapse in share prices on markets around the world. Needless to say neither I nor any of my colleagues in the Chicago Board of Trade share this point of view. Immediately following last Fall's market collapse, a number of studies, and I use the word studies very loosely, were undertaken by various government agencies, exchanges, and a presidential task force in the United States. The obvious flaw which runs across the lines of all of these studies is the very short time frame within which they were conceived and subsequently produced. The public outcry and industry finger pointing seemed to warrant immediate response on the part of all the parties concerned. As I have already pointed out, I don't believe that such an immediate response has done justice to the subject at hand. It is useful first to recap the chronology of events, up to and immediately following

NATO ASI Series, Vol. F54
A Reappraisal of the Efficiency of Financial Markets
Edited by Rui M.C. Guimaraes et al.

last October 19, to highlight a number of questions which warrant further in depth research.

All market participants agree on one thing concerning the events surrounding last October 19th: never had they witnessed the breadth of market movement or the volatility level that they saw during that time period. Many market participants agree on an additional point: the futures and futures options markets performed their function during that period admirably and efficiently.

Most people with any degree of financial market expertise have learned that "the market" is never wrong. The movement and direction of the overall market corresponds to factors which are at some point quantifiable. With the benefit of hindsight and rational analysis, market fundamentals and market behavior were telling us what was about to happen. Remember that prior to October 19th many market analysts were claiming that the stock markets were overvalued. All major stock markets around the world were bumping up against all time record high levels as measured by their respective indices. The historic market declines should not, once again in hindsight, have been a surprise to anyone.

On Wednesday, October 14, 1987 an unfavourable trade imbalance of $15.8 billion was announced for the United States. In addition to that being a huge trade imbalance in and of itself, the figure was significantly greater than the majority of market analysts' predictions. On that same day, the Dow Jones Industrial Average fell by an alarming 95.45 points. On Thursday, the same indicator declined by an additional 57.61 points, and on Friday, just to insure that no one enjoyed their weekend, the Dow Jones average fell another 108.35 points. This amounted to approximately a 10% decline in market value in only three days! Over that weekend, both the trade balance and the United States budget deficit were cited over and over as the culprits which led to the decline in the market. While the unacceptable trade imbalance may have triggered the sell-off, most observers felt the more serious issue was the United States budget deficit. No signs were forthcoming that the deficit problem would be corrected. Foreign investors were financing the United States deficit and trends towards higher interest rates, coupled with a perceived tightening of the money supply by the Federal Reserve System threatened to exacerbate the deficit problem. Over that same weekend of October 17/18 the continued weakness of the U.S. dollar and its slide against other major currencies again began to impact those foreign investors holding dollar denominated U.S. bonds and equities. If there was even the slightest question of whether we are all now part of a global economy and a global marketplace, all doubt was in the process of being removed. On Monday morning October 19, in Tokyo (which was Sunday evening in the United States), the Nikkei Stock index fell 620.18 points. In Hong Kong at about the same time, the Hang-Seng index fell 420.81 points. Similarly, on Monday morning in London, the leading indicator on the London exchange, the Financial Times stock index, fell 248.60 points. All of the fundamental factors I've cited coupled with the reaction on the leading stock exchanges of the world to the declines in New York on the past Wednesday, Thursday, and Friday, fueled recessionary fears by Monday morning New York time. Certainly October 19 was one of the most turbulent days ever at the New York Stock Exchange. Monday's decline in the Dow Jones Industrial Average amounted to some 508 points. But once again, with the benefit of hindsight, Monday's events should not have come as a total surprise to anyone.

This brief summary of the events of those several days brings me to the situation at hand. Some would like us to believe that the futures markets caused the stock markets to decline. Program trading, portfolio insurance, dividend capture strategies, and computers all used in conjunction with the futures markets are said to be the villains. In the United States critics are calling for higher margin requirements for futures contracts in order to tame this wild market. In addition, they prescribe that stock index futures contracts and other such products be brought under the jurisdiction of the Securities and Exchange Commission and/or the Federal Reserve Board. However, for the most part, these critics do not themselves understand the basic foundation of the futures markets, nor do they understand the difference between futures margin requirements (performance bonds) and securities market margin requirements (credit or loan requirements).

The Board offers those who own stocks and bonds a way to manage or transfer the risk of owning such instruments in order that they may meet the objectives of their particular investment philosophy. It offers them price insurance.

By way of example, let's look at a property owner or potential property owner. Because he is able to purchase insurance on his house or factory building, he is much more willing and able to make the purchase of such a house or factory, knowing that he is protected against loss in that investment to some degree. The cost of his insurance is affordable relative to the risks he needs to cover. But if the cost of that insurance, that protection, were fifty percent of the value of his investment in the home or factory, (which is what we would face if regulators raise futures margin requirements) he would be much less likely to purchase either the insurance or the actual home or factory buildings for that matter. Very simply the costs involved would be too high for the protection level he needs. But in reality, the affordability of property and casualty insurance makes the real property market more efficient and less risky.

Using a similar analogy, look at the securities markets and the futures markets and their respective margin functions.

The United States Treasury Bond market is an excellent example. When the forty firms designated as primary dealers purchase debt from the United States Government, they immediately manage the risk of holding that debt until it is resold, by hedging their position in the U.S. Treasury Bond futures market at the Chicago Board of Trade. By hedging, they insure themselves against the risk of adverse price movement. Because they can cost-effectively purchase this price insurance, due to the fact that margin requirements for futures contracts are at their current levels, the primary dealers are willing to pay a higher price for the debt than they otherwise would be willing to pay. This allows the United States Government and subsequently the taxpayers the ability to borrow at cheaper rates.

Conversely, the primary dealer can offer the debt for sale to the long-term investor at a lower price which translates to a higher yield, simply because the dealer has managed his risk exposure and can work on narrower bid/asks spreads. These spreads have tightened by as much as 8/32nds of a point since Treasury Bond futures were initiated just over ten years ago. Putting that into perspective, 8/32nds of a point amounts to $250 for each $100,000 in Government Bonds. Knowing the level of U.S. Government debt, I don't think I need to carry the computation any further for you to understand the impact of narrowing the bid/ask Spreads!

These efficiencies have been achieved once again because the cost of procuring the protection for bond inventories has been minimal compared to the risk averted. This cost is largely a function of the margin requirements for holding futures positions. The research needed is that research which can demonstrate the efficiencies achieved by a market-place where the cost of the insurance does not approach the cost of the asset itself. Furthermore, the research needs to demonstrate the very important difference between futures margins (performance bonds) and securities margins (downpayments on the actual purchase of securities).

There have been a number of studies undertaken to examine the pricing efficiencies of the Treasury Bond Futures Market and of other futures markets for that matter. I will cite two such studies here to give you some reference to the type of work that has been done. But I re-emphasize that the futures marketplace must be cost efficient to use in order to achieve the pricing efficiencies demonstrated by the examples I have cited relative to the narrowing of bid/ask spreads, and subsequent offering of a lower cost to issuer and higher return to investor. The researh to date has taken the level of margin requirements for granted and hasn't examined the potential for the loss of these efficiencies given drastic changes in the level of margin requirements. Perhaps those studies which examine varying levels of margin requirements can be re-worked to examine the drastic changes being proposed in some circles.

Resnick and Hennigar (1983) found a high degree of efficiency in relative pricing in the Treasury Bond futures contract relative to the cash market. Klemkosky and Lasser (1985) however conclude that the T-Bond futures market may not be as efficient in cash/futures pricing relationships as claimed by Resnick and Hennigar, due to the effects of tax law changes in the United States as well as to the impact of borrowing costs on financing hedged positions. These are but two of many studies on the pricing efficiency of futures markets. As they illustrate, different research studies do not always come to the same conclusion. However, they do very thoroughly investigate the available data relative to their stated research objectives, and they present the facts from which market users can draw a number of conclusions about pricing efficiencies, depending on the users particular posture in the cash/futures Treasury Bond Market. The futures industry would ask for a similar objectivity and depth of research on the pressing questions concerning margin requirements and regulatory structure before changes are imposed.

If it can be established that significantly changing the margin requirements would significantly hamper the ability of the futures market to function efficiently, perhaps the regulatory authorities would re-think their current course of action. However, this scenario pre-supposes that the regulatory structure remains one of an agency knowledgeable about the futures and futures options industry. The present regulatory structure in the United States gives outright jurisdiction to separate agencies which have expertise over the economic activity that they are to regulate. The Commodity Futures Trading Commission understands the differences between capital formation products and risk-transferring products. They understand the important function of the futures markets and the purposes they serve. Throughout the entire volatile period last October, all of these agencies performed their respective duties without mishap. What efficiencies are to be gained by combining agencies or creating even more agencies to do what is already being done? Another question for some serious research consideration. In today's global markets, competition exists between regulators as well as between market participants and markets. The world markets have demanded and will be provided such tools as stock index futures contracts, whether these tools are offered in the United States or some other country. The success of the futures markets in the United States is due largely to the ability of the current system of futures regulation to assure market integrity without unnecessarily inhibiting market activity and innovation. The futures industry worldwide suffers as a result of Tin market defaults in London or Malaysian palm oil defaults in Kuala Lumpur. We are not looking for non-regulation, simply consistent, knowledgeable regulation that sustains that integrity of the industry. How does the perception of reality of regulation impact the efficiency in exchange for greater regulation? Two more important questions that need to be researched.

Finally, in keeping with the theme of the conference, I would like to briefly discuss the efficiencies of the current trading systems available in the futures and futures options markets.

Most of the futures and futures options contracts traded around the world today are traded in an open outcry auction market setting. This system, while maybe not the most efficient in terms of order flow, seems to be the most efficient in terms of price discovery. There is a very important distinction between these two types of efficiency: order flow and price discovery.

Price discovery is the basis for the very existence of our marketplace. The ability of the marketplace to digest relevant data and translate that into a willingness to buy or sell at a given price level is instantaneous and on going.

Several entities have tried to automate this price discovery function with little success. For example, the International Futures Exchange of Bermuda, INTEX, of which I was the director of market development from 1982 - 1983, has been unable to attract a significant number of users to offer the liquidity required by the users of any marketplace. In fact, many of the initial users of this computerised trading system used the price discovery mechanisms of the New York and Chicago Futures markets to determine their bid and offer prices for any business that was transacted on the automated system.

In terms of order flow efficiencies, the events of October 1987 placed extreme burdens on the equities markets and the futures markets. The equities markets buckled under the pressure as customers' calls went unanswered and orders went unfilled. The futures markets handled record volume on the same days, as money moved from equities to U.S. Government Bonds and tangible assets. Although the futures markets did absorb the record volume efficiently, it did point out that we were nearing even our existing capacities. This fact has resulted in a number of studies looking at order entry automation, that is, bringing the order to the open outcry arena.

What are the researchable issues relative to trading systems? Clearly, as I develop and maintain industry contacts around the world, the question of computer trading always enters the discussions. The problem is that most market participants accept the concept of computerized trading as a foregone conclusion, given our highly automated environment. To date, I have seen no research which examines the potential for increased efficiencies from such a system. Remember, I'm referring specifically to increased efficiencies in the realm of price discovery, not in order execution. Order execution efficiencies have been and are being studied, but price discovery efficiency is not.

As indicated at the start, this paper has raised more questions than it has answered. The areas of margin requirements, regulatory barriers, and trading systems are certainly substantial issues for further research.

To the degree that you believe that the growth and impact of the futures and futures options markets are indicative of their importance to world financial markets, I hope my remarks will encourage your investigation and analysis of these dynamic and intriguing markets.

References

Resnick B. and E. Hennigar, 1983, The relationship between futures and cash prices for U.S. Treasury Bonds, Review of Research in Futures markets volume 2.

Klemkosky R. and D. Lasser, 1985, An efficiency analysis of the T-Bond futures market, Journal of Futures Markets volume 5.

THE STABILITY OF SPECULATIVE PROFITS IN THE FOREIGN EXCHANGES*

Richard J. Sweeney, Claremont McKenna College and Claremont Graduate School, and

Patchara Surajaras, Claremont Graduate School, Claremont, CA 91711, USA

Keywords: speculation/ foreign exchange/ profits/ beating the market/risk premia/performance measurement/technical trading/ filter rules/X-statistics

Abstract: There is evidence that simple trading rules can make measured profits in the foreign exchange markets. Are these profits stable in the sense of not going to zero as time goes on, and not changing radically from period to period? This paper uses the X-statistic to measure risk-adjusted profits, on the assumption that risk premia are not time-varying, or more generally are approximately the same on the days the speculator is in the asset as for the whole period. It appears that profits are not approaching zero in later periods, and the volatility of profits appears reasonable in light of the noisiness of foreign exchange markets.

1. Introduction

A number of papers in the 1970s asked whether technical trading rules could make speculative profits in the foreign exchange market. The results were somewhat inconclusive (Dooley and Shafer (1976), Logue, Sweeney and Willett (1978), Cornell and Dietrich (1978)). In part, it was not clear how to measure performance, in particular, how to take account of risk; in part, there were real issues of the stability of the measured profits.[1] Later, however, Dooley and Shafer (1983) presented evidence of continued profitability, while Sweeney (1986) proposed a risk-adjusted performance measure and argued that statistically significant speculative profits could be made in the late 1970s and into the very early 1980s on the basis of patterns detectable in previous data. There is, however, some evidence of declining profitability of the technical rules previously studied (Surajaras (1987)). Further, it is not clear that speculative profits are stable, or insensitive, with regard to changes in the amount of data used to select strategies or the frequency with which strategies are changed.

NATO ASI Series, Vol. F54
A Reappraisal of the Efficiency of Financial Markets
Edited by Rui M. C. Guimaraes et al.

Stability of profits is clearly an issue of great interest to anyone who intends to use technical analysis to beat the market. For efficient markets advocates, the measured profits detected in some studies can be reconciled with market efficiency by assuming time-varying risk premia, so that the measured profits are not economic profits but simply a reward for bearing risk. Nevertheless, the concept of efficiency is more easily preserved if the measured profits of the past seem no longer available. Hence, the stability of profits is of substantial interest both to practitioners and to academic researchers. This paper investigates the stability of speculative profits over time, and their stability relative to changes in data used to select rule parameters and to change parameters.

Sweeney (1986) uses 1830 observations, from mid-1973 until early 1980. He uses the first 610 observations to look for profitable technical rules of the sort used by Alexander (1961, 1964), and then applies the most promising of them on the remaining 1220 observations as a test of whether profits could be earned by using patterns previously detected in the data. While the measured profits are on average lower in the test period than in the sample period (or prior period) where the rules were generated, the profits seemed large and statistically significant. Still, even assuming that these measured profits are economic profits, these results might be a fluke. Further, there is always the very real possibility that the market will catch on and eliminate any genuine speculative opportunities. Do these measured profits show some degree of stability over time after the period Sweeney examines?

Work by Surajaras (1987) casts some doubt on the stability of speculative profits. He looks at a number of technical approaches on 2000 out-of-sample observations, from mid-1978 to mid-1986, thus overlapping to some extent with Sweeney's 1220-observation test period, but including about five years' or 1250 observations' worth of fresh data. The Alexander rules work well on individual currencies in the first 1000 out-of-sample observations (overlapping substantially with Sweeney's (1986) test period), but not nearly as well in the final 1000, roughly mid-1982 to mid-1986. This is so even though Surajaras changes his filters between the two 1000-observation samples, the changes based always on prior data, in order to catch any changes in whatever underlying process is allowing measured speculative profits.

The issue is confused, however, by Surajaras' rather more successful results on alternative speculative techniques. The purpose of his work is, in fact, more to assess the relative power of various technical approaches than to address the stability of speculative profits. Surajaras considers not only Alexander filter rules, but also double moving average and single moving average rules. For each of these rules, he considers a number of different approaches to combining speculations on individual currencies into a portfolio. One of the techniques he considers focuses on finding a separate rule for each currency, as in Sweeney (1986); here, speculation on each currency is treated as a separate mutual fund, with overall results being judged as an equally-weighted portfolio of such funds. Another technique uses more integrated speculation, where in effect these mutual funds can borrow from one another, with the final results depending on the performance of a portfolio with <u>variable</u> rather than equal weights over time. If the currency speculation is indeed profitable, it turns out that this variable-weight approach should tend to give higher profits than the equal-weight approach, as section 3 discusses.

Tables 1 and 2 raise the issue of the stability of speculative profits. Both report results using Alexander rules. The first (based on Sweeney (1986)) shows at least some fall off in performance in the mid-1975 to mid-1980 period of the 1% and particularly the 2% filters, both of which looked very promising in the prior period from April, 1973, to mid-1975.[2] Table 2 (based on Surajaras (1987)) does not show prior period results but instead shows test results for "best" rules for each currency in two separate test periods, where the "best" rules were chosen based on prior period performance. The first column in Table 2 is comparable to the approach in Table 1 in using an equally-weighted portfolio of independent mutual funds, and shows a fall off in performance in the later period. This fall-off in performance in the later period raises the suspicion that technical trading rules may be losing their effectiveness. The second column in Table 2 shows an even more alarming fall off for the speculations carried out under the variable weight, integrated multi-currency speculation described above. This fall off in the second approach is particularly striking, since this approach should tend to give larger profits if indeed there are profits there to be made from the rules used. The average of the two portfolio approaches shows a fall of more than two thirds (column (3), from 4.89% to 1.63%/year).

Table 1

Alexander Filter Rules, Equally-Weighted Portfolios
Profits in %/Year

	1%	2%	Average of 1%, 2%
April 1973 to Mid-1975 (Prior Period)	3.69% (4.31)	4.41% (5.31)	4.05%
Mid-1975 to Mid-1980 (Test Sample)	3.36% (6.35)	1.99% (3.48)	2.65%

Notes: Based on Sweeney (1986). These results for an equally-weighted portfolio of currencies. Profits are net of transaction costs. The t-statistics in parenthesis assume that the profit measures across currencies are uncorrelated; this may overstate the t-statistics. For comparison of t-statistics across the two subperiods, multiply the t-statistics of the shorter period by 1.414 (= $2^{1/2}$), since the longer period has twice as many observations.

Table 2

Alexander Filter Rules, Equally- and Variably-Weighted Portfolios
Profits in %/Year

	(1) Equally-Weighted Portfolio	(2) Variably Weighted Portfolio	(3) Average of (1) and (2)
Mid-1978 to Mid-1982 (Test Sample)	3.58% (2.94)	6.20% (3.03)	4.89%
Mid-1982 to Mid-1986 (Test Sample)	2.56% (1.47)	0.69% (0.24)	1.63%
Whole period (average of the two subperiods)	3.07% (2.88)	3.45% (1.97)	3.26%

Notes: Based on Surajaras (1987). Profits are net of transaction costs. The t-statistics in parenthesis assume the population covariances of the profit measures across currencies are equal to the sample covariances; this may understate the t-statistics.

The Alexander rule, however, is the worst approach Surajaras considers over the whole 2000-observation period. Hence, it may not be important that the Alexander results in the second 1000-observation period are less impressive than in the first.

Surajaras' (1987) changes trigger values between the two test periods for virtually every currency. Well-chosen changes in rules can lead to enhanced profits, unwise changes can reduce profits. Table 3 gives some insights by looking at how the 1% and 2% Alexander filters, which Table 1 shows looked promising in Sweeney (1986), perform after Sweeney's test period for an equally-weighted portfolio of currencies. For the following six years, the two together average 2.06%, not too much below the average of 2.65% in Sweeney's test period and better than the 1.63% found for the second subperiod in Table 2. This suggests these simple rules give persistent profits, and switching rules may reduce performance.

This paper specifically considers the stability of speculative profits. While we use no new data beyond Surajaras', we make special efforts to avoid data-mining that might be viewed as trying to get around the instability of Alexander-type results as revealed in Surajaras (1987). Section 2 briefly discusses the performance measure used in this study, a generalized version of that used in Sweeney (1986). Section 3 lays out the rules investigated, and discusses whether to treat the speculations as one independent mutual fund per currency, as Sweeney (1986) does, or as mutual funds that can in effect lend and borrow from each other (Surajaras, 1987).

Section 4 and 5 discuss the stability of speculative profits. They use the final 1500 observations used by Surajaras, dividing them into two 750-observation periods, and also into six 250-observation periods (or "years"). The main stability issues considered are these. First, does there seem to be an optimum amount of prior data to use in selecting filters and lag lengths to use in speculating in a test period? Here, the results are somewhat inconclusive. Second, does there seem to be an optimum period after which the trigger values in a particular rule should be altered? Again the answer is somewhat inconclusive, though there is little support for mechanically altering triggers on a yearly basis as opposed to sticking with the same triggers for the entire test period. Third, do measured profits persist? The answer is a strong "Yes." Fourth, does there seem to be

Table 3

Alexander Filter Rules, Equally-Weighted Portfolios
Profits in %/Year

	1%	**2%**	**Average of 1% and 2%**
Mid-1980 to Mid-1983 (Test Sample)	0.84% (1.04) [0.46]	1.43% (1.82) [0.78]	1.14%
Mid-1983 to Mid-1986 (Test Sample)	2.38% (2.47) [1.05]	3.59% (3.75) [1.58]	2.99%
Whole Period (average of two subperiods)	1.61% (2.56) [1.11]	2.51% (4.05) [1.72]	2.06%

Notes: These are results for equally-weighted portfolios of currencies. Profits are net of transactions costs. The t-statistics in parenthesis assume that the profit measures across currencies are uncorrelated; this may overstate the t-statistics. The t-statistics in brackets assume that the population covariances of the profit measures across currencies are equal to the sample covariances; this may understate the t-statistics.

an approach that gives stability of speculative profits across periods? Not surprisingly, it turns out that simultaneously employing a basket of approaches gives fairly stable results.

Section 6 explicitly returns to the issues that started this paper, Has there been a decline in profits over time? Are speculative profits vanishing? It seems clear that profits are not vanishing. Surajaras' (1987) results in earlier chapters may through randomness, however, overstate the average level of profits one can expect over time. Section 7 offers a summary of results and some conclusions.

2. The Measurement of Performance

The profit measure used here is based on Sweeney (1987b) and is a generalization of the one used in Sweeney (1986, 1988). The profits reported here are risk-adjusted economic profits on the assumption that assets' risk premia are conditionally constant through time and the efficient markets hypothesis (EMH) that expected excess returns equal these risk premia. This joint assumption implies that there is no serial correlation in assets' returns and no lead/lag cross correlations across assets' returns. Given conditionally constant risk premia, any significant net measured profits are inconsistent with the EMH. Alternatively, measured profits and EMH are consistent only if there are time-varying risk premia.

Over T periods, the fund under consideration keeps its wealth fully invested across N different assets, with w_{jt} the share of wealth in asset j in period t. One of the N assets can be risk-free asset, if this exists. In some periods $w_{jt} \gtrless \bar{w}_j$, where $\bar{w}_j$ is the sample mean of w_{jt}, $\bar{w}_j \equiv \frac{1}{T} \Sigma_t^T w_{jt}$. A natural view is that the fund tries to make profits by the deviations of w_{jt} around $\bar{w}_j$, to take advantage of insights about fluctuations of rates of return around their means. An EMH counterview is that, relative to an unmanaged fund that just happened to choose constant weights $\bar{w}_j$, these fluctuations in w_{jt} around $\bar{w}_j$ will not ex ante improve measured returns <u>if</u> the performance evaluator believes the processes generating excess returns have conditionally constant means, equal to constant risk premia, and hence have zero serial correlation and only contemporaneous cross correlation; virtually all performance tests assume these conditions. Significant profits then lead to rejection of one or more of the joint hypotheses.

Asset pricing theories typically assume the expected excess rate of return on asset j equals its risk premium pr_j; this is the content of the EMH under such theories. In turn, if there are K economy-wide priced risk factors each with a premium PR_k, then $pr_j = \sum_{k=1}^{K} B_{jk} PR_k$, where the B_{jk} are the betas of j on the kth risk factor. This follows from the Sharpe-Lintner CAPM, the Black CAPM, the Merton intertemporal CAPM, the Breeden consumption-based asset pricing model or a Ross APM, and hence the test proposed here is consistent with all these theories. Assume the betas and the factor risk premia are conditionally constant, or less restrictively, that the pr_j are conditionally constant. With all expected returns conditionally constant, there is no serial correlation in returns nor any lead-lag patterns of cross correlation among assets' returns. The informed investor may claim, however, to be able to detect fluctuations in the expected return on j even though pr_j is constant. The tests developed here measure the investor's ability to do this. Significant measured profits then lead to a rejection either of the EMH or of constant risk premia pr_j.

More concretely, the rate of return on the fund's portfolio in t, R_{Ft}, is

$$R_{Ft} = \Sigma_j^N w_{jt} R_{jt}$$

and the average rate of return on the fund's portfolio over the period 1, T is

$$\bar{R}_F = \frac{1}{T} \Sigma_t^T R_{Ft} = \frac{1}{T} \Sigma_t^T \Sigma_j^N w_{jt} R_{jt},$$

where R_{jt} are returns in excess of either the risk-free rate (as in Sharpe-Lintner CAPM), the return on a minimum-variance zero-beta portfolio (in a Black CAPM) or the return on a portfolio with zero betas on all factors (in the APT). The fund's manager is allowed to choose any sequences $\{w_{jt}\}$ s/he likes. The average rate of return on a comparable buy-and-hold portfolio is

$$\bar{R}_{BH} = \frac{1}{T} \Sigma_t^T \Sigma_j^N \bar{w}_j R_{jt}.$$

At the end of T, the observer <u>constructs</u> the buy-and-hold portfolio to have the same $\bar{w}_j$ in every t that the manager averaged over the T periods; the comparison is then between the managed fund and some other constant-weight unmanaged fund that chooses the same $\bar{w}_j$.

Form the statistic

$$(1)\quad X \equiv \bar{R}_F - \bar{R}_{BH} = \frac{1}{T}\Sigma_t^T\Sigma_j^N w_{jt} R_{jt} - \frac{1}{T}\Sigma_t^T\Sigma_j^N \bar{w}_j R_{jt}$$

$$= \frac{1}{T}\Sigma_t^T\Sigma_j^N(w_{jt} - \bar{w}_j) R_{jt} = \frac{1}{T}\Sigma_t^T\Sigma_j^N u_{jt} R_{jt},$$

where $u_{jt} \equiv w_{jt} - \bar{w}_j$ so $\Sigma_t^T u_{jt} = 0$ (from the definition of $\bar{w}_j$) for all j, and $\Sigma_j^T w_{jt} = 1$ for all t). A non-zero X gives profits measured in the same dimensions as the Rs, for example, percent per day or decimal percent per year.

Next, evaluate X conditional on the observed, realized values of u_{jt}. The joint hypotheses of the EMH plus constant risk premia imply

$$EX = \frac{1}{T}\Sigma_t^T\Sigma_j^N u_{jt} ER_j = \frac{1}{T}\Sigma_j^N ER_j \Sigma_t^T u_{jt} = 0$$

since $\Sigma_t^T u_{jt} = 0$ for all j. Adding the hypothesis of conditionally constant contemporaneous variances and covariances implies that conditional on the observed us

$$(2)\quad \sigma_X^2 = E[\frac{1}{T}\Sigma_t^T\Sigma_j^N u_{jt} (R_{jt} - ER_j)]^2$$

$$= \frac{1}{T}\frac{1}{T}\Sigma_t^T[\Sigma_j^N u_{jt}^2 \sigma_{R_j}^2 + \Sigma_j^N \Sigma_{h, j\neq h}^N u_{jt} u_{ht} \operatorname{cov}(R_j, R_h)]$$

$$= \frac{1}{T}\frac{1}{T}\Sigma_t^T \operatorname{Var} P_t$$

$$= \frac{1}{T}\overline{\operatorname{Var} P}.$$

Thus,

$$(3)\quad \sigma_X = (\overline{\operatorname{Var} P})^{1/2}/T^{1/2},$$

where one can interpret

$$\operatorname{Var} P \equiv \Sigma_j^N u_{jt}^2 \sigma_{Rj}^2 + \Sigma_j^N \Sigma_{h, j\neq h}^N u_{jt} u_{ht} \operatorname{cov}(R_j, R_h)$$

as the variance in period t of a portfolio P_t that uses the weights u_{jt}, and $\overline{\operatorname{Var} P}$ is the average over time of this variance. (In principle, the covariance matrix can vary over time; see Sweeney (1987b).

Since the null hypothesis is (i) all pr_j are conditionally constant and (ii) the EMH holds so $ER_j = pr_j$, by construction X has the investor bear exactly the same ex ante risk (both systematic and unsystematic) in

$\bar{R}_F$ and $\bar{R}_{BH}$. In this sense X measures risk-adjusted profits. Whatever adjustment to $\bar{R}_F$ that should be made for risk is the same as for $\bar{R}_{BH}$, and hence is included in X by subtracting $\bar{R}_{BH}$ from $\bar{R}_F$.

The test allows for the possibility of superior ability either in market timing or in assessing firm characteristics. For example, in terms of the Sharpe-Lintner CAPM (though the example could be rephrased in terms of any asset-pricing model),

$$R_{jt} = B_j (ER_{Mt}) + B_j (R_{Mt} - ER_M) + e_{jt},$$

where B_j is the asset's beta, R_{Mt} the excess return on the market proxy used, and e_j the specific risk term. Conditional on the uniformed investor's information set, $E(R_{Mt} - ER_M) = 0 = Ee_{jt}$ for all j, t, and $ER_{jt} = B_j(ER_{Mt})$. The informed investor, however, may have superior ability in judging either $R_{Mt} - ER_M$ or e_{jt} (or both).

In principle, the returns on foreign assets are measured as the appreciation of the foreign currency plus the foreign risk-free rate, less the home-country risk-free rate. Since overnight risk-free rates are difficult to collect, in practice this interest-rate differential is omitted. Sweeney (1986) shows that this omission makes no difference to measured performance if the differential is on average the same on the days the investor is in the foreign asset as it is for the overall period; further, he shows for the dollar-DM rate for his sample that the empirical impact of neglecting the differential is small.

Any non-zero X has the dimension of profits per day (though the tables report them as profits per year by multiplying by 250). These profits are risk-adjusted in the sense that risk premia are reflected in the return on buy-and-hold.

3. Approaches to Technical Trading

This paper uses four different trading rules and two approaches to combining speculations in different currencies.

Alternative Rules. The Alexander rule is based on the early work of Alexander (1961, 1964). It says, "Buy when the price of the currency rises Y% above its past local low, and sell when it falls Z% from its past local high." The X and Z are the trigger values. The single moving average rule compares the price of the currency to an average of its current value and its latest Y - 1 values, a Y-period moving average. When the actual price rises above the moving average from below, this is a buy signal, and when price falls below the moving average from above, this is a sell signal. The double moving average rule uses two moving averages, one shorter than the other. The rule says to buy when the shorter rises above the longer moving average from below, to sell when the shorter falls below the longer from above.

Finally, the mixed rule for any period uses for a given currency the rule that appears best of the three just discussed, where "best" is based on results from data in a period prior to the test period. For a portfolio of currencies following a mixed strategy, then, some will likely use the Alexander, others the DMA or SMA in the same period.

Forming Portfolios. Sweeney (1986) assumes in effect that each currency speculation is a separate mutual fund, with each fund's assets fully invested in a home-country riskless asset when not fully invested in a foreign country asset that is riskless in terms of the foreign currency. He then forms an equally-weighted portfolio of the individual funds to allow an aggregate test.

In some of his work, Surajaras (1987) assumes that when one fund gets a sell signal, its assets go into a common pool that can be used by the other funds; assets in this common pool are invested at the risk-free rate for the dollar. If a sell signal arrives for the DM, for example, on the same day as a buy signal for the Swiss franc, the proceeds from the sale of the DMs are used along with any other idle assets to buy Swiss francs, which are then invested at the Swiss franc risk-free rate. If buy signals for several currencies arrive on the same day, all available assets are divided equally across these currencies. If no assets are available, no new buys can be made. This approach results in assets lying idle a smaller percentage of the time (approximately 11% of the time for Surajaras, 50% for Sweeney). If the risk-taking on average pays off in risk-adjusted profits, then the speculator wants to hold idle assets as small a percentage of time as possible. Further, Surajaras' approach results in fewer transactions and hence lower transactions costs, since some buy signals are met with no available assets to use and hence no transaction is made. This overall portfolio can be thought of as one where the currencies have variable weights and where the individual funds can borrow from and lend to each other.

Choosing Trigger Values and Lag Lengths. In all cases, trigger values for the Alexander rules and lag lengths for the moving averages for any period are chosen by examining, for each currency, performance in prior periods. Following Surajaras, we use as a criterion the highest transactions-costs adjusted X-statistic in the prior period. Similarly, we change the triggers and lengths in the second subperiod based on data that become available in the first subperiod. For each test period, he used the 900 preceding observations to search for the "best" triggers and lengths; work reported below uses from 250 to 1400 observations. The rule parameters are the same for both the equally-weighted and variably-weighted portfolio approaches; the difference between the two approaches is how much is invested in a currency that gets a buy signal.

Estimated Standard Errors. In finding the standard error of measured rates of profit, it is unclear how much weight to put on the covariance terms in (2). These terms are of the form

$$u_{jt}u_{ht}\ \mathrm{cov}(R_j,\ R_h),$$

where (2) takes the "u"s as given. Patterns of us that show positive cross correlation lead to a higher standard error in (2), since most covariances are positive. The variance σ_X^2 is calculated conditional on the us. There may well be a difference, however, in the pattern of us expected under efficiency and the pattern actually observed. To the extent that positive cross correlations of the us are due to inefficiencies (positive cross correlations of divergences between expected returns and conditionally constant risk premia) and are higher than would be expected under efficiency (no divergences and hence no cross correlations from this source), the standard error is artificially high. In this way, it makes sense to view the estimate from (2) as an upper bound. A truncated version that ignores the covariance terms may serve as a lower bound.

For these reasons, it is unclear exactly how to report standard errors and t-statistics. In Sweeney (1987a), the t-statistics for results for US equities are relatively insensitive to whether the covariance terms are included or not. In Surajaras (1987), the difference can be substantial for the foreign exchange market. (A feel for this difference is given by the two sets of t-statistics reported in Table 3). To conserve on space, t-statistics are generally omitted in the tables below. Table 4, based on Surajaras (1987), gives a good feel, however, for what the t-statistics are when the upper bound standard error is used or lower bound t-statistics are reported.

4. Choosing Trigger Values and Lag Lengths, and the Stability of Profits over Time

A number of possibilities are consistent with the fall off that Surajaras (1987) observed in the profitability of the Alexander rule.

Table 4

Profits in %/Year
(1) Equally-Weighted Portfolio of Individual Funds
(2) Variably-Weighted Portfolio of Interdependent Funds

Test Periods	Alexander		Double Moving Average		Single Moving Average		Mixed		Average	
	(1)	(2)	(1)	(2)	(1)	(2)	(1)	(2)	(1)	(2)
Mid-1978 to Mid-1982	3.5783% (2.9348)	6.1990%** (3.0297)	4.4943%** (2.9643)	5.8138%** (2.2181)	3.4668%** (2.1883)	6.5696%** (2.4526)	4.6528%** (3.2771)	4.3673%** (1.6374)	4.0480%** (3.2650)	5.7374%** (2.9864)
Mid-1982 to Mid-1986	2.5605% (1.4655)	0.6942%** (0.2242)	2.7113% (1.4269)	5.0161% (1.7782)	3.0908%** (1.6716)	5.9676%** (2.1936)	2.6635% (1.5439)	5.3122%** (1.9773)	2.7565% (1.7020)	4.2475%** (2.0342)
Whole period (average of the two subperiods)	3.0695%** (2.8813)	3.4466%** (1.9682)	3.6028%** (2.9642)	54150%** (2.8125)	3.2788%** (2.6932)	6.2686%** (3.2838)	3.6850%** (3.2745)	4.8398%** (2.5568)	3.4023%** (3.3361)	4.9925%** (4.8954)

Notes: From Surajaras (1987). To compare t-statistics for the subperiods with those of the whole period, multiply by 1.414.

**Significant at the 95% confidence level.

First, any non-zero measured profits may be wholly spurious or fluky, with the fall off meaning nothing. For the sake of discussion, assume that the results are not merely spurious or accidental. Second, the market may be catching on over the sample and acting in ways that reduce, and perhaps eventually eliminate, the measured profits. This interpretation would assume that the measured were economic profits that learning behavior was eliminating. The time over which the profits persisted would be impressive, and perhaps inconsistent with the EMH, even if they were being reduced and ultimately eliminated. Third, the process generating profits may change over time, and the trigger values and lag lengths used may not be suitable for the changed process. One way that inappropriate triggers and lengths can be chosen is by using inappropriate amounts of data in prior periods to select rules to use for speculation in the test periods. Fourth, the process may be changing rapidly enough that the 1000 observation test samples that Surajaras used are inappropriately long, as might have been Sweeney's 1220 observation test period. Fifth, the process may be changing in such a way that the best class of rules varies over time. Sixth, in a world in which the unknown best rule may come from changing classes of rules and changing amounts of prior data, the best ex ante approach may be to stick with one class and one amount of data. For example, using 500 days and a DMA may not be best in any period, but may give the best average over time. This paper casts some light on the third through sixth points.

Stability of Profits for Differing Prior Periods. Table 5 shows results for the four classes of rules and two portfolio approaches for various prior periods. The test sample runs from mid-1980 to mid-1986, and thus takes up where Sweeney's (1986) test sample leaves off. Several results seem clear.

First, the Alexander rules seem to have dropped off in performance from what Sweeney found with an equally-weighted portfolio (an average of 2.62%; see Table 1), whether we use the equally-weighted (2.30%) or variably-weighted (1.20%) portfolio approach.

Second, comparing column (1) for the Alexander rule in Table 5 with the average in Table 3 for the 1% and 2% rules, the tailored trigger values give a superior performance, 2.30% versus 2.06%, as opposed to sticking with the 1% and 2% trigger values that might have been picked based on Sweeney (1986). This difference in profitability is not, however, significant.

Table 5

Adjusted X-Statistics--Profits in %/Year
(1) Equally-Weighted Portfolio of Individual Funds, 1500 OBS
(2) Variably-Weighted Portfolio of Interdependent Funds, 1500 OBS
Mid-1980–Mid-1986

Prior Period*	Alexander		Double Moving Average		Single Moving Average		Mixed		Average	
	(1)	(2)	(1)	(2)	(1)	(2)	(1)	(2)	(1)	(2)
500	2.2950	3.0940	2.6600	4.4445	2.5225	3.0573	2.3275	2.1677	2.4513	3.1909
600	2.3200	2.9776	2.9225	3.0802	3.0650	5.9354	2.4900	3.1444	2.6994	3.7844
700	2.1875	-1.7301	2.9825	3.4492	3.1775	5.4112	2.9275	3.7814	2.8188	2.7281
800	2.3000	-1.3460	2.8300	3.9657	3.0650	4.7606	3.0775	4.2382	2.8871	2.9045
900	2.0975	- .6384	2.7300	2.2551	3.4025	5.2982	3.1950	4.0987	2.8563	2.7534
1,000	2.0300	1.5331	2.6775	2.1206	3.1600	4.3573	2.8950	4.1755	2.7331	3.0466
1,100	1.9675	1.4147	2.4550	1.7284	3.3250	5.4854	2.6875	3.6667	2.6088	3.0730
1,200	2.5650	2.4018	2.5575	1.7524	3.2450	6.2080	2.9450	3.7669	2.8281	3.5323
1,300	2.5775	1.9939	2.5775	2.5587	3.1775	6.3340	2.9250	3.1411	2.8144	3.5070
1,400	2.6875	2.3305	2.4475	2.3900	3.1925	6.7408	2.9250	3.6030	2.8131	3.7661
Average	2.3028	1.2031	2.6840	2.7745	3.1333	5.3588	2.8395	3.5794	2.7399	3.2287

*Number of observations used to choose filters and lag lengths ranges from 500 to 1400. These results are <u>not</u> the average of two 750-observation sub-periods.

Third, neglecting the Alexander rule, it is clear from the "Average" row in Table 5 that the variably-weighted beats the equally-weighted portfolio approach for the average of the columns for each rule. Even including the Alexander rule, the averages of the averages in Table 5 show that the variably-weighted beats the equally-weighted approach by almost half a percentage point (0.489%), though this is not statistically significant.

Fourth, for most sizes of the prior period, say 500, profits to the variably-weighted approach are on average (and sometimes substantially) larger than to the equally-weighted approach, as shown by comparing the "Average" columns.

Fifth, based on the "Average" row, the SMA variably-weighted portfolio approach dominates by far. Of course, this may be highly sample dependent. There are good, intuitive reasons, however, why this approach works. The equally-weighted approach works for the SMA, and thus the variably-weighted approach that keeps money busier on average should do even better. Further, as Surajaras (1987) pointed out, the SMA runs up sizable transactions costs with the equally-weighted approach, costs that the variably-weighted approach ends up reducing, since sometimes a transaction is signalled but there are no funds available and hence it is not carried out.

Sixth, in comparing average results in Tables 4 and 5, it is clear that a major reason for the lower average profits in the 1500-observation period is the fall off in performance of the double moving average and Alexander filter rules. In turn, the superior performance of these rules seems to have come in the first 500 observations of the 2000-observation period. One possibility is that these were particularly fortunate 500 observations. Another is that there is a trend to decreasing profits over time. We can check on this by splitting the 1500-observation period, as we do below.

Seventh, it is hard to see a clear advantage to any particular sample size used in the prior period to select rules for the test sample in Table 5. The "Average" columns show no very clear pattern for the equally-weighted portfolio approach, while for the variably-weighted portfolio approach the short prior periods (500 or 600) and the long prior periods (1300 or 1400) seem to work better than intermediate lengths. Both of these possible patterns suggested by averages suffer at least some contradiction from results from specific rules. For example, for variably-weighted portfolios, the DMA roughly does better with short prior periods, the SMA with long.

Eighth, the "Average" row and columns show the advantages of diversification across the fifteen currencies, four rules, and ten lengths of prior periods. For the variably-weighted portfolio, the average return is 3.22%/year, with a deviation of 3.78% above and 2.73% below. For the equally-weighted portfolio, the average return is 2.67%/year, with a deviation of 2.88% above and 2.45% below.

Temporal Stability of Profits.

Turn now to the two sub-periods of the 1500-observation test period.

The Equally-Weighted Portfolio. Table 6 sheds some light on the temporal stability of profits by looking at two subperiods of 750 observations each. The general picture, supported by the "Average" row, is very clear. There is a substantial increase in profits from the first subperiod to the second. This is in contrast to Surajaras' (1987) results where the first subperiod had substantially larger profits than the second, especially for the Alexander rules as Table 2 shows, but also for the DMA and SMA rules, as Table 4 shows. Since the test period here is the last 1500 observations of Surajaras' 2000 observation test period, there is clearly something of a puzzle here, to which we return below. At this point, we merely want to stress the obvious, that for the three years up to mid-1986, there seems to be little difference from the results Sweeney (1986) found for the average of the 1% and 2% triggers (2.65%—see Table 1 above) and the results in Table 6 (2.73% for the Alexander rule on average, 2.93% for the average of all the rules' averages).

The Variably-Weighted Portfolio Approach. Results here are much more mixed than for the equally-weighted portfolio approach. Table 7 shows that there is substantial instability over the two halves of the 1500-observation test period, with the first half giving substantially poorer results for the Alexander filter rule and somewhat poorer for the single moving average rule. This should be contrasted to Surajaras' (1987) results where his first period gave better results than the second period, as happens in Table 7 for the other two rules.

Switching Parameters After 750 Observations.

Comparing Tables 5 and 6 reveals an important point about the performance of the rules. For example, the Alexander rule equally-weighted portfolio in Table 5 gives an average of 2.30%. The average of the two periods in Table 6 (1.46% and 2.73%) is only 2.09% for the

Table 6

Adjusted X-Statistics--Profits %/Year
(1) Equally-Weighted Portfolio of Individual Funds, First 750 OBS
(2) Equally-Weighted Portfolio of Individual Funds, Second 750 OBS

Prior Period	Alexander		Double Moving Average		Single Moving Average		Mixed		Average	
	(1)	(2)	(1)	(2)	(1)	(2)	(1)	(2)	(1)	(2)
500	1.6500	3.0775	1.6075	2.8200	1.7150	3.4300	1.4075	3.0875	1.5950	3.1038
600	1.7475	2.7525	1.7200	2.4475	1.6525	3.2000	1.3775	2.8250	1.6244	2.8063
700	1.2175	2.6775	1.7875	2.3300	1.7100	3.8150	2.0800	2.2773	1.3944	2.7750
800	1.2475	2.7800	1.8475	2.9425	1.6225	3.6675	2.5900	2.5375	1.8269	2.9819
900	0.9900	3.0200	1.6275	2.7975	1.5550	3.6625	2.2575	2.5500	1.6075	3.0075
1,000	1.0175	2.6725	1.6125	2.8400	1.5625	3.3375	1.9300	2.8100	1.5306	2.9150
1,100	1.2125	2.4275	1.4225	2.5475	1.5200	3.4825	1.3675	2.5725	1.3806	2.7575
1,200	1.7725	2.8500	1.6100	3.1225	1.7075	3.2450	2.0225	3.1400	1.7781	3.0869
1,300	1.7675	2.5275	1.2700	3.1625	1.7325	3.2850	1.9200	2.4575	1.6725	2.8581
1,400	1.9425	2.4900	1.2800	3.2350	1.0650	3.3425	2.0175	3.0375	1.5763	3.0263
Average	1.4565	2.7265	1.5285	2.8245	1.5843	3.4468	1.8970	2.7295	1.6291	2.9318

Table 7

Adjusted X-Statistics--Profits %/Year
Variably-Weighted Portfolios of Interdependent Funds
(1) First 750 OBS
(2) Second 750 OBS

Prior Period	Alexander		Double Moving Average		Single Moving Average		Mixed		Average	
	(1)	(2)	(1)	(2)	(1)	(2)	(1)	(2)	(1)	(2)
500	2.7769	3.9045	6.8768	5.1526	4.7365	4.4030	5.0512	3.8526	4.8604	4.3282
600	2.4419	3.0270	7.3475	0.7179	4.5632	3.2004	0.9281	0.1666	3.8202	1.7405
700	-4.9096	6.3768	7.4739	-0.0053	4.1369	4.3329	0.5609	3.2878	1.8155	3.4981
800	-5.2962	4.4145	6.5714	-1.3408	3.4942	4.5321	1.3844	-3.5735	1.5385	1.0081
900	-0.2969	1.7236	6.1946	-0.4446	2.7164	5.8868	1.5650	2.3660	2.5448	2.3830
1,000	0.7137	2.5489	6.1897	-1.7902	3.5233	2.8253	3.3447	-1.9577	3.4439	.4066
1,100	1.1050	2.0248	5.6963	-1.6976	3.5758	5.5694	2.7957	-0.0016	3.2932	1.4738
1,200	0.7934	3.7824	5.5059	-0.8716	3.6938	3.9510	2.1286	2.0449	3.0304	2.2267
1,300	0.2874	3.3038	3.8256	-0.2358	4.8850	4.4493	3.2522	2.6103	3.0626	2.5319
1,400	0.7491	2.7226	2.6155	-0.1225	5.6049	5.2408	3.2388	0.3797	3.0521	2.0552
Average	-0.1635	3.3602	5.8297	0.0047	4.0930	4.4391	2.2930	0.9175	2.2998	2.1804

Alexander rule. Comparing Tables 5 and 6 shows that there are major, consistent difference across the two ways of measuring performance. The averages of averages show a difference of 0.45%.

There are two differences that account for the change. First, Table 5 uses the same rule throughout, while Table 6 switches rules. Second, whenever any rule starts, the program begins with the investor in the foreign currency, and when the period ends, the program forces the investor to sell out. Thus, breaking the 1500 observations into two periods may force the investor at the end of the first 750 and start of the next 750 to make transactions s/he would not otherwise make. If the investor is in the DM, say, and would like to stay there, forcing him to sell out on day 750 and buy back in on day 751 should have trivial impact. But if the investor is out of the DM, forcing him to buy in on day 751 and to hold until receiving a sell signal can be quite costly if the rule being used has some genuine predictive power.

It is of some interest to see how much difference these forced sales and purchases make. Assume that the same triggers and lengths are used in each 750 observation period as in the overall period, but that the investor is forced to make a fresh start after 750 observations. Comparing the averages of averages, the fresh-start approach (2.37%) relative to the constant approach (2.74%) costs the investor 0.38%. The difference between Tables 5 and 6 is the net of the impacts of the changes in triggers and rules and of the forced sales and purchases due to the fresh-start approach. Since this net difference is 0.45%, and the impact of the forced sales is 0.38%, it appears that the forced sales and purchases are the only important cause of the difference in performance between pursuing the same triggers and lengths over the entire 1500 observations versus switching triggers and lengths half-way through. This is bad news, however, for the belief that mechanically switching triggers and lengths can produce superior performance.

For the variably-weighted portfolio approach, comparing the average of the results in Table 6 to the results from using the same triggers and lengths throughout the 1500 observation test period shows superiority for using the same rule throughout rather than switching rules (though the results for the Alexander and Double Moving Average rules show some advantage to switching triggers and lengths). Recalling the above discussion of the cost to the investor of being forced to start over in the middle of the sample, it seems that a reasonable conclusion is that there is no clear cut superiority of sticking to triggers and lengths or switching them.

5. When to Change Filter Sizes and Lag Lengths?

The results so far apply to using long test periods (from three to six years in this paper, and up to eight years in Surajaras (1987)) and to using long prior periods to form guesses about promising strategies (from 500 to 1400 observations here, and 750 observations in Surajaras). It is not at all clear that such long periods are at all optimal, either in applying rules or searching for them. In using a 1/2 of 1% filter rule on U.S. equities, Sweeney (1987a) reports that changing stocks on a trading list every year gives superior performance compared to changing every two years, though the list maintained for two years gives positive measured profits. Of course, changing the composition of a trading list while maintaining the same trigger is not the same as holding constant the list of currencies traded but changing the rules used. The next step, however, is to consider shorter holding periods, in particular, 250 trading days (approximately one trading year).

Changing Rule Parameters Every Year. For equally-weighted portfolios of independent funds, the results are extremely discouraging, with the Alexander rule giving average profits of only 0.13%/year and the rules averaging only 0.09%/year overall. These results are particularly discouraging in comparison to holding the triggers and lengths constant throughout the six-year period, with the Alexander rule giving 2.30%/year and the rules averaging 2.74%/year. Recall from section 4, though, that we should expect some fall-off in performance because the program forces the investor to sell off at the end of each year and to buy at the beginning of the next year. In particular, the program may be forcing the investor to buy at a time when the rule would otherwise be strongly signalling that he should be out of the currency, and the program also forces the buyer to hold the currency until a sell signal.

Compare the results of using the same triggers from the initial prior period, but forcing the investor to start over at the beginning of each period versus simply keeping on with the same rule for the entire period. The average of results for all prior periods and all four rules is 0.5153% per year when the investor is forced to start over each year, versus 2.7393% when exactly the same trigger values are used but the investor is not forced to make a fresh start each year. On the other hand, forcing the investor not only to make a fresh start each year but also use a new set of triggers pays 0.0925% per year. In other words, the fresh start approach reduces profits by 2.224% (= 2.7393% - 0.5153%), while the combined impact of switching trigger values or lag lengths and the fresh start approach is to reduce profits by 2.6468% (= 2.7393% - 0.0925%). Thus, the additional effect of changing trigger values each year is to reduce profits by another 0.4228% per year (= 2.6468% - 2.2240%).

Forcing the investor to make a fresh start every year reduces profits by 2.224% per year, or since there are five fresh starts, by 0.4448%/year per fresh start. An earlier estimate of the costs of one fresh start after 750 observations was that it cost the investor 0.38%/year per that one fresh start. These two estimates of the costs of plunging in on investments, without considering market timing, are remarkably consistent.

The reduction due to switching triggers and lengths each year is not statistically significant. Nevertheless, as a point estimate, it costs the investor more than 0.4% per year to switch triggers and lengths. Further, this result is a warning that switching triggers and lengths relatively frequently, in this case on a yearly basis, may have very low value. This conclusion holds, though, only for relatively long prior periods, in this case periods of from 500 to 1400 observations.

Using Shorter Prior Periods. Table 8 shows the dismal results in columns (1) from using shorter prior periods, of from 250 to 500 observations, along with changing filters and lag lengths each year. The average across these prior-period lengths and the rules is -0.364%/year. It is clear by now that some major part of these poor results is due to forcing the investor to sell at the end of each year and to buy at the start of the next and then hold until a sell signal. However, these results are poor relative to switching rules every year but using longer prior periods. For example, above we found an average profit of 0.0925%/year for prior periods of from 500 to 1400 observations even though the filters and lag lengths are changed each year in both cases and both cases require a fresh start. Thus, the shorter prior periods cost the investor an average of 0.4565%/year as a best guess as compared to longer prior periods (though the difference is not significant). Further, compare the averages in Table 8 for the columns (1) and (2). This shows that the effect of changing the filters and lag lengths every period is to reduce profits by 0.8806%/year, from 0.5166% to -0.3640%.

Table 8

Adjusted X-Statistics--Profits %/Year
Equally-Weighted Portfolio of Independent Funds
(1) Filters and Lag Lengths Are Changed Each 250 OBS
(2) Same Filters and Lag Lengths Throughout, Fresh Start
Each 250 OBS

Prior Period	Alexander		Double Moving Average		Single Moving Average		Mixed		Average	
	(1)	(2)	(1)	(2)	(1)	(2)	(1)	(2)	(1)	(2)
250	-0.1025	0.5625	-0.2700	0.3150	-0.4150	0.5800	-0.3975	0.3300	-0.2963	0.4469
300	-0.4750	0.5300	-0.9450	0.2815	-0.3700	0.7550	-0.9425	0.3375	-0.6831	0.4760
400	0.3575	0.1575	-0.8850	0.4050	-0.0550	0.6950	-0.5000	0.6475	-0.2706	0.4763
450	-0.2675	0.6300	-0.4525	0.2125	-0.0500	0.5735	-0.6775	0.9450	-0.3619	0.5813
500	-0.1025	0.7825	-0.3625	0.2325	-0.1775	0.3550	-0.1900	1.0400	-0.2081	0.6025
Average	-0.1180	0.5235	-0.5830	0.2893	-0.2135	0.5845	-0.5415	0.6600	-.3640	0.5166

6. Have Speculative Profits Declined Over Time?

This paper began by noting Surajaras (1987) results that found declining profits for the Alexander filter rule for the four years ending in mid-1986 as compared to the preceding four years. One interpretation is that speculative profits are vanishing over time. On the other hand, for the equally-weighted portfolio approach Table 6 above found larger average profits for every technical trading rule for the three years ending in mid-1986 than for the three preceding years under the equally-weighted portfolio approach. The variably-weighted portfolio approach shows very similar average profits over the two 750-observation subperiods, with two rules showing larger profits and two smaller profits in the second subperiod. On this evidence, then, profits do not seem to show a downward trend as time goes on.

These results raise another problem, however, since they show a decline in average profits for the 1500-observation test period in comparison to average profits in Table 4 for the 2000-observation period. The equally-weighted portfolio approach gives 2.67% versus 3.40%. Similarly, comparisons for the variably-weighted portfolio approach shows that average profits are 4.99% in the 2000-observation period and only 3.23% in the 1500-observation period. For 900-observation prior periods, there is an even more substantial fall in moving from 2000 to 1500 test observations, from an average of 4.99% to 2.46% for the variably-weighted and from 3.40% to 2.31% for the equally-weighted portfolio approach. (Note that 900-observation prior periods do not perform very well in the 1500-observation test period as compared to different-sized prior periods.)

Clearly, the 500-observation difference in the two test periods matters substantially. Its importance might arise for three reasons. First, the 500 observations gone from the sample might be particularly profitable. Second, the deletion of these observations changes both prior periods and the rules they generate for use in the subperiods. Third, the new first subperiod overlaps only for 500 observations with the old first subperiod and overlaps for the first 250 observations of the old second subperiod, while the new second subperiod is simply the last 750 observations of the old second subperiod; simple redivision of periods may introduce random fluctuations in profits.

Table 9 sheds some light on these possibilities by showing the results from running Surajaras' (1987) filters and lag lengths on the

Table 9

Adjusted X-Statistics--Profits in %/Year
1500 OBS, Divided into Two Subperiods
(1) Filters and Lag Lengths Used by Surajaras (1987)
(2) Filters and Lag Lengths Developed Here

	Alexander		**Double Moving Average**		**Single Moving Average**		**Mixed**		**Average**	
	(1)	(2)	(1)	(2)	(1)	(2)	(1)	(2)	(1)	(2)
Variably-Weighted Interdependent Mutual Funds										
Sub-period 1	3.2762	-0.2969	4.0517	6.1946	1.8512	2.7164	4.6114	1.5650	3.4476	2.5448
Sub-period 2	-1.1192	1.7236	-4.0516	-0.4446	3.7735	5.8868	1.4451	2.3660	0.1195	2.4830
Whole Period	1.0785	0.7134	0.0001	2.8750	2.8123	4.3016	3.0282	1.9655	1.7297	2.4639
Equally-Weighted Independent Mutual Funds										
Sub-period 1	5.2600	.9900	5.7550	1.6275	4.3975	1.5550	6.0150	2.2575	5.3794	1.6075
Sub-period 2	2.7300	3.0200	2.8250	2.7975	3.5125	3.6625	2.9950	2.5500	3.0156	3.0075
Whole Period	3.9950	2.0050	4.2900	2.2125	3.9550	2.6088	4.5050	2.4038	4.1863	2.3075

Note: All rule parameters are from 900-observation prior periods.

periods used here as compared with the results of the 900-observation prior periods used. The difference, then, is due simply to the subperiod rules being chosen from prior periods that are 500 observations apart.

From Table 9, there is no clear superiority of one set of filters and lag lengths over the other when both the equally-weighted and variably-weighted portfolio approaches are considered. Looking at the approaches separately, however, shows some interesting differences.

For the equally-weighted portfolio approach, the filters and lag lengths from Surajaras (1987) work better on average in each subperiod (though only by a very small amount in the second subperiod) and hence overall than the new filters and lag lengths. On the other hand, the new parameters show increasing profits in the second subperiod relative to the first, while Surajaras' parameters show decreasing profits between the two subperiods. The old parameters give better results than the new in the first subperiod for every rule, while the new outperform the old for two of the four rules in the second subperiod. The results for the second subperiod are so close, however, that the big superiority of the old parameters in the first subperiod makes it appear that it was a mistake not to stick with the old parameters overall. For the equally-weighted portfolio approach, then, one may want to ascribe the decline in whole-period profits to a bad but random change in rule parameters.

For the variably-weighted approach, the new parameters give better average performance for the whole period than Surajaras' (2.46% versus 1.73%). The average performance of the new parameters is about constant over subperiods (2.55% versus 2.48%) while the performance of parameters from Surajaras (1987) shows substantial decline across subperiods (3.45% versus 0.12%). The profits from the new parameters rise between the two subperiods for all of the rules save the double moving average rule, where the fall between subperiods is large—but smaller than the fall under Surajaras' rule parameters.

It is worthwhile to compare the results of the old parameters for the new subperiods (in Table 9) and for the old subperiods (in Table 4) to show the effect of altering the subperiods. The equally-weighted portfolio's excellent performance in the shorter whole period is even better than in the longer whole period. It is tempting to put this improvement down to sheer randomness. By the same token, one might view the difference in whole-period results for the 2000- and 1500-observation periods when different 900-observation prior periods are used, 3.40% and 2.31%, as essentially random.

For the variably-weighted portfolio approach, changing the length of subperiods while keeping the same parameters is very costly—the whole-period average falls from 4.99% to 1.73%. Further, the fall off in profits between subperiods is accentuated by the shift to the shorter subperiods. Recall that Table 9 shows essentially no fall off in profits between subperiods for the new parameters. One reasonable view is that there is no ongoing tendency for profits to fall between subperiods, but that the 500-observation difference in the two different whole periods considered has a big though random effect on profits under the variably-weighted portfolio approach.

How can there be so much randomness with the variably-weighted portfolio approach? Recall that the standard errors from this approach tend to be large relative to those from the equally-weighted portfolio approach, as can be seen from Table 4 for the first subperiod, where the implied ratio of standard errors is 1.5496 (=1.9212/1.2398). This is so even though both approaches use exactly the same rule parameters and hence get exactly the same buy and sell signals for the individual currencies. Intuitively, the variably-weighted portfolio approach is subject to more randomness because it allows the possibility of more extreme positions. The equally-weighted portfolio approach never lets the fraction of total wealth invested in any one currency rise above roughly 1/15th, since each currency is treated essentially as an independent mutual fund. Under the variably-weighted portfolio approach, however, the funds can be thought of as borrowing and lending to each other. Suppose, for example, that all currencies get a sell signal—the funds realized from the sales are all put in Euro-dollar accounts and the investor is completely out of foreign currencies. Several days later, there is a buy signal for one currency and no others. All of the funds are then put in this one currency—the weight on this currency is unity. If things go well, they go really well--and if they go badly, they go really badly.

If one is willing to ascribe to randomness the different average performances of rules in the 2000- and 1500-observation periods, the question arises of the best estimate of true underlying performance. The longer period seems to say 3.40% and 4.99% for the equally-weighted and variably-weighted portfolio approaches (Table 4), while the shorter seems to say 2.67% and 3.23% (Table 5). The real message of this paper seems to be that while there is not a clear change in the level of profits over subperiods, it is unclear what level of profits to expect.

7. Conclusions

Speculative profits in the foreign exchanges show a degree of stability across periods that is perhaps somewhat surprising in light of the volatility of these markets. This paper began with the observation that profits seem to have fallen off for the Alexander filter rule from levels found earlier, leading to the possibility that the speculative potential of these markets was drying up and might ultimately vanish. Instead, the profitability of speculation could be argued to be roughly the same over, say, the past twelve years, based on the results in Sweeney (1986) and this paper. It seems, however, that the first 500 observations in Surajaras' (1987) 2000-observation sample give particularly favorable results for the Alexander filter and double moving average rules, enhancing the impression that later profits fall off. Whether one wants to estimate average profits for the future on the basis of the more favorable average results Surajaras (1987) finds or the more conservative results this paper finds is a problematic issue.

The Alexander rule does seem to be either the most profitable or stable. Moving average rules appear to be superior, with some evidence that the single moving average rule gives best performance.

The variably-weighted portfolio approach, seems to raise profits (especially for the single moving average rules) at the cost of greater variability.

Changing filters or lag lengths on a yearly basis does not seem to improve profits. Indeed, the point estimate says this reduces profits.

There does not seem to be a clear advantage across all rules to using larger or smaller amounts of data to select filters or lag lengths.

Finally, looking across the tables, diversification pays—diversification across rules and across amounts of data used to select filters and lag lengths.

Footnotes

*Thanks are due to L. Peter Jennergren for helpful comments.

[1] Praetz (1976) argues that the filter rule test of Fama and Blume (1966) was substantially biased against filter rules. Levich (1982), in a comment on Sweeney (1982), argues that risk may be different on average in the periods a technical rule has the speculator in the asset as opposed to out of the asset.

[2] Profits in this paper are measured in percent per year, using one or another version of the X-statistic discussed in section 2 below. All profits discussed here are reported net of transactions costs. Transactions costs of 1/8 of 1% per round trip are assumed; see Sweeney (1986) for a discussion of transactions costs.

[3] Suppose that there are fourteen currencies, and that for every period seven have positive us and seven have negative us. Let u_{it} be negative. Then, $u_{1t}u_{it}$ for all not equal to 1 shows six negative values and five positive values. If the covariances across currencies are roughly the same or is there is no systematic pattern of u-products and covariances, then the net impact of the covariance terms on the standard error will be negative.

REFERENCES

Alexander, S. S., 1961, Price Movements in Speculative Markets: Trends or Random Walks, Industrial Management Review 2, 7-26.

__________, 1964, Price Movements in Speculative Markets: Trends or Random Walks, Number Two, Industrial Management Review 5, 25-46.

Cornell, W.B., and J. K. Dietrich, 1978, The Efficiency of the Market for Foreign Exchange Under Floating Exchange Rates, Review of Economics and Statistics 60, 111-20.

Dooley, M., and J. Shafer, 1976, Analysis of Short-Run Exchange Rate Behavior, March 1973 to September 1975, International Finance Discussion Paper No. 76, Federal Reserve Board.

__________, 1983, Analysis of Short-Run Exchange Rate Behavior: March 1973 to November 1981, in: D. Bigman and T. Taya, eds., Exchange Rate and Trade Instability (Ballinger,Cambridge, MA) 43-69.

Fama, E. F., and M. Blume, 1966, Filter Rules and Stock-Market Trading, Journal of Business 39, 226-41.

Levich, R., 1982, Commentary, in: J. S. Dreyer, G. Haberler, and T. D. Willett, eds., The International Monetary System: A Time of Turbulence (American Enterprise Institute, Washington, D.C.) 128-35.

Logue, D. E., R. J. Sweeney, and T. D. Willett, 1978, The Speculative Behavior of Foreign Exchange Rates During the Current Float, Journal of Business Research 6, 159-74.

Praetz, P., 1976, Rates of Return of Filter Tests, Journal of Finance 31, 71-75.

Surajaras, Patchara, 1987, Technical Speculations and the Efficiency of the Foreign Exchange Market, Ph. D. dissertation, The Claremont Graduate School.

Sweeney, R. J., 1986, Beating the Foreign Exchange Market, Journal of Finance 41, 163-82.

__________, 1987a, Evidence on Short-Term Trading Strategies, Claremont Working Paper.

__________, 1987b, Testing Portfolio Performance with Observable Asset Weights, Claremont Working Paper.

__________. 1988, Some New Filter Rule Tests: Methods and Results, Journal of Financial and Quantitative Analysis, forthcoming.

__________, 1982, Intervention Strategy: Implications of Purchasing Power Parity and Tests of Spot Exchange Market Efficiency, in: J. S. Dreyer, G. Haberler, and T. D. Willett, eds., The International Monetary System: A Time of Turbulence (American Enterprise Institute, Washington, D.C.) 65-109.

FURTHER EVIDENCE AGAINST THE EFFICIENCY OF FUTURES MARKETS

Stephen J. Taylor and Abdelkamel Tari*
School of Management
University of Lancaster
Lancaster LA1 4YX
England

KEYWORDS/ABSTRACT: market efficiency/futures/currency markets/ commodity markets/price models/stochastic processes/ time series analysis/forecasting/price trends/speculation/ portfolios/risk/simulation

The efficiency of futures markets is explored by applying trend-following trading rules to simulated prices and to the prices of currency and commodity futures. The simulation results prove that the rules can exploit price trends consistent with the small autocorrelations observed for futures returns. Out-of-sample net excess returns are reported for IMM sterling, deutschemark and Swiss franc futures (1982-87) and for London cocoa and sugar futures (1982-85). Assuming futures have zero or negative "betas" the excess returns provide persuasive evidence against market efficiency.

* A. Tari, National Institute of Computing, Algiers.

NATO ASI Series, Vol. F54
A Reappraisal of the Efficiency of Financial Markets
Edited by Rui M. C. Guimaraes et al.

FURTHER EVIDENCE AGAINST THE EFFICIENCY OF FUTURES MARKETS

1. Trading rules and futures

1.1 Introduction

Results for trading rules applied to futures prices have frequently raised doubts about the weak-form efficiency of futures markets. Early studies by Stevenson and Bear (1970) and Leuthold (1972) document apparently high profits for U.S. agricultural futures but these have been criticised, for example by Praetz (1976a, 1976b). Recent studies by Taylor (1983, 1986), Bird (1985) and Lukac, Brorsen and Irwin (1988) also document apparent profits for various U.S. and U.K. forward and futures markets. Similar work by Sweeney (1986) for spot foreign exchange provides additional evidence against market efficiency.

This paper presents further evidence on the efficiency of the currency futures market operated by the International Monetary Market in Chicago and agricultural futures markets situated in London. Results are presented for sterling, deutschemark, and Swiss franc contracts from 1982 to 1987 inclusive, and for cocoa, coffee and sugar contracts from 1982 to 1985 inclusive. We show that published trading rules continue to be profitable.

We use rules first described in Taylor (1983) and emphasise that these rules are based upon optimal forecasts for time series models. Popular technical and academic trading rules, such as the filter rule of Alexander (1961), are not constructed from explicit price models. Rather popular rules are based upon a general concept, for example the filter rule aims to exploit trends. Taylor's rules are effective if there are trends in prices, a point of view supported by relevant tests and empirical evidence, see Taylor (1986). It should be noted that the prices considered here, from 1982 onwards, were collected after the publication of profitable results in Taylor (1986) for the rules applied to prices for earlier years.

Section 2 describes our trading assumptions. Price models, similar to ARIMA(1,1,1) models, are summarised in Section 3 and used to motivate two trading rules. In Section 4 we use simulated prices to show and stress that very little autocorrelation among returns is required to make a futures market inefficient. Our trading results for 1982 onwards follow in Section 5 and conclusions are presented in Section 6.

1.2 Spot/futures contrasts

Futures can be traded cheaply and this, together with the margin system, makes them attractive for technical traders and hence researchers. However futures contracts differ from spot contracts in a number of important ways.

First, the margin system prevents a clear description of the capital invested in a futures position. As Treasury Bills are acceptable margin for some traders it can be argued that no capital is required to finance a position.

Second, the benchmark for comparison with trading results is controversial with some researchers (e.g. Bodie and Rosansky, 1980) claiming a positive risk premium for commodity futures. Hence there is a case for the buy-and-hold benchmark. Risk-free investment provides another and logical benchmark.

Third, corrections for the risk incurred by trading commodity and currency futures are problematic. Asset pricing models can imply that risk adjustments are not required as (a) futures risks can be diversified away (Black, 1976), and (b) futures betas are empirically close to zero, see Dusak (1973),

Bodie and Rosansky (1980) and Elton, Gruber and Rentzler (1987). However, Lukac et al (1988) claim significant negative betas for technical rules applied to futures. Recent work on time-varying risk premia (e.g. Wolff, 1987) complicates the issue. We describe an intuitive approach to risk adjustments in Section 2.

Fourth, the seasonal anomalies found in spot prices are either absent or are less pronounced for futures prices. The well-known day-of-the-week seasonal pattern in U.S. share index returns is absent from index futures (Cornell, 1985, Finnerty and Park, 1987). Results for other futures are given by Roll (1984) and Taylor (1986).

1.3 Efficiency defined

Following Taylor (1986, pp. 197-9) we adopt a practical definition of the efficient market hypothesis. The hypothesis is said to be true if the risk-adjusted return, net of all costs, from the best trading rule is not more than the comparable figure when assets are traded infrequently. This is essentially the definition given by Jensen (1978). It assumes trading rules buy and sell the same goods, here futures, fairly often, typically more than once per futures contract. In comparison, goods should be traded at efficient markets as little as possible to minimize costs. Of course investors and institutions may never want to trade futures when they believe such markets are efficient.

Trading rules generate more business for brokers than efficient market policies and therefore have higher transaction costs. Further costs for traders arise from differing bid and ask prices, the acquisition of information and interpretation thereof. We use daily closing prices which effectively cost nothing to acquire. Our rules produce decisions using negligible time and computer resources.

Developing useful trading systems requires, we contend, specialist skills. The associated costs cannot be measured with any accuracy. Only the inventor or purchaser of a system can compare development or acquisition costs with net returns and of necessity such costs are here ignored. Risk has to be considered and ideally this should be done in a portfolio context involving alternative investments such as shares. We offer a way to do this in Section 2.

Our definition of an efficient market has the advantage of being practical at the cost of being person dependent. Resources, costs, opportunities to diversify and attitudes to risk vary between people. In particular transaction costs are very low for floor traders, are higher for most companies and are often higher for individual speculators.

Ball (1988) is highly critical of Jensen's definition of an efficient market. However it has been shown beyond reasonable doubt that futures markets are weak-form inefficient if the definition of Fama (1976, p.140) favoured by Ball is adopted. Random walk and related tests (e.g. Taylor, 1986, Chapter 6) show that futures prices do not adjust fully and instantaneously when new information becomes available. When a market is not "Fama" efficient we contend that it is of interest to discover if transaction costs prevent exploitation of the "Fama" inefficiencies. The Jensen definition is then relevant.

2. Trading assumptions

2.1 The trader

It will be supposed that the trader has substantial assets or acts on behalf of an organisation possessing substantial assets. These assets form a portfolio which is supposed to be well-diversified and to include cash on deposit, short-term bills and stocks. We consider such a trader to try and circumvent the problem of correcting trading results for risk. We return to risk corrections in Section 2.3. It is reasonable to concentrate on results for traders commanding substantial resources. Small speculators should probably keep out of futures and instead seek a reward for risk by trading stocks.

2.2 Transactions with the broker

The trader is assumed not to be a floor trader. When a futures position is opened the trader sends a bill to some broker as a margin deposit. The bill will be a risk-free government security and is chosen to have a maturity date after the futures contract expires. Furthermore the face value of the bill is equated with the value of the goods when the position is opened. This ensures in practise that no further margin deposit is required even if a short position is taken.

To illustrate suppose we consider trading Sterling December 1988 futures from 1 June to 30 November 1988. Then there might be a bill in the portfolio purchased for $100,000 on 1 January 1988 and repaying $110,000 on 1 January 1989. This bill is used for all trades involving the £ Dec 88 contract. Our first decision might be to go long on 15 June by buying at a price of $1.8 per £. Then we contract to pay $100,000 for £100,000/1.8 = £55,556 in December (buy 2.2222 futures contracts at the IMM, 1 contract is for £25,000) and send the broker the bill and some commission. Later, on 8 August we might be so fortunate as to close the trade by selling £55,556 for delivery in December at $1.9 (sell 2.2222 contracts). The broker then returns our gross profit of $1.9*55,556 - $100,000 = $ 5,556 and the bill. If we open another position before 30 November then we use the same bill and the same method to find the number of contracts. We ignore the fact that this number is usually not an integer. Transaction costs, being commission and the costs due to bid-ask spreads, are assumed for simplicity to be proportional to the value of the goods traded and to be paid when the trade commences. So if the proportional rate c is 0.002 then the above trade costs $200 to open and close. The trader uses cash on deposit to pay the broker and likewise gross trading gains and losses are paid into and out of cash on deposit. Gains and losses are settled immediately by the broker and trader when the trade is closed. Settlement delays have negligible financial consequences.

Unlike previous work in Taylor (1986), we suppose the trader can deal with the broker at published closing prices. We have been assured that this is feasible when trading currency futures using our strategies. The consequences of a short delay in taking decisions is in any case shown not to be severe in Section 4.2.

2.3 Excess returns

If we consider all the cash flows associated with the risk-free bill (commission, trading gains and losses, interest on the bill) we can construct a new security which we call a risky bill. At maturity the value of the risky bill is taken to be the value of the risk-free bill plus the gross trading profit less transaction costs. So for our illustration, supposing only one trade in the £ Dec 88 contract, we have a value for the risky bill of $110,000 + 5,556 - 200 = $115,356 on 1 January 1989. We ignore the time value of the cash flows to and from the broker which is negligible.

We define the excess return on the risky bill at maturity to be its maturity value less the maturity value of the risk-free bill divided by the face value of the risk-free bill (5.356% for the illustration). Likewise we can define an excess return for any subperiod of a bill's life. Note that excess returns on risky bills are positive over some time interval if and only if gross trading profits exceed transaction costs for the same time interval. We claim the futures market is inefficient for the trader if expected excess returns on risky bills are positive. We are here assuming that the beta (systematic risk) of the trading rule used is either zero or negative. This assumption is consistent with the studies cited in Section 1.2. In due course we hope to calculate betas for our rules and prices.

The futures market will be inefficient if expected excess returns on risky bills are positive and our beta assumption applies because the trader can then arrange a portfolio including risky bills that is better than a benchmark portfolio that does not include risky bills. By better we mean a lower variance without any decrease in the expected return of the portfolio. A numerical example is presented in Section 4.

We ignore the possibility of taking geared positions in the futures market because gearing is irrelevant when assessing efficiency. Gearing has no effect on the least portfolio variance obtainable for a specified expected return.

3. Price models and trading rules

3.1 Models

We now outline the models used to motivate trading rules (Section 3.3) and to provide simulated prices (Section 4). Supporting empirical evidence and simple parameter estimation methods can be found in Taylor (1986).

Let Z_t be the closing price on day t for some price model and let

$$X_t = \log(Z_t) - \log(Z_{t-1})$$

be the so-called return on day t. Let $\{X_t\} = \{X_1, X_2, \ldots\}$ be a set of random variables. Then, if the model is to be of value observed market returns $\{x_t\} = \{x_1, x_2 \ldots\}$ must be reasonably consistent with the generating process $\{X_t\}$. It is well known that the volatility of returns is stochastic and we are also interested in modelling trends in prices. We will only describe stationary models here but are aware that non-stationary models can be appropriate (Taylor, 1988).

To motivate our final models we begin with two special cases. Firstly, trends can be modelled and stochastic volatility ignored by supposing:

$$X_t = \mu_t + e_t \tag{1}$$

and
$$\mu_t - \mu = p\ (\mu_{t-1} - \mu) + \omega_t \tag{2}$$

with $\{e_t\}$ and $\{\omega_t\}$ stochastically independent noise processes. All our noise processes will be stationary, have zero mean and have Normal distributions. Throughout μ and σ^2 will be the mean and variance of X_t. For (1) and (2), $\{\mu_t\}$ is AR(1) and $\{X_t\}$ is ARMA(1,1). Let $\mathrm{var}(\mu_t) = A\sigma^2$ and $\mathrm{var}(e_t) = (1-A)\sigma^2$. Then the X_t have autocorrelations

$$\rho_{\tau,X} = \mathrm{cor}(X_t, X_{t+\tau}) = Ap^{\tau},\ \tau \geqslant 1.$$

Empirical evidence favours $0<A<0.05$ and $0.8<p<1$ for commodity and currency futures.

Secondly, volatility can be modelled and trends ignored by supposing:

$$X_t = \mu + e_t, \tag{3}$$

$$e_t = V_t \epsilon_t, \tag{4}$$

and
$$\log (V_t) - \alpha = \phi\ \{\log(V_{t-1}) - \alpha\} + \eta_t \tag{5}$$

with stochastically independent noise processes $\{\epsilon_t\}$ and $\{\eta_t\}$. Here $var(\epsilon_t) = 1$ and V_t is a conditional standard deviation for X_t. Equation (5) supposes log-volatility is AR(1). Similar models (but with $\phi = 1$) have been considered by Hull and White (1987) and Johnson and Shanno (1987). An alternative and important class of volatility models has been described by Engle and Bollerslev (1986) and Bollerslev (1987).

Mixing trend and volatility effects is necessary but it is not obvious how this should be done. Following Taylor (1986) we describe two plausible possibilities.

For both models:

$$X_t = \mu_t + e_t \qquad \text{as in (1)}$$
$$e_t = V_t \epsilon_t \qquad \text{as in (4)}$$
and $$\log (V_t) \text{ is AR(1)} \qquad \text{as in (5)}$$

with $var(\mu_t) = A\sigma^2$, $var(e_t) = (1-A)\sigma^2$ but now $var(\epsilon_t)$ is $1-A$. The <u>linear trend model</u> supposes trends $\{\mu_t\}$ are stochastically independent of volatility $\{V_t\}$ with:

$$\mu_t \text{ is AR(1) as in (2).}$$

The alternative <u>non-linear trend model</u>, however, lets the trend magnitude depend directly on volatility:

$$\mu_t = \mu + V_t T_t \tag{6}$$
and $$T_t \text{ is AR (1)} \tag{7}$$

with the variables T_t having zero mean, variance A and autocorrelations p^τ. Now $\{T_t\}$, $\{V_t\}$ and $\{\epsilon_t\}$ are assumed to be stochastically independent.

We let β^2 be the variance of $\log(V_t)$. Then both models have six parameters: μ, A, p, α, β and ϕ with σ^2 given by exp(2α +

$2\beta^2$). Also the autocorrelations of the X_t are Ap^{τ} for the linear trend model and very close to Ap^{τ} for the non-linear trend model. (Slightly different notation is used in Taylor (1986) for the linear trend model but the model structure is the same).

The trend term μ_t could be called a time-varying risk premium if its magnitude is consistent with observed premia estimates. We claim however that the variances of μ_t for our futures are far higher than the variance of observed premia estimates. For example, consider currencies and suppose μ_t is merely a time-varying risk premium. From Wolff (1987) we may suppose the absolute premium for one year is less than 5% so $|\mu_t|<0.05/250 = 0.0002$. Assuming μ_t has a uniform distribution over the range -0.0002 to 0.0002 gives $\text{var}(\mu_t) = (0.0004)^2/12$ (a generously high estimate). Also, from Taylor (1986) the variance of currency returns is more than $(0.005)^2$. Thus the proportion of returns variance attributable to time-varying risk premia is less than

$$(0.0004)^2/[12(0.005^2)] = 0.0005 \text{ approximately.}$$

This very small proportion is a small fraction of the proportion of variance here attributed to trends and denoted by A. Empirical estimates of A for currencies exceed 0.02 (Taylor, 1986). To explain A = 0.02 using time-varying risk premia would require the premium in annual terms to have a standard deviation greater than 17%. The comparable annual standard deviation given by Pope and Peel (1988) for their variable $P^*(t)$ is approximately 5%.

3.2 Forecasts

The trading rules make use of standardised forecasts k which are a function of volatility and return forecasts. As in Taylor (1986, Chapter 8), at time t the latest return x_t (calculated from closing prices z_{t-1} and z_t) is used to forecast the next day's volatility and return using simple updating equations.

The volatility forecast $\hat{v}_t$ made at time t is a function of the return x_t and the forecast $\hat{v}_t$ made at time t-1:

$$\hat{v}_{t+1} = 0.9\ \hat{v}_t + 0.1\ (1.253|x_t|). \tag{8}$$

Likewise the return forecast $f_{t,1}$ made at time t is a function of x_t and the forecast $f_{t-1,1}$ made at time t-1:

$$f_{t,1} = (\hat{v}_{t+1}/\hat{v}_t)\ [(p-q)x_t + qf_{t-1,1}]. \tag{9}$$

In equation (9), q is the moving average parameter when an ARMA(1,1) process has autocorrelations Ap^{τ}. It is the number solving

$$q^2 - q\{1 + (1-2A)p^2\}/\{(1-A)p\} + 1 = 0 \text{ and } q<1.$$

An estimate of the standard deviation of $F_{t,1}$, the variable that generates $f_{t,1}$, conditional upon the observed volatility forecast is

$$\hat{\sigma}_F = \hat{v}_{t+1}\ \{Ap(p-q)/(1-pq)\}^{½}$$

Dividing the forecast $f_{t,1}$ by its estimated standard deviation gives the standardised forecast

$$k = f_{t,1}/\hat{\sigma}_F. \tag{10}$$

The variable k is intended to have zero mean and unit variance.

The definition of k first appeared in Taylor (1983) except we have now used 1.253 in equation (8) instead of 1.333. The definition is based upon optimal forecasts for the non-linear trend model. Initial values are needed for the various forecasts and we have followed the methods used before.

3.3 Two strategies

The rules, also called strategies, have two parameters. The first (k_1) controls opening market positions and the second (k_2) their closure. The trader will have one of three possible market commitments when the market opens on some day t: long, short or none. Later the market will close at z_t giving a return x_t and hence k and the trader may buy or sell at the closing price.

Strategy 1 is an alternative to buy-and-hold intended to save money when a substantial downtrend is predicted. The trader buys on the first day for which $k > k_1$. Thereafter decisions can be summarised by the table:

Position at start of day t	Forecast has	Decision	Position after decision
Long	$k \geq k_2$	Do nothing	Long
"	$k < k_2$	Sell	None
None	$k > k_1$	Buy	Long
"	$k \leq k_1$	Do nothing	None

Strategy 2 is an alternative to risk-free investments. It aims to profit from substantial trends in either direction. Initially the position is none and decisions are then given by the table:

Postition at start of day t	Forecast has	Decision	Position after decision
None	$k>k_1$	Buy	Long
"	$k_1 \geqslant k \geqslant -k_1$	Do nothing	None
"	$k<-k_1$	Sell	Short
Long	$k \geqslant k_2$	Do nothing	Long
"	$k<k_2$	Sell	None
Short	$k \leqslant -k_2$	Do nothing	Short
"	$k>k_2$	Buy	None

For both strategies trades are never started during the final 15 days considered for a contract. Also, if necessary, positions are closed on the final day of the month preceding the contract's delivery month. We have used Strategy 1 for commodity futures and strategy 2 for currency futures.

4. Small autocorrelations can cause inefficient pricing

4.1 Simulations

We now consider trading results for simulated prices generated by a trend model. Our purpose is to show that small positive autocorrelations can, in theory, be exploited by a trend-seeking trading strategy. As small positive autocorrelations are observed empirically the simulation results encourage us to investigate trend-seeking strategies for real prices.

The simulated prices are intended to resemble real currency futures prices. Based upon the empirical results of Taylor (1986) we report results for the linear trend model with:

$\mu = 0$, $\alpha = -5.263$, $\beta = 0.46$, $\Phi = 0.987$,
$A = 0.021$ and $p = 0.95$.

These parameter values give $\sigma = 0.0064$. Also the returns have autocorrelations $(0.021)(0.95^{\tau})$, so, for example,

$\rho_{1,X} = 0.020$, $\rho_{10,X} = 0.013$,
$\rho_{20,X} = 0.008$ and $\rho_{30,X} = 0.005$.

Clearly these are very small autocorrelations. Potential trading profits arise because the total autocorrelation over all positive lags is relatively substantial:

$$\sum_{t=1}^{\infty} \rho_{\tau,X} = 0.399$$

The trend component μ_t has standard deviation equal to $\sigma\surd A$ = 0.00093 for the parameter values considered. So if the trend equals its standard deviation then the expected return over one trading day measured in annual terms is about $250\sigma\surd A$ = 23%. This high figure is far greater than published estimates of time-varying risk premia for exchange rates (recall the maximum estimate of Wolff (1987) is less than 5%). The expected long-run change in price when μ_t is the above value equals $\sigma\surd A/(1-p)$ = 1.9%. Clearly trading profits are possible if the trend can be forecast with sufficient accuracy.

The price model has been simulated for 800 years each made up of 250 trading days. The transaction rate c has been set at 0.2%. This is probably higher than the rate charged to speculators trading at the IMM (for 1 IMM contract of £25,000 with £1 = \$ 1.8 the assumed transaction costs would be \$90). As in Taylor (1983, 1986) we consider Strategy 2 with $k_1 = 0.8$ and $k_2 = -0.3$.

4.2 Results

For convenience suppose the risk-free bill used as a margin deposit has face value $100,000. Then our results are:

	Average per annum	Standard deviation
Gross trading profit	$7,503	$9,712
Trades	6.20	1.72
Transaction costs	$1,240	$ 344
Net trading profit	$6,263	$9,969
Days long or short	80%	9%

The estimated average excess return is 6.3% per annum and the standard error of this figure is 0.35%. Excess returns would be positive even if the transaction rate was increased from 0.2% (which is reasonable) to 1% (which is not). We have also evaluated trading results with a delay of one day between prices being known and trades being executed. This only reduces the estimated average excess return to 6.0%.

4.3 Portfolio examples

Suppose risk-free bills pay 10% interest per annum. Then the annual return from risky bills (using the simulation results) has approximately a mean equal to 16% and a standard deviation equal to 10%. Suppose the trader is considering incorporating risky bills into a portfolio made up equally of risk-free bills and stocks. If a diversified stock portfolio returns 20% on average (a generous estimate) with standard deviation 10% then the annual return from the portfolio

$$P = 0.5 \text{ (risk-free bills)} + 0.5 \text{ (diversified stocks)}$$

has mean 15% and standard deviation 5%. However,

Q = 0.411 (risk-free bills) + 0.221 (risky bills)
+ 0.368 (diversified stocks)

also has mean 15% but its standard deviation is only 4.3%. Also,

R = 0.396 (risk-free bills) + 0.258 (risky bills)
+ 0.346 (diversified stocks)

has standard deviation 5% (like P) but a higher mean equal to 15.8%.

4.4 Discussion

We have shown that profits can be extracted from very small autocorrelations. Note however that popular random walk tests may often fail to detect significant autocorrelation, furthermore optimal price forecasts will not apear to be much better than random walk forecasts. With trend model parameters A = 0.021 and p = 0.95 the probability of rejecting the random walk hypothesis using six years of daily data is probably less than one-third if the test statistic is based on the sum of squared sample autocorrelations r_1^2, $r_2^2,\ldots r_k^2$ (see Taylor, 1986, Section 6.10). Higher power to detect dependence is given by the tests introduced in Taylor (1982). Forecasts one day ahead based on trend models have mean square error about ½% less than the comparable figure for random walk forecasts when A=0.021 and p=0.95 (cf. Taylor, 1986, p. 187). Thus profit opportunities may be missed if conventional tests and forecasting appraisals are performed.

5. Trading results for recent years

5.1 Currency futures

We report results for sterling (BP), duetschemark (DM) and Swiss franc (SF) contracts traded at the IMM, for delivery in June and December commencing with the June 1979 contract and concluding with the December 1987 contract. The results for 1979-81 are not new, this being the out-of-sample period of Taylor (1986). This paper reports results for 1982-7 for the first time. Each futures contract is traded for six months, either from December to May or from June to November, using Strategy 2 with

$$A = 0.028,\ p = 0.95,\ k_1 = 0.8 \text{ and } k_2 = -0.3.$$

These constants are based upon a study of prices for contracts traded from 1974 to 1978 inclusive performed in 1982. We might of course obtain better results by updating the trading constants. However our purpose here is merely to see whether or not a published trading rule is profitable after publication.

Table 1 presents excess returns over six month periods with transaction costs assumed to be 0.2% of contract value. It is clear from the averages (expressed as percentage excess returns per annum) that the trading rule was less successful from 1982 to 1987 than from 1979 to 1981. Note that including results for 1987 has raised the overall average from a paltry 0.36% per annum for 1982-6 to 2.82% per annum for 1982-7. The results for 1987 (like 1981 and 1984) are very good for all three currencies. Without the 1987 results we might conclude that the rule has lost its value yet with them we favour the opposite conclusion. The results are further evidence against market efficiency for currency futures but it is not claimed (at present) that they prove inefficient pricing.

Standard t-tests on the data in the columns of Table 1 for a null hypothesis of zero or negative population mean are inconclusive because of the relatively small samples. Considering all 18 contracts from June 1979 to December 1987

Table 1 Excess returns for IMM futuress

Figures are percentage excess returns over six months

Contract	BP	DM	SF	
June 1979	-1.19	0.77	-4.35	
Dec. 1979	4.55	-0.71	-1.87	
June 1980	4.84	1.96	3.16	
Dec. 1980	-1.84	5.65	2.59	
June 1981	6.78	16.34	15.15	
Dec. 1981	0.55	1.62	12.16	
June 1982	-7.25	3.15	-8.61	
Dec. 1982	-5.66	-9.34	-13.61	
June 1983	11.93	-5.59	-0.73	
Dec. 1983	-11.19	6.34	-3.91	
June 1984	1.02	4.80	2.62	
Dec. 1984	6.31	8.33	10.63	
June 1985	11.39	-1.67	1.49	
Dec. 1985	-8.22	7.59	10.69	
June 1986	-2.90	2.33	3.28	
Dec. 1986	-1.54	-3.07	-3.19	
June 1987	14.96	1.33	2.97	
Dec. 1987	8.75	8.94	8.42	
Averages per annum	**BP**	**DM**	**SF**	**Overall**
1979-81	4.56	8.54	8.95	7.35
1982-87	2.93	3.86	1.68	2.82
1982-86	-1.22	2.57	-0.27	0.36
1979-87	3.48	5.42	5.10	4.34

the statistic $t = \sqrt{18}\bar{x}/s$ equals 0.99 for BP, 1.95 for DM, 1.16 for SF and 1.75 for the portfolio average excess return over all three currencies ($\bar{x}$ = sample mean, s = standard deviation). The t-values for DM and the portfolio exceed 1.74 and so are significant at the 5% level. For the latter 12 contracts from 1982 to 1987 t equals 0.57, 1.15, 0.39 and 0.90 for BP, DM, SF and the portfolio average. We tentatively conclude that the null hypothesis can be rejected for 1979-87 but not for 1982-7. The t-test requires independent observations and this assumption is not challenged by the figures in any column. The DM and SF excess returns are highly correlated (r=0.721, rank correlation = 0.606, 1979), BP and SF are slightly correlated, whilst BP and DM appear to be uncorrelated.

5.2 Commodity futures

Results are presented for cocoa, coffee and sugar contracts traded in London, for delivery in various Septembers, Novembers and Decembers respectively, commencing with 1977 contracts and concluding with 1985 contracts. Prices for 1986 and 1987 are not yet available for analysis at Lancaster. The results for 1977-81 are not new whilst those for 1982-5 are given for the first time. Each futures contract is traded for twelve months using Strategy 1. The trading constants are as used in previous publications and are as follows.

	A	**P**	k_1	k_2
Cocoa	0.0440	0.933	0	-1.6
Coffee	0.1220	0.833	0	-1.6
Sugar	0.0395	0.952	0.4	-1.0

Strategy 1 is intended to outperform the buy-and-hold strategy. Accordingly, Table 2 presents excess returns for Strategy 1 minus excess returns for buy-and-hold. The figures tabulated are for twelve month periods with transaction costs assumed to be 1% of contract value. Such costs are realistic.

Table 2 Excess returns for London futures

Figures are excess returns for Strategy 1 minus excess returns for buy-and-hold expressed as percentages per annum.

Delivery year	Cocoa	Coffee	Sugar
1977	0.00	-18.57	22.24
1978	5.85	30.24	24.78
1979	2.37	-11.93	1.40
1980	7.04	-5.08	24.51
1981	10.75	-9.21	33.34
1982	11.75	-11.40	20.52
1983	0.00	-19.79	-14.69
1984	-2.27	-8.81	20.86
1985	9.65	23.37	48.66
Averages			
1977-81	5.20	-2.91	26.57
1982-85	4.78	-4.16	18.84

It is perfectly clear from Table 2 that Strategy 1 is better than buy-and-hold for cocoa and sugar but not coffee. The samples are too small for informative tests. The excess returns for buy-and-hold for 1982-5 were 9.76% (cocoa), 28.24% (coffee) and -25.91% (sugar). Thus although the sugar results are much better than the appropriate benchmark, following Strategy 1 would have lost money for the four years 1982-5. The coffee results are poor for both 1977-81 and 1982-5. Certainly coffee trading would not have been recommended after seeing the results for 1977-81. However, cocoa and sugar trading would have appeared attractive given the results to 1982 and the subsequent results are highly satisfactory when compared with buy and hold. We claim that Table 2 provides very strong evidence against the efficiency of the London cocoa and sugar markets.

5.3 Comparisons with filter rule results

Tari (1987) compares the trend trading rules described here with the filter rule of Alexander (1961) for prices from 1982 to 1985. Strategy 2 outperforms the filter rule (with filter size 4%) for the currencies whilst strategy 1 is a little worse than a modified filter rule (filter size 12%) for the commodities. We do not yet have sufficient evidence to offer firm conclusions about the relative value of the trend strategies and the filter rule.

6. Concluding remarks

We have shown that published trading rules continue to be profitable.

Adopting a Bayesian approach to the evidence our own prior belief before this present study was against efficiency because futures prices up to 1981 supported three conclusions: (a) prices are not random walks, (b) the detected autocorrelation is theoretically enough to permit profitable trading rules, and (c) out-of-sample excess returns are positive. The results of this study are more in favour of inefficient pricing than efficient pricing so our posterior belief is even more strongly against efficient futures markets. Researchers with prior beliefs favouring efficiency for futures should, we contend, have posterior beliefs less committed to the efficiency paradigm because of the evidence presented here. We consider existing evidence for time-dependent risk premia is not sufficient to outweigh our evidence against market efficiency.

It would be helpful to have formal statistical tests for the significance of our results. We know of no rigorous tests of the null hypothesis that a market is efficient using the efficiency definition of Jensen (1978). Tests such as are given by Sweeney (1986) are merely tests of the more specific random walk hypothesis. The figures given in Tables 1 and 2 define small samples from which it is difficult to reach definite conclusions. It has been seen that increasing a sample by only one year (here 1987) can change our interpretation of the evidence.

Inspection of our results and those of Sweeney and Surajaras (1988) in this volume strongly suggests that institutions commanding substantial resources and committed to managing risk by extensive diversification may benefit by trading currencies using trend-seeking strategies. There could be much to gain if inefficiencies persist and little to lose in terms of expectations if they do not. Thus the present evidence may inhibit rather than encourage the publication of better strategies and parameter values along with clearer evidence about the efficiency of futures markets.

References

Alexander, S.S., 1961, Price movements in speculative markets: trends or random walks?, Industrial Management Review 2, 7-26.

Ball, R., 1988, What do we know about stock market "efficiency", published in these proceedings.

Bird, P.J.W.N., 1985, The weak form efficiency of the London Metal Exchange, Applied Economics 17, 571-587.

Black, F., 1976, The pricing of commodity contracts, Journal of Financial Economics 3, 167-179.

Bodie, Z. and V.I. Rosanksy, 1980, Risk and return in commodity futures, Financial Analysts Journal May/June, 27-39.

Bollerslev, T., 1987, A conditionally heteroskedastic time series model for security prices and rates of return data, Review of Economics and Statistics 59, 542-547.

Cornell, B., 1985, The weekly pattern in stock returns: cash versus futures: a note, Journal of Finance 40, 583-588.

Dusak, K., 1973, Futures trading and investors returns: an investigation of commodity market risk premiums, Journal of Political Economy 81, 1387-1406.

Elton, E.J., Gruber, M.J. and J.C. Rentzler, 1987, Professionally managed, publicly traded commodity funds, Journal of Business 60, 175-199.

Engle, R.F. and T. Bollerslev, 1986, Modelling the persistence of conditional variances, Econometric Reviews 5, 1-50.

Fama E.F., 1976, Foundations of Finance (Basis Blackwell, Oxford).

Finnerty, J.E. and H.Y. Park, 1987, Intraday return and volatility patterns in the stock market: futures versus spot, Working paper, University of Illinois at Urbana-Champaign.

Hull, J. and A. White, 1987, The pricing of options on assets with stochastic volatilities, Journal of Finance 42, 281-300.

Jensen, M.C., 1978, Some anomalous evidence regarding market efficiency, Journal of Financial Economics 6, 95-101.

Johnson, H. and D. Shanno, 1987, Option pricing when the variance is changing, Journal of Financial and Quantitative Analysis 22, 143-151.

Leuthold, R.M., 1972, Random walks and price trends: the live cattle futures market, Journal of Finance 27, 879-889.

Lukac, L.P., Brorsen, B.W. and S.H. Irwin, 1988, A test of futures market disequilibrium using twelve different trading systems, Applied Economics, forthcoming.

Pope P.F. and D.A. Peel, 1988, Analysts expectations and risk premia in the forward foreign exchange market: an empirical investigation, published in these proceedings.

Praetz, P.D., 1976a, Rates of return on filter tests, Journal of Finance 31, 71-75.

Praetz, P.D., 1976b, On the methodology of testing for independence in futures prices, Journal of Finance 31, 977-979.

Roll, R., 1984, Orange juice and weather, American Economic Review 74, 861-880.

Stevenson, R.A. and R.M. Bear, 1970, Commodity futures: trends or random walks?, Journal of Finance 25, 65-81.

Sweeney, R.J., 1986, Beating the foreign exchange market, Journal of Finance 41, 163-182.

Sweeney, R.J. and P. Surajaras, 1988, The stability of speculative profits in the foreign exchanges, published in these proceedings.

Tari, A., 1987, A comparison between two trading strategies, M.Sc. dissertation, University of Lancaster.

Taylor, S.J., 1982, Tests of the random walk hypothesis against a price-trend hypothesis, Journal of Financial and Quantitative Analysis 17, 37-61.

Taylor, S.J., 1983, Trading rules for investors in apparently inefficient markets, in: M.E. Streit, ed., Futures markets - modelling, managing and monitoring futures trading (Basil Blackwell, Oxford) 165-198.

Taylor, S.J., 1986, Modelling financial time series (John Wiley, Chichester).

Taylor, S.J., 1988, Forecasting the volatility of the DM/$ rate using the prices of futures and options on futures, Submitted for publication.

Wolff, C.C.P., 1987, Forward foreign exchange rates, expected spot rates, and premia: a signal - extraction approach, Journal of Finance 42, 395-406.

Comments on Stephen J. Taylor and Abdelkamel Tari "Further Evidence Against the Efficiency of Futures Markets"

by Ray Ball

Taylor and Tari apply a clever technique for filtering economic time series to a small sample of currency and commodity futures. The technique exploits information at all lags in the time series. Simulations reported by the authors show that apparently-small autocorrelations at individual lags can aggregate into exploitable dependence in the time series taken as a whole, the implication being that researchers must deal with the autocovariance function rather than with individual-lag statistics. The technique allows for a time-varying variance of price change, which recent history tells us is important. Fitting the models involves estimating six parameters, so the work is in the spirit of (but is more sophisticated than) Alexander's classic filter study. The models appear to earn abnormally high returns from trading in the three commodities and three currency futures, over post-fitting periods of four to six years. Taylor and Tari conclude that this is "strong" and "persuasive" evidence against market efficiency. Perhaps predictably, I believe the conclusion to be premature, for reasons enumerated below.

1. Prior beliefs. First and foremost, the Chicago currency futures market and the London agricultural futures market seem to me to be fiercely competitive markets. My priors are peaked on efficiency. I also believe that there are binding limitations in our understanding of what price sequences would look like in efficient markets. Two interpretations of the evidence presented in this paper therefore are feasible: (1) there are no systematic biases in the calculation of abnormal returns and the markets are inefficient; and (2) systematic biases exist and the evidence is inconclusive. In this case, I am inclined toward the second interpretation, because of my strong prior beliefs concerning both markets and our knowledge.

2. Is this genuinely "public" information? In a competitive market, we expect reward for effort. This is what market "efficiency" is about: an efficient market is one in which rewards from using information (in the form of expected returns) are in line with costs of using it. Stephen Taylor has been working on these filter rules for a decade; surely one would expect a return on his time, his computer costs, etc. If many other researchers have worked on but failed to develop successful models, then the expected rewards for the survivors surely should exceed their own costs. While the cost of obtaining the past price information used by these models might be negligible, the cost of generating the sequence of trading decisions from that information thus might be sufficiently high to influence the underlying economics. We should have no trouble accepting that physical scientists working in the universities occasionally uncover valuable ideas. Why cannot this be true for financial economists?

This is a difficult issue for the researcher to handle, and I do not wish to imply criticism of Taylor and Tari for not tackling it. In this type of research it is difficult to estimate the costs of producing a set of trading rule decisions and it therefore is difficult to know what level of

NATO ASI Series, Vol. F54
A Reappraisal of the Efficiency of Financial Markets
Edited by Rui M. C. Guimaraes et al.

expected return to predict. The problem is complicated by expressing rewards in terms of rates of return: over what amount of investment in futures are the information costs to be amortized? These difficulties helps explain the attractiveness of simpler research designs, in which the cost of obtaining information (such as changes in earnings) is known, to a close approximation, to be zero. In any event, I feel uncomfortable with the assumption, implicit in this paper, that the authors' own work is costless.[1]

3. Separating "normal" and "abnormal" returns. The appropriate benchmark for evaluating the trading rule returns is not clear. Does the trading rule hunt for periods in which the *equilibrium* expected return is high? Or does it simply hunt for high *abnormal* returns? These questions are central to our interpretation of the trading rule's profits, but a perfect answer seems to require a perfect theory of price equilibrium. Since we are never going to achieve perfection, we must recognize that we cannot perfectly separate normal and abnormal returns. In turn, we must admit the possibility that the trading rule's profitability arises from it being more likely to invest when investors are demanding a higher expected return.[2]

4. Definition and calculation of rates of return. Trading rule profits are converted to rates of return by expressing them as a percentage of the value of the Treasury bills deposited with the broker as a security bond. There are at least two problems with defining returns in this fashion. First, the monetary amount of the required bond is not an economically interesting divisor. Imagine that the broker (or whoever determines the trading rules) reduced the required security bond by a factor of (say) ten. Then the calculated *rate* of return would increase, also by a factor of ten. But would the market be any less efficient? In my way of looking at it, the market remains the same (I assume that it generates the same set of prices, despite the change in bonding requirements) and therefore it cannot possibly be more or less efficient as a simple consequence of changing the amount of the bond. If we are going to use rates of return to judge the market as efficient or otherwise, then we cannot possibly define them in terms of the amount of the required bond. Second, rates of return cannot be defined in terms of the amount invested under the strategy itself (i.e., ignoring the bond), because they then are undefined when the trading rule triggers a short position. This arises because the amount invested during short positions is negative. No combination of *rates* of return on long and short positions makes any definitional sense, whenever those rates are defined in terms of the amount invested under the trading rule.

If the monetary amount of the trading rule return cannot meaningfully be expressed as a

---

[1] The anomaly then shifts to be the unexplained motive for a researcher to place valuable research results in the public domain. I have heard two answers: (1) the abnormal returns since have been bid away in the market, so no harm is lost in publishing; and (2) academic glory.

[2] Within the restricted context of the CAPM, this issue reduces to whether the trading rule in effect searches for periods when the risk premium is high. Note that the authors explicitly assume that the systematic risk (beta) of the trading rule returns is non-positive. However, I am not convinced that the CAPM is sufficient for this task.

percentage of either the amount of the required bond or the amount of the futures purchased, how *can* a rate of return be expressed? This question forces us to consider how we make judgments about efficiency from rate of return data. In my view, the underlying economics is the prediction of reward-for-effort in the economic activity of information production. In this case, the information being produced is a complex function of price data: it is information on when and how to trade in currency and commodity futures. The underlying economics would tie the expected amount of the reward from trading to the amount of costs incurred *in producing the information on how and when to trade.* We therefore are not in a good position to evaluate market efficiency until we have a precise notion of the resources expended in earning a given amount of monetary return.

5. *How profitable are these trading rules anyway?* Even when taken at face value, the data in Tables 1 and 2 are far from convincing evidence of inefficiency. I shall focus on the post-1981 results because, as the authors observe, this is the out-of-sample period (the models were fitted over prior data). During this period, Tables 1 and 2 report that the trading rules earned positive abnormal profits, on average, of 2.82% (currencies) and 18.84% (commodities). But the averages appear to be dominated by outlying observations. A sign test tells a different story: in Table 1, the abnormal returns are positive in 21 of the 36 half-yearly periods; and in Table 2, they are positive in 6 of the 12 yearly periods. These can be crudely aggregated to produce a total across both currencies and commodities of positive abnormal returns in 16.5 years out of 30 (only 10% greater than expected). Note that the trading strategies and thus the abnormal returns are unlikely to be independent across futures contracts, whose prices presumably are positively correlated, so a correctly conducted sign test seems unlikely to produce a significant result. While this could be due to the sign test failing to utilize all of the information in the data, it does raise the issue of whether the average abnormal return is a sufficient and even interesting statistic when the trading rule generates a skewed distribution of abnormal returns.

Conclusions. The research in this paper is well done. Taylor and Tari update Alexander's classic study by fitting sophisticated filter models to currency and commodity futures. They claim evidence that strongly suggests market inefficiency. For a variety of reasons, I believe this conclusion to be premature. Nevertheless, the paper forces us to reconsider the results of the classic filter studies and raises several very interesting issues.

percentage of what the amount of the return [illegible] for the 'future' portion, how [illegible] are of return be expected [illegible] how [illegible] we make judgements about efficiency from the [illegible] data [illegible] economists [illegible] of rewards for [illegible] in the economy [illegible] information [illegible] the information being produced [illegible] information we [illegible] to trade in correctly and [illegible] would [illegible] expected earnings of the reward from trading in the market [illegible] information [illegible] and when [illegible] therefore [illegible] good [illegible] evaluate [illegible] efficiency until we [illegible] the nature of the [illegible] earning [illegible] return.

In [illegible] we [illegible] the data in Tables 1 and 2 [illegible] we shall focus [illegible] 1981 results [illegible] authors [illegible] over [illegible] days. During this period [illegible] trading rules earned positive abnormal returns on average, [illegible] .82 [illegible] the averages [illegible] Table [illegible] the [illegible] are positive [illegible] and [illegible] positive in [illegible] yearly [illegible] greater than [illegible] abnormal returns [illegible] presumably are positively [illegible] a significant result. [illegible] this could be due [illegible] the data, it [illegible] statistic when the trading rule generates [illegible] distribution [illegible].

Conclusions. The research in this paper [illegible] study by [illegible] evidence that strongly suggests [illegible] of rules [illegible] conclusion to be premature. Nevertheless [illegible] classic [illegible] and raises several very [illegible] issues.

ANALYST EXPECTATIONS AND RISK PREMIA IN THE FORWARD FOREIGN EXCHANGE MARKET: AN EMPIRICAL EXAMINATION

Peter F Pope

Department of Accounting and Finance
Strathclyde Business School
University of Strathclyde
100 Cathedral Street
Glasgow G4 0LN
Scotland

and

David A Peel

Department of Economics
University College of Wales
Aberystwyth SY23 3DB
Wales

The authors are grateful to Dot Jones for her assistance with computing.

KEYWORDS : forward exchange rate / survey data / exchange rate expectations / time-varying premium / rational expectations / bias / efficiency

ABSTRACT

This paper analyses the properties of the forward exchange rate in conjunction with a new source of survey data on spot exchange rate expectations. The empirical results suggest that over the sample period investigated the market was probably typified by both non-rational expectations and the existence of a time-varying premium component in the forward rate.

NATO ASI Series, Vol. F54
A Reappraisal of the Efficiency of Financial Markets
Edited by Rui M. C. Guimaraes et al.

Equilibrium models of international asset pricing indicate that the forward exchange rate will, in general, be a biased predictor of the future spot exchange rate due to the existence of a premium, or spread, contained within the forward rate (see, for example, Adler and Dumas (1983), Fama and Farber (1979), Hodrick and Srivastava (1984) and Roll and Solnic (1977)). If the premium varies over time then this has serious implications for researchers interested in the relationship between forward rates and future spot rates from the perspective of examining either the predictive ability of forward rates or the efficiency of the foreign exchange market. Since typically the premium (i.e. the difference between the expected future spot rate and the forward rate) is not readily observable, the focus of attention has been on the *ex post* forecast error (i.e. the difference between the actual future spot rate and the forward rate). Specifically, tests of forecast bias have frequently concluded that the forward exchange rate is not a rational expectations predictor of the future spot rate but have generally been unable to show whether the results are due to the existence of a time-varying premium, transactions costs, market inefficiency or a combination of these influences.[1]

The possibility that a time-varying premium exists has been addressed in recent papers by Fama (1984), Hodrick and Srivastava (1986) and Wolff (1987). All these papers involve a maintained assumption of efficient or rational expectations. In light of the accumulated evidence of expectational bias in some financial markets (see, for example, Figlewski and Wachtel (1981), Carlson and Parkin (1975)) and bearing in mind the fundamental nature of the rational expectations assumption in the work on time-varying risk premia, there seems to be a clear case for examining the properties of any observable market expectations for exchange rates. The limited evidence so far available on exchange rate expectations suggests that the rationality assumption might not be descriptively valid (see, for example, Frankel and Froot, 1987; Blake *et al*, 1986) but there is a need for further examination of this result, given the central role that expectations are playing in empirical identification and measurement of premia and the reappraisal of literature that would be necessary should the rationality assumption be generally rejected.

The primary objective of this paper is to analyse the properties of directly

---

1 See, for example, Cornell (1977), Geweke and Feige (1979), Levich (1978) and Hansen and Hodrick (1980).

observed spot exchange rate expectations for nine currencies. The analysis is based on a new source of survey data on spot exchange rate expectations, and this provides the potential for further empirical testing of the hypotheses of unbiasedness and efficiency of exchange rate expectations. We also use the expectations data to estimate directly the properties of the (risk) premium contained within the forward rate. The availability of a proxy for the market expectation provides an opportunity to analyse the properties of *ex ante* forward exchange premia. Since *a priori* we can expect survey forecasts of future spot rates not to include a premium component we can obtain directly a proxy measure of the premium by subtracting from the forward rate the proxy of the expected future spot rate. We can then look for the existence and the properties of the premium across currencies, conditional on the assumption that the survey forecasts reflect market expectations.[2] In this case it is not necessary to assume that the foreign exchange market is efficient or rational in order to identify and measure the premium component.

Our results indicate (1) that the market is typified by biased and inefficient expectations and (2) that the directly observed premia frequently follow a serially correlated process. Moreover, we show that the data are consistent with some of the results obtained by Fama (1984) and Hodrick and Srivastava (1986). This is of concern in light of the central role played by the rationality assumption in that work.

The paper is organised as follows. In Section 1 the basic relationships between expectations, the forward rate and the premium term are presented and the methodology of the empirical tests is described. Section 2 reports the empirical results and Section 3 contains a discussion. Finally in Section 4 we present our concluding comments.

---

2 Since this paper was written we have become aware that Frankel and Froot have written a working paper that apparently adopts a similar approach to analysing premia to our own, although they use different sources of expectations data (Frankel and Froot, 1986).

1. Basic Relationships and Empirical Methodology

1.1 Origin of forward exchange rate premium

The forward foreign exchange rate observed at time t for currency to be delivered at time t+n can be decomposed into the sum of two components: the market's expectation of the future spot rate and a premium term

$$F(t,t+n) = E[S(t+n)|t] + P(t) \tag{1}$$

where F(t,t+n) is the forward rate at time t for delivery at time t+n, E[S(t+n)|t] is the market expectation at time t of the spot exchange rate at time t+n and P(t) is a premium. In equilibrium it has been demonstrated in the context of an international capital asset pricing model and invoking the covered interest parity condition that the premium P(t) will in fact be the sum of two separate terms (Adler and Dumas, 1983). The first term will be due to the covariance between the exchange rate and inflation and will be present even under zero risk aversion because it is real returns which are assumed to influence portfolio decisions and the expected real return on holding an asset (e.g. deposits in a particular currency) depends on the expected value of the nominal return, the expected value of inflation and the covariance between the nominal return and inflation. The second term will be a risk premium linked to the covariance of the exchange rate with the real return on the world market portfolio, calculated using a weighted average worldwide inflation rate.

Thus, in general there can be a difference between the forward exchange rate and the market's expected future spot exchange rate and this is defined as the premium P(t). As a result there will be an expected cost, equal to P(t), associated with hedging a currency position in the forward market. Conversely, for the speculator who expects the future spot exchange rate to be E[S(t+n)], P(t) will be the expected return to forward market speculation. When P(t) is positive (i.e. F(t,t+n) > E[S(t+n)]) speculators will sell the foreign currency forward at a rate F(t,t+n) and expect to buy n periods later at E[S(t+n)|t] earning an expected return equal to the difference between the forward and expected future spot rates, i.e. P(t). If P(t) is negative (i.e. F(t,t+n) < E[S(t+n)]) then speculators will sell domestic currency forward at a rate F(t,t+n) and buy foreign assets which after n periods will be sold and the proceeds used to buy domestic currency at the expected spot rate E[S(t+n)]. The expected return in this case will be equal to the difference between the expected future spot rate and the forward rate, i.e.

$-P(t)$. In both cases the return can be viewed as the premium earned by the speculator for bearing risk.

1.2 Testing for expectational bias

The standard test of whether a predictor $\hat{Y}$, e.g. the forward rate, is an unbiased predictor of the future spot exchange rate, as employed by Frenkel (1981), Blake *et al* and others, is to run the following regression

$$S(t+n) = \alpha + \beta \hat{Y}(t,t+n) + u(t) \qquad (2)$$

where $u(t)$ is a disturbance term which will follow a moving average error process of order $(n-1)$. If, after selecting an appropriate technique for dealing with the MA error process, the joint hypothesis that α equals zero and β equals unity cannot be rejected then the inference will be drawn that $\hat{Y}(t,t+n)$ is an unbiased forecast. However there are two difficulties with the unbiasedness test in (2). First, it can be shown that this test is susceptible to Type I error if the forecast which enters as an independent variable is not an optimal (i.e. minimum variance) predictor (Holden and Peel, 1987). Thus there is a possibility that the researcher might conclude from the regression (2) that an unbiased forecast is biased simply because the forecast error variance is not minimised. A second difficulty with (2) is that $E(\beta) \neq 1$ if the predictor is the forward rate and if the premium term $P(t)$ is time-varying (Fama, 1984); or if $F(t,t+n)$ is correlated with the forecast error $u(t)$.[3] A more appropriate test of unbiasedness is to estimate

$$S(t+n) - \hat{Y}(t,t+n) = B + \epsilon(t) \qquad (3)$$

where B is a constant and $\epsilon(t)$ is the error term following a MA(n-1) process.
If (3) is used as the basis for testing for bias in a forecast then the difficulties described above will be avoided. However, in the case of the forward rate being interpreted as a predictor, a significant B will be ambiguous because in general it will reflect the difference between two components: the mean forecast error, $S(t+n)-E[S(t+n)]$, and the mean premium, $P(t)$. With survey data this abiguity can be resolved by isolating the proxy *ex ante* premium as the difference between the forward rate and the proxy market expectation, i.e.

$$P^*(t) = F(t,t+n) - M(t,t+n) \qquad (4)$$

---

3 For instance $F(t,t+n)$ could embody rational expectations but be subject to measurement error (Jacobs, 1982).

where M(t,t+n) is the proxy market expectation at time t of the spot exchange rate at time t+n derived from the survey. We can then treat M(t,t+n) itself as a proxy for the market expectation and use equation (3) to assess the biasedness property of the market expectation.

1.3 *Testing for expectational efficiency*

We examine forecast efficiency using the methods employed by Frenkel (1981) and others. The focus of analysis is the *ex post* forecast error of the expectations S(t+n)-M(t,t+n). In an efficient market the forecast error should be uncorrelated with any information known at time t, the date on which the market expectation is formed. To test the efficiency hypothesis we estimate the following regression

$$S(t+n)-M(t,t+n) = \alpha_0 + \beta_0 P^*(t) + \beta_1[F(t,t+n)-S(t)] + \epsilon_0(t) \qquad (5)$$

where α_0 and β_i, i=0,1 are regression coefficients and the ϵ_0 is the error term. This regression relates the *ex post* forecast error to respectively our estimate of the premium in the forward rate $P^*(t)$ and the forward-spot differential at time t, F(t,t+n)-S(t). Both these terms contain only information known at time t and therefore if they are found to be significantly correlated with the forecast error, i.e. if β_1 or β_2 are found to be significantly different from zero, then this would constitute *prima facie* evidence of market inefficiency, conditional on the hypothesis that the survey mean is a good proxy for the market expectation underlying the forward rate. In other words, the test of efficiency is founded on the predictability of forecast errors made by "the market" from publicly available information. Additionally, a non-zero α_0 coefficient would reflect any constant expectational bias that might be present in the proxy expectations after controlling for the magnitude of the premium and the forward-spot differential.

1.4 *Examining the premium component*

The estimating equations used by Fama (1984) are as follows

$$F(t,t+n) - S(t+n) = \alpha_3 + \beta_3[F(t,t+n) - S(t)] + \epsilon_3(t) \qquad (7)$$

$$S(t+n) - S(t) = \alpha_4 + \beta_4[F(t,t+n) - S(t)] + \epsilon_4(t) \qquad (8)$$

where the α_i and β_i, i=3,4 are regression coefficients and the ϵ are error terms. The relationship between the regression coefficients β_3 and β_4 is examined to make inferences about the behaviour of the premium. In particular, if β_3 is significantly different from zero *and* if market expectations are formed rationally, i.e. $E\{S(t+n)-E[S(t+n)]\} = 0$, then this can be interpreted as evidence of a time-varying premium component in the regressor. Since by construction $\beta_3+\beta_4 = 1$, the extent of deviation of β_4 from unity is an indicator of the extent of variation of the premium in the forward rate, conditional on the efficiency or rationality assumption. However, the two regression coefficients do not measure the proportions of the variance in F(t,t+n)-S(t) due to the the variance of the premium and the variance of the expected change in the spot rate except when Cov(P(t),E[S(t+n)-S(t)])=0. This leads Fama to analyse instead the difference β_3-β_4 which can be used to estimate the difference between the two variances as a proportion of the the total variance in F(t,t+n)-S(t). Using this approach and assuming rational expectations Fama establishes that the variance of P(t) is significantly greater than the variance of E[S(t+n)-S(t)] and that the two components of the spot-forward differential are negatively correlated.

The availablity of a direct estimate of the premium component enables more direct testing of some of the properties of the premium underlying the forward rate and its relationship with exchange rate expectations. This does not require the assumption of rational expectations but we must recognise that the analysis is conditional on the assumption that the survey mean expectation measure is representative of the market expectation. Some further discussion of this assumption is presented in Section 3.

In the empirical analysis of the premium measure we first examine the mean of the series and the most parsimonious time series representation. We then examine the variances of the components of the forward discount, including our premium measure, and the correlations between them. This analysis can be viewed as a direct test of the descriptive validity of the inferences drawn in the Fama (1984) analysis. As a final stage to the analysis we estimate the following regression

$$S(t+3)-F(t,t+3) = \tau_0 + \tau_1 P^*(t) + \tau_2[M(t,t+3)-S(t)] + \epsilon_5(t) \qquad (9)$$

where τ_i, i=0..2 are regression coefficients and $\epsilon_5(t)$ is an error term. Equation (9) is based on the Fama (1984) test in equation (7) and involves a decomposition of the regressor F(t,t+3)-S(t) into the premium and the expected depreciation terms. One useful interpretation of equation (9) is think of it as equivalent to a regression estimating the optimal linear combination of predictors for S(t+3), where the predictors include F(t,t+3), M(t,t+3) and S(t). Rearranging (9) and substituting F(t,t+3)-M(t,t+3) for $P^*(t)$ gives

$$S(t+3) = \tau_0 + (1+\tau_1)F(t,t+3) + (\tau_2-\tau_1)M(t,t+3) - \tau_2 S(t) + \epsilon_5(t) \qquad (10)$$

Substituting F(t,t+3) by M(t,t+3)+P(t) gives

$$S(t+3) = \tau_0 + (1+\tau_1)P(t) + (1+\tau_2)M(t,t+3) - \tau_2 S(t) + \epsilon_5(t) \qquad (11)$$

When the predictors in regression (10) embody different information then they can be combined to form an optimal predictor and can be expected to be given non-zero weights in the regression. However, if the survey expectation is a rational expectations predictor then from (11) we would expect τ_1 to be equal to -1 and τ_2 to equal zero in the presence of a time-varying premium.[4] If the forward rate is rational and there is no time-varying premium then we would expect both τ_1 and τ_2 to be zero.

1.5 Overlapping forecast horizons

In the empirical analysis that follows the measures of expectations and the forward rate are for a 3-month horizon and the frequency of the data is monthly. Therfore the sample observations overlap and this introduces a moving average error error process of order two in regressions where the regressand contains information which only becomes available after the end of the sampling interval t. Thus, for example, the *ex post* forecast error in equation (3) if entered as the dependent variable in a regrssion such as (3) will induce a moving average error term. The OLS coefficient estimates are consistent despite the serially correlated residuals. However, the OLS standard error estimates are biased. The method we employ to correct for the inefficiency in OLS parameter estimates expected under such

---

4 In regressions such as (9) the independent variables are either proxying for some unobservable variable, eg. true market expectations, or might embody rational expectations but be subject to measurement error, eg. F(t,t+3) (Jacobs, 1982). Statistically there is therefore a potential errors-in-variables problem. To examine the importance of this to our results we conducted tests using the instrumental variables estimation technique, where the instruments were taken to be lagged values of the variables. We found that our results were not qualitatively different after implementing this change. Hence we report only results based on the OLS regressions.

conditions is the method of moments estimator due to Hansen and Hodrick (1980).[5,6] A second method which is appropriate for estimating equation (3), is to jointly estimate, using non-linear least squares, the model parameter B and the moving average error process.

2. Empirical Tests

2.1 The data

Our data is based on a monthly survey of the three-month ahead spot exchange rate forecasts of up to 54 market analysts conducted by *Euromoney Treasury Report*.[7] The survey covers nine currencies over the 46 month sample period which extends from March 1984 to December 1987.[8] Analysts are polled at the beginning of each month and asked to forecast the level of the relevant spot exchange rate on the first trading day three months ahead. Thus, for example, the survey on Monday, January 4th 1988 records expected spot exchange rates for Friday April 1st 1988. The proxy measure of market expectation derived from the survey and used in this study is the

---

5 We wish to thank David Blake for supplying us with the software for implementing the Hansen and Hodrick method.

6 In an earlier version of this paper we employed an alternative technique which involved using OLS estimates and employing tables which give t-statistic confidence bounds for MA(2) processes to test the significance of coefficients. The tables are derived using methods outlined by Vinod (1976). They give lower and upper bounds for the t-values obtained from a least squares regression for all the combinations of the moving average parameters that are estimated from the regression residuals. If the t-value lies outside the bounds then it is appropriate to make inferences. Generally the results obtained from this method were consistent with those found using the Hansen and Hodrick method and therefore only the latter are reported in this paper.

7 We wish to thank Ken Ferris and Brian Martin of *Euromoney* for their assistance with the data.

8 For two currencies, the Belgian franc and the Swedish krona, forecasts are available from April 1984. Hence the sample size for these two currencies is 45.

mean forecast of the participating analysts.[9]

For each survey month we also collected the closing spot and 90-day forward exchange rates on the survey date and the closing spot exchange rate on the forecast horizon date.[10] All exchange rate data were obtained from *Datastream* and to be consistent with the survey U.S. dollars are defined as the base currency with the exception of the U.K. where rates are expressed as U.S. dollars to the pound. In common with previous research in the area (e.g. Fama (1984)) all levels of exchange rates (spot, forward and survey forecasts) are restated in natural logarithms so as to make the analysis independent of the assumed base currency.

2.2 Relative accuracy of alternative forecasts

The first stage in the empirical analysis is to calculate the accuracy of the various available predictors by examining the properties of the forecast errors. In Table 1 we report the root mean square forecast errors for the following predictors: the forward rate, F(t,t+3); the survey mean expectation, M(t,t+3); the spot exchange rate at the forecast date, S(t); and a naive composite forecast equal to the simple average of the forward rate, survey mean and spot rate. The data indicate that the spot rate was a superior predictor of the three month ahead spot rate for five of the nine currencies. In two instances the survey mean performed best and in a further two cases the composite predictor was superior. On no occasion was the forward exchange rate found to be superior as a predictor.

The superior forecasting performance of the spot rate relative to the forward rate has been a feature of many other empirical studies (eg Fama (1984)) and could, of course, be due to the presence of a time-varying risk premium in the forward rate. However, the inferior performance of the survey expectation relative to the spot rate provides *prima facie* evidence that the survey expectations are not rational. Table 1 shows that for only three currencies is the root mean square forecast error lower for the survey mean than for the spot exchange rate. Thus the Fama (1984)

---

9 Additional tests using the survey median showed that the results were not sensitive to the choice of consensus measure.

10. Generally there is not an exact correspondence between the forecast horizon and the 90-day forward contract period, but the difference is minor in relation to the length of the forecast horizon.

TABLE 1

ROOT MEAN SQUARE FORECAST ERRORS

	F(t,t+3)	M(t,t+3)	S(t)	Composite
Japan	0.0790	0.0726	0.0775	0.0756
Germany	0.0741	0.0745	0.0754	0.0740
U.K.	0.0804	0.0800	0.0751	0.0782
Switzerland	0.0814	0.0784	0.0821	0.0799
Belgium	0.0718	0.0723	0.0715	0.0704
Sweden	0.0589	0.0580	0.0531	0.0559
Italy	0.0704	0.0678	0.0648	0.0670
France	0.0719	0.0701	0.0692	0.0698
Canada	0.0242	0.0256	0.0226	0.0237

suggestion that the inaccuracy of the forward rate as predictor of the future spot rate could be attributable to variation in the premium component of the forward rate is not generally supported by our data, if the survey mean is accepted as a valid proxy for market expectations.

2.3 Tests of unbiasedness of expectations

In Table 2 we report the results of estimating equation (3), taking as forecasts the forward rate, the survey mean and the spot rate. Estimates of B are found by regressing respectively S(t+3)-F(t,t+3), S(t+3)-M(t,t+3) and S(t+3)-S(t) on a constant and a moving average process of order two, employing non-linear least squares. This is the correct method to test for bias, given our earlier discussion.

The empirical results in Table 2 indicate that the for all nine currencies the hypothesis of unbiasedness is rejected for the forward rate with the coefficient B having highly significant t-statistics in all cases. In the case of the survey mean the forecasts are unbiased for Germany, Switzerland and Canada and biased for the other six currencies. Also, the results for the spot exchange rate indicate that over the sample period there was non-zero mean drift in the spot rate for all currencies except the Canadian dollar. The Box-Pierce statistics indicate that the residuals are white noise in all regressions and no individual autocorrelations were found to be significant.

2.4 Test of efficiency of survey expectations

In order to test the efficiency of expectations we estimate equation (5) using the Hansen and Hodrick (1980) method. The results are reported in Table 3. They indicate very clearly that the *Euromoney* expectations are inefficient over our sample period. In particular the forecast error is highly correlated with the estimated risk premium, $P^*(t)$ for all countries except Japan, U.K. and Switzerland and with the forward-spot differential F(t,t+n)-S(t) for all currencies except Belgium, Italy and France.

2.4 Properties of the estimated premium

In Table 4 we report the mean and time series properties of our measure of the risk premium $P^*(t)$. There is clear evidence of an on average positive premium in the

TABLE 2

TEST OF UNBIASEDNESS: $S(t+n) - \hat{Y}(t,t+n) = B + \epsilon(t)$

	Forward rate			Survey mean			Spot rate		
	B	$\bar{R}^2$	BP_8	B	$\bar{R}^2$	BP_8	B	$\bar{R}^2$	BP_8
Japan	-0.0339 (4.50)	0.52	2.55	-0.0183 (2.84)	0.64	4.12	-0.0359 (5.24)	0.55	2.92
Germany	-0.0208 (2.87)	0.55	7.56	-0.0107 (1.60)	0.65	9.30	-0.0291 (4.07)	0.53	7.16
U.K.	0.0205 (2.76)	0.61	3.59	0.0142 (2.00)	0.65	4.51	0.0144 (1.99)	0.59	3.87
Switzerland	0.0202 (2.53)	0.56	5.34	-0.0100 (1.43)	0.65	6.42	-0.0301 (3.78)	0.52	5.29
Belgium	-0.0297 (4.12)	0.48	4.60	-0.0202 (2.98)	0.59	6.95	-0.0330 (4.22)	0.36	2.44
Sweden	-0.0272 (5.12)	0.56	4.41	-0.0114 (2.06)	0.60	7.73	-0.0192 (3.77)	0.54	4.99
Italy	-0.0307 (4.93)	0.57	5.43	-0.0143 (2.45)	0.67	7.66	-0.0184 (2.88)	0.54	6.64
Canada	-0.0054 (2.22)	0.56	3.23	0.0023 (0.94)	0.60	3.18	-0.0016 (0.70)	0.56	1.33
France	-0.0298 (4.34)	0.52	7.56	-0.0150 (2.40)	0.63	7.90	-0.0239 (3.38)	0.48	7.22

Notes: 1. Estimated using non-linear least squares and MA(2) error process.

2. t-values in parenthesis

3. Critical value for Box-Pierce Statistic with 8 lags at 5% level is 12.6

TABLE 3

TEST OF EFFICIENCY OF SURVEY DATA

$$S(t+3)-M(t,t+3) = \alpha + \beta_1 P^*(t) + \beta_2[F(t,t+3)-S(t)]$$

	α	β_1	β_2	$\bar{R}^2$
Japan	-0.06 (2.41)	-1.77 (1.71)	-3.43 (2.66)	0.18
Germany	-0.10 (3.29)	1.67 (2.06)	-8.67 (2.81)	0.31
U.K.	-0.05 (2.97)	-0.04 (0.06)	10.92 (5.37)	0.58
Switzerland	-0.12 (3.93)	-0.01 (0.01)	-10.85 (4.13)	0.42
Belgium	-0.04 (2.52)	1.89 (2.48)	-0.59 (1.47)	0.21
Sweden	0.01 (0.31)	1.67 (2.65)	4.11 (3.02)	0.40
Italy	-0.02 (0.36)	1.93 (2.06)	2.67 (0.98)	0.18
Canada	0.02 (2.19)	1.10 (2.31)	-6.01 (3.61)	0.42
France	-0.40 (1.53)	1.97 (1.99)	-1.26 (0.56)	0.14

first column of Table 4. For the U.K. signs are reversed because of the reversal of the base currency. The time series representations of the premia series show that the premium is serially correlated for all countries except Japan and Switzerland. Furthermore, the estimated constant component is highly significant for all countries.

In Table 5 we report the standard deviations of the various components of the forward discount, F(t,t+3)-S(t). The table shows the total variablility of the forward rate prediction error in the first column and these are consistent with the root mean square errors reported in Table 1. The fourth column of Table 5 gives the total variability in the forward discount. It is this total variability that Fama (1984) decomposes into the premium and expectational error components. Our direct estimates of these two components of the total variation are reported in columns three and four of Table 5.

It is immediately noticeable that the standard deviations of both of the forward discount components is higher than the overall total variability for all countries with the exception of Belgium where the premium measure has the lowest standard deviation. This finding coroborates the result of Fama (1984) with regard to the relative magnitude of the total variance in the forward discount. However, in contrast to Fama's results there is no evidence in our data that the variance of the premium term $P^*(t)$ is significantly greater than the variance of the expected change in the spot exchange rate (M(t,t+3)-S(t)). Indeed, whilst the two component variances are of the same order of magnitude the variance of the premium is lower in eight of the nine cases. In two cases (U.K. and Sweden) the difference between the expected depreciation variance and the premium variance is in fact approximately twice the total variance in the forward discount with the depreciation component being the greater.

In Table 6 we report correlation coefficients between $P^*(t)$ and respectively F(t,t+3), F(t,t+3)-S(t) and M(t,t+3)-S(t). The first column indicates that there is no strong correlation between the premium and the forward rate itself. More interesting is the weak correlation between the premium and the forward discount. The final column shows the very strong negative correlation between the premium and the expected depreciation which explains the results in Table 5 relating to the components of the forward discount variability, thus confirming Fama's findings.

TABLE 4

PROPERTIES OF THE SURVEY RISK PREMIUM MEASURE $P^*(t)$

	Mean	Constant	ARMA
Japan	0.0157	0.0157 (7.99)	(0,0)
Germany	0.0108	0.0077 (2.99)	(1,0)
U.K.	-0.0068	-0.0064 (3.49)	(0,2)
Switzerland	0.0110	0.0110 (5.07)	(0,0)
Belgium	0.0097	0.0059 (2.27)	(1,0)
Sweden	0.0162	0.0078 (2.69)	(1,0)
Italy	0.0173	0.0103 (3.33)	(1,0)
Canada	0.0075	0.0075 (7.59)	(0,2)
France	0.0151	0.0093 (3.28)	(1,0)

TABLE 5

STANDARD DEVIATIONS OF COMPONENTS OF F(t,t+3)-S(t)

	S(t+3)-F(t,t+3)	M(t,t+3)-S(t)	$P^*(t)$	F(t,t+3)-S(t)
Japan	0.0718	0.0113	0.0135	0.0109
Germany	0.0712	0.0139	0.0132	0.0039
U.K.	0.0785	0.0150	0.0127	0.0056
Switzerland	0.0791	0.0153	0.0143	0.0046
Belgium	0.0652	0.0289	0.0147	0.0243
Sweden	0.0524	0.0157	0.0133	0.0059
Italy	0.0631	0.0137	0.0124	0.0047
Canada	0.0241	0.0075	0.0069	0.0024
France	0.0654	0.0138	0.0126	0.0053

TABLE 6

CORRELATION COEFFICIENTS BETWEEN $P^*(t)$ AND $F(t,t+3)$, $F(t,t+3)-S(t)$, $M(t,t+3)-S(t)$

	F(t,t+3)	F(t,t+3)-S(t)	M(t,t+3)-S(t)
Japan	0.05	-0.14	-0.62
Germany	0.12	-0.46	-0.96
U.K.	0.27	0.05	-0.93
Switzerland	0.22	-0.39	-0.95
Belgium	-0.04	-0.14	-0.54
Sweden	0.20	0.23	-0.93
Italy	0.24	0.19	-0.94
Canada	0.04	0.71	-0.94
France	0.08	-0.07	-0.92

In Table 7 we report the results of estimating equation (9) using the Hansen and Hodrick (1980) methodology. For all countries except France, Belgium and Italy the joint hypothesis τ_1=-1, τ_2=0 can be rejected as can the joint hypothesis τ_1=0, τ_2=0. In the case of France, Belgium and Italy we find the data are consistent with both joint hypotheses, that is τ_1 is less than two standard errors from both-1 and 0. However, viewed alongside our previous results the evidence points to expectations being at least biased and generally inefficient as well.

3. Discussion

The empirical results reported in this paper suggest that the consensus expectation of foreign exchange analysts , as proxied by the survey mean expectations, does not display the properties of rational expectations. We find that the survey mean expectation was generally biased and inefficient for our data set, thus confirming the results of Blake *et al* (1986) and Frankel and Froot (1986). The results on the unbiasedness property are obtained after allowing for technical problems with the standard unbiasedness test applied in the literature.

The results denying the rationality of expectations are potentially important for tests of forward exchange market behaviour. As general evidence on the behaviour market agents they are entirely consistent with other recent findings based on different surveys and thus they act as external validation of the non-rationality findings reported elsewhere. In general therefore they tend to increase confidence levels in the other survey-based results.

It should be noted that doubts have been expressed about the ability of surveys such as the one used here to reflect the unobservable "true" market expectation (see, e.g. Koedijk and Ott, 1987). These doubts are based on both technical and incentive considerations. At the technical level it is possible that the naive weighting of individual forecasts (in this case the equal weighting involved in using the arithmetic mean) is inappropriate. Theoretically and intuitively the appropriate weights to be given to individual forecasts should reflect the value weights of positions taken in a market (Figlewski, 1980). Thus in general a survey-based measure, whatever the statistical weighting scheme employed, will measure the true market expectation with error. Furthermore, if the distribution of exchange rate changes is assymetric then the choice of measure of central

TABLE 7

$$S(t+3)-F(t,t+3) = \tau_0 + \tau_1 P^*(t) + \tau_2[M(t,t+3)-S(t)] + \epsilon_5(t)$$

	τ_0	τ_1	τ_2	$\bar{R}^2$
Japan	-0.0612 (2.41)	-2.6583 (2.94)	-3.4291 (2.66)	0.20
Germany	-0.1019 (3.29)	-8.0014 (2.57)	-8.6711 (2.81)	0.25
U.K.	-0.0523 (2.97)	-11.9621 (5.62)	-10.9283 (5.37)	0.58
Switzerland	-0.1188 (3.93)	-11.8569 (4.39)	-10.8507 (4.13)	0.43
Belgium	-0.0412 (2.52)	0.2972 (0.34)	-0.5916 (1.47)	0.09
Sweden	-0.0057 (0.32)	-3.4359 (2.27)	-4.1106 (3.02)	0.28
Italy	-0.0151 (0.36)	-1.7390 (0.59)	-2.6738 (0.98)	0.08
Canada	0.0181 (2.19)	-5.9073 (3.47)	-6.0075 (3.61)	0.35
France	-0.0388 (1.53)	-0.2916 (0.12)	-1.2572 (0.58)	0.05

tendency (e.g. the mean or median expectation) will be potentially important, although this point did not seem to be applicable to our data. With regard to the incentive difficulty, in might be argued that analysts' responses are not disciplined by having to bear a penalty on inaccurate forecasts, as market agents would. Although there is some truth in the assertion that there is no direct cost associated with forecast errors, in the case of the *Euromoney* survey at least there is some incentive to be accurate introduced through the publication of a periodic "league table" ranking analysts by their accuracy. To the extent that the reputation of the forecasting institution depends upon the quality of its forecasts and is perceived as being important, we can expect survey reponses to reflect "best expectations".[11]

To the extent that the survey data can be accepted as a proxy for market expectations, the properties of the expectations can potentially explain why the forward rate itself has been found in previous work not to possess the properties of rational expectations forecasts. The results reported here suggest that the foreign exchange market, over the period of our analysis, was typified by both non-rational expectations and the existence of time-varying risk premia. Our results are consistent with those of Fama (1984) and Hodrick and Srivastava (1986) to the extent that we can confirm the existence of a premium component in the forward rate. We also find negative covariation between the premium and the expected change in the spot exchange rate over the forecast horizon is present in our data. This effect also seems to drive the results of Fama. However, the potentially damaging result in this paper as far as the Fama (1984) and subsequent similar tests are concerned is that the central assumption of rational expectations is not present. Also, the results on the relative magnitudes of the variability in components of the forward discount are problematic because they show that the inaccuracy in the forward rate as a forecast of the future spot rate is attributable to expectational errors as much as to the time-varying premium

[11] It is interesting to note at this juncture that there has been considerable willingness to accept as inputs to tests of financial market behaviour other surveys of financial forecasts such as the Money Market Services survey of money expectations. The apparent distinguishing feature of exchange rate expectation surveys is that they seem to be biased and inefficient and the question which must then be addressed is whether these properties automatically disqualify the survey data from further use.

component.

4. Conclusion

Of the "stories" offered by Fama (1984) as explanations of the perverse relationship he observes between future spot and forward exchange rates, our results suggest that the suggestion that the market is non-rational or inefficient must be considered as a serious contender. As Frankel and Froot (1987) have observed, it is possible that the nature of any *ex post* market non-rationality is highly time-dependent. In particular, if the true data-generating process underlying the spot exchange rate changes over time then the observed bias and inefficiency of expectations could simply be due to optimal learning (De Canio, 1979) as typified by, for example, a Kalman Filter.

REFERENCES

Adler, M and B Dumas, 'International Portfolio Choice and Corporation Finance: A Synthesis', *Journal of Finance* 38, July 1983, pp.925-84.

Blake, D, Beenstock, M and Brasse, V, 'The Performance of UK Exchange Rate Forecasters', *The Economic Journal*, 1986, 96, pp 986-999.

Carlson, J A and M Parkin, 'Inflation Expectations', *Economica* 42, 1975, pp.123-38.

De Canio, S J, 'Rational Expectations and Learning from Experience', *Quarterly Journal of Economics* 93, 1979, pp.47-57

Fama, E F, 'Forward and Spot Exchange Rates', *Journal of Monetary Economics*, 1984, 2, pp 319-338.

Fama, E F and A Farber, 'Money, Bonds and Foreign Exchange', *American Economic Review* 69, September 1979, pp.269-82.

Figlewski, S, 'Market efficiency in a market with heterogeneous information', *Journal of Political Economy* 86, 1980, pp.581-97.

Figlewski, S and P Wachtel, 'The Formation of Inflationary Expectations', *Review of Economics and Statistics* 63, 1981, pp.1-10.

Frankel, J A and Froot, K, 'Interpreting Tests of Forward Discount Bias Using Survey Data on Exchange Rate Expectations', *National Bureau of Economic Research*, Working Paper No.1963, 1986

________________________, 'Using Survey Data to Test Some Standard Propositions Regarding Exchange Rate Expectations', *American Economic Review*, March 1987, pp.133-53

Hansen, L P and Hodrick, R J, 'Forward Exchange Rates as Optimal Predictors of Future Spot Rates: An Econometric Analysis', *Journal of Political Economy*, 1980, 88, pp 829-853.

Hodrick, R J and Srivastava, S, 'An Investigation of Risk and Return in Forward Foreign Exchange', *Journal of International Money and Finance*, 1984, 3, pp 5-29.

____________________________, 'The Covariation of Risk Premiums and Expected Future spot Exchange Rates', *Journal of International Money and Finance* 5, Supplement, March 1986, pp.5-21.

Holden K and D A Peel, 'On Testing for Unbiasedness and Efficiency of Forecasts',*UCW Aberystwyth*, Discussion Paper No.11, 1987.

Jacobs, R L, 'The Effect of Errors in Variables on Tests for a Risk Premium in Forward Exchange Rates', *Journal of Finance*, June 1982, pp 667-77.

Koedijk, K G and M Ott, 'Risk Aversion, Efficient Markets and the Forward Exchange Rate', *Federal Reserve Bank of St Louis Review*, December 1987, pp.5-13

Murfin, A and Ormerod, P, 'The Forward Rate and the US Dollar and the Efficient Markets Hypothesis, 1978-1983', *The Manchester School*, 1984, 56, pp 292-299.

Roll R and B Solnic, 'A Pure Exchange Asset Pricing Model', *Journal of International Economics* 7, May 1977, pp.161-79.

Vinod, H D, 'Effects of ARMA Errors in the Significance Tests', *Journal of the American Statistical Association*, 1976, 71, pp 929-933.

Wolff, C C P, 'Forward Foreign Exchange Rates, Expected Spot Rates, and Premia: A Signal Extraction Approach', *Journal of Finance*, June 1987, pp.395-406.

Comments on Peter Pope and David Peel "Analyst Expectations and Risk Premia in the Forward Foreign Exchange Market: An Empirical Examination,"

by

Richard J. Sweeney

The authors have an important issue, some new data—and a highly interesting paper. Like the authors, I focus first on the literature and the general issues, then on their specific contributions.

Much of the literature is very confusing. First, it becomes ever clearer that the forward premium is a biased predictor of coming spot rate appreciation, and that this bias is time varying. Second, some define the bias between the forward premium and the rational expectation of appreciation as "the risk premium." I believe that the bias very likely is a risk premium, rather than being due to transactions costs, measurement errors, econometric problems, or some of the other candidates, but still think the name "risk premium" is a bad choice because it calls to mind the theoretical asset pricing literature that predicts a bias based on risk premia. The evidence for the existence of a bias is not the same thing as evidence that the bias arises because of the premia in the theory. Third, even if this bias is a risk premium, there is no presumption that it is a systematic risk premium as required by asset pricing theories, and still less that the time-varying bias is due to a time-varying systematic risk premium. The bias might instead be based on unsystematic risk.

As the authors point out, the ex ante profit rate to forward speculation is the bias (or its negative, depending on the side of the market taken). Bilson (1981) and Sweeney and Lee (1988) report success in simulations in forecasting the bias and taking profitable speculative positions on portfolios of currencies. Sweeney and Lee's measured profits are risk-adjusted or true economic profits if the systematic risk premia are all constant over time. Alternatively, if there are time-varying systematic risk premia, they may but need not be able to explain fully these measured profits.

Hodrick and Srivastava (1984) use an intertemporal asset pricing model to investigate time varying risk premia. They assume that the betas on all forward speculations have the same sign and are constant, while the risk premium on a benchmark portfolio is time varying, and reject the model. The rejection may be due to the fact that they had to put very

NATO ASI Series, Vol. F54
A Reappraisal of the Efficiency of Financial Markets
Edited by Rui M. C. Guimaraes et al.

strong restrictions on the betas—namely, constant and all with the same sign—to test the model. Sweeney and Lee (1988) report that often the speculator will be long in one currency but short in another in the same period, which cannot happen with betas of the same sign. Further, the speculator is sometimes long in a currency and then later short in the same currency, which cannot happen with a constant beta and a positive risk premium on the benchmark portfolio.

In Sweeney (1988), I assume time-varying betas with a constant risk premium on the benchmark portfolio. I use a simple one factor model, with the factor the CRSP value-weighted return on the market. This can be motivated by the CAPM, the APT if there is one factor or any omitted factors are orthogonal to the market, or by an intertemporal asset pricing model where the market index proxies for the return on the benchmark portfolio. The model fails dismally when applied to explaining the speculative returns to ten foreign currencies. This failure may be due to misspecification, of course, but we are still left with no convincing evidence that the bias in the forward premium arises from time-varying systematic risk premia.

My discussion of the paper's original contributions can be organized around its tables. Table 2's conventional test, of whether the realized future spot rate less its predictor equals zero on average, is somewhat weak. Suppose there is a very large positive bias in the first half of the sample and an offsetting negative bias in the second half. The test would detect a problem only in the serial correlation of the residuals. This raises another issue. A second order MA is imposed on the residuals to take care of the overlapping forecast period problem, but the authors do not impose any further restrictions on this MA2. There are, however, MA patterns not at all consistent with reasonable models, for example, coefficients of 0.1 and 0.8 for the first two lags. It would be good to test for or impose the restrictions on the MA2 that can be derived from theory.

As for the ability of the mean survey response to predict the coming spot rate, Table 3 is much more satisfying—M seems pretty clearly not to be an efficient predictor. It might be useful to report also SUR results, with and without cross-equation restrictions of equal slopes and intercepts, though the estimation problems are non-trivial with the MA2 error terms. In Table 4, it would be useful to know about the time-series models that were fitted.

Since P* is stationary (I prcsume), it is not appropriate to regress it on the nonstationary F series in Table 6—plims do not exist. As for the regression of P* on M(t,t+3) - S(t), the results in the Table 3 are pretty much to be expected; think of S(t) = F(t, t+3) + e, where e is an error, so M - S = M - F - e.

The speculative profit rate investigated in Table 7 seems to have some predictable component. Bilson (1981) and Sweeney and Lee (1988) report some success in forecasting this rate using the forward premium, F - S. Do the two predictors here work better than the forward premium? Note that if the slopes are equal, then the two predictors collapse to the forward premium, since P* + (M - S) = (F - M) + (M - S) = F - S. Do the data reject the restriction? Can the coefficients can be assumed the same across countries?

References

Bilson, J.F.O., 1981, The "Speculative Efficiency" Hypothesis, Journal of Business, 54, 435-51.

Hodrick, R.J., and S. Srivastava, 1984, An Investigation of Risk and Return in Forward Foreign Exchange, Journal of International Money and Finance, 3, 5-29.

Sweeney, R.J., 1988, Risk Premia in Forward Exchange Rates, Claremont Working Paper.

____________, and E.J.Q. Lee, 1988, Trading Strategies in Forward Exchange Markets.

MONETARY AND ECONOMIC INFLUENCES IN ECONOMETRIC MODELS OF INTERNATIONAL COMMODITY PRICE BEHAVIOUR

Walter C. Labys*
Harmon C. Thomas
Daniel J. Gijsbers

Keywords: Commodity price behaviour, impact of monetary influences on commodity prices, econometric commodity price models.

Abstract:

This paper investigates the applicability of reduced form commodity price models at the individual commodity level. Studied are cocoa, coffee, cotton, lead, rubber, silver, sugar, tin and zinc prices. Of particular significance is the role played by monetary and economic influences in commodity price adjustments. Interest rates, exchange rates and liquidity have been recently cited as important in this regard. Empirical results based on econometric price equations confirm their importance.

1. Introduction

This paper examines several of the relations thought to exist between international monetary factors and the price behaviour of primary commodities. The violent nature of the swings which have occurred in commodity prices since the early 1970s has caused researchers to suspect that any fluctations due to physical or real factors have been amplified by economic and monetary factors. The fluctuations due to real factors already were pronounced because of limited expansion of productive capacities in the 1960s, and several years of crop deficits and surpluses, together with

---

*Professor of Resource Economics, Department of Mineral and Energy Resource Economics, West Virginia University, Morgantown WV, 26506-6070; Economic Affairs Officer, Commodities Division, United Nations Conference on Trade and Development, Palais des Nations, 1211 Geneva; and Graduate Research Assistant, Department of Mineral and Energy Resource Economics, West Virginia University, respectively. Thanks are due to Mailika Theeravanilia and Duangjai Intarapravich for their help with the data.

NATO ASI Series, Vol. F54
A Reappraisal of the Efficiency of Financial Markets
Edited by Rui M.C. Guimaraes et al.

subsequent low stocks at the beginning of cyclical upswings and high stocks at the cyclical declines. The economic and monetary factors which amplified these fluctuations included the sharp increases and more recent declines in petroleum prices, synchronization of business cycles in the major industrial countries, speculative demand for commodities brought about by the float and resulting instability of major currencies, and accelerating inflation and subsequent rising production costs. Recent attempts made to explain price fluctuations thus have examined changes in economic activity, inflation, interest rates, exchange rates and international liquidity in addition to real or demand-supply factors.

The purposes of this study are several. First, it provides an explanation of commodity price fluctuations based on a more comprehensive range of price determinants compared to prior studies. Second, it goes beyond aggregate price index analysis to evaluate the importance of these determinants for selected major commodities, i.e., those for which futures trading exists in London and/or New York: cocoa, coffee, cotton, lead, rubber, silver, sugar, tin and zinc. Third, the inclusion of futures markets captures the role of speculative demand in addition to physical demand.

This study consists of the following parts: 2. Past Models of Commodity Price Behaviour, 3. Determinants of Commodity Demand, 4. Determinants of Commodity Supply, 5. The Resulting Commodity Price Relation, 6. Empirical Framework, and 7. Interpretation of Results.

2. Past Models of Commodity Price Behaviour

Past attempts to explain commodity price behaviour have employed econometric models of a single equation or a multiple equation nature. The single equation approach has involved time-series methods ranging from tests of stochastic behaviour (Kendall, 1953) to the application of exponential smoothing and mixed autoregressive and moving average models (Labys and Granger, 1970; and Chu, 1978). The multiple equation approach has involved the construction of dynamic commodity models which concentrate on the demand, supply and inventory determinants of price behaviour (Labys, 1973). An extensive view of these models and their commodity price applications can be found in Labys and Pollak (1984).

However, three events have occurred in particular since 1972 which require a somewhat broader approach to explain commodity price behaviour.

These include the sudden jumps in petroleum prices from 1973 as well as changes in the world monetary system (caused by a transition from pegged to floating exchange rates for the major currencies). During this period the world also experienced several sharp increases in inflation which led many investors to consider commodity futures contracts as well as commodities themselves as a hedge against inflation.

To postulate a causal model of commodity price behaviour, price analysts thus began to consider the relation of financial and macroeconomic factors to important commodity variables. This influence was seen as: (1) acting through commodity demand such as changes in industrial activity, prices (own) and prices of substitutes, monetary or liquidity conditions, and exchange rates, (2) acting through supply such as factors of production and their relative efficiency, prices (own lagged), financial and capital conditions reflected in interest rates, exogenous supply conditions such as weather and exchange rates, (3) acting through international economic conditions such as inflation, recession and changes in relative purchasing power, and (4) acting through related commodity futures market activity such as speculation and hedging. Particularly in providing short run explanations of this type, the monetary, foreign exchange and futures market conditions would appear to be most important.

Among the studies which have served as a background for testing the importance of these determinants, Labys and Granger (1970) separated commodity price influences according to whether they originated in the physical market or in an accompanying futures exchange. Employing cross-spectral as well as step-wise regression techniques, they found that both futures and financial market conditions exerted a significant influence on commodity price fluctuations, particularly in the short run. With the floating of the major currencies and the rising of inflation in the early 1970's, Labys and Thomas (1975) again sought to decipher the price impact of futures, financial and inflationary conditions. Like Labys and Granger, they dealt with the behaviour of individual commodities and concentrated on the importance of financial factors interacting with price formation on futures exchanges. But they considered in addition financial variables such as exchange rates, money stocks, treasury bills, and the Euro-dollar and Euro-sterling rates. The impact of these variables on commodity price behaviour was found to be important.

More recently price analysts have been concerned with the impact of macroeconomic factors on commodity prices and thus have been concerned only with aggregate price indices. Cooper and Lawrence (1975) were among the first to discover the importance of the influence of international economic conditions and industrial activity on aggregate prices, particularly as these influences affected commodity demand. Bosworth and Lawrence (1982) also confirmed the significance of positive relationships between international economic activity and commodity prices. Supply-side variables such as production and inventories were also shown to influence aggregate price behaviour, a result also pointed out earlier by Labys and Granger (1970).

As this research has expanded, more attention has been placed on formulating more complete models of price formation based on the theory of excess demand which viewed price determination as a consequence of market equilibrium adjustments between demand and supply. Variations on this approach have included disequilibrium theories which emphasize either the presence of inventories (Hwa, 1979) or of dynamic expectations, learning and lagged adjustments (Labys, 1981). The most important stylistic feature of this approach was the transformation of the original structural relationships to a single reduced form price equation. Enoch and Panic (1981) were among the first to apply such a model to aggregate commodity price behaviour. Interest rates were theorized to affect commodity demand because of their influence on holding inventories and on the relative returns from alternative forms of asset holding. However, econometric tests of their price equation did not prove interest rates to be significant.

Grilli and Yang (1981) employed a similar reduced form approach but included a greater variety of monetary influences. As a long run influence, increases in international liquidity were theorized to deter commodity producing countries from "distress sales" at times of low market demand and also to stimulate other market participants to hold commodities as assets which adds to the industrial demand for them. As a short run influence, interest rates were hypothesized to increase the opportunity costs of inventory holding and variations in exchange rates were thought to create shifts between liquid and commodity assets. Econometric tests revealed that only the share of international liquidity held in private hands was significant in explaining relative commodity price movements and only for aggregate metal prices. Interest rates proved to be an important determinant only for aggregate agricultural raw material and metal price indices, while the variability in exchange rates was stronger in explaining aggregate food and metal price indices. They concluded that the greater the instability in foreign exchange markets, the stronger the hedging demand for commodities as diversifying assets seems to be.

Chu and Morrison (1984) examined longer run price behaviour also employing a reduced form approach. They found that variations in commodity prices were influenced by variations in industrial production, dollar exchange rates _vis_ à _vis_ other currencies, and supply shocks. However, only the level of interest rates influenced commodity prices significantly, and this occurred during the early 1980s and not during the mid-1970s. Their approach was later adopted by the Federal Reserve Bank of New York (1985) who tested its applicability to four of the major aggregate commodity price indices, i.e. the IMF, Economist, UNCTAD and World Bank indices. Econometric regression tests confirmed the importance of interest rates in explaining commodity prices. In addition, they showed that supply-side factors became important when market conditions return to long run "normality".

Gilbert (1986) in concentrating on the explanation of fluctuations in the World Bank commodity price indices developed a more rigorous analysis of the impact of exchange rates in these indices, introducing the role played by the indebtedness of developing countries in this linkage. Aggregate non-food agricultural and metal price indices were found to respond rapidly to exchange rate adjustments. Here the econometric method employed simulated the impact of interest rate shocks, instead of testing the statistical significance of coefficients in regression equations. Aggregate food price indices were found to lag behind these shocks, with an appropriate lag of almost two years.

Few of the studies, however, provided econometric tests of the importance of commodities and commodity futures contracts as a means of hedging to diversify international portfolio asset holding. Labys and Thomas (1975) did examine commodities as assets and considered the returns from holding commodities compared to other financial investments as part of the overall commodity price determination process. Labys and Cohen (1980) went one-step further to compare actual risk-return ratios of a single commodity to that of other assets. The importance of commodities as a hedge against inflation was also suggested by Bosworth and Lawrence (1982). Empirical evidence was provided by Bird (1981) who performed a number of statistical tests that confirmed that commodities provided a very favourable alternative to asset holding during the period 1973–1980.

In conclusion all of the above studies have verified the importance of macroeconomic and liquidity factors in addition to real factors as determinants of commodity prices. Our present concern as will be shown, is to test the importance of these factors at the individual commodity level, to explore the role of futures market activity, and to conduct the test based on short run or quarterly data.

3. Determinants of Commodity Demand

The demand for a primary commodity can be divided into the demand for current use (consumption or industrial processing) and the demand for inventory stocks. Inventory demand can be attributed to transactions, precautionary and speculative motives. In order to provide customers with a steady supply of a product (so as to maintain market share) and in order to avoid breaks in the production process, businesses normally carry a certain level of stocks for transactions and precautionary reasons. However, because considerable uncertainty may exist about future price movements, there will also be a demand (by speculators) for inventories for purely speculative reasons.

Factors which determine these different types of demand for a commodity are likely to be different. Economic theory suggests that for utility maximizing consumers and profit maximizing industrial users of commodities, the flow demand for current utilization of a commodity will depend primarily on prices (of the commodity in question and its substitutes) and a shift variable which for consumers is income, and for industrial users, economic activity. Inventory demand can best be explained by dividing it into its non-speculative and speculative components. Non-speculative demand reflects the theory of the accelerator. Inventories are held for production or transactions purposes and to this must be added a precautionary minimum quantity to prevent stock-out. The functional determinants of this demand are the cost of storage and even more importantly the inventory costs of financing the stock, i.e. interest charges associated with, and the opportunity cost of, holding stocks. Finally, the speculative demand for a commodity will depend largely upon the price expectations of speculators (given their attitude toward risks) and the consequent expected rate of return on holding commodities compared to other assets.

Total flow demand

Let the total flow demand for a commodity D^T be defined as the sum of consumption flows D^C and of changes in non-speculative demand D^{NI} and of speculative inventories D^{SI}.

$$D^T = D^C + \Delta D^{NI} + \Delta D^{SI} \tag{1}$$

Consumption demand

$$D^C = f\,[\underset{-}{P}, \underset{+}{PS}, \underset{-}{E}, \underset{+}{Y}] \tag{2}$$

where:

P = Spot price of the commodity

PS = Average price of substitute commodities

E = Effective exchange rate

Y = Level economic or industrial activity

Non-speculative inventory demand

$$D^{NI} = f\,[\underset{+}{D^T}, \underset{-}{R}] \tag{3}$$

where R = Interest Rate adjusted for inflation

Speculative Inventory Demand

$$D^{SI} = f[\underset{-}{R}, \underset{-}{PF}, \underset{+}{F}, \underset{+}{M}] \tag{4}$$

where:

PF = Three month commodity futures price

F = Measure of the volume of future market activity (e.g., turnover, futures/physical ratio). This variable is included here since inventory demand is expected to increase to cover long market positions.

M = Amount of liquidity in private hands (i.e. money supply).

It should be noted that futures and forward market prices are assumed to be the rational expectations prices, that is, they fully reflect all available information about the future course of prices.

4. Determinants of Commodity Supply

The theory of commodity supply as distinct from production theory views supply as a function of producers' profit expectations (where producers maximize profits based on the relation of a commodity's price to its cost of production. In the short-run production capacity is fixed and this places a limit on potential supply. However, in the long-run production capacity can be varied. Given the producers' optimizing choice of the rate of capacity utilization, short-run supply may also be influenced by supply shocks such as unusually good or bad weather (especially in the case of agricultural products), labour strikes, and technological innovations. The functional relationship for the short-run supply of a commodity can thus be specified as follows:

$$S = f[\underset{+}{P}, \underset{+}{E}, Z, T] \qquad (5)$$

where:

P = Spot price of the commodity

E = Effective exchange rate

Z = Exogenous supply shocks such as unusual weather, strikes, etc.

T = Time-trend, reflecting the rigidity of capital stock in the short-run production function.

For empirical investigation, these variables can be combined in the following functional form based on conventional Cobb-Douglas assumptions

$$S = B_0 \, (PE)^{\alpha_3} \, PS^{\alpha_4} \, Z^{\alpha_1} \, T^{\alpha_2} \qquad (6)$$

Because of the low short-run price elasticities (α_2, α_3) of commodity supply, the above supply equation can be more simply approximated by

$$S = B_0 Z^{\alpha_1} \, T^{\alpha_2} \, . \qquad (7)$$

5. The Resulting Commodity Price Model

Based on the above model, the reduced form solution for the price relation can be obtained as follows.

Total flow demand

$$D^T = D^C + \Delta D^I \qquad (1)$$

Consumption demand

$$D^C = A_0 \, (PE)^{-\beta_1} \, PS^{\beta_2} \, Y^{\beta_3} \qquad (2)$$

Nonspeculative inventory demand

$$\Delta D^{NI} = a_1\Delta R + a_2\Delta D^T \quad (3)$$

Speculative demand

$$\Delta D^{SI} = a'_1\Delta R + a + a_3\Delta PF + a_4\Delta F + a_5\Delta M \quad (4)$$

Change in inventory demand

$$\Delta D^I = \Delta D^{NI} + \Delta D^{SI} = a_1\Delta R + a_2\Delta D^T + a_3\Delta PF + a_4\Delta F + a_5\Delta M \quad (5)$$

Therefore (following Chu and Morrison, 1984):

$$D^T = D^C + \Delta D^I$$

$$= A_0 (PE)^{-\beta_1} PS^{\beta_2} Y^{\beta_3} \times e^{-[a_1\Delta R + a_2\Delta D^T + a_3\Delta PF + a_4\Delta F + a_5\Delta M]} \quad (6)$$

Supply

$$S = B_0 Z^{\alpha_1} T^{\alpha_2} \quad (7)$$

Prices

$D^T = S$ implies (taking logs):

$$\beta_1 P = a_0 - \beta_0 + \beta_2 PS + (\beta_2 - \beta_1)E + \beta_3 Y - a_1\Delta R - a_2\Delta D^T - a_3\Delta PF - a_4\Delta F - a_5\Delta M - \alpha_1 Z - \alpha_2 T \quad (8)$$

6. Empirical Framework

Rather than develop the above price relation as a complete commodity price model, we restrict the present empirical analysis to the testing of the importance of each of the determinants in explaining commodity prices. The most suitable price relation which could be employed in this capacity is the following:

$$\Delta P = b_0 + b_1\Delta E + b_2\Delta Y + b_3\Delta R + b_4\Delta F + b_5\Delta M + b_6\Delta PF$$

Regarding the choice of those commodities, we adopt a group of commodities possessing futures exchanges in London and New York. This makes the present analysis directly comparable to Labys and Thomas (1975). This list includes cocoa, coffee, copper, cotton, lead, rubber, silver, sugar, tin and zinc. These two locations permit commodity asset adjustments to be compared across two areas in which meaningful financial and macroeconomic data exist.

The overall time period selected began in 1970 (which coincides with the Labys and Thomas data) and ends in 1983, the limit of availability of certain data. Although the period since 1983 is interesting for observing price behaviour, the previous period does feature two complete international price and economic cycles, 1972-75 and 1976-78, together with the cycle beginning 1980.

The selection of the empirical variables for the evaluation of the resulting price relation was accomplished separately for London and for New York. The definitions of the variables employed in each case appear in Appendix Table A.1. The use of extremely large number of explanatory variables contained in the price relation required careful consideration of econometric validity. Particularly it appears that problems of multicollinarity could well be present in some cases. However, this effect is to some extent minimized. The independent as well as the dependent variables appear in first-difference form. The estimation method employed also corrected for autocorrelation in the equation errors. Concerning other data, the futures volume data were obtained from the respective exchanges in London and in New York. Financial and macroeconomic data derive from official IMF and OECD sources.

Figures 1 and 2 which follow provide a hint at some of the variable relations discussed earlier. The Figures feature the Economist commodity price index, Treasury bill rates, effective exchange rates, industrial share prices, and the Eurosterling and Eurodollar rates for the London and New York markets, respectively. Both Figures show a rough positive relationship between commodity prices and industrial share prices, but a sometimes negative relationship between commodity prices and the effective exchange rates, treasury bill rates, and the Eurodollar and Eurosterling rates.

7. Interpretation of Results

Tables 1 and 2 feature the first difference equations for the real or deflated commodity price variables in the London and New York markets, respectively. The wholesale price indices of the two countries have been used as the corresponding deflators. These equations proved to perform better than the first difference equations with prices in nominal form for all commodities in both markets, excepting sugar. Estimation methods employed assure the absence of autocorrelation in any of the equations.

Concerning the London market, some of the coefficients of the independent variables in the nine equations possess an incorrect sign. In

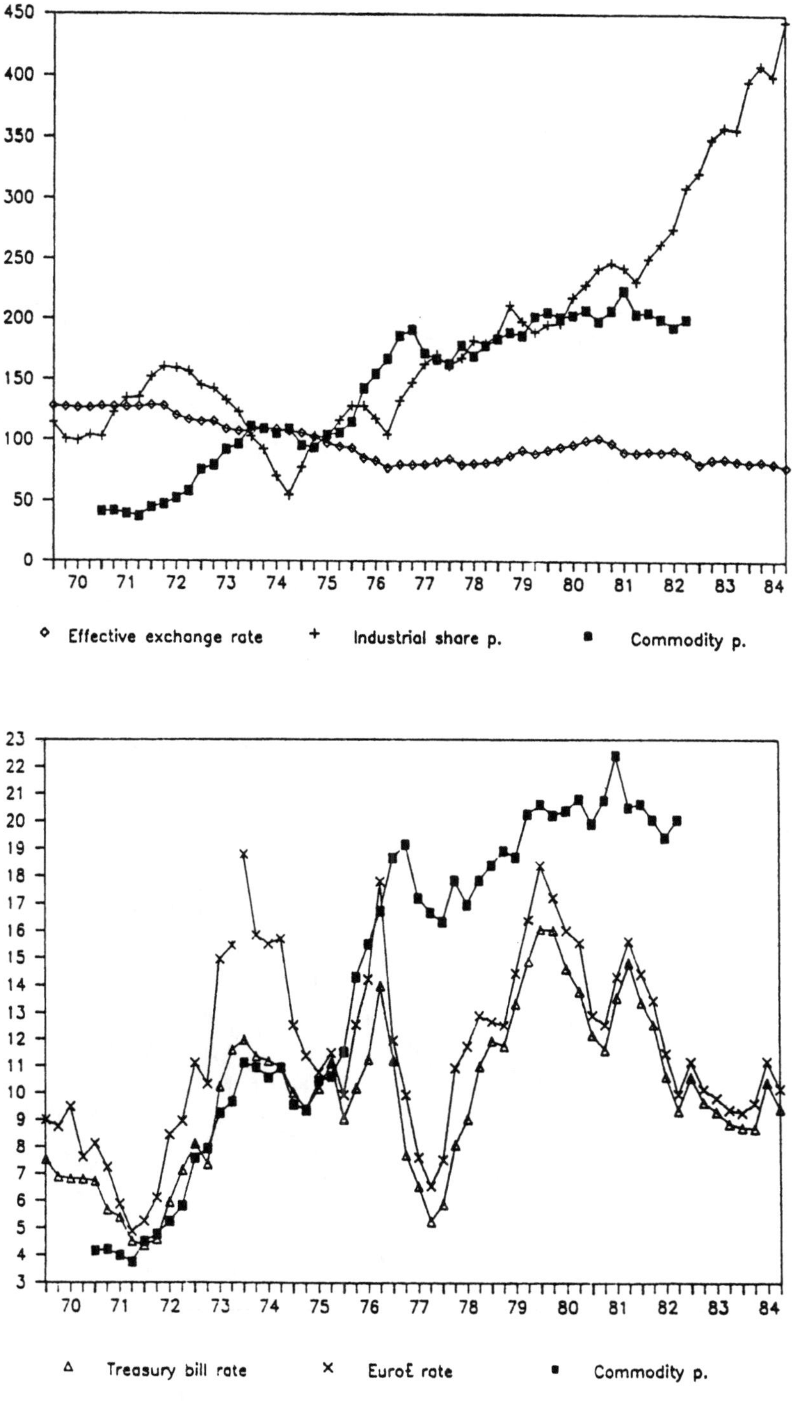

Figure 1

LONDON COMMODITY PRICE RELATIONS

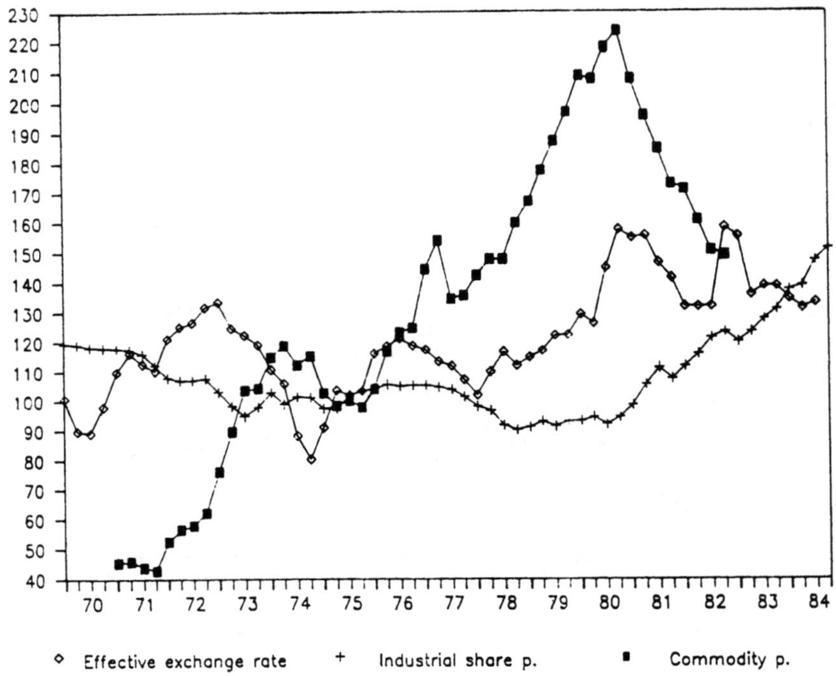

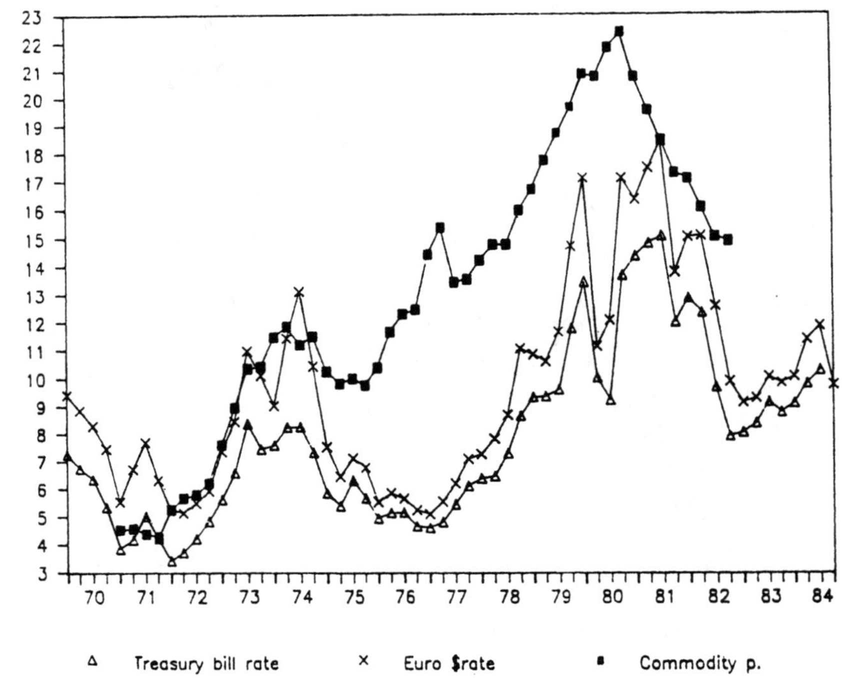

Figure 2

NEW YORK COMMODITY PRICE RELATIONS

Table 1

UK DEFLATED COMMODITY PRICE EQUATIONS

Intercept	dE	dY	d(TBR)	%d(F)	d(M)	ar(1)	R^2	F	DW [1)]
	Independent Variables and Expected Sign								
	-	+	-	+	-				
				COPPER (72.3-83.2)					
-0.1484	-0.0960	0.2428	0.0004	0.4117	-0.0298		0.1892	1.7773	1.62
(-0.397)	(-1.434)	(1.931)[b]	(0.002)	(0.915)	(-0.184)				
				SILVER (72.3-83.2)					
-0.0512	0.0024	0.1524	0.0563	0.4512	-0.0031		0.1097	0.8870	2.27
(-0.182)	(0.046)	(1.547)	(0.420)	(1.032)	(-0.025)				
				SUGAR (70.3-82.4)					
0.1264	0.0285	0.0958	0.0158	0.0198	-0.0844		0.1843	1.9878	1.93
(0.999)	(1.072)	(2.057)[b]	(0.251)	(0.098)	(-1.497)				
				COFFEE (71.3-82.4)					
0.6290	-0.1285	-0.0592	-0.0344	0.3810	-0.3899	0.4461	0.3357	3.2856	1.73
(0.927)	(-1.136)	(-0.336)	(-0.124)	(0.981)	(-1.601)	(2.861)[a]			
				COCOA (72.3-82.4)					
0.4770	-0.3207	0.0244	-0.3743	-0.4247	0.1894	0.2219	0.3274	2.8394	1.85
(0.744)	(-2.593)[a]	(1.170)	(-1.329)	(-1.665)	(0.169)	(1.293)			
				RUBBER (75.2-83.4)					
0.2561	-0.0875	0.1544	-0.0177	-0.0462	-0.1224	0.4067	0.4970	4.6116	1.99
(1.188)	(-3.062)[a]	(2.992)[a]	(-0.232)	(-0.775)	(-1.830)[b]	(2.233)[b]			
				ZINC (72.3-83.2)					
0.1893	-0.0566	0.0607	-0.0141	0.1300	-0.1247	0.4347	0.2766	2.3582	1.91
(0.631)	(-1.215)	(0.793)	(-0.113)	(0.434)	(-1.160)	(2.800)[a]			
				TIN (72.3-83.2)					
-0.0252	-0.8704	1.1311	-0.6498	2.2150	-0.2516		0.2757	2.8927	1.61
(-0.014)	(-2.772)[a]	(1.921)[b]	(-0.777)	(1.216)	(-0.338)				
				LEAD (72.3-83.2)					
-0.0734	-0.0356	0.0976	-0.0235	0.1408	-0.0065		0.2712	2.8279	1.62
(-0.7265)	(-1.969)[b]	(2.820)[a]	(-0.498)	(1.041)	(-0.154)				

1: Note that in first difference regression equations the explanatory power is less important than the correctness of the sign of the regressors.
a: t-statistic significant at 99% level , b: t-statistic significant at 95% level

Table 2

US DEFLATED COMMODITY PRICE EQUATIONS

Intercept	dE	dY	d(TBR)	%d(F)	d(M)	ar(1)	R^2	F	DW [1)]
	-	+	-	+	-				
				COPPER (70.4-83.3)					
-0.0025	0.0011	0.0150	0.0129	0.0402	-0.0003	-0.0332	0.3814	4.6242	1.98
(-0.269)	(0.468)	(2.276)[b]	(2.189)[b]	(1.726)[b]	(-2.429)[a]	(-0.210)			
				SILVER (70.4-83.3)					
0.0899	-0.0699	0.2223	0.7520	0.4056	-0.0030		0.2234	2.6465	2.18
(0.205)	(-0.656)	(1.075)	(2.880)[a]	(0.504)	(-0.543)				
				SUGAR (70.4-84.2)					
-0.0070	0.0011	0.0073	0.0010	-0.0024	0.00005	0.2767	0.1303	1.1982	1.95
(-0.656)	(0.500)	(1.768)[b]	(0.209)	(-0.161)	(0.447)	(1.833)[b]			
				COFFEE (73.3-84.3)					
0.0244	0.0062	-0.0124	-0.0119	0.00004	-0.00036	0.3298	0.1563	1.1734	1.85
(0.474)	(0.629)	(-0.633)	(-0.527)	(0.895)	(-0.715)	(2.102)[b]			
				COCOA (70.4-83.3)					
0.0232	-0.0037	0.0218	0.0254	-0.1133	-0.0006		0.1298	1.3725	1.95
(0.684)	(-0.438)	(1.299)	(1.218)	(-0.713)	(-1.285)				

1: Note that in first difference regression equations the explanatory power is less important than the correctness of the signs of the regressors

a: t-statistic significant at 99% level , b: t-statistic significant at 95% level the copper, silver and sugar equations the sign of the treasury bill rate is wrong. In the latter two equations the exchange rate variable is wrong as well. In the coffee equation the activity variable has the wrong sign but it is also insignificant. In the cocoa and rubber equations some inconsistency is found in the sign of the futures trading variable. In the zinc, tin and lead equations all signs are correct. While the treasury bill rate has the correct sign in six out of the nine equations, the variable lacked statistical significance.

Concerning the New York market, the treasury bill variable has the wrong sign in all equations except that for coffee. However, the coefficient is signficant in all cases. The exchange rate variable has the wrong sign in the copper and coffee equations. In the cocoa equation the volume of trading variable has the wrong sign. As can be seen from Table 2, the suguar equation did not yield any meaningful results.

There does appear to be however, a preponderance of equations in which the importance of monetary and economic influences on short run commodity price behaviour is confirmed. These results thus confirm that these influences are important not only in explaining aggregate commodity price indices but also individual commodity prices. The implications of these results are that a more general theoretical model could be formulated which reflects more accurately the influence of monetary conditions in individual commodity markets. It is this research which the authors are currently pursuing.

Appendix Table A.1

DATA DEFINITIONS

Variables	London	New York
E:	UK pound effective exchange rate: exchange rate between UK pound and 20 other major currencies weighted by the IMF's Multilateral Exchange Rate Model	US dollar effective exchange rate: exchange rate between US dollar and 20 other major currencies weighted by the IMF's Multilateral Exchange Rate Model
Y:	OECD GDP in US dollars, OECD	OECD GDP in US dollars, OECD
TBR:	UK treasury bill rate, three months tender rate, Bank of England	US treasury bill rate, three months tender rate, Federal Reserve Board
M:	UK M1, seasonally adjusted, Bank of England	US M1, seasonally adjusted, Federal Reserve Board
Deflator:	Consumer price index, IMF series	Producer price index, US Department of Labour
Cocoa P:	UK pounds per metric ton, UNCTAD Commodity Price Bulletin	Spot cocoa bean prices (ACCR) cents/lb, Commodity Yearbook
Cocoa F:	Cocoa volume of trade, International Commodity Clearing House	Cocoa volume of trade, Futures Industry Association
Coffee P:	UK pounds per metric ton, UNCTAD Commodity Price Bulletin	Weighted average of prices for unwashed arabica, robusta, other mild arabica and Columbian milds arabica, cents/lb, Commodity Yearbook
Coffee F:	Coffee volume of trade, International Commodity Clearing House	Coffee volume of trade, Futures Industry Association
Sugar P:	UK pounds per metric ton, UNCTAD Commodity Price Bulletin	Average price of raw sugar, contract 11, cents/lb, Commodity Yearbook
Sugar F:	Sugar volume of trade, International Commodity Clearing House	Sugar volume of trade, Futures Industry Association

Silver P:	Average price of silver, .999 fine, cents/troy oz, IMF, IFS	Average price of silver delivered to US destinations, .999 fine, cents/troy oz, IMF, IFS
Silver F:	Silver volume of trade, International Commodity Clearing House	Silver volume of trade, Futures Industry Association
Copper P:	LME price for electrolytic (wirebar) copper, UK pounds per metric ton, Metal Statisitics	Producer's price of electrolytic (wirebar) copper, Commodity Yearbook
Copper P^f:	Copper three months forward price, idem	
Copper F:	Copper volume of trade, International Commodity Clearing House	Copper volume of trade, Futures Industry Association
Lead P:	LME price for pig lead, min. 99.9%, UK pounds per metric ton, Metal Statistics	
Lead P^f:	Lead three months forward price, idem	
Lead F:	Lead volume of trade, International Commodity Clearing House	
Tin P:	LME price for high grade tin, min, 99.85%, UK pounds per metric ton, Metal Statistics	
Tin P^f:	Tin three months forward price, idem	
Tin F:	Lead volume of trade, International Commodity Clearing House	
Zinc P:	LME price for virgin zinc, min. 99.85%, UK pounds per metric ton, Metal Statistics	
Zinc P^f:	Zinc three months forward price, idem	
Zinc F:	Zinc volume of trade, International Commodity Clearing House	
Rubber P:	Natural rubber price, UK pounds per metric ton, Rubber Statistical Bulletin, The International Rubber Study Group, London	
Rubber P^f:	Rubber three months forward price, idem	
Rubber F:	Rubber volume of trade, idem	

REFERENCES

Bird, P.J. (1982). "Commodity Futures as a Store of Value." Discussion Paper No. 96, University of Stirling, Scotland.

Bird, P.J. (1981). "An Investigation of the Role of Speculation in the 1972 to 1975 Commodity Price Boom." Unpublished Ph.D. Thesis, University of Cambridge.

Bird, P.J. (1984). "Commodities as a Hedge Against Inflation." Applied Economics 16: 855-67.

Bodie, V. and Rosansky, I.V. (1980). "Risk, Return in Commodity Futures." Financial Analyst Journal, 27-39.

Bordo, D. (1980). "The Effects of Monetary Changes on Relative Commodity Prices and Role of Long-Term Contracts." Journal of Political Economy, 88: 1088-1109.

Bosworth, B. and Lawrence, R.Z. (1982). Commodity Prices and the New Inflation, Washignton: The Brookings Institution.

Breener, M. and Landskroner, Y. (1983). "Inflation Uncertainties and Returns on Bonds," Economica 50: 463-468.

Brown, R.L., Durbin, J., and Evans, J.M. (1975). "Techniques for Testing the Constancy of Regression Relationships over Time," Journal of the Royal Statistical Society, Series B, 149-192.

Chu, K.Y. and Morrison, T.K. (1984). "The 1981-82 Recession and Non-Oil Primary Commodity Prices," IMF Staff Papers 31: 93-140.

Chu, K., Hwa, E.C. and Krishnamurty, K. (1983). "Export Instability and Adjustments of Imports, Capital Inflows and External Reserves: A Short-Run Dynamic Model," in Bigman and Taya (eds.) Exchange Rate and Trade Instability: Causes, Consequences and Remedies, Cambridge, MA: Ballinger Publishing, pp. 195-214.

Chua J. and Woodward, R.S. (1982). "Gold as an Inflation Hedge," Journal of Business Finance and Accounting, 9: 191-7.

Cooper, R.M. and Lawrence, R.Z. (1975). "The 1972-75 Commodity Boom," with comments and discussion, Brookings Paper on Economic Activity, 3: 671-723.

Crockett, A. (1981). "Determination of Exchange Rate Movements: A Review," Fincance and Development, 18: 33-37.

Darby, R. (1982). "The Price of Oil and World Inflation and Recession," American Economic Review, 72: 738-51.

Edwards, S. (1985). "Commodity Export Prices and the Real Exchange Rate in Developing Countries: Coffee in Colombia," WP No. 1579, National Bureau of Economic Research, Cambridge, MA.

Enoch, C.A. and Panic, M. (1981). "Commodity Prices in the 1970's, Bank of England Quarterly Bulletin, 1: 42-53.

Fama, F.E. and Schwert, W.G. (1977). "Asset Returns and Inflation," Journal of Financial Economics, 5: 115-46.

Fama, F.E. (1979). "Inflation, Interest, and Relative Prices," Journal of Business, 52: 183-209.

Farrell, S.V., De Rosa, A.D. and McCowan, A.T. (1983). "Effects of Exchange Rate Variability on International Trade and Other Economic Variables: Review of Literature," Federal Reserve Bulletin.

Federal Reserve Bank of New York (1985). "Commodity Prices in the Current Recovery." FRBNY Quarterly Review 1: 11-19.

Fisher, S. (1977). "Long-Term Contracts, Rational Expectation and the Optimal Money Supply Rule," Journal of Political Economy, 85: 191-205.

Firth, (1979). "The Relationship Between Stock Market Returns and Rate of Inflation," Journal of Finance, 34: 743-49.

Fratianni, M. and Savona, P. (1972). La Liquidita Internazionale, (Bologna: Il Mulino).

French, M.W. (1984). "Should Policy Making Account for Market Expectations: An Estimate of Their Impact on Commodity Policy," Journal of Policy Modelling, 10: 243-58.

Gandolf, E.A. and Lothian, R.J. (1982). "International Price Behaviour and the Demand for Money," Economic Inquiry, 21: 295-311.

Garner, C.A. (1985). "Commodity Prices and Monetary Policy Reform," Federal Reserve Bank of Kansas City Economic Review, 70: 7-21.

Gay, D.G. and Manaster, S. (1981). "Hedging Against Commodity Price Inflation: Stocks and Bills as Substitutes for Futures Contracts," Journal of Business, 55: 317-43.

Gilbert, C.L. (1984). "A Rational Expectations Price Model for a Continuously Produced Primary Commodity," Discussion Paper, Institute of Economics and Statistics, Oxford.

Gilbert, C.L. (1986). "Exchange Rates, LDC Debt and Commodity Prices: A Model of the World Bank Commodity Price Index." Discussion Paper, Commodity Studies and Projections Division, World Bank, Washigton, D.C.

Goldstein, M. (1977). "International Liquidity: An Analytical and Empirical Reinterpretation," Ente Einaudi Wuaderni di Richerche, 11: 47-121.

Goreux, L.M. (1975). "Commodity Prices and Business Cycle," Discussion Paper, Research Department, International Monetary Fund, Washington, D.C.

Grilli, E. (1975). "Commodity Price Movements Before and After the Oil Crisis," The World Bank, draft mimeo.

Grilli, R.E. and Yang, C.M. (1981). "Real and Monetary Determinants of Non-Oil Primary Commodity Price Movement," Commodities Division Working Paper, No. 1981-6, World Bank, Washington, D.C.

Hwa, E.C. (1979). "Price Determination in Several International Primary Commodity Markets," IMF Staff Papers, 1: 157-88.

Jastram, R.W. (1982). "The Golden Constant in the Gold Standard and Commodity Price Behaviour," in A. Quadrio-Curzio (ed.), The Gold Problem: Economic Perspectives, Oxford: Oxford University Press for the Banca Nazionale del Lavoro.

Johnson, L.L. (1969). "The Theory of Hedging and Speculation in Commodity Futures," Review of Economic Studies, 3: 139-51.

Kaldor, N. (1976). "Inflation and Recession in the World Economy," Economic Journal, 86: 703-714.

Kendall, M.A. (1953). "Statistical Time-Series Analysis of Prices," Journal of the Royal Statistical Society, Series A.

Kravis, R.B. and Lipsey, R.E. (1978). "Price Behaviour in the Light of Balance of Payments Theories," Journal of International Economics, 8: 193-246.

Labys, W.C. (1973). Dynamic Commodity Models: Specification, Estimation and Simulation, Lexington: Heath Lexington Books.

Labys, W.C. and Granger, C.W.J. (1979). Speculation, Hedging and Commodity Price Forecasts, Lexington: Heath Lexington Books.

Labys, W.C. and Cohen, B.C. (1980). "Wine as a Medium-Term Investment Vehicle," European Agricultural Review.

Labys, W.C. and Pollak P. (1984). Commodity Models for Forecasting and Policy Analysis, Lovden: Croom-Helm.

Labys, W.C. and Thomas, H.C. (1975). "Speculation, Hedging and Commodity Price Behaviour: An International Comparison," Applied Economics, 7: 287-0301.

Labys, W.C. (1981). "A Disequilibrium Model of Commodity Market Adjustments," Report submitted to the National Science Foundation, Department of Mineral and Energy Resource Economics, West Virginia University.

Long, J.B. (1974). "Stock Prices, Inflation, and the Term Structure of Interest Rates," Journal of Financial Economics, 7: 131-70.

Manking, H.J. (1978). "Anticipated Inflation and Interest Rates in an Open Economy," Journal of Money, Credit and Banking, 10: 275-89.

Markowitz, H. (1959). Portfolio Selection: Efficient Diversification of Investment, John Wiley, New York.

Newberry, D.M. and Stiglitz (1981). The Theory of Commodity Price Stabilisation, Oxford: Oxford University Press.

Ram, R. and Spencer, E.D. (1983). "Stock Returns, Real Activity, Inflation, and Money: Comment," The American Economic Review, 73: 463-69.

Ray, G.F. (1977). "The Real Price of Primary Products," National Institute Economic Review 3: 76-79.

Ridler, D. and Yandle, C.A. (1972). "A Simplified Method for Analyzing the Effects of Exchange Rate Changes on Exports of a Primary Commodity," IMF Staff Papers, 19: 559-578.

Roll, R. (1973). "Assets, Money and Commodity Price Inflation Under Certainty," Journal of Money, Credit and Banking, 5: 903-23.

Rutledge, D.J.S. (1974). "Trading Volume and Price Variability: New Evidence of the Price Effects of Speculation," International Futures Trading Seminar Proceedings, 5: 161-74.

Schwert, W.G. (1981). "The Adjustment of Stock Prices to Information About Inflation," Journal of Finance, 36: 15-29.

Tobin, J. (1965). "The Theory of Portfolio Selection," in The Theory of Interest Rates, F.H. Hahn and F.P.E. Brechling, (eds.), London: MacMillan and Co.

Vittas, H. (1984). "Effects of Changes in EEC Currency Exchange Rates on Prices, Production and Trade of Agricultural Commodities in the Community," IMF Staff Papers, 31: 447-65.

Comments on W. Labys, H. Thomas and D. Gijsbers "Monetary and Economic Influences in Econometric Models of International Commodity Price Speculation"

by Robert J. Shiller

This paper treats very interesting questions: what accounts for the enormous fluctuations observed in recent years in commodity prices. Past research has apparently not been highly successful at explaining these movements. The commodity prices apparently present a difficult modeling problem, which the authors make a serious effort to solve.

The preliminary results reported here are a useful beginning, though as the authors admit, there are still some problems. In my view, the biggest shortcoming of this paper comes from the choice the authors made for the theoretical framework. The framework is of the flow equilibrium variety. A conventional demand curve for the final uses of the commodity is proposed, as well as a demand curve for the stock of inventories. Equilibrium requires that the demand for final uses plus the <u>change</u> in the demand for final inventories equals new production. Now, I won't quarrel with that equilibrium condition, which is, after all, a tautology. But I feel there is something suspicious about the resulting reduced form equation that relates the <u>level</u> or commodity prices to the quarterly <u>change</u> in interest rates. This makes price today depend on lagged interest rates. Why should lagged interest rates matter? And then if they do, why the one-quarter lagged interest rates, and not the one-week lagged or one-year lagged interest rates? Obviously, the choice the authors made has something to do with the data sampling interval, when in fact it should be specified in terms of parameters of economic behavior.

A better theoretical framework might possibly be derived by setting up the optimization problem faced by holders of inventories. Solving the problem would seem to suggest that commodity prices today would relate to expectations of <u>future</u> interest rates, though not <u>lagged</u> interest rates.

I also doubt that the interpretation of the lagged dependent variable on the regression, is right. Certainly, commodity prices, quoted as they are in very active speculative markets are not just "sluggish."

The authors claim this is a "short run" model. But they apply it over a dozen years of data where prices should some rather long swinger.

The estimated equations don't link up closely to the theory developed. For example, ordinary interest rates are used, not R, or Π,. The exchange

NATO ASI Series, Vol. F54
A Reappraisal of the Efficiency of Financial Markets
Edited by Rui M. C. Guimaraes et al.

rate does not enter as part of R, but separately, and no lagged exchange rates enters. The left-hand variable in the regression is in money (nominal) terms, but the only right hand variable there to pick up the inflation experienced over these years is the income measure Y. I think that these problems could easily be fixed by the authors in their future work.

I am not sure why separate UK and US estimates are made. I would expect that the log futures prices would differ only by the log of the exchange rate, the regression results would be essentially the same between the UK and US if the same variables were on the right-hand side of both the US equations, and if lagged exchange rate E were included to purge the lagged price from the exchange rate effect.

MARKET EFFICIENCY AND COMMODITY PRICES - FORECASTING SOYABEAN PRICES ON THE CHICAGO MARKET.

B.G. Kingsman.

Department of Operational Research and Operations Management. The Management School, University of Lancaster. Bailrigg, Lancaster LA1 4YX, U.K.

ABSTRACT.

This paper considers market efficiency in commodity markets. The semi-strong form of the efficiency hypothesis implies that the current prices, futures or cash, contain all the current knowledge of the state of supply and demand factors. It is therefore impossible to use econometric models, based only on known published information, to produce better forecasts of forward cash prices than the current futures prices. The development of a medium term price forecasting model for predicting prices up to about four months ahead is described. Because of the problem context in which the model was derived, the emphasis is on forecasting forward Chicago cash prices. The performance in using the models to forecast in practice over two and a half crop years is analysed and compared with the use of the futures price as a predictor. The results show that a combined predictor would give forecasts superior in every regard to the futures prices alone. The results of the error analysis, analysis of variance and the Theil Inequality Coefficient, indicate that neither the current cash nor futures prices take into account fully the current publicly known information. The soyabean market is thus inefficient to some degree.

KEYWORDS: commodity prices, soyabeans, expectations, econometric models, market efficiency.

NATO ASI Series, Vol. F54
A Reappraisal of the Efficiency of Financial Markets
Edited by Rui M.C. Guimaraes et al.

1. INTRODUCTION.

Defining a precise operational measure to test whether a market is efficient or not is a difficult problem. It is particularly so for raw material commodities since the market situation is continually changing under the impact of new information.

The semi-strong form of the Efficient Market Hypothesis implies that the current futures prices and/or cash price should have taken into account fully the implications of all the currently publicly available economic information concerning the commodity. Further to quote from Giles and Goss (1980): 'In the case of an efficient market for a continuous inventory commodity, the predictive interpretation of both futures prices and spot prices seems to be clear ...... both spot and futures prices may be interpreted as predictors of maturity date spot prices'. Soyabeans are a commodity that is stored in quantity continously. It should not therefore be possible to improve upon the current futures price as a predictor of the forward cash soyabean prices on Chicago, by the use of any econometric model for prices based only on currently available public information.

Let P_t and P_{t+h} be the cash prices at time t and t+h, $F_{t+h,t}$ be the futures price at time t for delivery at time t+h and I_t the information set at time t. Then the E.M.H. implies either

$$F_{t+h,t} = E(P_{t+h}|I_t) \quad \text{for } h>0 \tag{1}$$

or

$$P_t = E(P_{t+h}|I_t) \quad \text{"} \tag{2}$$

$$F_{t+h,t} = P_t + r_{t+h,t}$$

where $r_{t+h,t}$ is some risk or storage premium that the supplier of futures requires to carry the commodity from t to t+h.

Let us assume that an econometric model has been devised that, using only information publicly available at time t, provides forecasts, $M_{t+h,t}$, of the forward cash prices at time t+h, which do not directly include current cash or futures prices. A general predictor of forward cash prices then has the form

$$P_{t+h} = w_1 F_{t+h,t} + w_2(M_{t+h,t} | I_t) + u_{t+h,t} \qquad (3)$$

where $u_{t+h,t}$ is the innovation in price between periods t and t+h and satisfies $E(u_{t+h,t}|I_t) = 0$. Alternatively the current cash price replaces the futures price.

Under the Efficient Market Hypothesis the null hypothesis is that $w_1=1$ and $w_2=0$. Assessing the performance of this model to demonstrate that w_2 is or is not significantly different to zero thus provides a test of the E.M.H. in its semi-strong form. If this is found to be true then it provides strong evidence of the existence of inefficiency in information processing in comodity markets.

During the late seventies, the author developed a series of models for forecasting soyabean prices to assist in purchasing decisions. These were empirical descriptive econometric models based on current publicly available estimates of supply and demand factors. Some months after this research was completed the author was asked to provide regular price forecasts for two UK companies. This continued over almost a four year period. The reports and forecasts from the early part of 1978 to the autumn of 1980 have been preserved. Because of the task undertaken, the emphasis was on forecasting future Chicago cash prices for up to four months ahead. Forecasts for further ahead were produced only on rare occasions and were more discursive and scenario analysis rather than precise forecasts. The Chicago cash prices were then converted to landed European prices. By comparing the current prices quoted by suppliers with the forecasts for up to four months ahead, the purchaser could decide whether to buy future months' requirements at the current time or wait until future opportunities at expected lower prices.

The first part of the paper briefly describes the approach taken and the models produced. The forecasting performance achieved in practice over two and a half crop years is then analysed. This is compared with the futures prices and current cash prices as predictors. The results show that a combined predictor would give forecasts superior in every regard to the futures prices or cash price alone.

2. OTHER EVIDENCE ON INEFFICIENCY IN COMMODITY MARKETS.

A further consequence of the E.M.H., in its weak form confining the information set to past prices alone, is that it is impossible to derive a decision rule based on past prices that enables an industrial purchaser to buy at better than the average price over a period of time.

Already published work has shown that it is possible to develop decision rules using time series statistical forecasts which enable purchasers to buy at better than the average market price, see Guimaraes and Kingsman (1986), Kingsman (1985), and Taylor (1986). One example from Kingsman (1985) showed that the use of a decision pricebreak purchasing rule, with an adaptive exponential smoothing forecasting model for the price forecasts, applied to purchasing copper in practice by an industrial user over an 18 month period gave a saving of just under 2% compared to a policy of buying hand to mouth at a regular daily rate. A policy based on Taylor's price trend model simulated over a 6 year period indicated that a saving of 1.6% on a hand to mouth policy would have been achieved. In Guimaraes and Kingsman, a day to day buying policy for maize purchasing based on a price trend model is described. It was derived from analysis over the years up to 1972. A simulation of this policy over the years 1973-76 gave a saving of between 1-2% of the average price.

These results cast considerable doubt on the efficient market hypothesis as regards commodity prices. However this paper concentrates on more direct tests of the semi-strong form of the hypothesis.

3. THE GENERAL APPROACH TO COMMODITY PRICE FORECASTING MODELLING.

3.1 Expectations.

Although economists have traditionally regarded commodity markets as examples of a classic 'pure economic system', little successful work of practical use has been published. The work of Working and Weymar's 'Supply of Storage' theory, (1968), are notable exceptions to this. Most economists have concerned themselves with the very long term market behaviour. Furthermore, the general approach taken requires knowledge of the real underlying values of supply and demand. These are impossible to determine accurately until some years after the event. Hence many researchers give up complaining of the problems of inaccuracy and inadequate data.

An alternative approach taken by this author is to turn this argument about the unreliability and inaccuracy of the data on its head, to assert that it is precisely this inaccuracy and ever changing view and knowledge of the state of the market that causes the medium term fluctuations in price, see Kingsman (1974) and (1985). Primarily it is the market's general belief or expectations of the state of supply and demand that determine price. The actual values are irrelevant since the people in the market can only make decisions based on their current expectations.

A commodity market is a dynamic system in that new information or more reliable estimates of market factors are continuously becoming available. The acceptance of new information by the market explicitly changes market expectations and gives rise to a new equilibrium price level. Because new information takes time to be absorbed and its effects evaluated by the totality of people in the market, and because of the natural inertia of any complex system such as a commodity market, prices do not usually jump immediately to the new price level. Rather, a change to market expectations gives a new impetus and direction to price movements. Prices after a greater or lesser immediate reaction begin to move towards this new level, with reversals and rallies on the way. Thus the current expectations can be used to predict prices in the future not the immediate current price. The idea that economic behaviour is primarily determined by expectations rather than the actual values is not in itself new. Weymar (1968) included expectations in some of his supply and demand models. The two classical models in economics for expectations are Nerlove's 'Partial Adjustment Model', (1956) and (1958), and Cagan's 'Adaptive Expectations Model', (1956). These are generally applied to annual data and tend to imply a relatively smooth transition from one year's expectations to the next. They are in fact merely different forms of simple exponential smoothing. However, discussions with market participants make it clear that there can be very large discontinuous changes in their expectations from one month to the next over a year. The classical models are thus much too rigid and simple to deal adequately with the commodity situation. Expectations must be measured more directly.

There are vast amounts of quantitative information freely circulating in the market for any commodity. In most markets, merchants and dealers attempt to provide advice on expected production, stocks and consumption etc., over the coming months. In addition, industry and government agencies as well as the FAO provide estimates and forecasts. In some markets a single source may have become dominant and gained participants' confidence, so that its estimates become the market view. For example, the United States Department of Agriculture (USDA) is such a source for estimates of the US soyabean production. Alternatively, estimates from different sources can be combined to give the best figure. A further approach, particularly for consumption factors, is to use extrapolation methods based on cumulative crop year monthly or quarterly usages, as many market participants tend to do, especially for the less common materials where published estimates are rare. Discussions with market participants and research will show whether such simple extrapolation or a weighted average of the forecasts produced by alternative organisations is best for a particular commodity. Clearly the estimates freely available at any time to market participants provide a source for the quantitative measurement of market expectations at any time.

The major accepted reliable source on US production of soyabeans, as mentioned, is USDA. It provides an estimate of the crop size usually in the middle of the month from July to the following January. The July estimate is fairly tentative, based on the aceage planted on an average projected yield and has only been provided since 1971. August is the first estimate based on the crop condition. By September growing is complete and harvesting is about to begin. July/August is a critical time when lack of rain, as in 64/65, 74/75 and 76/77, can seriously reduce the yield per acre. Thus major changes can occur between the August and September estimates. The various estimates made by USDA for the crop years 63/64 to 77/78 are given in Table 1, from which it can be seen that large changes can occur at almost any time. The final column of the table gives the actual harvest returns only known much later. The differences between the September estimate and the actual harvest ranged between +105 to -101 million bushels.

Estimates of the carryover stock, the other supply factor, also change over time. Table 2 gives USDA's estimates as made in May and August of the crop year and November of the succeeding crop year.

USDA also provides a regular series of forecasts of crop year usages. These are published on a regular basis in November, January/February, April/May and August, following the end of quarter total stocks survey. These are given in Tables 3 and

Table 1 - USDA's Crop Estimates (million bushels).

Crop Year	Jul	Aug	Sep	Oct	Nov	Dec	Jan	Final
63/4	-	723	728	727	718	701	-	699
64/5	-	748	704	699	702	700	-	700
65/6	-	864	867	862	853	844	-	846
66/7	-	860	926	927	929	931	-	929
67/8	-	999	1003	994	985	973	-	976
68/9	-	1064	1080	1065	1079	1079	1080	1107
69/0	-	1060	1055	1070	1095	1117	-	1133
70/1	-	1114	1133	1135	1134	1136	-	1127
71/2	1177	1235	1186	1175	1200	1169	1169	1176
72/3	1180	1270	1286	1317	1351	1276	1276	1271
73/4	1588	1540	1599	1578	1575	1567	1567	1547
74/5	1433	1314	1316	1262	1244	1233	1233	1215
75/6	1450	1458	1442	1474	1520	1521	-	1547
76/7	1350	1344	1274	1250	1252	-	1265	1288
77/8	1595	1602	1644	1647	1683	-	1716	1762

Table 2 - USDA's Carryover Stock Estimates (million bushels).

Crop Year	May	Aug	Nov	Final
65/6	48	30	36	36
66/7	81	102	91	90
67/8	150	160	166	166
68/9	315	322	322	326
69/0	262	229	229	230
70/1	111	105	97	99
71/2	60	60	71	72
72/3	50	40	60	60
73/4	200	160	172	171
74/5	235	220	186	185
75/6	230	200	244	245
76/7	65	75	103	103

4. These show that large changes in the forecasts can occur over the crop year, either upwards or downwards, both in the domestic crush and export values. The crop years 69/70, 73/74, 74/75 and 75/76 all show particularly large changes.

Tables 5 and 6 show the cumulative monthly crush and cumulative monthly exports as a percentage of the crop year total. These are relatively consistent from one year to the next. The monthly values are published regularly, hence they provide an alternative method of predicting the expected annual values. For example, the crush from September to November 1971 was 186.0 million bushels; table 5 indicates that on average the crush for this period is 24.1% of the crop year total; hence the expected crop year crush for 70/71 would be 772 million bushels (100*186/24.1). This approach can give very different values to USDA's estimates. For example, in April of the 72/73 crop year it gave an expected total usage of 1327 million bushels compared to USDA's 1225 million bushels. In fact the expected demand exceeded significantly the estimated total supply indicating a very severe crisis in the market. It is perhaps not surprising that prices soared from $6.50 in April to over $11 per bushel in June. In most years the forecasts by this method are better predictors that USDA's estimates.

Viewing market expectations in this way means that we know in advance when changes in expectations will tend to occur and more importantly that large discontinuous changes in expectations are perfectly possible. The critical times for the flow of new information to the market, when major changes to market expectations are likely to occur, are August/September, November, January, April and June/July.

3.2 Price Determination Models.

Each buyer and seller individually sees and acts on the vast amount of information circulating in the market. Buyers and sellers make rational decisions based on their "expectations",

Table 3 - USDA's Forecasts of US Domestic Crush (million bushels)

Crop Year	Aug	Nov	Jan/Feb	Apr/May	Aug	Final
65/66	-	515	528	525	537	538
66/7	-	593	580	570	560	559
67/8	-	590	584	585	575	576
68/9	-	575	585	586	602	606
69/0	-	660	675	700	725	737
70/1	-	-	775	775	757	760
71/2	-	750	730	720	720	721
72/3	730*	765	-	750	735	722
73/4	790*	785	786	801	831	822
74/5	780	765	740	695	685	701
75/6	750	775	800	825	865	965
76/7	800	790	810	820	800	800

* Issued in September.

Table 4 - USDA's Forecasts of US Exports. (million bushels)

Crop Year	Aug	Nov	Jan/Feb	Apr/May	Aug	Final
65/66	-	230	245	245	255	251
66/7	-	275	275	275	255	262
67/8	-	290	280	280	270	267
68/9	-	280	285	285	287	287
69/0	-	335	340	375	415	433
70/1	-	-	450	450	433	433
71/2	-	410	400	414	425	417
72/3	499*	500	-	475	490	479
73/4	600*	550	525	550	560	539
74/5	525	500	450	425	420	421
75/6	450	475	500	535	565	555
76/7	540	540	540	545	570	570

* Issued in September.

Table 5 - Cumulative Monthly Crush as Percentage of Crop Year Total.

Crop Year	Sep	Oct	Nov	Dec	Jan	Feb	Mar	Apr	May	Jun	Jul
65/6	5.7	13.9	22.8	31.9	41.3	49.7	58.8	67.0	76.3	84.7	92.5
66/7	6.3	14.4	23.3	32.0	41.0	48.8	57.1	65.5	74.3	83.0	91.5
67/8	7.3	16.1	25.0	33.8	42.7	51.1	59.5	67.3	75.7	83.9	92.2
68/9	6.3	15.3	24.5	33.1	41.4	48.8	57.8	66.1	75.1	83.5	92.1
69/0	6.4	14.8	23.2	31.8	40.3	48.3	56.8	65.3	74.5	83.1	91.6
70/1	7.0	15.8	24.5	33.4	42.3	50.2	58.6	67.0	75.4	83.4	91.6
71/2	7.6	15.8	24.1	33.0	41.9	50.2	59.1	67.2	76.0	83.9	92.0
72/3	7.2	16.5	26.3	35.9	45.6	54.6	63.5	71.6	80.2	87.4	93.6
73/4	5.0	12.7	21.4	30.3	39.4	48.0	57.2	65.7	74.4	82.9	91.6
74/5	7.6	16.4	25.1	33.7	42.7	50.4	59.1	67.3	74.8	82.4	90.9
75/6	6.5	14.8	23.0	32.0	40.7	48.7	57.7	66.6	75.8	84.4	92.6
76/7	8.6	17.8	26.9	36.0	45.0	54.0	63.3	71.6	79.3	86.3	92.6

Table 6 - Cumulative Monthly Exports as Percentage of Crop Year Total.

Crop Year	Sep	Oct	Nov	Dec	Jan	Feb	Mar	Apr	May	Jun	Jul
65/6	1.9	14.8	30.5	43.0	50.9	57.7	66.3	74.4	82.9	90.7	95.6
66/7	2.1	13.3	28.9	40.3	48.6	56.4	63.1	71.4	79.7	87.4	93.8
67/8	3.9	15.0	30.0	40.2	48.3	55.4	64.4	72.5	80.1	87.1	93.5
68/9	4.8	16.3	33.7	47.1*	47.6*	51.5*	64.3	76.3	84.6	89.4	95.8
69/0	3.1	15.2	27.6	36.9	43.5	50.8	59.9	69.4	78.0	86.9	92.7
70/1	6.9	17.1	27.6	38.4	46.5	54.1	62.2	69.8	76.8	84.9	92.8
71/2	7.0	14.1	25.5	37.6	47.8	56.3	63.8	72.7	80.3	87.8	94.1
72/3	3.1	14.4	27.2	37.6	47.4	58.8	71.1	80.6	89.2	94.7+	97.7+
73/4	1.3	9.9	23.7	34.5	43.5	54.0	64.7	76.2	84.3	91.0	96.1
74/5	5.4	13.0	28.0	37.9	49.7	57.6	66.7	75.2	81.2	84.5	91.9
75/6	4.4	15.7	26.8	35.7	45.0	54.4	63.9	73.0	81.9	90.4	95.6
76/7	3.9	14.6	26.5	36.6	45.6	56.2	66.6	76.7	86.5	92.0	96.8

* Serious US Dock Strike. + Export Controls Imposed.

which are changing over time, and their current stocks and forward purchases/sales. At any time, several buyers and sellers the world over are agreeing to transactions at the same price or levels very close to it. As this is happening continuously, market participants must clearly have formed a common collective market expectation, a majority view, of the relative state of supply and demand. There must also exist a common mechanism to convert these expectations to a price acceptable to the buyers and sellers. If this were not so then the prices on any day, or within a week, would be fluctuating as much as prices do over a month or a quarter, as differing participants made deals based on vastly different views. One would expect large variations in price regularly between different parts of the world. The fact that neither of these circumstances occurs in practice confirms the general hypothesis. This does not of course prevent the existence of a few participants who take a different view and act upon it.

Price is a result of the interplay of supply and demand. In a general model of a market economy for a raw material there will be feedback and feedforward loops between price and supply and demand factors. However these are really long term; it takes several years for newly planted cocoa trees to bear fruit or for a new copper mine to be opened. With annual crops like cereals or oilseeds, high or low prices around planting time may motivate farmers to increase or decrease their sown acreage aiming for a higher or lower crop at harvesting time. Thereafter, the direct control of the amount that will grow and ripen for harvest is small. Late spring frosts, heavy rainfall or drought whilst the crop is growing and ripening, and insect or disease damage can lead to enormous variations in yield from year to year. These stochastic effects impose a large uncertainty on the likely crop size that generally obscures any systematic reaction to the earlier prices at planting. At harvest time, the farmer, having invested time and money, always feels it is worthwhile harvesting and selling his whole crop whatever the price in the market. Over the 25 years to the mid seventies, for example, US farmers always harvested 98% of the soya acreage planted, whether there were ample supplies or a shortage.

On the other side of the equation, the distinction between demand and consumption is important to modelling behaviour. Consumption in any year is what user companies or individuals actually used. Demand is the amount, based on their own economic and financial situation generally over the year, they would like to use. If there are ample supplies of material and prices remain at reasonable levels, then consumption will reach the demand level. Shortages of material mean that all demands cannot physically be met. Prices will increase and act as a rationing device which temporarily removes certain parts of demand. A few months of high prices will not remove the demand, nor necessarily reduce the future demands. However, a year or two of high prices, particularly if for several commodities, may reduce future demand as the shortages may bring about or be accompanied by recession in economies generally or consumers become accustomed to cheaper substitutes. For modelling and forecasting future prices it is quite feasible for the expectations of demand to exceed the expectations of total supply, although the amount actually consumed will be less than the supply.

Thus for agricultural materials, production and demand within the crop year are not significantly and continuously adaptive to prices over the period. This implies that in terms of modelling medium term price movements within the crop year, expectations of supply and demand factors can be treated as exogenous variables in econometric relationships to determine prices for future periods.

As outlined earlier, for decision making to be rational, there must exist some common way of assessing the relative state of supply and demand and then a common mechanism to translate this into a price. A useful analogy is that of a market barometer that measures the state of the market and indicates the general level of prices to expect, rather like the air pressure gives an indication of the likely future weather conditions. Since market participants generally talk of supply and demand in relative terms the market barometer must be a non linear function of supply and demand factors. There must then exist a (1-1) relationship between each particular value of the market barometer and the price level to expect. Thus if the same market conditions apply in two different years then the same prices will prevail. However, with floating currency exchange rates, the price factor may itself be changing in some fashion, independently of what is happening to that particular commodity.

4. SOYABEAN PRICE MOVEMENTS.

The major world soyabean market is Chicago. Most of the business in Chicago is in futures prices although a cash market exists. Analysis showed that other cash markets closely follow the Chicago prices. USDA calculated average monthly seasonal deviations as a percentage of the annual average cash price for the crop years 69/70 to 75/76 as given below, showing that prices fell to an annual low in November followed by a continuous rise to a peak in August.

Oct	Nov	Dec	Jan	Feb	Mar	Apr	May	Jun	Jul	Aug	Sep
-8.2	-9.3	-8.4	-4.9	-5.5	-4.3	-4.3	2.1	9.8	13.0	13.6	6.6

However, such averaging can disguise completely different patterns of seasonal price behaviour from one year to the next. This is apparent from Table 7, which shows the average monthly cash prices on Chicago for 63/64 to 76/77.

A. The Period November to August.

There are four alternative patterns of price behaviour.

1) Prices increase from their annual low in October to reach their maximum around March/April, where they stay for

Table 7 - Average Monthly Cash Prices of No. 1 Yellow Soyabeans at Chicago (Cents per Bushel).

Crop Year	Sep	Oct	Nov	Dec	Jan	Feb	Mar	Apr	May	Jun	Jul	Aug	Av
63/4	278	279	278	278	270	269	262	256	252	252	258	270	267
64/5	273	281	291	296	303	301	304	286	297	289	275	268	288
65/6	249	245	266	284	291	286	298	308	338	359	373	319	298
66/7	296	299	300	296	291	291	288	287	290	283	281	269	293
67/8	260	261	264	269	273	271	271	274	271	271	272	261	269
68/9	246	253	259	263	264	264	269	272	269	270	261	249	263
69/0	238	242	247	253	259	258	264	270	281	290	279	281	263
70/1	295	300	293	303	306	304	291	303	321	338	329	312	308
71/2	312	300	308	309	318	337	349	349	347	351	355	355	324
72/3	333	364	413	449	581	624	653	899	1087	860	908	650	622
73/4	562	565	595	617	634	623	556	542	547	697	755	757	621
74/5	833	758	728	633	568	556	576	523	515	558	597	555	617
75/6	497	470	459	465	474	466	471	521	625	664	630	659	535
76/7	623	658	686										

Sources: Economic Research service, USDA, and Commodity Year Book prior to 1966

Note: Some sources have prices post 1972 differing by up to 10 cents per bushel at times from the above values.

the rest of the crop year. This applies to 67/68, 68/69, 69/70 and also 71/72 but at a much higher level.

2) Prices increase through December to reach a peak around February, not necessarily a very marked peak, fall back through March and April and then increase rapidly over the final 3 months to reach a much higher level than the February peak. This pattern applies to the years 65/66, 70/71, 73/74 and 75/76.

3) The highest prices are for 72/73, where prices increased rapidly to their highest level over May and June,

before falling back strongly over July and August.

4) Finally, 63/64, 66/67 and 74/75 have prices falling continuously from November to March and then again to a minimum in June.

B. The Period May to December - the Old/New Crop Transition.

Here there are only two different patterns

1) The most common pattern is where prices peak in June to August, fall to their lowest level in October, well below the May price, and then increase through November and December. This group includes 65/66, 67/68, 68/69, 69/70 and 73/74 with the peak in June, 71/72 with its peak in July, and 66/67, 72/73 and 75/76 with the peak in August.

2) The other years, 63/64, 64/65, 70/71, 74/75 and 76/77, all show a continuous increase from May to October.

Note that for period (B), the two patterns of price behaviour are completely opposite to each other. In one, October is the lowest price of the year, well below the prices at the end of the old crop year, whilst in the other October can be the highest price over the crop year. This analysis clearly demonstrates that using a simple average pattern of seasonal price movement would be extremly misleading.

Examining Table 7 and the results described in the discussion above shows that there are certain critical months for determining price levels. If the prices for these months are known, then the prices for intermediate months can be obtained by simple interpolation. These critical months are October, January, March/April and June/July.

One particularly noticeable point is that prices since 1973 have been much higher than in earlier years, often twice as high. However, the relative state of supply and demand was similar for some years before and after 1973. Obviously some dramatic change occured in the soyabean market about that time. One possible explanation is the devaluation of the dollar relative to other currencies post 1971, falling to around 75% of its pre 1971 value in 1973. This is insufficient to explain the doubling of prices that has occurred. Further, if devaluation were the prime cause then we would expect similar sized jumps in prices when there were large changes in the dollar value, e.g. Dec 1971, Feb 1973 and July 1975 when the dollar changes were a fall of 2.2%, 7.5% and a rise of 4.2% respectively. The changes in soyabean prices in the same months were very different, rises of 31%, 33.5% and 7%. Thus we must conclude that some other factor accounts for most of the doubling of soya prices after 1973.

Soyabeans are mainly used for animal feed. The ability of the livestock farmer to buy soya at particular prices will clearly depend upon the prices he receives for his meat products. If meat prices are high and meat demand is stong then he is willing to pay high prices. However, although he can carry losses for a short period, if meat prices are low then he can only afford low prices for soya or must make do with a much lower amount than he would ideally wish.

Livestock meat prices tend to run in four year cycles. A high demand for meat initially results in high prices which causes increased production of cattle etc., resulting in excess production followed by lower prices causing decreased production. The cycle then starts all over again. Occasionally there are step changes so the situation does not return to the earlier conditions.

Historically there appears to be strong links between the general level of livestock product prices and oilseed prices. Over the years 1921-30, the livestock price index, published by USDA, on average was 141.6, within a range 122-153. The oilseed price index, also published by USDA, averaged 138.3. In 1931 the livestock index fell to 96, well below the normal range of variation of the previous 10 years. The oilseed index fell to 73. Over the subsequent 10 years the livestock index averaged 101, whilst the oilseed index averaged 94. In 1941 the livestock index rose to 133, well above the range of variation of the thirties. Oilseed prices also rose well above their earlier levels. From 1945-49 a new range of livestock prices was established about an average level of 266. The oilseed index also rose to a new higher level, an average of 289. Throughout the fifties and sixties the livestock price index remained within the range of variation set in the late forties, as did the oilseed price index. Over 1969-1971 the livestock index varied around 323. It broke out of this range during 1972 and into 1973 under the influence of the large price increases in feedgrains and oilseeds following the shortages of the 72/73 crop year.

Over 1973 the livestock index averaged 502, whilst the oilseed index rose to an average of 608 compared to a value of 250 in 1969. This transitional period is illustrated in Figure 1 which gives the average quarterly values for the two indices over 1965 to 1977. Soya prices rose over 1971 as did livestock prices. Soya prices reached 11 dollars per bushel in 72/73 before settling down to a new level. When ample supplies of soya returned in 75/76, prices did not fall back to the earlier levels but remained high because of the new higher level of livestock product prices. Since 1973, the livestock price index has averaged 480, 1.8 times the level of the previous 25 years.

The above suggests a chicken-egg-chicken argument, rather than a simple chicken-egg one. As oilseed prices increase livestock prices increase to cover the extra feeding costs. If the resulting higher livestock product prices are acceptable to the retail market so that the producer can sell a reasonable quantity of product, he is able to continue paying the higher prices for his feed. When a geater surplus of oilseeds comes about, he may not press so hard on the oilseed producers to reduce their prices compared to before

FIGURE 1 QUARTERLY SOYA PRICES AND LIVESTOCK PRICE INDICES

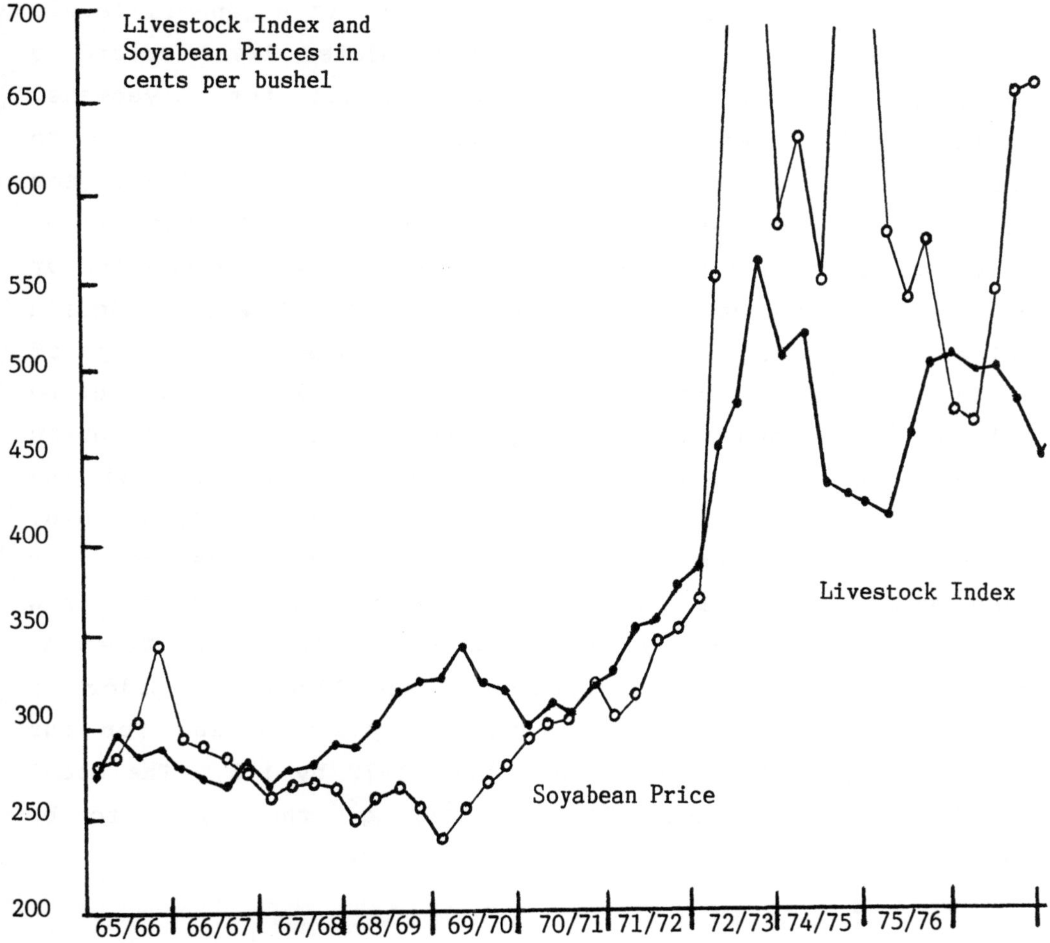

the sustained livestock product price increase.

The general model resulting from this analysis takes the following form. A level of livestock prices is set. Within a permitted normal range of variation about this general level, soyabean prices fluctuate about some related level according to variations in the supply and demand for soyabeans. Variations in livestock prices both within and from year to year will not be a significant factor influencing within year and year to year variations in soya prices. If, because of sustained increases or decreases in retail meat prices and/or sustained increases or decreases in oilseed and feedgrain prices, the livestock prices move out of the normal range of variation, they change to a new general level for future prices. This produces a new general level for soyabean prices. Any relationship between soyabean prices and the relative supply and demand factors is moved bodily up or down, depending on whether the price level is increased or decreased. For the particular data period analysed, this means that we expect soya prices post 1972 to be 1.8 times as high, for the same supply/demand conditions, as prior to 1972. Hence we obtain a consistent price series for our modelling by dividing all prices post 1972 by 1.8. The model predictions, when used for forecasting, thus have to be multiplied by 1.8 to give present day prices.

5. A MARKET BAROMETER FOR SOYABEANS.

The overall US soyabean situation from 1963 to 1977 is illustrated diagramatically in Figure 2, where the hindsight values for the US total supply, US domestic use and exports are shown by the different shadings. The unshaded area is the final crop year carryover stocks, representing the surplus of soyabeans in any crop year. From 64/65 to 68/69 the total supply of beans increased faster than the total usage so that the surplus, the carryover stocks, increased year by year. Prices fell continously. In 69/70 this came to a halt.

FIGURE 2 - THE GENERAL U.S. SOYA SITUATION

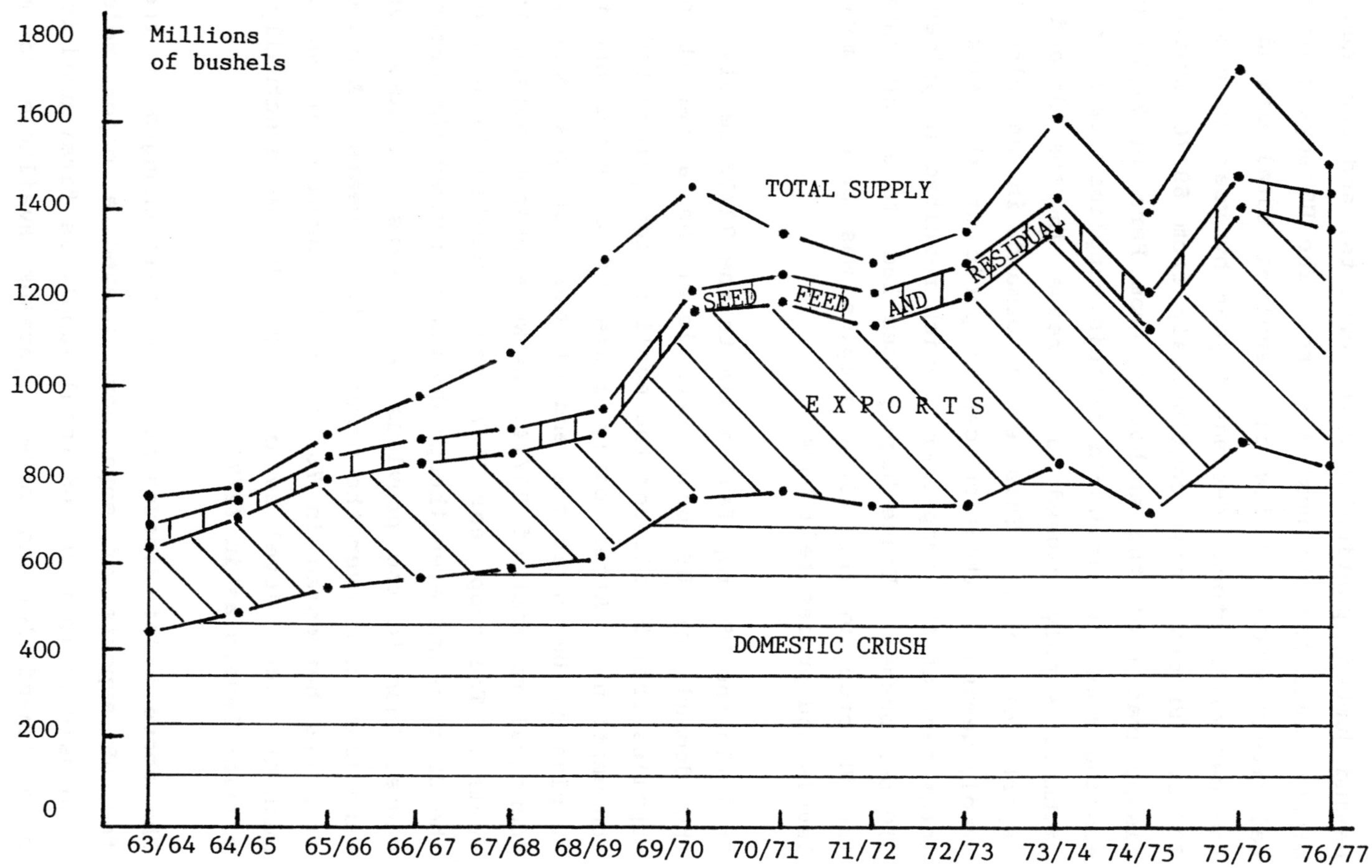

Demand jumped, particularly for exports, and remained at this higher level for the next 4 years. The US soya crop remained relatively stable, below the level of total demand, so that the carryover stocks decreased year by year to a minimum in 72/73. Prices rose continuously from 69/70 onwards. The disappearance of the anchovies from Peru in 72/73 with the ensuing reduction in world protein supplies from the reduced fishmeal supply caused an increase in the demand for US exports of soya. This extra demand in an already tight supply/demand situation caused panic in the market in the later part of the crop year, which resulted in prices of over $10 per bushel. These high prices led to a vast increase in the US crop so the 73/74 surplus was back to more normal levels and prices fell back.

In 74/75 the US crop fell again to the 72/73 levels. However, the demand for US beans was lower as a result of extra supplies from Brazil and the earlier high prices reducing meat consumption. After early fears of a world shortage the surplus of beans at the end of the crop year was virtually identical to that of 73/74, as were prices during the early summer. The crop year 75/76 saw a further large increase in the US crop and even though demand increased the carryover was higher than in the previous two years. Prices over 75/76 were lower than over the previous three years. A much reduced crop was harvested in 76/77 so the surplus of beans was at much the same level as in 72/73. Prices eventually rose to similar levels as in 72/73.

The above brief discussion shows that changes in the demand for US exports of soya have played a major role. The hypothsis is that the US total supply is first used to satisfy home demand leaving some soyabeans available to meet the demand for US exports as

$$\text{Potential Export Supply} = \text{Open.Stock} + \text{Crop} - \text{Domestic Use}$$

A market barometer can then be defined as the percentage that the export demand is of this potential supply, the 'Export Ratio';

$$\text{Export Ratio} = \frac{100 \times \text{Export Demand}}{\text{Potential Export Supply}}$$

It is worthy of note that the US government interferred in the market to impose an export embargo in 72/73 to ensure that home demand was fully satisfied.

The values for this ratio for each crop year, using hindsight values and taking actual exports for the export demand, are given in Figure 3. The figure also displays the average crop year cash prices. It indicates that a very good correlation betwen the two time series exists. The export ratio and the prices go up and down together, both reaching local maximums in 65/66, 72/73 and 76/77 and local minimums in 68/69 and 75/76. The export ratio has very similar values for 64/65, 65/66 and 72/73, whilst the prices in 72/73 were very much higher than in the earlier two years. However, although in hindsight the three years had virtually identical export ratios, the values based on market expectations were very much higher in the early part of the 72/73 crop year.

One advantage of this market barometer is that it is relatively easy to include the effect of changes in the Brazilian soya crop from year to year. Brazil has grown to be a substantial producer and exporter. However, Brazil rarely has large carryover stocks. Thus as Brazil's crop increases or decreases from year to year the demand for US exports will be changed pro rata, so the Export Ratio can be easily updated, in March or April, the time of Brazil's harvest.

6. THE ACTUAL PRICE DETERMINATION MODELS.

The final stage in the modelling process is to regress the prices at the critical times of the crop year identified in section 4 against the Export Ratio values calculated from the

FIGURE 3 EXPORT RATIO AND AVERAGE APRIL/JUNE SOYABEAN PRICES (ADJUSTED)

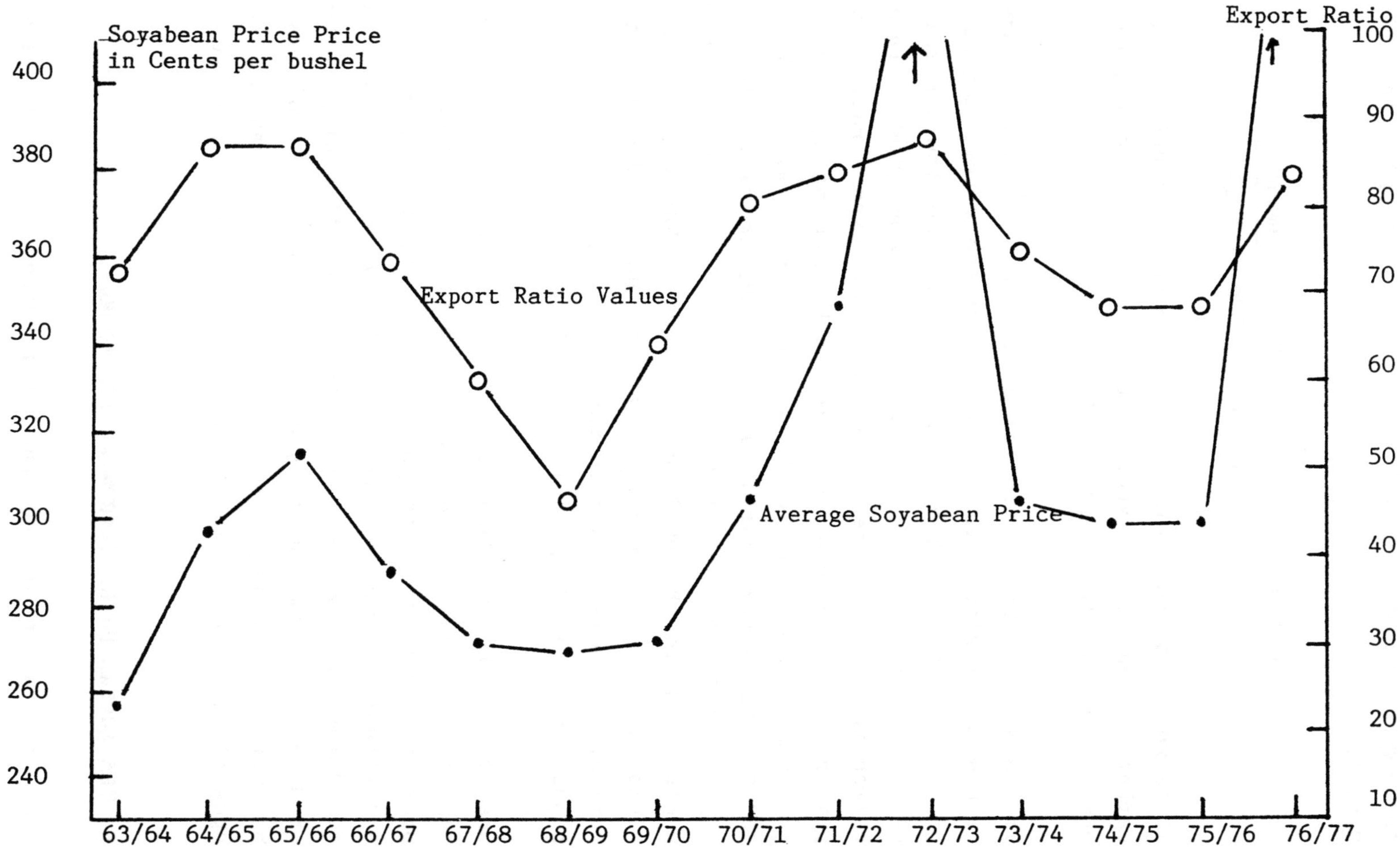

expectations of the supply and demand factors at the earlier times of the year identified as critical in the flow of information to the market in section 3.1. August is the first month when crop forecasts taking account of the actual crop conditions are made and September is the month when the first 'reliable' forecasts are available. October/November is the first critical point for prices for it is usually the lowest time of the year. Figure 4 shows the relationship between the lowest of the average prices over October or November against the expected Export Ratio values calculated in September. These values are generally taken directly from USDA estimates. However prior to 1971, USDA did not publish any forecasts of any sort for expected future domestic crush or exports. Prior to then a modified extrapolation method is used based, on the previous crop year usages over the first 9 months of the crop year. The continuous line drawn on the graph indicates a possible relationship. It has an equation

$$\text{Price (cents per bushel)} = 153 + 8400/(135.0 - \text{Export Ratio})$$

The prices in the figure and relationship are adjusted to pre 1972 values. The crop years 65/66, 66/67 and 73/74 are outlier points. In 66/67 there was a large increase in the crop estimate from August to September. On the August Export Ratio value, the equation would predict a price of $3.20 per bushel, the actual September average price. It could be that the market was sceptical of the increased crop estimate so prices did not fall as much as one would have expected. The crop year 73/74 may have had higher prices because of a residual effect of the very high prices of 72/73.

In August 1977, USDA forecast a crop of 1602 and an opening stock of 75 million bushels. They predicted a domestic usage of 922 and an export of 610 million bushels. The export ratio value is thus 610/(75+1602-922) = 80.8. The price predicted is thus 308, which multiplied by 1.8 gives a forecast of $5.545 per bushel for October. Revised forecasts in September

FIGURE 4 - OCTOBER/NOVEMBER PRICES VERSUS AUGUST/SEPTEMBER EXPORT RATIO

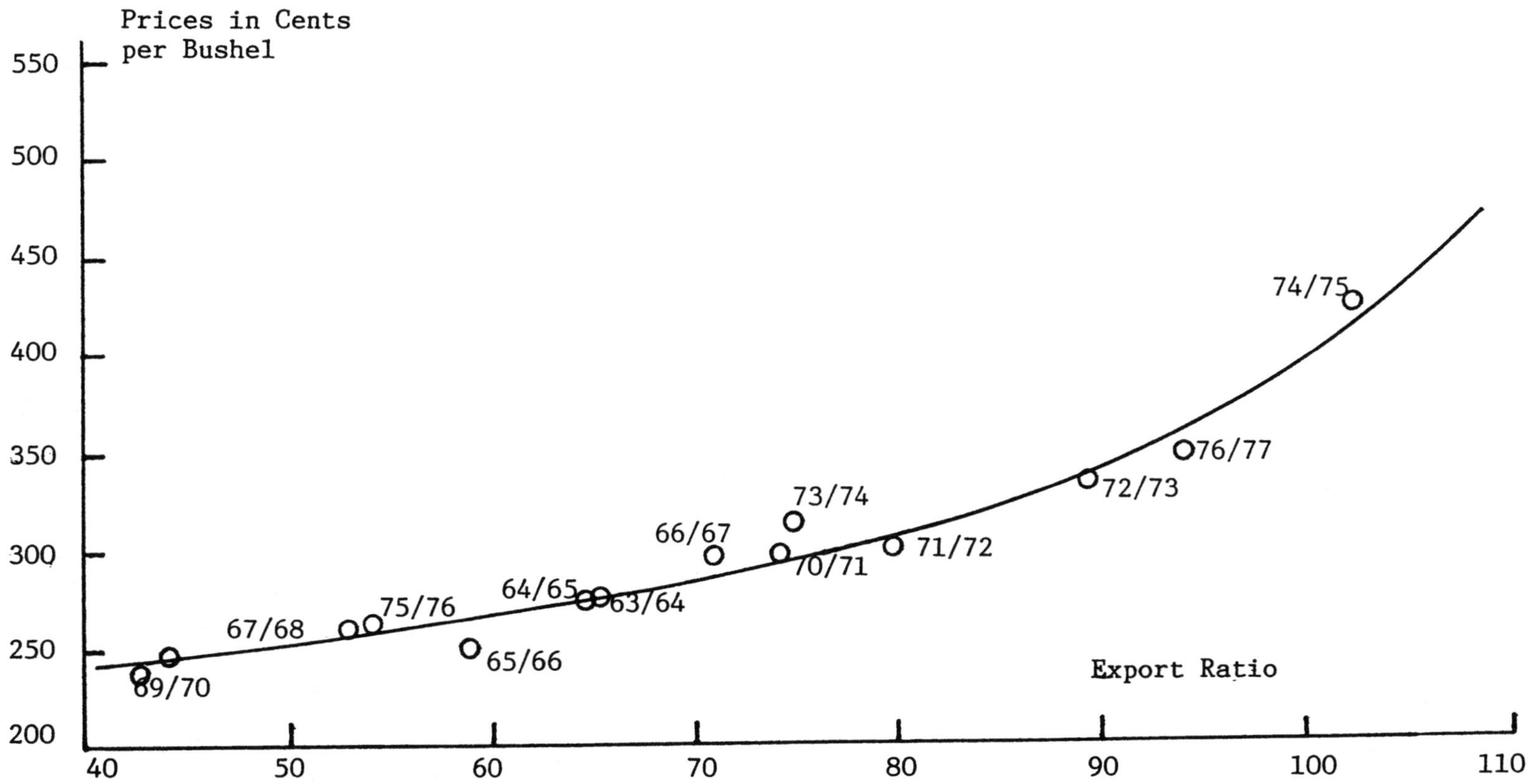

gave an export ratio of 75.3, which implies a forecast price for October of $5.28 per bushel. Prices rose to around $5.40 over the first half of September before falling back to around $5.28 per bushel. So the first prediction beyond the estimation period was fairly good.

The next example is for the April expected Export Ratio against the end of year price, June/July. This is shown in Figure 5. As shown in section 4, prices normally reach a peak in June or July followed by a decline through August. This appears to happen whenever the new crop acreage was up by 9% or more on the previous crop year's planted acreage. However if it was less than an increase of 2%, August prices tended to be higher than those of June. Thus we can conclude that Jume/July is the end of the period influenced by the state of the current crop. Thereafter the new crop recently planted becomes the major influence. In three years there was a significant difference between the June and July price, so both prices are shown on the figure. The year 72/73 causes some problems because the difference is so large. Hence two possible relationships are drawn on the figure. The one through the 72/73 June price has an equation

$$\text{Price (cents per bushel)} = 203 + 4100/(117.6 - \text{Export Ratio})$$

The other line is virtually identical except for export ratios larger than 95%. The first two years in the sample, 63/64 and 64/65, have been excluded from the graph as they did not fit the relationship at all. Similar relationships were derived for all the other combinations of critical price times and earlier critical information times. Except for the August export ratio, it was found that the extrapolations of current rates of usage method were better than USDA's estimates. Except for the situation of Figure 5, the points for the 73/74 crop year were always outliers above the relationships deduced. This may imply that after a year of severe shortage and high prices the market takes a more pessimistic view of prospects and tends to keep prices higher than they would be

FIGURE 5 - JUNE/JULY PRICE VERSUS APRIL EXPORT RATIO

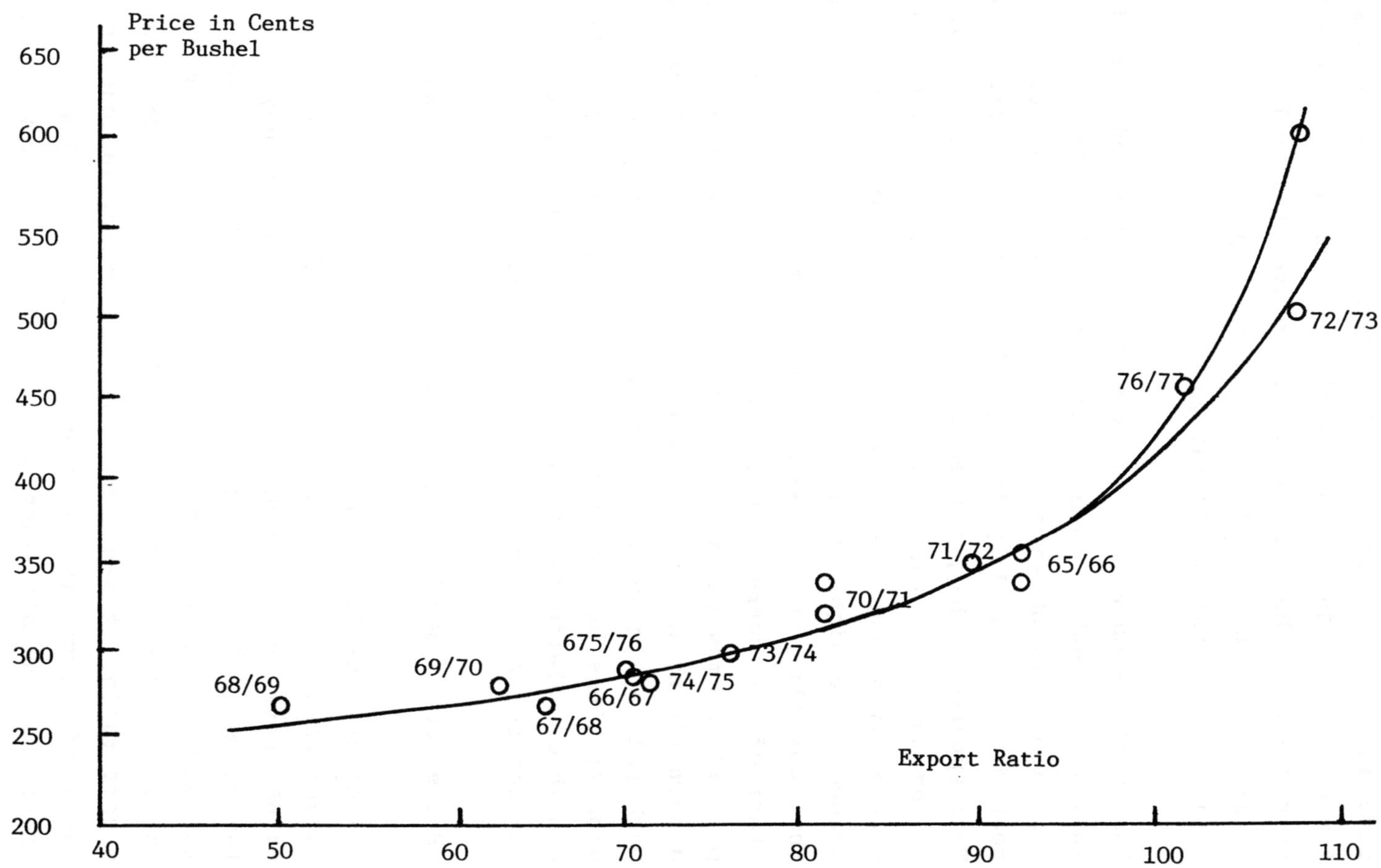

in other circumstances. The market perhaps requires the assurance of a second reasonable crop before bringing prices down to more normal levels consistent with the new situation.

7. THE FORECASTING AND ASSESSMENT SCENARIO.

A major point to bear in mind is that, as demonstrated in the modelling described above, the market situation and market expectations are continually changing. Hence we must ensure we compare the forecasts of the models with the futures prices at the time the models' forecasts are made.

The forecasts provided were of two types. A report with forecasts was routinely produced at the end of each month and normally issued at the start of the following month. It usually took 3 or 4 days to produce the report. Because of this and since there is a great deal of apparent white noise in the prices with, sizeable fluctuations from day to day, the average closing prices over the last week of the month was used as the comparative predictor. On some occasions there was a piece of news causing discontinuous changes in expectations, i.e. a large change in the crop estimate. A special forecast was issued on the same day that the news was published, or alternatively it had been anticipated by providing a range of forecasts for possible crop estimates in the previous end of month report. On these occasions, the closing prices on the day the news was published were used; the closing price in preference to the average of the highs and lows since it has given the market a full day to work out the implications of this new piece of information.

Futures are only quoted for a subset of months, January, March, May, July, August, September and November. A 'futures price' predictor for intermediate months was derived by simple interpolation between adjacent quoted months. This might introduce some bias into the predictors since the margins between successive futures are not necessarily linear.

The futures and cash prices used in the analysis are taken from the Chicago Board of Trade's Statistical Annuals for 1978, 1979 and 1980. The source of economic news was the trade press, such as The Public Ledger, and the Reuters Commodity Service provided by one of the companies involved in the project. This was processed as described earlier to give current expectations of the various supply and demand factors. The various models were then used to convert these into price forecasts. This assessment of supply and demand factors possibly included some judgement, but it was based only on currently publicly available market information and could have been performed by any other market participant.

The period concerned in this analysis turned out to be quite a hectic one, with the economic circumstances prevailing being very different to any encountered during the estimation period. The major change was, for the very first time, a disaster to the Brazilian crop. The 1978 Brazilian crop had initally been expected to be 13 million tonnes. In the event, because of drought conditions, it was eventually reduced to 8.5 million tonnes. Prior to this time, the Brazilian crop had increased consistently from year to year and the final outurn was usually quite close to the early estimates. The period covered in the forecasts was thus a very severe test of the models and approach.

8. THE RESULTS OF THE ANALYSIS.

The details of the actual forecasts made together with the futures prices and the average Chicago cash prices for the months of interest are given in Table 8. On three occasions, April, August and November of 1978, mid month forecasts were produced for the identical periods as in the previous end of month forecasts. This was because there was a significant change to the production estimates leading to a significant change in market expectations and hence likely prices. Since the model forecasts and the market prices, in an efficient market, reflect the current market information and the information set is different to the previous end of month forecasts, it is argued that these are valid different forecasts to be used in the assessment. In all cases the model forecasts of future prices are improved, so it would bias the assessment of the model and market efficiency to leave out the prior end of month forecasts.

The overall results for the 26 forecasts provided over the period from the 30th March 1978 to the 28th June 1980 are shown in Table 9. This gives the average error, the Root Mean Squared average error and the Maximum and Minimum range of errors for the model and the futures price predictor. The first indicates whether there is any persistent bias in the forecasts. However a zero average forecasting error could disguise very large positive and negative errors over time. This is covered in the second and third measures. All errors are measured as a percentage of the actual price. A positive error means over- and a negative error under-forecasting.

The one month ahead forecasts of the model are fairly good. However the model has a strong downward bias, underestimating the values for months further ahead. The particularly bad forecasts are for 3 and 4 months ahead in the early summer, covering the period when the market is affected by the new crop development but made at a time when it has just been planted and no information on real yield prospects is available. The assumption of an average yield suggested a reasonable surplus for the new crop indicating lower prices. The futures prices tended to be more conservative staying high. In many ways the results are similar to those in the estimation period for 73/74. It appears that following a panic situation of potential shortages the market keeps prices up. The model needs some revision to incorporate this factor. It should be noted, however, that the daily prices have sizeable fluctuations about the monthly average price. In the purchasing context, the forecasts are a guide to the buyer whether to purchase now or wait until later. Thus a small

TABLE 8 - THE FORECASTING DATA (Prices are in cents per bushel.)

DATE	CURRENT	MODEL FORECAST				FUTURES PRICES				ACTUAL PRICES			
		Months Ahead				Months Ahead				Months Ahead			
		1	2	3	4	1	2	3	4	1	2	3	4
30 Mar 1978	679	683	663	643	643	714	717	718	719	681	709	679	654
14 Apr 1978	719	693	693	679	665	735	735	732	730	681	709	679	654
27 Apr 1978	665	695	670	630	600	698	693	688	665	709	679	654	643
30 May 1978	715	695	660	605	605	732	722	712	681	679	654	643	647
5 Jul 1978	717	645	620	585	585	682	674	652	642	654	643	647	676
2 Aug 1978	637	620	590	590	615	631	613	607	603	643	647	676	666
15 Aug 1978	650	635	625	630	650	649	643	639	635	643	647	676	666
30 Aug 1978	665	623	613	633	660	655	650	645	648	647	676	666	679
29 Sep 1978	637	650	650	675	700	652	648	652	655	676	666	679	685
3 Nov 1978	698	690	695	695	712	703	710	715	721	666	679	685	729
15 Nov 1978	642	660	675	680	692	643	648	653	659	666	679	685	729
8 Dec 1978	670	680	697	680	640	670	675	682	688	679	685	729	746
26 Jan 1979	695	700	700	680	663	702	707	712	717	729	746	730	716
16 Feb 1979	734	740	740	740	710	752	759	766	770	746	730	716	767
23 Mar 1979	749	750	750	715	670	753	763	761	759	730	716	767	749
26 Apr 1979	722	720	695	653	630	733	740	747	746	716	767	749	717
30 May 1979	723	715	675	650	650	729	739	743	734	767	749	717	704
1 Jul 1979	784	740	630	650	655	797	803	794	791	749	717	704	652
1 Aug 1979	720	675	660	670	675	730	729	728	732	717	704	652	638
8 Sep 1979	697	670	640	650	660	700	700	700	713	704	652	638	640
30 Oct 1979	620	635	650	660	660	643	655	666	677	638	640	622	638
31 Jan 1980	634	650	630	600	600	656	666	674	683	638	606	580	602
6 Mar 1980	638	630	600	600	580	638	650	662	685	606	580	602	613
1 Apr 1980	579	580	580	570		599	606	619		580	602	613	
2 May 1980	588	605	605			593	605			602	613		
28 Jun 1980	632	680	680			651	654			719	736		

Table 9 - Comparison of Model and Futures Prices as Forecasts.

	MODEL FORECASTS			FUTURES PRICE 'FORECASTS'		
Months Ahead	Average Error	RMS Error	Range of Errors	Average Error	RMS Error	Range of Errors
1	-1.08	3.10	-6.78 to 3.96	1.06	4.11	-9.46 to 7.93
2	-2.93	5.53	-12.13 to 4.75	1.70	5.74	-11.14 to 12.07
3	-3.70	6.37	-12.82 to 6.11	3.17	6.81	-10.21 to 16.21
4	-4.21	6.90	-14.21 to 5.80	3.16	8.26	-9.60 to 21.32

Table 10 - Theil Inequality Coefficients.

Months Ahead	Model Forecasts	Futures Prices	Combined Predictor
1	0.69	1.01	0.73
2	0.97	1.08	0.76
3	1.03	1.20	0.83
4	0.93	1.14	0.80

Table 11 - Performance of Combined Models as Predictors.

	50/50 WEIGHTED AVERAGE			40/60 WEIGHTED AVERAGE		
Months Ahead	Average Error	RMS Error	Range of Errors	Average Error	RMS Error	Range of Errors
1	0.08	3.35	-7.44 to 5.08	0.31	3.54	-7.84 to 6.17
2	-0.52	4.50	-9.38 to 7.76	-0.04	4.68	-9.73 to 8.62
3	-0.17	5.34	-11.46 to 9.83	0.53	5.62	-11.21 to 11.10
4	-0.48	6.15	-10.99 to 11.89	0.26	6.50	-10.35 to 14.17

underforecasting of the forward average monthly prices is rather desirable as it increases the chances of paying no more than the average price over the month of delivery, which is a standard often used in assessing purchasing performance.

The results for the futures price predictor show an upward bias, tending to overestimate the prices, increasing the further ahead the forecasts are made. This could indicate the existence of a risk premium as mentioned earlier. However on almost half the occasions, the futures price predictor underestimates the forward cash price, often by large amounts. It is thus doubtful whether the whole of the positive bias can be explained as a risk premium.

The model forecasts are better in terms of the Root Mean Squared error values and the range of errors. Indeed the model is better on all counts for the one month ahead forecast.

A good test of the accuracy of the forecasts produced by any model, a standard test in econometrics, is Theil's Inequality Coefficient (1966). Let A_i be the actual realised change in the variable forecast, let C_i be the forecast change and n the number of forecasts, then the inequality coefficient is

$$U = +\sqrt{\frac{(C_i - A_i)^2/n}{A_i^2/n}}$$

U can lie between zero and infinity. The smaller its value the better is the forecasting performance. If $C_i = A_i$, then U = 0 so the model gives perfect forecasts, whilst if $C_i = 0$, then U = 1, and the forecasts are no better than a 'naive' zero-change prediction, which in our case means that the current cash price at time t is the best predictor of forward prices, implying that all information is taken into account in the current cash price, P_t.

The values of Theil's Inequality Coefficient are given in

Table 10, calculated for the actual rather than the percentage errors. On this criterion, the futures prices are not good predictors of the forward prices; they are very much worse than a no change in price prediction. The results suggest that the new information is taken into account in the current cash price. Futures prices are then the cash price plus some risk premium. The model forecasts are good for the one month ahead prediction but only slightly better than the no change in price prediction for further ahead.

The opposite biasses shown suggest that combining the model forecasts and the futures prices would improve the performance. Two simple examples are shown in Table 11, a simple arithmetic average and a 40% model and 60% futures weighted average. Both are superior to the model or futures prices alone on all counts. Using the simple arithmetic average for the one month ahead and the weighted average for 2 to 4 months ahead gives an unbiassed forecast. The RMS and the range of errors are also improved. Two thirds of the errors of the combined models are within one RMS of the average value. Theil's Inequality Coefficients for the simple arithmetic average forecast were given in the final column of Table 10. These range between 0.73 and 0.83, significantly better than the no change in price prediction. This demonstrates that there is public market information available affecting forward prices that is not fully taken into account in the current cash prices, as would be expected under the E.M.H.

A simple form of the general model, equation (3), is the unbiassed weighted average predictor, which for a general weight w, has the form

$$\begin{aligned} P_{t+h} &= wF_{t+h,t} + (1-w)M_{t+h,t} \\ &= F_{t+h,t} + (1-w)(M_{t+h,t} - F_{t+h,t}) \end{aligned} \qquad (4)$$

This can be regarded as a regression equation and the significance of the extra amount of variation explained by the addition of the model forecasts, represented by the ($M_{t+h,t}$ - $F_{t+h,t}$) term, which is uncorrelated with $F_{t+h,t}$, tested by analysis of variance. For the one step ahead forecast the residual sum of squares for the futures price alone is 23,966. The residual sum of squares for the combined model is 12,637. There are 26-2 degrees of freedom so the relevant F ratio is

$$F^* = \frac{(23{,}966 - 12{,}637)/1}{12{,}637/24} = 21.52$$

The equivalent F^* ratios for the 2, 3 and 4 months ahead forecasts are 23.56, 23.95 and 22.40. These all greatly exceed the 1% F value for 22 degrees of freedom of 7.94, showing that the inclusion of market information via the econometric models significantly improves the predictive power of the futures alone.

However the prediction errors in the weighted forecast are serially correlated. This is only to be expected in econometric models of raw materials, since an under/ overestimate in the expectations of a supply or demand factor is likely to be present for a major part of the crop year. The first order correlation coefficient in the errors is 0.56, but the serial correlation at higher lags is negligible. The analysis of variance must be corrected for this serial correlation as the normal methods underestimate the standard error. According to Keeping (1962), if a variable x has first order serial correlation ρ then

$$V(\bar{x}) = \sigma^2\{1 + 2\rho(1-1/N)\}/N$$

With ρ=0.56 then

$$V(\bar{x}) = 2.07\ \sigma^2/N$$

Hence in the analysis of variance the denominator in the F ratio must be multiplied by 2.07 to allow for the effect of the serial correlation in the errors. The resulting F ratios are all greater than 10.0 for all months ahead forecasts, so they are still significant at the 1% level.

9. CONCLUSIONS.

The econometric model is a simple empirical descriptive model rather than based on some assumed general theory of participant's behaviour, as for example Working and Weymar's Supply of Storage theory. It may be criticised for this. It assumes no supply or demand adjustment to price but only a stock adjustment. An important property is that it allows the possibility of total expected demand rates to exceed the total expected supply, implying that the expected end of crop year inventory can be negative. Weymar's supply of storage model has the logarithm of the ratio of price at time t+h to the price at time t related to the logarithm of the end of crop year inventory ratio. Thus negative values of the inventory ratio are not allowed.

The model could perhaps be expressed in an 'inventory ratio' form. However the equivalent 'inventory' in the model is the amount available to meet export demand after expected home demand has been satisfied. The demand part in the inventory ratio is replaced by the demand from overseas for the import of US soyabeans. It is suggested that the combined effects of the floating of international currency rates and the large growth in overseas demand for US soyabeans in the seventies changed the market radically. It was found that this model fitted much better than the standard inventory ratio of the supply of storage theory.

Further research to evaluate what the model implies in terms of a theory of individual market participants' behaviour would clearly be useful. Further analysis is also required to determine whether there was any price effect of the decline in the value of the dollar post the modelling period. It is possible that the step change in general price level post 1972 explained as due to the change in livestock prices also compounds in it a change in the relative value of the dollar.

Nevertheless, the models formed the basis for forecasts of future prices in real time based on currently available public market information. The forecasts are a proper basis for testing market efficiency. The analysis of variance and the Theil Inequality Coefficient results all demonstrate that neither the current cash price nor the futures prices take into account fully the currently and publicly known market information. The inclusion of known market information via the models described later improves the predictions of prices at future times. Hence it must be concluded that commodity markets, at least for soyabeans, do not fully reflect all the current publicly known information and hence are inefficient to some degree.

REFERENCES

Cagan P. (1956). 'The monetary dynamics of hyperinflation', in Friedman M (ed), 'Studies in the quantity theory of money', Chicago University Press.

Giles and Goss B. (1980). 'The predictive quality of futures prices, with an application to the Sydney Wool Futures market.' Australian Economic Papers. 19. pp291-300.

Guimaraes R.M.C. and Kingsman B.G. (1986). 'Tactical day to day buying policies for maize and measures for purchasing performance.' Paper presented to EURO VIII conference, Lisbon, Portugal. Submitted to JORS.

Keeping E.S. (1962). 'Introduction to Statistical Inference'. D. Van Nostrand Co., Inc. Princeton, New Jersey.

Kingsman B.G. (1974). 'Forecasting and research for supply markets - commodity buying systems'. Long Range Planning, Vol 7, pp24-38.

Kingsman B.G. (1974). 'Purchasing Strategy and tactical buying for linseed oil'. Paper presented at UK Operational Research Society Annual Conference, Brighton.

Kingsman B.G. (1985). 'Raw Materials Purchasing - an Operational Research Approach.' in the series: Frontiers of Operational Research and Applied Systems Analysis, Volume 4, Pergamon Press. Oxford-New York.

Nerlove M. (1956). 'Estimates of the elasticities of supply of selected agricultural commodities'. Journal of Farm Economics, 38.

Nerlove M. (1958). 'Distributed lags and demand analysis'. USDA Agricultural Handbook no 141, Washington.

Taylor S.J. (1986). 'Modelling Financial Time Series'. John Wiley, Chichester.

Theil H. (1966). 'Applied Economic Forecasting'. North Holland.

Weymar F.H. (1968). 'The dynamics of the world cocoa market'. M.I.T. Press.

PURCHASING MAIZE FUTURES UNDER A DEADLINE: TESTING AND RISK-YIELD EVALUATION OF A PRICE-TREND BUYING POLICY

José Sarsfield Cabral
Rui Campos Guimarães

GEIN, Department of Mechanical Engineering
University of Porto, Rua dos Bragas
4099 PORTO CODEX, PORTUGAL

KEYWORDS/ABSTRACT: purchasing/commodities/futures markets/ forecasting/buying policies/measures of performance/ risk-yield/market efficiency.

A purchasing rule based on short-term forecasts derived from Taylor's price-trend model was developed in previous research, for the scenario described as 'purchasing under a deadline'. Such a rule, when applied to the purchasing of maize futures, was shown to lead to purchasing costs significantly lower than the average market price.

This paper describes subsequent research carried out using artificially generated prices and aimed at improving and further testing the previous results. The purchasing rule was refined and, in particular, a new parameter was included to accommodate different attitudes of the buyers towards risk.

Finally, the appropriateness of the rescaled relative saving as a measure of purchasing performance was verified, by showing that its distribution is almost invariant over time.

NATO ASI Series, Vol. F54
A Reappraisal of the Efficiency of Financial Markets
Edited by Rui M. C. Guimaraes et al.

1. INTRODUCTION

The volatility of prices is a major source of difficulty in a commodity purchasing decision process, inducing most buyers to adopt passive management policies. In these policies the objective is to transfer the risks associated with price changes to third parties (e.g. their customers) or to buy consistently at or close to the average market price.

This paper focuses on an alternative type of policy, which is applicable to the day-to-day commodity buying decisions and aims at improving the purchasing performance (i.e. at reducing the long run purchasing costs within acceptable risk limits). The type of policy that will be addressed here is based on short-term price forecasts, derived from the price-trend models proposed by Taylor (1980, 1986), and on the refinement of an heuristic rule proposed by Guimarães (1981) and described in Guimarães and Kingsman (1985). This type of policy can be uccessfully used only if departures from the market efficiency hypothesis occur.

For the purpose of this paper, the efficient market hyphothesis will be stated in a weak form: within the context of a given purchasing process, a market is considered to be efficient if the results obtained by using adequately the information available in the present and past prices are, from the purchaser's point of view, not better than those obtainable in the absence of any information. According to this definition, the efficiency of a market depends not only on the way in which the information is reflected by the prices but also on the constraints inherent to the purchasing process and on the criteria by which the buyer evaluates each alternative policy. This means that, on the one hand, for a given buyer, the market may be efficient or not depending on the characteristics of the purchasing process and, on the other hand, for a given purchasing process, a market may be efficient for one buyer and inefficient for another.

In the next section the scenario described as 'purchasing under a deadline' is defined and its relevance in the purchasing of maize through the futures market will be briefly discussed. This will be followed, in section 3, by a description of Taylor's price-trend models and forecasting procedure. Section 4 includes a summary of previous results obtained by Guimarães (1981) concerning the day-to-day buying of maize futures under that scenario.

The subsequent sections of the paper describe further research carried out using artificial price series and aimed at testing and improving those results. The buying policy is refined, in particular to accommodate different attitudes of the buyer towards risk. The measure of purchasing performance proposed by Guimarães (1981) - the Rescaled Relative Saving (RRS) - is analysed and its appropriateness to conduct formal statistical tests on the purchasing savings is confirmed.

2. THE PURCHASING SCENARIO: PURCHASING MAIZE FUTURES UNDER A DEADLINE

There are several components to the actual commodity purchasing decisions, all of which must be covered to produce an overall purchasing policy. According to Kingsman (1985), these include determining the future consumption requirements for the commodity in question, defining a delivery-inventory policy for future purchase orders, specifying the start and finish of the active buying period for each order and finally deriving a tactical day-to-day buying policy for use within the active buying period.

The problem situation considered in this paper concerns the final stage, i.e. the tactical buying problem. In particular, it covers the purchasing under a deadline scenario, defined by Kingsman (1985) as the Type 2 tactical buying situation: 'Purchasing a known amount of raw material before a known deadline with many alternative opportunities to make a purchase. At each opportunity there is a single price offer at which the buyer can purchase all or only part of his total requirement or wait until the next buying opportunity and price offer'.

One practical application of this scenario was studied by Guimarães (1981) in the context of the feed grain purchasing operations by the Portuguese Government Importing Agency. Essentially the problem situation can be summarized as follows:

(i) A purchaser has to buy a known amount of maize futures over a specified period of time. Typically the length of such a period ranges from one month to two months and its start and finish are set previously, taking into account the last opportunity at which the futures have to be converted into physical, the medium term futures price forecasts available and the attitude of senior management towards risk and uncertainty.

(ii) At each buying opportunity the purchaser can buy any number of futures as long as at the end of the active buying period he holds the total number of futures envisaged initially (for the grain shipments handled by the importing agency, this number varied usually between two and four hundred).

(iii) At the end of the buying period, all the futures contracts are converted into physical (since this convertion is regarded as an inevitable part of the overall operation, the corresponding costs become irrelevant when comparing alternative buying policies).

Guimarães (1981) showed that this policy of buying futures first and then converting them into physical is clearly advantageous in relation to a policy of buying physical grains directly.

It should be noted that in the scenario just described no

sales of futures can be made during the active buying period. This constraint arose from the code of conduct of the importing agency. Buying and selling futures without restrictions, in a way unrelated to the actual requirements of grain, was considered too risky and speculative, therefore difficult to fit to the agency's corporate objectives.

3. TAYLOR'S PRICE-TREND MODELS AND FORECASTING PROCEDURE

The general price-trend model proposed by Taylor (1980) for a price series $\{z_t\}$ is defined by

$$\log(z_t) - \log(z_{t-1}) = x_t - \mu = \mu_t + e_t$$

$$E(e_t) = 0,\ \mathrm{var}(e_t) = \zeta_t^2,\ E(e_t . e_{t+i}) = 0 \quad (i \neq 0)$$

$$E(\mu_t) = 0,\ \mathrm{cov}(\mu_s, e_t) = 0 \quad (\text{all } s,t)$$

together with a stochastic process generating autocorrelated trends, $\{\mu_t\}$.

The term

$$x_t = \log(z_t) - \log(z_{t-1})$$

is called price return and is an accurate approximation of the relative price change between t-1 and t. In practice, the mean return, μ, is indistinguishable from zero.

In its simplest version, the trend process is defined as follows:

$$\text{(i) } \mu_t = \begin{cases} \mu_{t-1} & \text{, with probability } p \\ \text{new value} & \text{, with probability } 1-p \end{cases}$$

(ii) each new trend value is independent of all the past

values and is drawn from a probability distribution with mean zero and variance ν_t^2

(iii) for all t,

$$A = var(\mu_t)/var(x_t) = constant$$

An alternative to the trend step process just introduced is an AR(1) process defined by

$$\mu_t = p \cdot \mu_{t-1} + \eta_t$$

where $E[\eta_t] = E[\eta_t \cdot \eta_{t+i}] = E[\eta_s \cdot e_t] = 0$ (all s, t and i > 0)

The term

$$m = (1-p)^{-1}$$

represents the mean trend duration for the step process and a measure of the trend stability for the AR(1) process.

Up to this point no reference has been made to the modelling of the stochastic process underlying the variance of the returns. This problem has been dealt with by Taylor (1982 and 1986), who proposes two basic models: linear and non-linear trend models.

In Taylor's non-linear trend model it is assumed that

$$\begin{cases} \mu_t = V_t \cdot T_t \\ e_t = V_t \cdot \varepsilon_t \end{cases}$$

Hence

$$x_t - \mu = V_t \cdot (T_t + \varepsilon_t)$$

where V_t is the volatility of the returns, T_t are the

standardized trends and ε_t are the standardized errors.

Making $U_t = T_t + \varepsilon_t$, the returns are expressed as a product process:

$$x_t - \mu = V_t \cdot U_t$$

where U_t are the standardized returns.

In this model it is also assumed that:

(i) the stochastic processes $\{V_t\}$, $\{T_t\}$ and $\{\varepsilon_t\}$ are stationary and independent;

(ii) $\{\varepsilon_t\}$ is a zero mean white noise with variance equal to (1-A), where $A = var(\mu_t)/var(x_t)$; and

(iii) $\{T_t\}$ has zero mean, its variance is equal to A and its autocorrelation function is $\rho_{i,T} = p^i$.

Under these conditions, the autocorrelation function of $\{U_t\}$ is $\rho_{i,U} = A.p^i$. These autocorrelations are very close to those of the returns $\{x_t\}$.

A detailed description of this non-linear trend model is given in Taylor (1982).

In Taylor's linear trend model the term e_t is given by

$$e_t = V_t^* \cdot \varepsilon_t$$

and hence

$$x_t - \mu = \mu_t + V_t \cdot \varepsilon_t^* \qquad \text{where} \quad \varepsilon_t^* = \varepsilon_t/\alpha \; .$$

In this model it is also assumed that:

(i) the stochastic processes $\{\mu_t\}$, $\{V_t^*\}$ and $\{\varepsilon_t\}$ are stationary and independent;

(ii) $\{\varepsilon_t\}$ is a zero mean strict white noise with variance equal to (1-A), where $A=var(\mu_t)/var(x_t)$

(iii) $\{\mu_t\}$ has zero mean and its autocorrelation function is $\rho_{i,u} = p^i$.

Under these conditions, the autocorrelation function of the returns $\{x_t\}$ is $\rho_{i,x} = A.p^i$.

A detailed description of this linear trend model can be found in Taylor (1986).

In the generation of the artificial price series considered in this study, it was further assumed that:

(i) for both models $\mu = 0$;

(ii) for both models, $\{\log(V_t)\}$ is a $N(\alpha, \beta^2)$ AR(1) process (with parameter denoted by ϕ);

(iii) for the non-linear trend model, $\{T_t\}$ is a N(0,A) process (either trend step or AR(1)); and

(iv) $\{\mu_t\}$ is a $N(0, \nu^2)$ process (either trend step or AR(1)), with $\nu^2 = A.\exp(2\alpha + 2\beta^2)/[1-A+A.\exp(4\beta^2)]$, for the linear trend model.

Provided that the ratio A is small, which is always true for commodity futures prices, the theoretical autocorrelation function of the returns x_t is negligeable and will not be identified by inspecting the sample coefficients individually. The estimation of these coefficients directly from daily returns, x_t, would be inefficient because of the fluctuating variance. This can be overcome by calculating the rescaled returns, $Y_t = x_t/s_t$, where s_t is an estimate of the mean absolute deviation of the random variable generating the returns, obtained from the following inductive procedure:

$$s_t = (1-\gamma) * s_{t-1} + \gamma * |x_{t-1}|$$

with $\gamma = 0.1$ (as recomended by Taylor (1986), for commodities)

In order to test

$$H_o : \text{all } \rho_{i,y} = 0 \qquad (i > 0)$$

$$H_1 : \rho_{i,y} = A.p^i \qquad (i > 0,\ A > 0 \text{ and } 0 < p < 1)$$

Taylor (1980) proposed the following statistic:

$$U^* = 0.465 \sqrt{M} \sum_{i=2}^{30} (0.92)^i . r_i$$

which is asymptotically distributed as N(0,1) and where r_i are the sample autocorrelation coefficients of the rescaled returns and M is the sample size.

If H_o is rejected, the parameters of the price-trend model, A and p(or m), are estimated by minimizing the sum

$$S(A,p) = M . \sum_{i=2}^{30} (r_i - A.p^i)^2$$

The purchasing rules which will be discussed further on are based on the estimates of the standardized trends. The estimate of the standardised trend for the day t+1, uptdated after the price quote on day t, is defined as

$$c_t = \hat{\mu}_{t+1} / \hat{\mu}_{t+1} \quad , \text{ where}$$

$\hat{\mu}_{t+1}$: new estimate of the price-trend for the day t+1, updated after the price offer on day t

$\hat{\nu}_{t+1}$: new estimate of the standard deviation of $\hat{\mu}_{t+1}$, updated after the price offer on day t

Regardless of which Taylor's price-trend models is used, $\hat{\mu}_{t+1}$ and $\hat{\nu}_{t+1}$ are derived from the following expressions:

$$\hat{\mu}_{t+1} = (s_{t+1}/s_t) \cdot [q_o \cdot \hat{\mu}_t + (p_o - q_o) \cdot x_t]$$

$$\hat{\nu}_{t+1} = \sqrt{\frac{p_o \cdot (p_o - q_o) \cdot A_o}{1 - p_o \cdot q_o}} \cdot (\lambda \cdot s_{t+1})$$

where

λ : ratio between the standard deviation and the mean absolute deviation of e_{t+1} (Taylor (1978) suggests that λ should be set equal to 1.333)

p_o, A_o : estimates of the model parameters

q_o : root of the equation $q^2 - q \cdot \left\{ \frac{1+(1-2A_o) \cdot p_o^2}{(1-A_o) \cdot p_o} \right\} + 1 = 0$ which satisfies $0 < q_o < 1$

4. A PRICE-TREND BUYING POLICY

The buying policy originally proposed by Guimarães (1981) and described in Guimarães and Kingsman (1985) is based on the price forecasts derived from Taylor's price-trend models.

Using the following notation

N : total number of days (or, in general, buying opportunities) included in the active buying period;

Q : total amount of material (or futures) that has to be bought over the active buying period;

n : subscript denoting each of the days of the active buying period; for each day, n is the number of buying opportunities remaining to the end of that period ($n = N, N-1,\ldots,1$);

B_n : amount that, according to the buying policy, should be acquired on day n;

q_n : amount left to be bought with n days remaining to the end of the deadline (note that $q_N=Q$ and $q_n=q_{n+1} - B_{n+1}$ for $n=N-1, N-2,\ldots,1$);

c_n : estimate obtained on day n of the standardized trend on the following day, n-1;

the buying policy specifies the amount that should be acquired on any day, according to the following expressions:

$$\text{for } n \geq 2 \quad : B_n = \begin{cases} 0 & , \text{ if } \quad 0 \geq B_n^* \\ B_n^* & , \text{ if } \quad 0 < B_n^* \leq q_n \\ q_n & , \text{ if } \quad B_n^* > q_n \end{cases}$$

$$\text{for } n = 1 \quad : B_1 = q_1$$

where

$$B_n^* = f(n) \cdot c_n \cdot q_n$$

and $f(n)$ is a function which has to be derived by experimentation over past data.

The rule underlying this policy was derived heuristically and entails the following features:

(i) for any day of the buying period, a purchase will be made only if the current estimate of the trend is positive;

(ii) if a purchase is made, the amount that will be bought will increase with the degree of confidence in the positiveness of the trend (measured by the standardized forecast $c_n = \hat{\mu}_{n-1}/\hat{\nu}_{n-1}$) up to the limit q_n;

(iii) the function f(n) reflects the influence of the number of buying opportunities left up to the deadline on the buying decision that is to be taken each day. A priori it can be said that f(n) decreases monotonically with n. In theory, f(2) shoud be infinite. In fact, when n=2 (i.e. with one day still left in addition to the current one) if c_2 is positive, however small, the amount left to be bought (q_2) should be entirely purchased.

The function f(n) is calibrated using past data and attempting to maximize some measure of purchasing performance, which relies on a comparison between the purchasing costs incurred under the proposed buying policy and those incurred under some 'bench-mark' policy (see Guimarães and Kingsman (1985)).

Guimarães (1981) proposed the adoption of the rescaled relative saving (RRS) as a measure of purchasing performance. Such a measure is defined as follows:

$$RRS = \frac{(\bar{\pi} - \pi)/\bar{\pi}}{VR}, \qquad \text{where}$$

$\bar{\pi}$: average futures price over the buying period

π : average futures purchasing cost

VR : volatility of returns , measured by the average value of the estimate of their absolute deviation over the buying period (VR is a measure of the volatility of the relative price movements over that period)

The numerator of RRS represents, when the costs of holding futures are neglected, the relative costs saving achieved by the proposed policy in relation to a bench-mark policy consisting of buying equal numbers of futures, Q/N, at every opportunity. The difference between the holding costs incurred under those policies is, in fact, negligeable for all practical purposes (at current interest rates and assuming 10% deposits, the difference between holding costs for one-month buying periods will not exceed 0.03% of the average futures prices).

The denominator of RRS represents a scaling factor, which is introduced in an attempt to stabilize the distribution of the purchasing performance measure over time, making it nearly independent of the ever changing volatility of prices.

5. RESULTS OBTAINED FOR MAIZE FUTURES REAL PRICE DATA

The data set used by Guimarães (1981) consisted of the daily closing prices of all maize futures contracts quoted on Chicago between the first trading day of 1963 and the last one of 1976. The data was divided into two subsets. The first one, 1963-72, was used to calibrate the parameters of both the price-trend model and the buying policy. The second one, 1973--76, was used to assess the performance of the chosen policy.

Figure 1 presents estimates of the different parameters involved and shows relevant indicators of purchasing performance during the calibration period. Within this period, Bartlett's test showed that the variance of the daily returns was homogeneous. Under these conditions the criterion for the

Figure 1 - The price-trend buying policy : estimation/calibration of parameters and evaluation of performance during the calibration period

(i) Estimation of the parameters of Taylor's price-trend model

(a) Significance of the U^* statistics :

Contract	U^* statistic ($U^*(\alpha=0.05) = 1.65$)
Mar	2.94 (sig.)
May	2.02 (sig.)
Jul	1.47 (not sig.)
Sep	2.33 (sig.)
Dec	2.06 (sig.)
Overall ($\bar{U}^*$)	2.16 (sig.)

(b) Parameter estimates :

$p_0' = 0.947$ $(m_0' = 19$ days)

$A_0' = 1.77$ %

(ii) Calibration of the function f(n) (maximization of $\overline{RS}$ during the calibration period)

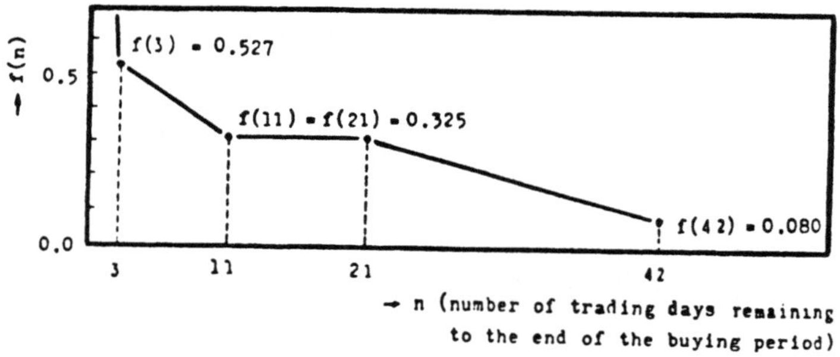

(iii) Summary of statistics concerning the buying performance over the calibration period

Length of buying period	Relative saving		Rescaled relative saving	
	Mean	S.E.	Mean	S.E.
N [trad.days]	$\overline{RS}$ [%]	$\hat{\sigma}(RS)$ [%]	$\overline{RRS}$	$\hat{\sigma}(RRS)$
21	0.42	1.48	0.65	2.55
42	0.48	1.81	0.78	3.03

calibration of f(n) consisted in the maximization of the mean relative saving. A summary of the purchasing performance results over the testing period is given in Table 1.

Table 1 - Results of the Price-Trend Buying Policy over the Testing Period

Lenght of buying period	Mean relative saving	Rescaled relative saving Mean	S.E.	Skew.	t-statistic ($\bar{t}(\alpha=0.05)\approx 1.65$)
N (trad.days)	$\overline{RS}$ (%)	$\overline{RRS}$	$\delta(RRS)$	$Sk^{(*)}$	
21	1.08	0.70	2.44	0.83	1.73 (sig.)
42	2.05	1.07	3.25	--	1.33 (not sig.)

(*) estimated as in Figure 2

The average rescaled relative saving, $\overline{RRS}$, was shown to be significant for buying periods of 21 trading days, i.e. a month. For two-month buying periods, although $\overline{RRS}$ was larger than that obtained for the one-month buying periods, its significance at 5% level could not be established. However the value shown in Table 1 is highly unlikely to be the result of pure chance, but more data would be required to establish statistically its significance.

The magnitude of the mean relative saving ($\overline{RS}$), aproximately proportional to the mean volatility of the returns, can, in times of unstable prices, become extremely attractive. For 1973-76, mean relative savings between 1% and 2%, depending on the length of the buying period were attainable.

The distributions of the relative savings (RS) and the relative rescaled savings (RRS) are shown in Figure 2. Both distributions have a near zero median an are considerably skewed. The number of times when losses are incurred is only slightly smaller than the number in which savings are made, 47.6% v. 52.4%. The implication of this is that the long term savings are made as result of 'savings larger than losses' rather than due to 'more successes than failures'.

Figure 2 - Sample distribution of the relative savings (RS) and rescaled relative savings (RRS) under the price-trend buying policy (one-month buying periods, all contracts, 1973-76)

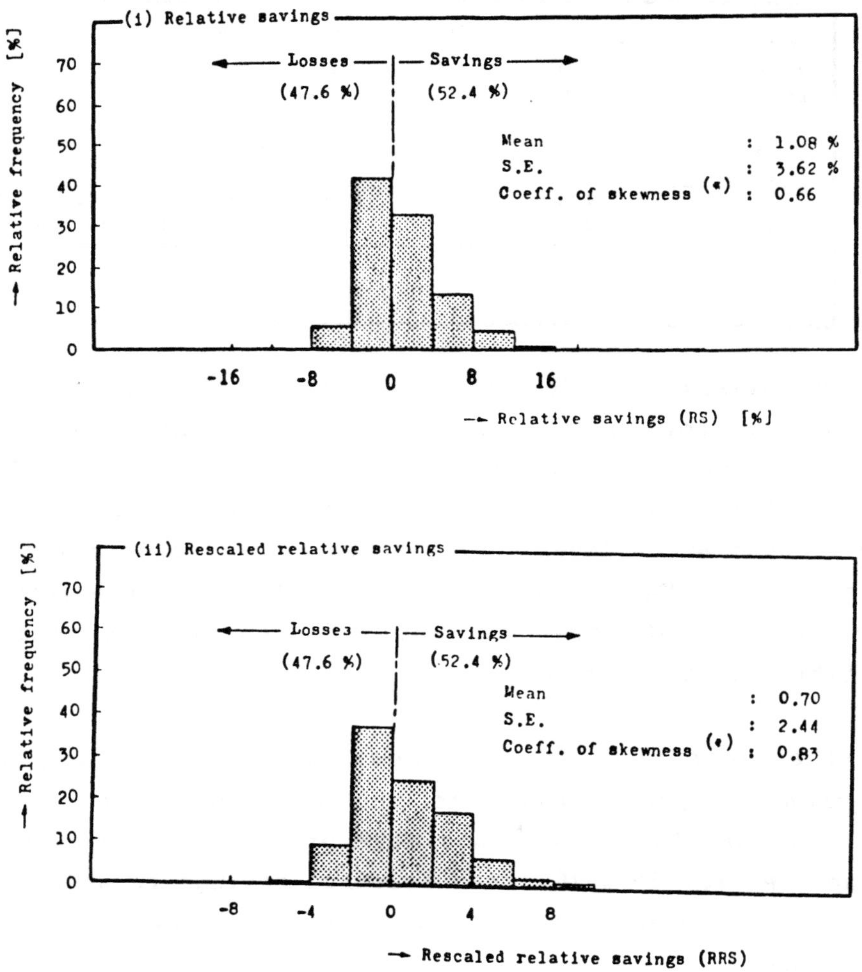

(*) estimated assuming that the distributions are Pearson

$$sk = \frac{\text{mean} - \text{mode}}{\sigma} = \frac{\beta_1 \cdot (\beta_2 + 3)}{2.(5\beta_2 - 6\beta_1 - 9)}$$

with

$\beta_1 = \mu_3^2 / \mu_2^3$

$\beta_2 = \mu_4 / \mu_2^2$ (μ_n is the nth moment about the mean)

The price-trend p (or m) and A parameters were reestimated from the entire 1963-76 dataset and the f(n) function was recalibrated over this period. Given the changes in the relative price volatility post 1972, the optimisation criterion was the maximization of the mean rescaled saving. The results are summarised in Figure 3.

Figure 3 - Price-trend buying policy: calibration of f(n) over the entire period (1963-76)

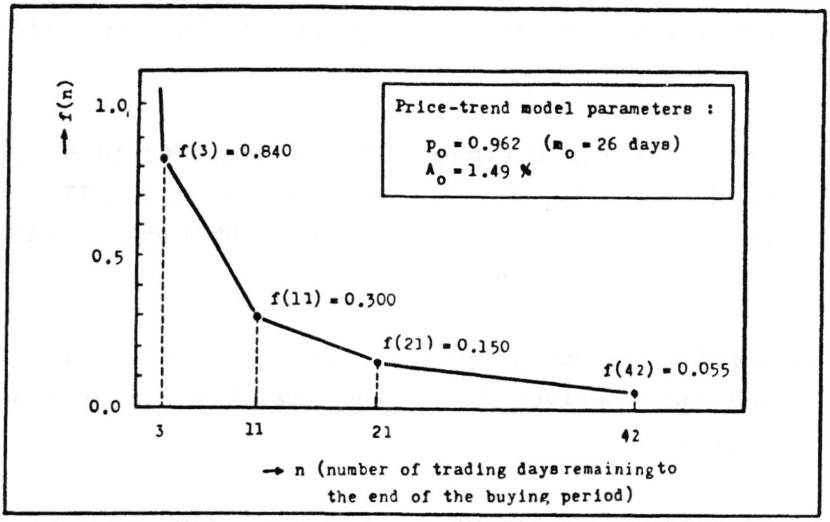

The differences between the new autocorrelation parameter estimates and the previous ones (see Figure 1(i)) are clearly insuficient to suggest any significant changes in the values of the parameters after 1972. More likely they are due to estimation errors. The comparison between the shape of the newly calibrated function f(n) and that of the original one (see Figure 1(ii)) reveals the difficulties arising in the estimation of the 'optimal' values of f(n).

6. REESTIMATION OF THE PARAMETERS OF THE RRS DISTRIBUTION

The results presented in the previous section were derived at the expense of a substantial data colletion effort. However their reliability should be questioned since the testing period was equivalent to only 48 one-month buying periods, which cannot be considered as a large sample. One of the objectives of this paper is to derive better estimates of the cost savings and to ascertain more confidently the statistical properties of the RRS measure of performance, by using artificially generated price series.

Table 2 shows parameter estimates of the RRS distribution derived from a sample of 1000 independent buying periods, under conditions which nearly replicate those prevailing in the buying operations over the testing period. Such conditions were as follows:

(i) The parameter estimates of the price-trend model, used to derive price forecasts, were set at A=1.77% and m=19 days (these estimates were those obtained from the 1963--72 calibration period).

(ii) The f(n) function adopted in the buying policy was the one derived from the calibration period (see Figure 1(ii)).

(iii) In the generation of prices, the values of the autocorrelation parameters A and m were set at 1.49% and 26 days, respectively (these values are the best estimates obtainable from the entire 1963-76 data set).

(iv) All the other parameters of the price-trend models were set at values so as to reflect the behaviour of maize futures prices over the testing period (these values are specified in Table 2).

Considering firstly the estimates of the mean rescaled relative saving, $\overline{RRS}$, it is noticiable that the values obtained from the linear trend model are significantly higher than those associated with the non-linear one. It is interesting to observe that the estimates obtained by Guimarães (1981) using real prices are approximately the average values of the estimates obtained from the linear and non-linear models. This

Table 2 - Parameter estimates of the RRS distribution

(i) 21 trading days

	RESULTS FROM TABLE 1	RESULTS BASED ON SIMULATED PRICES: NON-LINEAR TREND MODEL STEP	NON-LINEAR TREND MODEL AR(1)	LINEAR TREND MODEL STEP	LINEAR TREND MODEL AR(1)
$\overline{RRS}$	0.70	0.53	0.52	0.82	0.85
S.E.	2.44	2.65	2.81	2.98	3.20
$Sk^{(*)}$	0.83	0.39	0.38	0.37	0.47

(ii) 42 trading days

	RESULTS FROM TABLE 1	RESULTS BASED ON SIMULATED PRICES: NON-LINEAR TREND MODEL STEP	NON-LINEAR TREND MODEL AR(1)	LINEAR TREND MODEL STEP	LINEAR TREND MODEL AR(1)
$\overline{RRS}$	1.07	0.70	0.74	1.20	1.19
S.E.	3.25	4.48	4.01	4.47	4.56
$Sk^{(*)}$	--	0.18	0.23	0.24	0.25

(*) estimated as in Figure 2

Parameters used in the generation of prices:

Non-Linear Trend Model	Linear Trend Model
A=1.49% m=26 μ=0	A=1.49% m=26 μ=0
ϕ=0.97 β=0.50 α=-4.16202	ϕ=0.97 β=0.50 α=-4.13689

result is in agreement with Taylor's suggestion (1986) that a model between the linear and non-linear ones is likely to be the best representation of the real prices. A final comment on $\overline{RRS}$ should be made: its value is nearly unaffected by the type of trend process (step or AR(1)) used in the generation of prices.

As far as the higher moments of RRS are concerned, the new estimates depart more significantly from those obtained by Guimarães (1981). However, the general shape of the RRS distribution is reasonably close to that presented earlier in Figure 2(ii) and, in particular, the results obtained from artificial prices confirm that the numbers of negative and positive values of RRS are nearly identical.

The results concerning the distribution of the RS were not shown in Table 2 since they depend on the price volatility and, therefore, they are not as general as those concerning the RRS. Considering one-month buying periods, values of $\overline{RS}$ around 0.7% (for the non-linear trend models) and around 0.9% (for the linear-trend models) were obtained. For buying periods of two months, the values of $\overline{RS}$ were around 1.0% and 1.4% for the non-linear and the linear trend models, respectively.

7. IMPROVEMENT IN THE PROCEDURE USED IN THE CALIBRATION OF f(n)

In the price-trend buying policy presented in section 4 the specification of the amount to be bought on each opportunity is based upon the expression

$$B_n^* = f(n).c_n.q_n$$

where the function f(n) reflects the influence of the number of buying opportunities remaining to the deadline.

The function f(n) has to be derived by experimentation over past data. All that can be said a priori, as discussed earlier, is that it will be monotonically decreasing with n, and that f(2) should be infinite.

Given the sequential nature of the tactical problem, any optimal value for f(n) can only be derived after all the optimal values of f(n-1), f(n-2),..., f(2) have been specified. Therefore, the sequence of optimisation should start on f(3) (assuming $f(2)=\infty$) and then proceed to f(4),...,f(N), successively. This procedure implies an excessively large computational effort. For this reason, Guimarães (1981) proposed a simplified procedure consisting of replacing the 'optimal' function f(n) by a piecewise linear approximation of it. This procedure was found to be acceptable in view of the low sensivity of RRS to changes in f(n) around its 'optimal' values. As shown ealier in Figure 1, for a 42-day buying period the function was replaced by three linear segments, so only four values of f(n) were optimised (for n=3, 11, 21 and 42).

Even for this simplified version, the calibration procedure is still rather cumbersome. A further simplification was introduced by replacing the piecewise linear approximation of f(n) by the curvilinear function

$$f(n) = \kappa.(n-2)^{-\omega} \quad \text{(with } \kappa, \omega > 0 \text{ and n integer} > 1\text{).}$$

This function has the interesting property of becoming infinitive for n=2 and having monotonically decreasing positive values for n>2. Its parameters must be derived by experimentation so as to maximise the $\overline{RRS}$ measure of performance.

In Figure 4(i), the piecewise linear function shown earlier in Figure 1(ii) is compared with a curvilinear function calibrated over a set of 1000 independent periods of 42 daily prices. These were generated by a trend step model with parameters A=1.77% and m=19 days and with homogeneous variance of returns. Such a model was chosen to replicate the behaviour of the maize futures prices over the 1963-72 calibration period. The parameters of the curvilinear function were derived by maximising $\overline{RRS}$ over a grid of κ and ω values with a progressively refined mesh.

The purchasing results obtained with the two functions are quite close, as shown in Figure 4(ii). The price sets and the forecasting parameters used in this comparison were those considered earlier when deriving the results presented in Table 2. The generated prices reproduce approximately the behaviour of the maize futures prices over the 1973-76 testing period and were produced with AR(1)/trend processes. The analysis was extended to prices generated using the trend step process and again the RRS measure was similar for both calibrated functions.

Figure 4 - Curvilinear v. Piecewise Linear calibration procedures

(i) Comparison betweeen the shape of a curvilinear and a piecewise linear approximation of f(n)

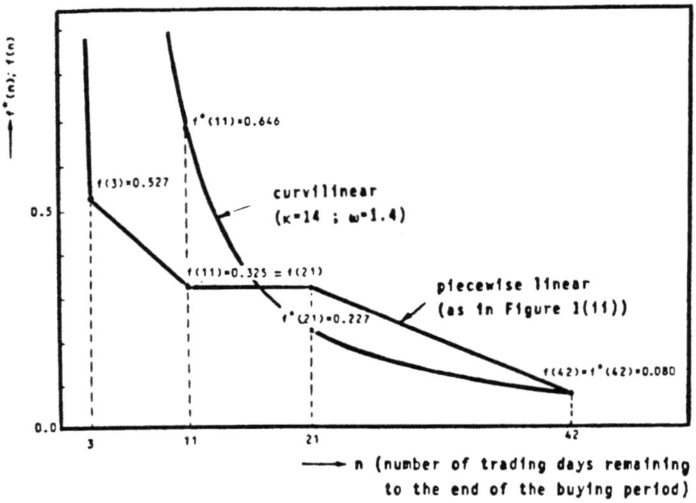

(ii) Comparison between the results obtained with the two calibrated functions

	Non-linear/AR(1)		Linear/AR(1)	
	Piecewise	Curvilinear	Piecewise	Curvilinear
(trad. days)	$\overline{RRS}$	$\overline{RRS}$	$\overline{RRS}$	$\overline{RRS}$
21	0.52	0.48	0.85	0.79
42	0.74	0.69	1.19	1.16

The curvilinear calibration procedure is much more efficient than the one previously considered. In fact, for an identical calibration precision, the computational effort involved in specifying the curvilinear function over a given data set is about 1/5 of that required to calibrate the piecewise linear function over the same data set.

One final point should be made about the shape of the calibrated f(n) functions. Because of the insensitivity of the buying performance to changes in the values of f(n), its calibration becomes rather unprecise, even for considerably sized sets of data.

8. REFORMULATION OF THE PRICE-TREND BUYING POLICY TO ACCOMMODATE DIFFERENT ATTITUDES OF THE BUYER TOWARDS RISK

8.1 The triggering parameter T

Under the price-trend buying policy presented earlier in section 4, the probability that the price paid for the commodity is higher than the average market price over each buying period is nearly 50%. For this reason, and irrespectively of the expected savings achievable, a buyer can find this policy unacceptable. In fact, in the long-term, its performance will be judged as negative by his management about half of the times the purchasing requirements are met. Furthermore, if the number of such requirements over, say, one year is small, the chances of having an overall negative performance during that year are considerable.

The recognition of this drawback led to the reformulation of the buying policy. The new buying procedure takes into account the following situations:

(i) c_n has a large positive value

In this situation, the positiveness of the trend is confidently ascertained and therefore a large proportion of q_n (the amount left to be bought) should be purchased. The larger c_n is the larger that proportion should be.

(ii) c_n has a large negative value

In this case since the negativeness of the trend is confidently ascertained, no purchase should be made.

(iii) c_n has a small absolute value

In this situation, since there is no confidence in the sign of the trend, the bench-mark buying policy (against which the performance is measured) will be adopted. This means that the amount q_n/n will be bought.

The distinction between any two of these situations is made through the triggering parameter, T. Adopting the notation previously introduced in section 4, the buying policy takes the following form:

$$B_n = \begin{cases} 0 \ , & \text{if} \quad -T > c_n \\ q_n/n \ , & \text{if} \quad -T \leq c_n \leq T \\ \text{Min}\ [q_n \ , \ \text{Max}(B_n^*, q_n/n)] \ , & \text{if} \quad c_n > T \end{cases}$$

where

$$B_n^* = f(n) \ . \ c_n \ . \ q_n$$

This new policy, which includes the original one as a special case (when T=0), deserves several comments. The first one concerns the potential infuence of the triggering parameter T on the purchasing results. If T is set at a very high value (e.g. T=3) then the stated policy will lead almost always to the same decisions as the bench-mark policy (i.e. a constant amount will be bought every day). This occurs because c_n is distributed approximately as N(0,1). As T is progressively reduced, the expected savings will increase, to reach a maximum at T=0, but the probability of obtaining a negative performance in any buying period will also raise, up to a limit of around 50% (again reached when T=0). The effect of changing T on the buying results is illustrated in Figure 5 considering buying periods of one month. The results were obtained from a sample of 1000 independent periods, with prices generated using a linear/AR(1) trend model. The parameters of this model and those used to derive price forecasts were set at the values considered earlier when deriving the results presented in Table 2. The buying decisions were based on the curvilinear f(n) function shown in Figure 4(i).

The second comment concerns the symmetry of the triggering points, +T and -T, at which the bench-mark policy is abandoned in favour of either buying more or not buying. Such symmetry is justifiable since the distribution of c_n is also symmetric.

Figure 5 - The influence of T on the purchasing results

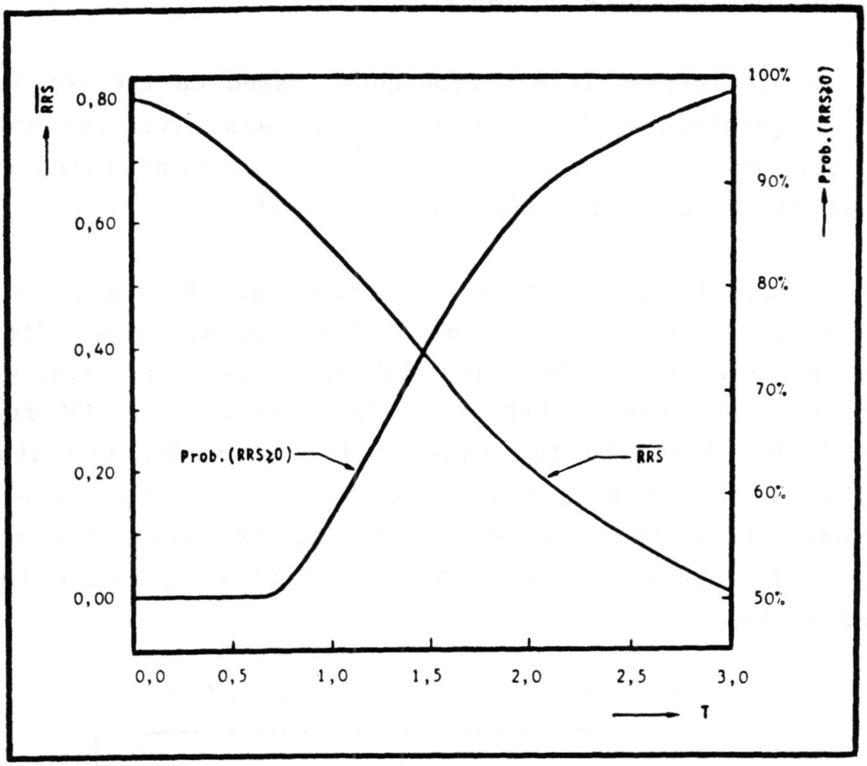

Finally, it should be observed that, in theory, the function f(n) should be recalibrated for each T. However, in practice, since $\overline{RRS}$ is rather insensitive to changes in the shape of f(n), that recalibration is not required.

8.2 A formal procedure for setting the value of T

The choice of an appropriate value for T depends on the way in which the buyer values both the positive and the negative buying results. An attempt to establish a tradeoff between yield and risk could be derived unformally by the buyer from the direct observation of the effect of T on those results, expressed either in terms of the rescaled relative savings (as in Figure 5) or in terms of the relative savings (i.e. $\overline{RS}$ and Prob(RS $\geq$ 0)). The former way of expressing the results is certainly more general. The latter is much easier to interpret by a buyer unfamiliarised with the RRS measure but, however, it can only be used in periods of constant and known (or estimated) price variance.

An alternative formal procedure, based on the Von Newmann and Morgenstern utility theory (1967), was developed and will be presented to show how different risk aversion buying attitudes reflect in different choices of T.

Figure 6 shows two utility functions which are identical for positive relative savings (U=RS%) but translate different degrees of aversion to the risk of incurring negative ones (for the "A" function $U=RS\%-(RS\%)^2/12$ and for the "B" function $U=RS\%-(RS\%)^2/6$). In the case of function 'B', the absolute value of the utility associated to RS=-12% is three times greater than that corresponding to RS=+12%. For the 'A' function, the value of |U(RS=-12%)| is only twice that of U(RS=+12%).

Figure 6 - Examples of risk-aversion utility functions

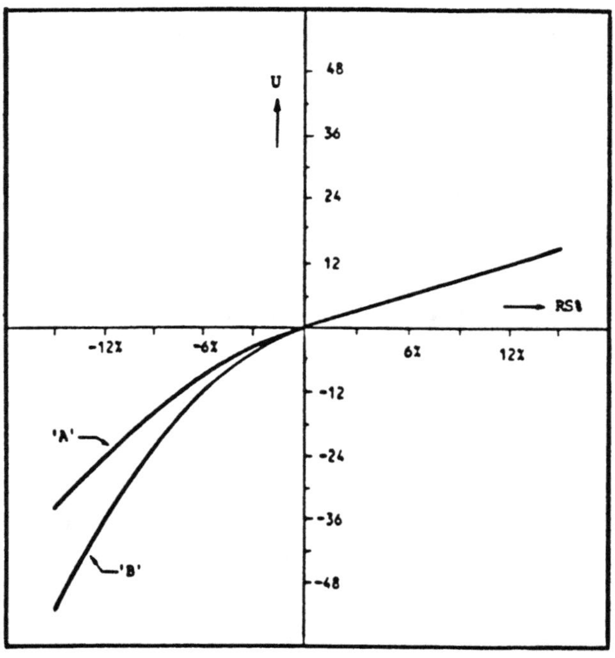

Considering the utility function 'B', Figure 7 shows how the expected utility is affected by the choice of T, for different values of σ_x, the standard deviation of the returns (other values were considered but the corresponding results were not shown, for the sake of clarity). Each of the curves presented in the diagramme was obtained from a sample of 1000 independent one-month buying periods of prices generated using a linear/AR(1) trend model with constant variance. The autocorrelation parameters of this model, the forecasting parameters and the f(n) function were set at the values considered earlier when deriving the results shown in Figure 5.

Figure 7 - The average utility ($\bar{U}$) as a function of T for different values of the standard deviation of the daily returns (σ_x)

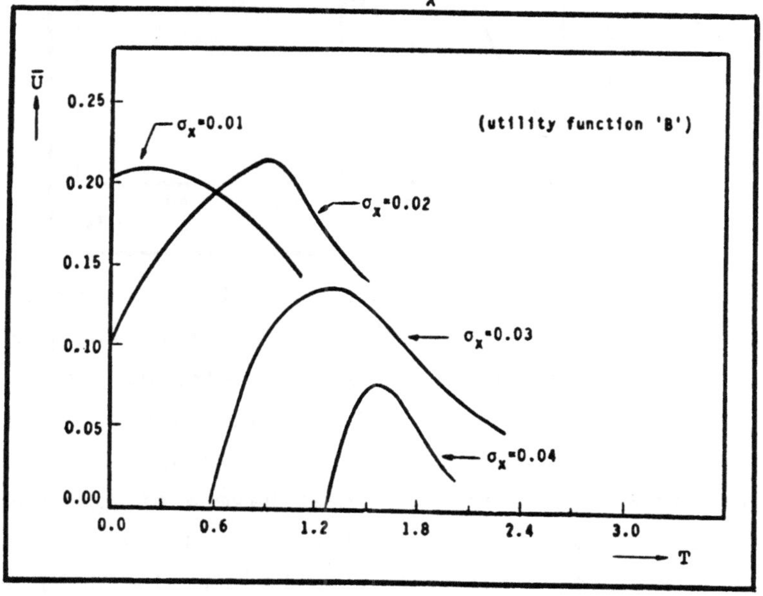

For each value of σ_x, the optimal value of T (i.e. the one which maximises the expected utility) can be derived from the corresponding curve shown in Figure 7.

Figure 8 presents the optimal values of T as a function of the standard deviation of the returns for both utility functions 'A' and 'B'. The range of annual estimates of the standard deviation of the daily returns for the Chicago maize futures prices over the period 1963-76 is marked on the diagramme.

Figure 8 - The optimal values of T as a function of the standard deviation of the daily returns (σ_x)

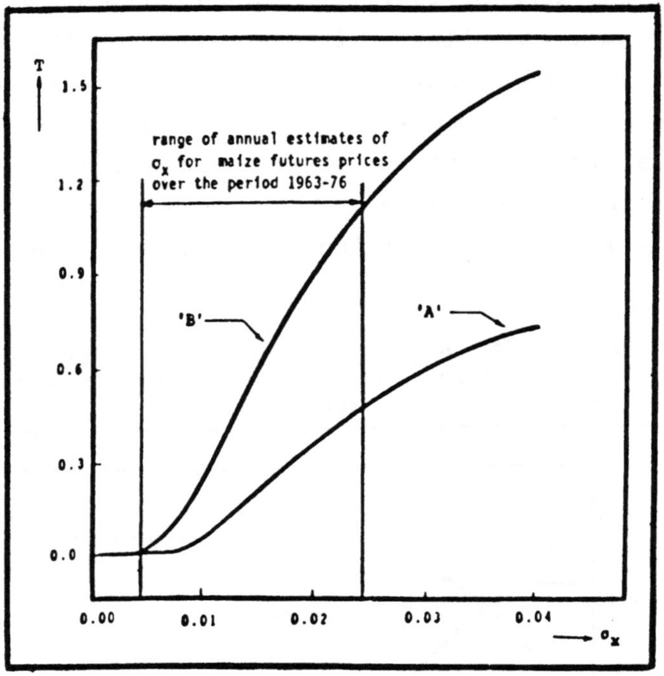

The interpretation of the results presented in the diagramme is quite simple. When σ_x is small, the probability of incurring in losses of a reasonable magnitude is very small (for σ_x=0.005, Prob(RS $\leq$ -2%) < 2.5%). Given the shape of the utility functions considered, the risk aversion is negligeable within the range of values of RS that have a significant chance of occuring. In this situation, the best buying policy is the original one (i.e. T=0) since this is the policy which maximises the yield, $\overline{RS}$. As σ_x increases, the greater will be the chances of incurring in large losses and, therefore, the optimal value of T will increase. The rate at which the optimal value of T increases is higher for the utility function 'B' than for 'A', since the former reflects a greater degree of risk avoidance than the latter.

Since the value of σ_x changes over time, T must be specified in a dynamic way. For each utility function reflecting the buyer's attitude towards risk (say, function 'B'), the corresponding curve shown in Figure 8 will be used on each buying opportunity to convert the current estimate of σ_x into the most appropriate value of T.

9. THE EFFECT OF DELAYING EACH PURCHASE BY ONE DAY

All the results presented in previous sections were obtained using either real daily closing prices of maize futures (in section 5) or prices generated artificially so as to simulate their behaviour (in all subsequent sections). The results were derived assuming that if the buyer decides to make a purchase based on the price quoted on any given day then he will pay the price quoted on that day. Taylor (1986), among others, criticises this assumption, since it demands that the buyer acts instantaneously upon the information received. An alternative procedure for evaluating the purchasing performance is to consider that if the buyer decides to make a purchase on any given day then he will pay the price quoted on the following day. This assumption, which implies that each purchase is delayed by one day in relation to the moment in which the price quote becomes known, may be realistic for the unsofisticated buyer who trades on the basis of information published on newspapers. However, for the professional buyers, such an assumption appears to be very pessimistic. Nevertheless it will be evaluated as a worst case situation.

Table 3 presents a comparison between the means and standard deviations of RRS shown earlier in Table 2 with those obtained when the purchases are delayed by one day.

The one-day purchasing delay implies reducing $\overline{RRS}$ by about 3% in relation to its previous values for buying periods of 21 days and by about 6% for 42-day buying periods (the corresponding percentage reductions observed in $\overline{RS}$ were of the same magnitude). The standard deviations are not significantly affected by the one-day delay. As mentioned above, the reductions in $\overline{RRS}$ (and in $\overline{RS}$) need not to be incurred if the buyer acts efficiently on the basis of information provided on line.

Table 3 - The effect of delaying each purchase by one day on the mean and standard deviation of RRS

(i) 21 trading days

	NON-LINEAR TREND MODEL				LINEAR TREND MODEL			
	STEP		AR(1)		STEP		AR(1)	
	No delay	1-day delay	No delay	1-day delay	No delay	1-day delay	No delay	1-day delay
$\overline{RRS}$	0.53	0.52	0.52	0.49	0.82	0.81	0.85	0.82
S.E.	2.65	2.68	2.81	2.79	2.98	2.98	3.20	3.17

(ii) 42 trading days

	NON-LINEAR TREND MODEL				LINEAR TREND MODEL			
	STEP		AR(1)		STEP		AR(1)	
	No delay	1-day delay	No delay	1-day delay	No delay	1-day delay	No delay	1-day delay
$\overline{RRS}$	0.70	0.69	0.74	0.67	1.20	1.08	1.19	1.12
S.E.	4.48	4.40	4.01	4.73	4.47	5.16	4.56	4.57

NOTE: the 'no delay' results are those presented in Table 2

Parameters used in the generation of prices :

Non-Linear Trend Model	Linear Trend Model
$A=1.49\%$ $m=26$ $\mu=0$	$A=1.49\%$ $m=26$ $\mu=0$
$\phi=0.97$ $\beta=0.50$ $\alpha=-4.16202$	$\phi=0.97$ $\beta=0.50$ $\alpha=-4.13689$

10. TESTING THE APPROPRIATENESS OF RRS AS A MEASURE OF PURCHASING PERFORMANCE

The calibration, testing and evaluation of the price-trend buying policy presented in this paper were based on the assumption that the distribution of the rescaled relative saving (RRS) is invariant over time. A first indication of the validity of this assumption was provided by the results presented in section 5. In fact, the estimates of the mean and standard deviation of RRS obtained for the calibration and testing periods (see Figure 1(iii) and Table 1) are reasonably similar, in spite of the marked change in the price volatility from the first period to the second one.

In order to test the stability of the distribution of RRS, the dependence of its moments on the standard deviation of the daily returns was studied using artificially generated price series. The results were obtained from sets of 1000 independent buying periods, with prices generated from alternative trend models. All the parameters of these models except those concerning the variance process and all the parameters used in the purchasing policy were set at the values considered earlier when deriving the results presented in Table 2. The buying decisions were based on the curvilinear f(n) function shown in Figure 4(i). For each set of 1000 periods, the standard deviation of the returns (σ_x) was kept constant and was set at different levels varying between 0.25% and 4.00%. The results derived for the one-month buying periods with prices generated from the linear/AR(1) trend model are summarised in Figure 9.

As shown in diagramme 9(i), $\overline{RRS}$ is approximately linearly dependent on σ_x. However, within the range of values of σ_x observed annually for the maize futures over the entire 1963-76 period, the variation of RRS is only about 2% of its average value. This value, which can be regarded as negligeable, contrasts markedly with that observed for $\overline{RS}$, as shown in the diagramme. The results obtained for the standard deviation of RRS, presented in the diagramme 9(ii), reveals a very similar influence of σ_x.

The analysis was extended to cover higher moments of the RRS distribution and other price models. In every case, the conclusion was that the RRS distribution is almost invariant with σ_x, which proves the appropriateness of using the rescaled relative saving as a measure of purchasing performance.

Figure 9 - The insensitivity of the RRS distribution to the volatility of the price returns

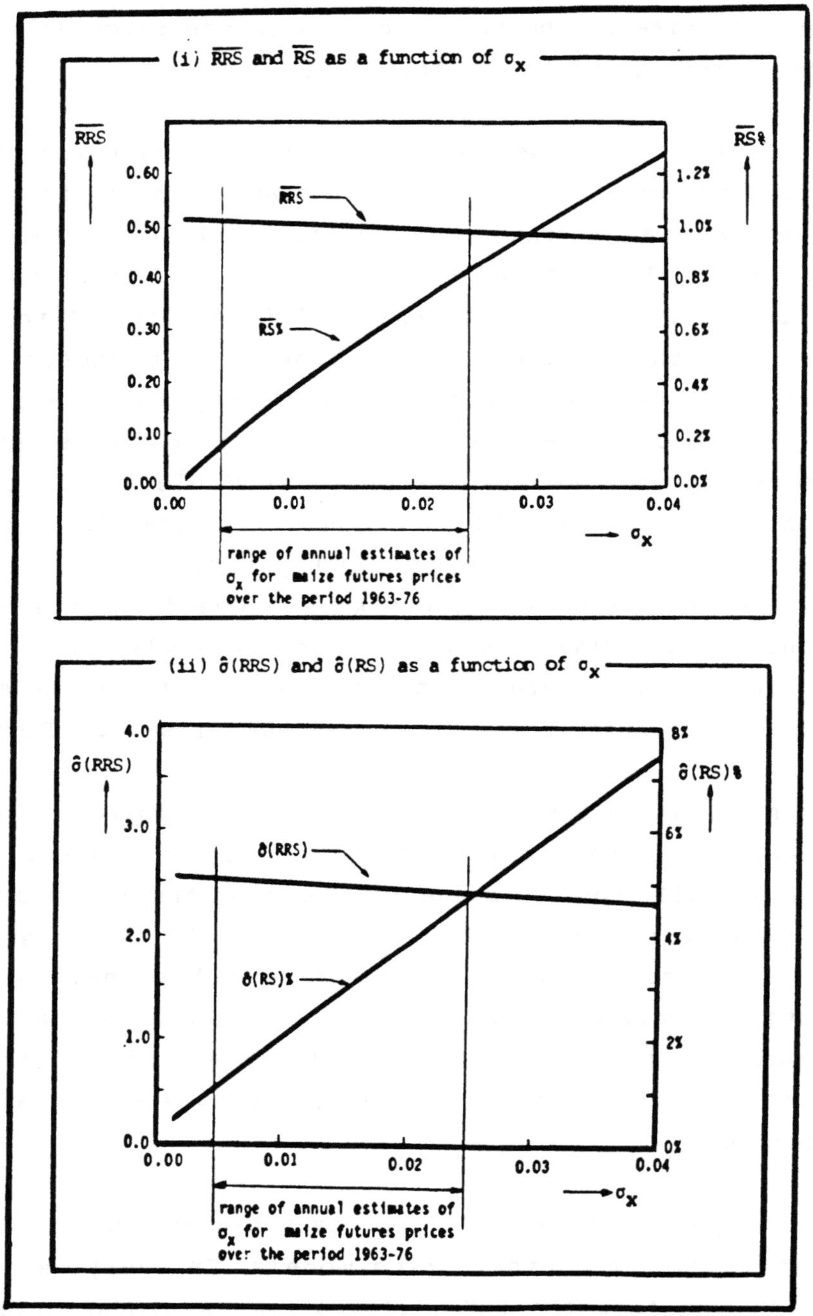

11. QUESTIONING THE EFFICIENCY OF THE MAIZE FUTURES MARKET

The results presented in previous sections call the market efficiency hypothesis in question, as far as the maize futures are concerned. For the purchasing scenario considered - purchasing futures under a deadline - it was confirmed that savings in relation to the average market price could be obtained consistently on the basis of information contained in the current and past prices. Such a confirmation is, by itself, insufficient to reject the efficiency hypothesis since risk considerations must be taken into account. However, if utility functions such us those presented in section 8.2 are thought to reflect realistically the attitude of some buyers towards risk (and the authors do believe in that) then, for such buyers, the market will not be efficient since the expected utility resulting from adopting the price-trend buying policy is positive.

12. CONCLUSIONS

The purchasing results obtained by Guimarães (1981) using real maize futures prices were tested on a large set of artificially generated prices. The test results confirm that the price-trend buying policy proposed by that author for the scenario described as 'purchasing under a deadline' leads to significant cost savings. Additionally, the results appear to corroborate the conjecture that the model which best describes the behaviour of futures prices is in between the linear and the non-linear trend models.

The original buying policy was refined in two ways. Firstly, the procedure adopted in the calibration of the f(n) function was improved by replacing the piecewise linear approximation of this function by a curvilinear one. Secondly, by introducing the triggering parameter T, the policy was enhanced to accomodate different attitudes of the buyers towards risk. A formal procedure based on the utility concept was developed to specify dynamically the optimal values of T.

The appropriateness of the rescaled relative saving as a measure of purchasing performance was verified, by showing that its distribution is almost invariant over time, irrespectively of the changing value of the standard deviation of the daily returns.

Although the efficiency of the maize futures market was not formally refuted for the scenario considered (it just cannot be done, according to the authors definition of market efficiency), strong evidence was provided against the efficiency dogma.

REFERENCES

Guimarães, R.M.C. (1981), National Planning of Commodity Import Operations: The Case of Portugal's Feed Grain Import's, Ph.D. Thesis, University of Lancaster.

Guimarães, R.M.C., and B.G. Kingsman (1985), A Day to Day Buying Policy for Maize, Paper presented at EURO VIII, Lisbon. Submitted to JORS.

Kingsman, B.G. (1985), Raw Materials Purchasing - An Operational Research Approach, Pergammom Press.

Taylor, S.J. (1978), Time Series Properties and Models of Commodity Prices, Ph.D. Thesis, University of Lancaster.

Taylor, S.J. (1980), Conjectured Models for Trends in Financial Prices, Tests and Forecasts, JRSS Series A, Vol. 143, No 3, 338-362.

Taylor, S.J. (1982), Financial Returns Modelled by the Product of Two Stochastic Processes: A Study of Daily Sugar Prices 1961-79, in O.D. Anderson (ed.), Time Series Analysis : Theory and Practice, Vol. 1, Amsterdam.

Taylor, S.J. (1986), Modelling Financial Time Series, John Wiley, Chichester.

Von Neumann, J., and O. Morgenstern (1967), Theory of Games and Economic Behavior, 3d ed., John Wiley, New York.

Comments on J.S. Cabral and R.M.C. Guimaraes: Purchasing maize futures under a deadline - testing and risk-yield evaluation of a price-trend buying policy

By S.J. Taylor

The paper by Cabral and Guimaraes lays the foundations for a study of maize futures prices from 1977 onwards. Guimaraes has already shown that prices from 1963 to 1976 possess exploitable inefficiences. Such results compiled with those in the present paper provide a sound methodological framework for exploring the issue of efficiency in recent years. Of course I look forward to purchasing results for prices from 1977 onwards with great interest.

My paper with Tari in these proceedings argues for inefficiencies in various futures markets. I imagine maize futures are as likely to be inefficient as are cocoa and sugar futures. My paper covers speculation. It is however less easy to demonstrate inefficiencies for purchasers than for speculators. Purchasers have to enter into commitments on a regular basis whereas speculators can wait for those days when their price forecasts are particularly attractive.

At a technical level the paper is fine. Price-trend models are suitable for maize futures. There are serious efforts in the paper to contend with two fundamental problems - first measuring performance and second taking account of risk. The paper neatly demonstrates the advantages of analysing simulated prices.

NATO ASI Series, Vol. F54
A Reappraisal of the Efficiency of Financial Markets
Edited by Rui M. C. Guimaraes et al.

A STATE-SPACE APPROACH TO FORECASTING COMMODITY PRICES

J. A. Assis Lopes
Centre of Urban and Regional Studies
Technical University of Lisbon
Av. Rovisco Pais
Lisbon 1000
Portugal

KEYWORDS/ABSTRACT : forecasting/Kalman filter/state-space/commodity prices/ random walk/dynamic linear model

Commodity spot prices have traditionally been modelled by a random walk. A state-space formulation is presented and used to forecast copper spot prices. This method and another advocated by S. J. Taylor are compared and conclusions presented.

1. Introduction

This paper describes a modelling alternative to the methodology developed by Taylor (1980, 1986) for short-term price forecasting and applies it to daily spot prices for copper. The random walk model for prices had been widely accepted until late in the 1970s, particularly in the work by Labys and Granger (1970). However this price model could not explain a number of empirical observations :

A. Statistical evidence against the random walk for time series of commodity prices (Cargill and Rausser, 1975, Taylor, 1980),

B. Successful results when applying trading rules (Praetz, 1976 and articles discussed therein),

NATO ASI Series, Vol. F54
A Reappraisal of the Efficiency of Financial Markets
Edited by Rui M.C. Guimaraes et al.

C. Results from medium-term price forecasts obtained from econometric models (Kingsman, 1974).

2. Taylor's methodology

To explain the evidence against the random walk model Taylor (1980) supposes there are trends in prices. When the variance is constant the model is :

$$x_t = \mu_t + u_t = \log(z_t) - \log(z_{t-1})$$

where :

z_t is price day t, u_t is white noise, μ_t is the trend term, $E[u_t] = E[\mu_t] = cov(u_t,u_j) = 0$, all t and all $j \neq t$, $V[u_t] = \sigma^2$, $V[\mu_t] = \nu^2$, $cov(u_t,\mu_j) = 0$ all t, j

and in the simplest case :

$$\mu_t = \mu_{t-1} \text{ with probability } p$$

$$= \text{a new value with probability } 1\text{-}p.$$

Modelling logarithms of prices as suggested by Fama (1965) instead of prices is intended to reduce the magnitude of changes in variance. The value of μ_t varies with time and is influenced by new information about supply and demand. To model trends with non-constant variance a step process is used for $\mu_t/V_t^{½}$ instead of μ_t where V_t is the variance of x_t at time t.

The standard deviation of returns can be estimated by a constant times the weighted average of the absolute values of present and past returns :

$$\hat{a}_t = \gamma \sum_{i=0}^{\infty} (1-\gamma)^i |x_{t-i-1}| = (1-\gamma)\hat{a}_{t-1} + \gamma|x_{t-1}|.$$

The best value of γ for copper is approximately 0.1. Taylor and Kingsman

(1978) showed that the autocorrelation coefficients for lags i depend on p and the trend and residual variances, thus :

$$\rho_i = \frac{p^i \nu^2}{\nu^2 + \sigma^2} = Ap^i$$

These correlations are characteristic of an ARMA(1,1) model which can be represented by

$$x_t - px_{t-1} = \varepsilon_t - q\varepsilon_{t-1}$$

where ε_t is a sequence of independent random variables. The ARMA(1,1) representation can also be applied to the rescaled returns.

Estimated values of A and p can be obtained by minimising, over A and p, the function

$$n \sum_{i=1}^{k} (r_i - Ap^i)^2$$

for r_i calculated from the y_t.

The value of q is given by solving a quadratic equation (see Taylor's paper in this volume). Given p and q a recursive forecast for the next return is given by

$$f_{t,1} = (\hat{a}_{t+1}/\hat{a}_t) \{qf_{t-1,1} + (p-q)x_t\}$$

and the forecast of the next price is

$$\hat{z}_{t+1} = z_t \exp (f_{t,1}).$$

3. State-space formulations

State-space formulations can incorporate variations in level and trend. Two models are used to forecast prices.

Model M1 (the dynamic linear model)

$$z_t = \beta_t + e_{1t}$$

$$\beta_t = \beta_{t-1} + \mu_t + \delta\beta_t$$

$$\mu_t = \mu_{t-1} + \delta\mu_t$$

with β_t the price level at time t, μ_t the price trend at time t, and with e_{1t}, $\delta\beta_t$, $\delta\mu_t$ zero-mean, white noise, level and trend disturbance terms, also

$$E[e^2_{1t}] = V_t,\ \mathrm{cov}(e_{1t}, e_{1j}) = 0 \text{ all } j \neq t,\ \mathrm{cov}(\delta\beta_t, \delta\mu_t) = 0 \text{ all } t.$$

The formulation of the model through the state-space approach is given by :

$$\begin{bmatrix} \beta_t \\ \mu_t \end{bmatrix} = \begin{bmatrix} 1 & 1 \\ 0 & 1 \end{bmatrix} \begin{bmatrix} \beta_{t-1} \\ \mu_{t-1} \end{bmatrix} + \begin{bmatrix} \delta\mu_t + \delta\beta_t \\ \delta\mu_t \end{bmatrix}$$

$$z_t = [1\ 0] \begin{bmatrix} \beta_t \\ \mu_t \end{bmatrix} + e_{1t}$$

with $W_t = E\,[w_t w_t']$ and $w_t = \begin{bmatrix} \delta\mu_t + \delta\beta_t \\ \delta\mu_t \end{bmatrix}$

The estimation of the parameters can be performed by using the Kalman filter and we can use recurrence relationships established for the determination of the V and W matrices.

Model M2 (random walk)

$z_t = z_{t-1} + e_{2t}$ where e_{2t} is white noise.

Combined forecasts

Combined forecasts at each instant are given by a weighted combination of the forecasts given by models M1 and M2 with weights (Granger, 1980) :

$$\alpha_1 = \frac{V(e_{1t}) - cov(e_{1t},e_{2t})}{V(e_{1t}) + V(e_{2t}) - 2cov(e_{1t},e_{2t})}$$

$$\alpha_2 = 1-\alpha_1$$

where e_{it} is the forecasting error for model i.

Cycles

A second approach to modelling the state consists of considering, besides the level and trend already considered, a cyclical component with stochastic characteristics, which can be represented by (Harvey, 1987) :

$$\begin{bmatrix} \psi_t \\ \psi_t^* \end{bmatrix} = \rho \begin{bmatrix} \cos\lambda & \sin\lambda \\ -\sin\lambda & \cos\lambda \end{bmatrix} \begin{bmatrix} \psi_{t-1} \\ \psi_{t-1}^* \end{bmatrix} + \begin{bmatrix} \delta\psi_t \\ \delta\psi_t^* \end{bmatrix}$$

with λ the frequency of the cycle in radians and ρ a damping factor ($0 \leqslant \lambda \leqslant \Pi$, $0 \leqslant \rho \leqslant 1$).

The terms $\delta\psi_t$ and $\delta\psi_t^*$ are white noise disturbances, mutually independent and normal with the same variance. The variable ψ_t^* appears by construction in order to obtain ψ_t.

The model is now

$$z_t = \beta_t + e_t$$

$$\beta_t = \beta_{t-1} + \mu_t + \psi_t + \delta\beta_t$$

$$\mu_t = \mu_{t-1} + \delta\mu_t$$

$$\psi_t = \rho\ (\psi_{t-1} \cos \lambda + \psi^*_{t-1} \sin \lambda) + \delta\psi_t$$

$$\psi_t^* = \rho(-\psi_{t-1} \sin \lambda + \psi^*_{t-1} \cos \lambda) + \delta\psi_t^*.$$

The existence of a cycle can be tested for using a procedure suggested by Harvey (1987).

4. Data and results

The prices used were daily closing prices for spot "wire-bars" copper traded at the London Metal Exchange between July 1978 and January 1984. Parameter estimates were obtained from the prices between July 1978 and July 1983 and the out-of-sample forecasting period was August 1983 to January 1984. The parameters obtained using the methodology of Taylor (1980, 1986) were:

$A = 0.0222$, $p = 0.8542$ and $q = 0.8362$

from which the average trend duration is $1/(1-p) = 7$ trading days.

For the first run of the state-space method (i.e. without cyclical effects):

$$\hat{\alpha}_2 = 0.887,\ E[e_{1t}^2] = 14.33,\ E[\delta\beta_t^2] = 120.4 \text{ and } E[\delta\mu_t^2] \approx 0.$$

The steady state was attained after 47 observations. For the second run, with cyclical effects :

$$\rho = 0.926,\ \lambda = 0.171,$$

$$E[e_t^2] = 19.69,\ E[\delta\beta_t^2] = 104.98,$$

$E[\delta\mu_t^2] \approx 0$ and $E[\delta\nu_t^2] \approx 0.69$.

The steady state was attained after 49 observations. Portmanteau and F tests were applied to the residuals to test for correlation and heteroscedasticity.

The values of the mean square forecasting errors for the out-of-sample period are shown in Table 1.

Table 1

Forecasting approach	MSE (one step forecasting)	MSE (% reduction from RW)
Taylor	102.57	0.55
Combined DLM	102.27	0.84
DLM with cyclical term	101.86	1.24
Random walk	103.14	

5. Conclusions

The forecasts one-step ahead give similar performances, but the best results are given by the formulation that includes cyclical, level and trend components. It must be noted that the out-of-sample assessment period is only five months and so too short for conclusive comparisons of the different forecasting methods.

The estimated cycle duration is 37 trading days and the cycle effect is significant using the Lagrange multiplier test.

The reduction in MSE obtained by the best forecast (1.24%) compared with the random walk forecast is relevant for any assessment of the efficiency of the copper market.

Convergence of the covariance matrices after few observations shows that the Kalman filter methodology can be applied to shorter datasets than are required by Taylor's methodology.

References

Cargill, T.F. and G.C. Rausser, 1975, Temporal price behaviour in commodity futures markets, Journal of Finance 30, 1043-1053.

Fama, E.F., 1965, The behaviour of stock market prices, Journal of Business 38, 34-105.

Granger, C.W.J., 1980, Forecasting in business and economics (Academic Press).

Harvey, A.C., 1987, Applications of the Kalman filter in econometrics, in : Advances in econometrics - Fifth world congress (Cambridge University Press).

Kingsman, B.G., 1974, Forecasting and research for supply markets, Long Range Planning 7, 24-38.

Labys, W.C. and C.W.J. Granger, 1970, Speculation, hedging and commodity price forecasts (Heath Lexington, Massachusetts).

Praetz, P.D., 1976, On the methodology of testing for independence in futures prices, Journal of Finance 31, 977-979.

Taylor, S.J., 1980, Conjectured models for trends in financial prices, tests and forecasts, Journal of the Royal Statistical Society 143A, 338-362.

Taylor, S.J., 1986, Modelling financial time series (John Wiley, Chichester).

Taylor, S.J. and B.G. Kingsman, 1978, Non-stationarity in sugar prices, Journal of the Operational Research Society 29, 971-980.

AN EMPIRICAL TEST OF THE OPM BASED ON EOE-TRANSACTIONS DATA

Angelien Kemna
Erasmus University
Department of Finance
P.O.Box 1738
3000 DR Rotterdam
The Netherlands

Keywords: Transaction data / European Options Exchange / Stock options / model testing / implied volatility / bid-ask spread / regression analysis

Abstract: Based on 4 months of EOE-transactions data of the 14 stock options, the option pricing model is tested on its validity. Differences between model and market prices are analyzed through the behaviour of the implied volatility. One important measurement error caused by the options bid-ask spread explains part of the differences in implied volatility per stock. Further, biases with respect to the time to maturity, the exercise price and dividend payments are found in addition to a time dependency of the implied volatility.

1. Introduction

During the last fifteen years numerous empirical tests of various versions of the option pricing model have been published[1]. In an excellent overview Galai [1983] summarizes the most important results. Testing the model validity with market data implies a joint test with market efficiency. If the option pricing model shows systematic biases with respect to the market prices, this can be due to model misspecifications, inefficiencies in both stock and/or options markets and lack of synchronization between stock and option quotations. One of the results from recent studies is that non-synchronization in stock and option data can substantially affect the results (see Rubinstein [1985] and Bhattacharya [1987]). In order to overcome part

[1] E.g. MacBeth and Merville [1979], Whaley [1982], Blomeyer and Klemkosky [1983], Sterk [1983], Rubenstein [1985].

NATO ASI Series, Vol. F54
A Reappraisal of the Efficiency of Financial Markets
Edited by Rui M.C. Guimaraes et al.

of this problem the analysis in this paper will be based on transactions data of the European Options Exchange (EOE) on stock call options from 13 August 1984 until 28 December 1984.

A direct comparison of model and market prices (see Macbeth and Merville [1979], Whaley [1982], Sterk [1983] and Blomeyer and Klemkosky [1983]) leads to the following three important results:

- The Black-Scholes pricing model does not consistently result in good predictions, especially for out-of-the-money, near-maturity calls.
- The standard deviation (or volatility) of the stock's rate of return is probably not constant over time.
- Alternative pricing models (like the compound option model of Geske [1977] do not yield consistently better predictions of market prices.

A disadvantage of this approach[2] is that when possible systematic biases are found between market and model prices it cannot be concluded whether they are caused by biases in the estimator of the volatility or by biases caused by misspecification of the model.

Another approach is based on the implied standard-deviation (ISD) which can be calculated by equating market and model prices[3]. The ISD approach investigates the behaviour of the ISD to determine the validity of the assumed model (see Beckers [1981], Brenner and Galai [1984] and Rubinstein [1985]). It is expected that the implied standard deviation per unit of time (ISD) is constant over time, across maturities and exercise prices. Deviations may be due to arrival of new information, market inefficiencies, lack of synchronization between options and stock markets or to the model being misspecified. The advantage of this approach above a direct comparison is that no estimate of the volatility is needed.

The forementioned results are based on CBOE daily closing and/or transactions data on stock options. In this paper the model validity will be tested based on EOE transactions data. Previous research on EOE stock options (Van der Hilst [1980]), or EOE gold options (Beckers [1984]) was

---

[2] A related disadvantage is that the deviations between model and market prices are not constant over time. It changes with time to maturity and stock price changes.

[3] We calculated the ISD using a Newton-Rhapson method (Bjorck and Dahlquist [1974]).

based on daily closing prices[4]. For the fourteen stocks concerned the model and market call option prices will be compared by studying the behaviour of the ISD. In case the underlying stock pays dividends during the life of the option contract, the binomial method will be used in order to incorporate the early exercise possibility[5]. Since only four or five stocks are actively traded, we also want to give insight in the differences in results between actively and inactively traded stocks. Therefore, data were gathered on the quoted bid-ask spread of option prices during three weeks of the sample period.

In section 2 the transactions and bid-ask data will be described in detail. The percentage bid-ask spread for the stocks shows that the percentage spread of inactively traded stocks is at least twice as much as the percentage spread of actively traded stocks.

In section 3 the average ISD and the standard deviation over the sample period will be presented. If the assumption of a constant volatility is valid, we would expect a degenerate distribution for the ISD. However, a substantial standard deviation around the average ISD over the sample period is found. In order to get an understanding of the possible measurement error caused by the fact that one transaction price will be closer to the bid price and another closer to the ask price, the average semi-difference between the ISD of the ask and bid price is calculated. This measure gives the maximum impact of the bid-ask spread on the standard deviation of the average ISD. It will be shown that the bid-ask spread in terms of spread in the ISD is not only different for the various stocks, but also for in-, at- and out-of-the-money options.

In section 4 the behaviour of the ISD with respect to the time to maturity and exercise price will be analyzed. From earlier work on CBOE transactions data (Blomeyer and Klemkosky [1983] and Rubinstein [1985]), it follows that the standard deviation of the average ISD is not only caused by data measurement errors or bid-ask spreads, but also by deviations of the ISD over time, across maturities and exercise prices. First, we will analyze the average ISD's for near-, middle- and long-termed options and for in-, at-

---

[4] Especially in thinly traded options markets the use of closing prices leads to limited results.

[5] Geske and Roll [1984] also report significant biases in the model prices due to the probability that dividend payments can be suspendend.

and out-of-the-money options. It turns out that for the various options classes there exists a significant difference in average ISD.

Further, we will test whether the time to maturity and the exercise price biases still exist in addition to the time dependency of the ISD by means of regression analysis. It shows that the inclusion of the time to maturity and the ratio between stock and exercise prices provides additional explanation to the ISD, implying significant biases with respect to time to maturity and exercise prices.

In section 5 differences between the average ISD's of transactions with and without dividend payments will be examined. Although the correct model is used to take into account the early exercise possibility, we still may expect that dividend payments cause systematically different ISD's (see Geske and Roll [1984]). Since realized dividends have been used as an estimator for the expected dividends, this bias can be caused by an unexpected level of the payment or an unexpected suspension of the payment. For various stocks there exists a significant difference in average ISD between transactions with and without dividend payments, and in a regression analysis we find that dividend payments provide additional explanation to the ISD besides time to maturity and the ratio between stock price and exercise price. However, the level of the dividend payments and the ex-dividend date are relatively constant over the years, which makes it more likely that the dividend bias is only a temporary effect caused by an inefficiency in the market.

2. Description of the data

The data used in this analysis are EOE-transactions data during the period 8/13/84 until 12/28/84. The total sample contains 20 weeks and approximately 140,000 transactions, of which about 75% (or some 105,000) call option transactions. The stocks on which the call options are written are presented in Table 1.

Call option transactions that did not satisfy the following requirements have been eliminated:

1. The call option price is more than one guilder[6].

---

[6] These are mostly near-term out-of-the-money options. Communications learned that these are very infrequently traded options.

2. The time to maturity is more than 20 days, because options of maturities with less than three weeks are insensitive to σ.
3. The premium is sufficiently high to calculate an implied volatility. This implies that for options without dividends the premium has to be more than the theoretical boundary: $\max(0, S-Ke^{-r(T-t)})$. For the boundary in case of dividend payments see Bhattacharya [1983] p.163.

Table 1 EOE stocks

Algemene Bank Nederland	ABN
AEGON	AGN
Albert Heijn	AH
AKZO	AKZ
Amsterdam Rotterdam Bank	ARB
Gist Brocades	GIS
Heineken	HEI
Hoogovens	HO
Koninklijke Luchtvaart Mij	KLM
Ned LLoyd Groep	NED
Nationale Nederlanden	NN
Philips	PHI
Koninklijke Olie	RD
Unilever	UNI

After elimination of the transactions that did not fulfill the above requirements, 88,069 call option transactions remained. This implies a decrease of about 15% in the number of transactions in our sample.
As an estimator for the risk-free rate we used the weekly quotation of the six month industry rate listed in "Het Financieële Dagblad".
Dividend information was gathered from "De Officiële Prijscourant", with the actual dividend declared during the life of the option contract used in the pricing model (we assume that taxes on dividends are zero[7]). Both newspapers are major Dutch financial newspapers. The data records contained the following information:

- present date
- stock price at the time of the transaction
- exercise price
- maturity date
- first dividend payment
- first dividend date

---

[7] For CBOE data Beckers [1981] uses an ad hoc percentage of 85% of the dividend payment. For the Dutch market no such percentage is known.

- second dividend payment
- second dividend date
- interest rate (annually)
- option price of the transaction

Information on the bid-ask spreads of the option prices has been gathered over three weeks (22-26 oct., 19-23 nov. and 24-28 dec.). The bid-ask sample has been screened similar as the sample containing transactions data. The bid-ask records contain the same information as the transactions records, except that the option price is replaced by the bid- and ask quote. Not available was the information whether the stock price at the time of the option transaction was a bid-, ask- or transaction price[8].

In table 2 we have given the number of transactions of the sample period, the number of bid-ask spreads and the percentage spread[9].

Table 2 Percentage spread

Stock	# of trans.	# of quotes	spread* in %
ABN	3,667	1,054	9.72
AGN	2,638	837	10.35
AH	1,124	396	14.94
AKZ	19,347	3,399	5.85
ARB	2,955	687	13.98
GIS	2,868	660	13.20
HEI	2,936	734	10.79
HO	7,403	1,477	10.77
KLM	9,619	2,477	7.40
NED	2,509	1,417	12.18
NN	1,018	660	9.59
PHI	16,188	2,497	7.45
RD	13,654	2,308	6.68
UNI	2,143	610	11.41
Total	88,069	19,213	8.83

*Average ask-bid/½(ask+bid)

8 This is not a very serious problem, since the Dutch stock market is not a market makers market and therefore no official bid- and ask prices are quoted.

9 The spreads of this sample can be seen as representative for the whole period since the addition of an extra week did not lead to changes of more than .1% in the average percentage spread.

The average percentage spread is defined as the average of the ask-bid/½(bid+ask) (see Phillips and Smith [1980]). It is expected that the liquidity of the options market will influence the bid-ask spread. A high liquidity in the options market is expected to lead to a low bid-ask spread. From table 2 it follows immediately that the actively traded stocks like AKZ, KLM, PHI and RD have a lower percentage spread than inactively traded stocks like AH, ARB, GIS, NED and UNI. Exceptions are HO with a relatively high and NN with a relatively low spread. The consequence of a high spread will be discussed in the next section. We can also conclude that the total percentage spread is above the 4.51% of the CBOE reported by Phillips and Smith [1980], but is below the 12.48% of the London market reported by Dickinson and Nisbet [1987].

Finally, in tabel 3 the frequency of the near-, middle- and long-term options and the out-, at- and in-the-money options for the transactions and the quotes are presented, as well as the percentages of the total. The boundaries for the options classes are the following:

time to maturity, T-t		
1	$T\text{-}t < .25$	near-term
2	$.25 \le T\text{-}t < .50$	middle-term
3	$.50 \le T\text{-}t$	long-term

ratio stock/exercise price, S/K		
1	$S/K < .95$	out-of-the-money
2	$.95 \le S/K < 1.05$	at-the-money
3	$1.05 \le S/K$	in-the-money

From table 3a and 3b it is clear that more than 50% of the transactions are at-the-money options, and almost 50% are near-term options. There are relatively more near-term in-the-money bid-ask quotes.

Table 3a Transactions

S/K	time to maturity 1	2	3	Total
1	10845 (12.3%)	10205 (11.6%)	2763 (3.1%)	23813 (27.0%)
2	23524 (26.7%)	19122 (21.7%)	4917 (5.6%)	47563 (54.0%)
3	8281 (9.4%)	6703 (7.6%)	1709 (1.9%)	16693 (19.0%)
Total	42650 (48.4%)	36030 (40.9%)	9389 (10.7%)	88069

Table 3b Quotes

S/K	time to maturity 1	2	3	Total
1	2337 (12.3%)	1738 (9.0%)	861 (4.5%)	4936 (25.7%)
2	4573 (23.8%)	2196 (11.4%)	928 (4.8%)	7697 (40.1%)
3	3571 (18.6%)	2595 (13.5%)	414 (2.2%)	6580 (34.2%)
Total	10481 (54.6%)	6529 (34.0%)	2203 (11.5%)	19213

3. The bid-ask spread

By using transactions data, it is possible to derive the empirical distribution of the implied standard deviation (ISD) for different stocks. If the model is correct and all variables are measured simultaneously and without error, a degenerate distribution for ISD should be expected. However, some variables are measured with error. One error will be caused by the bid-ask spread of the option price. This impact spread will be studied in this section. Another source of error can be caused by the estimator of the dividends, since realized dividends are used as an estimator for the expected dividends. This will be studied in section 5. Other measurement errors are included in the estimator for the interest rate, the fact that it is assumed that the stock price is a transaction price and the difference in accuracy between market and model prices.

If one assumes that the market price is equal to the model price, the ISD can be calculated by means of a Newton-Raphson procedure (Bjorck and Dahlquist [1974]). To account for the early exercise possibility due to dividend payments, the binomial model, in which we approximate the discrete payments by yields is used. Note that the market price on the EOE is given with one decimal accuracy, while the model prices are calculated with eight decimals accuracy. This can cause a difference in ISD for in-the-money and out-of-the-money options compared to at-the-money options[10]. In table 4 the number of transactions, the average ISD and the standard deviation for the sample period is presented.

Stocks with a high average implied volatility are KLM, HO and AKZ. NN and UNI have a low average implied volatility. The standard deviation of the average ISD of KLM is extraordinairy high. The next section shows that this is caused by a substantial decrease of the average ISD in the first 10 weeks followed by a substantial increase in the next 10 weeks.

Some of the standard deviation can be explained by the bid-ask spread of the option price, since transactions prices can be either close to the

---

[10] The influence of this accuracy difference can be illustrated as follows. For out-of-the-money and at-the-money middle-term call options the difference in accuracy leads to a range of approximately + and -.002 around a volatility of .20. For in-the-money call options this leads to a larger range of + and -.003.

Table 4 Average ISD per stock

Stock	Number of transactions	Average ISD	Standard deviation
ABN	3,667	.2393	.0432
AGN	2,638	.2211	.0408
AH	1,124	.2245	.0284
AKZ	19,347	.3203	.0378
ARB	2,955	.2878	.0491
GIS	2,868	.2247	.0396
HEI	2,936	.2125	.0429
HO	7,403	.3514	.0412
KLM	9,619	.3742	.0743
NED	2,509	.2658	.0446
NN	1,018	.1327	.0369
PHI	16,188	.2678	.0386
RD	13,654	.2014	.0393
UNI	2,143	.1498	.0368

bid or close to the ask price[11]. It is expected that the liquidity of the options market and the volatility of the stock will influence the bid-ask spread. As shown in the previous section, a high liquidity in the options market leads to a low bid-ask spread. It also may be expected that a low volatility of the stock leads to a low bid-ask spread. We see that this can be the explanation for the relatively low percentage spread found for NN and the relatively high percentage spread for HO.

The consequence of a large bid-ask spread will be a large standard deviation of the average ISD. In order to show the impact of the bid-ask spread on the standard deviation of the average ISD, the ISDs for the bid and ask quotes have been calculated. The semi-difference between the ISD of the ask and bid, $\frac{1}{2}(ISD_{ask} - ISD_{bid})$, gives the *maximum* measurement error of the ISD caused by the bid-ask spread. Since the transaction will always take place within the bid-ask spread, this percentage will be an upper boundary. Table 5 gives the number of quotes, the semi-difference in spread in terms of the ISD and the percentage by which the standard deviation of the average ISD can be explained by the bid-ask spread. There is a difference between the bid-ask quote sample and the transactions sample. From table 3b it followed that there is a relatively large number of quotes for in-the-money options compared to the number of transactions in this class. Since especially these options have a large spread in terms of the ISD, the spread for the whole sample will be rela-

[11] I thank Stan Beckers for this suggestion.

Table 5 Average spread in terms of the ISD

Stock	Number of obs.	spread* in ISD	%bid-ask of ISD**	Ratio S/K 1	2	3
ABN	1,054	.016	37%	.007	.012	.027
AGN	837	.024	59%	.012	.012	.040
AH	396	.015	53%	.011	.012	.041
AKZ	3,399	.012	32%	.007	.008	.025
ARB	687	.027	55%	.015	.020	.039
GIS	660	.020	51%	.011	.011	.047
HEI	734	.017	40%	.009	.010	.039
HO	1,477	.026	63%	.015	.018	.044
KLM	2,477	.026	35%	.014	.017	.035
NED	1,417	.029	65%	.015	.014	.053
NN	660	.024	65%	--***	.009	.036
PHI	2,497	.014	36%	.009	.010	.022
RD	2,308	.013	33%	.005	.007	.032
UNI	610	.017	46%	.007	.007	.033

* Average $\frac{1}{2}(ISD_{ask} - ISD_{bid})$
** (spread in ISD/standard deviation ISD)x100%
*** No observations

tively high. In table 5 the spread in terms of the ISD for out-, at- and in-the-money options has been given (detailed information is available at the authors request). This implies that this effect will also lead to an overestimation of the bid-ask spread effect. In conclusion, the bid-ask spread can explain only part of the standard deviation of the ISD.

4. Time to maturity and exercise price biases

In many papers[12] the option pricing model resulted in systematic biases for in- and out-of-the-money options and for different times to maturity. Geske and Roll [1984] have examined these biases theoretically and concluded that most of the biases were due to the early exercise feature of American call options. In order to deal with the early exercise problem the binomial approach has been used in case the stock pays one or two dividends during the life of the options contract.

Since not all the standard deviation of the average ISD can be explained by the bid-ask spread, possible systematic biases caused by differences in time to maturity and exercise prices will be examined (information on the frequency, the average and the standard deviation for the options classes are available at the authors request). In order to show the influence of

[12] MacBeth and Merville [1979], Beckers [1981], Blomeyer and Klemkosky [1983], Brenner and Galai [1984] and Rubinstein [1985].

the bid-ask spread for the various option classes, we have also given in appendix A the bid-ask spread in terms of the ISD. We want to point out the high standard deviation of the average ISD in case of near-term in-the-money options, which can be partly explained by the bid-ask spread and by the difference in accuracy between model and market prices, mentioned earlier. Further, for most stocks the near-term out-of-the-money call options have a higher average ISD than other classes, implying an overpricing of these options.

In table 6 the average ISD's for the six main options classes and the whole sample are presented. With the number of transactions and the standard deviation of each class the Z-value has been derived. The Z-value can be used to test on differences between means of two samples with a sufficient number of observations (see Hogg and Craig [1973]).
The asterix given for the Z-value implies a significant difference between the two means at at 5%-significance level. We test on the separate influence of both variables and ignore possible interaction effects between the time to maturity and the ratio between the stock price and the exercise price[13]. In table 6 each average ISD is marked with an asterix whenever the statistic exceeded |1.96|. For example .2514* implies that this ISD is significantly different from the second and third ISD within the different stock/exercise price ratio group.

Table 6 Average ISD for different T-t and S/K

Stock	Total	Time to maturity			Stock/Exercise price		
		1	2	3	1	2	3
ABN	.2393	.2457*	.2333*	.2244*	.2514*	.2312	.2340
AGN	.2211	.2245*	.2185	.2165	.2427*	.2158*	.2225*
AH	.2245	.2317*	.2119	.2128	.2305*	.2226	.2084
AKZ	.3203	.3260*	.3159*	.3080*	.3274*	.3161	.3143
ARB	.2878	.2936*	.2894*	.2593*	.2887*	.2771*	.3132*
GIS	.2247	.2294*	.2181	.2120	.2520*	.2196*	.1964*
HEI	.2125	.2248*	.2004*	.1728*	.2243	.2058*	.2263
HO	.3514	.3470*	.3533*	.3622*	.3547*	.3509	.3493
KLM	.3742	.3790*	.3694*	.3593*	.3748*	.3562*	.4040*
NED	.2658	.2731*	.2589*	.2414*	.2810*	.2663*	.2571*
NN	.1327	.1480*	.1199*	.1127*	- **	.1298*	.1632*
PHI	.2678	.2649*	.2688*	.2706*	.2840*	.2615*	.2648*
RD	.2014	.2091*	.1963*	.1848*	.2150*	.1961*	.2103*
UNI	.1498	.1654*	.1294*	.1153*	.1684*	.1419*	.1853*

** No observations

[13] Since the number of observations differs per cell we might expect that some interaction exist.

If all averages within one group are marked with an asterix, it means that all are significantly different from each other.

We see that the near-term average ISD is always significantly different from the middle- and long-term average ISD and that the middle-term is almost always significantly different from the long-term ISD (except for AGN, AH and GIS). Also, an increase in the time to maturity leads to a decrease in the average ISD. This implies that the longer termed options are relatively undervalued compared to shorter termed options. Exceptions are the stocks HO and PHI, where the average ISD increases when the time to maturity increases. The picture for the exercise price is less clear. Again for almost all stocks the three average ISD's are significantly different from each other. However, in many cases the at-the-money options have the lowest average ISD (see ABN, AGN, ARB, HEI, KLM, NN, PHI, RD and UNI). For the remaining stocks AH, AKZ, GIS, HO and NED we see that the ISD has a tendency to decrease when the exercise price with respect to the stock price decreases. This implies that in-the-money options are underpriced relative to at-the-money and out-of-the-money options.

This analysis holds only in case the basic assumption of the Black Scholes model, a known and constant volatility, holds. When the volatility is changing over time, systematic biases with respect to time to maturity and exercise price can partly be caused by a changing volatility. In order to study the time series behaviour more closely, an average ISD has been calculated every ten days, resulting in 14 average ISD's. Some of the figures are presented here to illustrate the difference in time series behaviour between stocks. In the figures 1 - 6 on the next page the line addressed with "all" contains the average ISD's of the whole sample. The same has been done for the subsample at-the-money middle-term options, which is addressed by "sub". The total number of observations for the whole sample and the subsample are given under the name of the stock. The overall averages of the two samples are drawn in the figure on day zero. The average given by * is the average of the whole sample and the one given by □ of the subsample.

In the figures two things can be noted. First, we see that the ISD is not constant over time, but the degree of change over time is different per stock. In figure 1 the average ISD of KLM shows a dramatic increase after approximately ten weeks. In contrast, the ISD of NED in figure 2 is more

Fig. 1 KLM
9619/1808 obs

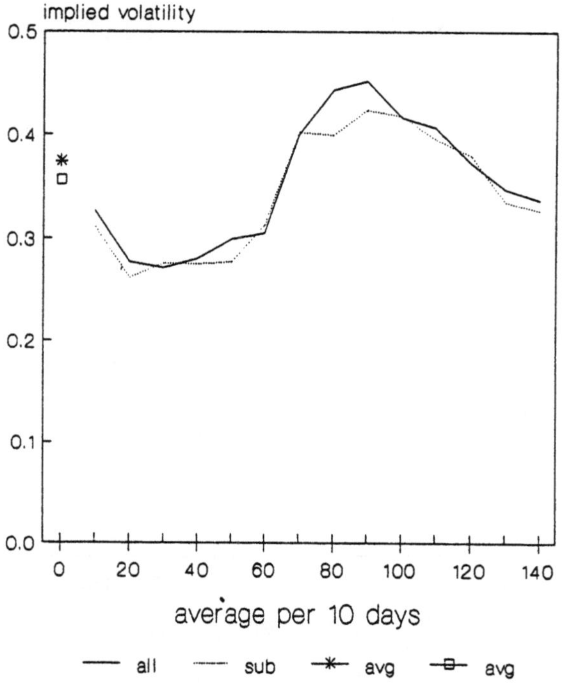

Fig. 2 NED
2509/581 obs

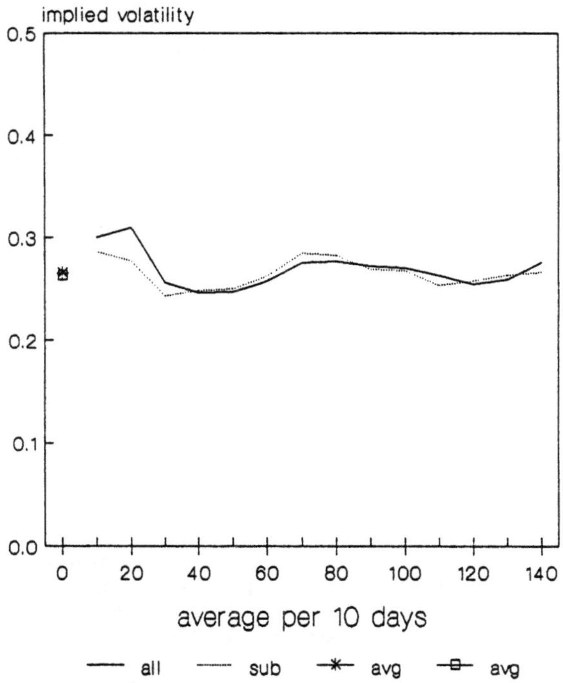

Fig. 3 HEI
2936/696 obs

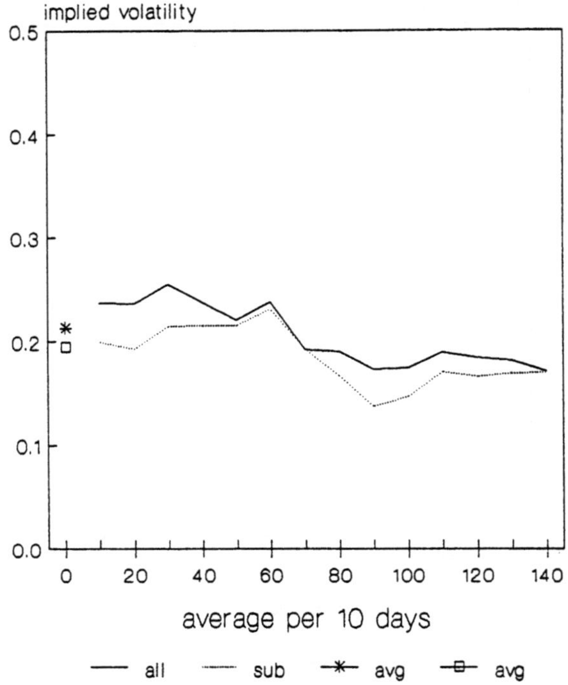

Fig. 4 UNI
2143/610 obs

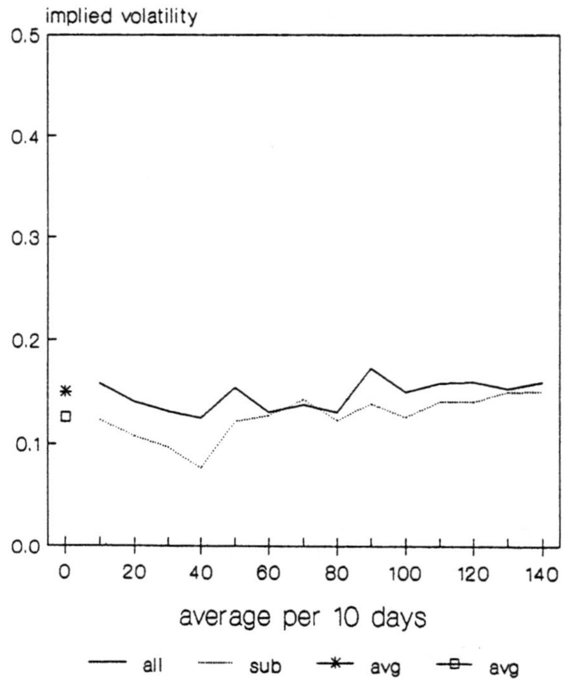

Fig. 5 AKZ
19347/3065 obs

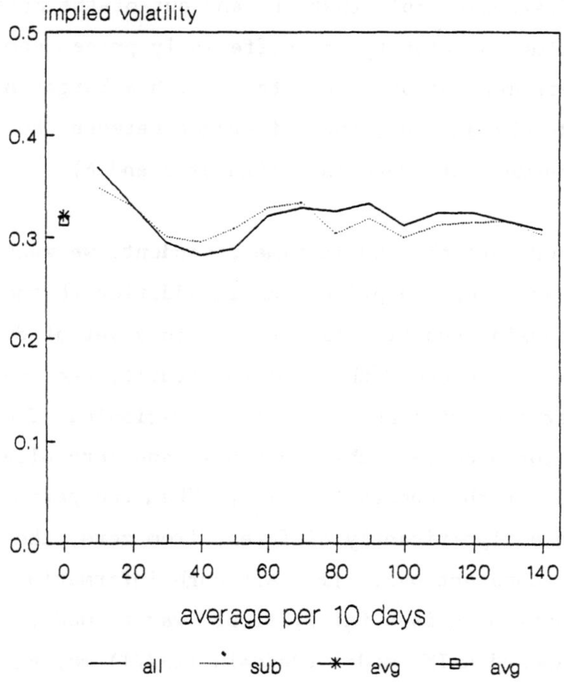

Fig. 6 PHI
16188/3422 obs

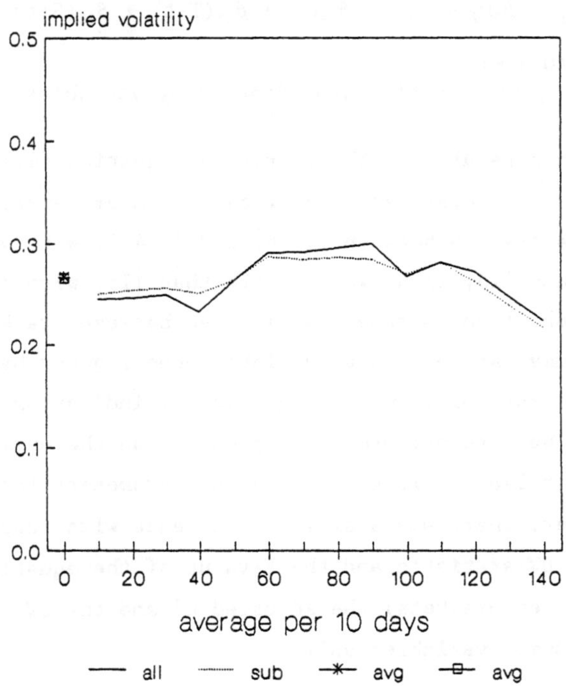

or less constant over time. Secondly, the difference in ISD for the whole sample and the subsample is large for the stocks HEI and UNI (see figures 3 and 4). Large differences imply that in- and out-of-the-money options with short or a long time to maturity are differently priced compared to at-the-money middle-termed options. For stocks with a larger number of transactions, like AKZ and PHI, the difference between the ISD's of the whole and the subsample are less (see figures 5 and 6).

Since we have found that the ISD is time dependent, we want to test on the time to maturity and exercise price bias in addition to the time factor. Therefore, a regression equation is set up with a set of dummy variables to deal with the time dependency, the time to maturity and the ratio between the stock and exercise price as explanatory variables. The dummy variables are equal to one for each ten subsequent days and zero elsewhere. The first ten days are used for the constant term β_1. When the parameters of the dummy variables are significantly different from zero, the implied volatility is not constant over time. Although information will get loss with this construction it is a fairly simple way to model the time dependency. A standard ARIMA model (Maddala [1977]) may give estimation problems due to the fact that time periods between subsequent observations are random. The regression equation is equal to:

$$(4.1)\quad ISD(t) = \beta_1 + \beta_2 D_2 + \ldots + \beta_{14} D_{14} + \beta_{15}(T-t) + \beta_{16}(S(t)/K) + e(t)$$

$e(t) \sim n(0,\sigma_e^2)$
$D_2, \ldots, D_{14}$ are the time dependent dummy variables

In table 7 the main results of the regression equation (4.1) are presented. Since most of the parameters are significant at a 5% level, the parameters are marked with a t-value between $|1.96|$ and $|4.417|$ with one asterix, between $|4.417|$ and $|15|$ with two and more than $|15|$ with three. The standard deviation of the parameters is given between brackets. The parameters of the dummy variables are available upon request by the author. Not surprisingly, most of them are significant, indicating a time dependency of the ISD's. We also performed a regression on the dummy variables only. This did not lead to largely different parameters for the dummy variables. However, there was a slight difference with respect to the adjusted R^2, the DW-statistic and the F-value of the equation. In table 7 we included (between brackets) the adjusted R^2 and the DW-statistic for the regression with dummy variables only.

In order to see whether including the time to maturity and the ratio leads to a better explanation of the ISD, we tested the H_0 hypothesis that $\beta_{15} = \beta_{16} = 0$ with an F-test. The value is given in table 7, where one asterix implies significance on a 5% level and two asterixes a 1% significance level. The F-value for a 5% significance level is given between brackets. Notice that AKZ and PHI have less observations due to the omission of the transactions with two dividend payments.

Table 7 Regression results

Stock	Number of Obs	T-t β_{15}	S/K β_{16}	adj. R^2	DW	F-test
ABN	3667	-.055** (.004)	-.012 (.009)	.477 (.451)	1.27 (1.31)	1.051 (1.055)
AGN	2638	-.019 (.005)	.128** (.013)	.321 (.289)	1.46 (1.52)	1.047 (1.065)
AH	1124	-.063** (.005)	-.186** (.017)	.354 (.209)	1.53 (1.53)	1.224** (1.101)
AKZ	19136	-.024*** (.001)	-.043** (.003)	.352 (.336)	1.50 (1.51)	1.025* (1.024)
ARB	2955	-.057** (.005)	.106** (.013)	.273 (.214)	1.52 (1.61)	1.081* (1.061)
GIS	2868	-.049** (.004)	-.216*** (.011)	.478 (.374)	1.63 (1.68)	1.200** (1.062)
HEI	2936	-.128*** (.004)	-.128** (.011)	.587 (.430)	1.41 (1.62)	1.378** (1.062)
HO	7403	.018** (.003)	.001 (.005)	.112 (.108)	1.58 (1.58)	1.004 (1.039)
KLM	9619	-.068*** (.003)	.049** (.005)	.688 (.669)	1.20 (1.26)	1.062** (1.034)
NED	2509	-.066** (.006)	.025* (.012)	.196 (.148)	1.49 (1.52)	1.060 (1.067)
NN	1018	-.073** (.007)	.170** (.031)	.269 (.152)	1.51 (1.58)	1.159** (1.106)
PHI	15565	.030*** (.002)	-.019** (.003)	.405 (.387)	1.64 (1.64)	1.026 (1.027)
RD	13654	-.048*** (.002)	-.045* (.006)	.276 (.239)	1.08 (1.10)	1.051** (1.028)
UNI	2143	-.144*** (.005)	-.131** (.017)	.417 (.161)	1.65 (1.75)	1.439** (1.072)

Despite of the dummy variables for the time dependency, the parameters for the time to maturity and the ratio S/K are significantly different from zero. From this regression it also follows that the time to maturity has a significant negative influence on the ISD, except for HO and PHI. The exercise price bias is less clear. In some cases the parameter of the ratio is significantly positive, in other cases it is significantly negative. There exists a substantial difference between various stocks with respect to the magnitude and level of significance of the regression parameters. The stocks HEI and UNI have large and very significant parameters for both the time to maturity and the ratio, an accordingly high adjusted R^2 and significant F-test value.
The significance results for the parameters will be slightly optimistic, since the DW-statistic is a bit too low. However, the DW-statistic has to be carefully interpreted, since the time series is not based on fixed points in time, but on subsequent random points in time. According to the F-test the ISD's of the stocks AH, GIS, HEI, KLM, NN, RD and UNI are significantly influenced by the time to maturity and the ratio stock/exercise price.

5. The dividend bias

An important measurement error can be caused by the estimator of the dividend payments, since the realized dividend payments are used as an estimator for the expected dividend payments. Instead of modelling the uncertainty surrounding the dividends explicitly, we only examine the difference in average ISD between transactions with and without dividend payments. Therefore, we divide our sample into transactions with and without dividend payments. In table 8 the number of transactions, the average and the standard deviation (between brackets) of the ISD for the transactions with no dividends and with one dividend payment are given. We omitted the few transactions which contained two dividend payments (only AKZ and PHI have these transactions).

Only AKZ, HEI, PHI and RD have a large subsample with one dividend payment. It also shows that for these stocks the average ISD is significantly higher for the subsample containing one dividend payment. However, as we have seen before, the ISD's are not constant over time, which means that a higher average ISD could also be caused by the fact that these transactions accidentely occur in times of high volatility.

Table 8 Average ISD for no and one dividend payment

Stock	No dividend # obs.	avg	(std)	One dividend # obs.	avg	(std)	Z-value
ABN	3,338	.2349	(.0391)	329	.2839	(.0561)	15.5*
AGN	2,313	.2165	(.0376)	325	.2541	(.0471)	13.8*
AH	1,092	.2245	(.0286)	32	.2243	(.0216)	-.1
AKZ	9,724	.3181	(.0450)	9,712	.3229	(.0285)	8.9*
ARB	2,822	.2880	(.0481)	133	.2842	(.0674)	-.6
GIS	2,832	.2248	(.0396)	36	.2218	(.0316)	-.6
HEI	2,009	.1971	(.0345)	927	.2460	(.0402)	32.0*
HO	7,196	.3512	(.0416)	207	.3597	(.0230)	5.1*
KLM	9,619	.3742	(.0743)	--	--	--	--
NED	2,454	.2661	(.0448)	55	.2482	(.0271)	-4.8*
NN	825	.1318	(.0374)	193	.1365	(.0343)	1.7
PHI	2,964	.2280	(.0459)	12,601	.2765	(.0307)	54.7*
RD	9,397	.1990	(.0296)	4,257	.2067	(.0546)	8.6*
UNI	2,112	.1497	(.0370)	31	.1546	(.0186)	1.4

We also examine the time series behaviour of the ISD's for the stocks AKZ, HEI, PHI and RD. In table 9 the average ISD for every ten days is given. The first series contains options without dividend payments during the life of the contract. The second series contains options with one dividend payment during the life of the contract. In general, the options in the second series will have a longer time to maturity[14]. The period in which a dividend payment (if any) took place is underlined.

Table 9 Times series of samples with and without dividend

Stock	Average ISD per ten days 10	20	30	40	50	60	70	80	90	100	110	120	130	140
	.38	.34	.29	.26	.27	-	-	-	-	.31	.32	.33	.32	.31
AKZ	.35	.32	.30	.30	.30	.32	.33	.33	.34	.32	.33	.32	.32	.31
	-	-	-	.22	.22	.24	.19	.19	.17	.18	.19	.19	.18	.17
HEI	.24	.24	.26	.27	-	-	-	.18	-	-	-	-	-	-
	.24	.24	.22	.20	.25	-	-	-	-	-	-	-	.23	.22
PHI	.25	.25	.26	.25	.27	.29	.29	.30	.30	.27	.28	.27	.27	.24
	-	-	-	.18	.17	.19	.21	.23	.23	.20	.20	.19	.17	.19
RD	.20	.19	.19	.23	-	-	-	.23	.22	.21	.21	.20	.19	.19

[14] Hence, there will exist some interaction effect between the dividend payments and the time to maturity.

From the time series behaviour we see that the average ISD of the subsample with one dividend payment tends to increase in the days before the ex-dividend date. After this date the average ISD is almost equal to the average ISD of the subsample without dividend payments. It seems that when the next dividend payment is far enough ahead, the average ISD's of both samples are equal. Stocks with less transactions including one dividend payment, like ABN and AGN, show the same behaviour. This implies that the bias caused by dividend payments is only temporary, especially concentrated before or on the actual dividend date.

In order to get a better understanding of the results, we have calculated the average ISD for the various options classes for the stocks AKZ, HEI, PHI and RD. The results are given in table 10. For AKZ and RD the in-the-money near-term options with one dividend payment have a high implied volatility. A closer look at the transactions data learned that especially for RD these were transactions were early exercise was very likely and many transactions took place just before the dividend date. HEI and PHI have a high volatility for all near-term options. Again it can be concluded that pricing is certainly out of line shortly before a dividend payment occurs. One reason might be that the on the dividend announcement date, the announced dividend was not equal to the expected dividend payment. However, for AKZ, HEI, RD and PHI the dividend

Table 10 Classification of average ISD

		No dividend Time to maturity			One dividend Time to maturity		
Stock	S/K	1	2	3	1	2	3
AKZ	1	.3428	.3098	--	.3363	.3180	.3106
	2	.3115	.3085	--	.3343	.3186	.3050
	3	.2883	.3110	--	.3534	.3228	.3142
HEI	1	.2148	.2122	.1793	.2692	.2187	.1900
	2	.1938	.1900	.1613	.2598	.2070	.1925
	3	.2216	.1845	.1799	.2692	.1985	.1653
PHI	1	--	.2323	--	.3118	.2818	.2686
	2	.2295	.2222	--	.2828	.2693	.2638
	3	.2230	.2432	--	.2918	.2653	.2757
RD	1	.2206	.2093	.2091	.2309	.2013	.2062
	2	.1961	.1948	.1771	.2111	.1900	.1834
	3	.2070	.1430	.1670	.3135	.2095	.1887

payments in the two years before the payment in 1984 were almost identical to the payment in 1984. It is unlikely that uncertainty on the level of the dividend payment would have been the reason for the high implied volatility of the near-term in-the-money options.

Another explanation for this behaviour might be that the parties who have written call options expect that these will be exercised early, forcing them to deliver the underlying stock. In order to prevent this, they have to close their position just before the dividend date. Due to these closing buy transactions the extra demand for call options might drive up the price of the options. On the other side, the party who has bought the options in the past has an extra reason to exercise just before the dividend date, since it takes three weeks before the party has to pay for the stock. In the meantime, the dividends can be collected and the stock sold, implying no investment outlay for the stock during this transaction.

In order to test the additional bias in the ISD caused by the dividend payments, we add a dividend correction to regression equation (4.1) as follows:

$$(5.1)\quad ISD(t) = \beta_1 + \beta_2 D_2 + \ldots + \beta_{14} D_{14} + \beta_{15}(T-t) + \beta_{16}(S(t)/K) + \text{dum}\times(D_1 + \beta_2 D_2 + \ldots + \beta_{14} D_{14} + \beta_{15}(T-t) + \beta_{16}(S(t)/K)) + e(t)$$

$e(t) \sim n(0,\sigma_e^2)$
$D_2, \ldots, D_{14}$ are the time dependent dummy variables
dum = 0 for no dividend and is equal to 1 for one dividend

The results are presented in table 11. In the column including the number of observations the first row of each stock contains the subsample without dividend payments and the second row the subsample with one dividend payment. The number of asterixes have the same interpretation as in the previous regression. The adjusted R^2 and DW-statistic of regression equation (4.1) are given between brackets. The value for the F-test is based on the MSE's of equation (4.1) compared to (5.1). If the value is significant, it implies that dividend payments offer a significant explanation to the level of the ISD's.

From the results it follows that the stocks with a significant higher ISD containing one dividend payment have a significant F-value (at the 1% level) here. All significant parameters for the time to maturity show a negative sign for the one dividend dummy ($\text{dum}\times\beta_{15}$). Noticable is the change in sign for PHI: the subsample containing one dividend payment has a negative bias with respect to the time to maturity. The change in sign for the time to maturity for PHI is mainly caused by the high ISD's of the near-term options. AKZ, HEI and RD show a remarkable positive bias for the ratio in case of one dividend payment (dumxβ_{16}). This is caused by the high ISD for the in-the-money options.

Table 11 Regression results including a dividend corrector

Stock	Number of Obs	T-t	S/K	dum*T-t	dum*S/K	adj R^2	DW	F-test
ABN	3,338 329	-.059** (.004)	.003 (.009)	-.126** (.014)	.042* (.018)	.564 (.477)	1.45 (1.27)	1.198** (1.055)
AGN	2,313 325	-.009 (.006)	.139** (.013)	-.160** (.015)	.082** (.014)	.395 (.321)	1.52 (1.46)	1.122** (1.065)
AH	1,092 31	-.096*** (.006)	-.199** (.016)	-.887** (.186)	.509** (.105)	.419 (.354)	1.47 (1.53)	1.113* (1.101)
AKZ	9,724 9,412	-.044** (.003)	-.072*** (.003)	-.072*** (.004)	.066*** (.004)	.440 (.352)	1.43 (1.50)	1.157** (1.024)
ARB	2,822 133	-.074** (.006)	.105** (.012)	-.065 (.053)	.012 (.039)	.297 (.273)	1.54 (1.52)	1.035 (1.061)
GIS	2,832 36	-.056** (.004)	-.220*** (.011)	-.997* (.087)	.056* (.055)	.486 (.478)	1.64 (1.63)	1.014 (1.062)
HEI	2,009 927	-.100*** (.005)	-.173** (.013)	-.110** (.008)	.162** (.020)	.662 (.587)	1.59 (1.41)	1.222** (1.062)
HO	7,196 207	.021** (.004)	.000 (.005)	-.093 (.093)	.046 (.051)	.114 (.112)	1.58 (1.58)	1.002 (1.039)
KLM	9,619	-.068*** (.003)	.049** (.005)	--	--	.688	1.20	--
NED	2,454 55	-.072** (.006)	.026* (.012)	.240 (.235)	-.137* (.132)	.198 (.196)	1.49 (1.49)	1.002 (1.067)
NN	825 193	-.080** (.009)	.180** (.031)	-.037* (.017)	-.007 (.031)	.327 (.269)	1.60 (1.51)	1.086 (1.106)
PHI	2,964 12,601	.020* (.008)	-.012* (.003)	-.034** (.008)	-.002 (.005)	.457 (.405)	1.65 (1.64)	1.095** (1.027)
RD	9,397 4,257	-.026** (.003)	.014* (.007)	-.096*** (.004)	.127*** (.008)	.353 (.276)	1.10 (1.08)	1.199** (1.028)
UNI	2,112 31	-.170*** (.005)	-.155** (.016)	-.053 (.195)	.064 (.111)	.459 (.417)	1.60 (1.65)	1.079* (1.072)

6. Conclusion

In this paper we have tested the model validity using EOE transactions data on stock call options. If the option pricing model shows systematic biases with respect to the market prices, this can be attributed to model misspecifications, inefficiencies in both stock and/or options market and nonsynchronous data. By using transactions data we have tried to eliminate the problem of nonsynchronous data. What remains is the joint test of market efficiency and model specification. In that sense the results of this paper are limited, since we did not test market efficiency separately.

In order to find systematic biases model and market prices have been compared through the implied volatility. If it is assumed that the Black-Scholes model and the required assumptions are valid, and that stock and options markets are synchronous and efficient, then the implied volatility should be equal across different transactions. This means that the ISD should be equal for various stock and exercise prices, for different times to maturity and for possible dividend payments.

An important measurement error is caused by the bid-ask spread of the option price. Part of the fluctuation in the ISD can be explained by the bid-ask spread. Further, it was shown that time to maturity leads to a systematic negative bias, whereas the sign of the ratio differs per stock. However, part of the results are biased, since there exists a strong time dependency among different ISD's over time. In the sample period the ISD's of most stocks were not constant over time, and, furthermore, are temporarely influenced by dividend payments. Especially near-term in-the-money options just before a dividend payment showed significantly higher ISD's.

We can conclude this paper with the rejection of the joint hypothesis of a correct model specification and market efficiency. There exist systematic biases, although not all of them are equally strong for each stock. Suggestions for further research will be in the direction of an ex-ante test on market efficiency, although some preliminary work suggests that the database should be extended in order to obtain more data. The same problem applies for possible interesting non-parametric tests as performed by Rubinstein [1985]. Although these tests are very attractive, they require more transactions than available in the database.

REFERENCES

Beckers, S., 1981, Standard Deviations Implied in Option Prices as Predictors of Future Stock Price Variability, *Journal of Banking and* Finance *5, 363-381.*
Beckers, S., 1984, On the Efficiency of the Gold Options Market, *Journal* of *Banking and Finance* **8**, 459-470.
Bhattacharya, M., 1980, Empirical Properties of the Black-Scholes Formula under Ideal Conditions, *Journal of Financial and Quantitative* Analysis *15, 1081-1105.*
Bhattacharya, M., 1987, Price Changes of Related Securities: The Case of Stock Call Options and Stocks, *Journal of Financial and Quantitative* Analysis *1, 1-15.*
Bjorck, A. and G. Dahlquist, 1974, *Numerical Methods*, Prentice Hall.
Black, F. and M. Scholes, 1973, The Pricing of Options and Corporate Liabilities, *Journal of Political Economics* **81**, 637-659.
Blomeyer, E.C. and R.C. Klemkosky, 1983, Test of Market Efficiency for American Call Options, in M. Brenner, ed., *Option Pricing*, Lexington, Mass.:D.C. Heath, 101-121.
Brenner, M. and D. Galai, 1984, On Measuring the Risk of Common Stocks Implied by Options Prices:A Note, *Journal of Financial and* Quantitative Analysis *19, 403-412.*
Dickinson, J.P. and M.J. Nisbet, 1987, Pricing in the London Traded Options Markt: An Empirical Study, *University of Glasgow* Workingpaper, presented at the EFA in Madrid.
Galai, D., 1977, Tests of Market Efficiency of the Chicago Board Option Exchange, *Journal of Business* **50**, 167-197.
Galai, D., 1983, A Survey of Empirical Tests of Option Pricing Models, in M. Brenner, ed., *Option Pricing*, Lexington, Mass.:D.C. Heath, 45-80.
Geske, R., 1977, The Valuation of Corporate Liabilities as Compound Options, *Journal of Financial and Quantitative Analysis* **4**, 541-552.
Geske, R. and R. Roll, 1984, On Valuing American Call options with the Black-Scholes European Formula, *Journal of Finance* **39**, 443-455.
Hogg, R.V. and A.T. Craig, 1973, *Introduction to Mathematical Statistics*, 3rd edition, Collier MacMillan Publishers London.
MacBeth, J. and L. Merville, 1979, An Empirical Examination of the Black-Scholes Call Option Pricing Model, *Journal of Finance* **34**, 1173-1186.
Maddala, G.S.,1977, Econometrics, McGraw-Hill, N.Y..
Phillips, S.M. and C.W. Smith, 1980, Trading Costs for Listed Options, *Journal of* Financial Economics *8, 179-201.*
Rubinstein, M., 1985, Nonparametric Tests of Alternative Option Pricing Models Using all Reported Trades and Quotes on the 30 Most Active CBOE Option Classes from August 23, 1976 through August 31, 1978 *Journal of* Finance *2, 455-480.*
Sterk, W.E., 1983, Comparative Performance of the Black-Scholes and the Roll-Geske-Whaley Option Pricing Models, *Journal of Financial and Quantitative Analysis* 3, 345-354.
Van der Hilst, J., 1980, Marktefficiency op de EOE te Amsterdam, F.J. Ballendux e.a., red., *Financiering en Belegging, stand van zaken anno* 1980, *Erasmus Universiteit Rotterdam, 128-138.*
Whaley, R.E., 1982, Valuation of American Call Options on Dividend-Paying Stocks, *Journal of Financial Economics* **10**, 29-58.

THE PRICING OF EUROMARKET WARRANTS ON JAPANESE STOCKS

A PRELIMINARY STUDY

Gordon Gemmill
City University Business School
Frobisher Crescent
Barbican Centre
London EC2Y 8HB

KEYWORDS/ABSTRACT: warrants/options/markets/efficiency/Japan/volatility/mean-reversion/arbitrage

From October 1981 to April 1988 Japanese companies made 671 issues, outside their domestic market, of bonds with warrants. Of these, 382 were in dollars and had a face value of $37 billion. This paper examines the motives for the issue and purchase of these warrants. It then develops a simple model for pricing them, taking account of the cost of shorting the stock. The prevailing view is that the warrants are (inefficiently) under-priced. Arbitrage tests on time-series for 54 warrants confirm some inefficiency, although this has declined through time. Use of the model on time-series for 6 warrants indicates that implied volatility declines siginificantly with time to maturity. However, the very wide deviations of implied from historic volatilities suggest either a mis-specified model or an inefficient market. Further research is needed to separate these two hypotheses.

This paper was begun while the author was visiting the University of Aix-Marseille II. He is grateful to Kevin Connolly and Jonathan Knight of James Capel Ltd for the provision of data and advice. He also acknowledges the contribution of Tetsu Ozaki in his MBA thesis of 1986.

NATO ASI Series, Vol. F54
A Reappraisal of the Efficiency of Financial Markets
Edited by Rui M. C. Guimaraes et al.

1. INTRODUCTION

Japanese companies have been issuing bonds with warrants since October 1981, following an amendment of Commercial Law. However, the Japanese Security Business Association decided that the warrants would not be detachable and only in November 1985 was that restriction removed. Thereafter there was a large increase in the number of issues. By 1.8.86 there had been 139 dollar issues, 108 Swiss Franc issues, and 31 DM issues, all in the euromarket, (see Table 1). Additionally, there were 27 Yen issues in the Japanese market. By April 1st 1988 the total of dollar issues had reached $37 billion.

Table 1 Issues of Japanese Equity Warrants

	At 1st August 1986		At 1st April 1988	
Denominated Currency	Outstanding Amount(mil.)	Number of issues	Outstanding Amount(mil.)	Number of issues
U.S. $	9200	139	36664	382
SF	6600	108	11168	239
DM	2600	31	3550	40
ECU	100	1	180	3
#	50	2	50	2
YEN	220000(1)	27(1)	20(2)	1(2)

Sources: 1986 Nomura International
1988 James Capel Ltd.

Notes:

(1) Domestic Yen issues, including 14 undetachables
(2) These were euromarket issues of Yen

In the first few years of trading there was a prevailing view among analysts in London that the warrants were greatly undervalued. If the warrants were undervalued at issue, the question arises of why companies were willing to write warrants? They must have been foregoing potential income, unless there were a mutual arbitrage gain for both the issuer and the buyer.

The main objective of this paper is to examine the hypothesis of inefficient pricing. In order to do that, it is first necessary to develop an appropriate pricing model, given the particular characteristics of Japanese warrants. We therefore begin by looking at the motives for issuing and for buying these warrants. We then develop an arbitrage-based model, which gives a lower bound for the warrant price. Arbitrage tests of the lower bound are made using a sample of 54 warrants observed weekly, spanning the period November 1983 to February 1988. The model is then used to examine the behaviour of the implied volatility relative to the historic volatility on a sample of 6 warrants, to see how well it fits the data and to test the hypothesis that volatility declines with time to maturity.

There appears to have been relatively little published research on warrant pricing. Early papers which used the Black and Scholes framework were concerned to show the impact of dividends (Schwartz, 1976) and the effect of dilution (Galai and Schneller, 1978). Green (1977) indicated the potentially beneficial impact on managerial incentives of warrants as compared with simple bonds. Emanuel (1984) and Constantinides (1984) both indicated that optimal exercise may not be at a single date. There have been almost no empirical studies of warrants. Patterson (1986) was concerned with the speed with which warrant prices adjusted to changed stock prices. Meier (1987) indicated that implied volatility declines with time to maturity, using a small sample of Swiss warrants observed at two dates.

It should be noted that this paper reports on the first stage of a larger piece of research. The results are therefore more suggestive than definitive, but their presentation should help to improve the further analyses.

2. MOTIVES FOR ISSUING WARRANTS (THE SUPPLY SIDE)

Since warrants have value, issuing debt with warrants reduces the cost of the debt. A risky company may prefer to issue warrants than to pay a very high coupon on its debt. On the other hand, the exercise of warrants dilutes the equity of the company, so issuing warrants may be against the interest of the existing shareholders. As shareholders are sensitive to dilution, one might expect that warrants would be issued by small and relatively risky companies, for whom warrants have a double benefit: the riskiness of the share increases the warrant value and so reduces the coupon required on the bond. As the warrants are attached to the bonds at issue, management may be signalling to the new bondholders that it intends to follow a more risky strategy than heretofore. The warrants then compensate for the lower bond value which this strategy implies.

These arguments cannot explain the issue of Japanese warrants, because small and speculative companies are not allowed to make issues. Underwriters have a rule which protects both them and investors from "improper" risk. This rule limits companies which can issue warrants to a minimum size, profitability, interest coverage and pay-out ratio. Japanese issuers are therefore large companies which are already capable of borrowing money at reasonable cost without any "sweetener". The shareholders are mainly banks, which have seldom intervened actively in the running of the companies and do not appear to have resisted the dilution of their shareholding via the issue (and exercise) of warrants and convertibles.

The warrants are issued just out-of-the-money, with a life of several years, so they are almost certain to be exercised. Issuing warrants is therefore somewhat like making a deferred rights issue, with payment of the present value today. The Japanese companies are however strong enough to make rights issues immediately, if they wish, so that does not explain the rash of warrants.

One reason for the issue of Japanese warrants may be an unusual law concerning new shares. If an existing company raises new funds by issuing shares at the current market price, the difference between the face value of the share and the current price is regarded as an "improper" cash inflow, which is not really the property of the company. The company must therefore return this improper "premium" to the existing shareholders gradually through time, usually by giving the shareholders extra shares at no cost.(1)

On closer inspection, however, the effect of the deferred payment of the "premium" would appear to be marginal in its impact. The gain is that the warrant value is obtained immediately, but that is small anyway relative to the value of the shares which are issued when the warrants are exercised.

If none of the above arguments for issuing warrants is persuasive, there remains the simple argument that the demand for these instruments is such that their issue does not affect the share price, whereas issuing shares directly would do so. This does not imply that the warrants are necessarily mispriced at issue, but that there is a clientele effect: buyers of warrants would not normally buy the shares directly. This leads us on to the next section in which we examine the motives for buying these instruments.

3. MOTIVES FOR BUYING WARRANTS (THE DEMAND SIDE)

There are no organised markets in options on Japanese stocks, so to obtain a levered position in such a stock one can either borrow in order to buy the stock, or one can buy a warrant on the stock. Buying warrants may be the cheaper and administratively more convenient of the two strategies . While the spreads on warrants are about 5% as compared with about 2 1/2% for Japanese equities, buyers of options gain the benefit of limited downside risk. Buyers of warrants therefore obtain a call on the diluted stock, a position which cannot be directly obtained in any other way, (but which can be replicated by a delta-ratioed position in the share).

4. AN EXAMPLE OF A DOLLAR DENOMINATED WARRANT

Before discussing in detail the "fair" price for a warrant, it is essential that the nature of the instrument be understood. Suppose that a Japanese company wishes to issue five-year debt with warrants. We assume that:

- the current share price is 439 yen;
- the current exchange rate is 150 yen per dollar;
- LIBOR is 7%.

It is customary to set the exercise price 2.5% above the current share price, so in this case it would be 1.025 x 439 = 450 yen.

In order to decide the value of the warrant, the issuer then typically reasons as follows. He begins by calculating the present value of the expected future pay-off. Firstly a growth rate for the value of the share is assumed, say 5% in our example. Thus the expected share price in five years' time is 439 x (1.05)^5 = 560.29 yen. The expected profit for buyers of warrants is therefore 560.29 - 450 = 110.29 yen in five years' time. If the appropriate discount rate for the company is 7%, the present value of the warrant is 78.63 yen.

Commercial Law requires that the value of the new shares issued via the warrant should not exceed the face value of the bond. Let us assume that the face value of the bond is $5,000 and that the "warrantability" is one, i.e. the capital raised from exercise of a warrant exactly equals the face value of the bond. We already know that the exercise price is 450 yen, but to convert this to dollars we need a fixed exchange rate, such as $150 per yen. The number of shares per warrant is then (5000 x 150)/450) = 1,667.

Now we can find the total yen value of a warrant: it is the warrant value per share (78.63 yen) times the number of shares per warrant (1,667), equalling 131076.2 yen . If the current exchange rate is 150 yen/$ then the "theoretical" value of the warrant at issue is $873.04, or about 17.5% of the face value of the $5,000 bond. It is quoted per $100 of bond, so the quoted price would be 17.5.

This procedure is expressed more formally in the Appendix, where we obtain,

$$w = W \times 100 \times Q \times (FF/E) \times (1/FC). \quad (6)$$

where w is the warrant price ($) per $100 of bond
W is the yen warrant value per share
Q is the warrantability (capital raised by exercise relative to bond capital)
FF is the fixed exchange rate
E is the yen exercise price
FC is the current exchange rate.

The above procedure for valuing a warrant at issue is consistent with the principles of options pricing in all but three aspects. The first is that it takes no account of the probability distribution of the pay-off. The second is that the exercise of the warrants will result in a dilution of the stock. The dilution on Japanese warrants is, however, small, seldom more than 2 or 3%, so this error is likely to be minor. The third aspect is that the warrant is priced in dollars and it is implicitly assumed that the exchange rate at maturity will be the same as at the time of issue. If the forward rate for the date of maturity were lower than at issue, e.g. 120 yen per dollar as compared with 150 at issue, then if the warrant were issued at par it would be possible to capture an expected gain of PV[(150 - 120)/ 150] x 100 percent by buying the warrant and selling dollars forward. Given that since 1985 the forward dollar has been weak relative to the yen, it is small wonder that the new issues quickly went to a premium over the issue price.

5. PRICING MODELS FOR DOLLAR WARRANTS ON JAPANESE SHARES

The lower bound to the price of a call on a Japanese stock, for which the currency is the yen, is,

$$C >= \max[0, S - PV(E)]. \quad (7)$$

For simplicity we will henceforth omit the zero condition and write,

$$C >= S - PV(E). \quad (8)$$

When the continuous interest rate is R we have,

$$C >= S - Ee^{-Rt}. \quad (9)$$

If the stock pays a continuous dividend d, then

$$C >= Se^{-dt} - Ee^{-Rt}. \quad (10)$$

There are significant costs of going short in Japanese stocks, which mean that the above will not be the true lower bound. These costs, or difficulties, include:

(i) proceeds from short selling are not paid-out, so the arbitrage involving the purchase of the call and the sale of the stock requires capital;

(ii) the rate of interest paid on the proceeds from the short sale is less than the market rate of interest. For example in September 1986 the rate on a short position was 2.25% while the rate on 6-month certificates of deposit was 4.85%. The rate on the short position is also variable and not known in advance. It is paid by Japan Security Finance and varies with market conditions with respect to supply and demand for short positions;

(iii) a short position can only be maintained for six months, after which it must either be eliminated or rolled over, incurring extra risk;

(iv) a short position is subject to margin calls, in the event of increased share prices.

These conditions are not uncommon in other markets, but they are probably more severe in Japan. The arbitrage bound may therefore need to be modified to take account of the difference between market rates and rates on short positions:

$$C >= Se^{(r-R-d)t} - Ee^{-Rt}, \quad (11)$$

where r is the rate paid on short positions, so that R-r is the rate foregone from shorting.

This revised bound is plotted in Figure 1. It starts on the share-price axis to the right of PV(E) and has a slope of $e^{(r-R-d)}$, which is less than one.

Whether the revised bound is to the left or right of (S-E) will depend on r and d. If r<d, i.e. the interest paid on short postions is less than the dividend yield, then (S-E) always exceeds the revised bound. To see this we may equate the two bounds and solve for S:

$$S - E = Se^{(r-R-d)} - Ee^{-Rt},$$

$$S = E[(1-e^{-Rt})/(1-e^{(r-R-d)t})]. \quad (12)$$

If r=d then the two bracketed parts of the equation are equal, so that S=E, implying that the revised bound would originate at E along the S axis. For values of d in excess of r, the revised bound will move further to the right along the S axis.

To put this in context, r is generally in the range 2-3%, while d for Japanese stocks is about 1%. This means that the revised bound is likely to originate to the left of E along the S axis and to cut the S-E bound, (as drawn in Figure 1).

We may now write a modified Black/Scholes formula based upon this bound, which will be:

$$C = Se^{(r-R-d)} N(d1) - Ee^{-Rt} N(d2), \quad (13)$$

where N(d1) and N(d2) are the usual standard normal values, d1 and d2 being adjusted by replacing S with the discounted S value.

The above equation should provide a "minimum" price in yen for the warrant. If the cost of shorting is assumed to

Figure 1 Lower Bounds to the Warrant Price

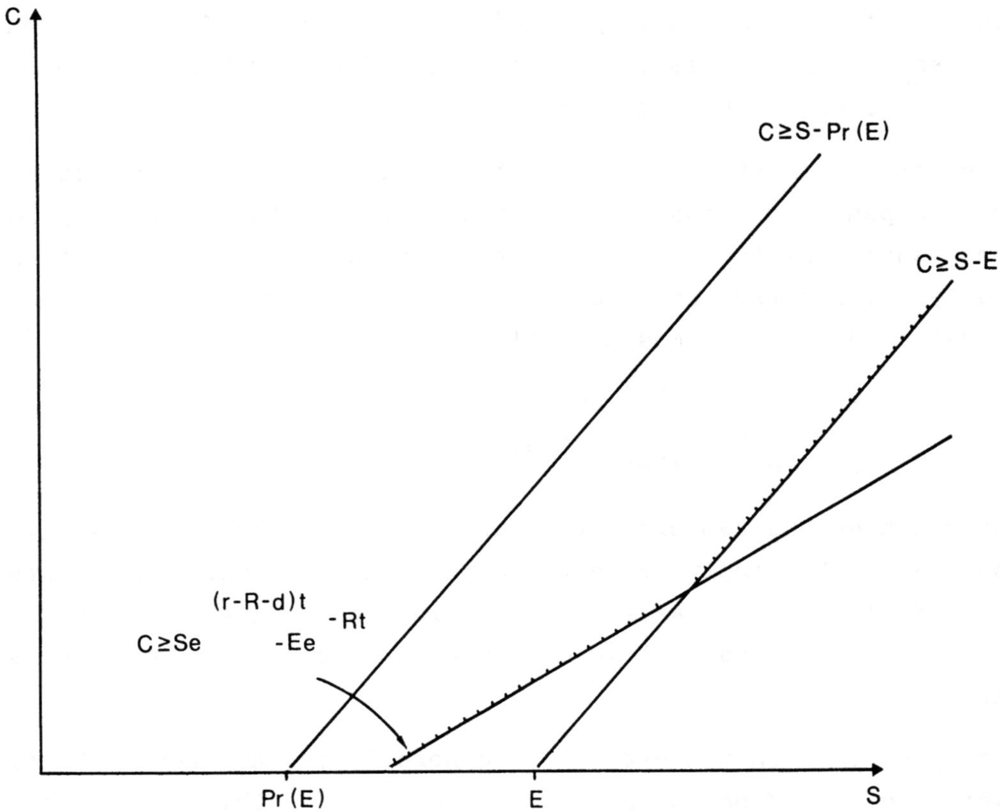

Note:

The effective bound is shown as

be zero, we obtain the standard Merton dividend-adjusted price, which might be considered the truly "fair" price. It is "fair" because the analysis so far has ignored the possibility that holders of the share decide to sell it and buy warrants instead. They experience no cost of shorting, so their "fair" price will be higher than the modified price from above. In the empirical analysis which follows we accordingly calculate both "minimum" and "fair" prices.

One final consideration is that the warrants are quoted in dollars, yet we have proceeded as if they were simple yen warrants. The fact that they are denominated in dollars is immaterial. While they call for yen-denominated assets at yen-denominated exercise prices, at any time the dollar and yen prices of the warrants must be equated via the spot exchange rate. Hence the interest rate to apply is a yen rate and the analysis is greatly simplified relative to one in which currency risks must be accommodated.

6. DATA

A sample of 54 warrants was obtained from James Capel Ltd, all of which had not expired by 15th February 1988. The sample consisted of Friday closing observations of warrant prices per $100 of bond and contemporaneous stock prices and exchange rates. The sample was chosen to give a spread of maturities and extent of "in-the-moneyness". The distribution of maturities is shown in Table 2.

Table 2 Information on Sample Warrants

Distribution by year of maturity:	88	89	90	91	92	93	94	95	96
	3	9	4	12	16	5	4	0	1

Distribution by S/E on 15.2.88	<.50	<.75	<1.00	<1.25	<1.50	>1.50
	0	3	18	11	11	11

7.ARBITRAGE TESTS

Two lower bound tests were made. The first took into account the cost of shorting and has already been presented as Equation (11). The second did not take account of the cost of shorting and has been presented as Equation (10). The second bound is the usual one for call options and is a more severe test.

The sample gave 4759 individual observations of warrant prices. Of these 454 (9.5%) failed to satisfy the first bound and 1262 (26.5%) failed to satisfy the second bound. Arbitrages were more prevalent in some series than in others and this is indicated by the finding that on average within a series 5.5% of the observations failed the first test and 17.0% failed the second test. Such a failure rate, even on the weaker test, is much higher than has been found in traded-options markets, (see e.g. Galai, 1978), and must cast doubt on the efficiency of this market.

Despite the above findings, it remains to explain why 25 of the series contained no arbitrages at all. Two alternative hypotheses were investigated. The first was that the existence of arbitages was associated with warrants for which we have more observations, indicating that inefficiency existed in early periods but not later periods. The second was that arbitrages were associated with a lack of foreign listing/ownership of the shares, resulting in liquidity problems. Cross-sectional regressions were used to test these hypotheses.

Beginning with the test of foreign listing/ownership, there was no significant association between these two variables and the existence of arbitrages. However, there were significant positive associations between both kinds of arbitrage and the length of series for each warrant.

The estimated relationships were,

$$\text{ARB1} = -3.415 + \underset{(5.08)}{0.101}\ \text{LENGTH} \qquad R^2 = 0.332$$

$$ARB2 = -3.547 + \underset{(6.82)}{0.233}\ LENGTH \qquad R^2 = 0.472$$

N=54

where ARB1 is the number of type 1 arbitrages
ARB2 is the number of type 2 arbitrages
LENGTH is the number of observations in a series
N is the number of observations (warrants)
and numbers in brackets are t values.

8. PRELIMINARY MODEL TESTS

Preliminary analyses of three warrants using the "lower-bound" and "fair" models, as defined above, gave rather mixed results. The three warrants were observed two-weekly over the period 10/85 to 8/86. They were Toray, with eighteen months to maturity, Mitsubishi Corporation with three years to maturity and Mitsubishi Estate with seven years to maturity. The volatilities used were based on three years of observations.

Figures 2 to 4 summarise the results. For Mitsubishi Corporation, (Figure 2), there was a very close relationship between the observed warrant price and the channel of model prices. Generally the warrant price was close to the model lower-bound price, (based upon the cost of shorting), but it also drifted up on occasion and breached the fair bound once in 1986.

The results for Toray (Figure 3) and Mitsubishi Estate (Figure 4) were not so encouraging. For Toray, the warrant which had only 18 months to maturity at the beginning of the sample period, the market price was usually (but not always) above the fair bound. In the last weeks of the period its behaviour was somewhat wild: sometimes near or above the fair bound and sometimes below the lower bound. For Mitsubishi Estate (Figure 4) the results were more

Figure 2: MITSUBISHI CORPORATION

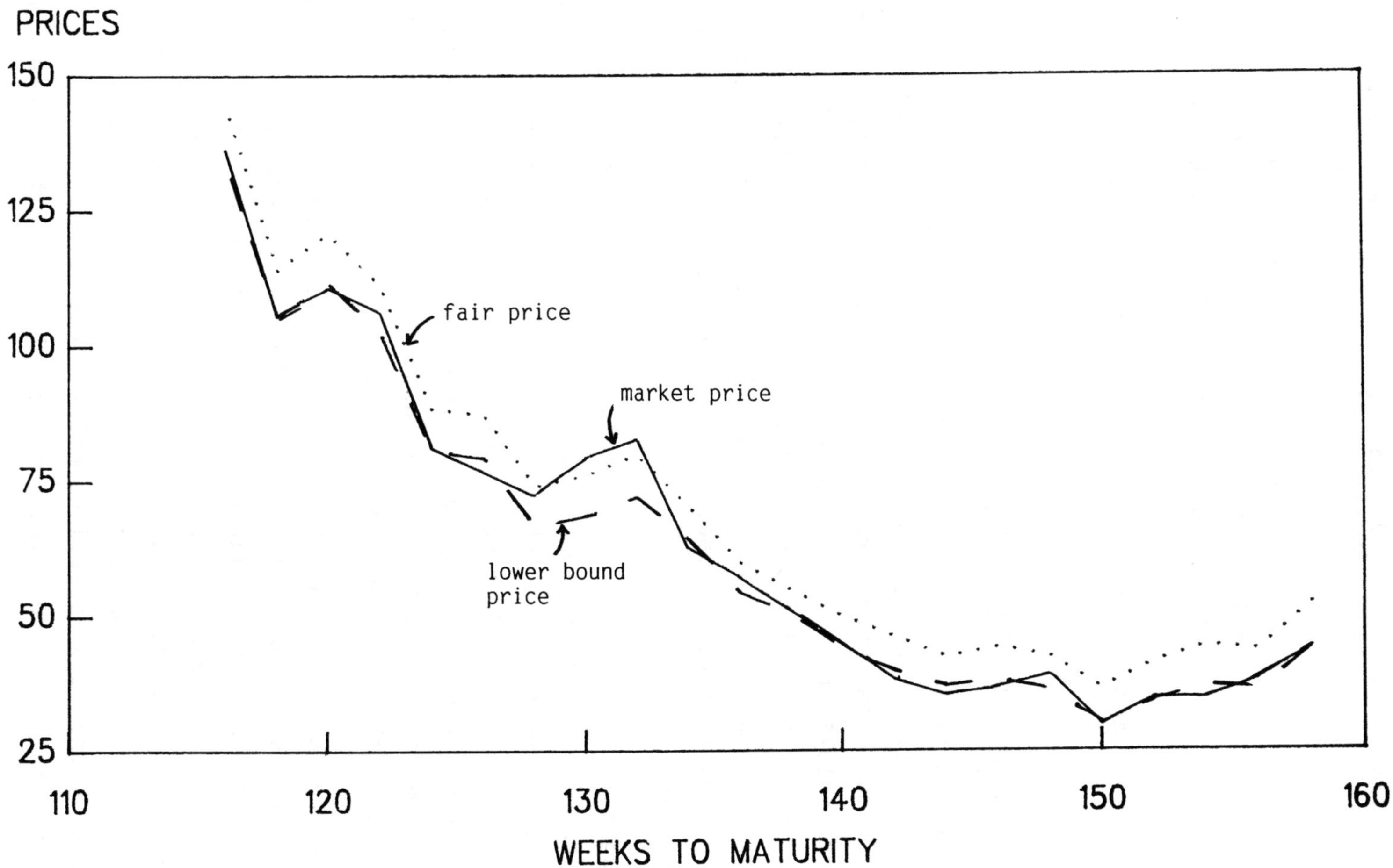

Figure 3: TORAY

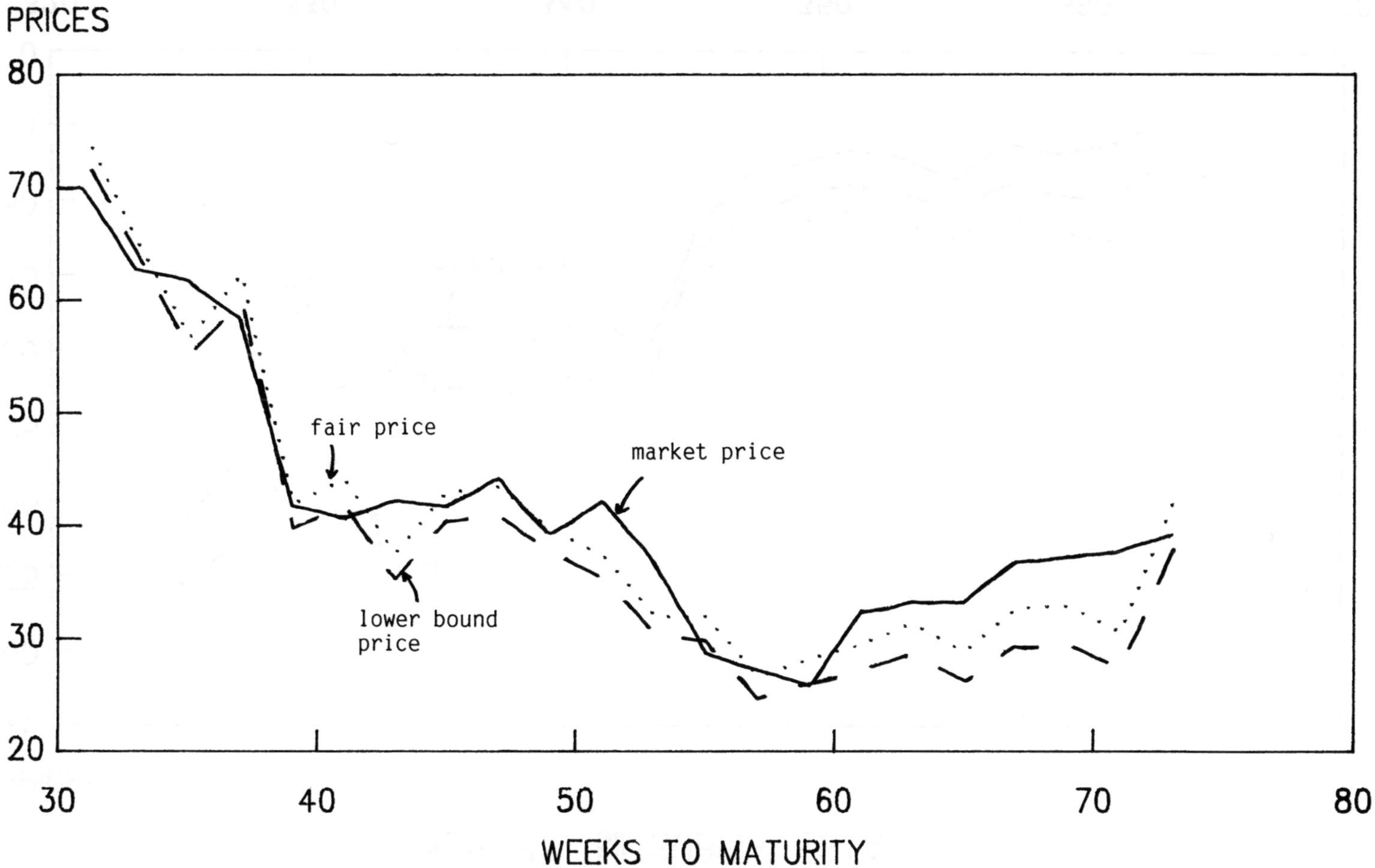

Figure 4: MITSUBISHI ESTATE

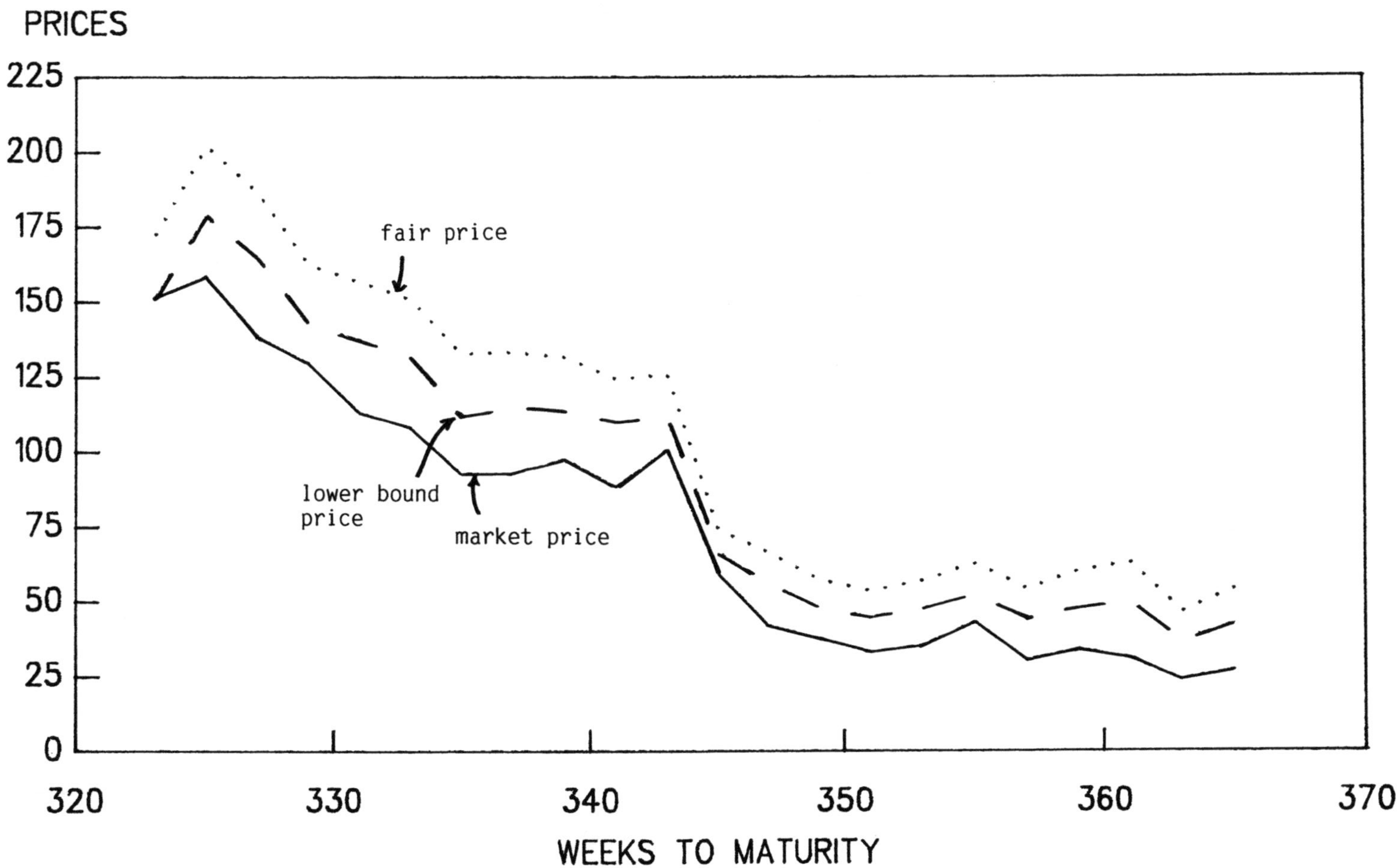

consistent: the market price was 10 to 30% below the model minimum price except in the last period.

The explanation of why we were able to model well the behaviour of Mitsubishi Corporation but not the other two warrants lies in the choice of volatility. Mitsubishi Corporation had about three years to maturity and we used a three-year estimated volatility. The Toray volatility was higher (but rather wild) than the three-year estimate, while the Mitsubishi Estate volatility was much lower. For example, the implied volatility of the latter was fairly consistently about 0.26, using the lower-bound model, whereas the three-year volatility which we used was 0.469.

The conclusion is that understanding how volatility is related to maturity is a crucial precursor to modelling warrant prices and then testing for market efficiency. The remainder of this paper is therefore concerned with examining this relationship.

9. ANALYSIS OF VOLATILITY

There are strong theoretical and empirical grounds for the view that variance will not increase linearly with time, i.e. that annualised volatility will decline with increasing maturity. The theory derives from papers by Samuelson (1965, 1976) in which it is argued that asset prices are determined by expectations. Information which affects these expectations arrives at random and so the asset prices will move randomly. However, at a sufficiently distant horizon expectations will reflect a "normal" level of price which will be rather stable, so that the expected price at that horizon will move very little. If these expectations are rational, then the subsequent spot-price distribution will show mean reversion. The paper by Poterba and Summers (1988) demonstrates this phenomenon in spot prices for various equity markets including that of Japan, (and reviews the recent work by others on this subject).

Studies of futures prices on commodities tend to confirm that distant expectations are stable, (see e.g. Rutledge, 1976, Grammatikos and Saunders, 1986). It has also been rather consistently observed that there is a tendency for Black/Scholes options prices to overvalue distant options, (see e.g. Galai, 1987, for a review of empirical work and Rubinstein (1985) for evidence on out-of-the-money options), indicating the possibility of declining volatility.[(2)] More recently Ball and Torous (1987) examined futures options on sugar, DM and gold at various maturities. They found the expected decline in implied volatility with maturity for sugar and DM, but not for gold. However, the latter result would appear to be spurious because they did not allow for the generally-rising volatility of spot-gold over the sample period. Meier (1987) found a significant decline in volatility for Swiss equity warrants with maturity, but he observed only two dates in cross-section.

We hypothesise that annualised volatility declines with time to maturity in the manner indicated in Figure 5. The Y-axis is implied annual volatility relative to volatility of the spot asset and the X-axis is time to maturity of the option. With no time remaining the volatility of the warrant equals that of the asset. At some very long maturity the volatility declines asymptotically to a lower bound. The figure has a dotted portion closer to maturity because our tests were only made for longer maturities. The reason for this is that closer to maturity the warrants were so far into the money that implied volatilities became meaningless.

10. VOLATILITY RESULTS

Initially ten warrants were chosen for this analysis. Of these four were eliminated: three because the series were too short to be useful and one (Komori Printing) because it is said to be grossly abnormal in its behaviour.[(3)] The six remaining warrants were (with expiry date): Mitsubishi 11/88, Sony 04/90, Toray 12/90, Itoh 07/92, Glory 06/93 and Mitsubishi Estate 10/88.

Figure 5 Hypothesised Relationship of Volatility to Maturity

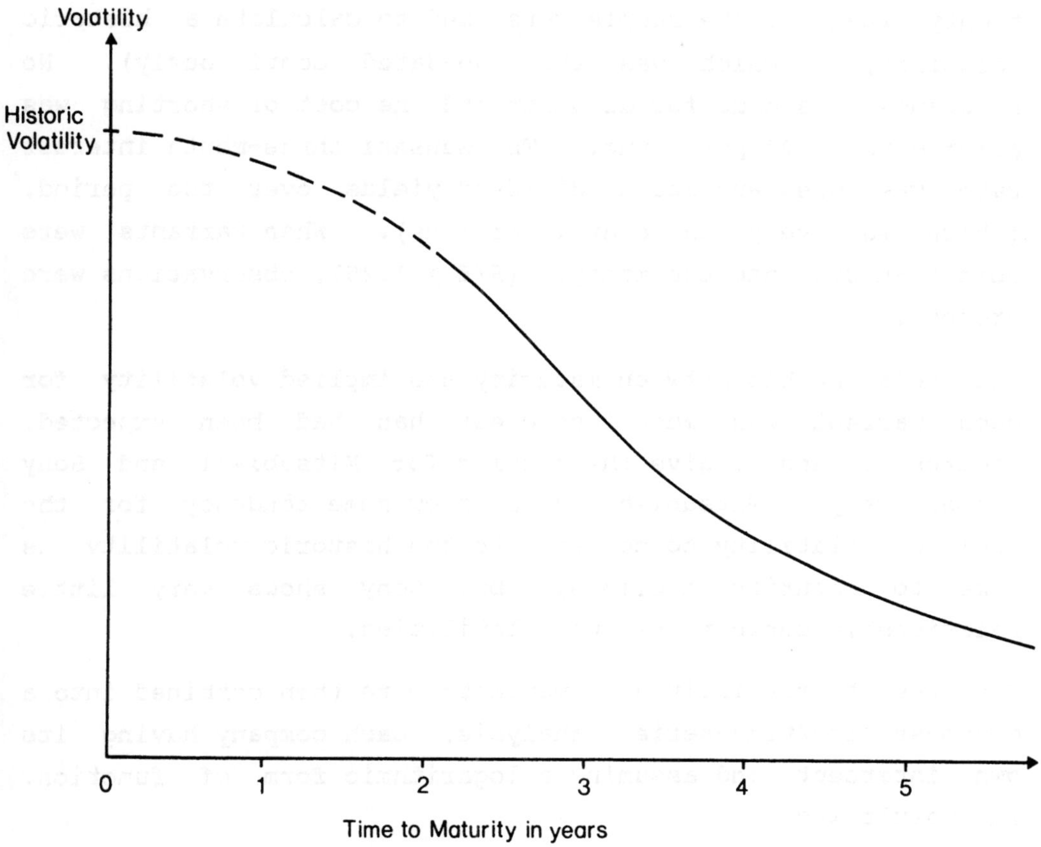

Implied volatilities were calculated weekly using a binomial model [4] over the whole sample period, except that the first twenty weeks of the sample were used to calculate a historic volatility, (which was then up-dated continuously). No allowance was made for dilution and the cost of shorting was assumed to be 2% per annum. The Gensaki three-month interest rate was used and actual dividend yields over the period, (which were very stable at 1% or less). When warrants were more than 25% into the money, (S/E > 1.25), observations were dropped.

The relationship between maturity and implied volatility for each warrant was much less clear than had been expected. Figures 6 and 7 give the results for Mitsubishi and Sony respectively. Mitsubishi does show some tendency for the implied volatility to converge to the historic volatility as time to maturity declines, but Sony shows very little relationship between the two volatilities.

The results for individual warrants were then combined into a cross-section/time-series analysis, each company having its own intercept and assuming a logarithmic form of function. The result was,

$$\log(SI/SH)_{it} = 2.359 + DUM_i - \underset{(9.17)}{1.860} \log(S/E)_{it} - \underset{(4.62)}{0.604} \log(t)$$

$$N = 355 \quad R^2 = 0.361$$

where SI is implied volatility

SH is historic volatility

DUM is company-specific dummy variable

S is share price

E is exercise price

t is time to maturity

i is company subscript.

Figure 6: MITSUBISHI VOLATILITY

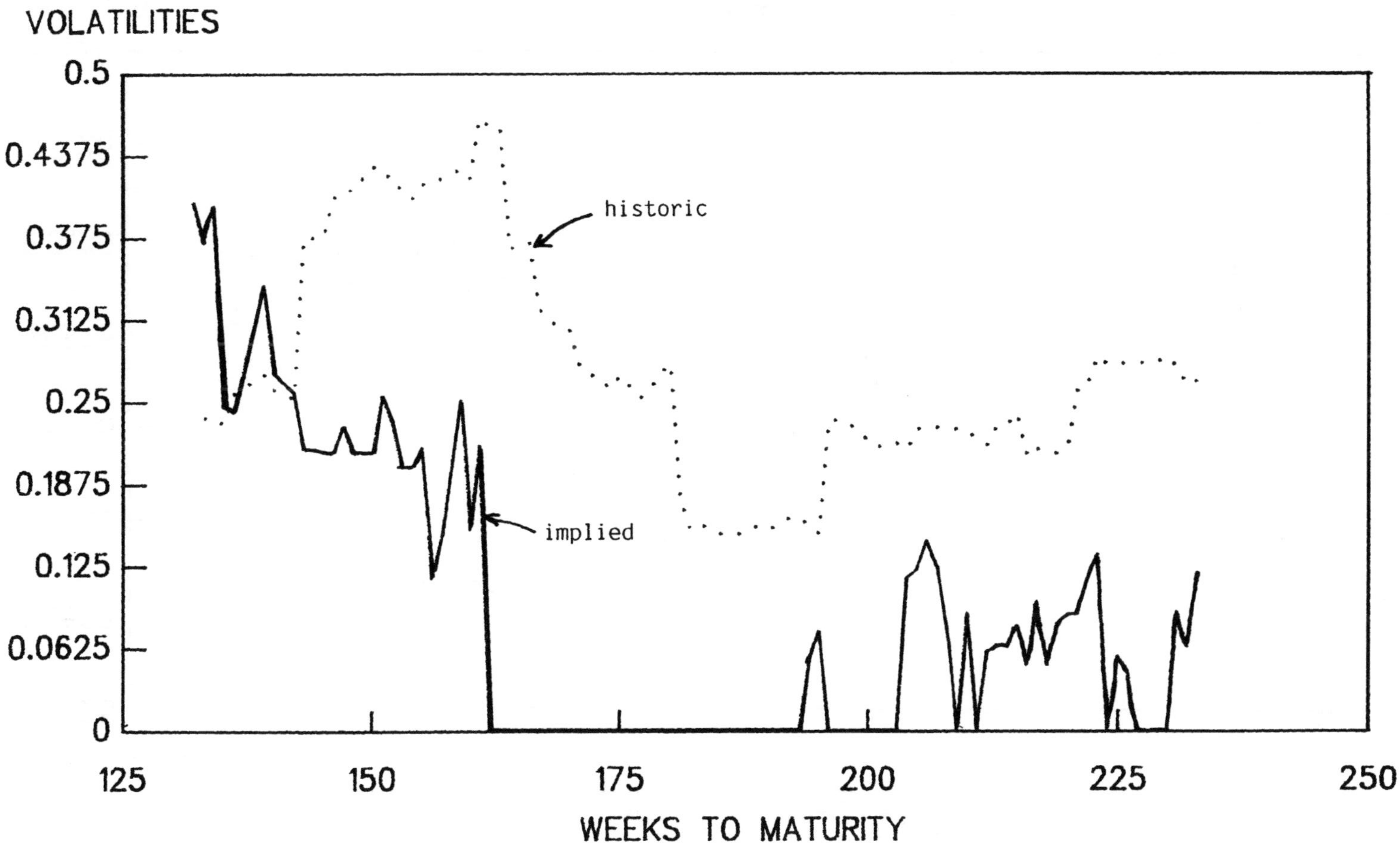

Figure 7: SONY VOLATILITY

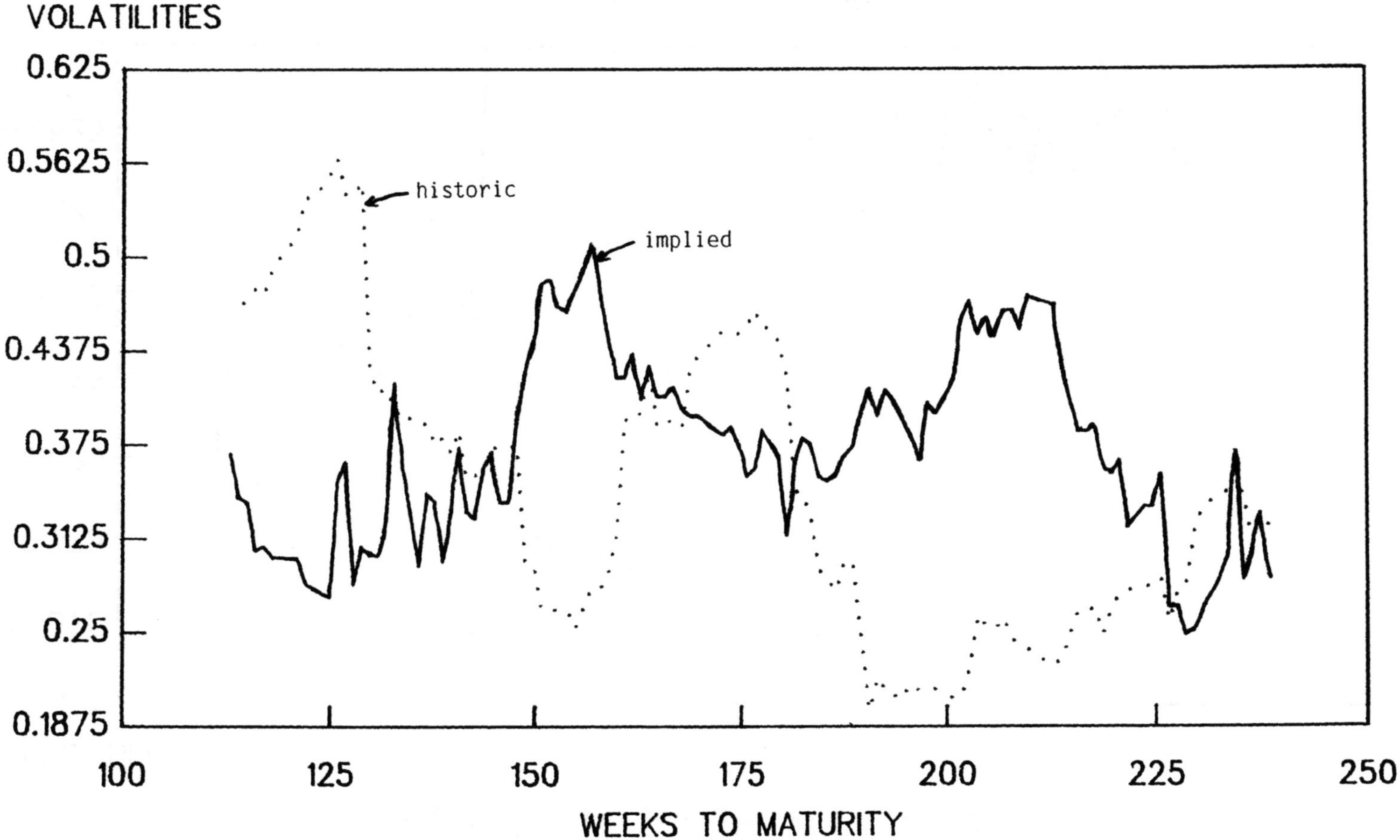

There was a significantly negative relationship between time to maturity and implied volatility of -0.604. This indicates that for each 1% increase in time to maturity the implied volatility declined by 0.604%. For example, if the implied volatility were 0.30 at 100 weeks it would be 0.17 at 200 weeks.

There was also a significantly negative relationship between "in-the-moneyness" (S/E) and the implied volatility. An increase of 1% in this variable resulted in a 1.86% decline in implied volatility. The reason for this remains to be explained.

11. CONCLUSIONS

1. The reasons why Japanese companies issue warrants remain unclear. The most plausible reason is that they prefer deferred to actual rights issues. Another reason is that warrants provide investors with call options which cannot easily be obtained in other ways, as there are no traded options on Japanese shares.

2. The warrant market showed some inefficiency. In a time-series sample of 4759 prices on 54 warrants arbitrage bounds were broken with a frequency much higher than for comparable traded options. The arbitrages were associated with the longer series, indicating greater inefficiency in the earlier periods. However, arbitrages were not negatively associated with liquidity proxies such as foreign listing or ownership.

3. An arbitrage-based model, allowing for the cost of shorting the stock, appeared to explain changes in warrant prices but not their levels.

4. A cross-section/time-series analysis of six warrants indicated that implied volatility declined significantly with time to maturity. A 1% increase in time resulted in approximately a 0.6% fall in volatility. This is consistent with Samuelson's (1965) view of "ergodic"

price behaviour and the Poterba and Summers (1988) observation of mean-reverting prices.

5. Finally, it remains in further research to allow for the behaviour of volatility in model-based efficiency tests.

FOOTNOTES

(1) For example, if the company issues new shares at a price of 2000 yen when the face value of a share is 50 yen, there is a premium of 1950 yen which will have to be repaid to shareholders in the future. The premium is accumulated and Commercial Law requires that 20% of the premium is distributed each year. An amendment of the law in 1981 limited the pay-out to 20% in each of the next three years, so the total pay-out is now 60% of the premium. If, however, the company issues warrants (or convertibles), no premium need be paid-out until the exercise ratio exceeds 50%. The company therefore may prefer to issue warrants to issuing shares, because at least in the former case there is a cash inflow immediately with no obligation to repay the "premium" until exercise occurs, probably at the maturity of the warrants.

(2) An alternative explanantion is that volatility is stochastic and this leads to a positive bias in the Black/Scholes model in relation to time. However, the effect is small (see Hull and White, 1987).

(3) It exhibits strong association with rumours of the Emperor's death, as that event would require large amounts of printing of new banknotes etc.

(4) A numerical method is required so that the S-E bound is not breached.

REFERENCES

Ball, C.A. and Torous, W.N. (1986), "Futures Options and the Volatility of Futures Prices", Journal of Finance, 41, pp.857-870.

Constantinides, G.M. (1984), "Warrant Exercise and Bond Conversion in Competitive Markets", Journal of Financial Economics, 13, pp.371-397.

Cox, J.C. and Rubinstein, M. (1985), Options Markets, Englewood Cliffs: Prentice Hall.

Emanuel, D.C. (1983), "Warrant Valuation and Exercise Strategy", Journal of Financial Economics, 11, pp.211-235.

Galai,D. (1978), "Empirical Tests of Boundary Conditions for CBOE Options", Journal of Financial Economics, 6, pp.187-211.

Galai, D. and Schneller, M. (1978), "Pricing of Warrants and the Value of the Firm", Journal of Finance, 33, pp.1333-1342.

Galai,D. (1987) "Empirical Tests of Options Pricing Models: An Updated Review", Hebrew University, Jerusalem, September.

Grammatikos, T. and Saunders, A. (1986), "Futures Price Variability: A Test of Maturity and Volume Effects", Journal of Business, 59, pp.319-330.

Green,R.C. (1984), "Investment Incentives, Debt and Warrants", Journal of Financial Economics, 11, pp.115-136.

Hull,J. and White,A. (1987), "The Pricing of Options on Assets with Stochastic Volatilities", Journal of Finance, 42, pp.281-300.

Meier,M. (1987), "Investment in the Swiss Franc Equity Warrant Market", Finanzmarkt und Portfolio Management, 3, pp.25-36.

Patterson, D.M. (1986), "The Speed of Adjustment of Warrant Prices to Changes in Stock Prices", Journal of Business and Economic Statistics, 4, pp.233-241.

Poterba,J. and Summers,L. (1988), "Mean Reversion in Stock Prices: Evidence and Implications", Working Paper, Department of Economics, Massachusetts Institute of Technology.

Rutledge, D. (1976), " A Note on the Variability of Futures Prices", Review of Economics and Statistics, 58, pp.118-120.

Samuelson, P. (1965), "Proof the Properly Anticipated Prices Fluctuate Randomly", Industrial Management Review, 6, pp.41-50.

Samuelson, P. (1976), "Is Real World Price a Tale Told by the Idiot of Chance?", Review of Economics and Statistics, 58, pp.120-123.

Schwartz, E. (1977), "The Valuation of Warrants: Implementing a New Approach", Journal of Financial Economics, 4, pp.79-93.

APPENDIX: MARKET PROCEDURE IN PRICING A WARRANT AT ISSUE

This procedure for deciding on the warrant value per share may be summarised as follows. The yen warrant value per share, W, is,

$$W = PV(S' - E), \qquad (1)$$

where $S' = S(1 + g)^T$

PV is the discount rate for the company
S is the share price in yen
S' is the expected future share price
E is the exercise price in yen
g is the annual growth rate of the share price
and T is the life in years of the warrant.

The capital raised in dollars equals the number of shares per warrant times the exercise price in yen converted to dollars at the fixed exchange rate,

$$K = N \times E/FF$$

so

$$N = K \times FF/E \qquad (2)$$

where N is the number of shares per warrant
K is the capital raised in dollars
and FF is the fixed exchange rate.

The yen value of a warrant is,

$$YV = W \times N \qquad (3)$$

where YV is yen value of a warrant.

Then the dollar value of the warrant is,

$$DV = W \times N/FC, \qquad (4)$$

where DV is dollar value of a warrant
FC is current exchange rate (Y/$).

Finally, the warrant is quoted per $100 of bond,

$$w = DV \times Q \times 100 \qquad (5)$$

where Q is the warrantability (capital raised on exercise per $1 of bond).

Substituting we obtain,

$$w = W \times 100 \times Q \times (FF/E) \times (1/FC). \qquad (6)$$

where w is the warrant price ($) per $100 of bond.

DISCUSSANT

PHELIM P. BOYLE,
UNIVERSITY OF WATERLOO
WATERLOO, ONTARIO
CANADA, N2L 3G1

Most of the studies of market efficiency have been carried out using United States price data. Since the Japanese capital market is now the largest in the world, and since it has been relatively neglected by finance scholars, Dr. Gemmil's paper is therefore welcome. The author noted that the paper is still somewhat preliminarily. I hope my comments will be useful to the author in subsequent revisions. I have a few general comments and then some specific ones.

Perhaps the first point is that warrants are not options although they have similarities with options. Warrants, it must be emphasized, are corporate securities and need not be exercised simultaneously in a block. Emanuel [1983] and Constantinides [1984] have examined the gaming aspect of strategic optimal exercise. Constantinides has shown that the theoretical price of the warrant may be lower under strategic exercise than by block exercise. Another implication of the fact that warrants are securities of the firm is that it complicates the valuation. Since the market value of the firm on which the warrants are written is usually obtained by summing the values of the firm's liabilities the warrant price which we want to obtain is a component of total firm value. There is a degree of circularity here.

My second general comment has to do with the tests of market efficiency. It would be useful to construct a hedged portfolio of the warrants and shorting the stock allowing for the actual short sale restrictions and compute the return to such a strategy.

My third comment raises a concern about how the short sale restriction is incorporated into the pricing model. It is not obvious that this is best approached via altered boundary conditions. Another approach might be to examine what happens if such a restriction is built right into the derivation of the pricing model. For work along these lines involving transactions costs, see Leland [1985]. Of course, this could be a difficult exercise.

My specific comments are as follows. In conducting his tests, the author uses end of day prices. This introduces a lack of simultaneity. Even if the model prices were exactly equal to market prices, the boundary conditions would appear to be violated in these circumstances.

The paper in its current form just records the numbers of violations. Of much more interest is the magnitude of the violations and their distribution.

In documenting alleged violations, a researcher needs to be careful to show that these represent feasible arbitrage possibilities for an actual investor. For careful work in this vein see Halpern and Turnbull (1985).

In the discussion of biases in the model, the author should relate his findings to the comprehensive results obtained by Rubinstein on U.S. stock option data. The author elected to discard some of the warrants in his analysis of the volatility issue. This can sometimes be a dangerous strategy.

In summary, the author has tackled an interesting problem, but there are several areas where the analysis could be improved.

References

Emanuel, D.C., (1983), "Warrant Valuation and Exercise Strategy", Journal of Financial Economics , pp. 211-233.

Constantinides, G., (1984), "Warrant Exercise and Bond Conversions in Competitive Markets," pp. 371-398.

Rubinstein, M., (1985), "Non-parametric Tests of Alternative Option Pricing Models", Journal of Finance, pp. 455-480.

Leland, H., (1985), "Option Pricing and Replication with Tranactions Costs", Journal of Finance, Vol. 40, No. 5, pp. 1283-1302.

Halpern, P. and Turnbull, S.M., (1985), "Empirical Tests for Boundary Conditions of Toronto Stock Exchange Options," Journal of Finance, Vol. 40. No. 2, pp. 481-500.

INDEX

Workshop participants

F. Amador, Escuela Superior de Tecnica Empresarial Agricola, Cordoba, Spain
R. Ball, University of Rochester, USA
P.P. Boyle, University of Waterloo, Canada
G. Bulkley, University of Exeter, UK
J.S. Cabral, Porto University, Portugal
C.M. Cadsby, University of Guelph, Canada
P.J. Catania, Chicago Board of Trade, USA
L. Condoyanni, University of Lancaster, UK
N.P. Crato, Universidade Tecnica de Lisboa, Portugal
W.F.M. De Bondt, University of Wisconsin-Madison, USA
A. De Ridder, Federation of Swedish Industries, Sweden
S. Ekern, Norwegian School of Economics and Business Administration, Norway
H.M. Fisunoglu, University of Cukurova, Turkey
A.J. Francfort, James Madison University, USA
D.R. Fraser, Texas A & M University, USA
G.T. Gemmill, City University, USA
R.M.C. Guimaraes, Porto University, Portugal
G. Hawawini, INSEAD, Fontainebleau, France
B. Jacquillat, Universite de Paris-Dauphine, France
L.P. Jennergren, Stockholm School of Economics, Sweden
S.M. Keane, University of Glasgow, UK
D.B. Keim, University of Pennsylvania, USA
A.G.Z. Kemna, Erasmus University, The Netherlands
B.G. Kingsman, University of Lancaster, UK
W.C. Labys, West Virginia University, USA
J. Lakonishok, University of Urbana-Champaign, USA
M. Levis, University of Bath, UK
J.A.A. Lopes, Universidade Tecnica de Lisboa, Portugal
S.M. McLeay, University College of North Wales, UK
J.F. O'Hanlon, University of Lancaster, UK
D.A. Peel, University College of Wales, UK

P.F. Pope, University of Strathclyde, UK

G.S. Shea, Pennsylvania State University, USA

R.J. Shiller, Yale University, USA

B.G. Sorensen, Odense Universitet, Denmark

R.J. Sweeney, Claremont McKenna College, USA

S.J. Taylor, University of Lancaster, UK

H. Uhlir, Justus-Liebig-Universitat Giessen, F.R. Germany

G. Verga, University of Parma, Italy

T. Vermaelen, INSEAD, Fontainebleau, France

L. Vinell, Federation of Swedish Industries, Sweden

R.E. Wessels, Erasmus University, The Netherlands

NATO ASI Series F

Including Special Programme on Sensory Systems for Robotic Control (ROB)

Vol. 1: Issues in Acoustic Signal – Image Processing and Recognition. Edited by C. H. Chen. VIII, 333 pages. 1983.

Vol. 2: Image Sequence Processing and Dynamic Scene Analysis. Edited by T. S. Huang. IX, 749 pages. 1983.

Vol. 3: Electronic Systems Effectiveness and Life Cycle Costing. Edited by J. K. Skwirzynski. XVII, 732 pages. 1983.

Vol. 4: Pictorial Data Analysis. Edited by R. M. Haralick. VIII, 468 pages. 1983.

Vol. 5: International Calibration Study of Traffic Conflict Techniques. Edited by E. Asmussen. VII, 229 pages. 1984.

Vol. 6: Information Technology and the Computer Network. Edited by K. G. Beauchamp. VIII, 271 pages. 1984.

Vol. 7: High-Speed Computation. Edited by J. S. Kowalik. IX, 441 pages. 1984.

Vol. 8: Program Transformation and Programming Environments. Report on a Workshop directed by F. L. Bauer and H. Remus. Edited by P. Pepper. XIV, 378 pages. 1984.

Vol. 9: Computer Aided Analysis and Optimization of Mechanical System Dynamics. Edited by E. J. Haug. XXII, 700 pages. 1984.

Vol. 10: Simulation and Model-Based Methodologies: An Integrative View. Edited by T. I. Ören, B. P. Zeigler, M. S. Elzas. XIII, 651 pages. 1984.

Vol. 11: Robotics and Artificial Intelligence. Edited by M. Brady, L. A. Gerhardt, H. F. Davidson. XVII, 693 pages. 1984.

Vol. 12: Combinatorial Algorithms on Words. Edited by A. Apostolico, Z. Galil. VIII, 361 pages. 1985.

Vol. 13: Logics and Models of Concurrent Systems. Edited by K. R. Apt. VIII, 498 pages. 1985.

Vol. 14: Control Flow and Data Flow: Concepts of Distributed Programming. Edited by M. Broy. VIII, 525 pages. 1985.

Vol. 15: Computational Mathematical Programming. Edited by K. Schittkowski. VIII, 451 pages. 1985.

Vol. 16: New Systems and Architectures for Automatic Speech Recognition and Synthesis. Edited by R. De Mori, C.Y. Suen. XIII, 630 pages. 1985.

Vol. 17: Fundamental Algorithms for Computer Graphics. Edited by R.A. Earnshaw. XVI, 1042 pages. 1985.

Vol. 18: Computer Architectures for Spatially Distributed Data. Edited by H. Freeman and G.G. Pieroni. VIII, 391 pages. 1985.

Vol. 19: Pictorial Information Systems in Medicine. Edited by K. H. Höhne. XII, 525 pages. 1986.

Vol. 20: Disordered Systems and Biological Organization. Edited by E. Bienenstock, F. Fogelman Soulié, G. Weisbuch. XXI, 405 pages.1986.

Vol. 21: Intelligent Decision Support in Process Environments. Edited by E. Hollnagel, G. Mancini, D.D. Woods. XV, 524 pages. 1986.

NATO ASI Series F

Vol. 22: Software System Design Methods. The Challenge of Advanced Computing Technology. Edited by J.K. Skwirzynski. XIII, 747 pages. 1986.

Vol. 23: Designing Computer-Based Learning Materials. Edited by H. Weinstock and A. Bork. IX, 285 pages. 1986.

Vol. 24: Database Machines. Modern Trends and Applications. Edited by A.K. Sood and A.H. Qureshi. VIII, 570 pages. 1986.

Vol. 25: Pyramidal Systems for Computer Vision. Edited by V. Cantoni and S. Levialdi. VIII, 392 pages. 1986. *(ROB)*

Vol. 26: Modelling and Analysis in Arms Control. Edited by R. Avenhaus, R.K. Huber and J.D. Kettelle. VIII, 488 pages. 1986.

Vol. 27: Computer Aided Optimal Design: Structural and Mechanical Systems. Edited by C.A. Mota Soares. XIII, 1029 pages. 1987.

Vol. 28: Distributed Operating Systems. Theory und Practice. Edited by Y. Paker, J.-P. Banatre and M. Bozyiğit. X, 379 pages. 1987.

Vol. 29: Languages for Sensor-Based Control in Robotics. Edited by U. Rembold and K. Hörmann. IX, 625 pages. 1987. *(ROB)*

Vol. 30: Pattern Recognition Theory and Applications. Edited by P.A. Devijver and J. Kittler. XI, 543 pages. 1987.

Vol. 31: Decision Support Systems: Theory and Application. Edited by C.W. Holsapple and A.B. Whinston. X, 500 pages. 1987.

Vol. 32: Information Systems: Failure Analysis. Edited by J.A. Wise and A. Debons. XV, 338 pages. 1987.

Vol. 33: Machine Intelligence and Knowledge Engineering for Robotic Applications. Edited by A.K.C. Wong and A. Pugh. XIV, 486 pages. 1987. *(ROB)*

Vol. 34: Modelling, Robustness and Sensitivity Reduction in Control Systems. Edited by R.F. Curtain. IX, 492 pages. 1987.

Vol. 35: Expert Judgment and Expert Systems. Edited by J.L. Mumpower, L.D. Phillips, O. Renn and V.R.R. Uppuluri. VIII, 361 pages. 1987.

Vol. 36: Logic of Programming and Calculi of Discrete Design. Edited by M. Broy. VII, 415 pages. 1987.

Vol. 37: Dynamics of Infinite Dimensional Systems. Edited by S.-N. Chow and J.K. Hale. IX, 514 pages. 1987.

Vol. 38: Flow Control of Congested Networks. Edited by A.R. Odoni, L. Bianco and G. Szegö. XII, 355 pages. 1987.

Vol. 39: Mathematics and Computer Science in Medical Imaging. Edited by M.A. Viergever and A. Todd-Pokropek. VIII, 546 pages. 1988.

Vol. 40: Theoretical Foundations of Computer Graphics and CAD. Edited by R.A. Earnshaw. XX, 1246 pages. 1988.

Vol. 41: Neural Computers. Edited by R. Eckmiller and Ch. v. d. Malsburg. XIII, 566 pages. 1988.

NATO ASI Series F

Vol. 42: Real-Time Object Measurement and Classification. Edited by A. K. Jain. VIII, 407 pages 1988. *(ROB)*

Vol. 43: Sensors and Sensory Systems for Advanced Robots. Edited by P. Dario. XI, 597 pages. 1988. *(ROB)*

Vol. 44: Signal Processing and Pattern Recognition in Nondestructive Evaluation of Materials. Edited by C.H. Chen. VIII, 344 pages. 1988. *(ROB)*

Vol. 45: Syntactic and Structural Pattern Recognition. Edited by G. Ferraté, T. Pavlidis, A. Sanfeliu, H. Bunke. XVI, 467 pages. 1988. *(ROB)*

Vol. 46: Recent Advances in Speech Understanding and Dialog Systems. Edited by H. Niemann, M. Lang, G. Sagerer. X, 521 pages. 1988.

Vol. 47: Advanced Computing Concepts and Techniques in Control Engineering. Edited by M.J. Denham, A.J. Laub. XI, 518 pages. 1988.

Vol. 48: Mathematical Models for Decision Support. Edited by Gautam Mitra. IX, 762 pages. 1988.

Vol. 49: Computer Integrated Manufacturing. Edited by I. Burhan Turksen. VIII, 568 pages. 1988.

Vol. 50: CAD Based Programming for Sensory Robots. Edited by B. Ravani. IX, 565 pages. 1988. *(ROB)*

Vol. 51: Algorithms and Model Formulations in Mathematical Programming. Edited by Stein W. Wallace. IX, 190 pages. 1989.

Vol. 52: Sensor Devices and Systems for Robotics. Edited by Alícia Casals. IX, 362 pages. 1989. *(ROB)*

Vol. 53: Advanced Information Technologies for Industrial Material Flow Systems. Edited by S.Y. Nof and C.L. Moodie. IX, 710 pages. 1989.

Vol. 54: A Reappraisal of the Efficiency of Financial Markets. Edited by R.M.C. Guimarães, B.G. Kingsman and S.J. Taylor. X, 804 pages. 1989.

MIX
Papier aus verantwortungsvollen Quellen
Paper from responsible sources
FSC® C105338

If you have any concerns about our products,
you can contact us on
ProductSafety@springernature.com

In case Publisher is established outside the EU,
the EU authorized representative is:
Springer Nature Customer Service Center GmbH
Europaplatz 3, 69115 Heidelberg, Germany

Printed by Libri Plureos GmbH
in Hamburg, Germany